PSYCH 2

Rathus

CENGAGE
Learning

Australia • Brazil • Japan • Korea • Mexico • Singapore • Spain • United Kingdom • United States

PSYCH 2

PSYCH, 2nd Edition
Rathus

Executive Editors:
  Maureen Staudt
  Michael Stranz

Senior Project Development Manager:
  Linda deStefano

Marketing Specialist:
  Courtney Sheldon

Senior Production/Manufacturing Manager:
  Donna M. Brown

PreMedia Manager:
  Joel Brennecke

Sr. Rights Acquisition Account Manager:
  Todd Osborne

Cover Image:
  Getty Images*

*Unless otherwise noted, all cover images used by Custom
Solutions, a part of Cengage Learning, have been supplied
courtesy of Getty Images with the exception of the Earthview
cover image, which has been supplied by the National
Aeronautics and Space Administration (NASA).

For product information and technology assistance, contact us at
Cengage Learning Customer & Sales Support, 1-800-354-9706

For permission to use material from this text or product,
submit all requests online at **cengage.com/permissions**
Further permissions questions can be emailed to
permissionrequest@cengage.com

This book contains select works from existing Cengage Learning resources and
was produced by Cengage Learning Custom Solutions for collegiate use. As such,
those adopting and/or contributing to this work are responsible for editorial
content accuracy, continuity and completeness.

Compilation © 2011 Cengage Learning
ISBN-13: 978-1-133-76997-2

ISBN-10: 1-133-76997-7

Cengage Learning
5191 Natorp Boulevard
Mason, Ohio 45040
USA

Cengage Learning is a leading provider of customized learning solutions with
office locations around the globe, including Singapore, the United Kingdom,
Australia, Mexico, Brazil, and Japan. Locate your local office at:
international.cengage.com/region.
Cengage Learning products are represented in Canada by Nelson Education, Ltd.
For your lifelong learning solutions, visit **www.cengage.com/custom.**
Visit our corporate website at **www.cengage.com.**

Printed in the United States of America

PSYCH
Brief Contents

SPEAK UP!

SHE DID

PSYCH2 was built on a simple principle: to create a new teaching and learning solution that reflects the way today's faculty teach and the way you learn.

Through conversations, focus groups, surveys, and interviews, we collected data that drove the creation of the current version of PSYCH2 that you are using today. But it doesn't stop there – in order to make PSYCH2 an even better learning experience, we'd like you to SPEAK UP and tell us how PSYCH2 worked for you.

What did you like about it? What would you change? Are there additional ideas you have that would help us build a better product for next semester's students?

At **www.CengageBrain.com** you'll find all of the resources you need to succeed – **videos, flash cards, interactive quizzes** and more!

Speak Up! Go to **www.CengageBrain.com**.

PSYCH Contents

DAVID BUFFINGTON/GETTY IMAGES

PETER CADE/GETTY IMAGES

ERIK ISAKSON / GETTY IMAGES

LARSEN & TALBERT/JUPITER IMAGES

© 2007 KEVIN ARNOLD/ JUPITERIMAGES CORPORATION

KEITH BROFSKY/GETTY IMAGES

© RUBBERBALL / ALAMY

SCOTT T. BAXTER/GETTY IMAGES

COCOON/GETTY IMAGES

PM IMAGES/GETTY IMAGES

PHOTOLINK/GETTY IMAGES

GETTY IMAGES

MIKE DUNNING/GETTY IMAGES

© IMAGE SOURCE BLACK/JUPITERIMAGES

What *is* Psychology?

Learning Outcomes

LO **1** Define psychology

LO **2** Describe the various fields and subfields of psychology

LO **3** Describe the origins of psychology and identify those who made significant contributions to the field

LO **4** Identify theoretical perspectives of modern psychologists toward behavior and mental processes

LO **5** Describe modern approaches to research and practice—critical thinking, the scientific method, and ethical considerations

> ## "What standards or rules should we apply when we are trying to sort out truth from fiction?"

Each week, supermarket tabloid headlines exclaim over the latest abductions by extraterrestrials. Isn't it strange that extraterrestrials have the technology to fly between the stars, and yet apparently still need to prod and poke us to figure out how we work? If you can believe the photos and drawings in the tabloids, aliens have been hopping around in the same flying saucers for half a century—a saucer-shaped silver disk with a hump on top. Meanwhile, we inferior humans have progressed. We have evolved our modes of transportation from sleek cars with tail fins to boxy Scions and Elements. We continuously update our iPods with the latest music and download the newest ringtones into our camera cell phones. But the aliens keep flying the same model flying saucers. They're nothing to text home about.

Although we can find some humor in these tales of abduction by aliens, psychologists and other scientists are very interested in the questions these tales raise about human nature and the distinction between sensationalism and science. What do we know about people who claim to have been abducted by aliens? What standards or rules should we apply when we are trying to sort out truth from fiction and decide whether we will believe the "kidnap victims"?

Truth or Fiction?

What do you think?

Folklore, common sense, or nonsense? Place a T for "True" or F for "False" on the lines provided (you'll learn the answers as you read through the text).

__ More than 2,000 years ago, Aristotle wrote a book on psychology, with contents similar to the book you are now holding.

__ The ancient Greek philosopher Socrates suggested a research method that is still used in psychology.

__ Men receive the majority of doctoral degrees in psychology.

__ Even though she had worked to complete all the degree requirements, the first female president of the American Psychological Association turned down the doctoral degree that was offered to her.

__ You could survey millions of voters and still fail to predict the outcome of a presidential election.

__ In many experiments, neither the study participants nor the researchers know who is receiving the real treatment and who is not.

Many psychologists have studied the reported alien kidnappings, and one of their conclusions is that the kidnappings never occurred. However, the people making the claims are not necessarily mentally ill, nor are they even lying (Newman & Baumeister, 1998). These are by and large people who have "remembered" their "experiences" while undergoing therapy, and often under hypnosis. Tales of alien abduction are widely known throughout our culture, so it is not at all surprising that the "memories" of "kidnap victims" would tend to coincide (Lynn & Kirsch, 1996; Patry & Pelletier, 2001).

"Abductees" generally claim that they are awakened in their sleep by the aliens and unable to move. Psychologists know that many of our voluntary muscles—the ones involved in movement—are "paralyzed" when we sleep, which is why we usually don't thrash about when we dream (McNally & Clancy, 2005). *Hallucinations*—that is,

psychology
the science that studies behavior and mental processes

theory
a formulation of relationships underlying observed events

seeing and hearing things that are not really there—are quite common as we are waking from a sleep-paralyzed state, and it seems that the reported experiences of "abductees" fit the pattern.

Psychologists also know that people are quite open to suggestion, especially when undergoing hypnosis (Clark & Loftus, 2004). Memories are not perfect snapshots. Sometimes the person interviewing the supposed kidnap victim asks leading questions—that is, questions that might encourage the witnesses to recall events in a certain way—looking for experiences with aliens.

All in all, "UFO memories may be constructed from bits and pieces of sleep-related hallucinations, nightmares, and media attention and fixed solidly into place with the suggestion of hypnosis and the validation of support groups" (Clark & Loftus, 1996). Abductees may also be trying to escape, temporarily, from their humdrum lives—just as buyers of the supermarket tabloids might be doing (Newman and Baumeister, 1998).

Psychologists have thus worked to "explain" how it can be that many people report being abducted by aliens and being subjected to tests by them. But is there evidence that people have been abducted by aliens? In sum, when we subject the stories in the supermarket tabloids to scientific analysis, we usually find that they fall short of any reasonable requirements of evidence.

This book will take you on a journey. It's not a journey into outer space. It's a journey into the inner space of thinking critically about the world around you, about stories and arguments made by other people, about human behavior and mental processes. In our overview of reported alien abductions, we touched on people's memories, the state of consciousness known as sleep, hallucinations, hypnosis, the search for stimulating events, social influences on witnesses, and the effects of social support and the media. All these, and much, much more, lie within the science of psychology. We will see who psychologists are, what they do, what they have learned, and perhaps most importantly, how they sort out truth from fiction. Let us begin by asking, *What is psychology?*

LO¹ Psychology as a Science

Psychology is the scientific study of behavior and mental processes. Topics of interest to psychologists include the nervous system, sensation and perception, learning and memory, intelligence, language, thought, growth and development, personality, stress and health, psychological disorders, ways of treating those disorders, sexual behavior, and the behavior of people in social settings such as groups and organizations.

Sciences have certain goals. Psychology, like other sciences, seeks to describe, explain, predict, and control the events it studies. Psychology thus seeks to describe, explain, predict, and control behavior and mental processes. "Controlling" behavior and mental processes doesn't mean to psychologists what it may sound like to most people. Psychologists are committed to a belief in the dignity of human beings, and human dignity requires that people be free to make their own decisions and choose their own behavior. Psychologists study the influences on human behavior, but they use this knowledge only on request and to help people meet their own goals. For example, a psychologist would wish to help someone who is suffering from anxiety and who asks for help.

When possible, descriptive terms such as *a threat* and concepts such as *anxiety* are interwoven into **theories**. Theories propose reasons for relationships among events, as in perception of *a threat* can arouse feelings of *anxiety*. They allow us to derive explanations and predictions, as in "Dwayne will feel *anxious* if he perceives *a threat*." A theory of hunger should allow us to predict when people will or will not eat. Many psychological theories combine statements about behavior (such as *evading a threat*), mental processes (such as *thinking that the threat may be harmful*), and biological processes (*rapid heart and respiration rates*). If our observations are not adequately explained by or predicted from a theory, we should consider revising or replacing it.

The remainder of this chapter presents an overview of psychology as a science. You will see that psychologists have diverse interests and fields of specialization. We discuss the history of psychology and the perspectives from which today's psychologists view behavior and mental process. Finally, we consider the research methods used by psychologists.

LO²What Psychologists Do

Psychologists share a keen interest in behavior, but in other ways, they may differ markedly. *Just what do psychologists do?* Psychologists engage in research, practice, and teaching. Some researchers engage primarily in basic, or pure research. Pure research has no immediate application to personal or social problems and, therefore, has been characterized as research for its own sake. Others engage in applied research, which is designed to find solutions to specific personal or social problems. Although pure research is sparked by curiosity and the desire to know and understand, today's pure research frequently has applications tomorrow. For example, pure research on learning and motivation in pigeons, rats, and monkeys done early in the 20th century has found applications in school systems. The research has shown, for example, that learning often takes time and repetition and profits from "booster shots" (that is, repetition even after the learning goal has been reached). Pure research into the workings of the nervous system has enhanced knowledge of disorders such as epilepsy, Parkinson's disease, and Alzheimer's disease.

Many psychologists *practice* psychology by applying psychological knowledge to help individuals change their behavior so that they can meet their own goals more effectively. Still other psychologists primarily teach. They share psychological knowledge in classrooms, seminars, and workshops. Some psychologists engage in all three: research, practice, and teaching.

Fields of Psychology

Psychologists are found in different specialties. Although some psychologists wear more than one hat, most of them carry out their functions in the following fields.

Many developmental, educational, and school psychologists observe children's behavior in the classroom—the "natural setting" for important behavior.

Clinical psychologists help people with psychological disorders adjust to the demands of life. Clinical psychologists evaluate problems such as anxiety and depression through interviews and psychological tests. They help clients resolve problems and change self-defeating behavior. For example, they may help clients face "threats," such as public speaking, by exposing the clients gradually to situations in which they make presentations to actual or virtual groups (see *virtual therapy* in Chapter 13). Clinical psychologists are the largest subgroup of psychologists (see Figure 1.1 on page 6). *Counseling psychologists,* like clinical psychologists, use interviews and tests to define their clients' problems. Their clients typically have adjustment problems but not serious psychological disorders. For example, clients may have trouble making academic or vocational decisions or making friends in college.

School psychologists help school systems identify and assist students who have problems that interfere with learning. They help schools make decisions about placing students in special classes. *Educational psychologists* research theoretical issues related to learning, measurement, and child development. They study how learning is affected by psychological factors such as motivation and intelligence, sociocultural factors such as poverty and acculturation, and teacher behavior. Some educational psychologists prepare standardized tests such as the SATs.

Developmental psychologists study the changes—physical, cognitive, social, and emotional—that occur across the life span. They try to sort out the effects of heredity and the environment on development.

Personality psychologists identify and measure human traits and determine influences on human thought processes, feelings, and behavior. They are particularly concerned with issues such as anxiety, aggression, and gender roles. *Social psychologists* are concerned with the nature and causes of individuals' thoughts, feelings, and behavior in social situations. Whereas personality psychologists tend to look within the person for explanations of behavior, social psychologists tend to focus on social influences.

Environmental psychologists study the ways in which people and the environment—the natural environment and the human-made environment—influence one another. For example, we know that extremes of temperature and loud noises interfere with learning in school. Environmental psychologists also study ways to encourage people to recycle

pure research research conducted without concern for immediate applications

applied research research conducted in an effort to find solutions to particular problems

OJO IMAGES / JUPITER IMAGES

Figure 1.1

New Doctorates in Psychology (median age = 32)

Demographic Factors	%
Women	78.1
Men	21.7
Asian American/Pacific Islander	4.8
African American	5.6
Latina or Latino American	6.3
Native American	<1.0
European American	76.4
Type of Degree	**%**
Ph.D.	52.9
Psy.D.	47.1
Work Setting	**%**
Academia	20.2
Hospitals	19.6
Other Human Service	16.0
Independent Practice	13.7
Business/Government	13.5
Schools/Educational	7.8
Managed Care	7.3
Primary Work Activity	**%**
Health Service	69.5
Education	13.7
Research	10.2
Administration	4.1
Other	2.5
Selected Subfields	**%**
Clinical Psychology	62.0
Counseling Psychology	11.1
School Psychology	9.5
Clinical Child Psychology	6.4
Other	10.7

Source: Adapted from american psychological association (2009a). Doctoral psychology workforce fast facts. Health service provider subfields. Center for workforce studies. http://research.apa.org/fastfacts-09.pdf. © Copyright 2009 APA center for workforce studies. Washington, DC.

and to preserve bastions of wild=erness.

Experimental psychologists specialize in basic processes such as the nervous system, sensation and perception, learning and memory, thought, motivation, and emotion. For example, experimental psychologists study which areas of the brain are involved in solving math problems or listening to music. They use people or animals such as pigeons and rats to study learning.

Industrial psychologists focus on the relationships between people and work. *Organizational psychologists* study the behavior of people in organizations such as businesses. *Human factors psychologists* make technical systems such as automobile dashboards and computer keyboards more user-friendly. *Consumer psychologists* study the behavior of shoppers in an effort to predict and influence their behavior. They advise store managers how to lay out the aisles of a supermarket in ways that boost impulse buying, how to arrange window displays to attract customers, and how to make newspaper ads and TV commercials more persuasive.

Health psychologists examine the ways in which behavior and attitudes are related to physical health. They study the effects of stress on health problems such as headaches, cardiovascular disease, and cancer. Health psychologists also guide clients toward healthier behavior patterns, such as exercising and quitting smoking.

Sport psychologists help athletes concentrate on their performance and not on the crowd, use cognitive strategies such as positive visualization (imagining themselves making the right moves) to enhance performance, and avoid choking under pressure.

Forensic psychologists apply psychology to the criminal justice system. They deal with legal matters such as whether a defendant was sane when

{ Aristotle }

How do we number Aristotle's contributions to psychology?

1 He argued that science could rationally treat only information gathered by the senses.

2 He numbered the so-called five senses of vision, hearing, smell, taste, and touch.

3 He explored the nature of cause and effect.

4 He pointed out that people differ from other living things in their capacity for rational thought.

5 He outlined laws of *associationism* that have lain at the heart of learning theory for more than 2,000 years.

6 He also declared that people are motivated to seek pleasure and avoid pain—a view that remains as current today as it was in ancient Greece.

he or she committed a crime. Forensic psychologists may also treat psychologically ill offenders, consult with attorneys on matters such as picking a jury, and analyze criminals' behavior and mental processes. Forensic psychologists, like other psychologists, may choose to conduct research on matters ranging from evaluation of eyewitness testimony to interrogation methods.

LO³ Where Psychology Comes From: A History

Have you heard the expression "Know thyself"? It was suggested by the ancient Greek philosopher, Socrates, more than 2,000 years ago. Psychology, which is in large part the endeavor to know ourselves, is as old as history and as modern as today. Knowledge of the history of psychology allows us to appreciate its theoretical conflicts, its place among the sciences, the evolution of its methods, and its social and political roles.

> **Truth**
>
> More than 2,000 years ago, Aristotle wrote a book on psychology, *Peri Psyches*, with contents similar to the book you are now holding. Like this book, *Peri Psyches* begins with a history of psychological thought and historical views of the mind and behavior.

Who were some of the ancient contributors to psychology? One of them is the ancient Greek philosopher Aristotle (384–322 BCE). Aristotle argued that human behavior, like the movements of the stars and the seas, is subject to rules and laws. Then he delved into his subject matter topic by topic: personality, sensation and perception, thought, intelligence, needs and motives, feelings and emotion, and memory.

> **introspection**
> deliberate looking into one's own cognitive processes to examine one's thoughts and feelings

Other ancient Greek philosophers also contributed to psychology. Around 400 BCE, Democritus suggested that we could think of behavior in terms of a body and a mind. (Contemporary psychologists talk about the interaction of biological and mental processes.) He pointed out that our behavior is influenced by external stimulation. Democritus was one of the first to raise the question of whether there is free will or choice. Putting the question another way, where do the influences of others end and "our own selves" begin?

Socrates (c. 470–399 BCE) suggested that we should rely on rational thought and introspection—careful examination of one's own thoughts and emotions—to achieve self-knowledge. He also pointed out that people are social creatures who influence one another.

Had we room enough and time, we could trace psychology's roots to thinkers even farther back in time than the ancient Greeks, and we could trace its development through the great thinkers of the Renaissance. As it is, we must move on to the development of psychology as a laboratory science during the second half of the 19th century. Some historians set the marker date at 1860. It was then that Gustav Theodor Fechner (1801–1887) published his landmark book *Elements of Psychophysics,* which showed how physical events (such as lights and sounds) are related to psychological sensation and perception. Fechner also showed how we can scientifically measure the effect of these events. Most historians set the debut of modern psychology as a laboratory science in the year 1879, when Wilhelm Wundt used scientific methods to investigate what were previously philosophical questions in his laboratory in Leipzig, Germany.

> **Truth**
>
> Socrates suggested a research method that is still used in psychology—introspection, which is based on Socrates' advice to "know thyself," which has remained a motto of psychology ever since.

> **I wished, by treating Psychology like a natural science, to help her become one.**
>
> —William James

Structuralism

The German psychologist Wilhelm Wundt (1832–1920) looked as if he were going to be a problem child. He did poorly in elementary school—his mind would wander—and he had to repeat a grade. Eventually he attended medical school because he wanted to earn a good living. But he did not like working with patients and dedicated himself to philosophy and psychology.

Like Aristotle, Wundt saw the mind as a natural event that could be studied scientifically, like light, heat, and the flow of blood. Wundt used introspection to try to discover the basic elements of experience.

Wundt and his students founded the school of psychology called structuralism. *What is structuralism?* Structuralism attempted to break down conscious experience into objective sensations, such as sight or taste, and subjective feelings, such as emotional responses, will, and mental images like memories or dreams. Structuralists believed that the mind functions by combining objective and subjective elements of experience.

Functionalism

Toward the end of the 19th century, William James became a major figure in the development of psychology in the United States. He focused on the relation between conscious experience and behavior. He argued, for example, that the stream of consciousness is fluid, and continuous. Introspection convinced him that experience cannot be broken down into objective sensations and subjective feelings as the structuralists maintained.

James was a founder of the school of functionalism. *What is functionalism?* The school of functionalism focused on behavior in addition to the mind or consciousness. Functionalists looked at how our experience helps us function more adaptively in our environments—for example, how habits help us cope with common situations. (When eating with a spoon, we do not create an individual plan to bring each morsel of food to our mouths.) They also turned to the laboratory for direct observations as a way to supplement introspection. The structuralists tended to ask, "What are the pieces that make up thinking and experience?" In contrast, the functionalists tended to ask, "How do behavior and mental processes help people adapt to the requirements of their lives?"

James was also influenced by Charles Darwin's (1809–1882) theory of evolution. Earlier in the 19th century, the British naturalist Darwin had argued that organisms with adaptive features—that is, the "fittest"—survive and reproduce. Functionalists adopted Darwin's theory and proposed that adaptive behavior patterns are learned and maintained. Maladaptive behavior patterns tend to drop out; only the "fittest" behavior survives. Adaptive behaviors tend to be repeated and become habits. James wrote, "habit is the enormous flywheel of society." Habit keeps the engine of civilization running.

Behaviorism

Imagine you have placed a hungry rat in a maze. It meanders down a pathway that ends in a T. It can turn left or right. If you consistently reward the rat with food for turning right, it will learn to turn right when it arrives there, at least when it is hungry. But what does the rat *think* when it is learning to turn right?

Does it seem absurd to try to place yourself in the "mind" of a rat? So it seemed to John Broadus Watson (1878–1958), the founder of American behaviorism. Watson was asked to consider the contents of a rat's "mind" as one of the requirements for his doctoral degree, which he received from the University of Chicago in 1903. Functionalism was the dominant view of psychology at the University of Chicago, and functionalists were concerned with the stream of consciousness as well as observable behavior. But Watson (1913) believed that if psychology was to be a natural science, like physics or chemistry, it must limit itself to observable, measurable events—that is, to behavior alone—hence, the term *behaviorism*.

Wilhelm Wundt

William James

Figure 1.2

The Power of Reinforcement

TOM MCHUGH/PHOTO RESEARCHERS, INC.

In the photo we see a feathered friend that has learned to drop shapes into their proper places through reinforcement. Behaviorists teach animals complex behaviors such as this by first reinforcing approximations to the goal (or target behavior). As time progresses, closer approximations are demanded before reinforcement is given.

What is behaviorism? **Behaviorism** is the school of psychology that focuses on learning observable behavior. The term "observable" includes behaviors that are observable by means of instruments, such as the heart rate, blood pressure, and brain waves. These behaviors are *public* in that they can be measured easily and multiple observers would agree about their existence and features. Given their focus on behavior, behaviorists define psychology as the scientific study of *behavior,* not of *behavior and mental processes.*

B. F. Skinner (1904–1990) also contributed to behaviorism. He believed that organisms learn to behave in certain ways because they have been **reinforced** for doing so—that is, their behavior has a positive outcome. He demonstrated that laboratory animals can be trained to carry out behaviors through strategic use of reinforcers, such as food. He trained rats to turn in circles, climb ladders, and push toys across the floor. Because Skinner showed that he could teach animals remarkable combinations of behaviors by means of reinforcement, many psychologists adopted the view that, in principle, one could explain complex human behavior in terms of thousands of instances of learning through reinforcement (see Figure 1.2).

Gestalt Psychology

In the 1920s, another school of psychology—**Gestalt psychology**—was prominent in Germany. In the 1930s, the three founders of the school—Max Wertheimer (1880–1943), Kurt Koffka (1886–1941), and Wolfgang Köhler (1887–1967)—left Europe to escape the Nazi threat. They carried on their work in the United States, giving further impetus to the growing American ascendance in psychology.

What is Gestalt psychology? Gestalt psychologists focused on perception and on how perception influences thinking and problem solving. The German word *Gestalt* translates as "pattern" or "organized whole." In contrast to the behaviorists, Gestalt psychologists argued that we cannot understand human nature by focusing only on observable behavior. In contrast to the structuralists, they claimed that we cannot explain human perceptions, emotions, or thought processes in terms of basic units. Perceptions are *more* than the sums of their parts: Gestalt psychologists saw our perceptions as wholes that give meaning to parts, as we see in Figure 1.3.

Gestalt psychologists showed that we tend to perceive separate pieces of information as integrated wholes, depending on the contexts in which they occur. In part A of Figure 1.3, the dots in the centers of the drawings are the same size, yet we may perceive them as being different in size because of their surroundings. The second symbol in each line in part B is identical, but in the top row we may perceive it as a *B* and in the bottom row as the number 13. The symbol has not changed, but its context

behaviorism
the school of psychology that defines psychology as the study of observable behavior and studies relationships, between stimuli and responses

reinforcement
a stimulus that follows a response and increases the frequency of the response

Gestalt psychology
the school of psychology that emphasizes the tendency to organize perceptions into wholes and to integrate separate stimuli into meaningful patterns

Figure 1.3

The Importance of Context

A. Are the dots in the center of the configurations the same size? Why not take a ruler and measure them?

B. Is the second symbol in each line the letter *B* or the number *13*?

C. Which of the gray squares is brighter?

Figure 1.4

Some Insight into Insight

At first, the chimpanzee cannot reach the bananas hanging from the ceiling. After some time has passed, the chimp has an apparent "flash of insight" and piles the boxes on top of one another to reach the fruit.

has. The inner squares in part C are equally bright, but they do not appear so because of their contrasting backgrounds.

Gestalt psychologists believed that learning could be active and purposeful, not merely responsive and mechanical as in Watson's and Skinner's experiments. They found that much learning, especially in problem solving, is accomplished by insight, not by mechanical repetition.

Consider Wolfgang Köhler's research with chimpanzees, as shown in Figure 1.4. At first, the chimpanzee is unsuccessful in reaching for bananas suspended from the ceiling. Then he suddenly stacks the boxes and climbs up to reach the bananas. It seems the chimp has experienced a sudden reorganization of the mental elements of the problem—that is, he has had a "flash of insight." Köhler's findings suggest that people, too, often manipulate the elements of problems until we group them in such a way that we believe we will be able to reach a goal. The manipulations may take quite some time as mental trial and error proceeds. But once the solution has been found, we seem to perceive it all of a sudden.

Psychoanalysis

What is psychoanalysis? **Psychoanalysis**—another school of psychology—is the name of the theory of personality and of the method of therapy developed by Sigmund Freud (1856–1939). As a theory of personality, psychoanalysis was based on the idea that much of our lives is governed by unconscious ideas and impulses that originate in childhood conflicts.

Psychoanalytic theory proposes that most of the mind is unconscious—a seething cauldron of conflicting impulses, urges, and wishes. People are motivated to satisfy these impulses, ugly as some of them are. But at the same time, people are motivated to see themselves as decent, and hence may delude themselves about their true motives. As a physician, Freud's goal was to help individuals who were suffering from various psychological and social problems. His method of psychotherapy, psychoanalysis, aims to help patients gain insight into many of their deep-seated conflicts and to find socially acceptable ways of expressing wishes and gratifying needs.

LO⁴ How Today's Psychologists View Behavior and Mental Processes

Today we no longer find psychologists who describe themselves as structuralists or functionalists. And, although the school of Gestalt psychology gave birth to current research approaches in perception and problem solving, few would label themselves Gestalt psychologists. But we do find Gestalt therapists who help clients integrate conflicting parts of their personality (making themselves "whole"). The numbers of behaviorists and psychoanalysts have been declining (Robins et al., 1999). Many contemporary psychologists in the behaviorist tradition look on themselves as social cognitive theorists, and many psychoanalysts consider themselves neoanalysts or ego analysts rather than traditional Freudians.

Sigmund Freud

MANSELL/TIME & LIFE PICTURES/GETTY IMAGES

The history of psychological thought has taken many turns, and contemporary psychologists differ in their approaches. Today there are several broad, influential perspectives in psychology: evolutionary and biological, cognitive, humanistic–existential, psychodynamic, learning, and sociocultural. Each emphasizes different topics of investigation. Each approaches its topics in its own way.

The Biological and Evolutionary Perspectives

Psychologists are interested in the roles of heredity and evolution in behavior and mental processes such as psychological disorders, criminal behavior, and thinking. Generally speaking, our heredity provides a broad range of behavioral and mental possibilities. Environmental factors interact with inherited factors to determine specific behavior and mental processes.

What is the biological perspective? Psychologists with a biological perspective seek the links between the activity of the brain, the activity of hormones, and heredity, on the one hand, and behavior and mental processes on the other. Psychologists assume that the thoughts, fantasies, and dreams—and the inborn or instinctive behavior patterns of many species, such as the songs and nest-building of birds—are made possible by the nervous system, and especially the brain. Some biological psychologists—also called *biopsychologists*—focus on evolution.

What is the evolutionary perspective? Evolutionary psychologists focus on the evolution of behavior and mental processes. Charles Darwin argued that in the age-old struggle for existence, only the "fittest" (most adaptive) organisms reach maturity and reproduce. For example, fish that swim faster or people who are naturally immune to certain diseases are more likely to survive and transmit their *genes* to future generations. Individuals die, but species tend to evolve in adaptive directions. Evolutionary psychologists suggest that much human social behavior, such as aggressive behavior and mate selection, has a hereditary basis. People may be influenced by social rules, cultural factors, even personal choice, but evolutionary psychologists believe that inherited tendencies also move us in certain directions. When we ask the question "What evolves?" our answer is the biological processes and structures that make behavior possible.

MARY EVANS/PHOTO RESEARCHERS, INC.

Charles Darwin

The Cognitive Perspective

What is the cognitive perspective? Psychologists with a cognitive perspective venture into the realm of mental processes to understand human nature. They investigate the ways in which we perceive and mentally represent the world, how we learn, remember the past, plan for the future, solve problems, form judgments, make decisions, and use language. Cognitive psychologists, in short, study those things we refer to as the *mind*.

The cognitive tradition has roots in Socrates' advice to "know thyself" and in his suggested method of introspection. We also find cognitive psychology's roots in structuralism, functionalism, and Gestalt psychology, each of which, in its own way, addressed issues that are of interest to cognitive psychologists.

cognitive
having to do with mental processes such as sensation and perception, memory, intelligence, language, thought, and problem solving

The Humanistic–Existential Perspective

The humanistic–existential perspective is cognitive in flavor, yet it emphasizes more the role of subjective (personal) experience. *What is the humanistic–existential perspective?* Let us consider each of the parts of this perspective: *humanism* and *existentialism*.

Humanism stresses the human capacity for self-fulfillment and the central roles of consciousness, self-awareness, and decision making. Humanists believe that self-awareness, experience, and choice permit us, to a large extent, to "invent ourselves" as we progress through life. Consciousness—our sense of being in the world—is seen as the force that unifies our personalities. *Existentialism* views people as free to choose and as being responsible for choosing ethical conduct. Grounded in the work of Carl Rogers (1951) and Abraham Maslow (1970), the humanistic–existential perspective has many contemporary adherents (Moss, 2002; Schneider et al., 2003).

The Psychodynamic Perspective

In the 1940s and 1950s, psychodynamic theory dominated the field of psychotherapy and influenced scientific psychology and the arts. Renowned artists and writers consulted psychodynamic therapists to liberate the expression of their unconscious ideas. Today, Freud's influence is still felt, although it no longer dominates psychotherapy. Contemporary psychologists who follow theories derived from Freud are likely to call themselves *neoanalysts*.

social-cognitive theory
a school of psychology in the behaviorist tradition that includes cognitive factors in the explanation and prediction of behavior; formerly termed *social learning theory*

sociocultural perspective
the view that focuses on the roles of ethnicity, gender, culture, and socioeconomic status in behavior and mental processes

Famous neoanalysts such as Karen Horney (1885–1952) and Erik Erikson (1902–1994) focused less on the unconscious and more on conscious choice and self-direction.

Perspectives on Learning

Many contemporary psychologists study the effects of experience on behavior. Learning, to them, is the essential factor in describing, explaining, predicting, and controlling behavior. The term *learning* has different meanings to psychologists of different persuasions, however. Some students of learning find roles for consciousness and insight. Others do not. This distinction is found today among those who adhere to the behavioral and social cognitive perspectives.

What are the two major perspectives on learning? Early proponents of **behaviorism**, like John B. Watson, viewed people as doing things because of their learning histories, their situations, and rewards, not because of conscious choice. Like Watson, contemporary behaviorists emphasize environmental influences and the learning of habits through repetition and reinforcement. Social-cognitive theorists, in contrast, suggest that people can modify and create their environments. They note that people engage in intentional learning by observing others. Since the 1960s, social cognitive theorists have gained influence in the areas of personality development, psychological disorders, and psychotherapy.

The Sociocultural Perspective

The profession of psychology focuses mainly on the individual and is committed to the dignity of the individual. However, many psychologists today believe we cannot understand people's behavior and mental processes without reference to their diversity.

What is the sociocultural perspective? The **sociocultural perspective** addresses many of the ways in which people differ from one another. It studies the influences of ethnicity, gender, culture, and socioeconomic status on behavior and mental processes. Studying cultures other than their own helps psychologists

understand the roles of culture in behavior, beliefs, values, and attitudes.

Ethnicity

One kind of diversity involves people's ethnicity. Members of an ethnic group share their cultural heritage, race, language, or history. The experiences of various ethnic groups in the United States highlight the impact of social, political, and economic factors on human behavior and development (Basic Behavioral Science Task Force, 1996b).

The most well-known African American psychologists may be Kenneth Clark (1914–2005) and Mamie Phipps Clark (1917–1983). The Clarks conducted research that showed the negative effects of school segregation on African American children. In one such study, African American children were shown white and brown dolls and asked to "Give me the pretty doll," or "Give me the doll that looks bad." Most children's choices showed that they preferred the white dolls over the brown ones. The Clarks concluded that the children had swallowed society's preference for European Americans. The Clarks' research was cited by the Supreme Court in 1954 when it

DAVID BUFFINGTON/GETTY IMAGES

overturned the "separate but equal" schools doctrine that had allowed inequalities in school services for various ethnic groups.

A Latino American psychologist, Jorge Sanchez, was among the first to show how intelligence tests are culturally biased—to the disadvantage of Mexican American children. A Latina American, Lillian Comas-Díaz (e.g., 2003), edits a journal on multicultural mental health. An Asian American psychologist, Richard Suinn (Jenkins et al., 2003), studies mental health and the development of identity among Asians and Asian Americans.

Gender

Gender refers to the culturally defined concepts of masculinity and femininity. Gender is not fully defined by anatomic sex. It involves a complex web of cultural expectations and social roles that affect people's self-concepts and hopes and dreams as well as their behavior. Just as members of ethnic minority groups have experienced prejudice, so too have women.

Although American women have attended college only since 1833—when Oberlin College opened its doors to women—most American college students today are, in fact, women. Women now receive nearly three-quarters of the undergraduate and doctoral degrees in psychology (American Psychological Association, 2009a; U.S. Department of Education, 2004).

© EUDORA WELTY/CORBIS

How did research by Kenneth Clark and Mamie Phipps Clark influence a Supreme Court decision?

gender
the culturally defined concepts of *masculinity* and *femininity*

Women have made indispensable contributions to psychology. Mary Whiton Calkins (1863–1930) introduced the method of paired associates to study memory (see Chapter 7), discovered the primacy and recency effects, and engaged in research into the role of the frequency of repetition in the vividness of memories. Calkins had studied psychology at Harvard University, which she had to attend as a "guest student," because Harvard was not yet admitting women. When she completed her Ph.D. requirements, Harvard would not award her the degree because of her sex. Instead, Harvard offered to grant her a doctorate from its sister school, Radcliffe. As a form of protest, Calkins declined the offer. Even without the Ph.D., Calkins went on to become president of the American Psychological Association.

In more recent years, Mary Salter Ainsworth (1913–1999) revolutionized our understanding of attachment between parents and children by means of her cross-cultural studies. Elizabeth Loftus (e.g., Loftus, 2004; Loftus & Bernstein, 2005) has shown that our memories are not snapshots of the past. Instead, they often consist of something old (what actually happened), something new (that is, influenced by more recent events), something borrowed (for example, further shaped by our biases and prejudices), and something blue (altered by tinges of color or emotion).

The contributions of members of diverse ethnic groups and women have broadened our understanding of the influences of ethnicity and gender on behavior and mental processes. They have also increased our knowledge of differences among Europeans. For example, Southern Europeans singles (from Italy, Greece, and Portugal, for example) are more likely than Northern European singles (from the United Kingdom, France, Germany, and Scandinavia) to live with their parents until they get married (Giuliano, 2007). The researcher suggests that the family ties of Southern Europeans seem to be relatively stronger.

LO⁵ How Psychologists Study Behavior and Mental Processes

Does alcohol cause aggression? Does watching violence on TV cause children to be violent? Why do some people hardly ever think of food, whereas others are obsessed with it and snack all day? Why do some unhappy people attempt suicide, whereas others don't? How does having people of different ethnic backgrounds collaborate in their work affect feelings of prejudice?

Many of us have expressed opinions—maybe strong opinions—on questions like these. But as we saw in our discussion of people who claim to be abducted by aliens from outer space, scientists insist on evidence. Psychologists, like other scientists, use careful means to observe and measure behavior and the factors that influence behavior.

The need for evidence is one of the keys to critical thinking. Critical thinking is a life tool for all of us as well as a pathway toward scientific knowledge.

Critical Thinking

Psychologists are guided by scientific principles, and one hallmark of science is critical thinking. *What is critical thinking?* Critical thinking has many meanings. On one level, it means taking nothing for granted. It means not believing things just because they are in print or because they were uttered by authority figures or celebrities. It means not necessarily believing that it is healthful to express all of your feelings just because a friend in "therapy" urges you to do so. On another level, critical thinking refers to a process of thoughtfully analyzing and probing the questions, statements, and arguments of others.

Principles of Critical Thinking

1 *Be skeptical.* Keep an open mind. Politicians and advertisers try to persuade you. Are some of your own attitudes and beliefs superficial or unfounded? Accept nothing as the truth until you have examined the evidence.

2 *Insist on evidence.* It is not sufficient that an opinion is traditional, that it appears in print or on the Internet, or it is expressed by a doctor or a lawyer. Ask for evidence.

3 *Examine definitions of terms.* Some statements are true when a term is defined in one way but not when it is defined in another way. Consider the statement, "Head Start programs have raised children's IQs." The correctness of the statement depends on the definition of "IQ." (You will see later in the text that *IQ* is not the same thing as *intelligence.*)

4 *Examine the assumptions or premises of arguments.* Consider the statement that one cannot learn about

human beings by engaging in research with animals. One premise in the statement seems to be that human beings are not animals. We are, of course.

5 *Be cautious in drawing conclusions from evidence.* For many years, studies had shown that most clients who receive psychotherapy improve. It was therefore generally assumed that psychotherapy worked. Then a psychologist named Hans Eysenck pointed out that most psychologically troubled people who did *not* receive psychotherapy also improved. The question thus becomes whether people receiving psychotherapy are *more* likely to improve than those who do not. Current research on the effectiveness of psychotherapy therefore carefully compares the benefits of therapy techniques to the benefits of other techniques or of no treatment at all. Be especially skeptical of anecdotes. When you hear "I know someone who...," ask yourself whether this one person's reported experience is satisfactory as evidence.

6 *Consider alternative interpretations of research evidence.* Does alcohol cause aggression? Later in the chapter we will report evidence that there is a clear *connection,* or correlation, between alcohol and aggression. For example, many people who commit violent crimes have been drinking. But does the evidence show that drinking causes aggression? Might other factors, such as gender, age, or willingness to take risks, account for both drinking and aggressive behavior?

7 *Do not oversimplify.* Most human behavior involves complex interactions of genetic and environmental influences. Also consider the issue of whether psychotherapy helps people with psychological problems. A broad answer to this question—a simple yes or no—might be oversimplifying. It is more worthwhile to ask, What *type* of psychotherapy, practiced by *whom,* is most helpful for *what kind of problem?*

8 *Do not overgeneralize.* Consider the statement that one cannot learn about human beings by engaging in research with nonhuman animals. Is the truth of the matter an all or nothing issue? Are there certain kinds of information we can obtain about people from research with animals? What kinds of things are you likely to be able to learn only through research with people?

9 *Apply critical thinking to all areas of life.*

The Scientific Method

What is the scientific method? The scientific method is an organized way of using experience and testing ideas in an effort to expand and refine knowledge. Psychologists do not necessarily follow the steps of the scientific method as we might follow a recipe in a cookbook, but research is guided by certain principles.

Psychologists usually begin by *formulating a research question.* Our daily experiences, psychological theory, even folklore all help generate questions for research. Consider some questions that may arise from daily experience. Daily experience in using daycare centers may motivate us to conduct research on whether day care affects the development of social skills or the bonds of attachment between children and mothers. Social cognitive principles of observational learning may prompt research on the effects of TV violence. Research questions may also arise from common knowledge. Consider adages such as "misery loves company," "opposites attract," and "seeing is believing." Psychologists may ask, *Does misery love company? Do opposites attract? Can* people believe what they see?

A research question may be reworded as a hypothesis (see Figure 1.5). A hypothesis is a statement about behavior or mental processes that is tested through research. One hypothesis about day care might be that preschoolers who are placed in day care will acquire greater social skills in relating to peers than preschoolers who are cared for in the home.

Psychologists next examine the research question or *test the hypothesis* through controlled methods such as the experiment. For example, we could take

a group of preschoolers who attend day care and another group who do not, and introduce each to a new child in a controlled setting such as a child research center. We could then observe how children in each group interact with the new acquaintance.

Psychologists draw conclusions on the basis of their observations or findings. When their observations do not bear out their hypotheses, they may modify the theories from which the hypotheses were derived. Research findings often suggest refinements to psychological theories and, consequently, new avenues of research. In our research on day care, we would probably find that children in day care show greater social skills than children who are cared for in the home (Belsky et al., 2001).

As psychologists draw conclusions from research evidence, they are guided by principles of critical thinking. For example, they try not to confuse correlations—or associations—between findings with cause and effect. Although more aggressive children apparently spend more time watching violent TV shows, it may be erroneous to conclude from this kind of evidence that TV violence *causes* aggressive behavior. A selection factor may be at work because the children studied choose (select) for themselves what they will watch. Perhaps more aggressive children are more likely than less aggressive children to tune in to violent TV shows.

hypothesis
in psychology, a specific statement about behavior or mental processes that is tested through research

correlation
an association or relationship among variables, as we might find between height and weight or between study habits and school grades

selection factor
a source of bias that may occur in research findings when participants are allowed to choose for themselves a certain treatment in a scientific study

Figure 1.5

The Scientific Method

The scientific method is a systematic way of organizing and expanding scientific knowledge.

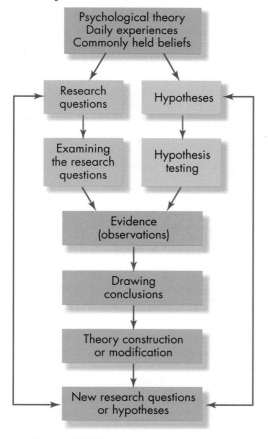

Go to CourseMate for PSYCH at www.cengagebrain.com to access an interactive version of this figure.

Samples and Populations

Consider a piece of history that never quite happened: The Republican candidate Alf Landon defeated the incumbent president, Franklin D. Roosevelt, in 1936. Or at least Landon did so in a poll conducted by a popular magazine of the day, the *Literary Digest*. In the actual election, however, Roosevelt routed Landon by a landslide of 11 million votes. In effect, the *Digest* accomplished something like this when they predicted a Landon victory. How was such a difference possible?

The *Digest*, you see, had surveyed voters by phone. Today telephone sampling is a widely practiced and reasonably legitimate polling technique.

All generalizations are dangerous, even this one.

—Alexandre Dumas

sample
part of a population

population
a complete group of organisms or events

random sample
a sample drawn so that each member of a population has an equal chance of being selected to participate

stratified sample
a sample drawn so that identified subgroups in the population are represented proportionately in the sample

volunteer bias
a source of bias or error in research reflecting the prospect that people who offer to participate in research studies differ systematically from people who do not

Truth

It is true that you could survey millions of voters and still not predict the outcome of a presidential election.

But the *Digest* poll was taken during the Great Depression, when people who had telephones were much wealthier than those who did not. People at higher income levels are also more likely to vote Republican. No surprise, then, that the overwhelming majority of those sampled said they would vote for Landon.

How do psychologists use samples to represent populations? The *Digest* poll failed because of its method of sampling. Samples must be drawn so that they accurately represent the population they are intended to reflect. Only representative samples allow us to generalize—or extend—our findings from research samples to populations.

In surveys such as that conducted by *Literary Digest,* and in other research methods, the individuals who are studied are referred to as a sample. A sample is a segment of a population (the group that is targeted for study). Psychologists and other scientists need to ensure that the people they observe represent their target population, such as U.S. voters, and not subgroups such as southern Californians or European American members of the middle class.

Does this telephone make me look rich?

Problems in Generalizing from Psychological Research

Many factors must be considered in interpreting the accuracy of the results of scientific research. One is the nature of the research sample. Later in the chapter we consider research in which the participants were drawn from a population of college men who were social drinkers. That is, they tended to drink at social gatherings but not when alone. Who do college men represent, other than themselves? To whom can we extend, or generalize, the results? For one thing, the results may not extend to women, not even to college women. In the chapter on consciousness, for example, we see that alcohol affects women more quickly than men.

Also, compared to the general adult male population, college men tend to be younger and score higher on intelligence tests. We cannot be certain that the findings extend to older men or to those with lower intelligence test scores. Social drinkers may even differ biologically and psychologically from alcoholics, who have difficulty controlling their drinking.

By and large, we must also question whether findings of research with men can be generalized to women and whether research with European American men can be extended to members of ethnic minority groups. For example, personality tests completed by European Americans and by African Americans may need to be interpreted in diverse ways if accurate conclusions are to be drawn.

Random and Stratified Sampling

One way to achieve a representative sample is by means of random sampling. In a random sample, each member of a population has an equal chance of being asked to participate. Researchers can also use a stratified sample, which is selected so that known subgroups in the population are represented proportionately in the sample. For instance, 13% of the American population is African American. A stratified sample would thus be 13% African American. As a practical matter, a large randomly selected sample will show accurate stratification. A random sample of 1,500 people will represent the broad American population reasonably well; a sample of 20,000 European Americans or men will not.

Large-scale magazine surveys of sexual behavior have asked readers to fill out and return questionnaires. Although many thousands of readers completed the questionnaires and sent them in, did the survey respondents represent the American population? Probably not. These studies and similar ones may have been influenced by volunteer bias. People

PHOTO BY H. ARMSTRONG ROBERTS/RETROFILE/GETTY IMAGES

who offer or volunteer to participate in research studies differ systematically from people who do not. In the case of research on sexual behavior, volunteers may represent subgroups of the population—or of readers of the magazines in question—who are willing to disclose intimate information and therefore may also be likely to be more liberal in their sexual behavior (Rathus et al., 2008). Volunteers may also be more interested in research than other people, as well as have more spare time. How might such volunteers differ from the population at large? How might such differences slant or bias the research outcomes?

Methods of Observation

Many people consider themselves experts in psychology. How many times have you or someone else been eager to share a life experience that "proves" some point about human nature?

We see much during our lifetimes, but our personal observations tend to be fleeting and unsystematic. We sift through experience for the things that interest us. We often ignore the obvious because it does not fit our assumptions about the way things ought to be. Scientists, however, have devised more controlled ways of observing others. *What methods of observation are used by psychologists?* In this section we consider three methods of observation widely used by psychologists and other behavioral scientists: the case study, the survey, and naturalistic observation.

Case Study

Case studies collect information about individuals and small groups. Many case studies are clinical; that is, they are detailed descriptions of a person's psychological problems and how a psychologist treated the problems. Case studies are sometimes used to investigate rare occurrences, as in the case of Chris Sizemore, who was diagnosed with multiple personalities (technically termed *dissociative identity disorder*). A psychiatrist identified three distinct personalities in Chris. Her story was made into a more theatrical movie called *The Three Faces of Eve.* One personality, "Eve White," was a mousy, well-meaning woman who had two other "personalities" inside her. One was "Eve Black," a promiscuous personality who emerged now and then to take control of her behavior. The third personality, "Jane," was a well-adjusted woman who integrated parts of Eve White and Eve Black.

Case studies have various sources of inaccuracy. People's memories have gaps and factual inaccuracies (Loftus, 2004). People may also distort their pasts to please the interviewer or because they want to remember things in certain ways.

Interviewers may also have certain expectations and subtly encourage participants to fill in gaps in ways that are consistent with these expectations. Psychoanalysts, for example, have been criticized for guiding people who seek their help into viewing their own lives from the Freudian perspective (Hergenhahn, 2005). No wonder, then, that many people provide "evidence" that is consistent with psychodynamic theory—such as, "My parents' strictness during toilet training is the source of my compulsive neatness." However, interviewers and other kinds of researchers who hold *any* theoretical viewpoint run the risk of indirectly prodding people into saying what they want to hear.

The Survey

Just as computers and pollsters predict election results and report national opinion on the basis of scientifically selected samples, psychologists conduct surveys to learn about behavior and mental processes that cannot be observed in the natural setting or studied experimentally. Psychologists conducting surveys may employ questionnaires and interviews or examine public records. One of the advantages of the survey is that by distributing questionnaires and analyzing answers with a computer, psychologists can study many thousands of people at a time.

The best-known surveys of all time, the so-called Kinsey reports, provided surprising information during the middle of the 20th century, a time of relative sexual repression in the United States. Alfred Kinsey and his colleagues published two surveys of sexual behavior based on extensive interviews: *Sexual Behavior in the Human Male* (1948)

case study
a carefully drawn biography that may be obtained through interviews, questionnaires, and psychological tests

survey
a method of scientific investigation in which a large sample of people answer questions about their atttudes or behavior

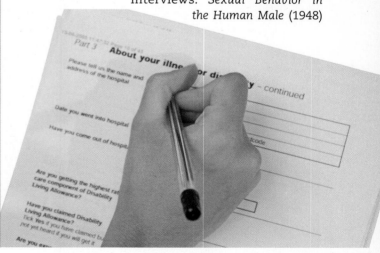

naturalistic observation a scientific method in which organisms are observed in their natural environments

correlation coefficient a number between +1.00 and −1.00 that expresses the strength and direction (positive or negative) of the relationship between two variables

and *Sexual Behavior in the Human Female* (1953). The nation was shocked to hear that masturbation among his sample of men was virtually universal in a day when masturbation was still widely thought to impair health. During this time, it was also widely believed that virtually all single women were virgins. Nonetheless, Kinsey found that about 1 woman in 3 who was still single at age 25 reported having engaged in sexual intercourse.

Surveys, like case studies, also have sources of inaccuracy. People may recall their behavior inaccurately or lie about it. Some people try to ingratiate themselves with their interviewers by answering in what they think to be the socially desirable direction. The Kinsey studies all relied on male interviewers, for example. It has been speculated that female interviewees might have been more open with female interviewers. Similar problems may occur when interviewers and the people surveyed are from different ethnic backgrounds. Other people may falsify their attitudes and exaggerate their problems to draw attention to themselves or to intentionally foul up the results.

Another bias in the case study and survey methods is social desirability. That is, many people involved in research studies tend to tell the interviewer what they think the interviewer would like to hear and not what they really think. For example, if people brushed their teeth as often as they claimed, and used the amount of toothpaste they indicated, three times as much toothpaste would be sold in the United States than is actually sold. People also appear to overreport church attendance and to underreport abortions (Barringer, 1993).

Naturalistic Observation

You use naturalistic observation—that is, you observe people in their natural habitats—every day. So do psychologists and other scientists. Naturalistic observation has the advantage of allowing psychologists and other scientists to observe behavior where it happens, or "in the field." Observers use unobtrusive measures to avoid interfering with the behaviors they are observing. For example, Jane Goodall has observed the behavior of chimpanzees in their natural environment to learn about their social behavior, sexual behavior, use of tools, and other facts of chimp life. Her observations have shown us that (1) we were incorrect to think that only humans use tools; and (2) kissing on the lips, as a greeting, is apparently used by chimpanzees as well as by humans (Goodall, 2000).

Correlation

Are people with higher intelligence more likely to do well in school? Are people with a stronger need for achievement likely to climb higher up the corporate ladder? What is the relationship between stress and health?

Such questions are often answered by the mathematical method of correlation. *What is the correlational method?* Correlation follows observation. By using the correlational method, psychologists investigate whether an observed behavior or a measured trait is related to, or correlated with, another. Consider the variables of intelligence and academic performance. These variables are assigned numbers such as intelligence test scores and academic averages. Then the numbers are mathematically related and expressed as a correlation coefficient (r). A correlation coefficient is a number that varies from $r = +1.00$ to $r = -1.00$.

In the film biography *Kinsey*, Liam Neeson played Alfred Kinsey, the scientist who investigated human sexuality during a time when even talking about sex was considered indecent.

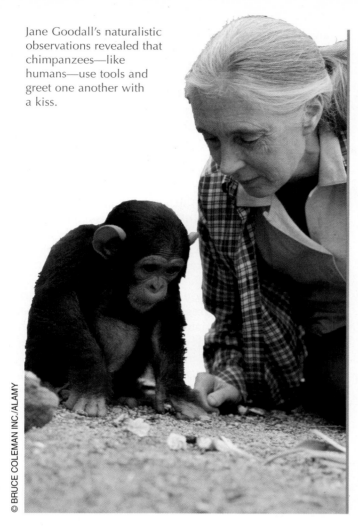

Jane Goodall's naturalistic observations revealed that chimpanzees—like humans—use tools and greet one another with a kiss.

© BRUCE COLEMAN INC./ALAMY

Studies report *positive correlations* between intelligence test scores and academic achievement, as measured, for example, by grade point averages. Generally speaking, the higher people score on intelligence tests, the better their academic performance is likely to be. The scores attained on intelligence tests tend to be positively correlated (about $r = +.30$ to $r = +.60$) with academic achievement (see the first panel in Figure 1.6) (Duckworth & Seligman, 2005; Mayes & Calhoun, 2007; Neisser et al., 1996). But factors *other* than performance on intelligence tests also contribute to academic success. These include achievement motivation, self-discipline, and adjustment (Duckworth & Seligman, 2005).

Many correlations are negative; that is, as one variable increases, the other variable decreases. There is a *negative correlation* between stress and health. As the amount of stress affecting us increases, the functioning of our immune system decreases (see Figure 1.6). Under high levels of stress, many people show poorer health.

What kinds of correlations (positive or negative) would you expect to find among behavior patterns such as the following: Churchgoing and crime? Language ability and musical ability? Level of education and incidence of teenage pregnancy? Grades in school and delinquency? Why?

Correlational research may suggest, but does not prove, cause and effect. For example, it may seem logical to assume that high intelligence makes it possible for children to profit from education. Research has also

JUPITERIMAGES

Figure 1.6

Positive and Negative Correlations

When there is a positive correlation between variables, as there is between intelligence and achievement, one increases as the other increases. By and large, the higher people score on intelligence tests, the better their academic performance is likely to be, as in the diagram on the left. (Each dot represents an individual's intelligence test score and grade point average.) But there is a negative correlation between stress and health. As the amount of stress we experience increases, the functioning of our immune system tends to decrease.

Positive correlation, as found between intelligence and academic achievement

Negative correlation, as found between stress and functioning of the immune system

What kind of correlation would you expect between teenagers' grades in school and their numbers of delinquent acts? Why?

experiment
a scientific method that seeks to confirm cause-and-effect relationships by introducing independent variables and observing their effects on dependent variables

independent variable
a condition in a scientific study that is manipulated so that its effects may be observed

dependent variable
a measure of an assumed effect of an independent variable

experimental groups
in experiments, groups whose members obtain the treatment

control groups
in experiments, groups whose members do not obtain the treatment, while other conditions are held constant

shown, however, that education contributes to higher scores on intelligence tests. Preschoolers who are placed in stimulating Head Start programs later attain higher scores on intelligence tests than age mates who did not have this experience. The relationship between intelligence and academic performance may not be as simple as we might think. What of the link between stress and health? Does stress impair health, or is it possible that people in poorer health encounter more stress?

The Experimental Method

What is the experimental method? Most psychologists agree that the preferred method for answering questions about cause and effect is the experiment. In an experiment, a group of subjects receives a *treatment,* such as a dose of alcohol, a change in room temperature, perhaps an injection of a drug. The subjects are then observed carefully to determine whether the treatment makes a difference in their behavior. Does alcohol alter the ability to take tests, for example? What about differences in room temperatures and level of background noise?

Experiments are used when possible because they allow psychologists to control the experiences of subjects and draw conclusions about cause and effect. A psychologist may theorize that alcohol leads to aggression because it reduces fear of consequences. She or he may then hypothesize that a treatment in which subjects receive a specified dosage of alcohol will lead to increases in aggression. Let us follow the example of the effects of alcohol on aggression to further our understanding of the experimental method.

Independent and Dependent Variables

In an experiment to determine whether alcohol causes aggression, subjects are given an amount of

Using an experimental group and a control group enhances researchers' ability to draw conclusions about cause and effect.

alcohol and its effects are measured. In this case, alcohol is an independent variable. The presence of an independent variable is manipulated by the experimenters so that its effects may be determined. The independent variable of alcohol may be administered at different levels, or doses, from none or very little to enough to cause intoxication or drunkenness.

The measured results, or outcomes, in an experiment are called dependent variables. The presence of dependent variables presumably depends on the independent variables. In an experiment to determine whether alcohol influences aggression, aggressive behavior would be a dependent variable. Other dependent variables of interest might include sexual arousal, visual motor coordination, and performance on cognitive tasks such as defining words.

In an experiment on the relationships between temperature and aggression, temperature would be an independent variable and aggressive behavior would be a dependent variable. We could set temperatures from below freezing to blistering hot, and study its effects on aggression. We could also use a second independent variable such as social provocation; we could insult some participants but not others and see whether insults affect their level of aggression. This method would allow us to study the ways in which two independent variables—temperature and social provocation—affect aggression, by themselves and together.

Experimental and Control Groups

Ideal experiments use "experimental groups" and "control groups." Participants in experimental groups obtain the treatment. Members of control groups do not. Every effort is made to ensure that all other conditions are held constant for both groups. This method enhances the researchers' ability to draw conclusions about cause and effect. The researchers can be more confident that outcomes of the experiment are caused by the treatments and not by chance factors or chance fluctuations in behavior.

For example, in an experiment on the effects of alcohol on aggression, members of the experimental group would ingest alcohol, and members of the control group would not. The researcher would then measure how much aggression was expressed by each group.

Blinds and Double Blinds

One classic experiment on the effects of alcohol on aggression (Boyatzis, 1974) reported that men at parties where beer and liquor were served acted more aggressively than men at parties where only soft drinks were served. But participants in the experimental group *knew* they had drunk alcohol, and those in the control group *knew* they had not. Aggression that appeared to result from alcohol might thus have reflected the participants' *expectations* about the effects of alcohol. People tend to act in stereotypical ways when they believe they have been drinking alcohol. For instance, men tend to become less anxious in social situations, more aggressive, and more sexually aroused. To what extent do these behavior patterns reflect the direct effects of alcohol on the body, and to what extent do they affect people's *beliefs* about the effects of alcohol?

In medicine, physicians sometimes give patients placebos (a fake treatment, often sugar pills, that has the appearance of being genuine) when the patient insists on a medical cure but the physician does not believe that one is necessary. When patients report that placebos have helped them, it is because they expected the pills to be of help and not because of the biochemical effects of the pills. Placebos are not limited to pills made of sugar. As we will see, participants in psychological experiments can be given placebos such as tonic water, but if the participants think they have drunk alcohol, we can conclude that

> The **men's** *belief* about what they drank affected their aggressive behavior more than what they actually consumed.

changes in their behavior stem from their beliefs about the effects of alcohol, not from the alcohol itself.

Well-designed experiments control for the effects of expectations by creating conditions under which participants are unaware of, or blind to, the treatment. Placebos are one way of keeping participants blind to whether they have received a treatment. Yet researchers may also have expectations. They may be "rooting for" a certain treatment. For example, tobacco company executives may wish to show that cigarette smoking is harmless. In such cases, it is useful if the people measuring the experimental outcomes are unaware of which participants have received the treatment. Studies in which neither the participant nor the experimenters know who has obtained the treatment are called double-blind studies. The Food and Drug Administration requires double-blind studies before it allows the marketing of new drugs. In a double-blind study, the drug and the placebo look and taste alike. Experimenters assign the drug or placebo to participants at random. Neither the participants nor the observers know who is taking the drug and who is taking the placebo. After the final measurements have been made, a neutral panel (a group of people who have no personal stake in the outcome of the study) judges whether the

placebo
a bogus treatment that has the appearance of being genuine

blind
in experimental terminology, unaware of whether or not one has received a treatment

double-blind study
a study in which neither the subjects nor the observers who has received the treatment

Figure 1.7

The Experimental Conditions in the Lang Study

The taste of vodka cannot be discerned when vodka is mixed with tonic water. For this reason, it was possible for subjects in the Lang study on the effects of alcohol to be kept "blind" as to whether or not they had actually drunk alcohol. Blind studies allow psychologists to control for the effects of subjects' expectations.

	Participants' beliefs	
Vodka and tonic water	Believed drinking vodka	Believed drinking tonic water only
Tonic water only	Believed drinking vodka	Believed drinking tonic water only

Participants' actual drinks

PURESTOCK/GETTY IMAGES

effects of the drug differed from those of the placebo.

In one classic double-blind study on the effects of alcohol, Alan Lang and his colleagues (1975) pretested a cocktail of vodka and tonic water to make certain that it could not be discriminated by taste from tonic water alone. They recruited college male social drinkers as participants. Some of the men drank vodka and tonic water. Others drank tonic water only. Of those who drank vodka, half were misled into believing they had drunk tonic water only (see Figure 1.7 on page 22). Of those who drank tonic water only, half were misled into believing their drink contained vodka. Thus, half the participants were blind to their treatment. Experimenters who measured the men's aggressive responses were also blind concerning which participants had drunk vodka.

The research team found that men who believed that they had drunk vodka responded "more aggressively" (that is, they chose a higher level of shock and pressed a lever to deliver it) to a provocation than men who believed that they had drunk tonic water only. The actual content of the drink was immaterial. That is, the men's *belief* about what they drank affected their aggressive behavior more than what they actually consumed. The results of the Lang study differ dramatically from those reported by Boyatzis, perhaps because the Boyatzis study did not control for the effects of expectations or beliefs about alcohol.

Truth

It is true that neither the participants nor the researchers know who is receiving the real treatment in many experiments.

Ethics of Research with Humans

If the Lang group were running their experiment today rather than in the 1970s, they might have been denied permission to do so by a university ethics review committee. Why? Because the researchers in the Lang study gave some participants alcohol to drink and deceived the entire group about the purposes and methods of the study. Was their method ethical? We'll return to this question, but let's first address a broader one. *What ethical issues affect research and practice with humans?*

Psychologists adhere to a number of ethical standards that are intended to promote individual dignity, human welfare, and scientific integrity. The standards are also intended to ensure that psychologists do not engage in harmful research methods or treatments. In virtually all institutional settings, including colleges, hospitals, and research foundations, ethics review committees help researchers consider the potential harm of their methods and review proposed studies according to ethical guidelines. When the committees find that proposed research might be unacceptably harmful to subjects, they may withhold approval. The committees also weigh the potential benefits of the research against the potential harm.

Today individuals must provide informed consent before they participate in research (American Psychological Association, 2002). A general overview of the research and the opportunity to choose not to participate apparently give potential participants a sense of control and decreases stress (Sieber, 2004). Is there a way in which participants in the Lang study could have provided informed consent? What do you think?

Psychologists keep the records of research participants and clients confidential because they respect people's privacy and because people are more likely to express their true thoughts and feelings when researchers or therapists keep them confidential (Smith, 2003a, 2003c). Sometimes conflicts of interest arise, as when a client threatens to harm someone and the psychologist feels obligated to warn the victim (Follingstad & McCormick, 2002).

Some studies could not be carried out if participants knew what the researchers were trying to learn, or which treatment they had received (e.g., a new medicine or a sugar pill). As you can imagine, psychologists have long debated the ethics of deceiving participants. According to the American Psychological Association's (2002) *Ethical Principles of Psychologists and Code of Conduct,* psychologists may use deception only when they believe the benefits of the research outweigh its potential harm, when they believe the individuals might have been willing to participate if they had understood the benefits of the research, and when participants are debriefed. Debriefing means that the purposes and methods of the research are explained afterward.

Return to the Lang (Lang et al., 1975) study on alcohol and aggression. In this study, the researchers (1) misinformed participants about the beverage they were drinking and (2) misled them into believing they were giving other subjects electric shock when they were actually pressing switches on an unconnected control board. (*Aggression* was defined as pressing these switches.) In the study, students who believed they had drunk vodka selected higher levels of shock than students who believed they had not.

Ethics of Research with Animals

Psychologists and other scientists may use animals to conduct research that cannot be carried out with humans. For example, experiments on the effects of early separation from the mother have been done with monkeys and other animals. Such research has helped psychologists investigate the formation of attachment bonds between parent and child.

What ethical issues affect research with animals? Experiments with infant monkeys highlight some of the ethical issues faced by psychologists and other scientists who contemplate potentially harmful research. Psychologists and biologists who study the workings of the brain destroy sections of the brains of laboratory animals to learn how they influence behavior. For example, a lesion in one part of a brain structure causes a rat to overeat. A lesion elsewhere causes the rat to go on a crash diet. Psychologists generalize to humans from experiments such as these in the hope of finding solutions to problems such as eating disorders. Proponents of the use of animals in research argue that many advances in medicine and psychology could not have taken place without them (Bekoff, 2002). For example, we would know less about how drugs affect tumors or the brain.

According to the ethical guidelines of the American Psychological Association, animals may be harmed only when there is no alternative and when researchers believe that the benefits of the research justify the harm (American Psychological Association, 2002; Smith, 2003b, 2003c).

Now that we have an overview of psychology as a science, we will move on to the connections between psychology and biology in Chapter 2. Psychologists assume that our behaviors and our mental processes are related to biological events. In Chapter 2 we consider the evidence for this assumption.

© BONKERSABOUTSCIENCE / ALAMY

Percent of new doctoral degrees in psychology earned by women > **78**

Percent of American population that is African American > **13**

Year that Wilhelm Wundt established the first psych lab > **1879**

Variation of a correlation coefficient > **−1.00 and +1.00**

0 < As a correlation coefficient, means that there is no linear relationship between the variables

---

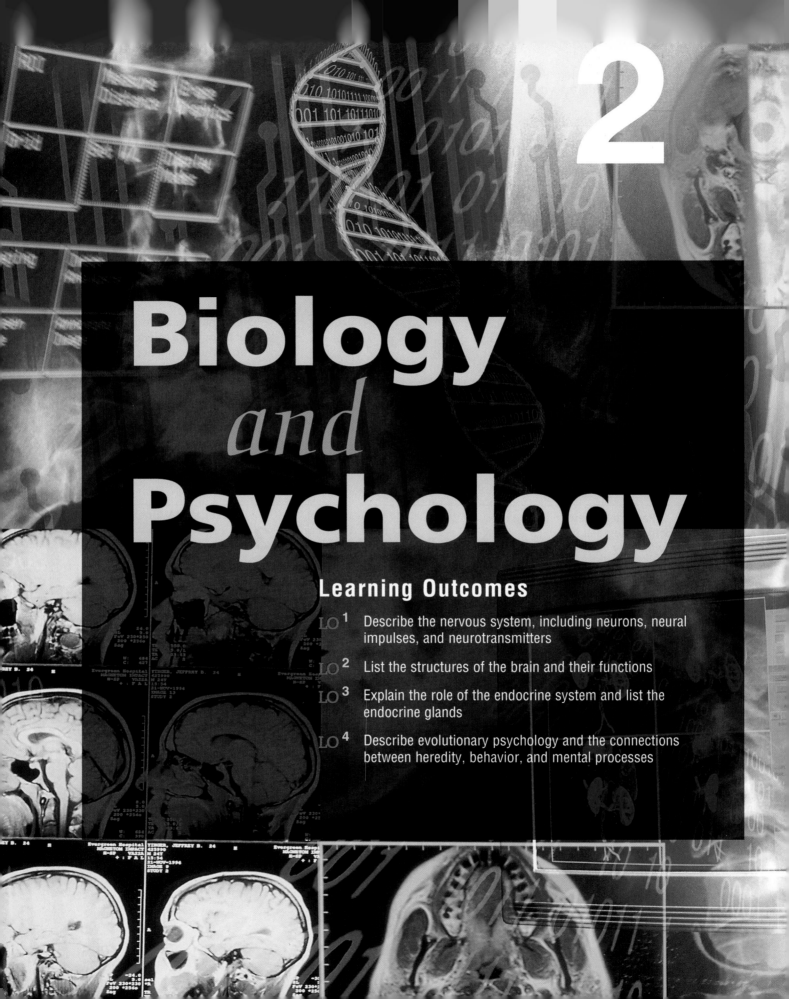

2

Biology *and* Psychology

Learning Outcomes

LO **1** Describe the nervous system, including neurons, neural impulses, and neurotransmitters

LO **2** List the structures of the brain and their functions

LO **3** Explain the role of the endocrine system and list the endocrine glands

LO **4** Describe evolutionary psychology and the connections between heredity, behavior, and mental processes

"*Gage is no longer Gage.*"

"Gage is no longer Gage," said those who had known him before the accident.

There are many key characters in the history of psychology, and some of them did not arrive there intentionally. One of these was a promising railroad worker who was helping our young nation stretch from coast to coast. His name was Phineas Gage. Gage was highly admired by his friends and his coworkers. But all that changed one day in 1848. While he was tamping down the blasting powder for a dynamite charge, Gage accidentally set the powder off. The inch-thick metal tamping rod shot upward through his cheek and brain and out the top of his head.

If the trajectory of the rod had been slightly different, Gage would have died. Although Gage fell back in a heap, he was miraculously alive. His coworkers watched in shock as he stood up a few moments later and spoke. While the local doctor marveled at the hole through Gage's head, Gage asked when he'd be able to return to work. Two months later, Gage's external wounds had healed, but the psychological aspects of the wound were now obvious. His former employer, who had regarded him as "the most efficient and capable foreman in their employ previous to his injury" (Harlow, 1868), refused to rehire him because he had changed so much:

The equilibrium or balance, so to speak, between his intellectual faculties and animal propensities, seems to have been destroyed. He is . . . irreverent, indulging at times in the grossest profanity (which was not previously his custom). [He showed little consideration for other people, was] impatient of restraint or advice when it conflicts with his desires . . . obstinate, yet capricious and vacillating, devising many plans of future operation, which are no sooner arranged than they are abandoned in turn for others . . . But all had not been lost in Gage's brain. In fact, many of his intellectual skills were just fine, apparently untouched.

Generations of researchers—psychologists, physicians, biologists, neuroscientists—have wondered how the changes in Gage's

Truth or Fiction?

What do you think?

Folklore, common sense, or nonsense? Place a T for "True" or F for "False" on the lines provided (you'll learn the answers as you read through the text).

__ A single cell can stretch all the way from your spine to your toe.

__ Messages travel in the brain by means of electricity.

__ A brain cell can send out hundreds of messages each second— and manage to catch some rest in between.

__ Fear can give you indigestion.

__ The human brain is larger than that of any other animal.

__ If a surgeon were to stimulate a certain part of your brain electrically, you might swear that someone had stroked your leg.

__ Charles Darwin was nearly excluded from the voyage that led to the development of his theory of evolution because the captain of the ship did not like the shape of his nose.

BSIP / PHOTO RESEARCHERS, INC.

PETE SALOUTOS / CORBIS

neuron
a specialized cell of the nervous system that transmits messages

glial cells
cells that nourish and insulate neurons, direct their growth, and remove waste products from the nervous system

personality might have been caused by the damage to his brain. Perhaps the trajectory of the rod spared parts of the frontal lobes that are involved in language and movement but damaged areas connected with personality and emotional response (Damasio, 2000; Wagar & Thagard, 2004).

In this chapter, we will learn about the frontal lobes of the brain and much more. We will travel from the small to the large—from the microscopic brain cells that hold and transmit information, to the visible structures that provide the basis for functions such as memory, speech, sensation, thought, planning, and voluntary movement.

LO¹ The Nervous System: On Being Wired

The nervous system is a system of nerves involved in thought processes, heartbeat, visual-motor coordination, and so on. The nervous system contains the brain, the spinal cord, and other parts that make it possible for us to receive information from the world outside and to act on that world.

The nervous system is composed of cells, most of which are neurons, which is where we will begin our study of the nervous system.

Neurons: Into the Fabulous Forest

Within our brains lies a fabulous forest of nerve cells, or neurons. *What are neurons?* Neurons are cells that can be visualized as having branches, trunks, and roots—something like trees. As we voyage through this forest, we see that many nerve cells lie alongside one another like a thicket of trees. But neurons can also lie end to end, with their "roots" intertwined with the "branches" of the neurons that lie below. Neurons receive "messages" from a number of sources such as light, other neurons, and pressure on the skin, and they can pass these messages along in a complex biological dance.

We are born with more than 100 billion neurons. Most of them are found in the brain. The nervous system also contains **glial cells**. Glial cells remove dead neurons and waste products from the nervous system, nourish and insulate neurons, and enable them to send messages in waves. But neurons occupy center stage in the nervous system. The messages transmitted by neurons somehow account for phenomena ranging from the perception of an itch from a mosquito bite to the coordination of a skier's vision and muscles to the composition of a concerto to the solution of an algebraic equation.

© KUS/PLAINPICTURE/CORBIS

SOURCE: FROM WEITEN. PSYCHOLOGY, 8E. COPYRIGHT © 2010 WADSWORTH, A PART OF CENGAGE LEARNING, INC. REPRODUCED BY PERMISSION. WWW.CENGAGE.COM.PERMISSIONS.

Figure 2.1

The Anatomy of a Neuron

"Messages" enter neurons through dendrites, are transmitted along the trunk-like axon, and then are sent from axon terminal buttons to muscles, glands, and other neurons. Axon terminal buttons contain sacs of chemicals called *neurotransmitters*. Neurotransmitters are released into the synaptic cleft, where many of them bind to receptor sites on the dendrites of the receiving neuron.

Go to CourseMate for PSYCH at www.cengagebrain.com to access an interactive version of this figure.

Neurons vary according to their functions and their location. Neurons in the brain may be only a fraction of an inch in length, whereas others in the legs are several feet long. Most neurons include a cell body, dendrites, and an axon (see Figure 2.1). The cell body contains the core or *nucleus* of the cell. The nucleus uses oxygen and nutrients to generate the energy needed to carry out the work of the cell. Anywhere from a few to several hundred short fibers, or dendrites, extend like roots from the cell body to receive incoming messages from thousands of adjoining neurons. Each neuron has an axon that extends like a trunk from the cell body. Axons are very thin, but those that carry messages from the toes to the spinal cord extend several feet.

Like tree trunks, axons can branch off in different directions. Axons end in small bulb-shaped structures called *terminals* or *terminal buttons*. Neurons carry messages in one direction only: from the dendrites or cell body through the axon to the axon terminals. The messages are then transmitted from the terminal buttons to other neurons, muscles, or glands.

As a child matures, the axons of neurons become longer, and the dendrites and terminals proliferate, creating vast interconnected networks for the transmission of complex messages. The number of glial cells also increases as the nervous system develops, contributing to its dense appearance.

Myelin

The axons of many neurons are wrapped tightly with white, fatty myelin that makes them look like strings of sausages under the microscope. The fat insulates the axon from electrically charged atoms, or ions, found in the fluids that surround the nervous system. The myelin sheath minimizes leakage of the electrical current being carried along the axon, thereby allowing messages to be conducted more efficiently.

Myelination is part of the maturation process that leads to the child's ability to crawl and walk during the first year. Infants are not physiologically "ready" to engage in visual–motor coordination and other activities until the coating process reaches certain levels. In people with the disease multiple sclerosis, myelin is replaced with a hard fibrous tissue that throws off the timing of nerve impulses and disrupts muscular control.

Afferent and Efferent Neurons

If someone steps on your toes, the sensation is registered by receptors or sensory neurons near the surface of your skin. Then it is transmitted to the spinal cord and brain through afferent neurons, which are perhaps two to three feet long. In the brain, subsequent messages might be conveyed by associative neurons that are only a few thousandths of an inch long. You experience the pain through this process and perhaps entertain some rather nasty thoughts about the perpetrator, who is now apologizing and begging for understanding. Long before you arrive at any logical conclusions, however, motor neurons (efferent neurons) send messages to your foot so that you withdraw it and begin an impressive hopping routine. Other efferent neurons stimulate glands so that your heart is beating more rapidly, you are sweating, and the hair on the back of your arms has become erect! Being a good sport, you say, "Oh, it's nothing." But considering all the neurons involved, it really is something, isn't it?

In case you think that afferent and efferent neurons will be hard to distinguish because they sound pretty much the SAME to you, remember that they *are* the "SAME." That is, Sensory Afferent, and Motor Efferent.

The Neural Impulse: "The Body Electric"[1]

In the 18th century, the Italian physiologist Luigi Galvani (1737–1798) conducted a shocking experiment in a rainstorm. While his neighbors had the sense to remain indoors, Galvani and his wife were out on the porch connecting lightning rods to the heads of dissected frogs whose legs were connected by wires to a well of water. When lightning blazed above, the frogs' muscles contracted. Galvani was demonstrating that the

⊛⊛⊛
[1] From Walt Whitman's *Leaves of Grass*.

> ### Truth
> It is true that a single cell can stretch all the way from your spine to your toe.

dendrites
rootlike structures, attached to the cell body of a neuron, that receive impulses from other neurons

axon
a long, thin part of a neuron that transmits impulses to other neurons from branching structures called *terminal buttons*

myelin
a fatty substance that encases and insulates axons, facilitating transmission of neural impulses

afferent neurons
neurons that transmit messages from sensory receptors to the spinal cord and brain. Also called *sensory neurons*

efferent neurons
neurons that transmit messages from the brain or spinal cord to muscles and glands. Also called *motor neurons*

messages (**neural impulses**) that travel along neurons are electrochemical in nature.

What are neural impulses? Neural impulses are messages that travel within neurons at somewhere between 2 (in nonmyelinated neurons) and 225 miles an hour (in myelinated neurons). This speed is not impressive when compared with that of an electrical current in a toaster oven or a lamp, which can travel at close to the speed of light—over 186,000 miles per second. Distances in the body are short, however, and a message will travel from a toe to the brain in perhaps 1/50th of a second.

An Electrochemical Voyage

The process by which neural impulses travel is electrochemical. Chemical changes take place within neurons that cause an electrical charge to be transmitted along their lengths. Neurons and body fluids contain ions—positively or negatively charged atoms. In a resting state—that is, when a neuron is not being stimulated by its neighbors—negatively charged chloride (Cl⁻) ions are plentiful within the neuron, contributing to an overall negative charge in relation to the outside. The difference in electrical charge readies (**polarizes**) a neuron for firing by creating an internal negative charge in relation to the

body fluid outside the cell membrane. The electrical potential across the neural membrane when it is not responding to other neurons—its **resting potential**—is about –70 millivolts in relation to the body fluid outside the cell membrane.

When an area on the surface of the resting neuron is adequately stimulated by other neurons, the cell membrane in the area changes its permeability to allow positively charged sodium ions to enter. Thus the area of entry becomes positively charged, or **depolarized** with respect to the outside (see Figure 2.2A). The permeability of the cell membrane then changes again, allowing no more sodium ions to enter (see Figure 2.2B).

The electrical impulse that provides the basis for the conduction of a neural impulse along an axon of a neuron is termed its **action potential**. The inside of the cell axon at the disturbed area has an action potential of 110 millivolts. This action potential, added to the –70 millivolts that characterizes the resting potential, brings the membrane voltage to a positive charge of about +30 to +40 millivolts (see Figure 2.3). This inner change causes the next section of the cell to become permeable to sodium ions. At the same time, other positively charged (potassium) ions are being pumped out of the area of the cell that was previously affected, which returns the area to its resting potential. In this way, the neural impulse is transmitted continuously along an axon. Because the impulse is created anew as it progresses, its strength does not change.

Firing: How Messages Voyage from Neuron to Neuron

The conduction of the neural impulse along the length of a neuron is what is meant by *firing*. When a rifle fires, it sends a bullet speeding through its barrel and discharges it at more than 1,000 feet per second. *What happens when a neuron fires?* Neurons also fire, but instead of a barrel, a neuron has an axon. Instead of discharging a bullet, it releases neurotransmitters.

Some neurons fire in less than 1/1,000th of a second. When they fire,

Figure 2.2

The Neural Impulse

When a section of a neuron is stimulated by other neurons, the cell membrane becomes permeable to sodium ions so that an action potential of about 40 millivolts is induced. This action potential is transmitted along the axon.

A. During an action potential, sodium gates in the neuron membrane open and sodium ions enter the axon, bringing a positive charge with them.

B. After an action potential occurs, the sodium gates close at that point, and open at the next point along the axon. When the sodium gates close, potassium gates open and potassium ions flow out of the axon, carrying a positive charge with them.

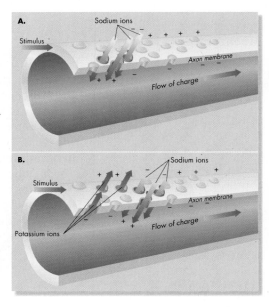

Truth

It is true that messages travel in the brain by means of electricity.
These are messages *within* neurons.
Communication *between* neurons, however, is carried out quite differently.

Figure 2.3

Changes in Electrical Charges as a Neural Impulse Is Transmitted Across an Axon

The resting potential of a segment of a cell axon is about −70 millivolts. But the inside of the cell axon at the disturbed area has an action potential of about 110 millivolts. When we add this figure to the −70 millivolts that characterizes the resting potential, we bring the membrane voltage to a positive charge of about +30 to +40 millivolts. This inner change causes the next section of the cell to become permeable to sodium ions. In this way, the neural impulse is transmitted continuously along an axon.

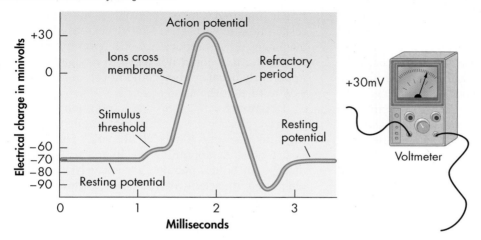

all-or-none principle
the fact that a neuron fires an impulse of the same strength whenever its action potential is triggered

refractory period
a phase following firing during which a neuron is less sensitive to messages from other neurons and will not fire

synapse
a junction between the axon terminals of one neuron and the dendrites or cell body of another neuron

neurotransmitters
chemical substances involved in the transmission of neural impulses from one neuron to another

neurons transmit messages to other neurons, muscles, or glands. However, neurons will not fire unless the incoming messages combine to reach a certain strength, which is defined as the *threshold* at which a neuron will fire. A weak message may cause a temporary shift in electrical charge at some point along the cell membrane, but this charge will dissipate if the neuron is not stimulated to its threshold.

Not only can a neuron fire in less than 1/1,000th of a second, but a neuron may also transmit several hundred messages each second. Every time a neuron fires, it transmits an impulse of the same strength. This occurrence is known as the **all-or-none principle**. That is, either a neuron fires or it doesn't. Neurons fire more often when they have been stimulated by larger numbers of other neurons. Stronger stimuli cause more frequent firing, but again, the strength of each firing remains the same.

For a few thousandths of a second after firing, a neuron is in a **refractory period**; that is, it is insensitive to messages from other neurons and will not fire. This period is a time of recovery during which sodium is prevented from passing through the neuronal membrane. Because such periods of "recovery" might occur hundreds of times per second, it seems a rapid recovery and a short rest indeed.

Truth

It is true that a single brain cell can send out hundreds of messages each second—and manage to catch some rest in between.

The Synapse: On Being Well-Connected

A neuron relays its message to another neuron across a junction called a **synapse**. *What is a synapse?* A synapse consists of an axon terminal button from the transmitting neuron, a dendrite, or the body of a receiving neuron, and a fluid-filled gap between the two that is called the *synaptic cleft* (see Figure 2.1). Although the neural impulse is electrical, it does not jump across the synaptic cleft like a spark. Instead, when a nerve impulse reaches a synapse, axon terminals release chemicals into the synaptic cleft like myriad ships being cast into the sea. Scientists have identified a few dozen of these chemicals to date. In the following section, we consider a few that are usually of the greatest interest to psychologists.

Neurotransmitters: The Chemical Keys to Communication

Sacs called synaptic vesicles in the axon terminals contain neurotransmitters. When a neural impulse (action potential) reaches the axon terminal, the vesicles release varying amounts of **neurotransmitters**—the chemical keys to communication—into the synaptic cleft. From there, they influence the receiving neuron. *Which neurotransmitters are of interest to psychologists? What do they do?*

Dozens of neurotransmitters have been identified. Each has its own chemical structure, and each can fit into a specifically tailored harbor, or receptor site, on the receiving cell. The analogy of a key fitting into a lock is often used to describe this process. Once released, not all molecules of a neurotransmitter find their way into receptor sites of other neurons. "Loose" neurotransmitters are usually either broken down or reabsorbed by the axon terminal (a process called *reuptake*).

Some neurotransmitters act to *excite* other neurons—that is, to cause other neurons to fire. Other neurotransmitters act to *inhibit* receiving neurons. That is, they prevent the neurons from firing. The sum of the stimulation—excitatory and inhibitory—determines whether a neuron will fire and, if so, when neurotransmitters will be released.

Neurotransmitters are involved in physical processes such as muscle contraction and psychological processes such as thoughts and emotions. Excesses or deficiencies of neurotransmitters have been linked to psychological disorders such as depression and schizophrenia. Let us consider the effects of some neurotransmitters that are of interest to psychologists: acetylcholine (ACh), dopamine, norepinephrine, serotonin, GABA, and endorphins.

Acetylcholine (ACh) controls muscle contractions. It is excitatory at synapses between nerves and muscles that involve voluntary movement but inhibitory at the heart and some other locations. The effects of *curare* highlight the functioning of ACh. Curare is a poison that is extracted from plants by South American indigenous people and used in hunting. If an arrow tipped with curare pierces the skin and the poison enters the body, it prevents ACh from binding to the receptor sites on neurons. Because ACh helps muscles move, curare causes paralysis. The victim is prevented from contracting the muscles used in breathing and therefore dies from suffocation. Botulism, a disease that stems from food poisoning,

prevents the release of ACh and has the same effect as *curare*.

ACh is also normally prevalent in a part of the brain called the hippocampus, a structure involved in the formation of memories (Louie & Wilson, 2001). When the amount of ACh available to the brain decreases, as in Alzheimer's disease, memory formation is impaired (Chu et al., 2005). In one experiment, researchers (Egawa et al., 2002) decreased the ACh available to the hippocampi of laboratory rats. As a result, the rats could not learn to navigate a maze, apparently because they could not remember which way to turn at the choice points.

Dopamine acts in the brain and affects ability to perceive pleasure, voluntary movement, and learning and memory (Davis et al., 2004; Heinz, 2004). Deficiencies of dopamine are linked to Parkinson's disease, in which people progressively lose control over their muscles (Olanow, 2000; Swerdlow et al., 2003). They develop muscle tremors and jerky, uncoordinated movements.

The psychological disorder *schizophrenia* is characterized by confusion and false perceptions, and it has been linked to dopamine. People with schizophrenia may have more receptor sites for dopamine in an area of the brain that is involved in emotional responding. For this reason, they may "overutilize" the dopamine available in the brain (Butcher, 2000; Kapur, 2003). Overutilization is connected with hallucinations and disturbances of thought and emotion. The phenothiazines, a group of drugs used in the treatment of schizophrenia, inhibit the action of dopamine by blocking some dopamine receptors (Lidow et al., 2001). Because of their action, phenothiazines may have Parkinson's-like side effects, which are usually treated by lowering the dose, prescribing additional drugs, or switching to another drug.

Norepinephrine is produced largely by neurons in the brain stem, and acts both as a neurotransmitter and as a hormone. It is an excitatory neurotransmitter that speeds up the heartbeat and other body processes and is involved in general arousal, learning and memory, and eating. Excesses and deficiencies of norepinephrine have

The boxer Muhammad Ali and the actor Michael J. Fox are two of the better-known individuals who are afflicted with Parkinson's disease.

Figure 2.4

The Divisions of the Nervous System

The nervous system contains two main divisions: the central nervous system and the peripheral nervous system. The central nervous system consists of the brain and spinal cord. The peripheral nervous system contains the somatic and autonomic systems. In turn, the autonomic nervous system has sympathetic and parasympathetic divisions.

Go to CourseMate for PSYCH at www.cengagebrain.com to access an interactive version of this figure.

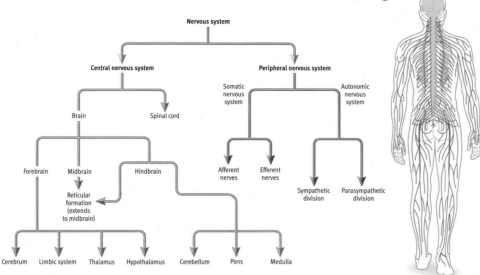

Endorphins occur naturally in the brain and in the bloodstream and are similar to the narcotic morphine in their functions and effects. They lock into receptor sites for chemicals that transmit pain messages to the brain. Once the endorphin "key" is in the "lock," the pain-causing chemicals are locked out. Endorphins may also increase our sense of competence, enhance the functioning of the immune system, and be connected with the pleasurable "runner's high" reported by many long-distance runners (Jonsdottir et al., 2000; Oktedalen et al., 2001).

been linked to mood disorders. Deficiencies of both ACh and norepinephrine particularly impair memory formation (Egawa et al., 2002).

The stimulants cocaine and amphetamine ("speed") boost norepinephrine (as well as dopamine) production, increasing the firing of neurons and leading to persistent arousal. Amphetamines both facilitate the release of these neurotransmitters and prevent their reuptake. Cocaine also blocks reuptake.

Serotonin is involved in emotional arousal and sleep. Deficiencies of serotonin have been linked to eating disorders, alcoholism, depression, aggression, and insomnia. The drug LSD decreases the action of serotonin and is also believed to increase the utilization of dopamine, which may be the mechanism by which it produces hallucinations.

Gamma-aminobutyric acid (GABA) is another neurotransmitter of great interest to psychologists. One reason is that GABA is an inhibitory neurotransmitter that may help calm anxiety reactions (Stroele et al., 2002). Tranquilizers and alcohol may quell anxiety by binding with GABA receptors and amplifying its effects. One class of antianxiety drug may also increase the sensitivity of receptor sites to GABA. Other studies link deficiencies of GABA to depression (Clénet et al., 2005).

Endorphins are inhibitory neurotransmitters. The word *endorphin* is the contraction of *endogenous morphine*. *Endogenous* means "developing from within."

There you have it—a fabulous forest of neurons in which billions upon billions of axon terminals are pouring armadas of neurotransmitters into synaptic clefts at any given time. The combined activity of all these neurotransmitters determines which messages will be transmitted and which ones will not. You experience your sensations, your thoughts, and your control over your body as psychological events, but the psychological events come from billions upon billions of electrochemical events.

We can think of neurons as the microscopic building blocks of the nervous system. Millions upon millions of these neurons gather together to form larger, visible structures that we think of as the parts of the nervous system. We discuss those parts next.

The Parts of the Nervous System

What are the parts of the nervous system? The nervous system consists of the brain, the spinal cord, and the **nerves** linking them to the sensory organs, muscles, and glands. As shown in Figure 2.4, the brain and the

SOURCE: FROM WEITEN. PSYCHOLOGY, 8E. COPYRIGHT © 2010 WADSWORTH, A PART OF CENGAGE LEARNING, INC. REPRODUCED BY PERMISSION. WWW.CENGAGE.COM.PERMISSIONS.

central nervous system
the brain and spinal cord

peripheral nervous system
the part of the nervous system consisting of the somatic nervous system and the autonomic nervous system

somatic nervous system
the division of the peripheral nervous system that connects the central nervous system with sensory receptors, skeletal muscles, and the surface of the body

autonomic nervous system (ANS)
the division of the peripheral nervous system that regulates glands and activities such as heartbeat, respiration, digestion, and dilation of the pupils

sympathetic
the branch of the ANS that is most active during emotional responses, such as fear and anxiety, that spend the body's reserves of energy

parasympathetic
the branch of the ANS that is most active during processes (such as digestion) that restore the body's reserves of energy

spinal cord
a column of nerves within the spine that transmits messages from sensory receptors to the brain and from the brain to muscles and glands throughout the body

spinal cord make up the central nervous system. If you compare your nervous system to a computer, your central nervous system would be your central processing unit (CPU).

The sensory (afferent) neurons, which receive and transmit messages to the brain and spinal cord, and the motor (efferent) neurons, which transmit messages from the brain or spinal cord to the muscles and glands, make up the peripheral nervous system. In the comparison of the nervous system to a computer, the peripheral nervous system makes up the nervous system's peripheral devices—keyboard, mouse, DVD drive, and so on. You would not be able to feed information to your computer's central processing unit without these *peripheral* devices. Other peripheral devices, such as your monitor and printer, allow you to follow what is happening inside your CPU and see what it has done.

The Peripheral Nervous System: The Body's Peripheral Devices

What are the divisions and functions of the peripheral nervous system? The peripheral nervous system consists of sensory and motor neurons that transmit messages to and from the central nervous system. Without the peripheral nervous system, our brains would be like isolated CPUs. There would be no keyboards, mouses, CDs, or other ways of inputting information. There would be no monitors, printers, modems, or other ways of displaying or transmitting information. We would be detached from the world. We would not be able to perceive it; we would not be able to act on it. The two main divisions of the peripheral nervous system are the *somatic nervous system* and the *autonomic nervous system*.

The somatic nervous system contains sensory (afferent) and motor (efferent) neurons. It transmits messages about sights, sounds, smells, temperature, body positions, and so on, to the central nervous system. Messages transmitted from the brain and spinal cord to the somatic nervous system control purposeful body movements such as raising a hand, winking, or running, as well as the tiny, almost imperceptible movements that maintain our balance and posture.

The autonomic nervous system (ANS) also has afferent and efferent neurons and regulates the glands and the muscles of internal organs. Thus, the ANS controls activities such as heartbeat, respiration, digestion, and dilation of the pupils. These activities can occur automatically, while we are asleep. But some of them can be overridden by conscious control. You can breathe at a purposeful pace, for example. Methods like biofeedback and yoga also help people gain voluntary control of functions such as heart rate and blood pressure.

The ANS also has two branches, or divisions: sympathetic and parasympathetic. These branches have largely opposing effects. Many organs and glands are stimulated by both branches of the ANS (see Figure 2.5). When organs and glands are simultaneously stimulated by both divisions, their effects can average out to some degree. In general, the sympathetic division is most active during processes that involve spending body energy from stored reserves, such as a fight-or-flight response to a predator or when you find out that your rent is going to be raised. The parasympathetic division is most active during processes that replenish reserves of energy, such as eating. When we are afraid, the sympathetic division of the ANS accelerates the heart rate. When we relax, the parasympathetic division decelerates the heart rate. The parasympathetic division stimulates digestive processes, but the sympathetic branch inhibits digestion. The ANS is of particular interest to psychologists because its activities are linked to various emotions such as anxiety and love.

The Central Nervous System: The Body's Central Processing Unit

What are the divisions and functions of the central nervous system? The central nervous system consists of the spinal cord and the brain. The spinal cord is a true "information superhighway"—a column of nerves as

> " Autonomic means automatic. "

Truth

It is true that fear can give you indigestion.

The Brain—is wider than the Sky—
For—put them side by side—
The one the other will contain
With ease—and you—beside—

—Emily Dickinson

thick as a thumb. It transmits messages from sensory receptors to the brain and from the brain to muscles and glands throughout the body. The spinal cord also carries out some "local government." That is, it responds to some sources of external stimulation through spinal reflexes. A spinal reflex is an unlearned response to a stimulus that may require only two neurons—a sensory neuron and a motor neuron (see Figure 2.6).

The spinal cord and brain contain gray matter and white matter. Gray matter consists of nonmyelinated neurons. Some of these are involved in spinal reflexes. Others send their axons to the brain. White matter is composed of bundles of longer, myelinated (and thus whitish) axons that carry messages to and from the brain. A cross section of the spinal cord shows that the gray matter, which includes cell bodies, is distributed in a butterfly pattern (see Figure 2.6).

The spinal cord is also involved in reflexes. We blink in response to a puff of air in our faces. We swallow when food accumulates in the mouth. A physician may tap below the knee to elicit the knee-jerk reflex, a sign that the nervous system is operating adequately. Sexual response involves many reflexes. Urinating and defecating are reflexes that occur in response to pressure in the bladder and the rectum. It is your central nervous system that makes you so special. Other species see more sharply, smell more keenly, and hear more acutely. Other species run faster, or fly through the air, or swim underwater—without the benefit of artificial devices such as airplanes and submarines. But it is your central nervous system that enables you to use symbols and language, the abilities that allow people not only to adapt to their environment but also to create new environments and give them names (Bandura, 1999).

spinal reflex
a simple, unlearned response to a stimulus that may involve only two neurons

gray matter
the grayish neurons and neural segments that are involved in spinal reflexes

white matter
axon bundles that carry messages from and to the brain

LO² The Brain: Wider Than the Sky

When I was a child, I was told that the human nervous system is more complex than that of any other animal and that our brains are larger than those of any other animal. Now, this last piece of business is not quite true. A human brain weighs about 3 pounds, but the brains of elephants and whales may be four times as heavy. Still, our brains account for a greater part of our body weight than do those of elephants or whales. Our brains weigh about 1/60th of our body weight. Elephant brains weigh about 1/1,000th of their total weight, and whale brains are a paltry 1/10,000th of their weight. Philosophers and scientists have wondered about the functions of the brain throughout history. Scientists today generally agree that the mind is a function of the brain (Bogen, 1998; Dietrich, 2004; Hohwy & Frith, 2004; Roser & Gazzaniga, 2004). Some engage in research that attempts to pinpoint exactly what

Figure 2.5

The Parasympathetic and Sympathetic Branches of the Autonomic Nervous System (ANS)

The parasympathetic branch of the ANS generally acts to replenish stores of energy in the body. The sympathetic branch is most active during activities that expend energy. The two branches of the ANS frequently have antagonistic effects on the organs they service.

Go to CourseMate for PSYCH at www.cengagebrain.com to access an interactive version of this figure.

> **Fiction**
>
> It is not true that the human brain is larger than that of any other animal.

happens in certain parts of the brain when we are listening to music or trying to remember someone's face. At other times—as in the case of Phineas Gage—knowledge has almost literally fallen into their laps. From injuries to the head—some of them minimal, some horrendous—we have learned that brain damage can impair consciousness, perception, memory, and abilities to make plans and decisions. In some cases, the loss of large portions of the brain may result in little loss of function. But the loss of smaller portions in particular locations can cause language problems, memory loss, or death. It has been known for about two centuries that damage to the left side of the brain is connected with loss of sensation or movement on the right side of the body, and vice versa. Thus it has been assumed that the brain's control mechanisms cross over from right to left, and vice versa, as they descend into the body.

Accidents provide unplanned—and uncontrolled—opportunities of studying the brain. Nevertheless, they remain useful (e.g., Baldo et al., 2004; Eslinger et al., 2004). Still, scientists learn more about the brain through methods like experimentation, electroencephalography, and brain scans. *How do researchers learn about the functions of the brain?*

Experimenting with the Brain

The results of disease and accidents (as in the case of Phineas Gage) have shown us that brain injuries can be connected with changes in behavior and mental

Figure 2.7

The Electroencephalograph (EEG)

The EEG detects brain waves that pass between electrodes that are attached to the scalp. It has been used to reveal electrical activity associated with relaxation and the stages of sleep.

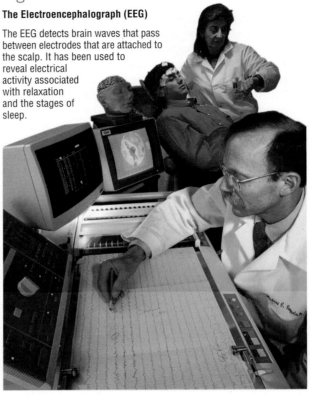

© RICHARD T. NOWITZ/CORBIS

processes. Scientists have also purposefully damaged part of the brain in laboratory animals to observe the results. For example, damaging one part of the hypothalamus causes rats to overeat. Damaging another part of the hypothalamus causes them to stop eating. It is as if parts of the brain contain on–off switches for certain kinds of behavior, at least in lower animals.

Because the brain has no receptors for pain, surgeon Wilder Penfield (1969) was able to stimulate parts of human brains with electrical probes. As a result, his patients reported perceiving certain memories. Electrical stimulation of the brain has also shown that parts of the brain are connected with specific kinds of sensations (as of light or sound) or motor activities (such as movement of an arm or leg).

The Electroencephalograph

Penfield stimulated parts of the brain with an electrical current and asked people to report what they experienced. Researchers have also used the electroencephalograph (EEG) to record the natural electrical activity

Figure 2.6

The Reflex Arc

Reflexes are inborn, stereotyped behavior patterns that have apparently evolved because they help individuals adapt to the environment even before they can understand and purposefully manipulate the environment. Here we see a cross-section of the spinal cord, highlighting a sensory neuron and a motor neuron, which are involved in the knee-jerk reflex. In some reflexes, interneurons link sensory and motor neurons.

Figure 2.8

Brain Imaging Techniques

Part A shows a CAT scan, part B shows a PET scan, and part C shows an MRI.

A. Computerized axial tomography (the CAT scan) passes a narrow X-ray beam through the head and measures structures that reflect the rays from various angles, enabling a computer to generate a three-dimensional image.

B. Positron emission tomography (the PET scan) injects a radioactive tracer into the bloodstream and assesses activity of parts of the brain according to the amount of glucose they metabolize.

C. Magnetic resonance imaging (MRI) places a person in a magnetic field and uses radio waves to cause the brain to emit signals that reveal shifts in the flow of blood, which, in turn, indicate brain activity.

A. CAT scan

Detectors · Moving X-ray source

B. PET scan

C. MRI

Coil

Magnetic rings

of the brain. The EEG (see Figure 2.7) detects minute amounts of electrical activity—called brain waves—that pass between the electrodes. Certain brain waves are associated with feelings of relaxation, with various stages of sleep, and with neurological problems such as epilepsy.

Brain-Imaging Techniques

When Phineas Gage had his fabled accident, the only ways to look into the brain were to drill holes or crack it open, neither of which would have contributed to the well-being of the subject. But in the latter years of the 20th century, researchers developed imaging techniques that tap the computer's capacity to generate images of the parts of the brain from sources of radiation.

Computerized axial tomography (CAT or CT scan), shown in Figure 2.8A, passes X-rays through the head and measures the structures that reflect the beams from various angles, generating a three-dimensional image. The CAT scan reveals deformities in shape and structure that are connected with blood clots, tumors, and other health problems.

A second method, positron emission tomography (PET scan), shown in Figure 2.8B, forms a computer-generated image of the activity of parts of the brain by tracing the amount of glucose used (or metabolized) by these parts. More glucose is metabolized in more active parts of the brain. To trace the metabolism of glucose, a harmless amount of a radioactive compound, called a *tracer*, is mixed with glucose and injected into the bloodstream. When the glucose reaches the brain, the patterns of activity are revealed by measurement of the positrons—positively charged particles—that are given off by the tracer. The PET scan has been used by researchers to see which parts of the brain are most active when we are, for example, listening to music, working out a math problem, using language, or playing chess.

A third imaging technique is magnetic resonance imaging (MRI), which is shown in Figure 2.8C.

computerized axial tomography (CAT or CT scan) a method of brain imaging that passes a narrow X-ray beam through the head and measures structures that reflect the rays from various angles, enabling a computer to generate a three-dimensional image

positron emission tomography (PET scan) a method of brain imaging that injects a radioactive tracer into the bloodstream and assesses activity of parts of the brain according to the amount of glucose they metabolize

magnetic resonance imaging (MRI) a method of brain imaging that places a person in a magnetic field and uses radio waves to cause the brain to emit signals that reveal shifts in the flow of blood, which, in turn, indicate brain activity

Figure 2.9

The Parts of the Human Brain

The view of the brain, split top to bottom, shows some of the most important structures. The "valleys" in the cerebrum are called fissures.

Go to CourseMate for PSYCH at www.cengagebrain.com to access an interactive version of this figure.

Corpus callosum
Thick bundle of axons that serves as a bridge between the two cerebral hemispheres

Cerebrum
Center of thinking and language; prefrontal area contains "executive center" of brain

Hypothalamus
Secretes hormones that stimulate secretion of hormones by the pituitary gland; involved in basic drives such as hunger, sex, and aggression

Pituitary gland
Secretes hormones that regulate many body functions, including secretion of hormones from other glands; sometimes referred to as the "master gland"

Thalamus
Relay station for sensory information

Cerebellum
Essential to balance and coordination

Reticular activating system
Involved in regulation of sleep and waking; stimulation of RAS increases arousal

Pons
Involved in regulation of movement, sleep and arousal, respiration

Medulla
Involved in regulation of heart rate, blood pressure, respiration, circulation

IMAGE SOURCE/© 2010 JUPITERIMAGES CORPORATION

In MRI, the person lies in a powerful magnetic field and is exposed to radio waves that cause parts of the brain to emit signals, which are measured from multiple angles. MRI relies on subtle shifts in blood flow. (More blood flows to more active parts of the brain, supplying them with oxygen.) MRI can be used to show which parts of the brain are active when we are, say, solving math problems (Rickard et al., 2000) or speaking (Dogil et al., 2002). Functional MRI (fMRI) enables researchers to observe the brain "while it works" by taking repeated scans while subjects engage in activities such as mental processes and voluntary movements.

Some researchers consider the prefrontal cortex to be the "executive center" of the brain, where decisions are made to keep information in working memory and to solve problems. The prefrontal cortex is the part of the frontal lobe (see Figure 2.11 on page 38) that is closest to the front of the brain. Research with the PET scan and MRI supports the view that the prefrontal cortex is where we process much of the information involved in making plans and solving problems (Kroger et al., 2002; Rowe et al., 2001).

A Voyage Through the Brain

What are the structures and functions of the brain? Let us begin our tour of the brain with the hindbrain, where the spinal cord rises to meet the brain (refer to Figure 2.9). Here we find three major structures: the medulla, the pons, and the cerebellum. Many pathways pass through the medulla to connect the spinal cord to higher levels of the brain. The medulla regulates basic functions such as heart rate, blood pressure, and respiration. (In fact, Gage survived his accident because his medulla escaped injury.) The medulla also plays roles in sleeping, sneezing, and coughing. The pons is a bulge in the hindbrain that lies forward of the medulla. *Pons* is the Latin word for "bridge"; the pons is so named because of the bundles of nerves that pass through it. The pons transmits information about body movement and is involved in functions related to attention, sleep and alertness, and respiration.

Behind the pons lies the cerebellum ("little brain" in Latin). The cerebellum has two hemispheres that are involved in maintaining balance and in controlling motor (muscle) behavior. You may send a command from your forebrain to get up and walk to the refrigerator, but your cerebellum is key to organizing the information that enables you to engage in these movements. The cerebellum allows you to place one leg in front of the other and reach your destination without tipping over. Injury to the cerebellum may impair motor coordination and cause stumbling and loss of muscle tone.

As we tour the hindbrain, we also find the lower part of the reticular activating system (RAS). That is where the RAS begins, but it ascends through the midbrain into the lower part of the forebrain. The RAS is vital in the functions of attention, sleep, and arousal. Injury to the RAS may result in a coma. Stimulation of the RAS causes it to send messages to the cerebral cortex (the large wrinkled mass that you think of as your brain), making us more alert to sensory information. In classic neurological research, Giuseppe Moruzzi and Horace Magoun (1949) discovered that electrical stimulation of the reticular formation of a sleeping cat caused it to awaken at once. But when the reticular formation was severed from higher parts of the brain, the cat fell into a coma from which it would not awaken. Drugs known as central nervous system depressants, such as alcohol, are thought to work, in part, by lowering RAS activity.

Key areas of the forwardmost part of the brain, or forebrain, are the thalamus, the hypothalamus, the limbic system, and the cerebrum (see Figure 2.10). The thalamus is located near the center of the brain, and could be said to lie between the forebrain and the midbrain. It consists of two joined egg-shaped structures. The thalamus serves as a relay station for sensory stimulation. Nerve fibers from sensory systems enter from below; their information is then transmitted to the cerebral cortex by fibers that exit from above. For example, the thalamus relays sensory input from the eyes to the visual areas of the cerebral cortex. The thalamus also regulates sleep and attention in coordination with other brain structures, including the RAS.

The hypothalamus lies beneath the thalamus and above the pituitary gland. It weighs only 4 grams, yet it is vital in the regulation of body temperature, concentration of fluids, storage of nutrients, and motivation and emotion. Experimenters learn many of the functions of the hypothalamus by implanting electrodes in parts of it and observing the effects of electrical stimulation. They have found that the

hypothalamus is involved in hunger, thirst, sexual behavior, caring for offspring, and aggression. Among lower animals, stimulation of various areas of the hypothalamus can trigger instinctual behaviors such as fighting, mating, or nest building.

Canadian psychologists James Olds and Peter Milner (1954) made a splendid mistake in the 1950s. They were attempting to implant an electrode in a rat's reticular formation to see how stimulation of the area might affect learning. Olds, however, was primarily a social psychologist and not a biological psychologist. He missed his target and found a part of the animal's hypothalamus instead. Olds and Milner dubbed this area the "pleasure center" because the animal would repeat whatever it was doing when it was stimulated. The term pleasure center is not used frequently, because it appears to attribute human emotions to rats. Yet the "pleasure centers" must be doing something right, because rats stimulate themselves in these centers by pressing a pedal several thousand times an hour, until they are exhausted (Olds, 1969).

The hypothalamus is important to humans as well as to lower animals. Unfortunately (or fortunately), our "pleasure centers" are not as clearly defined as those of the rat. Then, too, our responses to messages from the hypothalamus are less automatic and relatively more influenced by higher brain functions—that is, cognitive factors such as thought, choice, and value systems.

The limbic system forms a fringe along the inner edge of the cerebrum and is fully evolved only in mammals (see Figure 2.10). It is made up of several structures, including the amygdala, hippocampus, and parts of the hypothalamus. It is involved in memory and emotion and in the drives of hunger, sex, and aggression. People with hippocampal damage can retrieve old memories but cannot permanently store new information. As a result, they may reread the same newspaper day in and day out without recalling that they read it before. Or they may have to be perpetually reintroduced to people they have met just hours earlier (Squire, 2004).

The amygdala is near the bottom of the limbic system and looks like two little almonds. Studies using lesioning and electrical stimulation show that the amygdala is connected with aggressive behavior

thalamus
an area near the center of the brain involved in the relay of sensory information to the cortex and in the functions of sleep and attention

hypothalamus
a bundle of nuclei below the thalamus involved in body temperature, motivation, and emotion

limbic system
a group of structures involved in memory, motivation, and emotion that forms a fringe along the inner edge of the cerebrum

amygdala
a part of the limbic system that apparently facilitates stereotypical aggressive responses

Figure 2.10

The Limbic System

The limbic system is made up of structures that include the amygdala, the hippocampus, and parts of the hypothalamus. It is evolved fully only in mammals and forms a fringe along the inner edge of the cerebrum. The limbic system is involved in memory and emotion, and in the drives of hunger, sex, and aggression.

Go to CourseMate for PSYCH at www.cengagebrain.com to access an interactive version of this figure.

cerebrum
the large mass of the forebrain, which consists of two hemispheres

cerebral cortex
the wrinkled surface area (gray matter) of the cerebrum

corpus callosum
a thick fiber bundle that connects the hemispheres of the cortex

in monkeys, cats, and other animals. Early in the 20th century, Heinrich Klüver and Paul Bucy (1939) lesioned part of the amygdala of a rhesus monkey. Rhesus monkeys are normally a scrappy lot and try to bite or grab at intruders, but destruction of this animal's amygdala made it docile. No longer did it react aggressively to people. It even allowed people to poke and pinch it. Electrical stimulation of the part of the amygdala that Klüver and Bucy had destroyed, however, triggers a "rage response." For example, it causes a cat to hiss and arch its back in preparation to attack. The amygdala is also connected with a fear response (LeDoux, 1998). If you electrically stimulate another part of the

amygdala, the cat cringes in fear when you cage it with a mouse.

The amygdala is also connected with vigilance. It is involved in emotions, learning, and memory, and it sort of behaves like a spotlight, focusing attention on matters that are novel and important to know more about.

Only in humans does the cerebrum make up such a large part of the brain. The cerebrum is responsible for thinking and language. The surface of the cerebrum—the cerebral cortex—is wrinkled, or convoluted, with ridges and valleys. The convolutions allow a great deal of surface area to be packed into the brain—and surface area is apparently connected with cognitive ability. Valleys in the cortex are called *fissures*. A key fissure almost divides the cerebrum in half, creating two hemispheres with something of the shape of a walnut. The hemispheres are connected by the corpus callosum (Latin for "hard body"), a bundle of some 200 million nerve fibers.

Figure 2.11

The Geography of the Cerebral Cortex

The cortex has four lobes: frontal, parietal, temporal, and occipital. The visual area of the cortex is in the occipital lobe. The hearing or auditory cortex lies in the temporal lobe. The motor and somatosensory areas— shown below—face each other across the central fissure. Note that the face and the hands are "super-sized" in the motor and somatosensory areas. Why do you think this is so?

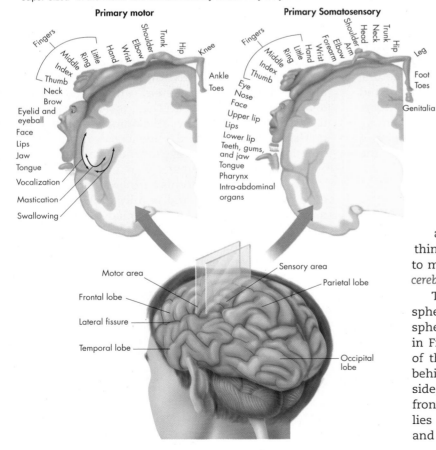

The Cerebral Cortex

The cerebral cortex is the part of the brain that you usually think of as your brain. *Cortex* is a Latin word meaning "bark," as in the bark of a tree. Just as the bark is the outer coating of a tree, the cerebral cortex is the outer coating of the cerebrum. Despite its extreme importance and its creation of a world of civilization and culture, it is only about 1/8" thick.

The cerebral cortex is involved in almost every bodily activity, including most sensations and most responses. It is also the part of the brain that frees people from the tyranny of genetic dictates and instinct. It is the seat of thinking and language, and it enables humans to think deeply about the world outside and to make decisions. *What are the parts of the cerebral cortex?*

The cerebral cortex has two hemispheres, left and right. Each of the hemispheres is divided into four lobes, as shown in Figure 2.11. The *frontal lobe* lies in front of the central fissure and the *parietal lobe* behind it. The *temporal lobe* lies below the side, or lateral, fissure—across from the frontal and parietal lobes. The *occipital lobe* lies behind the temporal lobe and behind and below the parietal lobe.

When light strikes the eyes, neurons in the occipital lobe fire, and as a result, we "see" (that is, the image is projected in the brain). Direct artificial stimulation of the occipital lobe also produces visual sensations. If neurons in the occipital region of the cortex were stimulated with electricity, you would "see" flashes of light even if it were pitch-black or your eyes were covered. The hearing or auditory area of the cortex lies in the temporal lobe along the lateral fissure. Sounds cause structures in the ear to vibrate. Messages are relayed from those structures to the auditory area of the cortex; when you hear a noise, neurons in this area are firing.

Just behind the central fissure in the parietal lobe lies an area called the somatosensory cortex, which receives messages from skin senses all over the body. These sensations include warmth and cold, touch, pain, and movement. Neurons in different parts of the sensory cortex fire, depending on whether you wiggle your finger or raise your leg.

Many years ago it was discovered that patients with injuries to one hemisphere of the brain would show sensory or motor deficits on the opposite side of the body below the head. This led to the recognition that sensory and motor nerves cross in the brain and elsewhere. The left hemisphere controls, acts on, and receives inputs from the right side of the body. The right hemisphere controls, acts on, and receives inputs from the left side of the body. The motor cortex lies in the frontal lobe, just across the valley of the central fissure from the somatosensory cortex. Neurons firing in the motor cortex cause parts of our body to move. More than 100 years ago, German scientists electrically stimulated the motor cortex in dogs and observed that muscles contracted in response (Fritsch & Hitzig, 1870/1960). Since then, neuroscientists have mapped the motor cortex in people and lower animals by inserting electrical probes and seeing which muscles contract. For example, José Delgado (1969) caused one patient to make a fist even though he tried to prevent his hand from closing. The patient said, "I guess, doctor, that your electricity is stronger than my will" (Delgado, 1969, p. 114).

Thinking, Language, and the Cortex

Areas of the cerebral cortex that are not primarily involved in sensation or motor activity are called *association areas*. They make possible the breadth

Truth

It is quite true that if an area of your somatosensory cortex is stimulated with an electrical probe, it might seem to you as if someone were touching your arm or leg.

and depth of human learning, thought, memory, and language. *What parts of the cerebral cortex are involved in thinking and language?* The association areas in the *prefrontal* region of the brain—that is, in the frontal lobes, near the forehead—are the brain's executive center. It appears to be where we solve problems and make plans and decisions (Baldo et al., 2004; Buchanan et al., 2004; Shimamura, 2002).

Executive functions like problem-solving also require memory, like the memory in your computer. Association areas also provide the core of your working memory (Chafee & Goldman-Rakic, 2000; Constantinidis et al., 2001). They are connected with various sensory areas in the brain and can tap whatever sensory information is needed or desired. The prefrontal region thus retrieves visual, auditory, and other memories and manipulates them; similarly, a computer retrieves information from files in storage and manipulates it in working memory.

Certain neurons in the visual area of the occipital lobe fire in response to the visual presentation of vertical lines. Others fire in response to presentation of horizontal lines. Although one group of cells may respond to one aspect of the visual field and another group of cells may respond to another, association areas put it all together. As a result, we see a box or an automobile or a road map and not a confusing array of verticals and horizontals.

Language Functions

In some ways, the left and right hemispheres of the brain duplicate each other's functions. In other ways, they differ. The left hemisphere contains language functions for nearly all right-handed people and for two out of three left-handed people (Pinker, 1994b). However, the brain remains "plastic," or changeable, through about the age of 13. As a result, children who lose the left hemisphere of the brain because of medical problems may transfer speech functions to the right hemisphere (Hertz-Pannier et al., 2002).

Two key language areas lie within the hemisphere of the cortex that contains language functions (usually the left hemisphere): Broca's area and Wernicke's area (see Figure 2.12). Damage to either area is likely to cause an aphasia—that is, a disruption of the ability to understand or produce language.

somatosensory cortex
the section of cortex in which sensory stimulation is projected. It lies just behind the central fissure in the parietal lobe

motor cortex
the section of cortex that lies in the frontal lobe, just across the central fissure from the sensory cortex; neural impulses in the motor cortex are linked to muscular responses throughout the body

aphasia
a disruption in the ability to understand or produce language

Wernicke's aphasia
a language disorder characterized by difficulty comprehending the meaning of spoken language

Broca's aphasia
a language disorder characterized by slow, laborious speech

Wernicke's area lies in the temporal lobe near the auditory cortex. It responds mainly to auditory information (sounds). As you are reading this page, however, the visual information is registered in the visual cortex of your occipital lobe. It is then recoded as auditory information as it travels to Wernicke's area. Broca's area is located in the frontal lobe, near the section of the motor cortex that controls the muscles of the tongue, throat, and other areas of the face used when speaking. Broca's area processes the information and relays it to the motor cortex. The motor cortex sends the signals that cause muscles in your throat and mouth to contract. If you are "subvocalizing"—saying what you are reading "under your breath"—that is because Wernicke's area transmits information to Broca's area via nerve fibers.

People with damage to Wernicke's area may show **Wernicke's aphasia**, which impairs their abilities to comprehend speech and to think of the proper words to express their own thoughts. Ironically, they usually speak freely and with proper syntax. Wernicke's area is essential to understanding the relationships between words and their meanings. When Broca's area is damaged, people usually understand language well enough but speak slowly and laboriously, in simple sentences. This pattern is termed **Broca's aphasia**.

Some people with Broca's aphasia utter short, meaningful phrases that omit small but important grammatical words such as *is, and,* and *the.* Such an individual may laboriously say "walk dog." The phrase can have various meanings, such as "I want to take the dog for a walk" or "Take the dog out for a walk."

Figure 2.12

Broca's and Wernicke's Areas of the Cerebral Cortex

The areas that are most involved in speech are Broca's area and Wernicke's area.

Broca's area

Wernicke's area

A part of the brain called the *angular gyrus* lies between the visual cortex and Wernicke's area. The angular gyrus "translates" visual information, as in perceiving written words, into auditory information (sounds) and sends it on to Wernicke's area. Brain imaging suggests that problems in the angular gyrus can seriously impair reading ability because it becomes difficult for the reader to segment words into sounds (Milne et al., 2002; Ruff et al., 2003).

Left Brain, Right Brain?

What would it mean to be "left-brained" or "right-brained"? The notion is that the hemispheres of the brain are involved in very different kinds of intellectual and emotional functions and responses. According to this view, left-brained people would be primarily logical and intellectual. Right-brained people would be intuitive, creative, and emotional. Those of us who are fortunate enough to have our brains "in balance" would presumably have the best of it—the capacity for logic combined with emotional richness.

Like many other popular ideas, the left-brain–right-brain notion is exaggerated. Research does suggest that in right-handed individuals, the left hemisphere is relatively more involved in intellectual undertakings that require logical analysis and problem-solving, language, and mathematical computation (Corballis et al., 2002; Shenal & Harrison, 2003). The other hemisphere (typically the right hemisphere) is usually superior in visual–spatial functions (it's better at putting puzzles together), recognition of faces, discrimination of colors, aesthetic and emotional responses, understanding metaphors, and creative mathematical reasoning. Despite these differences, the hemispheres of the brain do not act independently such that some people are truly left-brained and others are right-brained (Colvin et al., 2005). The functions of the left and right hemispheres overlap to some degree, and they tend to respond simultaneously as we focus our attention on one thing or another.

Whether we are talking about language functions or being "left-brained" or "right-brained," we are talking about people whose hemispheres of the cerebral cortex communicate back and forth.

Handedness

Being left-handed was once seen as a deficiency. Left-handed students were made to learn to write with their right hands. We are usually labeled right-handed or left-handed on the basis of our handwriting preferences, yet some people write with one hand and pass a football with the other.

Being left-handed appears to provide a somewhat- greater-than-average probability of language problems, such as dyslexia and stuttering, and health problems such as migraine headaches and allergies (Andreou et al., 2002; Geschwind & Galaburda, 1987; Habib & Robichon, 2003). But there may also be advantages to being left-handed. Left-handed people are more likely than right-handed people to be numbered among the ranks of gifted artists, musicians, and mathematicians (Kilshaw & Annett, 1983; Ostatníková et al., 2002).

The origins of handedness have a genetic component. If one of your parents is left-handed, your chances of being right-handed drop to about 80%. And if both of your parents are left-handed, your chances of also being left-handed are about 1 in 2 (Rosenbaum, 2000).

Split-Brain Experiments

A number of people with severe cases of **epilepsy** have split-brain operations in which much of the corpus callosum is severed (refer back to Figure 2.9). The purpose of the operation is to confine seizures to one hemisphere of the cerebral cortex rather than allowing a neural tempest to reverberate. Split-brain operations do seem to help people with epilepsy. *What happens when the brain is split in two?*

People who have undergone split-brain operations can be thought of as winding up with two brains, yet under most circumstances their behavior remains ordinary enough. Still, some aspects of hemispheres that have stopped talking to each other are intriguing.

As reported by pioneering brain surgeon Joseph Bogen (1969, 2000), each hemisphere may have a "mind of its own." One split-brain patient reported that her hemispheres frequently disagreed on what she should be wearing. What she meant was that one hand might undo her blouse as rapidly as the other was buttoning it.

Another pioneer of split-brain research, Michael Gazzaniga (2002), found that people with split brains whose eyes are closed may be able to verbally describe an object such as a key when they hold it in one hand, but not when they hold it in the other hand. If a person with a split brain handles a key with his left hand behind a screen, tactile impressions of the key are projected into the right hemisphere, which has little or no language ability (see Figure 2.13). Thus, he will not be able to describe the key. If he holds it in his right hand, he will have no trouble describing it because sensory impressions are projected into the left hemisphere of the cortex, which contains language functions. To further confound matters, if the word *ring* is projected into the left hemisphere while the person is asked what he is handling, he will say "ring," not "key."

This discrepancy between what is felt and what is said occurs only in people with split brains. Even so, people who have undergone split-brain operations tend to lead largely normal lives. And for the rest of us, the two hemispheres work together most of the time, such as when we are playing the piano or solving math problems.

epilepsy
temporary disturbances of brain functions that involve sudden neural discharges

Figure 2.13

A Divided-Brain Experiment

In the drawing on the left, we see that visual sensations in the left visual field are projected in the occipital cortex of the right hemisphere. Visual sensations from the right visual field are projected in the occipital cortex in the left hemisphere. In the divided-brain experiment diagrammed on the right, a person with a severed corpus callosum handles a key with his left hand and perceives the written word *key* in his left visual field. The word "key" is projected in the right hemisphere. Speech, however, is usually a function of the left hemisphere. The written word "ring," perceived by the right visual field, is projected in the left hemisphere. So, when asked what he is handling, the divided-brain subject reports "ring," not "key."

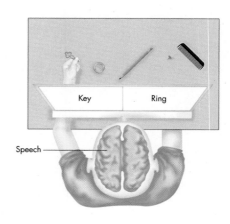

gland
an organ that secretes one or more chemical substances such as hormones, saliva, or milk

endocrine system
the body's system of ductless glands that secrete hormones and release them directly into the bloodstream

hormone
a substance secreted by an endocrine gland that regulates various body functions

pituitary gland
the gland that secretes growth hormone, prolactin, antidiuretic hormone, and other hormones

LO³ The Endocrine System

What is the endocrine system? The body contains two types of glands: glands with ducts and glands without ducts. A *duct* is a passageway that carries substances to specific locations. Saliva, sweat, tears, and breast milk all reach their destinations through ducts. Psychologists are interested in the substances secreted by a number of *ductless* glands because of their effects on behavior and mental processes. The ductless glands make up the endocrine system (see Figure 2.14), and they release hormones into the bloodstream. Hormones are then picked up by specific receptor sites and regulate growth, metabolism, and some forms of behavior. That is, they act only on receptors in certain locations.

Much hormonal action helps the body maintain steady states—fluid levels, blood sugar levels, and so on. Bodily mechanisms measure current levels; when these levels deviate from optimal, they signal glands to release hormones. The maintenance of steady states requires feedback of bodily information to glands. This type of system is referred to as a *negative feedback loop.* When enough of a hormone has been secreted, the gland is signaled to stop.

The Pituitary and the Hypothalamus

The pituitary gland and the hypothalamus work in close cooperation. The pituitary gland lies below the hypothalamus. Although the pituitary is only about the size of a pea, it is so central to the body's functioning that it has been dubbed the "master gland." The anterior (front) and posterior (back) lobes of the pituitary gland secrete hormones that regulate the functioning of many other glands. *Growth hormone* regulates the growth of muscles, bones, and glands. Children whose growth patterns are abnormally slow may catch up to their age-mates when they obtain growth hormone. *Prolactin* regulates maternal behavior in lower mammals such as rats and stimulates production of milk in women. As a water conservation measure, *vasopressin* (also called *antidiuretic hormone*) inhibits production of urine when the body's fluid levels are low. Vasopressin is also connected with stereotypical paternal behavior in some mammals. *Oxytocin* stimulates labor in pregnant women and is connected with maternal behavior (cuddling and caring for young) in some mammals (Insel, 2000; Taylor et al., 2000b). Obstetricians can induce labor by injecting pregnant women with oxytocin. During nursing, stimulation of the nerve endings of the nipples signals the brain to secrete oxytocin, which then causes the breasts to eject milk.

Although the pituitary gland may be the "master gland," the master has a "commander": the hypothalamus. We know today that the hypothalamus regulates much pituitary activity. The hypothalamus secretes a number of releasing hormones, or "factors," that stimulate the pituitary gland to secrete related hormones. For example, growth hormone releasing factor (hGRF) causes the pituitary to produce growth hormone. Blood vessels between the hypothalamus and the pituitary gland provide a direct route for these factors.

The Pineal Gland

The pineal gland secretes the hormone *melatonin,* which helps regulate the sleep–wake cycle and may affect the onset of puberty. Melatonin may also be connected with aging. In addition, it appears that melatonin is a mild sedative, and some people use it as a sleeping pill (Arendt, 2000; Nagtegaal et al., 2000). Melatonin may also help people adjust to jet lag (Takahashi et al., 2002).

Figure 2.14

The Endocrine Glands

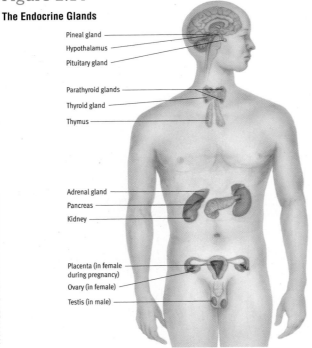

Pineal gland
Hypothalamus
Pituitary gland

Parathyroid glands
Thyroid gland

Thymus

Adrenal gland
Pancreas
Kidney

Placenta (in female during pregnancy)
Ovary (in female)
Testis (in male)

The Thyroid Gland

The thyroid gland could be considered the body's accelerator. It produces *thyroxin,* which affects the body's *metabolism*—the rate at which the body uses oxygen and produces energy. Some people are overweight because of *hypothyroidism,* a condition that results from too little thyroxin. Thyroxin deficiency in children can lead to *cretinism,* a condition characterized by stunted growth and mental retardation. Adults who secrete too little thyroxin may feel tired and sluggish and may put on weight. People who produce too much thyroxin may develop *hyperthyroidism,* which is characterized by excitability, insomnia, and weight loss.

The Adrenal Glands

The adrenal glands, located above the kidneys, have an outer layer, or cortex, and an inner core, or medulla. The adrenal cortex is regulated by the pituitary hormone ACTH (adrenocorticotrophic hormone). The adrenal cortex secretes hormones known as *corticosteroids,* or cortical steroids. These hormones regulate the heartbeat, increase resistance to stress, promote muscle development, and cause the liver to release stored sugar, making more energy available in emergencies, such as when you see another car veering toward your own. Epinephrine and norepinephrine are secreted by the adrenal medulla. *Epinephrine,* also known as adrenaline, is manufactured exclusively by the adrenal glands, but norepinephrine (noradrenaline) is also produced elsewhere in the body. (Norepinephrine acts as a neurotransmitter in the brain.) The sympathetic branch of the autonomic nervous system causes the adrenal medulla to release a mixture of epinephrine and norepinephrine that helps arouse the body to cope with threats and stress. Epinephrine is of interest to psychologists because it has emotional as well as physical effects. It intensifies most emotions and is central to the experience of fear and anxiety.

The Testes and the Ovaries

The testes and ovaries also produce steroids, among them testosterone and estrogen. If it were not for the secretion of the male sex hormone *testosterone* about six weeks after conception, we would all develop the external genital organs of females. Testosterone is produced not only by the testes but also in smaller amounts by the adrenal glands. A few weeks after conception, testosterone causes the male's sex organs to develop. During puberty, testosterone stokes the growth of muscle and bone and the development of primary and secondary sex characteristics. *Primary sex characteristics* are directly involved in reproduction and include the increased size of the penis and the sperm-producing ability of the testes. *Secondary sex characteristics* such as the presence of a beard and a deeper voice differentiate males from females but are not directly involved in reproduction.

The ovaries produce *estrogen* and *progesterone* as well as small amounts of testosterone. Estrogen is also produced in smaller amounts by the adrenal glands. Estrogen fosters female reproductive capacity and secondary sex characteristics such as accumulation of fatty tissue in the breasts and hips. Progesterone stimulates growth of the female reproductive organs and prepares the uterus to maintain pregnancy. Estrogen and testosterone have psychological effects as well as biological effects, which we will explore further in Chapter 3.

} Steroids, Behavior, and Mental Processes {

Steroids increase the muscle mass, heighten resistance to stress, and increase the body's energy supply by signaling the liver to release sugar into the bloodstream. The steroid testosterone is connected with the sex drive in both males and females (females secrete some testosterone in the adrenal glands) (Davis, 2000). Anabolic steroids (synthetic versions of the male sex hormone testosterone) have been used, sometimes in tandem with growth hormone, to enhance athletic prowess. Not only do these steroids enhance athletic prowess, but they are also connected with self-confidence, aggressiveness, even memory functioning (Janowsky et al., 2000). Anabolic steroids are generally outlawed in sports, however, the lure of steroids is understandable. Sometimes the difference between an acceptable athletic performance and a great one is rather small. Thousands of athletes try to make it in the big leagues, and the edge offered by steroids—even if minor—can spell the difference between a fumbling attempt and a smashing success. If steroids help, why the fuss? Some of it is related to the ethics of competition—the idea that athletes should "play fair." But steroid use is also linked to liver damage and other health problems.

natural selection
a core concept of the theory of evolution that holds that adaptive genetic variations among members of a species enable individuals with those variations to survive and reproduce

mutation
a sudden variation in an inheritable characteristic, as distinguished from a variation that results from generations of gradual selection

evolutionary psychology
the branch of psychology that studies the ways in which adaptation and natural selection are connected with mental processes and behavior

LO⁴ Evolution and Heredity

Charles Darwin almost missed the boat. Literally. Darwin had volunteered to serve on an expeditionary voyage on the H.M.S. *Beagle,* but the captain, Robert Fitz-Roy, objected to Darwin because of the shape of his nose. Fitz-Roy believed that you could judge a person's character by the outline of his facial features, and Darwin's nose didn't fit the . . . bill. But Fitz-Roy relented, and in the 1830s, Darwin undertook the historic voyage to the Galápagos Islands that led to the development of his theory of evolution.

In 1871 Darwin published *The Descent of Man,* which made the case that humans, like other species, were a product of evolution. He argued that the great apes (chimpanzees, gorillas, and so on) and humans shared a common primate ancestor. Evidence from fossil remains suggests that such a common ancestor might have lived about 13 million years ago (Moyà-Solà et al., 2004). Many people ridiculed Darwin's views because they were displeased with the notion that they might share ancestry with apes. Others argued that Darwin's theory contradicted the Bible's book of Genesis, which stated that humans had been created in one day in the image of God.

What is Darwin's theory of evolution? The concept of a *struggle for existence* lies at the core of Darwin's theory of evolution. At the Galápagos Islands, Darwin found himself immersed in the unfolding of a huge game of "Survivor," with animals and plants competing for food, water, territory, even light. But here the game was for real, and the rewards had nothing to do with fame or fortune. The rewards were reaching sexual maturity and transmitting one's genes into subsequent generations.

As described by evolutionary theory, some creatures have adapted successfully to these challenges, and their numbers have increased. Others have not met the challenges and have fallen back into the distant mists of time. Evidence suggests that 99.99% of all species that ever existed are now extinct (Gould, 2002). Which species prosper and which fade away are determined by natural selection; that is, species that are better adapted to their environment are more likely to survive and reproduce.

When we humans first appeared on Earth, our survival required a different sort of struggle than it does today. We fought or fled from predators such as leopards. We foraged across parched lands for food. But because of the evolution of our intellect, we prevailed. Our numbers have increased. We continue to transmit the traits that led to our selection down through the generations by means of genetic material whose chemical codes are only now being cracked.

Just what is handed down through the generations? The answer is biological, or physiological, structures and processes. Our biology serves as the material base for our behaviors, emotions, and cognitions (our thoughts, images, and plans). Biology somehow gives rise to specific behavioral tendencies in some organisms, such as the chick's instinctive fear of the shadow of the hawk. But the behavior of many species, especially higher species such as humans, is flexible and affected by experience and choice, as well as by heredity.

> **Individuals whose traits are better adapted to change are more likely to survive to transmit their traits to the next generation.**

According to the theory of evolution, species and individuals compete for the same resources. Natural variations from individual to individual, along with sudden changes in genes (see page 46) called mutations, lead to differences among individuals, differences which affect the ability to adapt to change. Those individuals whose traits are better adapted are more likely to survive (that is, to be "naturally selected"). Survival permits them to reach sexual maturity, to reproduce, and to transmit their features or traits to the next generation. What began as chance variation becomes embedded over the generations—if it fosters survival. Chance variations that hinder survival are likely to disappear from the gene pool.

Evolutionary Psychology: Doing What Comes Naturally

These same concepts of *adaptation* and *natural selection* have also been applied to psychological traits and are key concepts in evolutionary psychology. *What is evolutionary psychology?* Evolutionary psychology studies the ways in which adaptation and natural selection are connected with mental processes and behavior (Buss, 2000; Cory, 2002). Over the eons evolution has provided organisms with advantages such as stronger fins and wings, sharper claws, and camouflage. Human evolution has given rise to various physical traits and also to such diverse activities as language, art, committed relationships, and warfare.

One of the concepts of evolutionary psychology is that not only physical traits but also many patterns of behavior, including social behavior, evolve and can be transmitted genetically from generation to generation. Behavior patterns that help an organism to survive and reproduce may be transmitted to the next generation. Such behaviors are believed to include aggression, strategies of mate selection, even altruism (that is, self-sacrifice of the individual to help perpetuate the family grouping) (Bruene & Ribbert, 2002; McAndrew, 2002). Such behavior patterns are termed *instinctive* or *species-specific* because they evolved within certain **species**.

What is meant by an "instinct"? An **instinct** is a stereotyped pattern of behavior that is triggered in a specific situation. Instinctive behavior is nearly identical among the members of the species in which it appears. It tends to resist modification, even when it serves no purpose (as in the interminable barking of some breeds of dogs) or results in punishment. Instinctive behavior also appears when the individual is reared in isolation from others of its kind and thus cannot learn the behavior from experience.

Consider some examples of instinctive behavior. If you place an egg from the nest of a goose a few inches in front of her, she will roll it back to the nest with her beak. However, she won't retrieve it if it's farther away—in the "not my egg" zone. If you rear a white-crowned sparrow in isolation from other sparrows, it will still sing a recognizable species-specific song when it matures. The male stickleback fish instinctively attacks fish (or pieces of painted wood) with the kinds of red bellies that are characteristic of other male sticklebacks. Many psychologists consider language to be "instinctive" among humans. Psychologists are trying to determine what other kinds of human behavior may be instinctive. However, even instinctive behavior can be modified to some degree by learning, and most psychologists agree that the richness and complexity of human behavior are made possible by learning.

Heredity, Genetics, and Behavioral Genetics

What is meant by "heredity"? **Heredity** defines one's *nature,* which is based on biological structures and processes. Heredity refers to the biological transmission of traits that have evolved from generation to generation. Fish are limited in other ways by their natural traits. Chimpanzees and gorillas can understand many spoken words and express some concepts through nonverbal symbol systems such as American Sign Language. Apes cannot speak, however, apparently because of limitations in the speech areas of the brain.

What is meant by "genetics"? The subfield of biology that studies heredity is called genetics. The field of **genetics** looks at both species-specific behavior patterns (instincts) and individual differences among the members of a species. *Behavioral genetics* focuses on the contribution of genes to behavior.

Behavioral genetics bridges the sciences of psychology and biology. It is concerned with the genetic transmission of traits that give rise to patterns of behavior. Psychologists are thinking in terms of behavioral genetics when they ask about the inborn reasons why individuals may differ in their behavior and mental processes. For example, some children learn language more quickly than others. Part of the reason may lie in behavioral genetics—their heredity. But some children also experience a richer exposure to language at early ages.

Heredity appears to be a factor in almost all aspects of human behavior, personality, and mental processes (Bouchard & Loehlin, 2001). Examples include sociability, shyness, social dominance, aggressiveness, leadership, thrill seeking, effectiveness as a parent or a therapist, happiness, even interest in arts and crafts (Johnson & Krueger, 2006; Knafo & Plomin, 2006; Leonardo & Hen, 2006).

Heredity is apparently involved in psychological disorders ranging from anxiety and depression to schizophrenia, bipolar disorder, alcoholism, and personality disorders (Farmer et al., 2007; Hill et al., 2007; Metzger et al., 2007; Riley & Kendler, 2005). These disorders are discussed in chapter 12, but here we can note that a study of 794 pairs of female twins by Kendler and his colleagues (2000a) found six aspects of psychological health that were connected with genetic factors: feelings of physical well-being, social relationships, anxiety and depression, substance abuse, use of social support, and self-esteem.

species
a category of biological classification consisting of related organisms who are capable of interbreeding; *homo sapiens*—humans—make up one species

instinct
a stereotyped pattern of behavior that is triggered by a particular stimulus and nearly identical among members of a species, even when they are reared in isolation

heredity
the transmission of traits from parent to offspring by means of genes

genetics
the area of biology that focuses on heredity

gene
a basic unit of heredity, which is found at a specific point on a chromosome

chromosome
a microscopic rod-shaped body in the cell nucleus carrying genes that transmit hereditary traits from generation to generation; humans normally have 46 chromosomes

DNA
acronym for deoxyribonucleic acid, the substance that forms the basic material of chromosomes; it takes the form of a double helix and contains the genetic code

polygenic
referring to traits that are influenced by combinations of genes

genotype
one's genetic makeup, based on the sequencing of the nucleotides we term A, C, G, and T

The Kendler group also found, however, that the family environment contributed strongly to social relationships, substance abuse, and social support. Although psychological health is influenced by environmental factors, our understanding of the role of heredity continues to expand. Unlocking these mysteries depends on how well we understand genes and chromosomes.

Genes and Chromosomes

Genes are the most basic building blocks of heredity. Genes regulate the development of specific traits. Some traits, such as blood type, are controlled by a single pair of genes. (One gene is derived from each parent.) Other traits are determined by combinations of genes. The inherited component of complex psychological traits, such as intelligence, is believed to be determined by combinations of genes. It is estimated that the cells within your body contain 20,000 to 25,000 genes (Human Genome Sequencing Consortium, 2004).

Genes are segments of chromosomes. That is, chromosomes are made up of strings of genes. Each cell in the body contains 46 chromosomes arranged in 23 pairs. Chromosomes are large complex molecules of DNA (short for *deoxyribonucleic acid*), which has several chemical components. The tightly wound structure of DNA was first demonstrated in the 1950s by James Watson and Francis Crick. DNA takes the form of a double helix—a twisting molecular ladder (see Figure 2.15). The "rungs" of the ladder are made up of chemicals whose names are abbreviated as A, T, C, and G. A always links up with T to complete a rung, and C always combines with G. Therefore, you can describe the *genetic code* in terms of the nucleotides you find along just one of the rungs—e.g., CTGAGTCAC and so on. A single gene can contain hundreds of thousands of base pairs. So if you think of a gene as a word, it can be a few hundred thousand letters long and completely unpronounceable. A group of scientists working together around the globe—referred to as the Human Genome Project—has learned that the sequencing of your DNA consists of about 3 billion DNA sequences spread throughout your chromosomes (Plomin & Crabbe, 2000). These sequences—the order of the chemicals we call A, T, C, and G—caused you to grow arms and not wings, and skin rather than scales. Psychologists debate the extent to which genes influence complex psychological traits such as intelligence, aggressiveness, and happiness, and the appearance of psychological disorders such as schizophrenia. Some traits, such as eye color, are determined by a single pair of genes. Other traits, especially complex psychological traits such as sociability and aggressiveness, are thought to be polygenic—that is, influenced by combinations of genes.

Your genetic code provides your genotype—that is, your full genetic potential, as determined by the sequencing of the chemicals in your DNA.

Figure 2.15

Cells, Chromosomes, and DNA

A. The nuclei of cells contain chromosomes. **B.** Chromosomes are made up of DNA. **C.** Segments of DNA are made up of genes. The genetic code—that is the order of the chemicals A, G, T, and C—determines your species and all those traits that can be inherited, from the color of your eyes to predispositions toward many psychological traits and abilities, including sociability and musical talent.

Cell
Nucleus
Chromosomes
DNA

A + T
C + G

But the person you see in the mirror was also influenced by your early experiences in the home, injuries, adequacy of nourishment, educational experiences, and numerous other environmental influences. Therefore, you see the outer appearance of your phenotype, including the hairstyles of the day. Your phenotype is the manner in which your genetic code manifests itself because of your experiences and environmental circumstances. Your genotype enables you to acquire language. Your phenotype reveals that you are likely to be speaking English if you were reared in the United States or Spanish if you were reared in Mexico (or both, if you are Mexican American).

Your genotype provides what psychologists refer to as your nature. Your phenotype represents the interaction of your nature (heredity) and your nurture (environmental influences) in the origins of your behavior and mental processes. Psychologists are especially interested in the roles of nature and nurture in intelligence and psychological disorders. Our genotypes provide us with physical traits that set the stage for certain behaviors. But none of us is the result of heredity alone. Environmental factors such as nutrition, learning opportunities, cultural influences, exercise, and (unfortunately) accident and illness also determine our phenotypes, and whether genetically possible behaviors will be displayed. Behavior and mental processes represent the interaction of nature and nurture. A potential Shakespeare who is reared in poverty and never taught to read or write will not create a *Hamlet*.

We normally receive 23 chromosomes from our father's sperm cell and 23 chromosomes from our mother's egg cell (ovum). When a sperm cell fertilizes an ovum, the chromosomes form 23 pairs. The 23rd pair consists of sex chromosomes, which determine whether we are female or male. We all receive an X sex chromosome (so called because of the X shape) from our mother. If we also receive an X sex chromosome from our father, we develop into a female. If we receive a Y sex chromosome (named after the Y shape) from our father, we develop into a male. In the following section, we observe the unfortunate results that may occur when people do not receive the normal complement of chromosomes from their parents.

When people do not have the normal number of 46 chromosomes (23 pairs), physical and behavioral abnormalities may result. Most persons with Down syndrome, for example, have an extra, or third, chromosome on the 21st pair. Persons with Down syndrome have a downward-sloping fold of skin at the inner corners of the eyes, a round face, a protruding tongue, and a broad, flat nose. They are cognitively impaired and usually have physical problems that cause death by middle age (Schupf, 2000).

Kinship Studies

What are kinship studies? Kinship studies are ways in which psychologists compare the presence of traits and behavior patterns in people who are biologically related or unrelated to help determine the role of genetic factors in their occurrence. The more *closely* people are related, the more *genes* they have in common. Identical twins share 100% of their genes. Parents and children have 50% of their genes in common, as do siblings (brothers and sisters). Aunts and uncles related by blood have a 25% overlap with nieces and nephews. First cousins share 12.5% of their genes. If genes are involved in a trait or behavior pattern, people who are more closely related should be more likely to show similar traits or behavior. Psychologists and behavioral geneticists are especially interested in running kinship studies with twins and adopted individuals (Plomin, 2002).

Twin Studies

The fertilized egg cell (ovum) that carries genetic messages from both parents is called a *zygote*. Now and then, a zygote divides into two cells that separate, so that instead of developing into a single person, it develops into two people with the same genetic makeup. Such people are identical, or monozygotic (MZ), twins. If the woman releases two ova in the same month and they are both fertilized, they develop into fraternal, or dizygotic (DZ), twins. DZ twins, like other siblings, share 50% of their genes. MZ twins are important in the study of the relative influences of nature (heredity) and nurture (the environment) because differences between MZ twins are the result of nurture. (They do

phenotype
one's actual development and appearance, as based on one's genotype and environmental influences

nature
the inborn, innate character of an organism

nurture
the sum total of the environmental factors that affect an organism from conception onward

sex chromosomes
the 23rd pair of chromosomes, whose genetic material determines the sex of the individual

Down syndrome
a condition caused by an extra chromosome on the 21st pair and characterized by mental deficiency, a broad face, and slanting eyes

monozygotic (MZ) twins
twins that develop from a single fertilized ovum that divides in two early in prenatal development; MZ twins thus share the same genetic code; also called *identical twins*

dizygotic (DZ) twins
twins that develop from two fertilized ova and who are thus as closely related as brothers and sisters in general; also called *fraternal twins*

not differ in their heredity—that is, their nature—because their genetic makeup is the same.)

Twin studies compare the presence of traits and behavior patterns in MZ twins, DZ twins, and other people to help determine the role of genetic factors in their occurrence. If MZ twins show greater similarity on a trait or behavior pattern than DZ twins, a genetic basis for the trait or behavior is suggested.

Twin studies show how strongly genetic factors influence physical features. MZ twins are more likely to look alike and to be similar in height, even to have more similar cholesterol levels than DZ twins. MZ twins also resemble one another more strongly than DZ twins in intelligence and personality traits like sociability, anxiety, friendliness, and conformity, even happiness (Markon et al., 2002; McCourt et al., 1999; McCrae et al., 2000). MZ twins are also more likely than DZ twins to share psychological disorders such as autism, depression, schizophrenia, and even vulnerability to alcoholism (McGue et al., 1992; Plomin, 2000; Veenstra-Vanderweele & Cook, 2003).

Of course, twin studies are not perfect. MZ twins may resemble each other more closely than DZ twins partly because they are treated more similarly. MZ twins frequently are dressed identically, and parents sometimes have difficulty telling them apart.

One way to get around this difficulty is to find and compare MZ twins who were reared in different homes. Then, any similarities between MZ twins reared apart could not be explained by a shared home environment and would appear to be largely a result of heredity. In the fascinating Minnesota Study of Twins Reared Apart (Bouchard et al., 1990; DiLalla et al., 1999; Markon et al., 2002), researchers have been measuring the physiological and psychologi-

PETER CADE/GETTY IMAGES

cal characteristics of 56 sets of MZ adult twins who were separated in infancy and reared in different homes.

Research shows that MZ twin sisters begin to menstruate about one to two months apart, whereas DZ twins begin to menstruate about a year apart. MZ twins are more alike than DZ twins in their blood pressure, brain wave patterns, even in their speech patterns, gestures, and mannerisms (Hansell et al., 2001; Lensvelt-Mulders & Hettema, 2001; Lykken et al., 1992).

In sum, MZ twins reared apart are about as similar as MZ twins reared together on a variety of measures of intelligence, personality, temperament, occupational and leisure-time interests, and social attitudes. These traits thus would appear to have a genetic underpinning.

Adoption Studies

The results of kinship studies can be confused when relatives share similar environments as well as genes. Adoption studies overcome some of this problem by comparing children who have been separated from their parents at an early age (or in which identical twins are separated at an early age) and reared in different environments. Psychologists look for similarities between children and their adoptive and natural parents. When children reared by adoptive parents are more similar to their natural parents in a particular trait, strong evidence exists for a genetic role in the development of that trait.

In later chapters we will see that psychologists have been particularly interested in the use of adoption studies to sort out the effects of nature and nurture in the development of personality traits, intelligence, and various psychological disorders. Such traits and disorders apparently represent the interaction of complex groupings of genes as well as environmental influences.

1/60 < human brain weight/body weight

1/1000 < elephant brain weight/body weight

2–225 mi/hr < speed of neural impulses

lobes in the cortex > **4**

percent of > **99.99** species now extinct

186,000 mi/sec < speed of light

200 million < approx. number of nerve fibers in the corpus callosum

23 < pairs of human chromosomes

100 < percent genes shared by monozygotic twins

REVIEW

HE DID

PSYCH2 puts a multitude of study aids at your fingertips.
After reading the chapters, check out these resources for further help:

- **Chapter in Review cards**, found in the back of your book, include all learning outcomes, definitions, and visual summaries for each chapter.

- **Online printable flash cards** give you three additional ways to check your comprehension of key concepts.

Other great ways to help you study include **interactive games and online tutorial quizzes with feedback**.

You can find it all at **www.CengageBrain.com**.

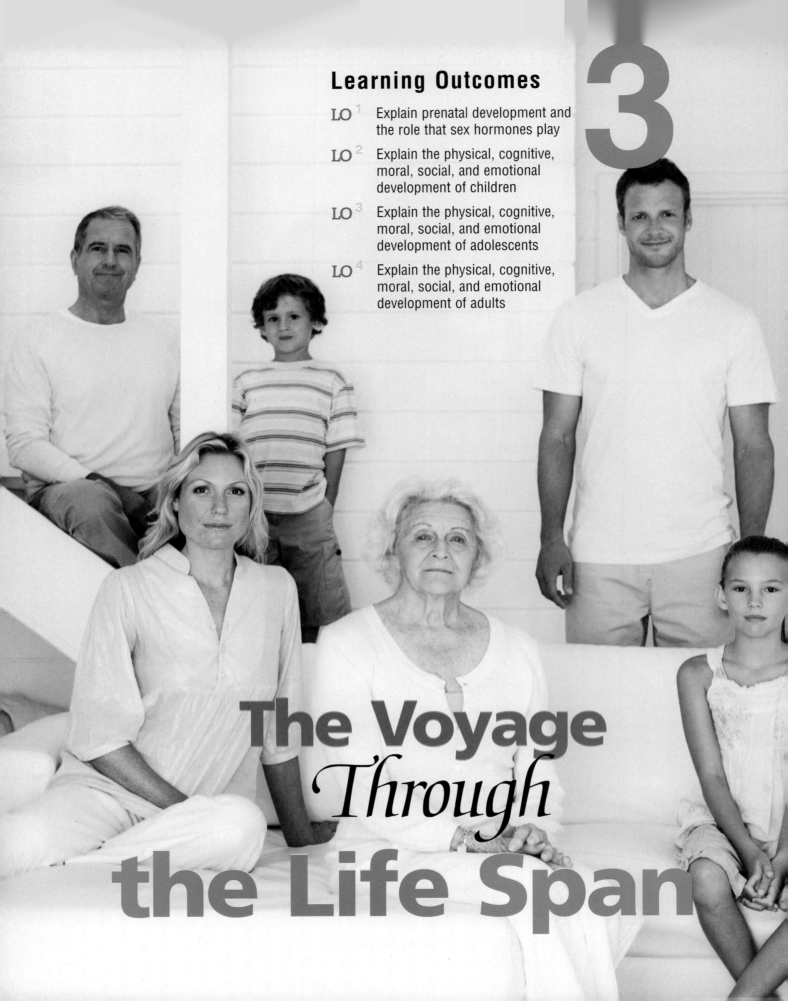

Learning Outcomes

LO¹ Explain prenatal development and the role that sex hormones play

LO² Explain the physical, cognitive, moral, social, and emotional development of children

LO³ Explain the physical, cognitive, moral, social, and emotional development of adolescents

LO⁴ Explain the physical, cognitive, moral, social, and emotional development of adults

3

The Voyage *Through* the Life Span

"Billions make the voyage, yet each is unique."

We have a story to tell. An important story. A fascinating story. It is your story. It is about the remarkable voyage you have already taken through childhood and adolescence. It is about the unfolding of your adult life. Billions have made this voyage before. You have much in common with them. Yet you are unique, and things will happen to you, and because of you, that have never happened before.

Developmental psychologists are interested in studying our voyage through the life span for several reasons. The discovery of early influences and developmental sequences helps psychologists understand adults. Psychologists are also interested in the effects of genetic factors, early interactions with parents and siblings, and the school and community on traits such as aggressiveness and intelligence.

Developmental psychologists seek to learn the causes of developmental abnormalities. For example, should pregnant women abstain from smoking and drinking? (Yes.) Is it safe for a pregnant woman to take aspirin for a headache or tetracycline to ward off a bacterial infection? (Perhaps not. Ask your obstetrician.) What factors contribute to child abuse? Some developmental psychologists focus on adult development. For example, what conflicts and disillusionments can we expect as we voyage through our thirties, forties, and fifties? The information acquired by developmental psychologists can help us make decisions about how we rear our children and lead our own lives.

Let us now turn to prenatal developments—the changes that occur between conception and birth. They are spectacular, but they occur "out of sight."

Truth or Fiction?

What do you think?

Folklore, common sense, or nonsense? Place a T for "True" or F for "False" on the lines provided (you'll learn the answers as you read through the text).

___ Your heart started beating when you were only one-fifth of an inch long and weighed a fraction of an ounce.

___ Prior to six months or so of age, "out of sight" is literally "out of mind."

___ The architect Frank Lloyd Wright designed New York's innovative spiral-shaped Guggenheim Museum when he was sixty-five years old.

___ Alzheimer's disease is a normal part of aging.

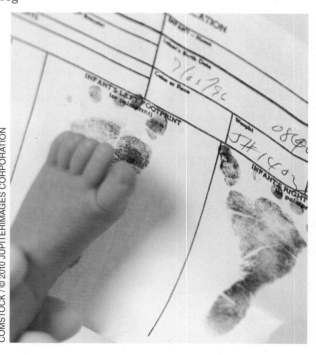

zygote
a fertilized ovum (egg cell)

germinal stage
the first stage of prenatal development, during which the dividing mass of cells has not become implanted in the uterine wall

amniotic sac
a sac within the uterus that contains the embryo or fetus

LO¹ Prenatal Development

The most dramatic gains in height and weight occur during prenatal development. *What developments occur from conception through birth?* Within nine months, the newly conceived organism develops from a nearly microscopic cell to a newborn child about twenty inches long. Its weight increases a billion-fold!

During the months following conception, the single cell formed by the union of sperm and egg—the **zygote**—multiplies, becoming two cells, then four, then eight, and so on.

Conception takes place in a fallopian tube. Following conception, the zygote divides repeatedly as it proceeds on its three- to four-day voyage to the

Figure 3.1

A Human Fetus at Twelve Weeks
By the end of the first trimester, formation of all the major organ systems is complete. Fingers and toes are fully formed, and the sex of the fetus can be determined visually.

A Human Fetus at Four Months
At this midway point between conception and birth, the fetus is covered with fine, downy hair, called *lanugo*.

> ## The heart will continue to beat without rest every minute of every day for most of a century, perhaps longer.

uterus. The ball-like mass of multiplying cells wanders about the uterus for another three to four days before beginning to implant in the uterine wall. Implantation takes another week or so. The period from conception to implantation is called the **germinal stage**.

The *embryonic stage* lasts from implantation until about the eighth week of development. During this stage, the major body organ systems take form. As you can see from Figure 3.1, the growth of the head precedes that of other parts of the body. The growth of the organs—heart, lungs, and so on—also precedes the growth of the extremities. The relatively early *maturation* of the brain and the organ systems allows them to participate in the nourishment and further development of the embryo. The heart will continue to beat without rest every minute of every day for most of a century, perhaps longer.

During the second month, the nervous system begins to transmit messages. By five to six weeks, the embryo is only a quarter-inch to a half-inch long, yet nondescript sex organs have formed. By about the seventh week, the genetic code (XY or XX) begins to assert itself, causing the sex organs to differentiate. If a Y sex chromosome is present, testes form and begin to produce *androgens* (male sex hormones), which further masculinize the sex organs. In the absence of these hormones, the embryo develops sex organs typical of the female, regardless of its genetic code. However, individuals with a male genetic code would be sterile. By the end of the second month, the head has become rounded and the facial features distinct—all in an embryo that is about one inch long and weighs one-thirtieth of an ounce.

As it develops, the embryo is suspended within a protective **amniotic sac** in the mother's uterus. The sac is surrounded by a clear membrane and contains amniotic fluid. The fluid is a sort of natural air bag, allowing the child to move or even jerk around without injury. It also helps maintain an even temperature.

Truth
During the fourth week, a primitive heart begins to beat and pump blood—in an organism that is one-fifth of an inch long.

From now until birth, the embryo exchanges nutrients and wastes with the mother through the placenta. The embryo is connected to the placenta by the umbilical cord. The placenta is connected to the mother by blood vessels in the uterine wall.

The *fetal stage* lasts from the beginning of the third month until birth. By the end of the third month, the major organ systems and the fingers and toes have formed. In the middle of the fourth month, the mother usually detects the first fetal movements. By the end of the sixth month, the fetus moves its limbs so vigorously that mothers often feel that they are being kicked. The fetus opens and shuts its eyes, sucks its thumb, alternates between periods of being awake and sleeping, and responds to light. It also turns somersaults, which can be perceived by the mother.

During the three months prior to birth, the organ systems of the fetus continue to mature. The heart and lungs become increasingly capable of sustaining independent life. The fetus gains about five-and-a-half pounds and doubles in length. Newborn boys average about seven-and-a-half pounds and newborn girls about seven pounds.

LO² Childhood

Childhood begins with birth. When my children are enjoying themselves, I kid them and say, "Stop having fun. You're a child, and childhood is the worst time of life." I get a laugh because they know that childhood is supposed to be the best time of life—a time for play and learning and endless possibilities. In this section we see that childhood is an exciting time of physical, cognitive, and social and emotional developments.

Physical Development

During infancy—the first two years of childhood—dramatic gains in height and weight continue. Babies usually double their birth weight in about five months and triple it by their first birthday (Kuczmarski et al., 2000). Their height increases by about ten inches in the first year. Children grow another four to six inches during the second year and gain some four to seven pounds. After that, they gain about two to three inches a year until they reach the adolescent growth spurt. Weight gains also remain fairly even at about four to six pounds per year until the spurt. Other aspects of physical development in childhood include reflexes and perceptual development.

Reflexes

Soon after you were born, a doctor or nurse probably pressed her fingers against the palms of your hands. Although you would have had no idea what to do

in response, most likely you grasped the fingers firmly—so firmly that you could have been lifted from your cradle!

Grasping at birth is inborn, an example of the importance of nature in human development. Grasping is one of the baby's reflexes. Reflexes are simple, unlearned, stereotypical responses elicited by specific stimuli. Newborn children do not know that it is necessary to eat to survive. Fortunately, rooting and sucking reflexes cause them to eat. They turn their head toward stimuli that prod or stroke the cheek, chin, or corner of the mouth. This is termed rooting. They suck objects that touch their lips. Reflexes are essential to survival and occur automatically—that is, without thinking about them.

Newborns use the withdrawal reflex to avoid painful stimuli. In the startle, or Moro, reflex, they draw up their legs and arch their backs in response to sudden noises, bumps, or loss of support while being held. They grasp objects that press against the palms of their hands (the grasp, or palmar, reflex). They fan their toes when the soles of their feet are stimulated (the Babinski reflex). Pediatricians test these reflexes to assess babies' neural functioning. Babies also breathe, sneeze, cough, yawn, blink, defecate, and urinate reflexively.

Motor Development

The motor development of the child refers to the progression from simple acts like lifting the head to running around. Maturation and experience both

fixation time
the amount of time spent looking at a visual stimulus

play key roles in motor development (Muir, 2000; Pryce et al., 2001; Roncesvalles et al., 2001). Maturation of the brain is a key to motor development. Motor development provides some of the most fascinating changes in infants, in part because so much seems to happen so quickly—and so much of it during the first year. Children go through a sequence that includes rolling over, sitting up, crawling, creeping, walking, and running. The ages at which infants first engage in these activities vary, but the sequence generally remains the same (see Figure 3.2). Invariant sequences suggest an unfolding of the genetic code (maturation).

The role of maturation in areas such as physical development (for example, gains in height and weight and the effects of puberty), language development, and motor development is clear. But environmental factors are also involved. Children may have certain genetic potentials for body size and growth rates, but they do not reach them unless environmental factors such as nutrition, relatively clean air, and so on are available. Children do not understand or produce language until their genetic codes spark the development of certain structures and processes in the brain. But the environment is also involved. Children learn the languages used in their homes and communities. They do not speak foreign tongues without being exposed to them.

Figure 3.2

Motor Development

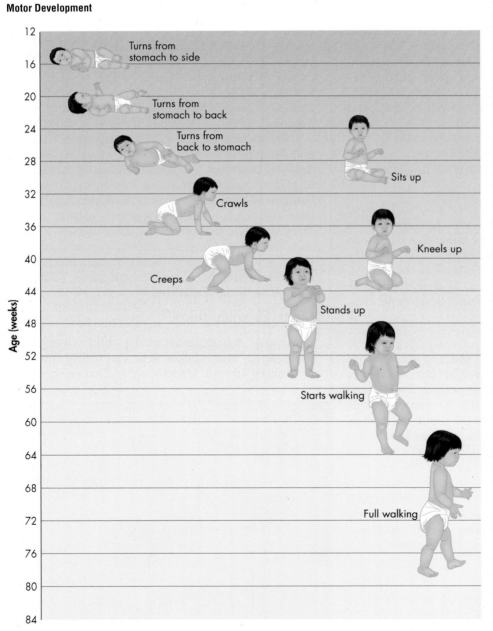

Perceptual Development

Newborn children spend about sixteen hours a day sleeping and do not have much opportunity to learn about the world. Yet they perceive the world reasonably well soon after birth. Within a couple of days, infants can follow, or "track," a moving light with their eyes (Kellman & von Hofsten, 1992). By three months, they can discriminate most colors (Banks & Shannon, 1993; Teller, 1998). Newborns are nearsighted, but by about four months, infants focus on distant objects about as well as adults do.

The visual preferences of infants are measured by the amount of time, termed **fixation time**, they spend looking at one stimulus instead of another. In classic research by Robert Fantz (1961), two-month-old infants preferred visual

Figure 3.3

Two-Month-Olds' Preferences for Visual Stimuli

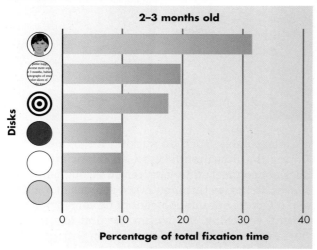

2–3 months old

Disks

Percentage of total fixation time

0   10   20   30   40

stimuli that resembled the human face to news print, a bull's eye, and featureless red, white, and yellow disks (see Figure 3.3).

Classic research has shown that infants tend to respond to cues for depth by the time they are able to crawl (at about six to eight months). Most also have the good sense to avoid crawling off ledges and table tops into open space (Campos et al., 1978).

Normal newborns hear well. Most newborns reflexively turn their heads toward unusual sounds. This finding, along with findings about visual tracking, suggests that infants are preprogrammed to survey their environments. Speaking or singing softly in a low-pitched tone soothes infants. This is why lullabies help infants fall asleep.

Three-day-old babies prefer their mother's voice to those of other women, but they do not show a preference for their father's voice (DeCasper & Prescott, 1984; Freeman et al., 1993). Babies, of course, have had months of "experience" in the uterus. For at least two or three months before birth, they have been able to hear. Because they are predominantly exposed to sounds produced by their mother, learning may contribute to newborn preferences.

Cognitive Development

The ways in which children mentally represent and think about the world—that is, their *cognitive development*—are explored in this section. Because cognitive functioning develops over many years, young children have ideas about the world that differ considerably from those of adults. Many of these ideas are charming but illogical—at least to adults. Let us consider three views of cognitive development. We will begin with Jean Piaget's stage theory of cognitive development. Then we will turn to the views of the Russian psychologist Lev Semenovich Vygotsky whose approach is quite different from Piaget's but is enjoying a rebirth in popularity. Then we will focus on Lawrence Kohlberg's theory of moral development.

Jean Piaget's Cognitive–Developmental Theory

Jean Piaget (1896–1980) earned his Ph.D. in biology. In 1920 he obtained a job at the Binet Institute in Paris, where work on intelligence tests was being conducted. His first task was to adapt English verbal reasoning items for use with French children. To do so, he had to try out the items on children in various age groups and see whether they could arrive at correct answers. The task was boring until Piaget became intrigued by the children's *wrong* answers. Another investigator might have shrugged them off, but Piaget perceived patterns in the children's "mistakes." The wrong answers reflected consistent, if illogical, cognitive processes. Piaget's observations led to his theory of cognitive development.

Assimilation Piaget described human thought, or intelligence, in terms of the concepts of assimilation and accommodation. **Assimilation** means responding to a new stimulus through existing cognitive structures.

assimilation
according to Piaget, the inclusion of a new event into an existing schema

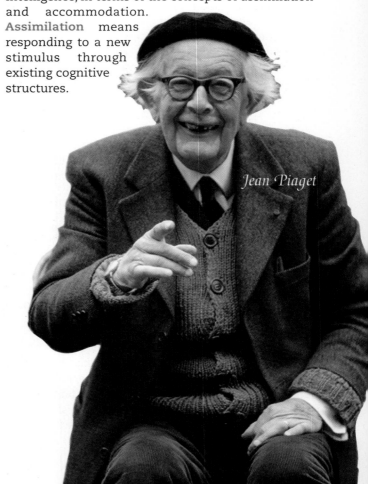

Jean Piaget

FARRELL GREHAN/CORBIS

DOUG GOODMAN/PHOTO
RESEARCHERS, INC.

schema
according to Piaget, a hypothetical mental structure that permits the classification and organization of new information

accommodation
according to Piaget, the modification of schemas so that information inconsistent with existing schemas can be integrated or understood

object permanence
recognition that objects removed from sight still exist, as demonstrated in young children by continued pursuit

Figure 3.4

Object Permanence

To this infant, who is in the early part of the sensorimotor stage, out of sight is truly out of mind. Once a sheet of paper is placed between the infant and the toy animal, the infant loses all interest in it. The toy is apparently not yet mentally represented.

Infants, for example, usually try to place new objects in their mouth to suck, feel, or explore. Piaget would say that the child is assimilating a new toy to the sucking schema. A schema is a pattern of action or a "mental structure" involved in acquiring or organizing knowledge.

Accommodation **Accommodation** is the creation of new ways of responding to objects or looking at the world. In accommodation, children transform existing schemas to incorporate new events. Children (and adults) accommodate to objects and situations that cannot be integrated into existing schemas. For example, children who study biology learn that whales cannot be assimilated into the "fish" schema. They accommodate by constructing new schemas, such as "mammals without legs that live in the sea." The ability to accommodate to novel stimuli advances as a result of maturation and experience. Let us apply these concepts to the stages of cognitive development.

Piaget's Stages of Cognitive Development

What are Piaget's stages of cognitive development? Piaget hypothesized that children's cognitive processes develop in an orderly sequence. Some children may be more advanced than others, but the sequence remains the same. Piaget (1963) identified four major stages of cognitive development: sensorimotor, preoperational, concrete operational, and formal operational.

The Sensorimotor Stage The newborn infant is capable of assimilating novel stimuli only to existing reflexes (or ready-made schemas) such as the rooting and sucking reflexes. But by the time an infant reaches the age of one month, he or she already shows purposeful behavior by repeating behavior patterns that

are pleasurable, such as sucking his or her hand. During the first month or so, an infant apparently does not connect stimuli perceived through different senses. Reflexive turning toward sources of auditory and olfactory stimulation cannot be considered purposeful searching. But within the first few months the infant begins to coordinate vision with grasping, to look at the object being held or touched.

A three- or four-month-old infant may be fascinated by her own hands and legs. The infant may become absorbed in watching herself open and close her fists. The infant becomes increasingly interested in acting on the environment to make interesting results (such as the sound of a rattle) last longer or occur again. Behavior becomes increasingly intentional and purposeful. Between four and eight months of age, the infant explores cause-and-effect relationships such as the thump made by tossing an object or the swinging that results from kicking a hanging toy.

For most infants younger than six months, objects are not yet represented mentally. For this reason, as you can see in Figure 3.4, a child makes no effort to search for an object that has been removed or placed behind a screen. By the age of eight to twelve months, however, infants realize that objects removed from sight still exist and attempt to find them. In this way, they show what is known as object permanence, thereby making it possible to play peekaboo.

Between one and two years of age, children begin to show interest in how things are constructed. It may be for this reason that they persistently touch and finger their parents' faces and their own. Toward the end of the second year, children begin to engage in mental trial and error before they try out overt behaviors. For example, when they look for an object you have removed, they will no longer begin their search in the last place they saw it. Rather, they may follow you, assuming you are carrying the object even though it is not visible. It is as though they are

Truth

It is true that "out of sight" is literally "out of mind" prior to the age of six months or so.

Table 3.1

Examples of Preoperational Thought

Type of Thought	Sample Questions	Typical Answers
Egocentrism	Why does it get dark out? Why does the sun shine? Why is there snow?	So I can go to sleep. To keep me warm. For me to play in.
Animism	Why do trees have leaves? Why do stars twinkle?	To keep them warm. Because they're happy and cheerful.
Artificialism	What makes it rain? Why is the sky blue? What is the wind?	Someone emptying a watering can. Somebody painted it. A man blowing.

anticipating failure in searching for the object in the place where they last saw it.

Because the first stage of development is dominated by learning to coordinate perception of the self and of the environment with motor activity, Piaget termed it the sensorimotor stage. This stage comes to a close with the acquisition of the basics of language at about age two.

The Preoperational Stage The preoperational stage is characterized by the use of words and symbols to represent objects and relationships among them. But be warned—any resemblance between the logic of children between the ages of two and seven and your own logic may be coincidental. Children may use the same words as adults, but this does not mean their views of the world are the same.

To a preoperational child, right is right and wrong is wrong. Why? "Because!"—that's why.

Preoperational children tend to think one-dimensionally—to focus on one aspect of a problem or situation at a time.

One consequence of one-dimensional thinking is egocentrism. Preoperational children cannot understand that other people do not see things the same way they do. When my daughter Allyn was two and a half. I asked her to tell me about a trip to the store with her mother. "You tell me," she replied. It seemed she did not understand that I could not see the world through her eyes.

To egocentric preoperational children, all the world's a stage that has been erected to meet their needs and amuse them. When asked, "What are television sets for?", they may answer, "To watch my favorite shows and cartoons." Preoperational children also show *animism*. They attribute life and consciousness to physical objects like the sun and the moon. They also show *artificialism*. They believe that environmental events like rain and thunder are human inventions. Asked what causes thunder, a four-year-old may reply 'A man grumbling.' Examples of egocentrism, animism, and artificialism are shown in Table 3.1.

To gain further insight into preoperational thinking, find a three- or four-year-old and try these mini-experiments:

- Pour water from a tall, thin glass into a low, wide glass. Now, ask the child whether the low, wide glass contains more, less, or the same amount of water that was in the tall, thin glass. If the child says that they hold the same amount of water, the child is correct. But if the child errs, why do you think this is so?

- Now flatten a ball of clay into a pancake, and ask the child whether you wind up with more, less, or the same amount of clay? If the child errs again, why do you think this is so?

To arrive at the correct answers to these questions, children must understand the law of conservation. This law holds that basic properties of substances such as mass, weight, and volume remain the same— that is, are *conserved*—when one changes superficial properties such as their shape or arrangement.

Conservation requires the ability to think about, or *center* on, two aspects of a situation at once, such as height and width. Conserving the mass, weight, or volume of a substance requires the recognition that a change in one dimension can compensate for a change in another. But the preoperational boy in Figure 3.5 focuses on only one dimension at a time. First he is shown two short, squat glasses of water and agrees that they contain the same amount of water. Then, while he watches, water is poured from a squat glass into a tall, thin glass. Now he is asked which glass contains more water. After mulling over the problem, he points to the tall glass. Why? Because when he looks at the glasses he is "overwhelmed" by the fact that the thinner glass is taller. The preoperational child focuses

sensorimotor stage
the first of Piaget's stages of cognitive development, characterized by coordination of sensory information and motor activity, early exploration of the environment, and lack of language

preoperational stage
the second of Piaget's stages, characterized by illogical use of words and symbols, spotty logic, and egocentrism

egocentrism
according to Piaget, the assumption that others view the world as one does oneself

conservation
according to Piaget, recognition that basic properties of substances such as weight and mass remain the same when superficial features change

COMSTOCK / © 2010 JUPITERIMAGES CORPORATION

objective responsibility according to Piaget, the assignment of blame according to the amount of damage done rather than the motives of the actor

concrete operational stage Piaget's third stage, characterized by logical thought concerning tangible objects, conservation, and subjective morality

decentration simultaneous focusing on more than one dimension of a problem, so that flexible, reversible thought becomes possible

subjective moral judgment according to Piaget, moral judgment that is based on the motives of the perpetrator

on the most apparent dimension of the situation—in this case, the greater height of the thinner glass. He does not realize that the increased width of the squat glass compensates for the decreased height. By the way, if you ask him whether any water has been added or taken away in the pouring process, he readily says no. But if you then repeat the question about which glass contains *more* water, he again points to the taller glass. If all this sounds rather illogical, that is because it is illogical—or, in Piaget's terms, preoperational.

Piaget (1997) found that the moral judgment of preoperational children is also one-dimensional. Five-year-olds tend to be slaves to rules and authority. When you ask them why something should be done in a certain way, they may insist, "Because that's the way to do it!" or "Because Mommy says so!" Right is right and wrong is wrong. Why? "Because!"—that's why.

According to most older children and adults, an act is a crime only when there is criminal intent. Accidents may be hurtful, but the perpetrators are usually seen as blameless. But in the court of the one-dimensional, preoperational child, there is **objective responsibility**. People are sentenced (and harshly!) on the basis of the amount of damage they have done, not their motives or intentions. To demonstrate objective responsibility, Piaget would tell children stories and ask them which character was naughtier and why. John, for example, accidentally breaks fifteen cups when he opens a door. Henry breaks one cup when he sneaks into a kitchen cabinet to find forbidden jam. The preoperational child usually judges John to be naughtier. Why? Because he broke more cups.

The Concrete Operational Stage By about age seven, the typical child is entering the stage of concrete operations. In this stage, which lasts until about age twelve, children show the beginnings of the capacity for adult logic. However, their logical thoughts, or *operations,* generally involve tangible objects rather than abstract ideas. Concrete operational children are capable of decentration; they can center on two dimensions of a problem at once. This attainment has implications for moral judgments, conservation, and other intellectual undertakings.

Children now become subjective in their moral judgments. When assigning guilt, they center on the motives of wrongdoers as well as on the amount of damage done. Concrete operational children judge Henry more harshly than John because John's misdeed was an accident.

Concrete operational children understand the laws of conservation. The boy in Figure 3.5, now a few years older, would say that the squat glass still contains the same amount of juice. If asked why, he might reply, "Because you can pour it back into the other one." Such an answer also suggests awareness of the concept of *reversibility*—the recognition that many processes can be reversed or undone so that things are restored to their previous condition. Centering simultaneously on the height and the width of the glasses, the boy recognizes that the loss in height compensates for the gain in width.

Figure 3.5

Conservation

Children in this stage are less egocentric. They are able to take on the roles of others and to view the world, and themselves, from other people's perspectives. They recognize that people see things in different ways because of different situations and different sets of values.

During the concrete operational stage, children's own sets of values begin to emerge and acquire stability. Children come to understand that feelings of love between them and their parents can endure even when someone is temporarily angry or disappointed. We continue our discussion of Piaget's theory—his stage of formal operations—later in the chapter in the section on adolescence.

Evaluation of Piaget's Theory A number of questions have been raised concerning the accuracy of Piaget's views. Among them are these:

- *Was Piaget's timing accurate?* Some critics argue that Piaget's methods led him to underestimate children's abilities (Bjorklund, 2000; Meltzoff & Gopnik, 1997). Other researchers using different methods have found, for example, that preschoolers are less egocentric and that children are capable of conservation at earlier ages than Piaget thought.

- *Does cognitive development occur in stages?* Cognitive events such as egocentrism and conservation appear to develop more continuously than Piaget thought—that is, they may not occur in stages (Bjorklund, 2000; Flavell, 2000). Although cognitive developments appear to build on previous cognitive developments, the process may be more gradual than stage-like.

- *Are developmental sequences always the same?* Here, Piaget's views have fared better. It seems there is no variation in the sequence in which cognitive developments occur.

In sum, Piaget's theoretical edifice has been rocked, but it has not been reduced to rubble. Now let us consider the views of Vygotsky.

Lev Vygotsky (1896–1934) was a Russian psychologist whose work was banned in communist Russia. Seventy years after his death, his work has been rediscovered. Unlike Piaget, Vygotsky was not a stage theorist. Instead, he saw the transmission of knowledge as cumulative, and focused on the ways in which children's interactions with their elders enhance their cognitive development.

Lev Vygotsky's Sociocultural Theory

The term *sociocultural theory* has different meanings. For example, the term can refer to the roles of factors such as ethnicity and gender in behavior and mental processes. Vygotsky's sociocultural theory focuses instead on the ways in which children's cognitive development is influenced by the cultures in which they are reared and the people who teach them.

Vygotsky's theory (1978) focuses on the transmission of information and cognitive skills from generation to generation. The transmission of skills involves teaching and learning, but Vygotsky was no behaviorist. He did not view learning as a mechanical process that can be described in terms of the conditioning of units of behavior. Rather, he focused more generally on how the child's social interaction with adults, largely in the home, organized a child's learning experiences in such a way that the child can obtain cognitive skills—such as computation or reading skills—and use them to acquire information. Like Piaget, Vygotsky saw the child's functioning as adaptive (Piaget & Smith, 2000), and the child adapts to his or her social and cultural interactions.

What are the key concepts of Vygotsky's theory of cognitive development? Key concepts in Vygotsky's theory include the zone of proximal development and *scaffolding*. The word *proximal* means "nearby" or "close," as in the words *approximate* and *proximity*. The zone of proximal development (ZPD) refers to a range of tasks that a child can carry out with the help of someone who is more skilled (Haenen, 2001). The "zone" refers to the relationship between the child's abilities and what she or he can do with help from others. Adults or older children best guide the child through this zone by gearing their assistance to the child's capabilities (Flavell et al., 2002).

Within the zone we find an apprenticeship in which the child works with, and learns from, others (Meijer & Elshout, 2001). When learning with others, the child tends to internalize—or bring inward—the conversations and explanations that help him or her gain skills (Prior & Welling, 2001; Vygotsky, 1962; Yang, 2000). Children not only learn the meanings of words from teachers but also learn ways of talking to themselves about solving problems within a cultural context (DeVries, 2000). Outer speech becomes inner speech. What was the teacher's becomes the child's. What was a social and cultural context becomes embedded within the child (Moro & Rodriguez, 2000); thus we have the term, *sociocultural theory*.

A *scaffold* is a temporary skeletal structure that enables workers to fabricate a building, bridge, or

zone of proximal development (ZPD) Vygotsky's term for the situation in which a child carries out tasks with the help of someone who is more skilled, frequently an adult who represents the culture in which the child develops

Proximal means "nearby" or "close."

other, more permanent, structure. Cognitive scaffolding refers to the temporary support provided by a parent or teacher to a child who is learning to perform a task. Guidance decreases as the child becomes more skilled and self-sufficient (Clarke-Stewart & Beck, 1999; Maccoby, 1992). In Vygotsky's theory, teachers and parents provide children with problem-solving methods that serve as cognitive scaffolding while the child gains the ability to function independently. A child's instructors may offer advice on sounding out letters and words that provide a temporary support until reading "clicks" and the child no longer needs the device. Children may be offered scaffolding that enables them to use their fingers to do calculations. Eventually, the scaffolding is removed and the cognitive structures stand alone.

Piaget's focus was largely maturational. It was assumed that maturation of the brain allowed the child to experience new levels of insights and suddenly develop new kinds of problem-solving. Vygotsky focused on the processes in the teacher–learner relationship. To Vygotsky, cognitive development was about culture and social interaction. Let us now turn to another aspect of cognitive development—the ways in

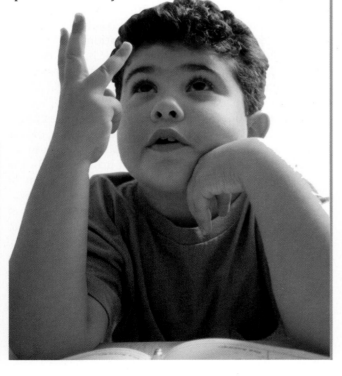

PURESTOCK / © 2010 JUPITERIMAGES CORPORATION

which children (and adults) arrive at judgments about what is right and what is wrong.

Lawrence Kohlberg's Theory of Moral Development

How do children reason about right and wrong? Cognitive–developmental theorist Lawrence Kohlberg (1981) used the following tale in his research into children's moral reasoning:

> In Europe a woman was near death from a special kind of cancer. There was one drug that the doctors thought might save her. It was a form of radium that a druggist in the same town had recently discovered. The drug was expensive to make, but the druggist was charging ten times what the drug cost him to make. He paid $200 for the radium and charged $2,000 for a small dose of the drug. The sick woman's husband, Heinz, went to everyone he knew to borrow the money, but he could only get together about $1,000, which was half of what it cost. He told the druggist that his wife was dying and asked him to sell it cheaper or let him pay later. But the druggist said: "No, I discovered the drug, and I'm going to make money from it." So Heinz got desperate and broke into the man's store to steal the drug for his wife (Kohlberg, 1969).

Heinz is caught in a moral dilemma. In such dilemmas, a legal or social rule (in this case, the law forbidding stealing) is pitted against a strong human need (his desire to save his wife). Children and adults arrive at yes or no answers for different reasons. According to Kohlberg, the reasons can be classified according to the level of moral development they reflect.

As a stage theorist, Kohlberg argues that the stages of moral reasoning follow a specific sequence. Children progress at different rates, and not all children (or adults) reach the highest stage. But the sequence is always the same: Children must go through stage 1 before they enter stage 2, and so on. According to Kohlberg, there are three levels of moral development and two stages within each level.

When it comes to the dilemma of Heinz, Kohlberg believed that people could justify Heinz's theft of the drug or his decision not to steal it by the reasoning of any level or stage of moral development. In other words, Kohlberg was not as interested in the eventual "yes" or "no" as he was in *how a person reasoned* to arrive at yes or no.

The Preconventional Level The **preconventional level** applies to most children through about the age of nine. Children at this level base their moral judgments on the consequences of behavior. For example, stage 1 is oriented toward obedience and punishment. Good behavior is obedient and allows one to avoid punishment. However, a child in stage 1 can decide that Heinz should or should not steal the drug.

In stage 2, good behavior allows people to satisfy their needs and those of others. (Heinz's wife needs the drug; therefore, stealing it—the only way of obtaining it—is not wrong.)

The Conventional Level In the **conventional level** of moral reasoning, right and wrong are judged by conformity to conventional (familial, religious, societal) standards of right and wrong. According to the stage 3 "good-boy orientation," moral behavior is that which meets the needs and expectations of others. Moral behavior is what is "normal"—what the majority does. (Heinz should steal the drug because that is what a "good husband" would do. It is "natural" or "normal" to try to help one's wife. *Or* Heinz should *not* steal the drug because "good people do not steal.")

In stage 4, moral judgments are based on rules that maintain the social order. Showing respect for authority and doing one's duty are valued highly. (Heinz *must* steal the drug; it would be his fault if he let his wife die. He would pay the druggist later, when he had the money.) Many people do not mature beyond the conventional level.

The Postconventional Level Postconventional moral reasoning is more complex and focuses on dilemmas in which individual needs are pitted against the need to maintain the social order and on personal conscience. We discuss the postconventional level later in the chapter in the section on adolescence.

Evaluation of Kohlberg's Theory

As Kohlberg's theory predicts, evidence supports the view that the moral judgments of children develop in an upward sequence (Boom et al., 2007). Postconventional thought, if found at all, first occurs in adolescence. Formal-operational thinking is apparently a prerequisite, and education is likely to play a role (Boom et al., 2007; Patenaude et al., 2003). Postconventional reasoning involves understanding of abstract moral principles and empathy with the views and feelings of others.

Kohlberg believed that the stages of moral development were universal, but he may have underestimated the influence of social, cultural, and educational institutions (Dawson, 2002). Parents are also important. Using reason in discipline and discussing the feelings of others advance moral reasoning (Dawson, 2002).

Social and Emotional Development

Social relationships are crucial to us as children. When we are infants, our very survival depends on them. Later in life, they contribute to our feelings of happiness and satisfaction. In this section we discuss aspects of social development, including Erikson's theory of psychosocial development, attachment, and styles of parenting.

Erik Erikson's Stages of Psychosocial Development

According to Erik Erikson, we undergo several stages of psychosocial development *What are Erikson's stages of psychosocial development?* During Erikson's first stage, **trust versus mistrust**, we depend on our primary caregivers (usually our parents) and come to expect that our environments will—or will not—meet our needs. During early childhood and the preschool years, we begin to explore the environment more actively and try new things. At this time, our relationships with our parents and friends can encourage us to develop *autonomy* (self-direction) and initiative, or feelings of shame and guilt. During the elementary school years, friends and teachers take on more importance, encouraging us to become industrious or to develop feelings of inferiority. We will return to Erikson's stages of development later in the chapter.

Attachment

Psychologist Mary D. Salter Ainsworth (1913–1999) defined **attachment** as an emotional tie that is formed between one animal or person and another specific individual. Attachment keeps organisms together—it is vital to the survival of the infant—and it tends to endure. The behaviors that define attachment include (1) attempts to maintain contact or nearness, and (2) shows of anxiety when separated. Babies and children try to maintain contact with caregivers to whom they are attached. They engage in eye contact, pull and tug at them, ask to be picked up, and may even jump in front of them in such a way that they will be "run over" if they are not picked up. *How do feelings of attachment develop? What kinds of experiences affect attachment?*

Mary D. Salter Ainsworth

conventional level according to Kohlberg, a period during which moral judgments largely reflect social conventions; a "law and order" approach to morality

trust versus mistrust Erikson's first stage of psychosocial development, during which children do—or do not—come to trust that primary caregivers and the environment will meet their needs

attachment the enduring affectional tie that binds one person to another

© MARVIN S. ROBERTS

The Strange Situation and Patterns of Attachment

The ways in which infants behave in strange situations are connected with their bonds of attachment with their caregivers. Given this fact, Ainsworth and her colleagues (1978) innovated the *strange situation method* to learn how infants respond to separations and reunions with a caregiver (usually the mother) and a stranger. Using this method, Ainsworth and her colleagues identified three major types of attachment, including secure attachment and two types of insecure attachment:

1 *Secure attachment.* Securely attached infants mildly protest their mother's departure, seek interaction upon reunion, and are readily comforted by her.

2 *Avoidant attachment.* Infants who show avoidant attachment are least distressed by their mother's departure. They play by themselves without fuss and ignore their mothers when they return.

3 *Ambivalent /resistant attachment.* Infants with ambivalent /resistant attachment are the most emotional. They show severe signs of distress when their mother leaves and show ambivalence upon reunion by alternately clinging to and pushing their mother away when she returns.

Attachment is connected with the quality of care that infants receive. The parents of securely attached children are more likely to be affectionate and reliable caregivers (Isabella, 1998; Posada et al., 2002). A wealth of research literature speaks of the benefits of secure attachment. For example, secure children are happier, more sociable, and more cooperative than insecure children (Bohlin et al., 2000). At ages five and six, securely attached children are liked better by their peers and teachers, are more competent, and have fewer behavior problems than insecurely attached children (Granot & Mayseless, 2001; Moss & St-Laurent, 2001). In this vein, we can also note that having the primary caregiver present during stressful situations, such as pediatric exams, helps children cope with these situations (Ybarra et al., 2000).

Stages of Attachment

Ainsworth and her colleagues observed infants in many societies, including the African country of Uganda. She noted the efforts of infants to maintain contact with the mother, their protests when separated from her, and their use of her as a base for exploring their environment. At first, infants show *indiscriminate attachment*. That is, they prefer being held or being with someone to being alone, but they are generally willing to be held by unfamiliar people. Specific attachment to the primary caregiver begins to develop at about four months of age and becomes intense by about seven months of age. Fear of strangers, which develops in some but not all children, follows one or two months later.

From studies such as these, Ainsworth identified three phases of attachment:

1 *The initial-preattachment phase,* which lasts from birth to about three months and is characterized by indiscriminate attachment.

2 *The attachment-in-the-making phase,* which occurs at about three or four months and is characterized by preference for familiar figures.

3 *The clear-cut-attachment phase,* which occurs at about six or seven months and is characterized by intensified depen-dence on the primary caregiver. Fear of strangers, which develops in some but not all children, follows one or two months later.

Theoretical Views of Attachment

Early in the 20th century, behaviorists argued that attachment behaviors are learned through experience. Caregivers feed their infants and tend to their other physiological needs. Thus, infants associate their caregivers with gratification of needs and learn to approach them to meet their needs. The feelings of gratification associated with the meeting of basic needs generalize into feelings of security when the caregiver is present.

However, classic research by psychologist Harry F. Harlow suggests that skin contact may be more important than learning experiences. Harlow noted that infant rhesus monkeys reared without mothers or companions became attached to pieces of cloth in their cages. They maintained contact with them and showed distress when separated from them. Harlow conducted a series of experiments to find out why (Harlow, 1959).

In one study, Harlow placed infant rhesus monkeys in cages with two surrogate mothers, as shown in Figure 3.6. One "mother" was made of wire mesh from which a baby bottle was extended. The other surrogate mother was made of soft, cuddly terrycloth. The infant monkeys spent most of their time clinging to the cloth mother, even though "she" did not gratify their need for food. Harlow concluded that monkeys—and perhaps humans—have an inborn need for contact comfort that is as basic as the need for food. Gratification of the need for contact comfort, rather than food, might be why infant monkeys (and humans) cling to their mothers.

Other researchers, such as ethologist Konrad Lorenz, argue that for many animals, attachment is an instinct—inborn. (Ethologists study the behavioral characteristics of various species of animals.) Attachment, like other instincts, is theorized to

Figure 3.6

Attachment in Infant Monkeys

occur in the presence of a specific stimulus and during a *critical period* of life—that is, a period during which the animal is sensitive to the stimulus.

Some animals become attached to the first moving object they encounter. The formation of an attachment in this manner is therefore called *imprinting*. Lorenz (1981) became well known when pictures of his "family" of goslings were made public. How did Lorenz acquire his following? He was present when the goslings hatched and during their critical period, and he allowed them to follow him. The critical period for geese and some other animals is bounded, at the younger end, by the age at which they first walk and, at the older end, by the age at which they develop fear of strangers. The goslings followed Lorenz persistently, ran to him when frightened, honked with distress at his departure, and tried to overcome barriers between them. If you substitute crying for honking, it all sounds rather human.

Ainsworth and Bowlby (1991) consider attachment to be instinctive in humans. However, among humans attachment is less related to issues such as locomotion and fear of strangers (which is not universal). Moreover, the critical period with humans is quite extended.

Konrad Lorenz and His Family of Goslings

Parenting Styles

Many psychologists have been concerned about the relationships between parenting styles and the personality development of the child. *What types of parental behavior are connected with variables such as self-esteem, achievement motivation, and independence in children?* Diana Baumrind (1973) has been particularly interested in the connections between parental behavior and the development of *instrumental competence* in their children. (Instrumental competence refers to the ability to manipulate the environment to achieve one's goals.) Baumrind has focused largely on four aspects of parental behavior: (1) strictness; (2) demands for the child to achieve intellectual, emotional, and social maturity; (3) communication ability; and (4) warmth and involvement. She labeled the three parenting styles the *authoritative, authoritarian,* and *permissive* styles. Other researchers also speak of the *uninvolved* style. These four styles are defined in the following ways:

1 *Authoritative parents.* The parents of the most competent children rate high in all four areas of behavior. They are strict (restrictive) and demand mature behavior. But they temper their strictness with desire to reason with their children and with love and support (Galambos et al., 2003). They expect much, but they explain why and offer help. Baumrind labeled these parents **authoritative parents** to suggest that they know what they want but are also loving and respectful to their children.

2 *Authoritarian parents.* **Authoritarian parents** view obedience as a virtue for its own sake. They have strict guidelines about what is right and wrong, and they demand that their children stick to them. Both authoritative and authoritarian parents have strict standards, but authoritative parents explain their demands and are supportive, whereas authoritarian parents rely on force and communicate poorly with their children. Authoritarian parents

critical period
a period of time when an instinctive response can be elicited by a particular stimulus

imprinting
a process occurring during a critical period in the development of an organism, in which that organism responds to a stimulus in a manner that will afterward be difficult to modify

authoritative parents
parents who are strict and warm; authoritative parents demand mature behavior but use reason rather than force in discipline

authoritarian parents
parents who are rigid in their rules and who demand obedience for the sake of obedience

permissive parents parents who impose few, if any, rules and who do not supervise their children closely

uninvolved parents parents who generally leave their children to themselves

adolescence the period of life bounded by puberty and the assumption of adult responsibilities

puberty the period of physical development during which sexual reproduction first becomes possible

secondary sex characteristics characteristics that distinguish the sexes, such as distribution of body hair and depth of voice, but that are not directly involved in reproduction

do not respect their children's points of view, and they may be cold and rejecting. When children ask them why they should do this or that, authoritarian parents often answer, "Because I say so!"

3 *Permissive parents.* **Permissive parents** are generally easygoing with their children. As a result, the children do pretty much what the children want. Permissive parents are warm and supportive, but poor at communicating.

4 *Uninvolved parents.* **Uninvolved parents** tend to leave their children on their own. They make few demands and show little warmth or encouragement.

Research evidence shows that the children of warm parents are more likely to be socially and emotionally well adjusted. They are also more likely to internalize moral standards—that is, to develop a conscience (Grusec, 2002; Rudy & Grusec, 2001).

Strictness seems to pay off, provided it is tempered with reason and warmth. Children of authoritative parents have the greatest self-reliance, self-esteem, social competence, and achievement motivation (Galambos et al., 2003; Grusec, 2002; Kim & Rohner, 2002). Children of authoritarian parents are often withdrawn or aggressive and usually do not do as well in school as children of authoritative parents (Kim & Rohner, 2002; Steinberg, 2001). Children of permissive parents seem to be less mature. They are often impulsive, moody, and aggressive. In adolescence, lack of parental monitoring is often linked to delinquency and poor academic performance. Children of uninvolved parents tend to obtain poorer grades than children whose parents make demands on them. The children of uninvolved parents also tend to be more likely to hang out with crowds who "party" a good deal and use drugs (Durbin et al., 1993). The message? Simple enough: Children profit when parents make reasonable demands, show warmth and encouragement, and spend time with them.

LO³Adolescence

Perhaps no other period of life is as exciting—and as bewildering—as adolescence. Adolescence is bounded by puberty and the assumption of adult responsibilities. Except for infancy, more changes occur during adolescence than during any other time. Like childhood, adolescence entails physical, cognitive, social, and emotional changes.

Physical Development

What physical developments occur during adolescence? One of the most noticeable physical developments of adolescence is a growth spurt that lasts two to three years and ends the gradual changes in height and weight that characterize most of childhood. Within this short span of years, adolescents grow some eight to twelve inches. Most boys wind up taller and heavier than most girls.

In boys, the weight of the muscle mass increases notably. The width of the shoulders and circumference of the chest also increase. Adolescents may eat enormous quantities of food to fuel their growth spurt.

Brain imaging studies show that adolescents' frontal lobes—the seat of executive functioning—are less active than those of adults. Their amygdalas, a part of the limbic system involved in emotions, are more active than adults'. These adolescent-adult differences in brain development may explain, at least in part, why many adolescents do not show the judgment, insight, and reasoning ability of adults.

Puberty: More Than "Just a Phase"?

Puberty is the period during which the body becomes sexually mature. It heralds the onset of adolescence. Puberty begins with the appearance of **secondary sex characteristics** such as body hair, deepening of the voice in males, and rounding of the breasts and hips in females. In boys, pituitary hormones stimulate the testes to increase the output of testosterone, which in turn causes enlargement of the penis and testes and the appearance of body hair. By the early teens, erections become common, and boys may ejaculate. Ejaculatory ability usually precedes the presence of mature sperm by at least a year. Ejaculation thus is not evidence of reproductive capacity.

In girls, a critical body weight in the neighborhood of 100 pounds is thought to trigger a cascade of hormonal secretions in the brain that cause the ovaries to secrete higher levels of the female sex hormone, estrogen (Frisch, 1997). Estrogen stimulates the growth of breast tissue and tissue in the hips and buttocks. The pelvis widens, rounding the hips. Small amounts of androgens produced by the adrenal glands, along with estrogen, spur the growth of pubic and underarm hair. Estrogen and androgens also stoke the development of female sex organs. Estrogen production becomes cyclical during puberty and regulates the menstrual cycle. The beginning of menstruation, or menarche, usually occurs between eleven and fourteen. Girls cannot become pregnant until they ovulate, however, and ovulation may begin two years after menarche.

Cognitive Development

The adolescent thinker approaches problems differently from the elementary school child. *What cognitive developments occur during adolescence?* Let us begin to answer this question by comparing the child's thought processes to those of the adolescent. The child sticks to the facts, to concrete reality. Speculating about abstract possibilities and what might be is very difficult. The adolescent, on the other hand, is able to deal with the abstract and the hypothetical. In this section we explore some of the cognitive developments of adolescence by referring to the views of Piaget and Kohlberg.

The Stage of Formal Operations

According to Piaget, children undergo three stages of cognitive development prior to adolescence: sensorimotor, preoperational, and concrete operational. The stage of formal operations is the final stage in Piaget's theory, and it represents cognitive maturity. For many children in Western societies, formal operational thought begins at about the beginning of adolescence—the age of eleven or twelve. Some people enter this stage later, however, and some never do.

The major achievements of the stage of formal operations involve classification, logical thought, and the ability to hypothesize. Central features are the ability to think about ideas as well as objects and to group and classify ideas—symbols, statements, entire theories. Adolescents can generally follow arguments from premises to conclusions and back again. They can generally appreciate both the outer environment and the world of the imagination: they engage in hypothetical thinking and deductive reasoning.

Formal operational adolescents (and adults) think abstractly. They solve geometric problems about circles and squares without reference to what the circles and squares may represent in the real world. Adolescents in this stage derive rules for behavior from general principles and can focus, or center, on multiple aspects of a situation at once to solve problems.

In this stage, adolescents tend to emerge as theoretical scientists—even though they may think of themselves as having little interest in science. That is, they can deal with hypothetical situations. They realize that situations can have different outcomes, and they think ahead, imagining those outcomes. Adolescents also conduct social experiments to test their hypotheses. They may try out various tones of voice and ways of treating others to see what works best for them.

Adolescent Egocentrism

Adolescents in the formal operational stage reason deductively. They classify objects or people and then draw conclusions about them. Adolescents can be proud of their new logical abilities, leading to a new sort of egocentrism: They demand acceptance of their logic without recognizing the exceptions or practical problems that may be considered by adults. Consider this example: "It is wrong to hurt people. Company A hurts people" (perhaps through pollution or economic pressures). "Therefore, Company A must be severely punished or shut down." This thinking is logical. But by impatiently demanding major changes or severe penalties, one may not fully consider various practical problems such as the thousands of workers who might be laid off. Adults have often had life experiences that encourage them to see shades of gray rather than black and white.

menarche
the beginning of menstruation

formal operational stage
Piaget's fourth stage, characterized by abstract logical thought and deduction from principles

PHILLIP JARRELL/GETTY IMAGES

imaginary audience an aspect of adolescent egocentrism; the belief that other people are as concerned with our thoughts and behaviors as we are

personal fable another aspect of adolescent egocentrism; the belief that our feelings and ideas are special and unique and that we are invulnerable

postconventional level according to Kohlberg, a period during which moral judgments are derived from moral principles and people look to themselves to set moral standards

The thought of preschoolers is characterized by egocentrism in which they cannot take another's point of view. Adolescent thought is marked by an egocentrism in which they can understand the thoughts of others but still have trouble separating things that are of concern to others and those that are of concern only to themselves (Elkind, 1967, 1985). Adolescent egocentrism gives rise to two interesting cognitive developments: the *imaginary audience* and the *personal fable.*

The concept of the **imaginary audience** refers to the belief that other people are as concerned with our thoughts and behavior as we are. Adolescents thus see themselves as the center of attention and assume that other people are also preoccupied with their appearance and behavior (Milstead et al., 1993). Adolescents may feel onstage with all eyes on them. The concept of the imaginary audience may drive the intense adolescent desire for privacy. It helps explain why adolescents are so self-conscious, why they worry about every facial blemish and spend hours grooming. Self-consciousness seems to peak at about thirteen and then decline. Girls tend to be more self-conscious than boys (Elkind & Bowen, 1979).

The **personal fable** is the belief that our feelings and ideas are special, even unique, and that we are invulnerable. The personal fable seems to underlie adolescent showing off and risk taking (Cohn et al., 1995).

The Postconventional Level of Moral Reasoning

Kohlberg's theory of moral reasoning involves three levels: preconventional, conventional, and postconventional. Individuals can arrive at the same decision as to whether or not Heinz should save his wife by taking the drug without paying for it for different reasons. Deciding not to steal the drug for fear of punishment is less complex than deciding not to because of the belief that doing so will weaken the social order.

None of Kohlberg's levels is tied to a person's age. Although postconventional reasoning is the highest level, most adolescents and adults never reach it. But if postconventional reasoning emerges, it usually does so in adolescence. Kohlberg's (1969) research found postconventional moral judgments were absent among seven- to ten-year-olds. But by age sixteen, stage 5 reasoning is shown by about 20% of adolescents, and stage 6 reasoning by about 5%.

At the **postconventional level**, moral reasoning is based on the person's own moral standards. Moral judgments are derived from personal values, not from conventional standards or authority figures. In the contractual, legalistic orientation characteristic of stage 5, it is recognized that laws stem from agreed-upon procedures and that the rule of law is in general good for society; therefore, laws should not be violated except under pressing circumstances. (Although it is illegal for Heinz to steal the drug, in this case it is the right thing to do.)

Stage 6 moral reasoning demands adherence to supposedly universal ethical principles such as the sanctity of human life, individual dignity, justice, and the Golden Rule ("Do unto others as you would have them do unto you"). If a law is unjust or contradicts the rights of the individual, it is wrong to obey it.

People at the postconventional level see their conscience as the highest moral authority. This point has created confusion. To some it suggests that it is right to break the law when it is convenient, but this interpretation is wrong. Kohlberg means that people at this level feel they must do what they think is right even if they break the law or must sacrifice themselves.

Are There Gender Differences in Moral Development?

A number of studies using Heinz's dilemma have found that boys show higher levels of moral reasoning than girls. But Carol Gilligan (1982; Gilligan et al., 1989) argues that this gender difference reflects different patterns of socialization for boys and girls—not differences in morality. Gilligan considers eleven-year-old Jake. Jake weighs the scales of justice like a math problem. He shows that life is worth more than property and concludes that it is Heinz's duty to steal the drug (stage 4 reasoning). Gilligan also points to eleven-year-old Amy. Amy vacillates. Amy says that stealing the drug and letting Heinz's wife die are both wrong. So Amy looks for alternatives, such as getting a loan, because it wouldn't help Heinz's wife if he went to jail.

Gilligan finds Amy's reasoning to be as sophisticated as Jake's, yet Amy would be rated as having a lower level of moral development in Kohlberg's scheme. Gilligan argues that girls are socialized to focus on the needs of others and forgo simple judgments of right and wrong. Amy is therefore more likely to show stage 3 reasoning, which focuses in part on empathy—or caring for others. Jake has been socialized to make judgments based on logic. He wants to derive clear-cut conclusions from premises.

We could argue endlessly about which form of moral reasoning—Jake's or Amy's—is "higher." Instead, let us note a review of the research that shows only slight tendencies for boys to favor Jake's "justice" approach and girls to favor Amy's "caring" approach (Jaffee & Hyde, 2000). Thus, the justice orientation does not "belong" to boys, and the care orientation does not "belong" to girls.

Social and Emotional Development

What social and emotional developments occur during adolescence? In terms of social and emotional development, adolescence has been associated with turbulence. In the 19th century, psychologist G. Stanley Hall described adolescence as a time of *Sturm und Drang*—storm and stress. Current views challenge the assumption that "storm and stress" is the norm (Griffin, 2001). Many adolescents experience a rather calm and joyous period of development. We need to consider individual differences and cultural variations (Arnett, 1999).

Certainly, many American teenagers abuse drugs, get pregnant, contract sexually transmitted infections, get involved in violence, fail in school, even attempt suicide (CDC, 2000b). The U.S. Centers for Disease Control and Prevention (CDC, 2000b) reported that 72% of all deaths among people aged ten to twenty-four years result from just four causes: motor vehicle crashes (31%), other accidents (11%), homicide (18%), and suicide (12%). Nevertheless, the majority of Americans make it through adolescence quite well.

Striving for Independence

As these biological changes take place, adolescents strive to become more independent from parents, which may lead to bickering (Smetana et al., 2003). Bickering usually concerns homework, chores, money, appearance, curfews, and dating. Disagreements about clothes and friends are common.

Adolescents and parents are often in conflict because adolescents experiment with things that can be harmful to their health. Yet—apparently because of the personal fable—adolescents may not perceive such activities to be as risky as their parents do. Cohn and his colleagues (1995) found, for example, that parents perceived drinking, smoking, failure to use seat belts, drag racing, and a number of other activities to be riskier than did their teenagers.

Some distancing from parents is beneficial (Smetana et al., 2003). After all, adolescents do have to form relationships outside the family. But greater independence does not necessarily mean that adolescents become emotionally detached from parents or fall completely under the spell of peers. Most adolescents continue to feel love, respect, and loyalty toward parents (Eberly & Montemayor, 1999). Adolescents who feel close to their parents actually show more self-reliance and independence than do those who distance themselves. They fare better in school and have fewer adjustment problems (Flouri & Buchanan, 2003). Despite conflict over issues of control, parents and adolescents tend to share social, political, religious, and economic views (Sagrestano et al., 1999). In sum, there are frequent differences between parents and adolescents on issues of personal control. However, there is apparently less of a "generation gap" on broader matters.

Ego Identity Versus Role Diffusion

According to Erik Erikson, we undergo eight stages of psychosocial development. Four of them, beginning with trust versus mistrust, occur in childhood. The fifth, that of *ego identity versus role diffusion,* occurs in adolescence. Ego identity is a firm sense of who one is and what one stands for. It can carry one through difficult times and lend meaning to achievements. Adolescents who do not develop ego identity may experience role diffusion. They spread themselves too thin, running down one blind alley after another and placing themselves at the mercy of leaders who promise to give them the sense of identity they cannot find for themselves.

The creation of an adult identity is a key challenge, involving learning about one's interests and abilities and connecting them with occupations and roles in life. Identity also involves sexual, political, and religious beliefs and commitments. Will the

ego identity
Erikson's term for a firm sense of who one is and what one stands for

role diffusion
Erikson's term for lack of clarity in one's life roles (due to failure to develop ego identity)

individual be monogamous or sexually active with several people? Will he or she lean left or right along the political spectrum? What role will be played by religion?

Adolescent Sexuality

The changes of puberty make the adolescent body ready for sexual activity. High hormone levels stir interest in sex. In today's world, many adolescents wrestle with issues of how and when to express their awakening sexuality. To complicate matters, Western culture sends mixed messages about sex. Teenagers may be advised to wait until they have married or entered into meaningful relationships, but they are also bombarded by sexual messages in films, TV, print advertising, and virtually every other medium.

About half of American high school students have engaged in sexual intercourse (CDC, 2000b). Adolescents usually obtain little advice at home or in school about how to handle their emerging sexuality. Peers also influence the sexual behavior of adolescents. When teenagers are asked why they do not wait to have sexual intercourse, the most common reason is peer pressure (Dickson et al., 1998). All in all, about 800,000 teenage girls get pregnant each year, resulting in 500,000 births ("Less Sex," 2004).

Still, there is encouraging news. Recent research shows a decline in the teenage pregnancy rate due largely to educational campaigns in the schools, the media, churches, and communities ("Less Sex," 2004).

LO⁴ Adulthood

Development continues throughout the life span. Many theorists believe that adult concerns and involvements follow observable patterns, so that we can speak of "stages" of adult development. Others argue that there may no longer be a standard life cycle with predictable stages or phases. Age now has an "elastic quality"—being fifty, sixty, seventy, eighty, or even ninety no longer necessarily means loss of cognitive or physical ability, or even wrinkling. People are living longer than ever before and are freer than ever to choose their own destiny.

Physical Development

The most obvious aspects of development during adulthood are physical. *What physical developments occur during adulthood?* Let us consider the physical developments that take place in young, or early, adulthood, which covers the ages between twenty and forty; the transition to middle adulthood, years forty to forty-five; middle adulthood, which spans the ages of forty-five to sixty-five; and late adulthood, which begins at sixty-five.

Young Adulthood

Most young adults are at their height of sensory sharpness, strength, reaction time, and cardiovascular fitness. On the other hand, women gymnasts find themselves lacking a competitive edge in their twenties because they are accumulating (normal) body fat and losing suppleness and flexibility. Other athletes, such as football, baseball, and basketball players, are more likely to experience a decline in their thirties. Most athletes retire by age forty. Sexually speaking, most people in early adulthood become readily aroused. They tend to attain and maintain erections as desired and to lubricate readily.

Middle Adulthood

In our middle years, we are unlikely to possess the strength, coordination, and stamina that we had during our twenties and thirties. The decline is most obvious in professional sports, where peak performance is at a premium.

The years between forty and sixty are reasonably stable. There is gradual physical decline, but it is minor and only likely to be of concern if a person competes with young adults—or with idealized memories of oneself. There are exceptions. The twenty-year-old couch potato occasionally becomes the fifty-year-old marathoner. By any reasonable standard, people in middle adulthood can maintain excellent cardiorespiratory condition. Because the physical decline in middle adulthood is gradual, people who begin to exercise and eat more nutritious diets (e.g., decrease intake of animal fats and increase intake of fruits and vegetables) may find themselves looking and feeling better than they did in young adulthood.

For women, menopause is usually considered to be the single most important change of life that occurs during middle adulthood. Menopause usually occurs during the late forties or early fifties. Menopause is the final phase of the *climacteric*, which is caused by a decline in secretion of female sex hormones. Ovulation comes to an end, and there is some loss of breast tissue and of elasticity of the skin. Loss of bone density can lead to osteoporosis (brittle bones). During the climacteric, many women experience hot flashes, loss of sleep, and some anxiety and depression. Women's experiences during and following the climacteric reflect the intensity of their physical symptoms—which vary considerably—and the extent to which their self-concept was wrapped up with their reproductive capacity (Dennerstein, 2003; Hvas et al., 2004).

Late Adulthood

An *agequake* is coming. With improved health care and knowledge of the importance of diet and exercise, more Americans than ever before are sixty-five or older (Nuland, 2005). In 1900, only one American in thirty was over sixty-five. By 2030, one American in five will be sixty-five or older.

Figure 3.7

The Relentless March of Time

Go to CourseMate for PSYCH at www.cengagebrain.com to access an interactive version of this figure.

Hair and nails
Hair often turns gray and thins out. Men may go bald. Fingernails can thicken.

Brain
The brain shrinks, but it is not known if that affects mental functions.

The senses
The sensitivity of hearing, sight, taste, and smell can all decline with age.

Skin
Wrinkles occur as the skin thins and the underlying fat shrinks, and age spots often crop up.

Glands and hormones
Levels of many hormones drop, or the body becomes less responsive to them.

Immune system
The body becomes less able to resist some pathogens.

Lungs
It doesn't just seem harder to climb those stairs; lung capacity drops.

Heart and blood vessels
Cardiovascular problems become more common.

Muscles
Strength usually peaks in the 20s, then declines.

Kidneys and urinary tract
The kidneys become less efficient. The bladder can't hold as much, so urination is more frequent.

Digestive system
Digestion slows down as the secretion of digestive enzymes decreases.

Reproductive system
Women go through menopause, and testosterone levels drop for men.

Bones and joints
Wear and tear can lead to arthritic joints, and osteoporosis is common, especially in women.

Various changes—some of them troublesome—do occur during the later years (see Figure 3.7). Changes in calcium metabolism increase the brittleness of the bones and heighten the risk of breaks due to falls. The skin becomes less elastic and subject to wrinkles and folds. Older people see and hear less acutely. Because of a decline in the sense of smell, they may use more spice to flavor their food. Older people need more time to respond to stimuli. Older drivers, for example, need more time to respond to changing road conditions. As we grow older, our immune system functions less effectively, leaving us more vulnerable to disease. Age-related changes impact sexual functioning, yet most people can enjoy sex for a lifetime if they remain generally healthy and adjust their expectations.

Cognitive Development

What cognitive developments occur during adulthood? As in the case of physical development, people are also at the height of their cognitive powers during early adulthood. Cognitive development in adulthood has many aspects—creativity, memory functioning, and intelligence.

People can be creative for a lifetime. At the age of eighty, Merce Cunningham choreographed a dance that made use of computer-generated digital images (Teachout, 2000). Hans Hofmann created some of his most vibrant paintings at eighty-five, and Pablo Picasso was painting in his nineties. Grandma Moses did not even begin painting until she was seventy-eight years old. Giuseppe Verdi wrote his joyous opera *Falstaff* at the age of seventy-nine.

Memory functioning does decline with age. But declines in memory are not usually as large as people assume and are often reversible (Villa & Abeles, 2000). Memory tests usually measure ability to recall meaningless information. Older people show better memory functioning in areas in which they can apply their experience, especially their specialties, to new challenges. For example, who would do a better job of learning and remembering how to solve problems in chemistry—a college history major or a retired professor of chemistry?

You might choose the chemistry professor because of his or her crystallized intelligence, not his or her fluid intelligence.

crystallized intelligence one's lifetime of intellectual achievement, as shown largely through vocabulary and knowledge of world affairs

fluid intelligence mental flexibility as shown in learning rapidly to solve new kinds of problems

Alzheimer's disease a progressive form of mental deterioration characterized by loss of memory, language, problem solving, and other cognitive functions

The Dream in this usage, Levinson's term for the overriding drive of youth to become someone important, to leave one's mark on history

Fiction

It is *not* true that the architect Frank Lloyd Wright designed New York's innovative spiral-shaped Guggenheim Museum when he was sixty-five years old. He was actually eighty-nine.

Crystallized intelligence represents one's lifetime of intellectual attainments. We are using the example of knowledge of chemistry, but crystallized intelligence is shown more generally by vocabulary and accumulated facts about world affairs. Therefore, crystallized intelligence can increase over the decades.

Fluid intelligence is defined as mental flexibility, demonstrated by the ability to process information rapidly, as in learning and solving problems in new areas. It is the sort of intellectual functioning that is typically measured on intelligence tests, especially with problems that have time limits.

Young adults obtain the highest intelligence test scores (Schaie et al., 2004). Yet people tend to retain verbal skills, as demonstrated by vocabulary and general knowledge, into advanced old age. The performance of older people on tasks that require speed and visual–spatial skills, such as piecing puzzles together, tends to decline (Schaie et al., 2004; Zimprich & Martin, 2002).

One of the most severe assaults on intellectual functioning, especially among older people, is Alzheimer's disease, a progressive form of mental deterioration that affects about 1% of people at age sixty and nearly half of people past age eighty-five (Brody, 2005). Although Alzheimer's is connected with aging, it is a disease rather than a normal progression (Yesavage et al., 2002).

Social and Emotional Development

Changes in social and emotional development during adulthood are probably the most "elastic" or fluid. These changes are affected by cultural expectations and individual behavior patterns. As a result, there is much variety. Nevertheless, many developmental theorists suggest that there are enough commonalities that we can speak of trends. One trend is that the outlook for older people has become more

Architect Frank Lloyd Wright with model of his Guggenheim Museum

optimistic over the past generation—not only because of medical advances but also because the behavior and mental processes of many older people are remaining younger than at any other time in history.

There is more good news. Research evidence suggests that people tend to grow psychologically healthier as they advance from adolescence through middle adulthood. Psychologists Constance Jones and William Meredith (2000) studied information on 236 participants in California growth studies who had been followed from early adolescence for about fifty years and found that they generally became more productive and had healthier relationships as time went on. Even some people with a turbulent adolescence showed better psychological health at age sixty-two than they had half a century earlier.

Young Adulthood

What social and emotional developments occur during young adulthood? Many theorists suggest that young adulthood is the period of life during which people tend to establish themselves as independent members of society.

At some point during their twenties, many people become fueled by ambition. Many strive to advance in their careers. Those who seek professional careers may spend much of their twenties acquiring the skills that will enable them to succeed (Levinson et al., 1978; Levinson, 1996). It is largely during the twenties that people become generally responsible for their own support, make their own choices, and are freed from parental influences. Many young adults adopt what theorist Daniel Levinson and his colleagues (1978) call the The Dream—the drive to "become" someone, to leave their mark on history—which serves as a tentative blueprint for life.

During young adulthood, people tend to leave their families of origin and create families of their own. Erik

Fiction

Alzheimer's disease is *not* a normal part of aging.

Erikson (1963) characterized young adulthood as the stage of intimacy versus isolation. Erikson saw the establishment of intimate relationships as central to young adulthood. Young adults who have evolved a firm sense of identity during adolescence are ready to "fuse" their identities with those of other people through marriage and abiding friendships. People who do not reach out to develop intimate relationships risk retreating into isolation and loneliness.

At age thirty or so, many people reassess their lives, asking themselves, "Where is my life going?" "Why am I doing this?" (Levinson et al., 1978). It is not uncommon for them to switch careers or form new intimate relationships. The later thirties are often characterized by settling down—planting roots. They become focused on career advancement, children, and long-term mortgages.

Middle Adulthood

A number of key changes in social and emotional development occur during middle adulthood. *What social and emotional developments occur during middle adulthood?* Consider Erikson's views on the middle years.

Erikson (1963) labeled the life crisis of the middle years generativity versus stagnation. *Generativity* involves doing things that we believe are worthwhile, such as rearing children or producing on the job. Generativity enhances and maintains self-esteem. Generativity also involves making the world a better place through joining church or civic groups. *Stagnation* means treading water, as in keeping the same job at the same pay for thirty years. Stagnation damages self-esteem.

According to Levinson and colleagues (1978), whose research involved case studies of forty men, there is a *midlife transition* at about age forty to forty-five. Previously, men had viewed their age in terms of the number of years that had elapsed since birth. Now they begin to think of their age in terms of the number of years they have left.

Research suggests that women may undergo a midlife transition sooner than men do (Zucker et al., 2002). Why? Much of it has to do with the winding down of the "biological clock"—that is, the abilities to conceive and bear children. For example, once they turn thirty-five women are usually advised to have their fetuses routinely tested for Down syndrome and other chromosomal disorders.

In both sexes, according to Levinson, the midlife transition may trigger a midlife crisis. The middle-level, middle-aged businessperson looking ahead to another ten to twenty years of grinding out accounts in a Wall Street cubbyhole may encounter severe depression. The homemaker with two teenagers, an empty house from 8:00 AM to 4:00 PM, and a fortieth birthday on the way may feel that she or he is coming apart at the seams. Both feel a sense of entrapment and loss of purpose.

Yet many Americans find that these years present opportunities for new direction and fulfillment. Many people are at the height of their productive powers during this period. Many, perhaps most, of today's robust forty-five- to fifty-five-year-olds can look forward to another thirty to forty healthy years.

Late Adulthood

What social and emotional developments occur during late adulthood? Generativity does not end with middle age. Research suggests that many individuals in late adulthood continue to be creative and also to maintain a firm sense of who they are and what they stand for (Webster, 2003). The Greek philosopher Plato was so optimistic about late adulthood that he argued that one could achieve great pleasure in one's later years, engage in meaningful public service, and also achieve wisdom (McKee & Barber, 2001).

According to psychologist Erik Erikson, late adulthood is the stage of ego integrity versus despair. The basic challenge is to maintain the belief that life is meaningful and worthwhile as one ages and faces the inevitability of death. Erikson, like Plato, spoke of the importance of wisdom. He believed that ego integrity derives from wisdom, which can be defined as expert knowledge about the meaning of life, balancing one's own needs and those of others, and pushing toward excellence in one's behavior and achievements (Baltes & Staudinger, 2000; Sternberg, 2000). Erikson also believed that wisdom enables people to accept their life span as occurring at a certain point in the sweep of history and as being limited. We spend most of our lives accumulating objects and relationships, and Erikson argues that adjustment in the later years requires the ability to let go of them. Other views of late adulthood stress the importance of creating new challenges; however, biological and social realities may require older people to become more selective in their pursuits.

intimacy versus isolation
Erikson's life crisis of young adulthood, which is characterized by the task of developing abiding intimate relationships

generativity versus stagnation
Erikson's term for the crisis of middle adulthood, characterized by the task of being productive and contributing to younger generations

midlife crisis
a crisis experienced by many people during the midlife transition when they realize that life may be more than halfway over and they reassess their achievements in terms of their dreams

ego integrity versus despair
Erikson's term for the crisis of late adulthood, characterized by the task of maintaining one's sense of identity despite physical deterioration

Sensation
and Perception

4

Learning Outcomes

"*Elephants detected the tsunami before the earth started shaking.*"

The tsunami that hit the coast of southern Asia in 2004 killed as many as a quarter of a million people. The people were caught off guard, but not the animals.

Along the western coast of Thailand, elephants giving rides to tourists began to trumpet agitatedly hours before the tsunami, just about when the earthquake that fractured the ocean floor sent the big waves rushing toward the shore. An hour before the waves slammed into the area, the elephants began wailing. Before the waves struck, they trooped off to higher ground. Elephants, tigers, leopards, deer, wild boar, water buffalo, monkeys, and reptiles in Sri Lanka's Yala National Park escaped the tsunami unharmed.

People have noticed that animals appear to detect earthquakes, hurricanes, volcanic eruptions, and tsunamis before the earth starts shaking. Some animals are apparently supersensitive to sound, others to temperature, touch, or vibration, which gives them advance warning.

Elephants are particularly sensitive to ground vibrations and probably sensed the earthquake that caused the tsunami in their feet and trunks. Some birds, dogs, tigers, and elephants can sense sound waves whose frequencies are too low for humans to hear. Dogs' superior sense of smell might detect subtle chemical changes in the air that warn them of calamities.

Different animals, then, have different sensory apparatuses, and many of them sense things that people cannot sense. Just how do humans sense the world around them?

Truth or Fiction?

What do you think?

Folklore, common sense, or nonsense? Place a T for "True" or F for "False" on the lines provided (you'll learn the answers as you read through the text).

— People have five senses.

— If we could see waves of light with slightly longer wavelengths, warm-blooded animals would glow in the dark.

— People sometimes hear what they want to hear.

— When we mix blue light and yellow light, we obtain green light.

— Many people experience pain "in" limbs that have been amputated.

— Some people can read other people's minds.

LO¹ Sensation and Perception

What are sensation and perception? Sensation is the stimulation of sensory receptors and the transmission of sensory information to the central nervous system (the spinal cord or brain). Sensory receptors are located in sensory organs such as the eyes and ears, the skin, and elsewhere in the body. Stimulation of the senses is an automatic process. It results from sources of energy, like light and sound, or from the presence of chemicals, as in smell and taste.

Perception is not automatic. Perception is an active process in which sensations are organized and interpreted to form an inner representation of the world. Perception may begin with sensation, but it also reflects our experiences and expectations as it makes sense of sensory stimuli. A person standing fifteen feet away and a twelve-inch-tall doll right next to you may cast similar-sized images on the back of your eye, but whether you interpret the size to be a foot-long doll or a full-grown person fifteen feet away is a matter of perception that depends on your experience with dolls, people, and distance.

In this chapter you will see that your perception of the world of changing sights, sounds, and other sources of sensory input depends largely on the so-called five senses: vision, hearing, smell, taste, and touch. But touch is just one of several "skin senses," which also include pressure, warmth, cold, and pain. There are also senses that alert you to your own body position without your having to watch every step you take. As we explore each of these senses, we will find that similar sensations may lead to different perceptions in different people—or to different situations in the same person.

Before we begin our voyage through the senses, let us consider a number of concepts that we use to talk about the relationships between sensations and perceptions: *absolute threshold, difference threshold, signal-detection theory,* and *sensory adaptation.* In doing so, we will learn why we can dim the lights gradually to near darkness without anyone noticing.

Fiction

People actually have many more than five senses.

We will also learn why we might become indifferent to the savory aromas of delightful dinners. *How do we know when something is there? How do we know when it has changed?*

Absolute Threshold

Nineteenth-century German psychologist Gustav Fechner used the term absolute threshold to refer to the weakest level of a stimulus that is necessary to produce a sensation. For example, the absolute threshold for light would be the minimum brightness (physical energy) required to activate the visual sensory system.

Psychophysicists look for the absolute thresholds of the senses by exposing individuals to progressively stronger stimuli until they find the minimum stimuli that the person can detect 50% of the time. These absolute thresholds are not all that absolute, however. Some people are more sensitive than others, and even the same person might have a slightly different response at different times. Nevertheless, under ideal conditions, our ability to detect stimuli is quite sensitive. (See the box feature, this page.)

How different our lives would be if the absolute thresholds for the human senses differed! If your ears were sensitive to sounds that are lower in pitch, you might hear the collisions among molecules of air. If you could see light with slightly longer wavelengths, you would see infrared light waves. Your world would be transformed because heat generates infrared light.

Difference Threshold

How much of a difference in intensity between two lights is required before you will detect one as being brighter than the other? The minimum difference in magnitude of two stimuli required to tell them apart

{ **Absolute Thresholds of the Senses** }

The following are measures of the absolute thresholds for the human senses of vision, hearing, taste, smell, and touch:

- *Vision:* a candle flame viewed from about 30 miles on a clear, dark night.
- *Hearing:* a watch ticking from about 20 feet away in a quiet room.
- *Taste:* 1 teaspoon of sugar dissolved in 2 gallons of water.
- *Smell:* about one drop of perfume diffused throughout a small house (1 part in 500 million).
- *Touch:* the pressure of the wing of a fly falling on a cheek from a distance of about 0.4 inch.

Truth

If we could see waves of light with slightly longer wavelengths, warm-blooded animals—including other people—would glow in the dark.

is their **difference threshold**. As with the absolute threshold, psychologists agree to the standard of a difference in strength that can be detected 50% of the time.

Psychophysicist Ernst Weber discovered through laboratory research that the threshold for perceiving differences in the intensity of light is about 2% (actually closer to 1/60th) of their intensity. This fraction, 1/60th, is known as **Weber's constant** for light. A related concept is the **just noticeable difference (jnd)**—the minimum difference in stimuli that a person can detect. For example, at least 50% of the time, most people can tell if a light becomes just 1/60th brighter or dimmer. Weber's constant for light holds whether we are comparing moderately bright lights or moderately dull lights. But it becomes inaccurate when we compare extremely bright or extremely dull lights.

Weber's constant for noticing differences in lifted weight is 1/53rd. (Round it off to 1/50th, or 2%.) That means if you are strong enough to heft a 100-pound barbell, you would not notice that it was heavier until about two pounds were added. Yet if you are a runner who carries one-pound dumbbells, you would definitely notice if someone slipped you dumbbells even a pound heavier because the increase would be 100%.

What about sound? People are most sensitive to changes in the pitch (frequency) of sounds. The Weber constant for pitch is 1/333, meaning that on average, people can tell when a tone rises or falls in pitch by an extremely small one-third of 1%. (Even a small error in pitch makes singers sound sharp or flat.) Remember this when friends criticize your singing. The sense of taste is much less sensitive. On average, people cannot detect differences in saltiness of less than 20%. That is why "low-salt" chips that have 15% less salt than your favorite chips do not taste so bad.

Signal-Detection Theory

From the discussion so far, it might seem that people are simply switched on by certain amounts of stimulation. This is not quite so. People are also influenced by psychological factors. **Signal-detection theory** considers these factors. *What is signal-detection theory?*

According to signal-detection theory, the relationship between a physical stimulus and a sensory response is not fully mechanical. People's ability to detect stimuli such as blips on a radar screen depends not only on the intensity of the blips but also on their training (learning), motivation (desire to perceive blips), and psychological states such as fatigue or alertness.

The intensity of the signal is one factor that determines whether people will perceive sensory stimuli (signals) or a difference between signals. Another is the degree to which the signal can be distinguished from background noise. It is easier to hear a friend speaking in a quiet room than in a room in which people are singing and clinking glasses. The sharpness of a person's biological sensory system is still another factor. Is sensory capacity fully developed? Is it diminished by age?

difference threshold the minimal difference in intensity required between two sources of energy so that they will be perceived as being different

Weber's constant the fraction of the intensity by which a source of physical energy must be increased or decreased so that a difference in intensity will be perceived

just noticeable difference (jnd) the minimal amount by which a source of energy must be increased or decreased so that a difference in intensity will be perceived

signal-detection theory the view that the perception of sensory stimuli involves the interaction of physical, biological, and psychological factors

Truth

It is true that people sometimes hear what they want to hear.

feature detectors
neurons in the sensory cortex that fire in response to specific features of sensory information such as lines or edges of objects

sensory adaptation
the processes by which organisms become more sensitive to stimuli that are low in magnitude and less sensitive to stimuli that are constant or ongoing in magnitude

sensitization
the type of sensory adaptation in which we become more sensitive to stimuli that are low in magnitude. Also called *positive adaptation*

desensitization
the type of sensory adaptation in which we become less sensitive to constant stimuli. Also called *negative adaptation*

That is, we tend to detect stimuli we are searching for. The place in which you are reading this book may be abuzz with signals. If you are focusing your attention on this page, the other signals recede into the background. One psychological factor in signal detection is focusing on signals one considers important.

Feature Detectors in the Brain

Imagine you are standing by the curb of a busy street as a bus approaches. When neurons in your sensory organs—in this case, your eyes—are stimulated by the approach of the bus, they relay information to the sensory cortex in the brain. Nobel Prize winners David Hubel and Torsten Wiesel (1979) discovered that various neurons in the visual cortex of the brain fire in response to particular features of the visual input. *What are feature detectors?* Many cells in the brain detect (i.e., fire in response to) lines presented at various angles—vertical, horizontal, and in between. Other cells fire in response to specific colors. Because they respond to different aspects or features of a scene, these brain cells are termed feature detectors. In the example of the bus, visual feature detectors respond to the bus's edges, depth, contours, textures, shadows, speed, and kinds of motion (up, down, forward, and back). There are also feature detectors for other senses. Auditory feature detectors, for example, respond to the pitch, loudness, and other aspects of the sounds of the bus.

> I think I can hear a watch ticking on the previous page.

Sensory Adaptation

Our sensory systems are admirably suited to a changing environment. *How do our sensory systems adapt to a changing environment?* Sensory adaptation refers to the processes by which we become more sensitive to stimuli of low magnitude and less sensitive to stimuli that remain the same, such as the background noises outside the window.

Consider how the visual sense adapts to lower intensities of light. When we first walk into a darkened movie theater, we see little but the images on the screen. As we search for our seats, however, we become increasingly sensitive to the faces around us and to the features of the theater. The process of becoming more sensitive to stimulation is referred to as sensitization, or *positive adaptation*.

But we become less sensitive to constant stimulation. When we live in a city, for example, we become desensitized to sounds of traffic except, perhaps, for the occasional backfire or siren. The process of becoming less sensitive to stimulation is referred to as desensitization, or *negative adaptation*.

Our sensitivities to stimulation provide our brains with information that we use to understand and influence the world outside. Therefore, it is not surprising that psychologists study the ways in which we sense and perceive this information—through vision, hearing, the chemical senses, and still other senses, as we see throughout the remainder of the chapter.

LO² Vision

Our eyes are our biological "windows on the world." Because vision is our dominant sense, blindness is considered by many to be the most debilitating sensory loss. To understand vision, let us first "look" at light.

Light

Light is fascinating stuff. It radiates. It illuminates. It dazzles. In almost all cultures, light is a symbol of goodness and knowledge. We speak of genius as "brilliance." People who aren't in the know are said to be "in the dark." *Just what is light?*

It is visible light that triggers visual sensations. Yet visible light is just one small part of a spectrum of electromagnetic energy that surrounds us (see Figure 4.1). All forms of electromagnetic energy

CORTIER CLAUDE/BELPRESS/ANDIA

move in waves, and different kinds of electromagnetic energy have signature wavelengths:

- *Cosmic rays:* The wavelengths of these rays from outer space are only a few *trillionths* of an inch long.
- *Radio waves:* Some radio signals extend for miles.
- *Visible light:* Roses are red, and violets are blue. Why? Different colors have different wavelengths, with violet the shortest at about 400-billionths of a meter in length and red the longest at 700-billionths of a meter.

Sir Isaac Newton, the British scientist, discovered that sunlight could be broken down into different colors by means of a triangular solid of glass called a *prism* (see Figure 4.1). You can remember the colors of the spectrum, from longest to shortest wavelengths, by using the mnemonic device *Roy G. Biv* (red, orange, yellow, green, blue, indigo, violet). The wavelength of visible light determines its color, or **hue**. The wavelength for red is longer than the wavelength for orange, and so on through the spectrum.

hue
the color of light, as determined by its wavelength

Figure 4.1

The Visible Spectrum

By passing a source of white light, such as sunlight, through a prism, we break it down into the colors of the visible spectrum. The visible spectrum is just a narrow segment of the electromagnetic spectrum. The electromagnetic spectrum also includes radio waves, microwaves, X-rays, cosmic rays, and many others. Different forms of electromagnetic energy have wavelengths that vary from a few trillionths of a meter to thousands of miles. Visible light varies in wavelength from about 400- to 700-billionths of a meter. (One meter = 39.37 inches.)

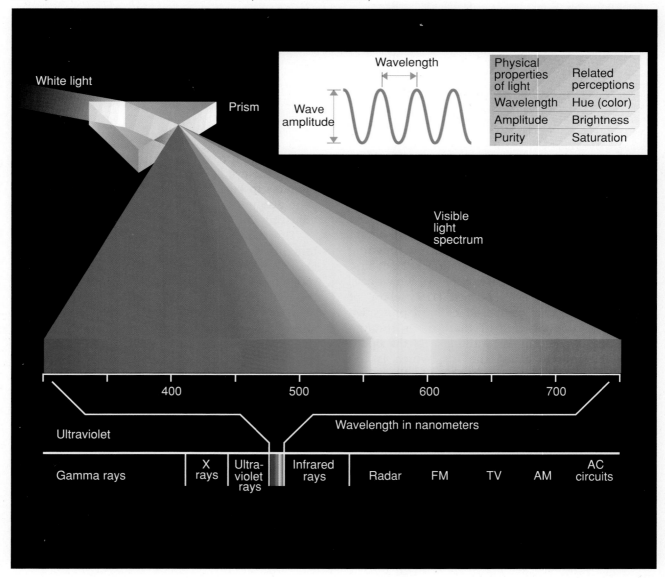

cornea
transparent tissue forming the outer surface of the eyeball

iris
a muscular membrane whose dilation regulates the amount of light that enters the eye

pupil
the black-looking opening in the center of the iris, through which light enters the eye

lens
a transparent body behind the iris that focuses an image on the retina

retina
the area of the inner surface of the eye that contains rods and cones

photoreceptors
cells that respond to light

bipolar cells
neurons that conduct neural impulses from rods and cones to ganglion cells

ganglion cells
neurons whose axons form the optic nerve

optic nerve
the nerve that transmits sensory information from the eye to the brain

Figure 4.2   *Go to CourseMate for PSYCH at www.cengagebrain.com to access an interactive version of this figure.* 🔄

The Human Eye

In both the eye and a camera, light enters through a narrow opening and is projected onto a sensitive surface. In the eye, the photosensitive surface is called the retina, and information concerning the changing images on the retina is transmitted to the brain. The retina contains photoreceptors called rods and cones. Rods and cones transmit sensory input back through the bipolar neurons to the ganglion neurons. The axons of the ganglion neurons form the optic nerve, which transmits sensory stimulation through the brain to the visual cortex of the occipital lobe.

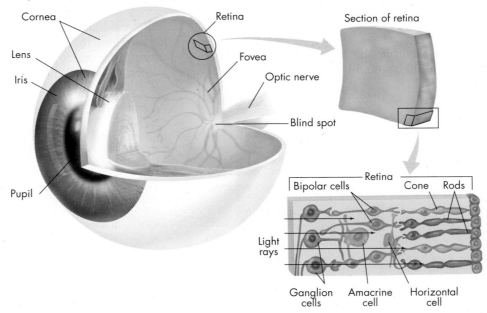

The Eye

How does the eye work? Look at the major parts of the eye, as shown in Figure 4.2. As with a camera, light enters through a narrow opening and is projected onto a sensitive surface. Light first passes through the transparent cornea, which covers the front of the eye's surface. (The "white" of the eye, or *sclera,* is composed of hard protective tissue.) The amount of light that passes through the cornea is determined by the size of the opening of the muscle called the iris, which is the colored part of the eye. The opening in the iris is the pupil. The size of the pupil adjusts automatically to the amount of light present. Therefore, you do not have to purposely open your eyes wider to see better in low lighting—the more intense the light, the smaller the opening. Pupil size is also sensitive to your emotions: We can be truly "wide-eyed with fear."

Once light passes through the iris, it encounters the lens. The lens adjusts or accommodates to the image by changing its thickness. Changes in thickness permit a clear image of the object to be projected onto the retina. These changes focus the light according to the distance of the object from the viewer. If you hold a finger at arm's length and

slowly bring it toward your nose, you will feel tension in the eye as the thickness of the lens accommodates to keep the retinal image in focus. When people squint to bring an object into focus, they are adjusting the thickness of the lens.

The retina consists of cells called photoreceptors that are sensitive to light (photosensitive). There are two types of photoreceptors: *rods* and *cones.* The retina (see Figure 4.2) contains several layers of cells: the rods and cones, the bipolar cells, and the ganglion cells. All of these cells are neurons. The rods and cones respond to light with chemical changes that create neural impulses that are picked up by the bipolar cells. These then activate the ganglion cells. The axons of the million or so ganglion cells in our retina converge to form the optic nerve. The optic nerve conducts sensory input to the brain, where it is relayed to the visual area of the occipital lobe. As if this were not enough, the eye has additional neurons to enhance this process. Amacrine cells and horizontal cells make sideways connections at a level near the rods and cones and at another level near the ganglion cells. As a result, single bipolar cells can pick up signals from many rods and cones, and, in turn, a single ganglion cell is able to funnel information from multiple bipolar cells. In fact, rods and cones outnumber ganglion cells by more than 100 to 1.

Rods and Cones

Rods and cones are the photoreceptors in the retina (see Figure 4.2). About 125 million rods and 6.4 million cones are distributed across the retina. The cones are most densely packed in a small spot at the center of the retina called the fovea (see Figure 4.2). Visual acuity (sharpness and detail) is greatest at this spot. The fovea is composed almost exclusively of cones. Rods are most dense just outside the fovea and thin out toward the periphery of the retina.

Rods allow us to see in black and white. Cones provide color vision. Rods are more sensitive to dim light than cones are. Therefore, as light grows dim during the evening hours, objects appear to lose their color before their outlines fade from view.

In contrast to the visual acuity of the fovea is the blind spot, which is insensitive to visual stimulation. It is the part of the retina where the axons of the ganglion cells converge to form the optic nerve (see Figure 4.2). Figure 4.3 will help you "view" your blind spot.

Visual acuity (sharpness of vision) is connected with the shape of the eye. People who have to be unusually close to an object to discriminate its details are *nearsighted*. People who see distant objects unusually clearly but have difficulty focusing on nearby objects are *farsighted*. Nearsightedness can result when the eyeball is elongated such that the images of distant objects are focused in front of the retina. When the eyeball is too short, the images of nearby objects are focused behind the retina, causing farsightedness. Eyeglasses or contact lenses help nearsighted people focus distant objects on their retinas. Laser surgery can correct vision by changing the shape of the cornea. Farsighted people usually see well enough without eyeglasses until they reach their middle years, when they may need glasses for reading.

Beginning in middle age—the late thirties to the mid-forties—the lenses of the eye start to grow brittle, making it more difficult to accommodate to, or focus on, objects. This condition is called presbyopia, from the Greek words for "old man" and "eyes." Presbyopia makes it difficult to perceive nearby visual stimuli. People who had normal visual acuity in their youth often require corrective lenses to read in middle adulthood.

Light Adaptation

When we walk out onto a dark street, we may at first not be able to see people, trees, and cars clearly. But as time goes on, we are better able to discriminate the features of people and objects. The process of adjusting to lower lighting is called dark adaptation.

The amount of light needed for detection is a function of the amount of time spent in the dark. The cones and rods adapt at different rates. The cones, which permit perception of color, reach their maximum adaptation to darkness in about ten minutes. The rods, which allow perception of light and dark only, are more sensitive to dim light and continue to adapt for forty-five minutes or so.

Adaptation to brighter lighting conditions takes place more rapidly. For instance, when you emerge from the theater into the brilliance of the afternoon, you may at first be painfully surprised by the featureless blaze around you. But within a minute or so of entering the street, the brightness of the scene dims and objects regain their edges.

Color Vision

For most of us, the world is a place of brilliant colors. Color is an emotional and aesthetic part of our everyday lives. In this section we explore

rods
rod-shaped photoreceptors that are sensitive only to the intensity of light

cones
cone-shaped photoreceptors that transmit sensations of color

fovea
an area near the center of the retina that is dense with cones and where vision is consequently most acute

blind spot
the area of the retina where axons from ganglion cells meet to form the optic nerve

visual acuity
sharpness of vision

presbyopia
a condition characterized by brittleness of the lens

dark adaptation
the process of adjusting to conditions of lower lighting by increasing the sensitivity of rods and cones

Figure 4.3

The Blind Spot

To try a "disappearing act," close your left eye, hold the book close to your face, and look at the boy with your right eye. Slowly move the book away until the pie disappears. The pie disappears because it is being projected onto the blind spot of your retina, the point at which the axons of ganglion neurons collect to form the optic nerve. Note that when the pie disappears, your brain "fills in" the missing checkerboard pattern, which is one reason that you're not usually aware that you have blind spots.

complementary
descriptive of colors of the spectrum that when combined produce white or nearly white light

afterimage
the lingering visual impression made by a stimulus that has been removed

some of the dimensions of color and then examine theories about how we manage to convert different wavelengths of light into perceptions of color. *What are some perceptual dimensions of color?* These include hue, value, and saturation.

The wavelength of light determines its color, or *hue*. The value of a color is its degree of brightness or darkness. The saturation refers to how intense a color appears to us. A fire-engine red is more saturated than a pale pinkish-red.

Colors also have psychological associations within various cultural settings. For example, in the United States a bride may be dressed in white as a sign of purity. In traditional India, the guests would be shocked, because white is the color for funerals. Here we mourn in black.

Warm and Cool Colors

If we bend the colors of the spectrum into a circle, we create a color wheel, as shown in Figure 4.4. Psychologically, the colors on the green–blue side of the color wheel are considered to be cool in temperature. Those colors on the yellow–orange–red side are considered to be warm.

Complementary Colors

The colors across from one another on the color wheel are labeled complementary. Red–green and blue–yellow are the major complementary pairs. If we mix complementary colors together, they dissolve into gray.

Figure 4.4

The Color Wheel

"But wait!" you say. "Blue and yellow cannot be complementary because by mixing pigments of blue and yellow we create green, not gray." True enough, but we have been talking about mixing *lights*, not *pigments*. Light is the source of all color. Pigments reflect and absorb different wavelengths of light selectively. The mixture of lights is an *additive* process. The mixture of pigments is *subtractive*. Figure 4.5 shows mixtures of lights and pigments of various colors.

Pigments gain their colors by absorbing light from certain segments of the spectrum and reflecting the rest. For example, we see most plant life as green because the pigment in chlorophyll absorbs most of the red, blue, and violet wavelengths of light. The remaining green is reflected. A red pigment absorbs most of the spectrum but reflects red. White pigments reflect all colors equally. Black pigments reflect very little light.

Afterimages

Try this experiment: Look at the strangely colored American flag on the next page for at least half a minute. Try not to blink as you are doing so. Then look at a sheet of white or light-gray paper. What has happened to the flag? If your color vision is working properly, and if you looked at the miscolored flag long enough, you should see a flag composed of the familiar red, white, and blue. The flag you perceive on the white sheet of paper is an afterimage of the first. (If you didn't look at the green, black, and yellow flag long enough the first time, try it again.) In afterimages, persistent sensations of color are followed by perception of the complementary color when the first color is removed. The same holds true for black and white. Staring at one will create an afterimage of the other. The phenomenon of afterimages has contributed to one of the theories of color vision, as we will see.

Theories of Color Vision

Adults with normal color vision can discriminate thousands of colors across the visible spectrum. Different colors have different wavelengths. Although we can vary the physical wavelengths of light in a continuous manner from shorter to longer, many changes in color are discontinuous. Our perception of a color shifts suddenly from blue to green, even though the change in

Fiction

It is not true that, when we mix blue light and yellow light, we obtain green light.

Figure 4.5

The mixture of lights is an *additive* process.

The mixture of pigments is *subtractive*.

wavelength may be smaller than that between two blues.

How do we perceive color? Why are roses red and violets blue? Our perception of color depends on the physical properties of an object and on the eye's transmission of different messages to the brain when lights with different wavelengths stimulate the cones in the retina.

There are two main theories of color vision: the trichromatic theory and the opponent-process theory (Gegenfurtner & Kiper, 2003). Trichromatic theory is based on an experiment conducted by the British scientist Thomas Young in the early 1800s. As in Figure 4.5, Young projected red, green, and blue-violet lights onto a screen so that they partly overlapped. He found that he could create any color in the visible spectrum by varying the intensities of the three

Figure 4.6

Place a sheet of white paper beneath the book and stare at the black dot in the center of the flag for at least thirty seconds. Then remove the book. The afterimage on the paper beneath will look familiar.

lights. When all three lights fell on the same spot, they created white light, or the appearance of no color at all.

The German physiologist Hermann von Helmholtz saw in Young's discovery an explanation of color vision. Helmholtz suggested that the retina in the eye must have three different types of color photoreceptors or cones. Some cones must be sensitive to red light, some to green, and some to blue. We see other colors when various color receptors are stimulated simultaneously. For example, we perceive yellow when the receptors for red and green are firing.

In 1870, another German physiologist Ewald Hering proposed the opponent-process theory of color vision: There are three types of color receptors, but they are not sensitive only to red, green, and blue, as Helmholtz had claimed. Hering suggested instead that afterimages (such as that of the American flag shown in Figure 4.6) are made possible by three types of color receptors: red–green, blue–yellow, and a type that perceives differences in brightness. According to Hering, a red–green cone cannot transmit messages for red and green at the same time. Therefore, staring at the green, black, and yellow flag for thirty seconds will disturb the balance of neural activity. The afterimage of red, white, and blue would represent the eye's attempt to reestablish a balance.

Research suggests that each theory of color vision is partially correct (Li & DeVries, 2004; Shapley & Hawken, 2002). For example, research shows that some cones are sensitive to blue, some to green, and some to red. However, cones appear to be connected by bipolar and ganglion neurons such that the messages produced by the cones are transmitted to the brain in an opponent-process fashion (Hornstein et al., 2004; Suttle et al., 2002).

A neural rebound effect apparently helps explain the occurrence of afterimages. That is, a green-sensitive ganglion that had been excited by green light for half a minute or so might switch briefly to inhibitory activity when the light is shut off. The effect would be to perceive red even though no red light is present (Hornstein et al., 2004).

trichromatic theory the theory that color vision is made possible by three types of cones, some of which respond to red light, some to green, and some to blue

opponent-process theory the theory that color vision is made possible by three types of cones, some of which respond to red or green light, some to blue or yellow, and some to the intensity of light

trichromat
a person with normal color vision

monochromat
a person who is sensitive to black and white only and hence color-blind

dichromat
a person who is sensitive to black–white and either red–green or blue–yellow and hence partially color-blind

closure
the tendency to perceive a broken figure as being complete or whole

Color Blindness

If you can discriminate among the colors of the visible spectrum, you have normal color vision and are labeled a trichromat. This means that you are sensitive to red–green, blue–yellow, and light–dark. *What is color blindness? Why are some people colorblind?* People who are totally color-blind, called **monochromats**, are sensitive only to lightness and darkness. Total color blindness is rare. Fully color-blind individuals see the world as trichromats would in a black-and-white movie.

Partial color blindness is a sex-linked trait that affects mostly males. Partially color-blind people are called **dichromats**. They can discriminate only between two colors—red and green or blue and yellow—and the colors that are derived from mixing these colors (Loop et al., 2003). Figure 4.7 shows the types of tests that are used to diagnose color blindness.

A dichromat might put on one red sock and one green sock, but would not mix red and blue socks. Monochromats might put on socks of any color. They would not notice a difference as long as the socks' colors did not differ in intensity—that is, brightness.

LO³ Visual Perception

What do you see in Figure 4.8—meaningless splotches of ink or a rider on horseback? If you perceive a horse and rider, it is not just because of the visual sensations provided by the drawing. Each of the blobs is meaningless in and of itself, and the pattern is vague. Despite the lack of clarity, however, you may still perceive a horse and rider.

Visual perception is the process by which we organize or make sense of the sensory impressions caused by the light that strikes our eyes. Visual perception involves our knowledge, expectations, and motivations. Whereas sensation may be thought of as a mechanical process (e.g., light stimulating the rods and cones of our retina), perception is an active process through which we interpret the world around us.

How do we organize bits of visual information into meaningful wholes? The answer has something to do with your general knowledge and your desire to fit incoming bits and pieces of information into familiar patterns. In the case of the horse and rider, your integration of disconnected pieces of information into a meaningful whole also reflects the principle of closure—that is, the tendency to perceive a complete or whole figure even when there are gaps in the sensory input.

Perceptual Organization

Early in the 20th century, Gestalt psychologists noted certain consistencies in the way we integrate bits and pieces of sensory stimulation into meaningful

Figure 4.7

Plates from a Test for Color Blindness

Can you see the numbers in these plates from a test for color blindness? A person with red–green color blindness would not be able to see the 6, and a person with blue–yellow color blindness would probably not discern the 12. (Caution: These reproductions cannot be used for actual testing of color blindness.)

Figure 4.8

Closure

Meaningless splotches of ink, or a horse and rider? This figure illustrates the Gestalt principle of closure.

Figure 4.9

The Rubin Vase: "In parts A, B, and C, is the vase the figure or the ground?"

Go to CourseMate for PSYCH at www.cengagebrain.com to access an interactive version of this figure.

A.

B.

C.

our perception may shift from seeing the vase to seeing two profiles. There is no such problem in part B. Because it seems that a blue vase has been brought forward against a colored ground, we are more likely to perceive the vase than the profiles. In part C, we are more likely to perceive the profiles than the vase, because the profiles are complete and the vase is broken against the background. Of course, if we wish to, we can still perceive the vase in part C, because experience has shown us where it is.

wholes. They attempted to identify the rules that govern these processes. As a group, these rules are referred to as the laws of perceptual organization.

Figure–Ground Perception

If you look out your window, you may see people, buildings, cars, and streets, or perhaps grass, trees, birds, and clouds. These objects tend to be perceived as figures against backgrounds. For instance, individual cars seen against the background of the street are easier to pick out than cars piled on top of one another in a junkyard.

When figure–ground relationships are *ambiguous*, or capable of being interpreted in various ways, our perceptions tend to be unstable and shift back and forth (Bull et al., 2003).

Figure 4.9 shows a Rubin vase, one of psychologists' favorite illustrations of figure–ground relationships. The figure–ground relationship in part A of the figure is ambiguous. There are no cues that suggest which area must be the figure. For this reason,

Other Gestalt Rules for Organization

Gestalt psychologists have noted that our perceptions are also guided by rules or laws of *proximity*, *similarity*, *continuity*, and *common fate*.

Let's try a mini-experiment. Without reading further, describe part A of Figure 4.10. Did you say it consists of six lines or of three groups of two parallel lines? If you said three sets of lines, you were influenced by the **proximity**, or nearness, of some of the lines. There is no other reason for perceiving them in pairs or subgroups: All lines are parallel and equal in length.

Now describe part B of Figure 4.10. Did you perceive the figure as a six-by-six grid, or as three columns

Figure 4.10

Some Gestalt Laws of Perceptual Organization

These drawings illustrate the Gestalt laws of proximity, similarity, continuity, and closure.

A. Proximity

B. Similarity

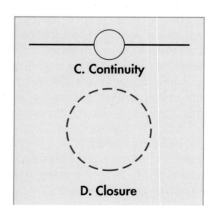

C. Continuity

D. Closure

similarity
the perceptual tendency to group together objects that are similar in appearance

continuity
the tendency to perceive a series of points or lines as having unity

common fate
the tendency to perceive elements that move together as belonging together

top-down processing
the use of contextual information or knowledge of a pattern in order to organize parts of the pattern

bottom-up processing
the organization of the parts of a pattern to recognize, or form an image of, the pattern they compose

illusions
sensations that give rise to misperceptions

stroboscopic motion
a visual illusion in which the perception of motion is generated by a series of stationary images that are presented in rapid succession

of 's and three columns of 's? According to the law of similarity, we perceive similar objects as belonging together. For this reason, you may have been more likely to describe part B in terms of columns than in terms of rows or a grid.

What of part C? Is it a circle with two lines stemming from it, or is it a (broken) line that goes through a circle? If you saw it as a single (broken) line, you were probably organizing your perceptions according to the rule of continuity. That is, we perceive a series of points or a broken line as having unity.

According to the law of common fate, elements seen moving together are perceived as belonging together. A group of people running in the same direction appears unified in purpose. Part D of Figure 4.10 provides another example of the law of closure. The arcs tend to be perceived as a circle (or a circle with gaps) rather than as just a series of arcs.

Top-Down Versus Bottom-Up Processing

Imagine that you are trying to put together a 1,000-piece jigsaw puzzle. Now imagine that you are trying to accomplish it after someone has walked off with the box showing the picture formed by the completed puzzle.

If you use the picture on the box, you're engaging in top-down processing—using the completed image to search for the proper pieces. Similarly, we may form more lasting relationships when we search with an idea of the qualities we will find compatible in another person. Or we may make better investments when we have a retirement financial goal and date in mind. With bottom-up processing, we begin with bits and pieces of information and try to assemble them in a pattern—in jigsaw puzzles and, perhaps, by being thrown into a social or vocational situation. In bottom-up processing, we do not have a clear idea of where we are going, and perhaps we try to make the best of things.

Perception of Motion

How do we perceive movement? To understand perception of movement, think of what it is like to be on a train that has begun to pull out of the station while the train on the next track stays still. If your own train does not lurch as it accelerates, it might seem that the other train is moving. Or you might not be sure whether your train is moving forward or the other train is moving back.

The visual perception of movement is based on change of position relative to other objects. To early scientists, whose only tool for visual observation was the naked eye, it seemed logical that the sun circled the earth. You have to be able to imagine the movement of the earth around the sun as seen from a theoretical point in outer space; you cannot observe it directly.

How, then, can you be certain which train is moving? One way is to look for objects that you know are still, such as platform columns, houses, signs, or trees. If your position does not change in relation to them, your train is not moving. You might also try to sense the motion of the train in your body. You probably know from experience how to do these things quite well.

We have been considering the perception of real movement. Psychologists have also studied several types of apparent movement, or illusions of movement. One of these illusions is stroboscopic motion.

Stroboscopic Motion

So-called motion pictures do not really consist of images that move. Rather, the audience is shown sixteen to twenty-two pictures, or *frames*, per second. Each frame differs slightly from the preceding one. Showing the frames in rapid succession provides the illusion of movement. This illusion of motion is termed stroboscopic motion.

At the rate of at least sixteen frames per second, the "motion" in a film seems smooth and natural. With fewer than sixteen or so frames per second, the movement looks jumpy and unnatural. That is why slow motion is usually achieved by filming 100 or more frames per second. When they are played back at about twenty-two frames per second, the movement seems slowed down, but still smooth and natural.

Depth Perception

How do we perceive depth? Monocular and binocular cues help us perceive the depth of objects—that is, their distance from us.

Monocular Cues

Artists use monocular cues called pictorial cues to create an illusion of depth. These cues can be perceived by one eye (*mono* means "one"). They include perspective, relative size, clearness, overlapping, shadows, and texture gradient, and they cause some objects to seem more distant than others even though they are all drawn or painted on a flat surface.

Distant objects stimulate smaller areas on the retina than nearby ones, even though they may be the same size. The distances between far-off objects also appear to be smaller than equivalent distances between nearby objects. For this reason, the phenomenon known as perspective occurs. That is, we tend to perceive parallel lines as coming closer together, or converging, as they recede from us. As we will see when we discuss *size constancy*, however, experience teaches us that distant objects that look small are larger when they are close. In this way, their relative size also becomes a cue to their distance.

Artists normally use *relative size*—the fact that distant objects look smaller than nearby objects of the same size—to suggest depth in their works.

The *clearness* of an object suggests its distance. Experience teaches us that we sense more details of nearby objects. For this reason, artists can suggest that objects are closer to the viewer by depicting them in greater detail.

We also learn that nearby objects can block our view of more distant objects. *Overlapping* is the placing of one object in front of another. Experience teaches us that partly covered objects are farther away than the objects that obscure them (see Figure 4.11).

Additional information about depth is provided by *shadowing* and is based on the fact that opaque objects block light and produce shadows. Shadows and highlights give us information about an object's three-dimensional shape and its relationship to the source of light. For example, in the right part of Figure 4.11, the left circle is perceived as a two-dimensional circle, but the right circle tends to be perceived as a three-dimensional sphere because of the highlight on its surface and the shadow underneath. In the "sphere," the highlighted central area is perceived as closest to us, with the surface receding to the edges.

Another monocular cue is texture gradient. (A gradient is a progressive change.) Closer objects are perceived as having rougher textures.

Motion cues are another kind of monocular cue. If you have ever driven in the country, you have probably noticed that distant objects such as mountains and stars appear to move along with you. Objects at an intermediate distance seem to be stationary, but nearby objects such as roadside markers, rocks, and trees seem to go by quite rapidly. The tendency of objects to seem to move backward or forward as a function of their distance is known as motion parallax. We learn to perceive objects that appear to move with us as being at greater distances.

Earlier we noted that nearby objects cause the lens of the eye to accommodate or bend more in order to bring them into focus. The sensations of tension in the eye muscles also provide a monocular cue to depth, especially when we are within about four feet of the objects.

monocular cues stimuli suggestive of depth that can be perceived with only one eye

perspective a monocular cue for depth based on the convergence (coming together) of parallel lines as they recede into the distance

texture gradient a monocular cue for depth based on the perception that closer objects appear to have rougher (more detailed) surfaces

motion parallax a monocular cue for depth based on the perception that nearby objects appear to move more rapidly in relation to our own motion

Figure 4.11

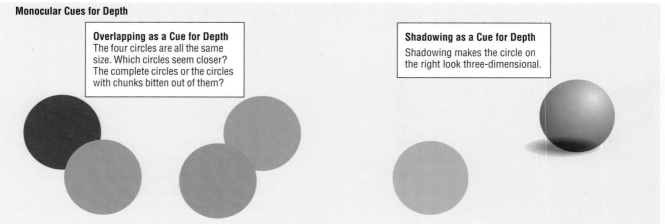

Monocular Cues for Depth

Overlapping as a Cue for Depth
The four circles are all the same size. Which circles seem closer? The complete circles or the circles with chunks bitten out of them?

Shadowing as a Cue for Depth
Shadowing makes the circle on the right look three-dimensional.

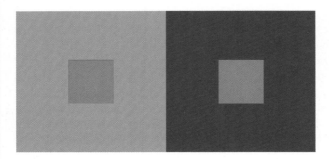

Figure 4.12

Brightness Constancy

The orange squares within the blue squares are the same hue, yet the orange within the dark blue square is perceived as brighter. Why?

binocular cues
stimuli suggestive of depth that involve simultaneous perception by both eyes

retinal disparity
a binocular cue for depth based on the difference in the image cast by an object on the retinas of the eyes as the object moves closer or farther away

convergence
a binocular cue for depth based on the inward movement of the eyes as they attempt to focus on an object that is drawing nearer

size constancy
the tendency to perceive an object as being the same size even as the size of its retinal image changes according to the object's distance

color constancy
the tendency to perceive an object as being the same color even though lighting conditions change its appearance

brightness constancy
the tendency to perceive an object as being just as bright even though lighting conditions change its intensity

Binocular Cues

Binocular cues, or cues that involve both eyes, also help us perceive depth. Two binocular cues are *retinal disparity* and *convergence*.

Try an experiment. Hold your right index finger at arm's length. Now hold your left index finger about a foot closer, but in a direct line. If you keep your eyes relaxed as you do so, you will see first one finger and then the other. An image of each finger will be projected onto the retina of each eye, and each image will be slightly different because the finger will be seen from different angles. The difference between the projected images is referred to as retinal disparity and serves as a binocular cue for depth perception. Note that in the case of the closer finger, the "two fingers" appear to be farther apart. Closer objects have greater retinal disparity.

If we try to maintain a single image of the closer finger, our eyes must turn inward, or converge on it, making us

cross-eyed. Convergence causes feelings of tension in the eye muscles and provides another binocular cue for depth. (After convergence occurs, try looking at the finger first with one eye closed, then the other. You will readily see how different the images are in each eye.) The binocular cues of retinal disparity and convergence are strongest when objects are close.

Perceptual Constancies

Think how confusing it would be if you believed that a door was a trapezoid and not a rectangle because it is ajar. Fortunately, perceptual constancies enable us to recognize objects even when their apparent shape or size differs. *What are perceptual constancies?*

Size Constancy

There are a number of perceptual constancies, including that of size constancy. The image of a dog seen from twenty feet away occupies about the same amount of space on your retina as an inch-long insect crawling on your hand. Yet you do not perceive the dog to be as small as the insect. Through your visual experiences you have acquired size constancy—that is, the tendency to *perceive* an object as the same size even though the size of its image on your retina varies as a function of its distance. Experience teaches us about perspective—that the same object seen at a distance appears to be smaller than when it is nearby.

Color Constancy

Color constancy is the tendency to perceive objects as retaining their color even though lighting conditions may alter their appearance. Your bright-yellow car may edge toward gray as the hours wend their way through twilight. But when you finally locate the car in the parking lot, you may still think of it as yellow. You expect to find a yellow car and still judge it to be "more yellow" than the (twilight-faded) red and green cars on either side of it.

Brightness constancy is similar to color constancy. Consider Figure 4.12. The orange squares within the blue squares are equally bright, yet the one within the dark-blue square is perceived as brighter. Why? Again,

© 2010 ENAMUL HOQUE/ JUPITERIMAGES CORPORATION

consider the role of experience. If it were nighttime, we would expect orange to fade to gray. The fact that the orange within the dark square stimulates the eye with equal intensity suggests that it must be much brighter than the orange within the lighter square.

Shape Constancy

Shape constancy is the tendency to perceive objects as maintaining their shape, even if we look at them from different angles so that the shape of their image on the retina changes dramatically. You perceive the top of a coffee cup or a glass to be a circle even though it is a circle only when seen from above. When seen from an angle, it is an ellipse. When the cup or glass is seen on edge, its retinal image is the same as that of a straight line. So why do you still describe the rim of the cup or glass as a circle? Perhaps for two reasons: First, experience has taught you that the cup will look circular when seen from above. Second, you may have labeled the cup as circular or round.

Let us return to the door that "changes shape" when it is ajar. The door is a rectangle only when viewed straight on. When we move to the side or open it, the left or right edge comes closer and appears to be larger, changing the retinal image to a trapezoid. Yet we continue to think of doors as rectangles. In the photo on the previous page, we see a woman with a very large hand, but because of experience, we recognize that the hand only appears to be out of proportion to the rest of her because it is pushed toward us.

Visual Illusions

The principles of perceptual organization make it possible for our eyes to "play tricks" on us. That is, the perceptual constancies trick the eye through *visual illusions*.

The Hering–Helmholtz and Müller–Lyer illusions (see Figure 4.13) are named after the people who devised them. In the Hering–Helmholtz illusion (part A), the horizontal lines are straight and parallel. However, the radiating lines cause them to appear to be bent outward near the center. The two lines in the Müller–Lyer illusion (part B) are the same length, but the line on the right, with its reversed arrowheads, looks longer.

Let us try to explain these illusions. Because of our experience and lifelong use of perceptual cues, we tend to perceive the Hering–Helmholtz drawing as three-dimensional. Because of our tendency to perceive bits of sensory information as figures against grounds, we perceive the blue area in the center as a circle in front of a series of radiating lines, all of which lie in front of a blue ground. Next, because of our experience with perspective, we perceive the radiating lines as parallel. We perceive the two horizontal lines as intersecting the "receding" lines, and we know that they would have to appear bent out at the center if they were to be equidistant at all points from the center of the circle.

Experience probably compels us to perceive the vertical lines in the Müller–Lyer illusion as the corners of a building (see Figure 4.13, part B). We interpret the length of the lines based on our experience with corners of buildings.

LO⁴ Hearing

Consider the advertising slogan for the classic science fiction film *Alien*: "In space, no one can hear you scream." It's true. Space is an almost perfect vacuum. Hearing requires a medium through which

Figure 4.13

The Hering–Helmholtz and Müller–Lyer Illusions

In the Hering–Helmholtz illusion, are the horizontal lines straight or curved? In the Müller–Lyer illusion, are the vertical lines equal in length?

Go to CourseMate for PSYCH at www.cengagebrain.com to access an interactive version of this figure.

A. The Hering–Helmholtz Illusion

B. The Müller–Lyer Illusion

hertz (Hz)
a unit expressing the frequency of sound waves. One hertz equals one cycle per second

decibel (dB)
a unit expressing the loudness of a sound

sound can travel, such as air or water. *What is sound?*

Sound, or auditory stimulation, is the vibration of molecules in a medium such as air or water. Sound travels through the medium like waves, or like ripples in a pond when you toss in a pebble. The molecules of the medium are alternately compressed and expanded like the movements of an accordion. If you were listening under water, you would also hear the splash because of changes in the pressure of the water. In either case, the changes in pressure are vibrations that approach your ears in waves. These vibrations—sound waves—can also be created by a ringing bell, your vocal cords, guitar strings, or the slam of a book thrown down on a desk. A single cycle of compression and expansion is one wave of sound. Sound waves can occur many times in one second. The human ear is sensitive to sound waves with frequencies of from twenty to 20,000 cycles per second.

Pitch and Loudness

Pitch and loudness are two psychological dimensions of sound. The pitch of a sound is determined by its frequency, or the number of cycles per second as expressed in the unit **hertz (Hz)**. One cycle per second is 1 Hz. The greater the number of cycles per second (Hz), the higher the pitch of the sound.

Figure 4.14

Sound Waves of Various Frequencies and Amplitudes

Which sounds have the highest pitch? Which are loudest?

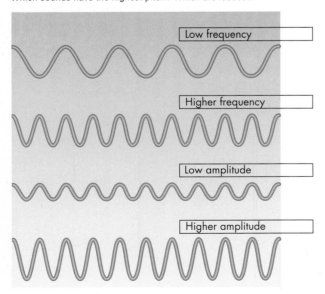

The pitch of women's voices is usually higher than that of men's voices because women's vocal cords are usually shorter and therefore vibrate at a greater frequency. Also, the strings of a violin are shorter than those of a viola or double bass. Pitch detectors in the brain allow us to tell differences in pitch.

The loudness of a sound roughly corresponds to the height, or amplitude, of sound waves. Figure 4.14 shows records of sound waves that vary in frequency and amplitude. Frequency and amplitude are independent. That is, both high- and low-pitched sounds can be either high or low in loudness. The loudness of a sound is expressed in **decibels (dB)**. Zero dB is equivalent to the threshold of hearing—the lowest sound that the typical person can hear. How loud is that? It's about as loud as the ticking of a watch twenty feet away in a very quiet room.

The decibel equivalents of familiar sounds are shown in Figure 4.15. Twenty-five dB is equivalent in

Figure 4.15

Decibel Ratings of Familiar Sounds

Zero dB is the threshold of hearing. You may suffer hearing loss if you incur prolonged exposure to sounds of 85 to 90 dB.

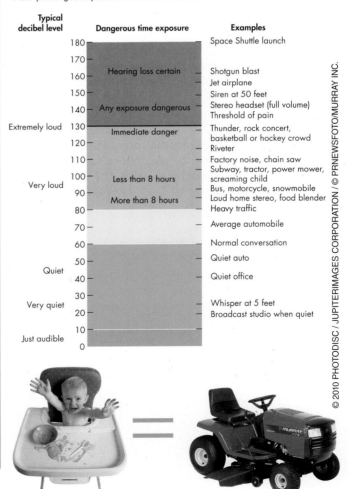

© 2010 PHOTODISC / JUPITERIMAGES CORPORATION / © PRNEWSFOTO/MURRAY INC.

loudness to a whisper at five feet. Thirty dB is roughly the limit of loudness at which your librarian would like to keep your college library. You may suffer hearing damage if you are exposed to sounds of 85 to 90 dB for long periods.

The Ear

How does the ear work? The ear is shaped and structured to capture sound waves, vibrate in sympathy with them, and transmit them to the brain. In this way, you not only hear something, you can also figure out what it is. The ear has three parts: the outer ear, the middle ear, and the inner ear (see Figure 4.16).

The outer ear is shaped to funnel sound waves to the *eardrum*, a thin membrane that vibrates in response to sound waves, and thereby transmits them to the middle and inner ears. The middle ear contains the eardrum and three small bones, which also transmit sound by vibrating. These bones were given their Latin names (*malleus, incus,* and *stapes* [pronounced STAYpeas]), which translate as "hammer," "anvil," and "stirrup") because of their shapes. The middle ear functions as an amplifier, increasing the pressure of the air entering the ear.

The stirrup is attached to another vibrating membrane, the *oval window*. The oval window works in conjunction with the round window, which balances the pressure in the inner ear (see Figure 4.16). The round window pushes outward when the oval window pushes in, and is pulled inward when the oval window vibrates outward.

The oval window transmits vibrations into the inner ear, the bony tube called the cochlea (from the Greek word for "snail"). The cochlea, which is shaped like a snail shell, contains two longitudinal membranes that divide it into three fluid-filled chambers. One of the membranes that lies coiled within the cochlea is called the basilar membrane. Vibrations in the fluids within the chambers of the inner ear press against the basilar membrane.

The organ of Corti, sometimes referred to as the "command post" of hearing, is attached to the basilar membrane. Some 25,000 receptor cells—called hair cells because they project like hair from the organ of Corti—are found in each ear. Hair cells "dance" in response to the vibrations of the basilar membrane. Their movements generate neural impulses, which are transmitted to the brain via the auditory nerve. Auditory input is then projected onto the hearing areas of the temporal lobes of the cerebral cortex.

Locating Sounds

How do we locate sounds? There is a resemblance between balancing a set of stereo speakers and

cochlea
the inner ear; the bony tube that contains the basilar membrane and the organ of Corti

basilar membrane
a membrane that lies coiled within the cochlea

organ of Corti
the receptor for hearing that lies on the basilar membrane in the cochlea

auditory nerve
the axon bundle that transmits neural impulses from the organ of Corti to the brain

Figure 4.16

The Human Ear

Go to CourseMate for PSYCH at www.cengagebrain.com to access an interactive version of this figure.

Organ of Corti

- Basilar membrane
- Tectorial membrane
- Hair cells

Section through cochlea

- Auditory nerve
- Hammer (malleus)
- Anvil (incus)
- Stirrup (stapes)
- Semicircular canals
- Oval window
- Cochlea
- Auditory nerve
- Outer ear (auditory canal)
- Eardrum
- Middle ear
- Round window
- Eustachian tube

locating sounds. A sound that is louder in the right ear is perceived as coming from the right. A sound coming from the right also reaches the right ear first. Both loudness and the sequence in which the sounds reach the ears provide directional cues.

But it may not be easy to locate a sound coming from in front or in back of you or above. Such sounds are equally distant from each ear and equally loud. So what do we do? Simple—we turn our head slightly to determine in which ear the sound increases. If you turn your head to the right and the loudness increases in your left ear, the sound is likely coming from in front.

Perception of Loudness and Pitch

Sounds are heard because they cause vibration in parts of the ear and information about these vibrations is transmitted to the brain. *How do we perceive loudness and pitch?* The loudness and pitch of sounds appear to be related to the number of receptor neurons on the organ of Corti that fire and how often they fire. Psychologists generally agree that sounds are perceived as louder when more of these sensory neurons fire.

It takes two processes to explain perception of color: *trichromatic theory* and *opponent-process theory*. Similarly, it takes at least two processes to explain perception of sound waves that vary in frequency from twenty to 20,000 cycles per second: *place theory* and *frequency theory*.

Hermann von Helmholtz helped develop the place theory of pitch discrimination as well as the trichromatic theory of color vision. Place theory holds that the pitch of a sound is sensed according to the place along the basilar membrane that vibrates in response to it. In research that led to the award of a Nobel Prize, Georg von Békésy (1957) found that receptors at different sites along the membrane fire in response to tones of differing frequencies. Receptor neurons appear to be lined up along the basilar membrane like piano keys. The higher the pitch of a sound, the closer the responsive neurons lie to the oval window (Larkin, 2000). However, place theory appears to apply only to pitches that are at least 5,000 Hz. But what about lower pitches? That's where frequency theory comes in.

Frequency theory notes that for us to perceive lower pitches, we need to match the frequency of the sound waves with our neural impulses. That is, in response to low pitches—say twenty to 1,000 cycles per second—hair cells on the basilar membrane fire at the same frequencies as the sound waves. However, neurons cannot fire more frequently. Therefore, frequency theory best explains perception of pitches between twenty and 1,000 cycles per second.

It takes at least two processes to explain how people perceive pitch. The perception of sounds between 1,000 and 5,000 cycles per second depends both on the part of the basilar membrane that vibrates (as in place theory), and the frequency with which it vibrates (as in frequency theory). The processes apparently work together to enable us to hear pitches in the intermediate range (Goldstein, 2004).

Deafness

More than one in ten Americans have a hearing impairment, and one in 100 cannot hear at all (Canalis & Lambert, 2000). *What is deafness? What can we do about it?*

Two major types of deafness are conductive deafness and sensorineural deafness. *Conductive deafness* stems from damage to the structures of the middle ear—either to the eardrum or to the bones that conduct (and amplify) sound waves from the outer ear to the inner ear (Canalis & Lambert, 2000). This is the hearing impairment often found among older people. Hearing aids amplify sound and often help people with conductive deafness.

Sensorineural deafness usually stems from damage to the structures of the inner ear, most often the loss of hair cells. Sensorineural deafness can also stem from damage to the auditory nerve, caused by such factors as disease or exposure to very loud sounds. In sensorineural deafness, people tend to be more sensitive to some pitches than others. In so-called Hunter's notch, the loss is limited to the frequencies of the sound waves generated by a gun firing. Prolonged exposure to 85 dB can cause hearing loss. People who attend rock concerts, where sounds may reach 140 dB, risk damaging their ears, as do workers who run pneumatic drills or drive noisy vehicles. The ringing sensation that often follows exposure to loud sounds probably means that hair cells in the inner ear have been damaged.

Cochlear implants, or "artificial ears," contain microphones that sense sounds and electronic equipment that transmits sounds past damaged hair cells to stimulate the auditory nerve. Such implants have helped many people with sensorineural deafness (Geers et al., 2002), but they cannot assume the functions of damaged auditory nerves.

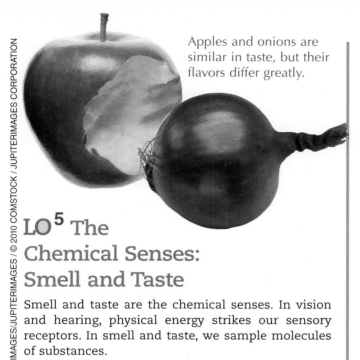

Apples and onions are similar in taste, but their flavors differ greatly.

LO⁵ The Chemical Senses: Smell and Taste

Smell and taste are the chemical senses. In vision and hearing, physical energy strikes our sensory receptors. In smell and taste, we sample molecules of substances.

Smell

Smell has an important role in human behavior. It contributes to the flavor of foods, for example. If you did not have a sense of smell, an onion and an apple might taste the same to you. People's sense of smell may be deficient when compared with that of a dog, but we can detect the odor of 1 one-millionth of a milligram of vanilla in a liter of air.

How does the sense of smell work? Smell detects odors. An *odor* is a sample of molecules of a substance in the air. Odors trigger firing of receptor neurons in the olfactory membrane high in each nostril. Receptor neurons can detect even a few molecules of the substance in gaseous form. The receptor neurons transmit information about odors to the brain via the olfactory nerve.

What's that SCENT you're wearing?

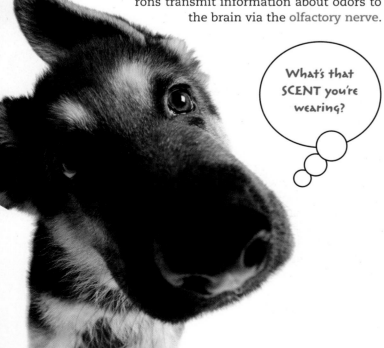

Taste

How does the sense of taste work? As in the case of smell, taste samples molecules of a substance. Taste is sensed through taste cells—receptor neurons located on taste buds. You have about 10,000 taste buds, most of which are located near the edges and back of your tongue. Some tastebuds are more responsive to sweetness, whereas others react to several tastes. Other taste receptors are found in the roof, sides, and back of the mouth, and in the throat. Buds in the mouth are evolutionarily adaptive because they can warn of bad food before it is swallowed (Brand, 2000).

Researchers generally agree on at least four primary taste qualities: sweet, sour, salty, and bitter. Some argue for a fifth basic taste, which is termed *umami* (pronounced *oohmommy*) in Japanese and means "meaty" or "savory." Regardless of the number of basic tastes, the flavor of a food is more complex than taste alone. *Flavor* depends on odor, texture, and temperature as well as on taste. Apples and onions are similar in taste, but their flavors differ greatly.

Just as some people see better than others, some people taste better than others—but their superiority may be limited to one or more basic tastes. Those of us with low sensitivity for sweetness may require twice the sugar to sweeten our food as those who are more sensitive. Those of us who claim to enjoy bitter foods may actually be taste-blind to them (Lanier et al., 2005). Sensitivities to various tastes have a genetic component (Bartoshuk, 2000; Duffy et al., 2004).

LO⁶ The Skin Senses

What are the skin senses? How do they work? The skin senses include touch, pressure, warmth, cold, and pain. We have distinct sensory receptors for pressure, temperature, and pain, but some nerve endings may receive more than one type of sensory input. Here let's focus on touch, pressure, temperature, and pain.

Touch and Pressure

Sensory receptors embedded in the skin fire when the surface of the skin is touched. There may

flavor
a complex quality of food and other substances that is based on their odor, texture, and temperature as well their taste

olfactory nerve
the nerve that transmits information concerning odors from olfactory receptors to the brain

taste cells
receptor cells that are sensitive to taste

taste buds
the sensory organs for taste. They contain taste cells and are located mostly on the tongue

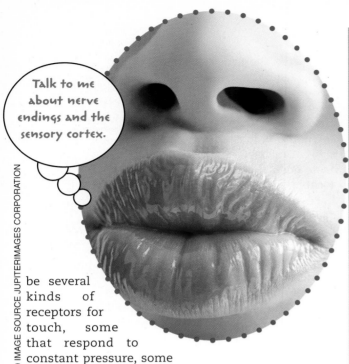

Talk to me about nerve endings and the sensory cortex.

be several kinds of receptors for touch, some that respond to constant pressure, some that respond to intermittent pressure, as in tapping the skin. *Active touching* means continually moving your hand along the surface of an object so that you continue to receive sensory input from the object (O'Dell & Hoyert, 2002). If you are trying to "get the feel of" a fabric or the texture of a friend's hair, you must move your hand over it. Otherwise the sensations quickly fade. If you pass your hand over the fabric or hair and then hold it still, the sensations of touching will fade. Active touching receives information concerning pressure, temperature, texture, and feedback from the muscles involved in movements of our hands.

Different parts of the body are more sensitive to touch and pressure than others. The parts of the body that "cover" more than their fair share of somatosensory cortex are most sensitive to touch. These parts include the hands, face, and some other regions of the body. Our fingertips, lips, noses, and cheeks are more sensitive than our shoulders, thighs, and calves. Why the difference in sensitivity? First, nerve endings are more densely packed in the fingertips and face than in other locations. Second, more sensory cortex is devoted to the perception of sensations in the fingertips and face (see Figure 2.11 on page 38).

Temperature

The receptors for temperature are neurons located just beneath the skin. When skin temperature increases, the receptors for warmth fire. Decreases in skin temperature cause receptors for cold to fire.

Sensations of temperature are relative. When we are at normal body temperature, we might perceive another person's skin as warm. When we are feverish, though, the other person's skin might seem cool. We also adapt to differences in temperature. When we enter a swimming pool, the water may seem cold because it is below body temperature. Yet after a few moments an 80°F pool may seem quite warm. In fact, we may chide a newcomer for not diving right in.

Pain

For most people, pain is a frequent visitor. Headaches, backaches, toothaches—these are only a few of the types of pain that most of us encounter from time to time. According to a national Gallup survey of more than 2,000 adults (Arthritis Foundation, 2000), 89% experience pain at least once a month. More than half (55%) of people aged sixty-five and above say they experience pain daily. People aged sixty-five and above are most likely to attribute pain to getting older (88%) and to assume they can do nothing about disabilities such as arthritis. By contrast, people aged eighteen to thirty-four are more likely to attribute pain to tension or stress (73%), overwork (64%), or their lifestyle (51%). When we assume that there is nothing we can do about pain, we are less likely to try. Yet 43% of Americans say that pain curtails their activities, and 50% say that pain puts them in a bad mood. *What is pain? What can we do about it?*

Pain results when neurons called *nociceptors* in the skin are stimulated. Evolutionary psychologists would point out that pain is adaptive, if unpleasant, because it motivates us to do something about it. For some of us, however, chronic pain—pain that lasts once injuries or illnesses have cleared—saps our vitality and interferes with the pleasures of everyday life (Turk & Okifuji, 2002).

We can sense pain throughout most of the body, but pain is usually sharpest where nerve endings are densely packed, as in the fingers and face. Pain can also be felt deep within the body, as in the cases of abdominal pain and back pain. Even though headaches may seem to originate deep inside the head, there are no nerve endings for pain in the brain.

Pain usually originates at the point of contact, as when you bang a knee. But it reverberates throughout the nervous system. The pain message to the brain is initiated by the release of chemicals such as prostaglandins, bradykinin, and *P* (yes, *P* stands for "pain"). *Prostaglandins* facilitate transmission of the pain message to the brain and heighten circulation to the injured area, causing the redness and swelling that we call inflammation. Inflammation attracts infection-fighting blood cells to the injury to protect it against invading germs. Pain-relieving drugs such as aspirin and ibuprofen help by inhibiting production of prostaglandins.

The pain message is relayed from the spinal cord to the thalamus and then projected to the cerebral cortex, making us aware of the location and intensity of the damage. Ronald Melzack (1999) speaks of a "neuromatrix" that includes these chemical reactions but involves other aspects of our physiology and psychology in our reaction to pain. For example, visual and other sensory inputs tell us what is happening and affect our interpretation of the situation. Our emotional response affects the degree of pain, and so do the ways in which we respond to stress. If, for instance, the pain derives from an object we fear, perhaps a knife or a needle, we may experience more pain. If we perceive that there is nothing we can do to change the situation, perception of pain may increase. If we have self-confidence and a history of successful response to stress, perception of pain may diminish.

Phantom Limb Pain

One of the more intriguing topics in the study of pain is phantom limb pain. About two out of three combat veterans with amputated limbs report feeling pain in such missing, or "phantom," limbs (Kooijman et al., 2000). Although the pain occurs in the absence of the limb, it is real enough. It sometimes involves activation of nerves in the stump of the missing limb, but local anesthesia does not always eliminate the pain. Researchers have found that many people who experience phantom limb pain have also undergone reorganization of the motor and somatosensory cortex that is consistent with the pain (Mackert et al., 2003).

> **Truth**
>
> Many people do appear to experience pain "in" limbs that have been amputated (Horgan & MacLachlan, 2004).

Gate Theory

Simple remedies like rubbing a banged knee frequently help relieve pain. Why? One possible answer lies in the *gate theory* of pain originated by Ronald Melzack and Patrick Wall (Sufka & Price, 2002). Gate theory proposes that the nervous system can process only a limited amount of stimulation at a time. Rubbing the knee transmits sensations to the brain that "compete" for the attention of neurons. Many nerves are thus prevented from transmitting pain messages to the brain. It is like shutting down a "gate" in the spinal cord, or like a switchboard being flooded with calls. Flooding prevents any calls from getting through.

Acupuncture

Thousands of years ago, the Chinese began mapping the body to learn where pins might be placed to deaden pain. This practice is termed acupuncture. Traditional acupuncturists believe that the practice balances the body's flow of energy, but research has shown that it stimulates nerves that reach the hypothalamus and may also cause the release of *endorphins* (Ulett & Wedding, 2003). Endorphins are neurotransmitters that are similar to the narcotic morphine in their chemical structure and effects.

LO⁷ Kinesthesis and the Vestibular Sense

Try an experiment. Close your eyes, and then touch your nose with your finger. If you weren't right on target, I'm sure you came close. But how? You didn't see your hand moving, and you didn't hear your arm swishing through the air. Humans and many other animals have senses that alert them to their movements and body position without relying on vision, including kinesthesis and the vestibular sense.

Kinesthesis

What is kinesthesis? **Kinesthesis** is the sense that informs you about the position and motion of parts of the body. The term is derived from the ancient Greek words for "motion" (kinesis) and "perception" (aisthesis). In kinesthesis, sensory information is fed back to the brain from sensory organs in the joints, tendons, and muscles. You were able to bring your finger to your nose easily by employing your kinesthetic sense. When you make a muscle in your arm, the sensations of tightness and hardness are also provided by kinesthesis.

kinesthesis
the sense that informs us about the positions and motion of parts of our bodies

vestibular sense
the sense of equilibrium that informs us about our bodies' positions relative to gravity

Imagine going for a walk without kinesthesis. You would have to watch the forward motion of each leg to be certain you had raised it high enough to clear the curb. And if you had tried the brief nose-to-finger experiment without the kinesthetic sense, you would have had no sensory feedback until you felt the pressure of your finger against your nose (or cheek, or eye, or forehead), and you probably would have missed dozens of times.

The Vestibular Sense

It is your vestibular sense that provides your brain with information as to whether or not you are physically upright.

How does the vestibular sense work? Sensory organs located in the semicircular canals and elsewhere in the ears monitor your body's motion and position in relation to gravity. They tell you whether you are falling and provide cues to whether your body is changing speed, such as when you are in an accelerating airplane or automobile.

LO⁸ ESP: Is There Perception Without Sensation?

Our sensory organs are the peripheral devices that feed information into our central processing units—our brains. What if there were such as thing as extra sensory perception (ESP)? What if sensation were bypassed, and we directly perceived things in the world outside? Although the actual research evidence comes down hard against ESP, 60% of the American public believes that some people have psychic powers or ESP (National Science Foundation, 2002). Therefore, it is useful to understand the issue and examine the type of research that psychologists conduct to determine whether it has validity. Let us begin by defining precognition and other topics in ESP.

Precognition, Psychokinesis, Telepathy, and Clairvoyance

Imagine the wealth you could amass if you had *precognition*, that is, if you were able to perceive future events in advance. Perhaps you would check the next week's stock market reports and know what to buy or sell. Or you could bet with confidence on who would win the next Super Bowl or World Series. Or think of the power you would have if you were capable of *psychokinesis*, that is, of mentally manipulating or moving objects. You may have gotten a glimpse of the possibilities in films like *The Matrix*, *The Sixth Sense*, and *Star Wars*. Precognition and psychokinesis are two concepts associated with ESP. Two other theoretical forms of ESP are *telepathy* or direct transmission of thoughts or ideas from one person to another, and *clairvoyance*, or the perception of objects that do not stimulate the sensory organs. An example of clairvoyance is "seeing" what card will be dealt next, even though it is still in the deck and unseen even by the dealer.

Many psychologists do not believe that ESP is an appropriate area for scientific inquiry. Other psychologists, however, believe that there is nothing wrong with investigating ESP. The issue for them is whether its existence can be demonstrated in the laboratory. *Does ESP really exist?*

A well-known ESP researcher was Joseph Banks Rhine of Duke University, who studied ESP for several decades, beginning in the 1920s. In a typical experiment in clairvoyance, Rhine would use a pack of twenty-five cards, which contained five sets of simple symbols. Pigeons pecking patterns at random to indicate which one was about to be turned up would be "correct" 20% of the time. Rhine found that some people guessed correctly significantly more often than the 20% chance rate. He concluded that these people might have some degree of ESP.

A more current method for studying telepathy is the *ganzfeld procedure* (Dalkvist, 2001; Parker, 2001). In this method, one person acts as a "sender" and the other as a "receiver." The sender views randomly selected visual stimuli such as photographs or videotapes, while the receiver, who is in another room and whose eyes are covered and ears are blocked, tries to mentally tune in to the sender. After a session, the receiver is shown four visual stimuli and asked to select the one transmitted by the sender. A person guessing which stimulus was "transmitted" would be correct 25% of the time (one time in four) by chance alone. An analysis of twenty-eight experiments using the ganzfeld procedure, however, found that receivers correctly identified the visual stimulus 38% of the time (Honorton, 1985), a percentage unlikely to be due to chance. A series of eleven more studies with the ganzfeld procedure obtained similar results (Bem & Honorton, 1994; Honorton et al., 1990).

Overall, however, there are reasons to be skeptical. First is the *file-drawer problem*. Buyers of supermarket tabloids tend to forget the predictions of "psychics" when the predictions fail to come true (that is, they have "filed" them away). Similarly, ESP researchers are more likely to "file away" research results that show failure. Therefore, we would expect unusual findings (for example, a subject with a high success rate on experimental tasks over a few days) to appear in the research literature. In other words, if you flip a coin indefinitely, eventually you will flip ten heads in a row. The odds against it are high, but if you report your eventual success and do not report the weeks of failure, you may give the impression that you have unique coin-flipping ability.

It has also been difficult to replicate experiments in ESP. People who have "demonstrated" ESP with one researcher have failed to do so with another, or they have refused to participate in other studies. Also, the findings in one study are usually absent in follow-ups or under careful analysis. For example, Milton and Wiseman (1999) reviewed the research reported by Bem and Honorton (1994). They weighed the results of thirty ganzfeld ESP studies from seven laboratories. They found no evidence—zero—that subjects in these studies scored above chance levels on the ESP task. From all of these studies, *not one person has emerged who can reliably show ESP from one occasion to another and from one researcher to another.* Research has not identified one single indisputable telepath or clairvoyant. In sum, most psychologists do not grant ESP research much credibility. They prefer to study perception that involves sensation. After all, what is life without sensation?

Fiction

There is no adequate scientific evidence that people can read other people's minds.

1/60 < Weber's constant for light	Weber's constant for lifted weight > **1/53**	Weber's constant for pitch > **1/333**
wavelength of violet light in nanometers > **400**	**700** < wavelength of red light in nanometers	**125** < million rods in the retina
6.4 < million cones in the retina	**16–22** < frames/second in movie film playback	**0** < equivalent to the threshold of hearing in dB

© 2010 IMAGE SOURCE PINK / JUPITERIMAGES CORPORATION

Consciousness

Learning Outcomes

LO[1]   Define consciousness

LO[2]   Explain the nature of sleep and various sleep disorders

LO[3]   Explain various uses of hypnosis, forms of meditation, and biofeedback techniques in altering consciousness

LO[4]   Explain the concepts of substance abuse; identify categories of drugs and how they alter consciousness

> ## "*When you talk to yourself, who talks, and who listens?*"

When you talk to yourself, who talks, and who listens?

This is the type of question posed by philosophers and scientists who study consciousness. Although it might seem that psychologists, who study the brain and mental processes, are best equipped to look into consciousness, they banished this topic from their field for many years. In 1904, for example, William James wrote an article with the intriguing title "Does Consciousness Exist?" James did not think consciousness was a proper area of study for psychologists because scientific methods could not directly observe or measure another person's consciousness.

John Watson, the "father of modern behaviorism," agreed. Watson insisted that only observable, measurable behavior is the province of psychology: "The time seems to have come when psychology must discard all references to consciousness" (1913, p. 163). When Watson became the president of the American Psychological Association in 1914, his view was further cemented in the minds of many psychologists.

But the past few decades have seen a cognitive revolution, and thousands of psychologists now believe we cannot capture the richness of human experience without referring to consciousness (Schultz & Schultz, 2008). We are flooded with studies of consciousness by psychologists, biologists, neuroscientists, physicists, even computer scientists. Yet we still cannot directly observe the consciousness of another person, and so we rely on self-reports of consciousness as we observe events such as neural activity in the brain.

Truth or Fiction?

What do you think?

Folklore, common sense, or nonsense? Place a T for "True" or F for "False" on the lines provided (you'll learn the answers as you read through the text).

___ We act out our forbidden fantasies in our dreams.

___ Insomnia can be caused by trying too hard to fall asleep.

___ It is dangerous to awaken a sleepwalker.

___ You can be hypnotized against your will.

___ You can teach a rat to raise or lower its heart rate.

___ Many health professionals calm down hyperactive children by giving them a stimulant.

___ Coca-Cola once "added life" to its signature drink through the use of a powerful—but now illegal—stimulant.

___ The number of people who die from smoking-related causes is greater than the number lost to motor-vehicle accidents, abuse of alcohol and all other drugs, suicide, homicide, and AIDS *combined.*

LO¹ What Is Consciousness?

Mental concepts such as consciousness acquire scientific status by being tied to observable behavior whenever possible. *What is consciousness?* The concept of consciousness has various meanings, and psychologists use it in many ways.

selective attention
the focus of consciousness on a particular stimulus

direct inner awareness
knowledge of one's own thoughts, feelings, and memories

preconscious
in psychodynamic theory, descriptive of material that is not in awareness but can be brought into awareness by focusing one's attention

Consciousness as Awareness

One meaning of consciousness is *sensory awareness* of the environment. The sense of vision enables us to see, or be *conscious* of, the sun gleaming on the snow. The sense of hearing allows us to hear, or be conscious of, a concert. Yet sometimes we are not aware of sensory stimulation. We may be unaware, or unconscious, of sensory stimulation when we do not pay attention to it. The world is abuzz with signals, yet you are conscious of or focusing on only the words on this page (I hope).

Therefore, another aspect of consciousness is selective attention. Selective attention means focusing one's consciousness on a particular stimulus. Selective attention is a key to self-control. To keep your car on the road, you must pay more attention to driving conditions than to your hunger pangs or a cell-phone call.

Adaptation to our environment involves learning which stimuli must be attended to and which can be safely ignored. Selective attention makes our senses keener (Vorobyev et al., 2004). This is why we can pick out the speech of a single person across a room at a

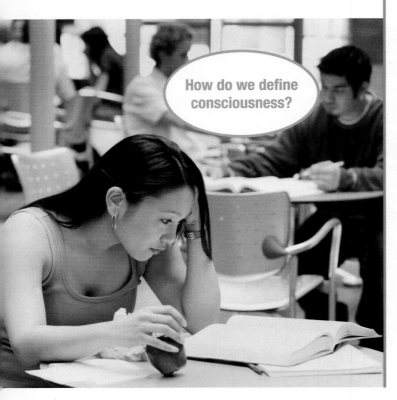

How do we define consciousness?

cocktail party, a phenomenon aptly termed the *cocktail party effect*. Selective attention also plays a role in the advertisements and marketing ploys we notice.

How do advertisers of running shoes, automobiles, or beer use these facts to get "into" our consciousness and, they hope, our pocketbooks? Think of some TV commercials that captured your attention. What kinds of stimuli made them front and center in your awareness?

Yet another meaning of consciousness is that of direct inner awareness. Close your eyes and imagine spilling a can of bright-red paint across a black tabletop. Watch it spread across the black, shiny surface and then spill onto the floor. Although this image may be vivid, you did not "see" it literally. Neither your eyes nor any other sensory organs were involved. You were conscious of the image through direct inner awareness.

We are conscious of—or have direct inner awareness of—thoughts, images, emotions, and memories. However, we may not be able to measure direct inner awareness scientifically. Nevertheless, many psychologists would argue that if you have it, you know it. Self-awareness is connected with the firing of billions of neurons hundreds of times per second. Even so, we detect psychological processes but not neural events (Roth, 2000).

Conscious, Preconscious, Unconscious, and Nonconscious

Sigmund Freud, the founder of psychoanalysis, differentiated between thoughts and feelings of which we are conscious and those that are preconscious and unconscious.

Preconscious material is not currently in awareness but is readily available. If you answer the following questions, you will summon up "preconscious"

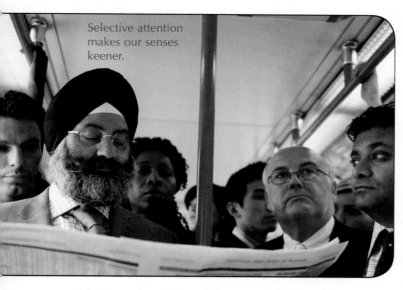
Selective attention makes our senses keener.

DIGITAL VISION/ JUPITER IMAGES

information: What did you eat for breakfast? What is your phone number? You can make these preconscious bits of information conscious by directing your attention to them.

Still other mental events are unconscious, or unavailable to awareness under most circumstances. Freud believed that some painful memories and sexual and aggressive impulses are unacceptable to us, so we *automatically* (unconsciously) eject them from awareness. That is, we *repress* them. Repression allows us to avoid feelings of anxiety, guilt, or shame.

Related, non-Freudian concepts include *suppression* and *nonconscious*. When people choose to stop thinking about unacceptable ideas or distractions, they are using suppression. When we consciously eject unwanted mental events from awareness, we are using suppression. We may suppress thoughts of an upcoming party when we need to study for a test. We may also try to suppress thoughts of the test while we are at the party!

Some bodily processes, such as the firing of neurons, are nonconscious. They cannot be experienced through sensory awareness or direct inner awareness. Growing hair and carrying oxygen in the blood are nonconscious. We can see that our hair has grown, but we have no sense receptors that provide sensations of growing. We feel the need to breathe but do not experience the exchange of carbon dioxide and oxygen.

Consciousness as Personal Unity

As we develop, we differentiate ourselves from that which is not us. We develop a sense of being persons, individuals. There is a totality to our impressions, thoughts, and feelings that makes up our consciousness—our continuing sense of self in the world. That self forms intentions and guides behavior. In this usage of the word, consciousness is self.

Consciousness as the Waking State

The word *conscious* also refers to the waking state as opposed, for example, to sleep. From this perspective, sleep, meditation, the hypnotic "trance," and the distorted perceptions that can accompany use of consciousness-altering drugs are considered *altered states of consciousness*.

In the remainder of this chapter, we explore various types of altered states of consciousness, including sleep and dreams; hypnosis, meditation, and biofeedback; and, finally, the effects of psychoactive drugs.

unconscious in psychodynamic theory, descriptive of ideas and feelings that are not available to awareness; also: without consciousness

repression in psychodynamic theory, the unconscious ejection of anxiety-evoking ideas, impulses, or images from awareness

suppression the deliberate, or conscious, placing of certain ideas, impulses, or images out of awareness

nonconscious descriptive of bodily processes such as growing hair, of which we cannot become conscious. We may "recognize" that our hair is growing, but we cannot directly experience the biological process

LO² Sleep and Dreams

Sleep is a fascinating topic. After all, we spend about one-third of our adult lives asleep. Sleep experts recommend that adults get eight hours of sleep a night, but according to the National Sleep Foundation (2008), adults in the United States typically get a bit less than seven. About one-third get six hours or less of sleep a night during the workweek. One-third admit that lack of sleep impairs their ability to function during the day, and nearly one in five admits to falling asleep at the wheel sometime during the past year.

Yes, we spend one-third of our lives in sleep—or would if we could. As you can see in Figure 5.1, on p. 100, some animals get much more sleep than we do, and some obtain much less. Why? It might have something to do with evolutionary forces. Animals who are most at risk of being hunted by predators tend to sleep less—an adaptive response to the realities of life and death. Individuals who slept more might have been killed by predators, eliminating their genes from the gene pool of their species.

Biological and Circadian Rhythms

Our lives are connected with the rhythms of the universe at large. Planet Earth rotates in about twenty-four hours. The earth revolves around the sun once a year.

We and other animals are also subject to rhythms,

circadian rhythm
a cycle that is connected with the twenty-four-hour period of the earth's rotation

alpha waves
rapid low-amplitude brain waves that have been linked to feelings of relaxation

nonrapid eye movement (NREM) sleep
stages of sleep 1 through 4

rapid eye movement (REM) sleep
a stage of sleep characterized by rapid eye movements, which have been linked to dreaming

and they are related to the rotation and revolutions of the planet. Many birds (and people who can afford it!) migrate south in the fall and north in the spring. A number of animals hibernate for the winter and emerge when buds are about to blossom again.

Alternating periods of wakefulness and sleep reflect an internally generated *circadian rhythm. What is a circadian rhythm?* A circadian rhythm is a cycle that is connected with the twenty-four-hour period of the earth's rotation. A cycle of wakefulness and sleep is normally twenty-four hours long. When people are removed from cues that signal day or night, however, a cycle tends to become extended to about twenty-five hours, and people sleep nearly ten of them (National Sleep Foundation, 2008). Why? We do not know. And during a night of sleep, we typically

undergo a series of ninety-minute cycles in which we run through the stages of sleep. In the morning, the shining sun adjusts the timing of the circadian clock by activating proteins in the retinas of the eyes. The proteins then signal tiny structures in the hypothalamus called the *suprachiasmatic nucleas (SCN)*. In turn, the SCN stimulates the pineal gland to decrease its output of the hormone melatonin, which promotes sleep.

Some of us, "morning people," function best in the morning, others in the afternoon. Some of us are "night owls," who are at our best when most neighbors are sound asleep.

Why do we sleep? Why do we dream? Let us explore the nature of sleep, dreams, and sleep disorders.

The Stages of Sleep

When we sleep, we slip from consciousness to unconsciousness. When we are conscious, our brains emit waves characterized by certain *frequencies* (numbers of waves per second) and *amplitudes* (heights—an index of strength). Brain waves indicate the activity of neurons. The strength or energy of brain waves is expressed in volts (an electrical unit). When we sleep our brain waves differ from those emitted when we are conscious. The electroencephalograph (EEG; see Figure 2.7 on page 34) has enabled researchers to measure brain waves. Figure 5.2 shows EEG patterns that reflect the frequency and strength of brain waves during the waking state, when we are relaxed, and when we are in the various stages of sleep. Brain waves, like other waves, are cyclical. The printouts in Figure 5.2 show what happens during a period of 15 seconds or so. *How do we describe the various stages of sleep?*

High-frequency brain waves are associated with wakefulness. When we move deeper into sleep, their frequency decreases and their amplitude (strength) increases. When we close our eyes and begin to relax before going to sleep, our brains emit **alpha waves**—low-amplitude brain waves of about eight to thirteen cycles per second.

Figure 5.2 shows five stages of sleep. The first four sleep stages are considered **nonrapid eye movement (NREM)** sleep. These contrast with the fifth stage, **rapid eye movement (REM)** sleep, so called because our eyes dart back and forth beneath our eyelids.

As we enter stage 1 sleep, our brain waves slow down from the alpha rhythm

Figure 5.1

Sleep Times for Mammals

Different mammals require different amounts of sleep. Reasons remain uncertain, but evolution apparently plays a role: Animals that are more prone to being attacked by predators sleep less.

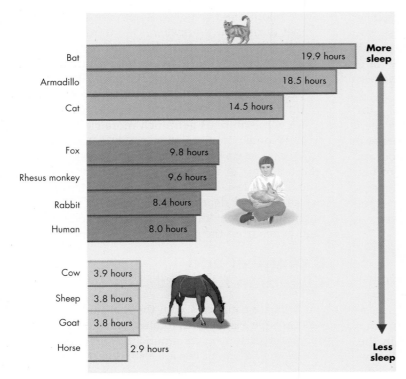

Bat	19.9 hours
Armadillo	18.5 hours
Cat	14.5 hours
Fox	9.8 hours
Rhesus monkey	9.6 hours
Rabbit	8.4 hours
Human	8.0 hours
Cow	3.9 hours
Sheep	3.8 hours
Goat	3.8 hours
Horse	2.9 hours

More sleep

Less sleep

Figure 5.2

The Stages of Sleep

This figure illustrates typical EEG patterns for the stages of sleep. During REM sleep, EEG patterns resemble those of the waking state. For this reason, REM sleep is often termed *paradoxical sleep*. As sleep progresses from stage 1 to stage 4, brain waves become slower, and their amplitude increases. Dreams, including normal nightmares, are most vivid during REM sleep. More disturbing sleep terrors tend to occur during deep stage 4 sleep.

Go to CourseMate for PSYCH at www.cengagebrain.com to access an interactive version of this figure. 🎧

theta waves
slow brain waves produced during the hypnagogic state

delta waves
strong, slow brain waves usually emitted during stage 4 sleep

Awake

Awake — beta waves (low amplitude, high frequency)

Drowsy — alpha waves (higher amplitude, slower frequency)

NREM Sleep

Stage 1 sleep — theta waves (low frequency, low amplitude)

Sleep spindle   K complex

Stage 2 sleep — sleep spindles and the K complex

Stage 3 sleep — beginning of delta waves (low frequency, high amplitude)

Stage 4 sleep — delta waves continue to increase in amplitude

REM Sleep

Occurs when we re-enter Stage 1, about ninety minutes after falling asleep (frequently called *paradoxical sleep*)

REM sleep — brain-wave patterns are very similar to those of initial NREM stage 1

and enter a pattern of theta waves. Theta waves, with a frequency of about six to eight cycles per second, are accompanied by slow, rolling eye movements. The transition from alpha waves to theta waves may be accompanied by a *hypnagogic state* during which we may experience brief but vivid dreamlike images. Stage 1 sleep is the lightest stage of sleep. If we are awakened from stage 1 sleep, we may feel we were not sleeping at all.

After thirty to forty minutes of stage 1 sleep, we undergo a steep descent into stages 2, 3, and 4 (see Figure 5.3 on page 102). During stage 2, brain waves are medium in amplitude with a frequency of about four to seven cycles per second, but these are punctuated by *sleep spindles*. Sleep spindles have a frequency of twelve to sixteen cycles per second and represent brief bursts of rapid brain activity.

During deep sleep stages 3 and 4, our brains produce slower delta waves, which reach relatively great amplitude. During stage 3, the delta waves have a frequency of one to three cycles per second. Stage 4 is the deepest stage of sleep, from which it is the most difficult to be awakened. During stage 4 sleep, the delta waves slow to about 0.5 to 2 cycles per second, and their amplitude is greatest.

After perhaps half an hour of deep stage 4 sleep, we begin a relatively rapid journey back upward through the stages until we enter REM sleep (see Figure 5.3). During REM sleep, we produce relatively rapid, low-amplitude brain waves that resemble those of light stage 1 sleep. REM sleep is also called *paradoxical sleep* because the EEG patterns observed suggest a level of arousal similar to that of the waking state (see Figure 5.2). However, it is difficult to awaken a person during REM sleep. When people are awakened during REM sleep, they report dreaming about 80% of the time. We also dream during NREM sleep but only about 20% of the time.

Each night we tend to undergo five cycles through the stages of sleep (see Figure 5.3). Five cycles include five periods of REM sleep. Our first journey through stage 4 sleep is usually the longest. Sleep tends to become lighter as the night wears on; periods of REM sleep lengthen and we may not enter the deepest stages of sleep. Toward morning our last period of REM sleep may last about half an hour.

The Functions of Sleep

Why do we sleep? Researchers do not have all the answers as to why we sleep, but sleep seems to serve several purposes: It rejuvenates the body, helps us recover from stress, helps us consolidate learning, and may promote development of infants' brains.

Consider the hypothesis that sleep helps rejuvenate a tired body. Most of us have had the experience of going without sleep for a night and feeling "wrecked" or "out of it" the following day. Perhaps the next evening we went to bed early to "catch up on our sleep." What happens to you if you do not

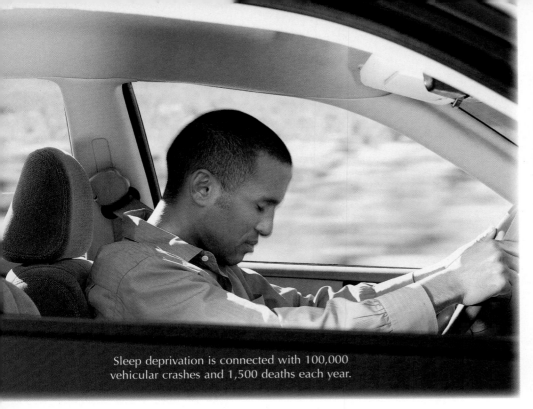

Sleep deprivation is connected with 100,000 vehicular crashes and 1,500 deaths each year.

Why Do You Need the Amount of Sleep You Need?

The amount of sleep we need seems to be in part genetically determined (National Sleep Foundation, 2008). People also need more sleep when they are under stress, such as a change of job or an episode of depression (National Sleep Foundation, 2008). Sleep helps us recover from stress.

Newborn babies may sleep sixteen hours a day, and teenagers may sleep "around the clock" (twelve hours or more). It is widely believed that older people need less sleep than younger adults do, but sleep in older people is often interrupted by physical discomfort or the need to go to the bathroom. To make up for sleep lost at night, older people may "nod off" during the day.

ADAM GAULT/GETTY IMAGES

sleep for one night? For several nights? Compare people who are highly sleep-deprived with people who have been drinking heavily. Sleepless people's abilities to concentrate and perform may be seriously impaired, but they may not recognize their limitations.

Many students can pull "all-nighters" during which they cram for a test through the night and perform reasonably well the following day (Horowitz et al., 2003). But they begin to show deficits in psychological functions such as learning and memory if they go sleepless for more than one night (Ohno et al., 2002; Taylor & McFatter, 2003). Sleep deprivation makes for dangerous driving (Stutts et al., 2003). The National Sleep Foundation (2008) estimates that sleep deprivation is connected with 100,000 vehicular crashes and 1,500 deaths each year. To combat sleep deprivation during the week, many people sleep late or nap on their days off (National Sleep Foundation, 2008).

Sleep, Learning, and Memory

REM sleep and deep sleep are both connected with the consolidation of learning and memory (Gais & Born, 2004; Ribeiro & Nicolelis, 2004). Fetuses have periods of waking and sleeping, and REM sleep may foster the development of the brain before birth (Fifer & Moon, 2003). In some studies, animals or people have been deprived of REM sleep. Under deprivation of REM sleep, animals and people learn more slowly and forget what they have learned more quickly (Kennedy, 2002; Ribeiro & Nicolelis, 2004). REM-sleep-deprived people and animals tend to show *REM rebound,* meaning that they spend more time in REM sleep during subsequent sleep periods. They "catch up."

Figure 5.3

Sleep Cycles

This figure illustrates the alternation of REM and non-REM sleep for the typical sleeper. There are about five periods of REM sleep during an eight-hour night. Sleep is deeper earlier in the night, and REM sleep tends to become prolonged toward morning.

11 PM	12 AM	1 AM	2 AM

Sleep stage	A	1	2	3	4	3	2	REM	1	2	3	4	3	2	3	2	REM

Dreams

What are dreams? Dreams are imagery in the absence of external stimulation and can seem real. In college I had repeated "anxiety dreams" the night before a test. I would dream that I had taken the test and it was all over. Imagine my disappointment when I awakened and realized the test still lay before me!

Dreams are most likely to be vivid during REM sleep. Images are vaguer and more fleeting during NREM sleep. If you sleep for eight hours and undergo five sleep cycles, you may have five dreams. Dreams may compress time the way a movie does, by skipping hours or days to a future time, but the actual action tends to take place in "real time." Fifteen minutes of events fills about fifteen minutes of dreaming (Hall, 1953). Furthermore, your dream theater is quite flexible. You can dream in black and white or in full color.

Some dreams are nightmares. One common nightmare is that you are falling. Another is that you are trying to run away from a threat but cannot gain your footing or coordinate your legs. Nightmares, like most pleasant dreams, are products of REM sleep.

Why do we dream what we dream? There are many theories about why we dream what we dream. Some are psychological, and others are more biologically oriented.

Dreams as "the Residue of the Day"

You may recall dreams involving fantastic adventures, but most dreams involve memories of the day gone by—or, poetically, "the residue of the day" (Domhoff, 2001, 2003). If we are preoccupied with illness or death, sex or aggression, or moral dilemmas, we are likely to dream about them. The characters in our dreams are more likely to be friends and neighbors than spies, monsters, and princes.

Traumatic events, however, can spawn nightmares, as reported in the aftermath of the terrorist attacks on the World Trade Center and Pentagon in 2001 (Gorman, 2001; Singareddy & Balon, 2002). People who have frequent nightmares are more likely than others to also have feelings of anxiety and depression (Blagrove et al., 2004; Levin & Fireman, 2002).

Dreams as the Expression of Unconscious Desires

In the Disney film *Cinderella*, a song lyric goes, "A dream is a wish your heart makes." Freud theorized that dreams reflect unconscious wishes and urges. He argued that dreams express impulses we would censor during the day. Moreover, he said that the content of dreams is symbolic of unconscious fantasized objects such as the genitals. In his method of psychoanalysis, Freud would interpret his clients' dreams. Dreams do, however, seem to be consistent with gender roles; that is, males are more likely than females to have dreams with aggressive content (Schredl et al., 2004).

The Activation–Synthesis Model of Dreams

There are also biological views of the "meanings" of dreams (Domhoff, 2003). According to the activation–synthesis model, acetylcholine (a neurotransmitter) and the pons (see Figure 2.11 on page 38) stimulate responses that lead to dreaming (Hobson, 2003; Ogawa et al., 2002). One is *activation* of the reticular activating system (RAS; see Figure 2.11), which arouses us, but not to waking. During the waking state, firing of these cells is linked to movement, particularly in walking, running, and other physical acts. But during REM sleep, neurotransmitters tend to inhibit activity so we usually do not thrash about

activation–synthesis model the view that acetylcholine and the pons activate the reticular activating system, which stimulates the cortex, but not to the point of waking; the cortex then pieces together (synthesizes) the cognitive activity into a dream

Fiction

There is no evidence that we act out forbidden fantasies in our dreams.

narcolepsy
a "sleep attack" in which a person falls asleep suddenly and irresistibly

(Bassetti et al., 2000). In this way, we save ourselves— and our bed partners—wear and tear. But the eye muscles are stimulated and show the REM activity associated with dreaming. The RAS also stimulates parts of the cortex involved in memory. The cortex then *synthesizes*, or pieces together, these sources of stimulation to yield the stuff of dreams (Anderson & Horne, 2004). Because recent events are most likely to be reverberating in our brains, we are most likely to dream about them. With the brain cut off from the world outside, learning experiences and memories are replayed and consolidated during sleep (Siegel, 2002; Stickgold et al., 2001). It's useful to get a night of sleep between studying and test-taking, if you can.

Sleep Disorders

Although nightmares are unpleasant, they do not qualify as sleep disorders. The term *sleep disorder* is reserved for other problems that can seriously interfere with our functioning.

What kinds of sleep disorders are there? Some sleep disorders, like insomnia, are all too familiar, experienced by at least half of American adults. Others,

like apnea (pauses in breathing) affect fewer than 10% of us (National Sleep Foundation, 2008). In this section we discuss insomnia and less common sleep disorders: narcolepsy, apnea, sleep terrors, bed-wetting, and sleepwalking.

Insomnia

According to the National Sleep Foundation (2008), more than half of American adults and about two-thirds of older adults are affected by insomnia in any given year. Trying to get to sleep compounds their sleep problems by creating autonomic activity and muscle tension. You cannot force or will yourself to go to sleep. You can only set the stage for sleep by relaxing when you are tired.

Narcolepsy

A person with narcolepsy falls asleep suddenly. Narcolepsy afflicts as many as 100,000 people in the United States and seems to run in families. The "sleep attack" may last fifteen minutes or so, after which

Truth

Many people have insomnia because they try too hard to fall asleep at night.

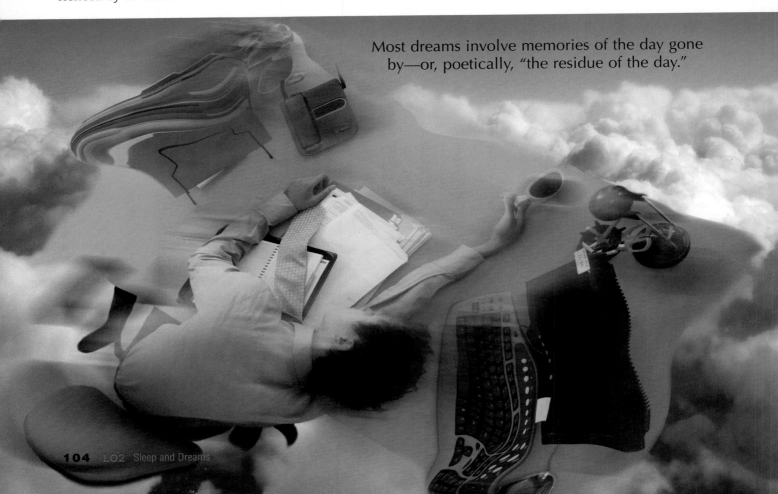

Most dreams involve memories of the day gone by—or, poetically, "the residue of the day."

the person feels refreshed. Nevertheless, sleep attacks are dangerous and upsetting. They can occur while driving or working with sharp tools. They may be accompanied by the collapse of muscle groups or the entire body—a condition called *sleep paralysis*. In sleep paralysis, the person cannot move during the transition from consciousness to sleep, and hallucinations (as of a person or object sitting on the chest) occur.

Narcolepsy is thought to be a disorder of REM-sleep functioning. Stimulants and antidepressant drugs have helped many people with the problem (Schwartz, 2004).

Apnea

Apnea is a dangerous sleep disorder in which the air passages are obstructed. People with apnea stop breathing periodically, up to several hundred times per night (National Sleep Foundation, 2008). Obstruction may cause the sleeper to sit up and gasp for air before falling back asleep. People with apnea are stimulated nearly, but not quite, to waking by the buildup of carbon dioxide. Some 10 million Americans have apnea, and it is associated with obesity and chronic snoring (National Sleep Foundation, 2008). Apnea can lead to high blood pressure, heart attacks, and strokes.

Causes of apnea include anatomical deformities that clog the air passageways, such as a thick palate, and problems in the breathing centers in the brain. Apnea is treated by such measures as weight loss, surgery, and *continuous positive airway pressure*, which is supplied by a mask that provides air pressure that keeps the airway open during sleep.

Deep-Sleep Disorders: Sleep Terrors, Bed-Wetting, and Sleepwalking

Sleep terrors, bed-wetting, and sleepwalking all occur during deep (stage 3 or 4) sleep. They are more common among children and may reflect immaturity of the nervous system (Kataria, 2004). Sleep terrors are similar to, but more severe than, nightmares, which occur during REM sleep. Sleep terrors usually occur during the first two sleep cycles of the night, whereas nightmares are more likely to occur toward morning. Experiencing a surge in the heart and respiration rates, the person may suddenly sit up, talk incoherently, and thrash about. He or she is never

Fiction

Contrary to myth, there is no evidence that sleepwalkers become violent if they are awakened, although they may be confused and upset.

fully awake, returns to sleep, and may recall a vague image as of someone pressing on his or her chest. (Memories of nightmares tend to be more detailed.) Sleep terrors are often decreased by a minor tranquilizer at bedtime, which reduces the amount of time spent in stage 4 sleep (Mason II & Pack, 2005).

Bed-wetting probably reflects immaturity of the nervous system. In most cases it resolves itself before adolescence, often by age eight. Methods that condition children to awaken when they are about to urinate have been helpful (Kainz, 2002; Mellon & McGrath, 2000). The drug imipramine often helps. Sometimes all that is needed is reassurance that no one is to blame for bed-wetting and that most children "outgrow" it.

Perhaps half of children talk in their sleep now and then. Adults occasionally do so, too. Surveys suggest that some 7% to 15% of children walk in their sleep (Neveus et al., 2002). Only 2% of adults do (Ohayon et al., 1999). Sleepwalkers may roam about nightly while their parents fret about possible accidents. Sleepwalkers typically do not remember their excursions, although they may respond to questions while they are up and about. Mild tranquilizers and maturity typically put an end to it.

apnea
temporary absence or cessation of breathing

sleep terrors
frightening dreamlike experiences that occur during the deepest stage of NREM sleep; nightmares, in contrast, occur during REM sleep

hypnosis
a condition in which people are highly suggestible and behave as though they are in a trance

LO³ Altering Consciousness Through Hypnosis, Meditation, and Biofeedback

Perhaps you have watched a fellow student try to place a friend in a "trance" after reading a book on hypnosis. Or perhaps you have seen an audience member hypnotized in a nightclub act. If so, chances are the person acted as if he or she had returned to childhood, imagined that a snake was about to have a nip, or lay rigid between two chairs for a while. In this section we deal with three altered states of consciousness: hypnosis, meditation, and biofeedback. In each of these, we focus on stimuli that are not common parts of our daily lives.

Hypnosis

Of these altered states, the one we hear of most is hypnosis. *What is hypnosis?* The word **hypnosis** is derived from the Greek word for sleep. It is an altered state of consciousness in which people are

role theory
a theory that explains hypnotic events in terms of the person's ability to act *as though* he or she were hypnotized

suggestible and behave as though they are in a trance. Modern hypnosis evolves from the ideas of Franz Mesmer in the 18th century. Mesmer asserted that everything in the universe was connected by forms of magnetism—which may not be far off the mark. However, he also claimed that people, too, could be drawn to one another by "animal magnetism." Not so. Mesmer used bizarre props to bring people under his "spell" and managed a respectable cure rate for minor ailments. Scientists now attribute his successes to the placebo effect, not animal magnetism.

Today hypnotism is more than a nightclub act. It is also used as an anesthetic in dentistry, childbirth, and medical procedures (Patterson, 2004; Shenefelt, 2003). Some psychologists use hypnosis to help clients reduce anxiety, overcome fears, or lessen the perception of chronic pain (Jensen et al., 2005; Pinnell & Covino, 2000). A study with 241 surgery patients shows how hypnosis can help people deal with pain and anxiety. The patients had procedures with local anesthetics (Lang et al., 2000). They could use as much pain medication as they wished. Patients who were hypnotized needed less additional pain medication and experienced less anxiety as measured by blood pressure and heart rate. The hypnotized patients focused on pleasant imagery rather than the surgery. Hypnosis helps people relax to cope with stress and enhance the functioning of their immune systems (Kiecolt-Glaser et al., 2001). Hypnosis can also be useful in helping people control their weight and stop smoking (Lynn et al., 2003). Some police departments use hypnosis to prompt the memories of witnesses.

The state of consciousness called the *hypnotic trance* has traditionally been induced by asking people to narrow their attention to a small light, a spot on the wall, an object held by the hypnotist, or the hypnotist's voice. The hypnotist usually suggests that the person's limbs are becoming warm, heavy, and relaxed. People may also be told that they are becoming sleepy or falling asleep. But hypnosis is *not* sleep, as shown by differences between EEG recordings for the hypnotic trance and the stages of sleep. (Subjects understand that the word *sleep* suggests a hypnotic trance.) Researchers are also studying changes in the brain that result from hypnosis. For example, Rainville and his colleagues (2002) used PET scans on people being hypnotized and found that mental absorption and mental relaxation are associated with changes in blood flow in the cerebral cortex (absorption) and parts of the brain involved in arousal and attention (relaxation).

Fiction

It is extremely unlikely that someone could be hypnotized against his or her will (Barber, 2000).

People who are easily hypnotized are said to have *hypnotic suggestibility*. Part of "suggestibility" is knowledge of what is expected during the "trance state." Generally speaking, suggestible people are prone to fantasy and want to cooperate with the hypnotist (Barber, 2000). As a result, they pay close attention to the instructions.

Explaining Hypnosis

Hypnotism is no longer explained in terms of animal magnetism, but others have offered explanations. According to Freud, hypnotized adults permit themselves to return to childish modes of responding that emphasize fantasy and impulse rather than fact and logic. Modern views of hypnosis are quite different. *How do psychologists explain the effects of hypnosis?*

Theodore Sarbin offers a **role theory** view of hypnosis (Sarbin & Coe, 1972). He points out that the changes in behavior attributed to the hypnotic trance can be successfully imitated when people are instructed to behave *as though* they were hypnotized.

> ❝ Hypnosis is *not* sleep, as shown by differences between EEG recordings for the hypnotic trance and the stages of sleep. ❞

For example, people can lie rigid between two chairs whether they are hypnotized or not. Also, people cannot be hypnotized unless they are familiar with the hypnotic "role"—the behavior that constitutes the trance. Sarbin is not saying that subjects *fake* the hypnotic role. Instead, Sarbin is suggesting that people *allow* themselves to enact this role under the hypnotist's directions.

The response set theory of hypnosis is related to role theory. It suggests that expectations play a role in the production of experiences suggested by the hypnotist (Kirsch, 2000). A positive response to each suggestion of the hypnotist sets the stage—creates a *response set*—in which the subject is more likely to follow further suggestions (Barrios, 2001).

Role theory and response set theory appear to be supported by research evidence that "suggestible" people want to be hypnotized, are good role players, have vivid imaginations, and know what is expected of them (Barber, 2000; Kirsch, 2000). By making suggestions that the subject follows, the hypnotist gets his or her "foot in the door," increasing the likelihood that the subject will follow additional suggestions. The fact that the behaviors shown by hypnotized people can be mimicked by people who know what is expected of them means that we need not resort to the concept of the "hypnotic trance"—an unusual and mystifying altered state of awareness—to explain hypnotic events.

Let us now consider two other altered states of consciousness that involve different ways of focusing our attention: meditation and biofeedback.

Meditation

What is meditation? The dictionary defines *meditation* as the act or process of thinking. But the concept usually suggests thinking deeply about the universe or about one's place in the world, often within a spiritual context. As the term is commonly used by psychologists, however, meditation refers to various ways of focusing one's consciousness to alter one's relationship to the world. In this use, ironically, *meditation* can also refer to a process by which people seem to suspend thinking and allow the world to fade away.

The kinds of meditation that helping professionals speak of tend to refer to rituals, exercises, even passive observation—activities that alter the normal relationship between the person and the environment. They are methods of suspending problem solving, planning, worries, and awareness of the events of the day. These methods alter consciousness —the normal focus of attention—and help people cope with stress by inducing feelings of relaxation.

One common form of meditation, transcendental meditation (TM), was brought to the United States by the Maharishi Mahesh Yogi in 1959. People practice TM by concentrating on *mantras*—words or sounds that are claimed to help the person achieve an altered state of consciousness. TM has some goals that cannot be assessed scientifically, such as expanding consciousness to encompass spiritual experiences, but there are also measurable goals, such as reducing anxiety and lowering blood pressure. For example, Herbert Benson (1975) found that TM lowered the heart and respiration rates and also produced what he labeled a *relaxation response*. The blood pressure of people with hypertension—a risk factor in cardiovascular disease—decreased.

A research program at the College of Maharishi Vedic Medicine in Fairfield, Iowa, has focused

response set theory the view that response expectancies play a key role in the production of the experiences suggested by the hypnotist

transcendental meditation (TM) the simplified form of meditation brought to the United States by the Maharishi Mahesh Yogi and used as a method for coping with stress on older African Americans, a group prone to hypertension (Ready, 2000). Two studies compared the effects of TM, muscle relaxation, and a "health education" placebo on high blood pressure (Alexander et al., 1996; Schneider et al., 1995). They found that TM was significantly more effective at reducing blood pressure than relaxation or the placebo. A third study reported that TM practiced regularly by African American adults was significantly more likely than the health education placebo to slow hardening of the arteries (Castillo-Richmond et al., 2000).

Psychologist Jon Kabat-Zinn, founder of the Stress Reduction Clinic at the University of Massachusetts Medical Center, has promoted the use of mindfulness meditation (MM) in cognitive and behavior therapy. MM, as opposed to TM, makes no pretense of achieving spiritual goals. Instead, MM provides clients with mantra-like techniques they can use to focus on the present moment rather than ruminate about problems (Heidenreich & Michalak, 2003; Salmon et al., 2004). MM holds promise for helping clients cope with problems such as depression as well as reducing stress (Ramel et al., 2004). Brain imaging also shows that meditation activates neural structures involved in attention and in control of the autonomic nervous system, helping produce feelings of relaxation (Lazar et al., 2000).

Biofeedback

Psychologist Neal E. Miller (1909–2002) trained laboratory rats to increase or decrease their heart rates. How? His procedure was simple but ingenious. As discovered by James Olds and Peter Milner (1954), there is a "pleasure center" in the rat's hypothalamus. A small burst of electricity in this center is strongly reinforcing: Rats learn to do what they can, such as pressing a lever, to obtain this "reward."

Miller (1969) implanted electrodes in the rats' pleasure centers. Some rats were then given a burst of electricity whenever their heart rates happened to increase. Other rats received the burst when their heart rates decreased. After a ninety-minute training session, the rats learned to alter their heart rates by as much as 20% in the direction for which they had been rewarded.

Truth

It is true that you can teach a rat to raise or lower its heart rate.

Biofeedback is a system that provides, or "feeds back," information about a bodily function to an organism. Through biofeedback training, people have learned to gain voluntary control over a number of functions that are normally automatic, such as heart rate and blood pressure.

© WILLIAM MCCOY/RAINBOW/GETTY IMAGE

Miller's research was an example of **biofeedback training (BFT)**. *What is biofeedback training?* Biofeedback is a system that provides, or "feeds back," information about a bodily function. Miller used electrical stimulation of the brain to feed back information to rats when they had engaged in a targeted bodily response—in this case, raised or lowered their heart rates. Somehow the rats used this feedback to raise or lower their heart rates voluntarily.

Similarly, people have learned to change some bodily functions voluntarily, including heart rate, that were once considered beyond conscious control. Electrodes are not implanted in people's brains. Rather, people hear a "blip" or receive some other signal that informs them when they are showing the targeted response.

How is biofeedback training used? BFT is used in many ways, including helping people combat stress, tension, and anxiety. For example, people can learn to emit alpha waves through EEG feedback and feel more relaxed. The psychologist asks the person to "make the blip go faster." A blip may blink faster whenever alpha waves are being emitted. An **electromyograph (EMG)** monitors muscle tension. The EMG can be used to help people become more aware of muscle tension in the forehead, fingers, and elsewhere and to learn to lower tension (Martin, 2002). Through the use of other instruments, people have learned to lower their heart rates, blood pressure, and sweating (Nagourney, 2002). Biofeedback is widely used by sports psychologists to teach athletes how to relax muscle groups that are unessential to the task at hand so that the athletes can control anxiety and tension.

LO⁴ Altering Consciousness Through Drugs

The world is a supermarket of drugs. The United States is flooded with drugs that distort perceptions and change mood—drugs that take you up, let you down, and move you across town. Some of these drugs are legal, others illegal. Some are used recreationally, others medically. Some are safe if used correctly and dangerous if they are not. Some people use drugs because their friends do or because their parents tell them not to. Some are seeking pleasure; others are seeking inner truth or escape.

Young people often become involved with drugs that impair their ability to learn at school and are connected with reckless behavior (Centers for Disease Control and Prevention, 2005). Alcohol is the most popular drug on high school and college campuses (Johnston et al., 2009). More than 40% of college students have tried marijuana, and one in six or seven smokes it regularly (Johnston et al., 2006). Many Americans take **depressants** to get to sleep at night and **stimulants** to get going in the morning. Cocaine was once a toy of the well-to-do, but price breaks have brought it into the lockers of high school students.

Substance Abuse and Dependence

Where does drug use end and abuse begin? *What are substance abuse and dependence?* The American Psychiatric Association (2000) defines **substance abuse** as repeated use of a substance despite the fact that it is causing or compounding social, occupational, psychological, or physical problems. If you are missing school or work because you are drunk or "sleeping it off," you are abusing alcohol. The amount you drink is not as crucial as the fact that your pattern of use disrupts your life.

Substance dependence is more severe than substance abuse and has behavioral and biological aspects (American Psychiatric Association, 2000). Behaviorally, dependence is characterized by loss of control over use of the sub-stance. Dependent people may organize their lives around getting and using a substance. Biological or physiological dependence is typified by tolerance, withdrawal symptoms, or both. **Tolerance** is the body's habituation to a substance so that, with regular usage, higher doses are needed to achieve similar effects. There are **withdrawal symptoms** when the level of usage suddenly drops off. Withdrawal symptoms for alcohol include anxiety, tremors, restlessness, rapid pulse, and high blood pressure.

When doing without a drug, people who are *psychologically* dependent show signs of anxiety such as shakiness, rapid pulse, and sweating that may be similar to withdrawal symptoms. Because of these signs, they may believe that they are physiologically dependent on—or addicted to—a drug when

electromyograph (EMG)
an instrument that measures muscle tension

depressant
a drug that lowers the rate of activity of the nervous system

stimulant
a drug that increases activity of the nervous system

substance abuse
persistent use of a substance even though it is causing or compounding problems in meeting the demands of life

substance dependence
loss of control over use of a substance; biologically speaking, dependence is typified by tolerance, withdrawal symptoms, or both

tolerance
habituation to a drug, with the result that increasingly higher doses of the drug are needed to achieve similar effects

withdrawal symptoms
a characteristic cluster of symptoms that results from sudden decrease in an addictive drug's level of usage

they are psychologically dependent. But symptoms of withdrawal from some drugs are unmistakably physiological. One is delirium tremens ("the DTs"), experienced by some chronic alcoholics when they suddenly lower their intake of alcohol. People with DTs have heavy sweating, restlessness, disorientation, and frightening hallucinations—often of crawling animals.

Causal Factors in Substance Abuse and Dependence

What are the causes of substance abuse and dependence? Substance abuse and dependence usually begin with experimental use in adolescence (Lewinsohn et al., 2000a). People experiment with drugs for various reasons, including curiosity, conformity to peer pressure, parental use, rebelliousness, escape from boredom or pressure, and excitement or pleasure (Griffin et al., 2004; Wilkinson & Abraham, 2004). Let us have a look at some theories of substance abuse.

Social–cognitive theorists suggest that people often try alcohol and tranquilizers such as Valium (the generic name is diazepam) on the basis of a recommendation or observation of others. Expectations about the effects of a substance predict its use (Cumsille et al., 2000).

Use of a substance may be reinforced by peers or by the drug's positive effects on mood and its reduction of anxiety, fear, and stress (Griffin et al., 2004). Many people use drugs as a form of self-medication for anxiety and depression, even

low self-esteem (Dierker et al., 2001). For people who are physiologically dependent, avoidance of withdrawal symptoms is also reinforcing. Carrying a supply of the substance is reinforcing because one need not worry about going without it. Parents who use drugs may increase their children's knowledge of drugs. They also, in effect, show their children when to use them—for example, by drinking alcohol to cope with tension or to lessen the anxiety associated with meeting people at parties and other get-togethers (Power et al., 2005).

Certain people apparently have a genetic predisposition toward physiological dependence on certain substances, such as alcohol, opioids, cocaine, and nicotine (Chen et al., 2004; Nurnberger et al., 2004; Radel et al., 2005). The biological children of alcoholics who are reared by nonalcoholic adoptive parents are more likely to develop alcohol-related problems than the biological children of the adoptive parents. An inherited tendency toward alcoholism may involve greater sensitivity to alcohol (that is, greater enjoyment of it) and greater tolerance (Pihl et al., 1990). Greater tolerance is shown by studies in which college students with alcoholic parents show better muscular control and visual–motor coordination when they drink than other college students do (Pihl et al., 1990). People with a family history of alcoholism are also more sensitive to the stimulating effects of alcohol, which occur at lower levels of intoxication (Conrad et al., 2001).

Now that we have learned about substance abuse

The amount you drink is not as crucial as the effects of drinking on your life in deciding whether or not you are abusing alcohol.

© NOBLE STOCK/JUPITERIMAGES

and dependence, let us turn to a discussion of the different kinds of psychoactive drugs. Some are depressants, others stimulants, and still others hallucinogens. Let us consider the effects of these drugs on consciousness, beginning with depressants.

Depressants

Depressants generally act by slowing the activity of the central nervous system. There are also effects specific to each depressant. In this section we consider the effects of alcohol, opiates, and barbiturates.

Alcohol—The Swiss Army Knife of Psychoactive Substances

No drug has meant so much to so many as alcohol. Alcohol is our dinnertime relaxant, our bedtime sedative, our cocktail-party social facilitator. We use alcohol to celebrate holy days, applaud our accomplishments, and express joyous wishes. The young assert their maturity with alcohol. Alcohol is used at least occasionally by the majority of high school and college students (Bachman et al., 2008). Alcohol even kills germs on surface wounds.

People use alcohol like a Swiss Army knife. It does it all. It is the all-purpose medicine you can buy without prescription. It is the relief from anxiety, depression, or loneliness that you can swallow in public without criticism or stigma (Bonin et al., 2000; Swendsen et al., 2000). A man who takes a Valium tablet may look weak. It is "macho" to down a bottle of beer.

But the army knife also has a sharp blade. No drug has been so abused as alcohol. Ten million to 20 million Americans are alcoholics. In contrast, 750,000 to 1 million use heroin regularly, and about 800,000 use cocaine regularly (O'Brien, 1996). Excessive drinking has been linked to lower productivity, loss of employment, and downward movement in social status. Yet, half of all Americans use alcohol regularly.

About four college students die *each day* from alcohol-related causes (Hingson et al., 2002). Binge drinking—having five or more drinks in a row for a male, or four or more for a female (Naimi et al., 2003b)—is connected with aggressive behavior, poor grades, sexual promiscuity, and accidents (Birch et al., 2007; Keller et al., 2007). Nevertheless, 44% of college students binge at least twice a month (Hingson et al., 2002). The media pay more attention to deaths due to heroin and cocaine overdoses, but more college students die each year from causes related to drinking, including accidents and overdoses (Hingson et al., 2002).

What are the effects of alcohol? The effects of alcohol vary with the dose and duration of use. Low doses may be stimulating because alcohol dilates blood vessels, which ferry sugar through the body. Higher doses have a sedative effect, which is why alcohol is classified as a depressant. Alcohol relaxes people and deadens minor aches and pains. Alcohol impairs cognitive functioning, slurs the speech, and impairs coordination.

Alcohol lowers inhibitions. Drinkers may do things they would not do if they were sober, such as having unprotected sex (Donohue et al., 2007). When drunk, people may be less able to foresee the consequences of their behavior. They may also be less likely to summon up their moral beliefs. Then, too, alcohol induces feelings of elation and euphoria that may wash away doubts. Alcohol is also associated with a liberated social role in our culture. Drinkers may place the blame on alcohol ("It's the alcohol, not me"), even though they choose to drink.

Men are more likely than women to become alcoholics. Why? A cultural explanation is that tighter social constraints are usually placed on women. A biological explanation is that alcohol hits women harder, discouraging them from overindulging. Alcohol "goes to women's heads" faster than to men's, because women metabolize less of it in the stomach (Lieber, 1990). Alcohol reaches women's bloodstreams and brains relatively intact. Asians and Asian Americans are less likely than Europeans and European Americans to drink to excess because they are more likely to show an unpleasant "flushing response" to alcohol, as evidenced by redness of the face, rapid heart rate, dizziness, and headaches (Fromme et al., 2004).

Regardless of how or why one starts drinking, regular drinking can lead to physiological dependence. People are then motivated to

opiates
a group of narcotics derived from the opium poppy that provide a euphoric rush and depress the nervous system

narcotics
drugs used to relieve pain and induce sleep. The term is usually reserved for opiates

opioids
chemicals that act on opiate receptors but are not derived from the opium poppy

barbiturate
an addictive depressant used to relieve anxiety or induce sleep

About four college students die *each day* from alcohol-related causes.

drink to avoid withdrawal symptoms. Still, even when alcoholics have "dried out"—withdrawn from alcohol—many return to drinking. Perhaps they still want to use alcohol as a way of coping with stress or as an excuse for failure.

Opiates

Opiates are a group of narcotics derived from the opium poppy, from which they obtain their name. The ancient Sumerians gave the opium poppy its name: It means "plant of joy." Opioids are similar in chemical structure but made in a laboratory. Opiates include morphine, heroin, codeine, Demerol, and similar drugs. *What are the effects of opiates?* The major medical application of opiates is relief from pain.

Heroin can provide a strong euphoric "rush." Users claim that it is so pleasurable it can eradicate thoughts of food or sex. High doses can cause drowsiness and stupor, alter time perception, and impair judgment. With regular use of opiates, the brain stops producing neurotransmitters that are chemically similar to opiates—the pain-relieving endorphins.

As a result, people can become physiologically dependent on opiates, such that going without them can be agonizing. Withdrawal syndromes may begin with flu-like symptoms and progress through tremors, cramps, chills alternating with sweating, rapid pulse, high blood pressure, insomnia, vomiting, and diarrhea. This information seems to have gotten through to high school students; most disapprove of using heroin (Johnston et al., 2006).

Heroin was once used as a cure for addiction to morphine. Now we have methadone, a human-made opioid that is used to treat physiological dependence on heroin. Methadone is slower acting than heroin and does not provide the thrilling rush, but it does prevent withdrawal symptoms.

Barbiturates

What are the effects of barbiturates? **Barbiturates** like Nembutal and Seconal are depressants with several medical uses, including relief from anxiety, tension, and pain, and treatment of epilepsy, high blood pressure, and insomnia. With regular use, barbiturates lead rapidly to physiological and psychological dependence. Physicians therefore provide them with caution.

Barbiturates are popular as street drugs because they are relaxing and produce mild euphoria. High doses result in drowsiness, motor impairment, slurred speech, irritability, and poor judgment. A highly physiologically dependent person who is withdrawn abruptly from barbiturates may experience convulsions and die. Because of additive effects, it is dangerous to mix alcohol and other depressants.

Stimulants

Stimulants increase the activity of the nervous system. Some of their effects can be positive. For example, amphetamines stimulate cognitive activity and apparently help people control impulses. Some stimulants are appealing as street drugs because they contribute to feelings of euphoria and self-confidence. But they also have their risks. In this section we discuss amphetamines, cocaine, and nicotine.

Amphetamines and Related Stimulants

What are the effects of amphetamines? **Amphetamines** were first used by soldiers during World War II to help them stay alert at night. Truck drivers also use them to drive through the night. Students use amphetamines for all-night cram sessions. Dieters use them because they reduce hunger.

Amphetamines are often abused for the euphoric rush high doses can produce. Some people swallow amphetamines in pill form or inject liquid Methedrine, the strongest form, into their veins. As a result, they may stay awake and high for days on end. But such highs must end. People who have been on prolonged highs sometimes "crash," or fall into a deep sleep or depression. Some commit suicide when crashing.

Although some critics believe that Ritalin is prescribed too freely, Ritalin has been shown to increase the attention span, decrease aggressive and disruptive behavior, and lead to academic gains (Evans et al., 2001; Pelham et al., 2002). Why should Ritalin, a stimulant, calm children? Hyperactivity may be connected with immaturity of the cerebral cortex, and Ritalin may stimulate the cortex to exercise control over more primitive parts of the brain.

Tolerance for amphetamines and Ritalin develops quickly, and users can become dependent on them, especially when they use them to self-medicate themselves for depression. Whether these stimulants cause physical addiction has been a subject of controversy (Shen et al., 2007). High doses can cause restlessness, insomnia, loss of appetite, hallucinations, paranoid delusions (e.g., false ideas that others are eavesdropping or intend them harm), and irritability.

Cocaine

Cocaine is derived from coca leaves—the plant from which the soft drink took its name. Do you recall commercials claiming that "Coke adds life"? Given its caffeine and sugar content, "Coke"—Coca-Cola, that is—should provide quite a lift. But Coca-Cola hasn't been "the real thing" since 1906, when the company stopped using cocaine in its formula.

> **Truth**
>
> It is true that many health professionals calm hyperactive children by giving them a stimulant—the stimulant methylphenidate (Ritalin).

What are the effects of cocaine? The stimulant cocaine produces euphoria, reduces hunger, deadens pain, and boosts self-confidence. As shown in Figure 5.4, cocaine apparently works by binding to sites on sending neurons that normally reuptake molecules of the neurotransmitters norepinephrine, dopamine, and serotonin. As a result, molecules of these transmitters remain longer in the synaptic cleft, enhancing their mood-altering effects and producing a "rush." But when cocaine levels drop, lower absorption of neurotransmitters by receiving neurons causes the user's mood to "crash." Cocaine may be brewed from coca leaves as a "tea," snorted in powder form, or injected in liquid form. Repeated snorting constricts blood vessels in the nose, drying the skin and sometimes exposing cartilage and perforating the nasal septum. These problems require cosmetic surgery. The potent cocaine derivatives known as "crack" and "bazooka" are inexpensive because they are unrefined.

Physical dangers include sudden rises in blood pressure, which constricts the coronary arteries and decreases the oxygen supply to the heart, and quickens the heart rate events that can lead to respiratory and cardiovascular collapse, as in the sudden deaths of some young athletes (Mitchell, 2006). Overdoses can cause restlessness and insomnia, tremors, headaches, nausea, convulsions, hallucinations, and delusions. Use of crack has been connected with strokes. Only about 4% of adolescents aged fifteen to nineteen use cocaine regularly, and most believe that it is harmful (Johnston et al., 2006). Cocaine causes physiological as well as psychological dependence.

Cocaine—also called *snow* and *coke*—has been used as a local anesthetic since the early 1800s. In 1884 it came to the attention of Sigmund Freud, who used it to fight his own depression and published an article about it: "Song of Praise." Freud's early ardor was tempered when he learned that cocaine is habit-forming and can cause hallucinations and delusions.

amphetamines stimulants derived from *alpha-methyl-beta-phenyl-ethylamine*, a colorless liquid consisting of carbon, hydrogen, and nitrogen

> IRONICALLY, HEROIN WAS ONCE USED AS A CURE FOR ADDICTION TO MORPHINE.

> **Truth**
>
> It is true that Coca-Cola once "added life" through the use of a powerful, then-legal but now-illegal stimulant: cocaine.

Figure 5.4

How Cocaine Produces Euphoria and Why People "Crash"

Go to CourseMate for PSYCH at www.cengagebrain.com to access an interactive version of this figure.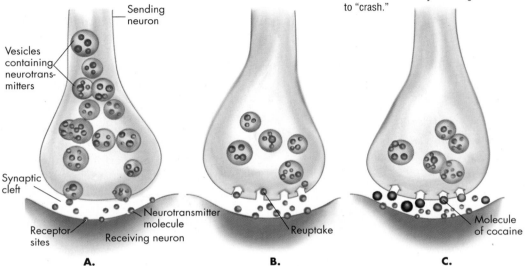

A. In the normal functioning of the nervous system, neurotransmitters are released into the synaptic cleft by vesicles in terminal buttons of sending neurons. Many are taken up by receptor sites in receiving neurons.

B. In the process called reuptake, sending neurons typically reabsorb excess molecules of neurotransmitters.

C. Molecules of cocaine bind to the sites on sending neurons that normally reuptake molecules of neurotransmitters. As a result, molecules of norepinephrine, dopamine, and serotonin remain longer in the synaptic cleft, increasing their typical mood-altering effects and providing a euphoric "rush." When the person stops using cocaine, the lessened absorption of neurotransmitters by receiving neurons causes his or her mood to "crash."

Sending neuron

Vesicles containing neurotransmitters

Synaptic cleft

Neurotransmitter molecule

Receptor sites

Receiving neuron

Reuptake

Molecule of cocaine

A.　　**B.**　　**C.**

Nicotine

Nicotine is the stimulant in tobacco smoke. *What are the effects of nicotine?* Nicotine stimulates discharge of the hormone adrenaline and the release of neurotransmitters, including dopamine, acetylcholine, GABA, and endorphins (Brody, 2008). Adrenaline creates a burst of autonomic activity that accelerates the heart rate and pours sugar into the blood.

Acetylcholine is vital in memory formation, and nicotine appears to enhance memory and attention; improve performance on simple, repetitive tasks; and enhance the mood (Gentry, et al., 2000; Rezvani & Levin, 2001). Although it is a stimulant, because of GABA and endorphins, nicotine has a relaxing effect. It depresses the appetite and raises the metabolic rate. Thus, some people smoke cigarettes to control their weight.

The perils of cigarette smoking are widely known today. One surgeon general declared that cigarette smoking is the chief preventable cause of death in the United States. The numbers of Americans who die from smoking are comparable to the number of lives that would be lost if two jumbo jets crashed *every day.* If flying were that unsafe, would the government ground all flights? Would the public continue to make airline reservations?

Table 5.1

Snapshot, U.S.A.: Gender, Level of Education, and Smoking		
Factor	**Group**	**Percent Who Smoke**
Gender	Women	18.3
	Men	23.1
Level of education	Fewer than 12 years	27.5
	16 years and above	10.6

Data based on reports of persons aged 18 and above.

Source: Dube, S. R., Asman, K., Malarcher, A., & Carabollo, R. (2009). Cigarette Smoking among adults and trends in smoking cessation—United States, 2008. *Morbidity and Mortality Weekly Report, 58*(44), 1227–1232.

© IAN NOLAN/ALAMY

Nicotine creates the physiological dependence on tobacco products (American Lung Association, 2008). Symptoms of withdrawal include nervousness, drowsiness, loss of energy, headaches, irregular bowel movements, lightheadedness, insomnia, dizziness, cramps, palpitations, tremors, and sweating.

It's no secret. Cigarette packs sold in the United States carry messages like "Warning: The Surgeon General Has Determined That Cigarette Smoking Is Dangerous to Your Health." Cigarette advertising has been banned on radio and television. Nearly 430,000 Americans die from smoking-related illnesses each year (American Lung Association, 2008). This number is greater than the equivalent of two jumbo jets colliding in midair each day with all passengers lost.

The carbon monoxide in cigarette smoke impairs the blood's ability to carry oxygen, causing shortness of breath. The **hydrocarbons** ("tars") in cigarette and cigar smoke lead to lung cancer (American Lung Association, 2008). Cigarette smoking also stiffens arteries (Mahmud & Feely, 2003) and is linked to death from heart disease, chronic lung and respiratory diseases, and other health problems. Women who smoke show reduced bone density, increasing the risk of fracture of the hip and back. Pregnant women who smoke have a higher risk of miscarriage, preterm births, stillborn babies, and children with learning problems (American Lung Association, 2008).

Secondhand smoke—smoke inhaled from other people's tobacco products—is also connected with respiratory illnesses, asthma, and other health problems.

Truth

The number of smoking-related deaths in the U.S. is higher than the number of people who die each year from motor vehicle accidents, alcohol and drug abuse, suicide, homicide, and AIDS *combined.*

hydrocarbons
chemical compounds consisting of hydrogen and carbon

second-hand smoke
smoke from the tobacco products and exhalations of other people

hallucinogen
a substance that causes hallucinations

marijuana
the dried vegetable matter of the *Cannabis sativa* plant

Prolonged exposure to secondhand smoke during childhood is a risk factor for lung cancer (American Cancer Society, 2008). Because of the effects of second-hand smoke, smoking has been banished from many airplanes and restaurants.

Why, then, do people smoke? For many reasons—such as the desire to look sophisticated (although these days smokers may be more likely to be judged foolish than sophisticated), to have something to do with their hands, and—of course—to take in nicotine.

The incidence of smoking is connected with gender and level of education (see Table 5.1). Better-educated people are less likely to smoke and more likely to quit if they do smoke.

Hallucinogens

Hallucinogens are so named because they produce hallucinations—that is, sensations and perceptions in the absence of external stimulation. Hallucinogens may also have additional effects such as relaxation, euphoria, or, in some cases, panic.

Marijuana

Marijuana is produced from the *Cannabis sativa* plant, which grows wild in many parts of the world. *What are the effects of marijuana?* Marijuana helps some people relax and can elevate their mood. It also sometimes produces mild hallucinations, which is why we discuss it as a hallucinogen. The major psychedelic substance in marijuana is delta-9-tetrahydrocannabinol, or THC. THC is found in the branches and leaves of the plant, but it is highly concentrated in the resin. *Hashish,* or "hash," is derived from the resin and is more potent than marijuana.

Marijuana carries a number of health risks. For example, it impairs the perceptual–motor coordination used in driving and operating machines. It impairs short-term memory and slows learning (Egerton 35 al., 2006).

Some users report that marijuana helps them socialize. Moderate to strong intoxication is linked to reports of sharpened perceptions, increases in self-insight, creative thinking, and empathy for

LSD
lysergic acid diethy-
lamide; a hallucinogen

flashbacks
distorted perceptions
or hallucinations that
occur days or weeks
after LSD usage
but mimic the LSD
experience

mescaline
a hallucinogen derived
from the mescal (pey-
ote) cactus

**phencyclidine
(PCP)**
another hallucinogen
whose name is an ini-
tialism for its chemical
structure

others. Time seems to slow. A song might seem to last an hour rather than minutes. There is increased aware-ness of bodily sensations such as heartbeat. Marijuana users also report that strong intoxication heightens sex-ual sensations. Visual hal-lucinations may occur, and strong intoxication may cause disorientation. If the smoker's mood is euphoric, disorientation may be inter-preted as "harmony" with the universe, but some users find disorientation threaten-ing and

fear they will not regain their identity (Bonn-Miller et al., 2007). Rapid heart rate and heightened awareness of bodily sen-sations lead some users to fear their hearts will "run away" with them. Strong intoxication can cause nausea and vomiting. Regular users may experience toler-ance and withdrawal symptoms (Budney et al., 2007). Brain imaging studies suggest that males who begin using mari-juana in adolescence may have smaller brains and less gray matter than other males (Ashtari et al., 2009). Both males and females who started mari-juana use early may be generally smaller in height and weight than other people. These differences may reflect the effect of marijuana on pituitary and sex hormones.

LSD is a hallucinogen that can give rise to a vivid parade of colors and visual distortions. Some users claim to have achieved great insights while "tripping," but typically they have been unable to recall or apply them afterward.

LSD and Other Hallucinogens

LSD is the abbreviation for lysergic acid diethylam-ide, a synthetic hallucinogen. *What are the effects of LSD and other kinds of hallucinogens?* Users of "acid" claim that it "expands consciousness" and opens up new worlds to them. Sometimes people say they have achieved great insights while using LSD, but when it wears off they cannot apply or recall them. LSD produces vivid, colorful hallucinations.

Some LSD users have **flashbacks**—distorted perceptions or hallucinations that mimic the LSD "trip" but occur days, weeks, or longer after usage. The experiencing of flashbacks is more technically termed hallucinogen persisting perception disorder (HPPD) by the American Psychiatric Association (2000). The psychological explanation of "flashbacks" is that people who would use LSD regularly are also more likely to allow flights of fancy. But research with 38 people with HPPD suggests that following extensive use of LSD, the brain may fail to inhibit internal sources of visionlike experiences when the eyes are closed (Abraham & Duffy, 2001).

Other hallucinogens inc-lude **mescaline** (derived from the peyote cactus) and **phen-cyclidine (PCP)**. PCP was devel-oped as an anesthetic and an animal tranquilizer. It goes by the street names "angel dust," "ozone," "wack," and "rocket fuel." The street terms "killer joints" and "crystal super grass" refer to PCP combined with marijuana.

Regular use of hallucinogens may lead to tol-erance and psychological dependence, but is not known to create physiological dependence. High doses may impair coordination, cloud judgment, change the mood, and cause frightening halluci-nations and delusions. Table 5.2 summarizes the effects of various psychoactive drugs.

Table 5.2

Drugs and Their Effects

Drug	Type	How Taken	Desired Effects	Tolerance	Abstinence Syndrome	Side Effects
Alcohol	Depressant	By mouth	Relaxation, euphoria, lowered inhibitions	Yes	Yes	Impaired coordination, poor judgment, hangover*
Heroin	Depressant	Injected, smoked, by mouth	Relaxation, euphoria, relief from anxiety and pain	Yes	Yes	Impaired coordination and mental functioning, drowsiness, lethargy*
Barbiturates and Methaqualone	Depressants	By mouth, injected	Relaxation, sleep, euphoria, lowered inhibitions	Yes	Yes	Impaired coordination and mental functioning, drowsiness, lethargy*
Amphetamines	Stimulants	By mouth, injected	Alertness, euphoria	Yes	†	Restlessness, loss of appetite, psychotic symptoms
Cocaine	Stimulant	By mouth, snorted, injected	Euphoria, self-confidence	Yes	Yes	Restlessness, loss of appetite, convulsions, strokes, psychotic symptoms
Nicotine (cigarettes)	Stimulant	By tobacco (smoked, chewed, or sniffed)	Relaxation, stimulation, weight control	Yes	Yes	Cancer, heart disease, lung and respiratory diseases
Marijuana	Hallucinogenic	Smoked, by mouth	Relaxation, perceptual distortions, enhancement of experience	†	†	Impaired coordination, learning, respiratory problems, panic
MDMA "Ecstasy"	Stimulant/ Hallucinogenic	By mouth	Alertness, self-confidence, hallucinations	?	?	Impaired memory, increased heart rate, anxiety, confusion, possible depression
LSD, PCP	Hallucinogenic	By mouth	Perceptual distortions, vivid hallucinations	Yes	No	Impaired coordination, psychotic symptoms, panic

*Overdose can result in death.
†Recent research suggests the answer is yes, although some might consider the "jury still to be out."

1/3 < portion of adult life spent in sleep

minutes/cycle in each of the sleep stages > **90**

cycles/second delta waves in stage 4 sleep > **0.5 to 2**

50 < percent American adults affected by insomnia

750,000–1,000,000 < the number of people in the U.S. who regularly use heroin.

10,000,000–20,000,000 < the number of alcoholics in the U.S.

1 to 3 < cycles/second delta waves in stage 3 sleep

100,000 < yearly vehicular crashes connected to sleep deprivation

6

Learning

Learning Outcomes

LO¹ Describe the learning process according to classical conditioning

LO² Describe the learning process according to operant conditioning

LO³ Describe cognitive factors in learning

"What do we learn from video games? Aggressive skills, violent thoughts?"

Dylan Klebold and Eric Harris were engrossed in violent video games for hours at a time. They were particularly keen on a game named *Doom*. Harris had managed to reprogram *Doom* so that he, the player, became invulnerable and had an endless supply of weapons. He would "mow down" all the other characters in the game. His program caused some of the characters to ask God why they had been shot as they lay dying. Later on, Klebold and Harris asked some of their shooting victims at Columbine High School in Colorado whether they believed in God. One of the killers also referred to his shotgun as Arlene, the name of a character in *Doom* (Saunders, 2003).

In the small rural town of Bethel, Alaska, Evan Ramsey shot four people, killing two and wounding two. Afterward, he said his favorite video games—*Doom, Die Hard,* and *Resident Evil*—taught him that being shot would reduce a player's "health factor" but probably not be lethal.

The debate about whether violence in media such as films, television, and video games fuels violence in the real world has been going on for more than forty years. Psychologist Craig A. Anderson (2003, 2004), who has carried out extensive research in this area, argues that studies show that media violence is a risk factor for increasing emotional arousal, aggressive behavior, and violent thoughts.

One reason to be particularly concerned about violent video games is that they require audience participation (Anderson et al., 2004). Players don't passively watch; they *participate*. Violent games like *Grand Theft Auto* have grown increasingly popular. Some games reward players for killing police, prostitutes, and bystanders. Virtual

Truth or Fiction?

What do you think?

Folklore, common sense, or nonsense? Place a T for "True" or F for "False" on the lines provided (you'll learn the answers as you read through the text).

___ A single nauseating meal can give rise to a taste aversion that lasts for years.

___ Psychologists helped a young boy overcome his fear of rabbits by having him eat cookies while a rabbit was brought closer and closer.

___ During World War II, a psychologist created a missile that would use pigeons to guide the missile to its target.

___ Slot-machine players pop coins into the machines most rapidly when they have no idea when they might win.

___ You can train a rat to climb a ramp, cross a bridge, climb a ladder, pedal a toy car, and do several other tasks—all in proper sequence.

___ You have to make mistakes to learn.

___ Despite all the media hoopla, no scientific connection has been established between violence in the media and real-life aggression.

learning
(1) according to behaviorists, a relatively permanent change in behavior that results from experience (2) according to cognitive theorists, the process by which organisms make relatively permanent changes in the way they represent the environment because of experience

classical conditioning
a simple form of learning in which a neutral stimulus comes to evoke the response usually evoked by another stimulus by being paired repeatedly with the other stimulus

weapons include guns, knives, flamethrowers, swords, clubs, cars, hands, and feet. Sometimes the player assumes the role of a hero, but it is also common for the player to assume the role of a criminal.

What do we *learn* from video games and other media, such as television, films, and books? The research suggests that we learn a great deal—not only aggressive skills, but also the idea that violence is the normal state of affairs.

We will return to this controversial issue later in the chapter. This is the chapter that deals with the psychology of learning. Most of what we learn may be helpful and adaptive. But there are exceptions, as in the case of violent video games.

What is learning? Learning as defined in psychology is more than listening to teachers, honing skateboard jumps, or mastering the use of an iPod. From the strict behaviorist perspective, **learning** is a relatively permanent change in behavior that arises from practice or experience. The behaviorist perspective plays down the roles of cognition and choice. It suggests that players of violent video games went on rampages because they had been rewarded or reinforced for similar behavior in games.

Cognitive psychologists define learning as a mental change that may or may not be associated with changes in behavior. These mental changes may affect, but do not directly cause, changes in behavior. From this perspective, the participants in the video games had acquired skills that enabled them to attack people, but they had then chosen to attack others. Learning, for cognitive psychologists, may be *shown* by changes in behavior, but learning itself is a mental process. Cognitive psychologists suggest that people choose whether or not to imitate the aggressive and other behaviors they observe, and that people are most likely to imitate behaviors that are consistent with their values.

Sometimes learning experiences are direct, as when we are praised for doing something properly. But we can also learn from the experiences of others—by watching their behavior and hearing their life stories. We learn, too, from books and audiovisual media. In this chapter we consider various kinds of learning, including conditioning and learning in which cognition plays a more central role.

BANANASTOCK/JUPITERIMAGES

What do we *learn* from violence in video games and other media? The research suggests that we learn a great deal—not only aggressive skills, but also the idea that violence is the normal state of affairs.

LO¹ Classical Conditioning: Learning What Is Linked to What

Classical conditioning involves ways in which we learn to associate events with other events. It is involuntary, automatic learning. For example, we generally prefer grades of A to grades of F and are more likely to stop for red lights than green lights. Why? We are not born with instinctive attitudes toward letter grades or stoplights. Rather, we learn the meanings of these symbols because they have been associated with other events. A's are associated with the approval of our teachers and caregivers. Because of experience in crossing streets or riding in cars, we associate green lights with the word "go" and red lights with "stop."

What is classical conditioning? **Classical conditioning** is a simple form of associative learning that enables organisms to anticipate events. If the name Ivan Pavlov rings a bell with us, it is most likely because of his research in learning with dogs. *What is the contribution of Ivan Pavlov to the psychology of learning?* Ivan Pavlov (1927) made his great contribution to the psychology of learning by accident. Pavlov was actually attempting to identify neural receptors in the mouth that triggered a response from the salivary glands. But his efforts were hampered by the dogs' annoying tendency to salivate at undesired times, such as when a laboratory assistant was clumsy and banged the metal food trays.

Just as you salivate after you've taken a big bite of cake, a dog salivates if meat powder is placed on its tongue. Pavlov was dosing his dogs with meat powder for his research because he knew that salivation in response to meat powder is a reflex. Reflexes are unlearned and evoked by certain **stimuli**. Pavlov discovered that reflexes can also be learned, or *conditioned,* by association. His dogs began salivating in response to clanging food trays because clanging, in the past, had been repeatedly paired with arrival of food. The dogs would also salivate when an assistant entered the laboratory. Why? In the past, the assistant had brought food.

Pavlov at first viewed the extra salivation of his dogs as a hindrance to his research. But then it dawned on him that this "problem" might be worth looking into. He found out that he could train, or condition, his dogs to salivate in response to any stimulus.

In his initial experiments, Pavlov trained dogs to salivate when he sounded a tone. Pavlov termed these trained salivary responses "conditional reflexes." The reflexes were *conditional* on the repeated pairing of a previously neutral stimulus (such as the clanging of a food tray) and a stimulus (in this case, food) that evoked the target response (in this case, salivation). Today, conditional reflexes are generally referred to as *conditioned responses*.

Pavlov demonstrated conditioned responses by showing that when meat powder was placed on a dog's tongue, the dog salivated. Pavlov repeated the process several times, with one difference. He preceded the meat powder by half a second or so with the sounding of a tone on each occasion. After several pairings of the meat powder and the tone, Pavlov sounded the tone but did **not** follow it with the meat powder. Still the dog salivated. It had learned to salivate in response to the tone.

stimulus
an environmental condition that elicits a response

Explaining Classical Conditioning

Behaviorists explain the outcome of *classical conditioning* in terms of the publicly observable conditions of learning. For them, classical conditioning is a simple form of learning in which one stimulus comes to evoke the response usually evoked by another stimulus. Why? Because the stimuli are paired repeatedly. In Pavlov's demonstration, the dog learned to salivate in response to the tone *because* the tone had been paired with meat powder. Behaviorists do *not* say that the dog "knew" food was on the way. How can we guess what a dog "knows"? We can only outline the conditions under which targeted behaviors occur.

Cognitive psychologists view classical conditioning as the learning of relationships among events. The relationships allow organisms to mentally represent their environments and make predictions (Pickens & Holland, 2004). In Pavlov's demonstration, the dog salivated in response to the tone *because* the tone became mentally connected with the meat. The cognitive focus is on *the information learned by the organism.* Organisms are seen as seekers of information that generate and test rules about relationships among events.

Ivan Pavlov and His Associates—Including a "Professional Furry Salivator" (the Dog).

© BETTMANN/CORBIS

Stimuli and Responses in Classical Conditioning

unconditioned stimulus (UCS) a stimulus that elicits an unconditioned response

unconditioned response (UCR) a natural, usually unvarying response elicited by a stimulus without learning or conditioning

orienting reflex an unlearned response in which an organism attends to a stimulus

conditioned stimulus (CS) a previously neutral stimulus that, after repeated association with an unconditioned stimulus, elicits the response elicited by the unconditioned stimulus.

conditioned response (CR) a response that becomes associated with a previously unrelated stimulus as a result of pairing the stimulus with another stimulus that normally elicits the response

In Pavlov's experiment, the meat powder is an **unconditioned stimulus (UCS)**. Salivation in response to the meat powder is an unlearned or **unconditioned response (UCR)**. The tone was at first a meaningless or neutral stimulus. It might have caused the dog to look in the direction of the sound—an **orienting reflex**. But the tone was not yet associated with food. Then, through repeated association with the meat powder, the tone became a learned or **conditioned stimulus (CS)** for the salivation response. Salivation in response to the tone (or conditioned stimulus) is a learned or **conditioned response (CR).** Therefore, salivation can be either a conditioned response or an unconditioned response, depending on the method used to evoke the response (see Figure 6.1).

Here is a mini-experiment that many adults have tried. They smile at infants, say something like "kitchie-coo" (don't ask me why), and then tickle the infant's foot. Perhaps the infant laughs and perhaps curls or retracts the foot. After a few repetitions—which psychologists call "trials"—the adult's simply saying "kitchie-coo" is likely to be enough to cause the infant to laugh and retract its foot.

Taste Aversion

When I was a child in the Bronx, my friends and I would go to the movies on Saturday mornings. One day my friends dared me to eat two huge containers of buttered popcorn by myself. I had no problem with the first

Figure 6.1

A Schematic Representation of Classical Conditioning

Prior to conditioning, food elicits salivation. The tone, a neutral stimulus, elicits either no response or an orienting response. During conditioning, the tone is sounded just before meat powder is placed on the dog's tongue. After several repetitions, the tone, now a CS, elicits salivation, the CR.

Go to CourseMate for PSYCH at www.cengagebrain.com to access an interactive version of this figure.

enormous basket of buttered popcorn. More slowly—much more slowly—I forced down the second basket. I felt bloated and nauseated. The taste of the butter, corn, and salt lingered in my mouth and nose, and my head spun. It was obvious to me that no one could talk me into even another handful of popcorn that day. But I was surprised that I couldn't face buttered popcorn again for a year.

Years later I learned that psychologists refer to my response to buttered popcorn as a *taste aversion*. Many decades have now passed, and the distinctive odor of buttered popcorn still turns my stomach.

What are taste aversions? Why are they of special interest to psychologists? Taste aversions are intriguing examples of classical conditioning. They are adaptive because they motivate organisms to avoid harmful foods. Taste aversions differ from other kinds of classical conditioning in a couple of ways. First, only one association may be required. A single overdose of popcorn left me with a lifetime aversion. Second, whereas most kinds of classical conditioning require that the unconditioned stimulus and conditioned stimulus be close together in time, in taste aversion the unconditioned stimulus (in this case, nausea) can occur hours after the conditioned stimulus (in this case, the flavor of food).

The Evolution of Taste Aversion

Research on taste aversion also challenges the view that organisms learn to associate any stimuli that are linked in time. In reality, not all stimuli are created equal. The evolutionary perspective suggests that animals

(and humans) would be biologically predisposed to develop aversions that are adaptive in their environments (Garcia et al., 1989). Those of us who acquire taste aversions quickly are less likely to eat bad food, more likely to survive, and more likely to contribute our genes to future generations.

In a classic study, Garcia and Koelling (1966) conditioned two groups of rats. Each group was exposed to the same three-part conditioned stimulus: a taste of sweetened water, a light, and a clicker. Afterward, one group of rats was induced to experience nausea by radiation or poison, and the other group received electric shock. After conditioning, the rats who had been nauseated showed an aversion for sweetened water but not to the light or clicker. Although all three stimuli had been presented at the same time, *the rats had acquired only the taste aversion*. After conditioning, the rats that had been shocked avoided both the light and the clicker, *but they did not show a taste aversion to the sweetened water*. For each group of rats, learning was adaptive. In the natural scheme of things, nausea is more likely to stem from poisoned food than from lights or sounds. So, for nauseated rats, acquiring the taste aversion was appropriate. Sharp pain, in contrast, is more likely to stem from natural events involving lights (e.g., fire, lightning) and sharp sounds (e.g., twigs snapping, things falling). Therefore, it was more appropriate for the shocked animals to develop an aversion to the light and the clicker than the sweetened water.

In classical conditioning, organisms learn to connect stimuli, such as the sounding of a tone with food. Now let us consider various

Formation of a Taste Aversion?
Taste aversions can be acquired by means of a single pairing of the US and the CS. Evolutionary psychologists point out that the rapid acquisition of a taste aversion makes it more likely that a human or an animal will survive and reproduce.

© JUPITERIMAGES

IMAGE COPYRIGHT GELPI 2010. USED UNDER LICENSE FROM SHUTTERSTOCK.COM factors in classical conditioning, beginning with what happens when the connection between stimuli is broken.

Extinction and Spontaneous Recovery

Figure 6.2

Learning and Extinction Curves

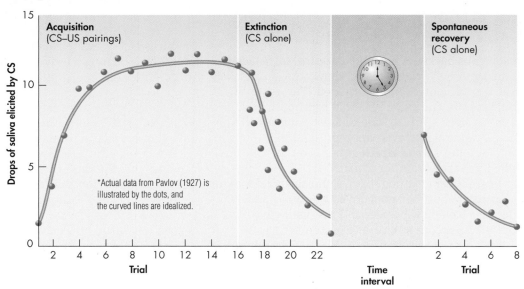

Acquisition (CS–US pairings)   Extinction (CS alone)   Spontaneous recovery (CS alone)

Drops of saliva elicited by CS

*Actual data from Pavlov (1927) is illustrated by the dots, and the curved lines are idealized.

Trial   Time interval   Trial

Extinction and spontaneous recovery are aspects of conditioning that help us adapt by updating our expectations or representations of a changing environment. For example, a child may learn to connect hearing a car pull into the driveway (a conditioned stimulus) with the arrival of his or her parents (an unconditioned stimulus). Thus, the child may squeal with delight when he or she hears the car.

What is the role of extinction in classical conditioning? Extinction enters the picture when times—and the relationships between events—change. After moving to a new house, the child's parents may commute by public transportation. The sound of a car in a nearby driveway may signal a neighbor's, not a parent's, homecoming. When a conditioned stimulus (such as the sound of a car) is no longer followed by an unconditioned stimulus (a parent's homecoming), the conditioned stimulus loses its ability to elicit a conditioned response. The organism adapts to change.

In classical conditioning, **extinction** is the process by which conditioned stimuli lose the ability to elicit conditioned responses, because the conditioned stimuli are no longer associated with unconditioned stimuli. That is, the toddler is no longer gleeful at the sounds of the car in the driveway. From the cognitive perspective, extinction changes the child's mental representation of its environment, because the conditioned stimulus no longer allows the child to make the same prediction.

In experiments on the extinction of conditioned responses, Pavlov found that repeated presentations of the conditioned stimulus (in this case, the

Evolution would favor the survival of animals that associate a water hole with the thirst drive from time to time so that they return to it when it once more holds water.

tone) without the unconditioned stimulus (in this case, meat powder) led to extinction of the conditioned response (salivation in response to the tone). Basically, the dog stopped salivating at the sound of the tone. Interestingly, Figure 6.2 shows that a dog was conditioned to begin to salivate in response to a tone after two or three pairings of the tone with meat powder. Continued pairings of the stimuli led to increased salivation (measured in number of drops of saliva). After seven or eight trials, salivation leveled off at eleven to twelve drops.

In the next series of experiments, salivation in response to the tone was extinguished by trials in which the tone was presented without the meat powder. After about ten extinction trials, the animal no longer salivated. It no longer showed the conditioned response when the tone was sounded.

What is the role of spontaneous recovery in classical conditioning? We asked what would happen if we were to allow a day or two to pass after we had extinguished salivation in Pavlov's dog and then again sounded the tone. Where would you place your bet? Would the dog salivate or not?

If you bet that the dog would again show the conditioned response (in this case, salivation in response to the tone), you were correct. Organisms tend to show **spontaneous recovery** of extinguished conditioned responses as a function of the passage of time. For this reason, the term *extinction* may be a bit misleading. When a species of animal becomes extinct, all members of that species capable of reproducing have died. The species vanishes. But the experimental extinction of conditioned responses does not lead to their permanent eradication. Rather, it seems to *inhibit* them. The response remains available for the future under the "right" conditions.

Evolutionary psychologists note that spontaneous recovery, like extinction, is adaptive. What would happen if the child heard no car in the driveway for several months? It could be that the next time a car entered the driveway the child would associate the sounds with a parent's homecoming rather than with the arrival of a neighbor. This expectation could be appropriate. After all, *something* had changed when no car entered the driveway for so long. In the wild, a water hole may contain water for only a couple of months during the year. Evolution would favor the survival of animals that associate the water hole with the thirst drive from time to time so that they return to it when it once more holds water.

As time passes and seasons change, things sometimes follow circular paths and arrive where they were before. Spontaneous recovery helps organisms adapt to situations that recur from time to time.

Generalization and Discrimination

No two things are exactly alike. Traffic lights are hung at slightly different heights, and shades of red and green differ a little. The barking of two dogs differs, and the sound of the same animal differs slightly from one bark to the next. Rustling sounds in the undergrowth differ, but evolution would favor the survival of rabbits and deer that flee when they perceive any one of many possible rustling sounds. Adaptation requires us to respond similarly (or *generalize*) to stimuli that are equivalent in function and to respond differently to (or *discriminate* between) stimuli that are not.

What is the role of generalization in classical conditioning? Pavlov noted that responding to different stimuli as though they were functionally equivalent—*generalizing*—is adaptive for animals. **Generalization** is the tendency for a conditioned response to be evoked by stimuli that are similar to the stimulus to which the response was conditioned. For example, Pavlov demonstrated generalization by getting his dog to salivate when it was shown a circle. Then later the dog salivated in response to being shown closed geometric figures—even squares. The more closely the figure resembled a circle, however, the greater the *strength* of the response (as measured by drops of saliva).

But what happens if food follows the presentation of a circle but not a square? *What is the role of discrimination in classical conditioning?* Organisms must also learn that (1) many stimuli perceived as being similar are functionally different, and (2) they must respond adaptively to each. During the first couple of months of life, for example, babies can discriminate their mother's voice from those of other women. They often stop crying when they hear their mother but not when they hear a stranger.

Pavlov showed that a dog conditioned to salivate in response to circles could be trained *not* to salivate in response to ellipses. After a while, the dog no longer salivated in response to the ellipses. Instead, it showed **discrimination**: It salivated only in response to circles. Pavlov found that increasing the difficulty of the discrimination task apparently tormented the dog. After the dog was trained to salivate in response to circles but not ellipses, Pavlov showed it a series of

spontaneous recovery the recurrence of an extinguished response as a function of the passage of time

generalization in conditioning, the tendency for a conditioned response to be evoked by stimuli that are similar to the stimulus to which the response was conditioned

discrimination in conditioning, the tendency for an organism to distinguish between a conditioned stimulus and similar stimuli that do not forecast an unconditioned stimulus

higher-order conditioning
a classical conditioning procedure in which a previously neutral stimulus comes to elicit the response brought forth by a *conditioned* stimulus by being paired repeatedly with that conditioned stimulus

progressively rounder ellipses. Eventually the dog could no longer distinguish the ellipses from circles. The animal was so stressed that it urinated, defecated, barked profusely, and snapped at laboratory personnel.

How do we explain the dog's belligerent behavior? In *Frustration and Aggression,* a classic work written more than sixty-five years ago, a group of behaviorally oriented psychologists suggested that frustration induces aggression (Dollard et al., 1939). Rewards—such as food— are usually contingent on correct discrimination. That is, if the dog errs, it doesn't eat. Cognitive theorists, however, disagree (Rescorla, 1988). They would say that in Pavlov's experiment, the dog's loss of the ability to adjust its mental map of the environment was frustrating.

Daily life requires generalization and discrimination. No two hotels are alike, but when we travel from one city to another it is adaptive to expect to stay in a hotel. It is encouraging that a green light in Washington has the same meaning as a green light in Paris. Returning home requires the ability to discriminate among our home from others. Imagine the confusion that would reign if we could not discriminate among our friends, mates, or coworkers from other people.

© 2010 COMSTOCK / JUPITERIMAGES CORPORATION

Higher-Order Conditioning

Consider a child who is burned by touching a hot stove. After this experience, the sight of the stove may evoke fear. And because hearing the word *stove* may evoke a mental image of the stove, just hearing the word may evoke fear.

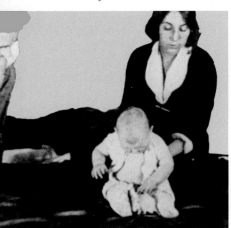

Watson and Rayner conditioned 'Little Albert' to fear a rat by clanging steel bars behind his head when he played with the rat.

Do you recall the mini-experiment in which an adult smiles, says "kitchie-coo," and then tickles an infant's foot? After a few repetitions, just smiling at the infant may cause the infant to retract its foot. In fact, just walking into the room may have the same effect! The experiences with touching the hot stove and tickling the infant's foot are examples of higher-order conditioning. *What is higher-order conditioning?*

In **higher-order conditioning**, a previously neutral stimulus (for example, hearing the word *stove* or seeing the adult who had done the tickling enter the room) comes to serve as a learned or conditioned stimulus after being paired repeatedly with a stimulus that has already become a learned or conditioned stimulus (for example, seeing the stove or hearing the phrase "kitchie-coo"). Pavlov demonstrated higher-order conditioning by first conditioning a dog to salivate in response to a tone. He then repeatedly paired the shining of a light with the sounding of the tone. After several pairings, shining the light (the higher-order conditioned stimulus) came to evoke the response (salivation) that had been elicited by the tone (the first-order conditioned stimulus).

Applications of Classical Conditioning

Some of the most important applications of classical conditioning involve the conditioning of fear and the counterconditioning or extinction of fear. The fear-reduction methods we discuss are part of behavior therapy, which we elaborate in Chapter 13.

"Little Albert": Classical Conditioning of Emotional Responses

In 1920, John B. Watson and his future wife, Rosalie Rayner, published an article describing their demonstration that emotional reactions such as fears can be acquired through principles of classical conditioning. The subject of their demonstration was a lad known in psychological literature by the name of Little Albert. Albert was a phlegmatic fellow at the age of eleven months, not given to ready displays of emotion. But prior to the study, the infant did enjoy playing with a laboratory rat.

Using a method that some psychologists have criticized as unethical, Watson startled Little Albert by clanging steel bars behind his head when he played with the rat. After seven pairings, Albert showed fear of the rat even though clanging was suspended. Albert's fear was also generalized to objects similar in appearance to the rat, such as a rabbit and the fur

© ARCHIVES OF THE HISTORY OF AMERICAN PSYCHOLOGY - THE UNIVERSITY OF AKRON collar on his mother's coat. Albert's conditioned fear of rats may never have become extinguished because extinction would have required perceiving rats (the conditioned stimuli) without painful consequences (in the absence of the unconditioned stimuli). But Albert's mother removed him from the laboratory before Watson and Rayner could attempt to countercondition the boy's acquired fear. And once outside the laboratory, fear might have prevented Albert from facing furry animals. And as we shall see in the section on operant conditioning, avoiding furry animals might have been *reinforced* by reduction of fear.

Counterconditioning

The reasoning behind counterconditioning is this: If fears, as Watson had shown, could be conditioned by painful experiences like a clanging noise, perhaps fears could be **counterconditioned** by substituting pleasant experiences. In 1924, Watson's protégé Mary Cover Jones attempted to countercondition fear in a two-year-old boy named Peter.

Peter had an intense fear of rabbits. Jones had a rabbit gradually brought closer to Peter while he munched candy and cookies. Jones first placed the rabbit in a far corner of the room while Peter munched and crunched. Peter cast a wary eye, but he continued to consume the treats. Gradually the animal was brought closer until Peter simultaneously ate and touched the rabbit. Jones theorized that the joy of eating was incompatible with fear and counterconditioned it.

Truth

It is true that psychologists helped a young boy overcome his fear of rabbits by having him eat cookies while a rabbit was brought progressively closer.

Flooding and Systematic Desensitization

If Mary Cover Jones had simply plopped the rabbit on Peter's lap rather than bring it gradually closer, she would have been using the method of

COPYRIGHT © MICHAEL NEWMAN / PHOTO EDIT

flooding. Flooding and systematic desensitization, like counterconditioning, are behavior therapy methods for reducing fears. They are based on the classical conditioning principle of extinction. In flooding, the client is exposed to the fear-evoking stimulus until fear is extinguished. Little Albert, for example, might have been placed in close contact with a rat until his fear had become extinguished. In extinction, the conditioned stimulus (in this case, the rat) is presented repeatedly in the absence of the unconditioned stimulus (the clanging of the steel bars) until the conditioned response (fear) is no longer evoked.

Although flooding is usually effective, it is unpleasant. (When you are fearful of rats, being placed in a room with one is no picnic.) For this reason, behavior therapists frequently prefer to use **systematic desensitization**, in which the client is gradually exposed to fear-evoking stimuli under circumstances in which he or she remains relaxed. For example, while feeling relaxed, Little Albert might have been given an opportunity to look at photos of rats or to see rats from a distance before they were brought closer. Systematic desensitization takes longer than flooding but is not as unpleasant.

In any event, people can learn by means of simple association. In terms of the evolutionary perspective, organisms that can learn by several routes—including conditioning and conscious reflection—would stand a greater chance of survival than organisms whose learning is limited to conditioning.

LO² Operant Conditioning: Learning What Does What to What

Through classical conditioning, we learn to associate stimuli. As a result, a simple, usually passive response made to one stimulus is then made in response to the other. In the case of Little Albert, clanging noises were associated with a rat. As a result, the rat came to elicit the fear caused by the clanging. However, classical conditioning is only one kind of learning that occurs in these situations. After Little Albert acquired his fear of the rat, his voluntary behavior changed:

counterconditioning
a fear-reduction technique in which pleasant stimuli are associated with fear-evoking stimuli so that the fear-evoking stimuli lose their aversive qualities

flooding
a behavioral fear-reduction technique based on principles of classical conditioning; fear-evoking stimuli (CSs) are presented continuously in the absence of actual harm so that fear responses (CRs) are extinguished

systematic desensitization
a behavioral fear-reduction technique in which a hierarchy of fear-evoking stimuli is presented while the person remains relaxed

reinforce
to follow a response with a stimulus that increases the frequency of the response

operant behavior
voluntary responses that are reinforced

operant conditioning
a simple form of learning in which an organism learns to engage in behavior because it is reinforced

Fiction

During World War II, Skinner *proposed* that pigeons be trained to guide missiles to their targets, but his proposal was never acted on.

He tried to avoid the rat. Thus, Little Albert engaged in another kind of learning—*operant conditioning*. In operant conditioning, organisms learn to do things—or *not* to do things—because of the consequences of their behavior. For example, I avoided buttered popcorn to prevent nausea. But we also seek fluids when we are thirsty, sex when we are aroused, and an ambient temperature of 68° to 70° F when we feel too hot or too cold. *Classical conditioning focuses on how organisms form anticipations about their environments. Operant conditioning focuses on what they do about them.* Let us consider the key contributions of B. F. Skinner to operant conditioning.

B. F. Skinner and Reinforcement

When it comes to unusual war stories, few will top that of B. F. Skinner. One of Skinner's wartime efforts was "Project Pigeon." *What is the contribution of B. F. Skinner to the psychology of learning?* In their training, the pigeons would be **reinforced** with food pellets for pecking at targets projected onto a screen (see Figure 6.3). Once trained, the pigeons would be placed in missiles. Their pecking at similar targets displayed on a screen would correct the missile's flight path, resulting in a "hit" and a sacrificed pigeon. Plans for building the necessary missile—for some reason called the *Pelican* and not the *Pigeon*—were scrapped, however. The pigeon equipment was too bulky, and Skinner's suggestion was not taken seriously.

Project Pigeon may have been scrapped, but Skinner's ideas have found wide

Figure 6.3

Project Pigeon

application. In operant conditioning, an organism learns to *do* something because of the effects or consequences of the behavior.

Skinner taught pigeons and other animals to engage in **operant behavior**, behavior that operates on, or manipulates, the environment. In classical conditioning, involuntary responses such as salivation or eyeblinks are often conditioned. In operant conditioning, *voluntary* responses such as pecking at a target, pressing a lever, or skills required for playing tennis are acquired, or conditioned. *What is operant conditioning?*

Operant conditioning is defined as a simple form of learning in which an organism learns to engage in certain behavior because of the effects of that behavior. In operant conditioning, we learn to engage in behaviors that result in presumably desirable consequences such as food, a hug, an A on a test, attention, or social approval. Some children learn to conform to social rules to earn the attention and approval of their parents and teachers. Ironically, other children may learn to "misbehave" because misbehavior also gets attention. In particular, children may learn to be "bad" when their "good" behavior is routinely ignored. Some children who do not do well in school seek the approval of deviant peers (Patterson et al., 2000).

Methods of Operant Conditioning

Skinner (1938) made many theoretical and technological innovations. Among them was his focus on discrete behaviors, such as lever pressing, as the *unit,* or type, of behavior to be studied. Other psychologists might focus on how organisms think or "feel." Skinner focused on measurable things they do. Many psychologists have found these kinds of behavior inconsequential, especially when it comes to explaining and predicting human behavior. But Skinner's supporters point out that focusing on discrete behavior creates the potential for helpful changes. For example, in helping people combat depression, one psychologist might focus on their "feelings." A Skinnerian would focus on cataloging (and modifying) the types of things that "depressed people" do. Directly modifying depressive behavior might also brighten clients' self-reports about their "feelings of depression."

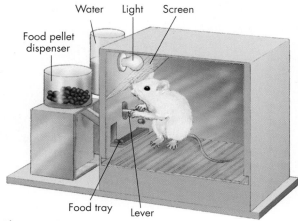

Water Light Screen

Food pellet
dispenser

Food tray   Lever

Figure 6.4

The Effects of Reinforcement

To study operant behavior, Skinner devised an animal cage (or "operant chamber") that has been dubbed the *Skinner box*. (Skinner himself repeatedly requested that his operant chamber *not* be called a Skinner box, but history has thus far failed to honor his wishes.) Such a box is shown in Figure 6.4. The cage is ideal for laboratory experimentation because experimental conditions can be carefully introduced and removed, and their effects on laboratory animals can be observed.

The rat in Figure 6.4 was deprived of food and placed in a Skinner box with a lever at one end. At first it sniffed its way around the cage and engaged in random behavior. The rat's first pressing of the lever was accidental. But because of this action, a food pellet dropped into the cage. The arrival of the food pellet increased the probability that the rat would press the lever again. The pellet is thus said to have *reinforced* lever pressing.

In operant conditioning, it matters little why or how the first "correct" response is made. The animal can happen on it by chance or be physically guided to make the response. You may command your dog to "Sit!" and then press its backside down until it is sitting. Finally you reinforce sitting with food or a pat on the head and a kind word. Animal trainers use physical guiding or coaxing to bring about the first "correct" response. Can you imagine how long it would take to train your dog if you waited for it to sit or roll over and then seized the opportunity to command it to sit or roll over?

People, of course, can be verbally guided into desired responses when they are learning tasks such as spelling, adding numbers, or operating a machine. But they need to be informed when they have made the correct response. Knowledge of results often is all the reinforcement people need to learn new skills.

Types of Reinforcers

A reinforcer is any stimulus that increases the probability that the responses preceding it— whether pecking a button in a Skinner box or studying for a quiz—will be repeated. *What are the various kinds of reinforcers?* Reinforcers include food pellets when an animal has been deprived of food; water when it has been deprived of liquid; the opportunity to mate; the sound of a tone that has previously been associated with eating. Skinner distinguished between positive and negative reinforcers.

Positive and Negative Reinforcers

Positive reinforcers increase the probability that a behavior will occur when they are applied. Food and approval usually serve as positive reinforcers. **Negative reinforcers** increase the probability that a behavior will occur when the reinforcers are *removed* (see Figure 6.5).

Skinner himself repeatedly requested that his operant chamber not be called a Skinner box, but history has thus far failed to honor his wishes.

primary reinforcer
an unlearned reinforcer

secondary reinforcer
a stimulus that gains reinforcement value through association with established reinforcers

conditioned reinforcer
another term for a secondary reinforcer

Figure 6.5

Positive Versus Negative Reinforcers

Procedure	Behavior	Consequence	Change in behavior
Use of positive reinforcement	Behavior (Studying)	Positive reinforcer (Teacher approval) is *presented* when student studies	Frequency of behavior *increases* (Student studies more)
Use of negative reinforcement	Behavior (Studying)	Negative reinforcer (Teacher disapproval) is *removed* when student studies	Frequency of behavior *increases* (Student studies more)

Go to CourseMate for PSYCH at www.cengagebrain.com to access an interactive version of this figure.

People often learn to plan ahead so that they need not fear that things will go wrong. In such cases fear acts as a negative reinforcer; *removal* of fear increases the probability that planning ahead will be repeated.

Immediate Versus Delayed Reinforcers

Immediate reinforcers are more effective than delayed reinforcers. Therefore, the short-term consequences of behavior often provide more of an incentive than the long-term consequences.

Some students socialize when they should be studying because the pleasure of socializing is immediate. Studying may not pay off until the final exam or graduation. (This is why younger students do better with frequent tests.) It is difficult to quit smoking cigarettes because the reinforcement of nicotine is immediate and the health hazards of smoking are more distant. Focusing on short-term reinforcement is also connected with risky sex, such as engaging in sexual activity with a stranger or failing to prevent pregnancy (Caffray & Schneider, 2000; Fuertes et al., 2002). One of the aspects of being human is the ability to foresee the long-range consequences of one's behavior and to make choices. But immediate reinforcers—such as those cookies staring in the face of the would-be dieter—can be powerful temptations indeed.

Nicotine Creates
Short-Term Reinforcement

It is difficult to quit smoking cigarettes because the reinforcement of nicotine is immediate and the health hazards of smoking are more distant.

Primary and Secondary Reinforcers

We can also distinguish between primary and secondary, or conditioned, reinforcers. **Primary reinforcers** are effective because of the organism's biological makeup. For example, food, water, warmth (positive reinforcers), and pain (a negative reinforcer) all serve as primary reinforcers. **Secondary reinforcers** acquire their value through being associated with established reinforcers. For this reason they are also termed **conditioned reinforcers**. We may seek money because we have learned that it may be exchanged for primary reinforcers.

Extinction and Spontaneous Recovery in Operant Conditioning

Keisha's teacher writes "Good" on all of her homework assignments before returning them. One day, her teacher no longer writes anything on the assignments—the reinforcement ends. Reinforcers are used to strengthen responses. What happens when reinforcement stops? *What is the role of extinction in operant conditioning?*

In Pavlov's experiment, the meat powder was the event that followed and confirmed the appropriateness of salivation. In Keisha's situation, seeing "Good" written on her assignments confirmed the appropriateness of the way in which she did her homework. In operant conditioning, the ensuing events are reinforcers. The extinction of learned responses results from the repeated performance of operant behavior without reinforcement. Keisha might stop doing her homework if she is not reinforced for completing it. In other words, reinforcers maintain operant behavior or strengthen habitual behavior in operant conditioning. With humans, fortunately, people can reinforce

Procedure	Behavior	Consequence	Change in behavior
Use of negative reinforcement	Behavior (Studying)	Negative reinforcer (Teacher disapproval) is *removed* when student studies	Frequency of behavior *increases* (Student studies more)
Use of punishment	Behavior (Talking in class)	Punishment (Detention) is *presented* when student talks in class	Frequency of behavior *decreases* (Student talks less in class)

Figure 6.6

Negative Reinforcers Versus Punishments

reward
a pleasant stimulus that increases the frequency of the behavior it follows

punishment
an unpleasant stimulus that suppresses the behavior it follows

discriminative stimulus
in operant conditioning, a stimulus that indicates that reinforcement is available

Go to CourseMate for PSYCH at www.cengagebrain.com to access an interactive version of this figure.

themselves for desired behavior by telling themselves they did a good job—or in Keisha's case, she may tell herself that she is doing the right thing regardless of whether her teacher recognizes it.

What is the role of spontaneous recovery in operant conditioning? Spontaneous recovery of learned responses occurs in operant conditioning as well as in classical conditioning. Spontaneous recovery is adaptive in operant conditioning as well as in classical conditioning. Reinforcers may once again become available after time elapses, just as there are new tender sprouts on twigs when the spring arrives.

Reinforcers Versus Rewards and Punishments

Reinforcers are defined as stimuli that increase the frequency of behavior. *Why did Skinner make a point of distinguishing between reinforcers on the one hand and rewards and punishments on the other?* Reinforcers are known by their effects, whereas **rewards** and punishments are known by how they feel. It may be that most reinforcers—food, hugs, having the other person admit to starting the argument, and so on—feel good, or are pleasant events. Yet things that we might assume would feel bad, such as a slap on the hand, disapproval from a teacher, even suspensions and detention may be positively reinforcing to some people—perhaps because such experiences confirm negative feelings toward teachers or one's belonging within a deviant subculture (Atkins et al., 2002).

Skinner preferred the concept of reinforcement to that of reward because reinforcement does not suggest trying to "get inside the head" of an organism (whether a human or lower animal) to guess what it would find pleasant or unpleasant. A list of reinforcers is arrived at scientifically and *empirically*—that is, by observing what sorts of stimuli increase the frequency of the behavior.

Punishments are defined as aversive events that suppress or decrease the frequency of the behavior they follow (see Figure 6.6). Punishment can rapidly suppress undesirable behavior (Gershoff, 2002) and may be warranted in "emergencies," such as when a child tries to run into the street.

Discriminative Stimuli

B. F. Skinner might not have been able to get his pigeons into the drivers' seats of missiles, but he had no problem training them to respond to traffic lights. Imagine yourself trying the following experiment.

Place a pigeon in a Skinner box with a button on the wall. Deprive it of food for a while. Drop a food pellet into the cage whenever it pecks the button. Soon it will learn to peck the button. Now you place a small green light in the cage and turn it on and off intermittently throughout the day. Reinforce button pecking with food whenever the green light is on, but not when the light is off. It will not take long for the pigeon to learn that it will gain as much by grooming itself or cooing and flapping around as it will by pecking the button when the light is off.

The green light has become a **discriminative stimulus**. *What are discriminative stimuli?* Discriminative stimuli, such as green or red lights, indicate whether behavior (in the case of the pigeon, pecking a button) will be reinforced (by a food pellet being dropped into the cage). Behaviors that are not reinforced tend to be extinguished. For the pigeon in our experiment, the behavior of pecking the button *when the light is off* is extinguished.

A moment's reflection will suggest many ways in which discriminative stimuli influence our behavior. Isn't it more efficient to answer the telephone when it is ringing? Do you think it is wise to ask someone for a favor when she or he is displaying anger and disapproval toward you?

We noted that a pigeon learns to peck a button if food drops into its cage when it does so. What if you want the pigeon to continue to peck the button, but

continuous reinforcement
a schedule of reinforcement in which every correct response is reinforced

partial zreinforcement
one of several reinforcement schedules in which not every correct response is reinforced

fixed-interval schedule
a schedule in which a fixed amount of time must elapse between the previous and subsequent times that reinforcement is available

variable-interval schedule
a schedule in which a variable amount of time must elapse between the previous and subsequent times that reinforcement is available

you're running out of food? Do not despair. As we see in the following section, you can keep that bird pecking away indefinitely, even as you hold up on most of the food.

Schedules of Reinforcement

In operant conditioning, some responses are maintained by means of **continuous reinforcement**. You probably become warmer every time you put on heavy clothing. You probably become less thirsty every time you drink water. Yet if you have ever watched people toss their money down the maws of slot machines, you know that behavior can also be maintained by means of **partial reinforcement**. *What are the various schedules of reinforcement? How do they affect behavior?*

Folklore about gambling is consistent with learning theory. You can get a person "hooked" on gambling by fixing the game to allow heavy winnings at first. Then you gradually space out the winnings (reinforcements) until gambling is maintained by infrequent winning—or even no winning at all. Partial reinforcement schedules can maintain gambling, like other behavior, for a great deal of time, even though it goes unreinforced (Pulley, 1998).

Responses that have been maintained by partial reinforcement are more resistant to extinction than responses that have been maintained by continuous reinforcement (Rescorla, 1999). From the cognitive perspective, we could suggest that organisms that have experienced partial reinforcement do not expect reinforcement every time they engage in a response. Therefore, they are more likely to persist in the absence of reinforcement.

There are four basic reinforcement schedules: *fixed-interval, variable-interval, fixed-ratio,* and *variable-ratio.*

Interval Schedules

In a **fixed-interval schedule**, a fixed amount of time—say, a minute—must elapse before the correct response will result in a reinforcer. With a fixed-interval schedule, an organism's response rate falls off after each reinforcement and then picks up again as the time when reinforcement will occur approaches. For example, in a one-minute fixed-interval schedule, a rat is reinforced with, say, a food pellet for the first operant—for example, the first pressing of a lever—that occurs after a minute has elapsed. After each reinforcement, the rat's rate of lever pressing slows down, but as the end of the one-minute interval draws near, lever pressing increases in frequency, as suggested in Figure 6.7. It is as if the rat has learned that it must wait a while before it is reinforced. The resultant record on the cumulative recorder shows a typical series of upward waves, or scallops, which are called *fixed-interval scallops.*

Car dealers use fixed-interval reinforcement schedules when they offer incentives for buying up the remainder of the year's line in summer and fall. In a sense, they are suppressing buying at other times, except for consumers whose current cars are in their death throes or those with little self-control. Similarly, you learn to check your e-mail only at a certain time of day if your correspondent writes at that time each day.

Reinforcement is more unpredictable in a **variable-interval schedule**. Therefore, the response rate is steadier but lower. If the boss calls us in for a weekly report, we probably work hard to pull things together just before the report is to be given, just as we might cram the night before a weekly quiz. But if we know that the boss might call us in for a report on the progress of a certain project at any time (variable-interval schedule), we are likely to keep things in a state of reasonable readiness at all times. However,

Truth

For gamblers, the unpredictability of winning also maintains a high response rate.

Figure 6.7

The Fixed-Interval Scallop

Response rate picks up as time of availability of reinforcement approaches

Response rate slacks off after reinforcement

Cumulative frequency of responses

0

Time

Fixed-interval schedule

our efforts are unlikely to have the intensity they would in a fixed-interval schedule (for example, a weekly report). Similarly, we are less likely to cram for unpredictable pop quizzes than to study for regular quizzes. But we are likely to do at least some studying on a regular basis. Likewise, if you receive e-mail from your correspondent regularly, you are likely to check your e-mail regularly, but with less eagerness.

Ratio Schedules

In a **fixed-ratio schedule**, reinforcement is provided after a fixed number of correct responses have been made. In a **variable-ratio schedule**, reinforcement is provided after a variable number of correct responses have been made. In a 10:1 ratio schedule, the mean number of correct responses that would have to be made before a subsequent correct response would be reinforced is ten, but the ratio of correct responses to reinforcements might be allowed to vary from, say, 1:1 to 20:1 on a random basis.

Fixed- and variable-ratio schedules maintain a high response rate. With a fixed-ratio schedule, it is as if the organism learns that it must make several responses before being reinforced. It then "gets them out of the way" as rapidly as possible. Consider the example of piecework. If a worker must sew five shirts to receive ten dollars, he or she is on a fixed-ratio (5:1) schedule and is likely to sew at a uniformly high rate, although there might be a brief pause after each reinforcement. With a variable-ratio schedule, reinforcement can come at any time. Slot machines tend to pay off on variable-ratio schedules, and players can be seen popping coins into them and yanking their "arms" with barely a pause. I have seen players who do

not even stop to pick up their winnings. Instead, they continue to pop in the coins, either from their original stack or from the winnings tray.

Shaping

If you are teaching hip-hop dancing to people who have never danced, do not wait until they have performed it precisely before telling them they're on the right track. The foxtrot will be back in style before they have learned a thing.

We can teach complex behaviors by **shaping**. *How can we use shaping to teach complex behavior patterns?* Shaping reinforces progressive steps toward the behavioral goal. At first, for example, it may be wise to smile and say, "Good," when a reluctant newcomer gathers the courage to get out on the dance floor, even if your feet are flattened by his initial clumsiness. If you are teaching someone to drive a car with a standard shift, at first generously reinforce the learner simply for shifting gears without stalling.

But as training proceeds, we come to expect more before we are willing to provide reinforcement. We reinforce **successive approximations** of the goal. If you want to train a rat to climb a ladder, first reinforce it with a food pellet when it turns toward the ladder. Then wait until it approaches the ladder before giving it a pellet. Then do not drop a pellet into the cage until the rat touches the ladder. In this way, the rat will reach the top of the ladder more quickly than if you had waited for the target behavior to occur at random.

fixed-ratio schedule a schedule in which reinforcement is provided after a fixed number of correct responses

variable-ratio schedule a schedule in which reinforcement is provided after a variable number of correct responses

shaping a procedure for teaching complex behaviors that at first reinforces approximations of the target behavior

successive approximations behaviors that are progressively closer to a target behavior

© 2007 JUPITERIMAGES CORPORATION

Have you ever driven home and suddenly realized that you couldn't recall exactly how you got there? Your entire trip may seem "lost." Were you in great danger? How could you allow such a thing to happen? Actually, your driving and your responses to the demands of the route may have become so habitual that you did not have to focus on them. As you drove, you were able to think about dinner, work, or the weekend. But if something unusual had occurred on the way, such as an engine problem or a rainstorm, you would have devoted as much attention to your driving as was needed to arrive home. Your trip was probably quite safe after all.

> **Truth**
>
> Through use of shaping, one can indeed train a rat to climb a ramp, cross a bridge, climb a ladder, and so on in a desired sequence.

Applications of Operant Conditioning

Operant conditioning, like classical conditioning, is not just an exotic laboratory procedure. We use it every day in our efforts to influence other people. Parents and peers induce children to acquire so-called gender-appropriate behavior patterns through rewards and punishments. Parents also tend to praise their children for sharing their toys and to punish them for being too aggressive. Peers participate in the socialization process by playing with children who are generous and nonaggressive and often by avoiding those who are not (Warman & Cohen, 2000).

Operant conditioning also plays a role in attitude formation. Adults often reward children for expressing attitudes that coincide with their own and punish or ignore them for expressing contradictory attitudes. Let us now consider some specific applications of operant conditioning.

Biofeedback Training

Biofeedback training (BFT) is based on principles of operant conditioning. BFT has enabled people and lower animals to learn to control autonomic responses to attain reinforcement (Miller, 1969; Vernon et al., 2003).

Through BFT, people can gain control of autonomic functions such as the flow of blood in a finger. They can also learn to improve their control over functions that can be manipulated voluntarily, such as muscle tension. When people receive BFT, reinforcement is given in the form of *information*. Perhaps

a sound changes in pitch or frequency of occurrence to signal that they have modified the autonomic function in the desired direction. For example, we can learn to emit alpha waves—the kind of brain wave associated with feelings of relaxation—through feedback from an electroencephalograph (EEG, an instrument that measures brain waves). People use other instruments to learn to lower their muscle tension, heart rates, and blood pressure.

BFT is also used with people who have lost neuromuscular control of parts of their body as a result of an accident. A "bleep" sound informs them when they have contracted a muscle or sent an impulse down a neural pathway. By concentrating on changing the bleeps, they may gradually regain voluntary control over the damaged function.

Behavior Modification in the Classroom: Accentuating the Positive

Remember that reinforcers are defined as stimuli that increase the frequency of behavior—not as pleasant events. Ironically, adults frequently reinforce undesirable behavior in children by paying attention to them, or punishing them, when they misbehave but ignoring them when they behave in desirable ways. Similarly, teachers who raise their voices when children misbehave may be unintentionally conferring hero status on those pupils in the eyes of their peers. To the teacher's surprise, some children may then go out of their way to earn disapproval.

Teacher preparation and in-service programs show teachers how to use behavior modification to reverse these response patterns. Teachers are taught to reinforce children when they are behaving

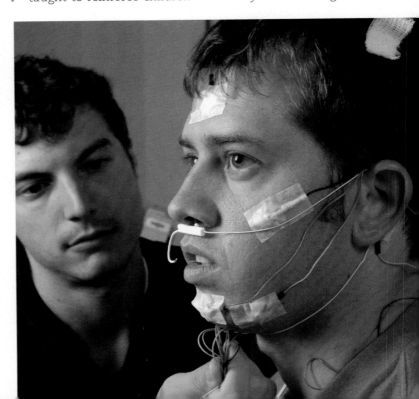

appropriately and, when possible, to extinguish misbehavior by ignoring it.

Among older children and adolescents, peer approval may be a more powerful reinforcer than teacher approval. Peer approval may maintain misbehavior, and ignoring misbehavior may only allow students to become more disruptive. In such cases it may be necessary to separate troublesome children.

Teachers also frequently use time out from positive reinforcement to discourage misbehavior. In this method, children are placed in a drab, restrictive environment for a specified period, usually about ten minutes, when they behave disruptively. While they are isolated, they cannot earn the attention of peers or teachers, and no reinforcers are present.

Programmed Learning: Step by Step

B. F. Skinner developed an educational method called *programmed learning* that is based on operant conditioning. This method assumes that any complex task involving conceptual learning as well as motor skills can be broken down into a number of small steps. These steps can be shaped individually and then combined in sequence to form the correct behavioral chain.

Programmed learning does not punish errors. Instead, correct responses are reinforced, usually with immediate feedback. Every child earns a 100, but at her or his own pace. Programmed learning also assumes it is the task of the teacher (or program) to structure the learning experience in such a way that errors will not be made.

Fiction

Actually, one can learn *without* making mistakes.

LO³ Cognitive Factors in Learning

Classical and operant conditioning were originally conceived of as relatively simple forms of learning. Much of conditioning's appeal is that it can be said to meet the behaviorist objective of explaining behavior in terms of observable events—in this case, laboratory conditions. Building on this theoretical base, some psychologists have suggested that the most complex human behavior involves the summation of a series of instances of conditioning. Many psychologists believe, however, that conditioning is too mechanical a process to explain all instances of learned behavior, even in laboratory rats. They turn to cognitive factors to describe and explain additional findings in the psychology of learning. *How do we explain what happens during classical conditioning from a cognitive perspective?*

In addition to concepts such as association and reinforcement, cognitive psychologists use concepts such as mental structures, schemas, templates, and information processing. Cognitive psychologists see people as searching for information, weighing evidence, and making decisions. Let us consider some classic research that points to cognitive factors in learning, as opposed to mechanical associations. These cognitive factors are not necessarily limited to humans—although, of course, people are the only species that can talk about them.

> Remember that **reinforcers** are defined as stimuli that increase the frequency of behavior—not as pleasant events.

Latent Learning: Forming Cognitive Maps

Many behaviorists argue that organisms acquire only responses for which they are reinforced. E. C. Tolman, however, showed that rats also learn about their environment in the absence of reinforcement. In doing so, he showed that rats must form cognitive maps of their surroundings. *What is the evidence that people and lower animals form cognitive maps of their environments?*

Tolman trained some rats to run through mazes for food goals. Other rats were allowed to explore the same mazes for several days without food goals or other rewards. After the unrewarded rats had been allowed to explore the mazes for ten days, food rewards were placed in a box at the far end of the

latent
hidden or concealed

contingency theory
the view that learning occurs when stimuli provide information about the likelihood of the occurrence of other stimuli

observational learning
the acquisition of knowledge and skills through the observation of others (who are called *models*) rather than by means of direct experience

maze. The previously unrewarded rats reached the food box as quickly as the rewarded rats after only one or two trials (Tolman & Honzik, 1930).

Tolman concluded that the rats had learned about the mazes by exploring them even when they went unrewarded by food. He distinguished between *learning* and *performance*. Rats apparently created a cognitive map of a maze. Even though they were not externally motivated to follow a rapid route through the maze, they would learn fast routes just by exploring it. Yet this learning might remain hidden, or **latent**, until food motivated them to take the rapid routes.

Contingency Theory

Behaviorists and cognitive psychologists interpret classical conditioning in different ways. Behaviorists explain it in terms of the pairing of stimuli. Cognitive psychologists explain classical conditioning in terms of the ways in which stimuli provide information that allows organisms to form or revise mental representations of their environment. Robert Rescorla's **contingency theory** suggests that learning occurs only when the conditioned stimulus (CS) provides *information* about the unconditioned stimulus (US).

In classical conditioning of dogs, Rescorla (1967) obtained some results that are difficult to explain without reference to cognitive concepts. Each phase of his work paired a tone (a CS) with an electric shock (a US), but in different ways. With one group of animals, the shock was consistently presented after the tone. The dogs in this group learned to show a fear response when the tone was presented.

A second group of dogs heard an equal number of tones and received an equal number of electric shocks, but the shock did not immediately follow the tone. In other words, the tone and the shock were not paired. Now, from the behaviorist perspective, the dogs should not have learned to associate the tone and the shock, because one did not predict the other. Actually, the dogs learned quite a lot: They learned that they had nothing to fear when the tone was sounded! They showed vigilance and fear when the laboratory was quiet—for the shock might come at any time—but they were calm in the presence of the tone itself.

The third group of dogs also received equal numbers of tones and shocks, but the stimuli were presented at random. Occasionally they were paired, but most often they were not. According to Rescorla, behaviorists might argue that intermittent pairing of the tones and shocks should have brought about some learning. Yet it did not. The animals showed no fear in response to the tone. Rescorla suggests that the animals in this group learned nothing because the tones did not allow them to make predictions about electric shock. Rescorla concluded that learning occurs only when the CS (in this case, the tone) provides information about the US (in this case, the shock).

Observational Learning

How many things have you learned from watching other people in real life, in films, and on television? From films and television, you may have gathered vague ideas about how to skydive, ride a surfboard, climb sheer cliffs, run a pattern to catch a touchdown pass in the Super Bowl, and dust for fingerprints, even if you have never tried them yourself. How do people learn by observing others?

In experiments on **observational learning**, Albert Bandura and his colleagues conducted experiments (e.g., Bandura et al., 1963) that show that we can acquire skills by observing the behavior of others. Observational learning occurs when, as children, we watch our parents cook, clean, or repair a broken appliance. Observational learning takes place when we watch teachers solve problems on the blackboard or hear them speak in a foreign language. Observational learning is not mechanically acquired

To what degree are gender roles learned by observation?

through reinforcement. We can learn through observation without engaging in overt responses at all. It appears sufficient to pay attention to the behavior. We may need some practice to refine the skills we acquire. We may also allow these skills to lie dormant or latent. For example, we may not imitate aggressive behavior unless we are provoked and believe that we are more likely to be rewarded than punished for it.

In the terminology of observational learning, a person who engages in a response that is imitated is a **model**. When we see modeled behavior being reinforced, we are said to be *vicariously* reinforced. Engaging in the behavior thus becomes more likely for us as well as for the model.

Violence in the Media and Aggression

We learn by observing parents and peers, attending school, reading books, and watching media such as television and films. Movies and the Internet are also key sources of informal observational learning. Children are routinely exposed to scenes of murder, beating, and sexual assault—just by turning on the TV set (Huesmann et al., 2003). If a child watches two to four hours of TV a day, she or he will have seen 8,000 murders and another 100,000 acts of violence *by the time she or he has finished elementary school* (Eron, 2000). Are kids less likely to be exposed to violence by going to the movies? No. One study found that virtually all G-rated animated films have scenes of violence, with a mean duration of nine to ten minutes per film (Yokota & Thompson, 2000). Other media with violent content include films, music, music videos, video games, the Internet, and comic books (Anderson, 2004).

Bandura: Effects of Violence in the Media

A classic experiment by Bandura, Ross, and Ross (1963) suggests the influence of aggressive models. One group of preschool children observed a film of an adult model hitting and kicking an inflated Bobo doll, while a control group saw an aggression-free film. The experimental and control groups were then left alone in a room with the same doll, as hidden observers recorded their behavior. The children who had observed the aggressive model showed significantly more aggressive behavior toward the doll themselves (see Figure 6.8 on the following page). Many children imitated bizarre attacks they would not have thought up themselves.

Violence tends to be glamorized in the media. Superheroes battle villains who are trying to destroy or take over the world. Violence is often portrayed as having only temporary or minimal effects. (How often

has Wile E. Coyote fallen from a cliff and been pounded into the ground by a boulder, only to bounce back and pursue the Road Runner once more?) In the great majority of violent TV shows, there is no remorse, criticism, or penalty for violent behavior. Few TV programs show harmful long-term consequences of aggressive behavior.

model
an organism that engages in a response that is then imitated by another organism

Seeing the perpetrator of the violence go unpunished increases the chances that the child will act aggressively (Krcmar & Cooke, 2001). Children may not even view death as much of a problem. As killer Evan Ramsey said, being shot might reduce a person's "health factor." How often do videogame characters "die"— only to be reborn to fight again?

Why all this violence? Simple: Violence sells. But does violence do more than sell? That is, does media violence *cause* real violence? If so, what can parents and educators do to prevent the fictional from spilling over into the real world?

Fiction

Actually, numerous scientific connections have been established between violence in the media and real-life aggression.

Consensus on the Effects of Violence in the Media?

In any event, most organizations of health professionals agree that media violence contributes to aggression (Anderson, 2004; Huesmann et al., 2003). Consider a number of ways in which depictions of violence make such a contribution:

- *Observational learning.* Children learn from observation. TV violence models aggressive "skills," which children may acquire. Media violence also provides viewers with aggressive scripts— that is, ideas about how to behave in situations like those they have observed.

- *Disinhibition.* Punishment inhibits behavior. Conversely, media violence may disinhibit aggressive behavior, especially when media characters "get away" with violence or are rewarded for it.

- *Increased arousal.* Media violence and aggressive video games increase viewers' emotional arousal. That is, media "work them up." We are more likely to be aggressive when we are aroused.

- *Priming of aggressive thoughts and memories.* Media violence triggers aggressive ideas and memories.

- *Habituation.* We become "habituated to," or used to, repeated stimuli. Repeated exposure to TV violence may decrease viewers' sensitivity to real violence. If children come to perceive violence as the norm, they may become more tolerant of it and place less value on restraining aggressive urges.

Figure 6.8

Classic Research on the Imitation of Aggressive Models

On the other hand, viewers are more likely to imitate media violence when they identify with the characters and when the portrayal of violence is realistic (Huesmann et al., 2003). Therefore, viewers may be more likely to imitate violence when the perpetrator looks like them and lives in a similar environment than when it is perpetrated by Wile E. Coyote.

Playing violent video games increases aggressive thoughts and behavior in the laboratory (Anderson, 2003, 2004). It is also connected with a history of juvenile delinquency. However, males are relatively more likely than females to act aggressively after playing violent video games and are more likely to see the world as a hostile place (Bartholow & Anderson, 2002). But students who obtain higher grades are *less* likely than their lower-achieving peers to act aggressively after exposure to violent media games. Thus, gender roles, possible biological gender differences, and psychological factors such as achievement motivation also figure into the effects of media violence.

There seems to be a circular relationship between exposure to media violence and aggressive behavior (Anderson & Dill, 2000; Anderson et al., 2003; Haridakis, 2002). Yes, violence in the media contributes to aggressive behavior, but aggressive youngsters are also more likely to seek out this kind of entertainment. Figure 6.9 explores the possible connections between media violence and aggressive behavior.

The family also affects the likelihood that children will imitate media violence. Studies find that parental substance abuse, paternal physical punishments, and single parenting contribute to the likelihood of aggression in early childhood (Brook et al., 2001; Gupta et al., 2001). Parental rejection and use of physical punishment further increase the likelihood of aggression in children (Eron, 1982). These family factors suggest that the parents of aggressive children may be absent or

unlikely to help young children understand that the kinds of socially inappropriate behaviors they see in the media are not for them. A harsh home life may also confirm the TV viewer's or game player's vision of the world as a violent place.

If children believe violence to be inappropriate for them, they will be less likely to act aggressively, even if they have acquired aggressive skills from exposure to the media or other sources. It would be of little use to talk about learning if we couldn't remember what we learn from second to second or from day to day. In the next chapter, we turn our attention to memory. In Chapter 8, we see how learning is intertwined with thinking, language, and intelligence.

Teaching Children *Not* to Imitate Media Violence

Children are going to be exposed to media violence—if not in Saturday-morning cartoon shows, then in evening dramas and in the news. Or they'll hear about violence from friends, watch other children get into fights, or read about violence in the newspapers. If all those sources of violence were somehow hidden from view, they would learn about violence in *Hamlet, Macbeth,* and the Bible. The notion of preventing children from being exposed to violent models may be impractical.

What, then, should be done? Parents and educators can do many things to tone down the impact of media violence. Children who watch violent shows may act less aggressively when they are informed that:

- The violent behavior they observe in the media does not represent the behavior of most people.

- The apparently aggressive behaviors they watch are not real. They reflect camera tricks, special effects, and stunts.

- Most people resolve conflicts by nonviolent means.

- The real-life consequences of violence are harmful to the victim and often to the aggressor.

Despite our history of evolutionary forces, and despite the fact that in most species, successful aggression usually wins individuals the right to transmit their genes to future generations, humans are thinking beings. If children consider violence to be inappropriate for them, they will be less likely to act aggressively, even when they have acquired aggressive skills from exposure to the media or other sources.

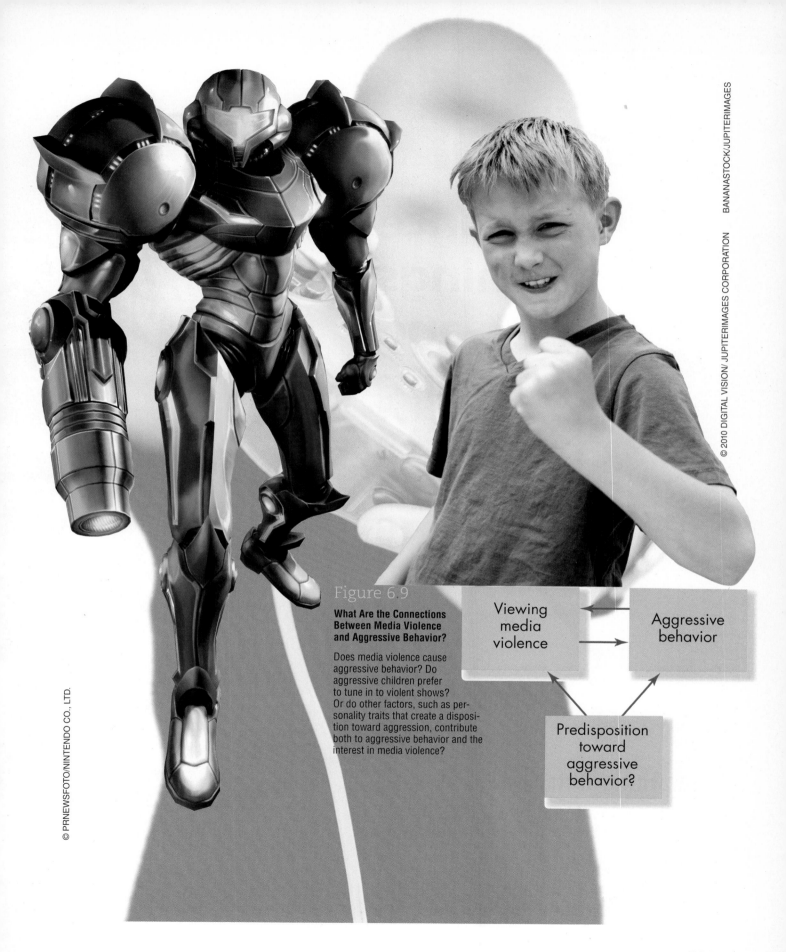

Figure 6.9

What Are the Connections Between Media Violence and Aggressive Behavior?

Does media violence cause aggressive behavior? Do aggressive children prefer to tune in to violent shows? Or do other factors, such as personality traits that create a disposition toward aggression, contribute both to aggressive behavior and the interest in media violence?

Viewing media violence

Aggressive behavior

Predisposition toward aggressive behavior?

Memory:
Remembrance of Things Past—and Future

Learning Outcomes

LO **1** Define memory and differentiate between types of memories

LO **2** Explain the process of memory

LO **3** Explain the stages of memory

LO **4** Identify contributors to forgetting

LO **5** Describe the biological aspects of memory

> **" Without your memory, there is no past. "**

Jeff would never forget his sudden loss of memory. He watched in horror as his flip phone slipped from his pocket and fell to the floor of the Blockbuster store in Boston. Before he could grab it, it shattered into pieces. A New York college student, Jeff experienced the trauma of phone loss on his winter break.

Why was the loss traumatic? Why was it a memory problem? Simple: There was no way for Jeff to retrieve his phone book. "I was at the store and it was snowing out and I suddenly realized that I had no way of getting in touch with anyone," he explains (Metz, 2005). Jeff now copies every cell-phone entry in a little black book—made of paper. Other people back up their phone books—and their pictures and downloads—on servers provided by cellular telephone operating companies or cell-phone manufacturers.

What's the problem with remembering all those phone numbers? The answer lies partly in their length. Psychologist George Miller (1956) researched the amount of information people can keep in mind at once, and he found that the average person is comfortable with digesting about seven digits at a time. Most people have little trouble recalling five pieces of information, as in a ZIP code. Some can remember nine, which is, for most, an upper limit. So seven pieces of information, plus or minus one or two, is the "magic" number.

This chapter is all about the "backup assistant" in your brain—your memory. Without your memory, there is no past. Without your memory, experience is trivial and learning is lost. Let us see what psychologists have learned about the ways in which we remember things—beyond keying them into our handheld device's memory storage.

Five Memory Challenges

Let's challenge your memory. This is not an actual memory test of the sort used by psychologists to determine whether people's memory functioning is within normal limits. Instead, it will provide you with some insight into how your memory works and may also be fun.

explicit memory memory that clearly and distinctly expresses (explicates) specific information

episodic memory memories of events experienced by a person or that take place in the person's presence

semantic memory general knowledge, as opposed to episodic memory

implicit memory memory that is suggested (implied) but not plainly expressed, as illustrated in the things that people *do* but do not state clearly

Directions: Find four sheets of blank paper and number them 1 through 4. Also use a watch with a second hand. Then follow these instructions:

1. Following are ten letters. Look at them for fifteen seconds. Later in the chapter I will ask you if you can write them on sheet number 1. (No cheating! Don't do it now.)

THUNSTOFAM

2. Look at these nine figures for thirty seconds. Then try to draw them in the proper sequence on sheet number 2, right after you have finished looking at them. (We'll talk about your drawings later.)

3. Look at the list of seventeen letters for sixty seconds and then see whether you can reproduce it on sheet number 3.

GMC-BSI-BMA-TTC-IAF-BI

4. Which of these pennies is an accurate reproduction of the Lincoln penny? This time there's nothing to draw on another sheet; just circle or put a check mark by the penny that you think resembles the ones you see every day.

5. Examine the following drawings for one minute. Then copy the *names* of the figures on sheet number 4. When you're finished, just keep reading. Soon I'll be asking you to draw those figures.

○—○	✕	⟨	▷—◁
Eyeglasses	Hourglass	Seven	Gun

LO¹ Memory Systems

Jeff remembered a thing he had personally done, like drop his cell phone in Boston on a blustery day in January. Remembering dropping one's cell phone is an *episodic memory*—a memory of an event in one's life. According to psychologists who have extensively researched memory, episodic memory is one kind of memory system (Dobbins et al., 2004; Schacter, 2000). There are several, most of which address information from the past, but one—prospective memory—which involves keeping the things we intend to do in mind. Let us begin by distinguishing between explicit memories and implicit memories. As you will see, for all practical purposes, implicit memories may last for a lifetime.

Explicit Versus Implicit Memories

Explicit Memory

What is meant by explicit memory? Explicit memory—also referred to as *declarative memory*—is memory for specific information. Things that are *explicit* are clear, or clearly stated or explained. The use of the term *declarative* indicates that these memories state or reveal (i.e., *declare*) specific information. The information may be autobiographical or refer to general knowledge.

Two kinds of explicit memories are described by psychologist Endel Tulving (1985): episodic and semantic. They are identified according to the type of information they hold.

Episodic Memory (I remember...) What is meant by episodic memory? Episodic memories are types of explicit memories. They are memories of the things that happen to us or take place in our presence. Episodic memory is also referred to as *autobiographical memory*. Your memories of what you ate for breakfast and of what your professor said in class today are episodic memories. We tend to use the phrase "I remember ..." when we are referring to episodic memories, as in "I remember the blizzard of 2004."

Semantic Memory (I know...) What is meant by semantic memory? General knowledge is referred to as **semantic memory**—another kind of explicit memory. *Semantics* concerns meanings. You can "know" that the United States has fifty states without visiting them and personally adding them up. You "know" who authored *Hamlet,* although you were not looking over Shakespeare's shoulder as he did so. These are examples of semantic memory.

Your future recollection that there are several memory systems is more likely to be semantic than episodic. In other words, you are more likely to "know" that there are several types of memory than to recall where you were and how you were sitting. We are more likely to say "I know ..." in reference to semantic memories, as in "I *know* about—" (or "I heard about—") "—the blizzard of 1898."

Implicit Memory

What is meant by implicit memory? Implicit memory—also referred to as *nondeclarative memory*—is memory of how to perform a procedure or skill; it is the act itself, doing something, like riding a bike, accessing your cell-phone contacts list, and texting a message (Schacter et al., 1993). Implicit memories are suggested (or implied) but not plainly stated or verbally expressed. Implicit memories are illustrated by the things that people *do* but not by the things they state clearly. Implicit memories involve procedures and skills, cognitive and physical, and are also referred to as *procedural* or *skill memories.*

Implicit memories can endure even when we have not used them for years. Getting to class "by habit"—without paying attention to landmarks or directions—is another instance of implicit memory. If someone asked you what two times two is, the number four would probably "pop" into mind without conscious calculation. After going over the alphabet or multiplication tables hundreds of times, our memory of them becomes automatic or implicit. We need not focus on them to use them.

Your memory of the alphabet or the multiplication tables reflects repetition that makes associations automatic. This phenomenon is called priming. Brain imaging shows that priming makes it possible for people to carry out mental tasks with less neural activity (Savage et al., 2001; Schacter et al., 2004). Years of priming help people make complete words out of the word fragments (Schacter et al., 1999). Even though the cues in the following fragments are limited, you might make them into words:

PYGY   TXT   BUFL

Sample answers are "pygmy," "text," and "buffalo." Can you think of others?

Daniel Schacter (1992) illustrates implicit memory with the story of a woman with amnesia who was wandering the streets. The police picked her up and found that she could not remember who she was and that she had no identification. After fruitless interviewing, the police hit on the idea of asking her to dial phone numbers—"any number at all." When asked for the phone numbers of people she knew, she had had no answer. She could not *declare* her mother's phone number. She could not make the number *explicit.* She could not even remember her mother's name, or whether she had a mother. But dialing her mother's phone number was a habit, and she did it "on automatic pilot."

ERIK ISAKSON / GETTY IMAGES

Retrospective Memory Versus Prospective Memory

Retrospective memory is the recalling of information that has been previously learned. *Episodic, semantic,* and *implicit memories* involve remembering things that were learned. Prospective memory refers to remembering to do things in the future, such as remembering to pay your bills or to withdraw some cash.

Most of us have had failures of prospective memory in which we feel we were supposed to do something but can't remember what. Prospective memory may fail when we are preoccupied, distracted, or "stressed out" about time (Schacter, 1999).

There are various kinds of prospective memory tasks. *Habitual tasks* such as getting to class on time are easier to remember than occasional tasks such as meeting someone for coffee at an arbitrary time (d'Ydewalle et al., 1999). Motivation also plays a role. You are more likely to remember the coffee date if the person you are meeting excites you. Psychologists also distinguish between event-based and time-based prospective memory tasks (Fortin et al., 2002). *Event-based tasks* are triggered by events, such as remembering to take one's medicine at breakfast or to brush one's teeth after eating. *Time-based tasks* are to be performed at a certain time or after a certain amount of time has elapsed between occurrences, such as tuning in to a favorite news program at 7:30 p.m. or taking a pill every four hours (Marsh et al., 2005).

An age-related decline takes place in retrospective and prospective memories (Brigman & Cherry, 2002; Reese &

priming
the activation of specific associations in memory, often as a result of repetition and without making a conscious effort to access the memory

retrospective memory
memory for past events, activities, and learning experiences, as shown by explicit (episodic and semantic) and implicit memories

prospective memory
memory to perform an act in the future, as at a certain time or when a certain event occurs

Truth

Although the woman did not "know" what she was doing, she dialed her mother's number.

encoding
modifying information so that it can be placed in memory; the first stage of information processing

storage
the maintenance of information over time; the second stage of information processing

maintenance rehearsal
mental repetition of information to keep it in memory

metamemory
self-awareness of the ways in which memory functions, allowing the person to encode, store, and retrieve information effectively

elaborative rehearsal
the kind of coding in which new information is related to information that is already known

Cherry, 2002). The decline in older adults may be related to their speed of cognitive processing rather than the "loss" of information per se. In the case of prospective memory, older adults take longer to respond to the cues or reminders (West & Craik, 1999).

Moods and attitudes affect prospective memory (Villa & Abeles, 2000). For example, depressed people are less likely to push to remind themselves to do what they intend to do (Rude et al., 1999).

Before moving to the next section, turn to sheet number 4 and draw the figures from memory. Hold onto the drawings. We'll talk about them soon.

LO² Processes of Memory

Both psychologists and computer scientists speak of processing information. Think of using a computer to write a term paper. Once the system is up and operating, you begin to enter information. You can enter information by, for example, typing alphanumeric characters on a keyboard or—in the case of voice recognition technology—speaking. But if you were to do some major surgery on your computer and open up its memory, you wouldn't find these characters or sounds inside it. This is because the computer is programmed to change the characters or sounds—the information you have entered—into a form that can be placed in its electronic memory. Similarly, when we perceive information, we must change it into a form that can be remembered if we are to place it in our memory.

Encoding

Information about the outside world reaches our senses in the form of physical and chemical stimuli. The first stage of information processing is changing information so that we can place it in memory: encoding. *What is the role of encoding in memory?* When we encode information, we transform it into psychological formats that can be

represented mentally. To do so, we commonly use visual, acoustic, and semantic codes.

Let us illustrate the uses of coding by referring to the list of letters you first saw in the section on challenges to memory. Try to write the letters on sheet number 1. Go on, take a minute and then come back.

If you had used a *visual code* to try to remember the list, you would have mentally represented it as a picture. That is, you would have maintained—or attempted to maintain—a mental image of the letters.

You may also have decided to read the list of letters to yourself—that is, to silently say them in sequence: "t," "h," "u," and so on. By so doing, you would have been using an *acoustic code*, or representing the stimuli as a sequence of sounds. You may also have read the list as a three-syllable word, "thun-sto-fam." This is an acoustic code, but it also involves the "meaning" of the letters, in the sense that you are interpreting the list as a word. This approach has elements of a semantic code.

Semantic codes represent stimuli in terms of their meaning. Our ten letters were meaningless in and of themselves. However, they can also serve as an acronym—a term made up of the first letters of a phrase that is pronounced as a word—for the familiar phrase "THe UNited STates OF AMerica." This observation lends them meaning.

Storage

The second memory process is *storage*. *What is the role of storage in memory?* Storage means maintaining information over time. If you were given the task of storing the list of letters—that is, told to remember it—how would you attempt to place it in storage? One way would be by maintenance rehearsal—by mentally repeating the list, or saying it to yourself. Our awareness of the functioning of our memory, referred to by psychologists as metamemory, becomes more sophisticated as we develop.

You could also encode the list of letters by relating it to something that you already know. This coding is called elaborative rehearsal. You are "elaborating" or extending the semantic meaning of the letters you are trying to remember. For example, as mentioned above, the list of ten letters is an acronym for "The United States of America." That is, you take the first two letters of each of the words in the phrase and string them together to make up the ten letters of THUNSTOFAM. If you had recognized this, storage of the list of letters might have been almost instantaneous, and it would probably have been permanent. But enough maintenance rehearsal can do the job.

Retrieval

The third memory process is *retrieval*. *What is the role of retrieval in memory?* The retrieval of stored information means locating it and returning it to consciousness. With well-known information such as our names and occupations, retrieval is effortless and rapid. But when we are trying to remember large amounts of information, or information that is not perfectly understood, retrieval can be difficult or fail. It is easiest to retrieve information stored in a computer by using the name of the file. Similarly, retrieval of information from our memories requires knowledge of the proper cues.

If you had encoded THUNSTOFAM as a three-syllable word, your retrieval strategy would involve recollection of the word and rules for decoding. In other words, you would say the "word" *thun-sto-fam* and then decode it by spelling it out. You might err in that "thun" sounds like "thumb" and "sto" could also be spelled "stow." However, using the semantic code, or recognition of the acronym for "The United States of America," could lead to flawless recollection.

I predicted that you would immediately and permanently store the list if you recognized it as an acronym. Here, too, there would be recollection (of the name of a nation) and rules for decoding. That is, to "remember" the ten letters, you would have to envision the phrase ("The United States of America") and read off the first two letters of each word. In this case, you are actually reconstructing the list of ten letters.

But what if you were not able to remember the list of ten letters? What would have gone wrong? In terms of the three processes of memory, it could be that you had (1) not encoded the list in a useful way, (2) not entered the encoded information into storage, or (3) stored the information but forgotten the cues for remembering it—such as the phrase "The United States of America" or the rule for decoding the phrase.

You may have noticed that we have come a long way into this chapter, but I have not yet *defined* memory. No apologies—we weren't ready. Now that we have explored some basic concepts, let us give it a try: Memory is the processes by which information is encoded, stored, and retrieved.

LO³ Stages of Memory

William James (1890) was intrigued by the fact that some memories are unreliable. They would "go in one ear and out the other," while other memories stuck for a lifetime. The world is a dazzling array of sights and sounds and other sources of sensory information, but only some of it is remembered. Psychologists Richard Atkinson and Richard Shiffrin (1968) suggested a model for how some information is lost immediately, other information is held briefly, and still other information is held for a lifetime. *What is the Atkinson–Shiffrin model of memory?* As shown in Figure 7.1 on page 146, they proposed three stages of memory that determine whether (and how long) information is retained: *sensory memory, short-term memory* (STM), and *long-term memory* (LTM).

Sensory Memory

When we look at a visual stimulus, our impressions may seem fluid enough. Actually, however, they consist of a series of eye fixations referred to as *saccadic eye movements*. These movements jump from one point to another about four times each second. Yet the visual sensations seem continuous, or stream-like, because of sensory memory. Sensory memory is the type or stage of memory that is first encountered by a stimulus. Although sensory memory holds impressions briefly, it is long enough so that a series of perceptions seem to be connected. *How does sensory memory function?*

To explain the functioning of sensory memory, let us return to our list of letters: THUNSTOFAM. If the list were flashed on a screen for a fraction of a second, the visual impression, or memory trace, of the stimulus would also last for only a fraction of a second afterward. Psychologists speak of the memory trace of the list as being held in a visual *sensory register*.

If the letters had been flashed on a screen for, say, a tenth of a second, your ability to remember them on the basis of sensory memory alone would be limited. Your memory would be based on a single eye fixation, and the trace of the image would vanish before a single second had passed. A century ago, psychologist William McDougall (1904) engaged in research in which he showed people one to twelve letters

retrieval
the location of stored information and its return to consciousness; the third stage of information processing

memory
the processes by which information is encoded, stored, and retrieved

sensory memory
the type or stage of memory first encountered by a stimulus

memory trace
an assumed change in the nervous system that reflects the impression made by a stimulus

arranged in rows—just long enough to allow a single eye fixation. Under these conditions, people could typically remember only four or five letters. Thus, recollection of THUNSTOFAM, a list of ten letters arranged in a single row, would probably depend on whether one had encoded it so that it could be processed further.

George Sperling (1960) modified McDougall's experimental method and showed that there is a difference between what people can see and what they can report. McDougall had used a *whole-report procedure,* in which people were asked to report every letter they saw in the array. Sperling used a modified *partial-report procedure,* in which people were asked to report the contents of one of three rows of letters. In a typical procedure, Sperling

flashed three rows of letters like the following on a screen for 50 milliseconds (1/20th of a second):

$$A\ G\ R\ E$$
$$V\ L\ S\ B$$
$$N\ K\ B\ T$$

Using the whole-report procedure, people could report an average of four letters from the entire display (one out of three). But if immediately after presenting the display Sperling pointed an arrow at a row he wanted viewers to report, they usually reported most of the letters in the row successfully.

If Sperling presented six letters arrayed in two rows, people could usually report either row without error. If people were flashed three rows of four letters

Figure 7.1

Three Stages of Memory: The Atkinson–Shiffrin Model

The Atkinson–Shiffrin model proposes that there are three stages of memory: (a) sensory memory, (b) short-term memory, and (c) long-term memory. Part A shows that sensory information impacts the registers of sensory memory. Memory traces are held briefly in sensory memory before decaying. If we attend to the information, much of it can be transferred to short-term memory (STM). Part B Information may be maintained in STM through maintenance rehearsal or elaborative rehearsal. Otherwise, it may decay or be displaced. Part C: Once information is transferred to long-term memory (LTM), it may be filed away indefinitely. However, if the information in LTM is organized poorly, or if we cannot find cues to retrieve it, it can be lost.

Go to CourseMate for PSYCH at www.cengagebrain.com to access an interactive version of this figure.

Sensory memory   Short-term memory   Long-term memory

Rehearsal

Sensory input   Attention   Storage   Retrieval

A. Forgetting occurs through decay

B. Forgetting occurs through decay or displacement

C. Forgetting occurs through retrieval failure

each—a total of twelve—they reported correctly an average of three of four letters in the designated row, suggesting that about nine of the twelve letters had been perceived.

Sperling found that the amount of time that elapsed before he pointed to the row to be reported affected people's memory. If he delayed pointing for a few fractions of a second after showing the letters, people were less successful in reporting the letters in the row. If he allowed a full second to elapse, the arrow did not help people remember at all. Sperling concluded that the memory trace of visual stimuli *decays* within a second (see Figure 7.1). With a single eye fixation, people can *see* most of a display of twelve letters clearly, as shown by their ability to immediately read off most of the letters in a designated row. Yet as fractions of a second are elapsing, the trace of the letters is fading. By the time a full second elapses, the trace is gone.

Iconic Memory

Psychologists believe we possess a sensory register for each sense. The mental representations of visual stimuli are referred to as icons. The sensory register that holds icons is labeled iconic memory. Iconic memories are accurate, photographic memories. But these memories are brief. What most of us usually think of as a photographic memory—the ability to retain exact mental representations of visual stimuli over long periods—is technically termed eidetic imagery. Only a few people are capable of eidetic imagery.

Iconic Memory and Saccadic Eye Movements

As mentioned previously, saccadic eye movements occur about four times a second. But iconic memory holds icons for up to a second. For this reason, the flow of visual information seems smooth and continuous. Your impression that the words you are reading flow across the page, rather than jumping across in spurts, is a product of your iconic memory. Similarly, motion pictures present sixteen to twenty-two separate frames, or still images, each second, but iconic memory allows you to perceive the imagery in the film as being seamless (G. R. Loftus, 1983).

Truth

Those of us who see and mentally represent visual stimuli do have "photographic memories."

Echoic Memory

Mental representations of sounds, or auditory stimuli, are called echoes. Echoic memory is the sensory register that holds echoes.

The memory traces of auditory stimuli—echoes—can last for several seconds, many times longer than the traces of visual stimuli (icons). This difference is one of the reasons that acoustic codes aid in the retention of information that has been presented visually—or why saying the letters or syllables of THUNSTOFAM makes the list easier to remember.

Short-Term Memory

Imagine that you are completing a writing assignment and you key or speak words and phrases into your word-processing program. They appear on your monitor as a sign that your computer has them in *memory*. Your word-processing program allows you to add words, delete words, check whether they are spelled correctly, add images, and move paragraphs from place to place. Although you can manipulate the information in your computer's memory, it isn't saved. It hasn't been entered into storage. If the program or the computer crashes, the information is gone. The computer's memory is a short-term affair. To maintain a long-term connection with the information, you have to save it. Saving it means naming it—hopefully with a name that you will remember so that you can later find and retrieve the information—and instructing your computer to save it (keep it in storage until told otherwise).

If you focus on a stimulus in the sensory register, you will tend to retain it in your own short-term memory—also referred to as working memory—for a minute or so after the trace of the stimulus decays. *How does short-term memory function?* As one researcher describes it, "Working memory is the

> The memory traces of auditory stimuli —echoes—can last for several seconds, many times longer than the traces of visual stimuli (icons).

icon
a mental representation of a visual stimulus that is held briefly in sensory memory

iconic memory
the sensory register that briefly holds mental representations of visual stimuli

eidetic imagery
the maintenance of detailed visual memories over several minutes

echo
a mental representation of an auditory stimulus (sound) that is held briefly in sensory memory

echoic memory
the sensory register that briefly holds mental representations of auditory stimuli

short-term memory
the type or stage of memory that can hold information for up to a minute or so after the trace of the stimulus decays

working memory
another term for *short-term memory*

serial-position effect
the tendency to recall more accurately the first and last items in a series

mental glue that links a thought through time from its beginning to its end" (Goldman-Rakic, 1995). When you are given a phone number by the information operator and write it down or immediately dial the number, you are retaining the number in your short-term memory. When you are told the name of someone at a party and then use that name immediately in addressing that person, you are retaining the name in short-term memory. In short-term memory, the image tends to fade significantly after ten to twelve seconds if it is not repeated or rehearsed. It is possible to focus on maintaining a visual image in the short-term memory, but it is more common to encode visual stimuli as sounds, or auditory stimuli. Then the sounds can be rehearsed, or repeated.

Once information is in our short-term memories, we can work on it. Like the information in the word-processing program, we can manipulate it. But it isn't necessarily saved. If we don't do something to save—such as write down a new telephone number or key it into your cell phone's contact list—it can be gone forever.

You need to rehearse new information to "save" it, but you may need only the proper cue to retrieve information from long-term memory.

Let us now return to the task of remembering the first list of letters in the challenges to memory at the beginning of the chapter. If you had encoded the letters as the three-syllable word THUN-STO-FAM, you would probably have recalled them by mentally rehearsing (saying

to yourself) the three-syllable "word" and then spelling it out from the sounds. A few minutes later, if someone asked whether the letters had been uppercase (THUNSTOFAM) or lowercase (thunstofam), you might not have been able to answer with confidence. You used an acoustic code to help recall the list, and uppercase and lowercase letters sound alike.

Because it can be pronounced, THUNSTOFAM is not too difficult to retain in short-term memory. But what if the list of letters had been TBXLFNTSDK? This list of letters cannot be pronounced as it is. You would have to find a complex acronym to code these letters, and do so within a fraction of a second—most likely an impossible task. To aid recall, you would probably choose to try to repeat the letters rapidly—to read each one as many times as possible before the memory trace fades. You might visualize each letter as you say it and try to get back to it (that is, to run through the entire list) before it decays.

Let us assume that you encoded the letters as sounds and then rehearsed the sounds.

When asked to report the list, you might mistakenly say T-V-X-L-F-N-T-S-T-K. This would be an understandable error because the incorrect V and T sounds are similar, respectively, to the correct B and D sounds.

The Serial-Position Effect

If asked to recall the list of letters TBXLFNTSDK, you would be likely to recall the first and last letters in the series, T and K, more accurately than the others. *Why are we most likely to remember the first and last items in a list?* The tendency to recall the first and last items in a series is known as the **serial-position effect.** This effect may occur because we

Memorizing a Script by Rehearsing Echoic Memories
As actors work on memorizing scripts, they first encode visual information (printed words) as echoes (their corresponding sounds within the brain). Then they commit the echoes to memory by rehearsing (repeating) them, referring back to the visual information as necessary. Eventually, the lines of other actors become cues that trigger memory of an actor's own lines.

pay more attention to the first and last stimuli in a series. They serve as the boundaries for the other stimuli. It may also be that the first items are likely to be rehearsed more frequently (repeated more times) than other items. The last items are likely to have been rehearsed most recently and hence are most likely to be retained in short-term memory.

Chunking

Rapidly rehearsing ten meaningless letters is not an easy task. With TBXLFNTSDK there are ten discrete elements, or **chunks**, of information that must be kept in short-term memory. When we encode THUNSTOFAM as three syllables, there are only three chunks to memorize at once.

As noted at the beginning of the chapter, psychologist George Miller (1956) found that the average person is comfortable with remembering about seven integers at a time, the number of integers in a telephone number. *Is seven a magic number, or did the phone company get lucky?*

Businesses pay the phone company hefty premiums so that they can attain numbers with two or three zeroes or repeated digits—for example, 592-2000 or 277-3333. These numbers include fewer chunks of information and so are easier to remember. Customer recollection of business phone numbers increases sales. One financial services company uses the toll-free number CALL-IRA, which reduces the task to two chunks of information that also happen to be meaningfully related (semantically coded) to the nature of the business.

Return to the third challenge to memory presented earlier. Were you able to remember the six groups of letters? Would your task have been simpler if you had grouped them differently? How about moving the dashes forward by a letter, so that they read GM-CBS-IBM-ATT-CIA-FBI? If we do this, we have the same list of letters, but we also have six chunks of information that can be coded semantically (according to what they mean). You may have also been able to generate the list by remembering a rule, such as "big corporations and government agencies."

Reconsider the second challenge to memory presented earlier. You were asked to remember nine chunks of visual information. Perhaps you could have used the acoustic codes "L" and "Square" for chunks three and five, but no obvious codes are available for the seven other chunks. Now look at Figure 7.2. If you had recognized that the elements in the challenge could be arranged as the familiar tic-tac-toe grid, remembering the nine elements might have required two chunks of information. The first would have been the men-

tal image of the grid, and the second would have been the rule for decoding: Each element corresponds to the shape of a section of the grid if read like words on a page (from upper left to lower right). The number sequence 1 through 9 would not in itself present a problem, because you learned this series by rote many years ago and have rehearsed it in countless calculations since then.

chunk
a stimulus or group of stimuli that are perceived as a discrete piece of information

Interference in Short-Term Memory

In a classic experiment with college students, Lloyd and Margaret Peterson (1959) demonstrated how prevention of rehearsal can wreak havoc with short-term memory. They asked students to remember three-letter combinations such as HGB—normally, three easy chunks of information. They then had the students count backward from an arbitrary number, such as 181, by threes (that is, 181, 178, 175, 172, and so on). The students were told to stop counting and to report the letter sequence after the intervals of time shown in Figure 7.3 on page 150. The percentage of correctly recalled letter combinations fell dramatically within seconds. After eighteen seconds of interference, counting had dislodged the letter sequences in almost all students' memories.

Figure 7.2

A Familiar Grid
The nine drawings in the second challenge to memory form this familiar tic-tac-toe grid when the numbers are placed inside them and they are arranged in order. This method for recalling the shapes collapses nine chunks of information into two. One is the tic-tac-toe grid. The second is the rule for decoding the drawings from the grid.

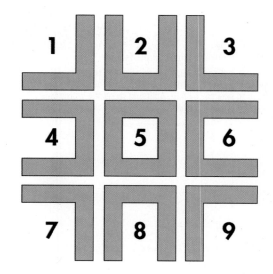

displace
in memory theory, to cause information to be lost from short-term memory by adding new information

long-term memory
the type or stage of memory capable of relatively permanent storage

repression
in Freud's psychodynamic theory, the ejection of anxiety-evoking ideas from conscious awareness

schema
a way of mentally representing the world, such as a belief or an expectation, that can influence perception of persons, objects, and situations

Psychologists say that the appearance of new information in short-term memory displaces the old information. Remember: Only a few bits of information can be retained in short-term memory at the same time.

Long-Term Memory

Long-term memory is the third stage of information processing (Refer back to Figure 7.1.). Think of your long-term memory as a vast storehouse of information containing names, dates, places, what Johnny did to you in second grade, and what Susan said about you when you were twelve. *How does long-term memory function?*

Some psychologists (Freud was one) used to believe that nearly all of our perceptions and ideas are stored permanently. We might not be able to retrieve all of them, however.

Some memories might be "lost" because of lack of proper cues, or they might be kept unconscious by the forces of **repression**. Adherents to this view often pointed to the work of neurosurgeon Wilder Penfield (1969). When parts of their brains were electrically stimulated, many of Penfield's patients reported the appearance of images that had something of the feel of memories.

Today most psychologists view this notion as exaggerated. Memory researcher Elizabeth Loftus,

for example, notes that the "memories" stimulated by Penfield's probes lacked detail and were sometimes incorrect (Loftus & Loftus, 1980; E. F. Loftus, 1983). Now let us consider some other questions about long-term memory.

How Accurate Are Long-Term Memories?

Psychologist Elizabeth Loftus notes that memories are distorted by our biases and needs—by the ways in which we conceptualize our worlds. We represent much of our world in the form of **schemas**. A *schema* is a way of mentally representing the world, such as a belief or expectation, that can influence our perception of persons, objects, and situations.

Now, retrieve sheet number 4. You drew the figures "from memory" according to instructions on page 142. Now look at Figure 7.4. Are your drawings closer in form to those in group 1 or to those in group 2? I wouldn't be surprised if they were more like those in group 1—if, for example, your first drawing looked more like eyeglasses than a dumbbell. After all, they were labeled like the drawings in group 1. The labels serve as *schemas* for the drawings—ways of organizing your knowledge of them—and these schemas may have influenced your recollections.

How Much Information Can Be Stored in Long-Term Memory?

How many "gigabytes of storage" are there in your most personal computer—your brain? Unlike a computer, the human ability to store information is, for all practical purposes, unlimited (Goldman-Rakic et al., 2000b). Even the largest hard drives fill up when we save Web pages, photos, songs, and movies. Yet how many "movies" of the past have you saved in your own long-term memory? How many thousands of scenes and stories can you rerun at will? And, assuming that you have an intact sensory system, the movies in your personal storage bins not only have color and sound, but also aromas, tactile sensations, and more. *Your long-term memory is a biochemical "hard drive" with no known limits on the amount of information it can store.*

New information may replace older information in short-term memory, but there is no evidence that long-term memories—those in "storage"—are lost by

> " Long-term memory is reconstructive rather than photographic. "

Figure 7.3

The Effect of Interference on Short-Term Memory

In this experiment, college students were asked to remember a series of three letters while they counted backward by threes. After just three seconds, retention was cut by half. Ability to recall the words was almost completely lost by fifteen seconds.

Fiction

It has *not* been shown that all our experiences are permanently imprinted on the brain.

Figures shown	Group 1	Group 2

Figure 7.4

Memory as Reconstructive

In their classic experiment, Carmichael, Hogan, and Walter (1932) showed people the figures in the left box and made remarks as suggested in the other boxes. For example, the experimenter might say, "This drawing looks like eyeglasses [or a dumbbell]." When people later reconstructed the drawings, they were influenced by the labels.

displacement. Long-term memories may endure a lifetime. Now and then it may seem that we have forgotten, or "lost," a long-term memory such as the names of elementary-school classmates, yet it may be that we cannot find the proper cues to retrieve them. However, if you drive by your elementary school (a cue) you might suddenly recall the long-lost names of schoolteachers.

Levels of Processing Information

People who use elaborative rehearsal to remember things are *processing information at a deeper level* than people who use maintenance rehearsal. *What is the levels-of-processing model of memory?* Fergus Craik and Robert Lockhart (1972) pioneered the levels-of-processing model of memory, which holds that memories tend to endure when information is processed *deeply*—attended to, encoded carefully, pondered, and related to things we already know. Remembering relies on how *deeply* people process information, not on whether memories are transferred from one *stage* of memory to another.

Think of all the math problems we solved in high school. Each problem is an application of a procedure and, perhaps, of certain formulas. By repeatedly applying the procedures and formulas in slightly different contexts, we rehearse them elaboratively. As a result, we are more likely to remember them.

Truth

It is true that it may be easier for you to recall the name of your first-grade teacher than the name of someone you just met at a party.

Biologically oriented research connects deep processing with activity in certain parts of the brain, notably the prefrontal area of the cerebral cortex (Constantinidis et al., 2001). One reason that older adults show memory loss is that they tend not to process information quite as deeply as younger people do (Grady et al., 1999). Deep processing requires sustained attention, and older adults, along with people who have suffered brain injuries and strokes, apparently cannot focus as well as they once did (Winocur et al., 2000).

Flashbulb Memories

Why is it that some events, like the attack of September 11, 2001, can be etched in memory for a lifetime? It appears that we tend to remember events that are surprising, important, and emotionally stirring more clearly. Such events can create "flashbulb memories," which preserve experiences in detail (Finkenauer et al., 1998; Otani et al., 2005). Why is the memory etched when the "flashbulb" goes off? One factor is the distinctness of the memory. It is easier to discriminate stimuli that stand out. Such events are striking in themselves. The feelings caused by them are also special. It is thus relatively easy to pick them out from the storehouse of memories. Major events such as the assassination of a president or the loss of a close relative also tend to have important effects on our lives. We are likely to dwell on them and form networks of associations. That is, we are likely to rehearse them elaboratively. Our rehearsal may include great expectations, or deep fears, for the future.

> **Stress hormones help carve events into memory—"as almost to leave a scar upon the cerebral tissues."**

Biology is intimately connected with psychology. Strong feelings are connected with the secretion of stress hormones, and stress hormones help carve events into memory—"as almost to leave a scar upon the cerebral tissues," as noted by William James.

Organization in Long-Term Memory

The storehouse of long-term memory is usually well organized. Items are not just piled on the floor or

thrown into closets. *How is knowledge organized in long-term memory?* We tend to gather information about rats and cats into a certain section of the storehouse, perhaps the animal or mammal section. We put information about oaks, maples, and eucalyptus into the tree section. Such categorization of stimuli is a basic cognitive function. It allows us to make predictions about specific instances and to store information efficiently.

We tend to organize information according to a *hierarchical structure*, as shown in Figure 7.5. A *hierarchy* is an arrangement of items (or chunks of information) into groups or classes according to common or distinct features. As we work our way up the hierarchy shown in the figure, we find more encompassing, or *superordinate*, classes to which the items below them belong. For example, all mammals are animals, but there are many types of animals other than mammals.

Figure 7.5

The Hierarchical Structure of Long-Term Memory

Where are whales filed in the hierarchical cabinets of your memory? Your classification of whales may influence your answers to these questions: Do whales breathe underwater? Are they warm-blooded? Do they nurse their young? A note to biological purists: This figure is not intended to represent phyla, classes, orders, and so on accurately. Rather, it shows how an individual's classification scheme might be organized.

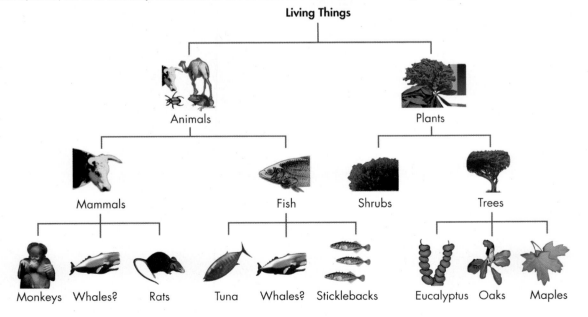

When items are correctly organized in long-term memory, you are more likely to recall—or know—accurate information about them. For example, do you "remember" whether whales breathe underwater? If you did not know that whales are mammals (or in Figure 7.5, *subordinate* to mammals), or if you knew nothing about mammals, a correct answer might depend on some remote instance of rote learning. That is, you might be depending on chancy episodic memory rather than on reliable semantic memory. For example, you might recall some details from a TV documentary on whales. If you *did* know that whales are mammals, however, you would also know—or remember—that whales do not breathe underwater. How? You would reconstruct information about whales from knowledge about mammals, the group to which whales are subordinate. Similarly, you would know, or remember, that because they are mammals, whales are warm-blooded, nurse their young, and are a good deal more intelligent than, say, tunas and sharks, which are fish. Had you incorrectly classified whales as fish, you might have searched your memory and constructed the incorrect answer that they do breathe underwater.

The Tip-of-the-Tongue Phenomenon

Having something on the tip of your tongue can be a frustrating experience. Psychologists term this experience the **tip-of-the-tongue (TOT) phenomenon**, or the *feeling-of-knowing experience*. *Why do we sometimes feel that the answer to a question is on the tip of our tongue?*

Research provides insight into the TOT phenomenon (Brown & McNeill, 1966; James & Burke, 2000). In classic research, Brown and McNeill (1966) defined some rather unusual words for students, such as *sampan*, a small riverboat used in China and Japan. The students were then asked to recall the words they had learned. Some of the students often had the right word "on the tip of their tongue" but reported words with similar meanings such as *junk, barge,* or *houseboat.* Still other students reported words that sounded similar, such as *Saipan, Siam, sarong,* and *sanching.* Why?

To begin with, the words were unfamiliar, so elaborative rehearsal did not take place. The students did not have an opportunity to relate the words to other things they knew. Brown and McNeill also suggested that our storage systems are indexed according to cues that include both the sounds and the meanings of words—that is, according to both acoustic and semantic codes. By scanning words similar in sound and meaning to the word on the tip of the tongue, we sometimes find a useful cue and retrieve the word for which we are searching.

Sometimes an answer seems to be on the tip of our tongue because our learning of the topic is incomplete. We may not know the exact answer, but we know something. (As a matter of fact, if we have good writing skills, we may present our incomplete knowledge so forcefully that we earn a good grade on an essay question on the topic!) At such times, the problem lies not in retrieval but in the original processes of learning and memory—that is, encoding and storage.

Context-Dependent Memory

The context in which we acquire information can also play a role in retrieval. I remember walking down the halls of the apartment building where I had lived as a child. Cooking odors triggered a sudden assault of images of playing under the staircase, of falling against a radiator, of the shrill voice of a former neighbor calling for her child at dinnertime. Odors, it turns out, are particularly likely to trigger related memories (Pointer & Bond, 1998).

My experience was an example of a **context-dependent memory**. My memories were particularly clear in the context in which they were formed. *Why might it be useful to study in the same room in which we will be tested?* One answer is that being in the proper context—for example, studying in the exam room or under the same conditions—can dramatically enhance recall (Isarida & Isarida, 1999).

According to a study with twenty bilingual Cornell students, the "context" for memory extends to language (Marian & Neisser, 2000). The students were in

PHOTODISC/GETTY IMAGES

state-dependent memory information that is better retrieved in the physiological or emotional state in which it was encoded and stored, or learned

nonsense syllables meaningless sets of two consonants, with a vowel sandwiched in between, that are used to study memory

their early twenties and had emigrated from Russia an average of eight years earlier. They were asked to recall the details of experiences in Russia and the United States. When they were interviewed in Russian, they were better able to retrieve experiences from their lives in Russia. Similarly, when they were interviewed in English, they were better able to recall events that happened in the United States.

State-Dependent Memory

State-dependent memory is an extension of context-dependent memory. We sometimes retrieve information better when we are in a biological or emotional state similar to the one in which we encoded and stored the information. Feeling the rush of love may trigger other images of falling in love. The grip of anger may prompt memories of incidents of frustration. The research in this area extends to states in which we are sober or inebriated.

LO⁴ Forgetting

What do DAL, RIK, BOF, and ZEX have in common? They are all **nonsense syllables**. Nonsense syllables are meaningless sets of two consonants with a vowel sandwiched in between. They were first used by Hermann Ebbinghaus (1885/1913) to study memory and forgetting. Because nonsense syllables

DIGITAL VISION/GETTY IMAGES

are intended to be meaningless, remembering them should depend on simple acoustic coding and maintenance rehearsal rather than on elaborative rehearsal, semantic coding, or other ways of making learning meaningful. They are thus well suited for use in the measurement of forgetting. *What types of memory tasks are used in measuring forgetting?*

Memory Tasks Used in Measuring Forgetting

Three basic memory tasks have been used by psychologists to measure forgetting: recognition, recall, and relearning. Nonsense syllables have been used in studying each of them. The study of these memory tasks has led to several conclusions about the nature of forgetting.

Recognition

One aspect of forgetting is failure to recognize something we have experienced. There are many ways of measuring *recognition*. In many studies, psychologists ask subjects to read a list of nonsense syllables. The subjects then read a second list of nonsense syllables and indicate whether they recognize any of the syllables as having appeared on the first list. Forgetting is defined as failure to recognize a syllable that has been read before.

In another kind of recognition study, Harry Bahrick and his colleagues (1975) studied high-school graduates who had been out of school for various lengths of time. They interspersed photos of the graduates' classmates with four times as many photos of strangers. Recent graduates correctly recognized former classmates 90% of the time. Those who had been out of school for forty years recognized former classmates 75% of the time. A chance level of recognition would have been only 20% (one photo in five was of an actual classmate). Thus, even older people showed rather solid long-term recognition ability.

Recognition is the easiest type of memory task. This is why multiple-choice tests are easier than fill-in-the-blank or essay tests.

> **Truth**
>
> If you study with the stereo on, you would probably do better to take the test with the stereo on.

Recall

In his own studies of *recall*, another memory task, Ebbinghaus (1885/1913) would read lists of nonsense syllables aloud to the beat of a metronome and then see how many he could produce from memory. After reading through a list once, he usually would be able to recall seven syllables—the typical limit for short-term memory.

Psychologists also often use lists of pairs of nonsense syllables, called **paired associates**, to measure recall. A list of paired associates is shown in Figure 7.6. Subjects read through the lists pair by pair. Later they are shown the first member of each pair and are asked to recall the second. Recall is more difficult than recognition. In a recognition task, one simply indicates whether an item has been seen before or which of a number of items is paired with a stimulus (as in a multiple-choice test). In a recall task, the person must retrieve a syllable, with another syllable serving as a cue.

Retrieval is made easier if the two syllables can be meaningfully linked—that is, encoded semantically—even if the "meaning" is stretched. Consider the first pair of nonsense syllables in Figure 7.6. The image of a WOMan smoking a CEG-arette may make CEG easier to retrieve when the person is presented with the cue WOM.

Relearning

Relearning is a third method of measuring retention. Do you remember having to learn all of the state capitals in grade school? What were the capitals of Wyoming and Delaware? Even when we cannot recall or recognize material that had once been learned, such as Cheyenne for Wyoming and Dover for Delaware, we can relearn it more rapidly the second time.

To study the efficiency of relearning, Ebbinghaus (1885/1913) devised the **method of savings**. First he recorded the number of repetitions required to learn a list of nonsense syllables or words. Then he recorded the number of repetitions required to relearn the list after a certain amount of time had elapsed. Next he computed the difference in the number of repetitions to determine the **savings**. If a list had to be repeated twenty times before it was learned, and twenty times again after a year had passed, there were no savings. Relearning, that is, was as tedious as the initial learning. If the list could be learned with only ten repetitions after a year had elapsed, however, half the number of repetitions required for learning had been saved.

Figure 7.7 on page 156 shows Ebbinghaus's classic curve of forgetting. As you can see, there was no loss of memory as measured by savings immediately after a list had been learned. However, recollection dropped quite a bit, by half, during the first hour after learning a list. Losses of learning then became more gradual. It took a month (thirty-one days) for retention to be cut in half again. Forgetting occurred most rapidly right after material was learned.

Figure 7.6

Paired Associates

WOM	CEG
GOR	NIF
XAR	MUP
JEK	BAC
HOK	MIB

Interference Theory

When we do not attend to, encode, and rehearse sensory input, we may forget it through decay of the trace of the image. Material in short-term memory, like material in sensory memory, can be lost through decay. It can also be lost through displacement, as may happen when we try to remember several new names at a party.

Why can learning Spanish make it harder to remember French? The answer may be found in **interference theory**. According to this view, we also forget material in short-term and long-term memory because newly learned material interferes with it. The two basic types of interference are retroactive interference (also called *retroactive inhibition*) and proactive interference (also called *proactive inhibition*).

paired associates
nonsense syllables presented in pairs in experiments that measure recall

method of savings
a measure of retention in which the difference between the number of repetitions originally required to learn a list and the number of repetitions required to relearn the list after a certain amount of time has elapsed is calculated

savings
the difference between the number of repetitions originally required to learn a list and the number of repetitions required to relearn the list after a certain amount of time has elapsed

interference theory
the view that we may forget stored material because other learning interferes with it

Figure 7.7

Ebbinghaus's Classic Curve of Forgetting

Recollection of lists of words drops precipitously during the first hour after learning. Loss of learning then becomes more gradual. Retention drops by half within the first hour. It takes a month (thirty-one days), however, for retention to be cut in half again.

Retroactive Interference

In **retroactive interference**, new learning interferes with the retrieval of old learning. For example, a medical student may memorize the names of the bones in the leg through rote repetition. Later he or she may find that learning the names of the bones in the arm makes it more difficult to retrieve the names of the leg bones, especially if the names are similar in sound or in relative location on each limb.

Proactive Interference

In **proactive interference**, older learning interferes with the capacity to retrieve more recently learned material. High-school Spanish may pop in when you are trying to retrieve college French or Italian words. All three are Romance languages, with similar roots and spellings. Previously learned Japanese words probably would not interfere with your ability to retrieve more recently learned French or Italian, because the roots and sounds of Japanese differ considerably from those of the Romance languages.

> ### Truth
> It is true that learning Spanish can make it harder to remember French—and vice versa.

Repression

According to Sigmund Freud, we are motivated to forget painful memories and unacceptable ideas because they produce anxiety, guilt, and shame. *What is the Freudian concept of repression?* Repression, according to Freud, is the automatic ejection of painful memories and unacceptable urges from conscious awareness. It is motivated by the desire to avoid facing painful memories and emotions.

Psychoanalysts believe that repression is at the heart of disorders such as **dissociative amnesia** (see Chapter 12). There is a current controversy in psychology about whether repression (motivated forgetting) exists and, if it does, how it works.

There is much research on repression, often in the form of case studies that are found in psychoanalytic journals (e.g., Eagle, 2000). Much has been made of case studies in which veterans have supposedly forgotten traumatic battlefield experiences, developed post-traumatic stress disorder (once called "battlefield neurosis"), and then "felt better" once they recalled and discussed the traumatic events (Karon & Widener, 1998). Critics argue that the evidence for such repression and recovery of memories is weak and that this kind of "memory" can be implanted by the suggestions of interviewers (Loftus, 2001). The issue remains controversial, as we see next.

Do People Really Recover Repressed Memories of Childhood?

Despite shaky scientific support, there are cases of so-called recovered memories, especially memories of childhood sexual abuse by a relative, teacher, or friend. The question is whether these memories are induced by therapists who foster beliefs that become so deeply ingrained they seem like authentic memories. "We don't know what percent of these recovered memories are real and what percent are pseudomemories," notes psychiatrist Harold Lief (cited in Brody, 2000), one of the first to challenge such memories.

Psychologist Elizabeth Loftus has engaged in numerous studies that show how easy it is to implant false memories through leading questions. In one study, researchers were able to readily convince half the subjects that they had been lost in a mall or hospitalized with severe pain as children.

Infantile Amnesia

Can children remember events from the first couple of years of life? When he interviewed people about their early experiences, Freud discovered that they could not recall episodes that had happened prior to the age of three or so and that recall was cloudy through the age of five. This phenomenon is referred to as infantile amnesia.

Infantile amnesia has little to do with the fact that the episodes occurred in the distant past. Middle-aged and older people have vivid memories from the ages of six through ten, yet the events happened many decades ago. But eighteen-year-olds show steep declines in memory when they try to recall episodes that occurred earlier than the age of six, even though they happened less than eighteen years earlier (Wetzler & Sweeney, 1986).

Freud believed that young children have aggressive impulses and perverse lusts toward their parents. He attributed infantile amnesia to repression of these impulses. The episodes lost to infantile amnesia, however, are not weighted in the direction of such "primitive" impulses. In fact, infantile amnesia probably reflects the interaction of physiological and cognitive factors. For example, a structure of the limbic system (the hippocampus) that is involved in the storage of memories does not become mature until we are about two years old (Squire, 2004). Also, myelination of brain pathways is incomplete for the first few years, contributing to the inefficiency of information processing and memory formation.

There are also cognitive explanations for infantile amnesia:

- Infants are not particularly interested in remembering the past (Neisser, 1993).

- Infants, in contrast to older children, tend not to weave episodes together into meaningful stories of their own lives. Information about specific episodes thus tends to be lost. Research shows that when parents reminisce about the past with children, the children's memories of being infants are strengthened (Peterson, 2002).

- Infants do not make reliable use of language to symbolize or classify events (Wang, 2003). Their ability to *encode* sensory input—that is, to apply the auditory and semantic codes that facilitate memory formation—is therefore limited. Yet research shows that young infants can recall events throughout the period when infantile amnesia is presumed to occur if they are now and then exposed to objects they played with or photos of events (Rovee-Collier, 1999).

> "We are unlikely to remember episodes from early childhood unless we are reminded of them from time to time."

In any event, we are unlikely to remember episodes from early childhood unless we are reminded of them from time to time as we develop. Many early childhood memories that seem so clear today might be reconstructed and hold many inaccuracies. They might also be memories of events that occurred later than we thought. Yet there is no evidence that such early memories are systematically repressed.

Anterograde and Retrograde Amnesia

Adults also experience amnesia, although usually for biological reasons, as in the cases of anterograde and retrograde amnesia (Kopelman, 2002). *Why do people frequently have trouble recalling being in accidents?* In so-called anterograde amnesia, there are memory lapses for the period following a trauma such as a

infantile amnesia inability to recall events that occur prior to the age of two or three; also termed *childhood amnesia*

hippocampus a structure in the limbic system that plays an important role in the formation of new memories

anterograde amnesia failure to remember events that occur after physical trauma because of the effects of the trauma

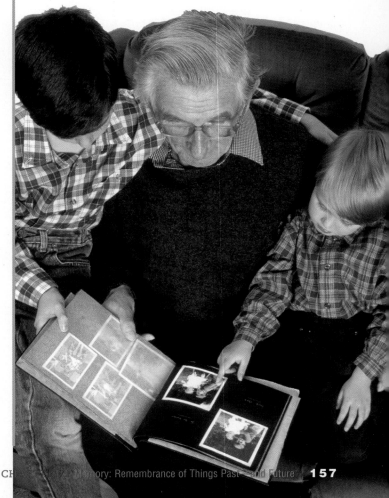

© CW IMAGES / ALAMY

retrograde amnesia
failure to remember events that occur prior to physical trauma because of the effects of the trauma

engram
(1) an assumed electrical circuit in the brain that corresponds to a memory trace (2) an assumed chemical change in the brain that accompanies learning (from the Greek *en-*, meaning "in" and *gramma,* meaning "something that is written or recorded")

Thalamus

Hippocampus

COURTESY OF DANA COPELAND

Forever 27

The hippocampus is essential to the formation of new memories. Consider the classic case of a man called "H. M." Parts of the brain are sometimes lesioned to help people with epilepsy. In H. M.'s case, a section of the hippocampus was removed (Milner, 1966). Right after the operation, H. M.'s mental functioning appeared normal. As time went on, however, it became clear that he had problems processing new information. For example, two years after the operation, H. M. believed he was twenty-seven—his age at the time of the operation. When his family moved to a new address, H. M. could not find his new home or remember the new address. He responded with appropriate grief to the death of his uncle, yet he then began to ask about his uncle and why he did not visit. Each time he was reminded of his uncle's passing, he grieved as if he were hearing it for the first time. H. M.'s operation apparently prevented him from transferring information from short-term to long-term memory.

blow to the head, an electric shock, or an operation. In some cases the trauma seems to interfere with all the processes of memory. The ability to pay attention, the encoding of sensory input, and rehearsal are all impaired. A number of investigators have linked certain kinds of brain damage—such as damage to the hippocampus—to amnesia (Eichenbaum & Fortin, 2003; Spiers et al., 2001).

In retrograde amnesia, the source of trauma prevents people from remembering events that took place before the accident (Wheeler & McMillan, 2001). In one well-known case of retrograde amnesia, a man received a head injury in a motorcycle accident (Baddeley, 1982). When he regained consciousness, he had lost memory for all events that had occurred after the age of eleven. In fact, he appeared to believe that he was still eleven years old. During the next few months he gradually recovered more knowledge of his past. He moved toward the present year by year, up until the critical motorcycle ride.

But he never did recover the events just prior to the accident. The accident had apparently prevented the information that was rapidly unfolding before him from being transferred to long-term memory. In terms of stages of memory, it may be that our perceptions and ideas need to consolidate, or rest undisturbed for a while, if they are to be transferred to long-term memory (Nader et al., 2000).

LO⁵ The Biology of Memory

Psychologists assume that mental processes such as the encoding, storage, and retrieval of information— that is, memory—are accompanied by changes in the

brain. Early in the 20th century, many psychologists used the concept of the engram in their study of memory. Engrams were viewed as electrical circuits in the brain that corresponded to memory traces—neurological processes that paralleled experiences. Yet biological psychologists such as Karl Lashley (1950) spent many fruitless years searching for such circuits or for the structures of the brain in which they might be housed. Much research on the biology of memory focuses today on the roles of stimulants, neurons, neurotransmitters, hormones, and structures in the brain.

Neural Activity and Memory

What neural events are connected with memory? Rats who are reared in stimulating environments provide some answers. The animals develop more dendrites and synapses in the cerebral cortex than rats reared in impoverished environments (Neisser, 1997a). Moreover, visually stimulating rats increases the number of synapses in their visual cortex (Battaglia et al., 2004; Bilkey, 2004). Therefore, the storage of experience does involve avenues of communication among brain cells.

Information received through other senses is just as likely to lead to corresponding changes in the cortical regions that represent them. For example, sounds may similarly cause changes in the auditory cortex. Experiences perceived by several senses are apparently stored in numerous parts of the cortex. The recall of sensory experiences apparently involves neural activity in related regions of the brain.

Research with sea snails such as *Aplysia* and *Hermissenda* offers more insight into the biology of memory. *Aplysia* has only some 20,000 neurons compared with humans' billions. As a result, researchers have been able to study how experience is reflected at the synapses of specific neurons. The sea snail will reflexively withdraw its gills when it receives electric shock, in the way a person will reflexively withdraw a hand from a hot stove or a thorn. In one kind of experiment, researchers precede the shock with a squirt of water. After a few repetitions, the sea snail becomes conditioned to withdraw its gills when squirted with the water. When sea snails are conditioned, they release more serotonin at certain synapses. As a consequence, transmission at these synapses becomes more efficient as trials (learning) progress (Kandel, 2001). This greater efficiency is termed long-term potentiation (LTP). As shown in Figure 7.8, dendrites can also participate in LTP by sprouting new branches that attach to the transmitting axon. Rats who are given substances that enhance LTP learn mazes with fewer errors; that is, they are less likely to turn down the wrong alley (Uzakov et al., 2005).

Serotonin and many other naturally occurring chemical substances, including adrenaline, noradrenaline, acetylcholine, glutamate, antidiuretic hormone, even the sex hormones estrogen and testosterone have been shown to play roles in memory.

The hippocampus is not a storage bin. It is involved in relaying sensory information to parts of the cortex.

Brain Structures and Memory

What structures in the brain are connected with memory? Memory does not reside in a single structure of the brain; it relies on complex neural networks that draw on various parts of the brain (Nyberg et al., 2000). However, some parts of the brain play more specific roles in memory. The hippocampus is vital in storing new information even if we can retrieve old information without it (Fields, 2005). But the hippocampus is not a storage bin. Rather, it is involved in relaying sensory information to parts of the cortex.

Where are the storage bins? The brain stores parts of memories in the appropriate areas of the sensory cortex. Sights are stored in the visual cortex, sounds in the auditory cortex, and so on. The limbic system is largely responsible for integrating these pieces of information when we recall an event. The frontal lobes apparently store information about where and when events occur (Goldman-Rakic et al., 2000a).

But what of the decision to try to recall something? What of the spark of consciousness that drives us to move

long-term potentiation (LTP) enhanced efficiency in synaptic transmission that follows brief, rapid stimulation

Figure 7.8

One Avenue to Long-Term Potentiation (LTP)

LTP can occur via the action of neurotransmitters such as serotonin and glutamate at synapses. Structurally, LTP can also occur as shown in Parts A and B, when dendrites sprout new branches that connect with transmitting axons, increasing the amount of stimulation they receive.

Part A.

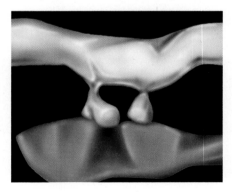

Part B.

Jean Piaget, the investigator of children's cognitive development, distinctly remembered an attempt to kidnap him from his baby carriage as he was being wheeled along the Champs Élysées. He recalled the excited throng, the abrasions on the face of the nurse who rescued him, the police officer's white baton, and the flight of the assailant. Although they were graphic, Piaget's memories were false. Years later, the nurse admitted that she had made up the tale.

Can eyewitness testimony be trusted? Is there reason to believe that the statements of eyewitnesses are any more factual than Piaget's? Legal professionals and psychologists are concerned about the accuracy of our long-term memories as reflected in eyewitness testimony (Cutler, 2009; Cutler & Kovera, 2010; Wright & Loftus, 2008). Let us consider what can go wrong—and what can go right—with eyewitness testimony.

One problem with eyewitness testimony is that the words chosen by an experimenter—and those chosen by a lawyer interrogating a witness—have been shown to influence the reconstruction of memories (Cutler & Kovera, 2010). For example, an attorney for the plaintiff might ask the witness, "How fast was the defendant's car going when it *smashed into* the plaintiff's car?" In such a case, the car might be reported as going faster than if the question had been: "How fast was the defendant's car going when the accident occurred?" Could the attorney for the defendant claim that use of the word *smashed* biased the witness? What about jurors who heard the word *smashed*? Would they be biased toward assuming that the driver had been reckless?

Children tend to be more suggestible witnesses than adults, and preschoolers are more suggestible than older children. But when questioned properly, even young children may be able to provide accurate and useful testimony (Ceci et al., 2007; Krähenbühl et al., 2009).

There are also problems in the identification of criminals by eyewitnesses. For one thing, witnesses may pay more attention to the suspect's clothing than to more meaningful characteristics such as facial features, height, and weight.

Other problems with eyewitness testimony include the following (Cutler & Kovera, 2010):

Identification is less accurate when suspects belong to ethnic or racial groups that differ from that of the witness.

Identification of suspects is compromised when interrogators make misleading suggestions.

TOM MERTON / OJO IMAGES / JUPITER IMAGES

"Psychologist Eilzabeth Loftus showed that our testimony can be affected by the concepts that attorneys use when they ask questions. For example, eyewitnesses assumed that cars were going faster if the attorney asked, "How fast were the cars going when they *smashed* into each other?" as opposed to "How fast were they going when they *hit* one another?"

Witnesses are seen as more credible when they claim to be certain in their testimony, but there is little evidence that claims of certainty are accurate.

There are thus many problems with eyewitness testimony. Yet even Elizabeth Loftus (e.g., Wright & Loftus, 2008), who has extensively studied the accuracy of eyewitness testimony, agrees that it is a valuable tool in the courtroom. After all, identifications made by eyewitnesses are frequently correct, and what, Loftus asks, would be the alternative to the use of eyewitnesses? If we were to prevent eyewitnesses from testifying, how many criminals would go free?

Sources: Ceci, S. J., Kulkofsky, S., Klemfuss, J. Z., Sweeney, C. D., & Bruck, M. (2007). Unwarranted assumptions about children's testimonial accuracy. *Annual Review of Clinical Psychology, 3*, 311–328.

Cutler, B. L. (2009). *Expert testimony on the psychology of eyewitness identification.* New York: Oxford University Press.

Cutler, B. L. & Kovera, M. B. (2010). *Evaluating eyewitness identification.* New York: Oxford University Press.

Krähenbühl, S., Blades, M., & Eiser, C. (2009). The effect of repeated questioning on children's accuracy and consistency in eyewitness testimony. *Legal and Criminological Psychology, 14*(2), 263–278.

Wright, D. B., & Loftus, E. F. (2008). In G. Cohen & M. A. Conway. (Eds.). *Memory in the real world, 3rd edition.* New York: Psychology Press.

backward in time or to strive to remember to do something in the future? The prefrontal cortex (see Figure 7.9 on page 161) is the executive center in memory (Buckner et al., 2001; Wheeler & Treisman, 2002). It appears to empower people with consciousness—the ability to mentally represent and become aware of experiences that occur in the past, present, and future. It enables people to mentally travel back

in time to reexperience the personal, autobiographical past. It enables people to focus on the things they intend to do in the future, such as mail a letter on the way to class or brush their teeth before going to bed.

The hippocampus is also involved in the where and when of things (Eichenbaum & Fortin, 2003). The hippocampus does not become mature until we are about two years old. Immaturity may be connected

Figure 7.9

The Prefrontal Cortex of the Brain

The prefrontal cortex comes in pairs. One is found in each hemisphere, a bit above the outer edge of the eyebrow. The prefrontal cortex is highly active during visual and spatial problem-solving. Your sense of self—your continuous sense of being in and operating on the world—may also reside largely in the prefrontal cortex.

Prefrontal cortex

© CORBIS

with infantile amnesia. Adults with hippocampal damage may be able to form new procedural memories, even though they cannot form new episodic ("where and when") memories (Fields, 2005). They can develop new skills even though they cannot recall the practice sessions (Reed & Squire, 1997).

The thalamus is involved in the formation of verbal memories. Part of the thalamus of an Air Force cadet known as N. A. was damaged in a fencing accident. Afterward, N. A. could no longer form verbal memories, but he could form visual memories (Squire, 2004). (One might measure visual memory by showing people pictures, allowing time to pass, and then asking them to point out those they have been shown.)

The encoding, storage, and retrieval of information thus involve biological activity. As we learn, new synapses are developed, and changes occur at existing synapses. Parts of the brain are also involved in the formation of memories. In the next chapter, we see how people manipulate information they have stored to adapt to the environment or create new environments.

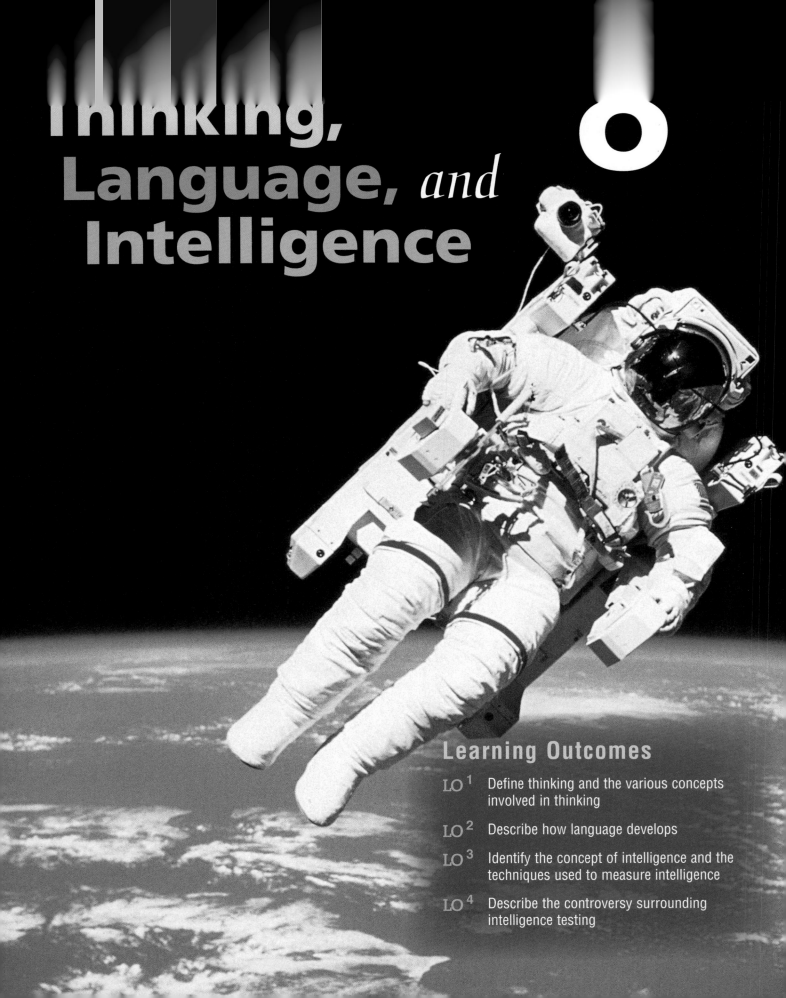

Thinking, Language, *and* Intelligence

Learning Outcomes

LO 1 Define thinking and the various concepts involved in thinking

LO 2 Describe how language develops

LO 3 Identify the concept of intelligence and the techniques used to measure intelligence

LO 4 Describe the controversy surrounding intelligence testing

"*Intelligence may be the most controversial topic in psychology.***"**

What form of life is so adaptive that it can survive in desert temperatures of 120°F or Arctic climes of –40°F? What form of life can run, walk, climb, swim, live underwater for months on end, and fly to the moon and back? I won't keep you in suspense any longer. We are that form of life. Yet our unclad bodies do not allow us to adapt to these extremes of temperature. Brute strength does not allow us to live underwater or travel to the Moon. Rather, it is our cognitive processes that allow us to adapt to these conditions and surpass our physical limitations.

In this chapter we explore thinking, language, and intelligence. Thinking enables us to pose problems and solve them, and to make judgments and decisions. Humans use language not only in communicating, but also in thinking. Humans attach words and sentences to the objects and concepts they think about, taking them into abstract realms. Intelligence may be the most controversial topic in psychology. Psychologists do not agree on exactly what intelligence is or exactly how people develop intelligence. By and large, however, psychologists view intelligence as the underlying ability to understand the world and cope with its challenges.

Truth or Fiction?

What do you think?

Folklore, common sense, or nonsense? Place a T for "True" or F for "False" on the lines provided (you'll learn the answers as you read through the text).

— Only humans can use insight to solve problems.

— Crying is an early form of language.

— Young children say things like "Daddy goed away" and "Mommy sitted down" because they *do* understand rules of grammar.

— "Street smarts" are a sign of intelligence.

— Creative people are highly intelligent.

— Highly intelligent people are creative.

— Two children can answer exactly the same items on an intelligence test correctly, yet one child can be above average in IQ, and the other can be below average.

— Intelligence tests measure many things other than intelligence.

LO¹ Thinking

The Greek philosopher Aristotle pointed out that people differ from lower organisms in their capacity for rational thinking. *What is thinking?* **Thinking** means paying attention to information, representing it mentally, reasoning about it, and making judgments and decisions about it. Thinking refers to conscious, planned attempts to make sense of and change the world. By contrast, mental processes such as dreaming and daydreaming do not represent thinking; they may be unplanned and proceed more or less on their own.

We begin with concepts, which provide many of the building blocks for thinking.

thinking
paying attention to information, mentally representing it, reasoning about it, and making decisions about it

Concepts

Concepts are mental categories used to group together
objects, relations, events,
abstractions, or qualities that
have common properties.
Concepts are crucial to cognition. Concepts can represent
objects, events, and activities—and visions of things
that never were or cannot
be measured, such as Middle
Earth in *The Lord of the Rings* or
the Land of Oz in *The Wizard of Oz.*

Labels for objects depend on experience with
them and on one's cultural setting (Sloman et al.,
2002). Squares, circles, and triangles are not all that
common in nature, and some peoples, such as the
Himba of northern Namibia, have no concepts of
them (Roberson et al., 2002). But these shapes are
concepts that are basic to geometry. Much thinking has to do with categorizing new concepts and
manipulating relationships among concepts, as in
problems in geometry.

We tend to organize concepts in *hierarchies.* For
example, the newspaper category includes objects
such as your school paper and the *Los
Angeles Times.* Newspapers, college textbooks, and catalogs
can be combined into
higher-order cat-
egories such as
printed matter or
printed devices

that store information. If you add hard drives and
DVDs, you can create a still higher category—*objects
that store information.* Now consider a question that
requires categorical thinking: How are a newspaper
and a DVD alike? Answers to such questions entail
supplying the category that includes both objects.
In this case, we can say that both objects store
information. Their functions are alike, even if their
technology differs.

Prototypes are good examples. They best match
the key features of categories. Which animal seems
more birdlike to you: a robin or an ostrich? Why?
Which better fits the prototype of a fish: a sea horse
or a tuna? Why?

Many simple prototypes, such as *dog* and *red,*
are taught by means of examples, or exemplars.
Research suggests that it is more efficient for most
of us to learn what *fruits* and *vegetables* are from
experience with exemplars of each, rather than by
working from definitions of them (Smits et al., 2002).
We point to a dog and tell a child "dog" or "This is a
dog." Dogs are *positive instances* of the dog concept.
Negative instances—things that are *not* dogs—are
then shown to the child while we say, "This is *not* a
dog." Negative instances of one concept may be positive instances of another. So, in teaching a child, we
may be more likely to say, "This is not a dog—it's a
cat" than simply, "This is not a dog."

Children may at first include horses and
other four-legged animals within the dog
concept until the differ-
ences between dogs
and horses are

Circles, squares, and triangles are found only
rarely in nature and not among the Himba of
northern Namibia. It is not surprising, then,
that they have no words for these concepts.

pointed out. In language development, such overinclusion of instances in a category (reference to horses as dogs) is labeled *overextension*.

Children's prototypes become refined after children are shown positive and negative instances and given explanations. Abstract concepts such as *bachelor* or *square root* tend to be formed through explanations that involve more basic concepts.

Problem-Solving

Problem-solving is an important aspect of thinking. Here's a problem for you to solve. What are the next two letters in this series?

> O T T F F S S E _ _ ?

How did you try to find the answer? Did you search your personal memory banks and ask yourself what O can stand for, then T, and so on? Did you try to think of some phrase the letters might represent? Perhaps the first letters of the stars in a constellation? [If you don't resort to a search engine answer and do not arrive at the answer on your own, I'll be discussing it within a few pages.]

Understanding the Problem

Successful understanding of a problem generally requires three features:

- *The parts or elements of our mental representation of the problem relate to one another in a meaningful way.* If we are trying to solve a problem in geometry, our mental triangles, like actual triangles, should have angles that total 180 degrees.

- *The elements of our mental representation of the problem correspond to the elements of the problem in the outer world.* If we are assessing a patient in the emergency room of a hospital, we want to arrive at a diagnosis of what might be wrong before we make a treatment plan. To do so, we take the patient's "vital signs," including heart rate, temperature, and blood pressure, so that our mental picture of the patient conforms to what is going on in his or her body.

- *We have a storehouse of background knowledge that we can apply to the problem.* We have the necessary experience or course work to solve the problem.

The Use of Algorithms

An **algorithm** is a specific procedure for solving a type of problem. An algorithm invariably leads to the solution—if it is used properly, that is. Mathematical formulas like the Pythagorean theorem are examples of algorithms. They yield correct answers to problems *as long as the right formula is used.* Finding the right formula to solve a problem may require scanning one's memory for all formulas that contain variables that represent one or more of the elements in the problem. The Pythagorean theorem concerns right triangles. Therefore, it is appropriate to consider using this formula for problems concerning right triangles, but not others.

If you are going to be meeting someone for the first time and want to make a good impression, you consider the nature of the encounter (for example, a job interview or a "blind date") and then consider how to dress and behave for the encounter. If it's a job interview, the algorithm may be to dress neatly, be well-groomed, and not to wear too much cologne or perfume. If it's a date, you may ditch the suit but hike up the cologne or perfume a notch. In either case, smile and make eye contact—it's all part of the formula.

Anagrams are scrambled words. *Korc* is an anagram for *rock* or *cork*. The task in anagram problems is to try to reorganize jumbles or groups of letters into words. Some anagram problems require us to use every letter from the pool of letters; others allow us to use only some of the letters. How many words can you make from the pool of letters *DWARG?* If you were to use the **systematic random search** algorithm, you would list every possible letter combination, using from one to all five letters. You could use a dictionary or a spell-checking program to see whether each result is, in fact, a word. The method might take awhile, but it would work.

The Use of Heuristic Devices

Is it best to use a tried-and-true formula to solve a problem? Sometimes people use shortcuts to "jump to conclusions"—and these are often correct conclusions. The shortcuts are called **heuristics**, or heuristic devices—rules of thumb that help us simplify and solve problems. Heuristics are often based on strategies that worked in the past (Klaczynski, 2001).

In contrast to algorithms, heuristics do not guarantee a correct solution. But when they work, they permit more rapid solutions. A heuristic device for solving the anagram problem would be to look for familiar letter combinations and then check the remaining letters for words that include these combinations. In *DWARG*, for example, we find some familiar combinations: *dr* and *gr*. We may then quickly find *draw, drag,* and *grad*. The drawback to this method is that we might miss some words.

One type of heuristic device is the **means–end analysis**. In using this heuristic device, we assess the difference between our current situation and our goals

algorithm
a systematic procedure for solving a problem that works invariably when it is correctly applied

systematic random search
an algorithm for solving problems in which each possible solution is tested according to a particular set of rules

heuristics
rules of thumb that help us simplify and solve problems

means–end analysis
a heuristic device in which we try to solve a problem by evaluating the difference between the current situation and the goal

mental set
the tendency to respond to a new problem with an approach that was successfully used with similar problems

insight
in Gestalt psychology, a sudden perception of relationships among elements of the "perceptual field," permitting the solution of a problem

and do what we can to reduce this difference. Let's say that you are out in your car and have gotten lost. One heuristic device based on analysis of what you need to do to get to where you want to go might be to ask for directions. This approach requires no "sense of direction." An algorithm might be more complicated and require some scientific knowledge. For example, if you know your destination is west of your current location you might try driving toward the setting sun.

The Use of Analogies

An *analogy* is a partial similarity among things that are different in other ways. The analogy heuristic applies the solution of an earlier problem to the solution of a new one. We use the analogy heuristic whenever we try to solve a new problem by referring to a previous problem (Halpern et al., 1990).

Let us see whether you can use the analogy heuristic to your advantage in the following number-series problem. Look at the following series of numbers and find the rule that governs their order:

8, 5, 4, 9, 1, 7, 6, 3, 2, 0

This is rather abstract and mathematical. Actually, you use the analogy heuristic regularly. For example, when you begin a new term with a new instructor, you probably consider who the instructor reminds you of. Then, perhaps, you recall the things that helped you get along with the analogous instructor and try them on the new one. We tend to look for things that helped us in the past in similar situations. When we considered OTTFFSSENT, we used the first letters of the numbers one through ten. When we consider the first ten digits in the following order—8, 5, 4, 9, 1, 7, 6, 3, 2, and 0—we can again think of their first letters when they are spelled out. It happens that they are in alphabetical order (*eight*, *five*, *four*, and so on).

Factors That Affect Problem-Solving

The way you approach a problem is central to how effective you are at solving it. Other factors also influence your effectiveness. *What factors make it easier or harder to solve problems?* Three such factors reside within you: your level of expertise, whether you fall prey to a mental set, and whether you develop insight into the problem.

Expertise To appreciate the role of expertise in problem-solving, unscramble the following anagrams, taken from Novick and Coté (1992). In each case use all of the letters to form an actual English word:

DNSUO
RCWDO
IASYD

How long did it take you to unscramble each anagram ("sound," "crowd," and "daisy")? Would a person whose native language is English—that is, an "expert"—unscramble each anagram more efficiently than a bilingual person who spoke another language in the home? Why or why not?

Experts solve problems more efficiently and rapidly than novices do. Generally speaking, people who are experts at solving a certain kind of problem share the following characteristics (Szala, 2002; Gorodetsky & Klavir, 2003):

- They know the particular area well.
- They have a good memory for the elements in the problems.
- They form mental images or representations that facilitate problem-solving.
- They relate the problem to similar problems.
- They are more goal-directed and have efficient methods for problem-solving.

These factors are interrelated. Art historians, for example, acquire a database that permits them to understand the intricacies of paintings. As a result, their memory for details of paintings mushrooms.

Novick and Coté (1992) found that the solutions to the anagram problems seemed to "pop out" in under two seconds among experts. The experts apparently used more efficient methods than the novices. Experts seemed to use *parallel processing*. That is, they dealt simultaneously with two or more elements of the problems. In the case of DNSUO, for example, they may have played with the order of the vowels (*UO* or *OU*) at the same time that they tested which consonant (D, N, or S) was likely to precede them, arriving quickly at *sou* and *sound*. Novices were more likely to engage in *serial processing*—that is, to handle one element of the problem at a time.

Mental Sets The tendency to respond to a new problem with the same approach that helped solve similar problems is termed a **mental set**. Mental sets usually make our work easier, but they can mislead us when the similarity between problems is illusory.

Insight To gain insight into the role of **insight** in problem-solving, consider the following problem, posed by Metcalfe (1986):

A stranger approached a museum curator and offered him an ancient bronze coin. The coin had an authentic appearance and was marked with the date 544 BCE. The curator had happily made acquisitions from suspicious sources before, but this time he promptly called the police and had the stranger arrested. Why?

I'm not going to give you the answer to this problem. But I'll make a guarantee. When you arrive at the solution, it will hit you all at once. You'll think "Of course!" It will seem as though the pieces of information in the problem have suddenly been reorganized so that the solution leaps out—in a flash.

Bismarck, one of psychologist N. R. F. Maier's rats, appeared to suddenly reorganize the pieces of information in a problem with which he was presented, showing evidence of insight in his species. (Maier & Schneirla, 1935). Bismarck had been trained to climb a ladder to a tabletop where food was placed. On one occasion, Maier used a mesh barrier to prevent the rat from reaching his goal. But, as shown in Figure 8.1, a second ladder was provided and was visible to the animal. At first Bismarck sniffed and scratched and tried to find a path through the mesh. Then he spent some time washing his face, an activity that may signal frustration in rats. Suddenly he jumped into the air, turned, ran down the familiar ladder and around to the new ladder, ran up the new ladder, and claimed his just desserts. Did Bismarck suddenly perceive the relationships between the elements of the problem so that the solution occurred by insight? He seems to have had what Gestalt psychologists have termed an "Aha! experience."

Incubation An incubator warms chicken eggs so that they will hatch. **Incubation** in problem-solving refers to standing back from the problem for a while as some process within may continue to work on it. Later, the answer may come to us in a flash of insight. Standing back from the problem may help by distancing us from unprofitable but persistent mental sets (Both et al., 2004; Segal, 2004).

Functional Fixedness **Functional fixedness** may hinder problem-solving. For example, first ask yourself what a pair of pliers is. Is it a tool for grasping, a paperweight, or a weapon?

A pair of pliers could function as any of these, but your tendency to think of it as a grasping tool is fostered by your experience with it. You have probably used pliers only for grasping things. Functional fixedness is the tendency to think of an object in terms of its name or its familiar function. It can be similar to a mental set in that it makes it difficult to use familiar objects to solve problems in novel ways.

incubation
in problem-solving, a hypothetical process that sometimes occurs when we stand back from a frustrating problem for a while and the solution "suddenly" appears

functional fixedness
tendency to view an object in terms of its name or familiar usage

Judgment and Decision-Making

How do people make judgments and decisions? You might like to think that people are so rational that they carefully weigh the pros and cons when they make judgments or decisions. Or you might think that they insist on finding and examining all the relevant information. Actually, people make most of their decisions on the basis of limited information. They take shortcuts. They use heuristic devices—rules of thumb—in judgments and decision-making just as they do in problem-solving (Gilovich et al., 2002). For example, they may let a financial advisor select stocks for them rather than research the companies themselves. Or they may see a doctor recommended by a friend rather than look at the doctor's credentials. In this section we consider various factors in judgment and decision-making.

Fiction

It appears that humans are not the only species who use insight to solve problems.

Figure 8.1

Bismarck Uses a Cognitive Map to Claim His Just Desserts

Bismarck has learned to reach dinner by climbing ladder *A*. But now the food goal (*F*) is blocked by a wire-mesh barrier *B*. Bismarck washes his face for a while, but then, in an apparent flash of insight, he runs back down ladder *A* and up new ladder *N* to reach the goal.

Heuristics in Decision-Making

Let us begin by asking you to imagine that you flip a coin six times. In the following three possible outcomes, H stands for heads and T for tails. Circle the most likely sequence:

> H H H H H H
> H H H T T T
> T H H T H T

Did you select T H H T H T as the most likely sequence of events? Most people do. Why? There are two reasons. First, people recognize that the sequence of six heads in a row is unlikely. (The probability of achieving it is $1/2 \times 1/2 \times 1/2 \times 1/2 \times 1/2 \times 1/2$, or 1/64th.) Three heads and three tails are more likely than six heads (or six tails). Second, people recognize that the sequence of heads and tails ought to appear random. T H H T H T has a random look to it, whereas H H H T T T does not.

People tend to select T H H T H T because of the **representativeness heuristic**. According to this decision-making heuristic, people make judgments about events (samples) according to the populations of events that they appear to represent (Kahneman & Frederick, 2002; Shepperd & Koch, 2005). In this case, the sample of events is six coin tosses. The "population" is an infinite number of random coin tosses. But guess what? *Each* sequence is equally likely (or unlikely). If the question had been whether six heads or three heads and three tails had been more likely, the correct answer would have been three and three.

If the question had been whether heads and tails would be more likely to be consecutive or in random order, the correct answer would have been random order. But each of the three sequences is a *specific* sequence. What is the probability of attaining the *specific* sequence T H H T H T? The probability that the first coin toss will result in a tail is 1/2. The probability that the second will result in a head is 1/2, and so on. Thus, the probability of attaining the exact sequence T H H T H T is identical to that of achieving any other specific sequence: $1/2 \times 1/2 \times 1/2 \times 1/2 \times 1/2 \times 1/2$ = 1/64th. (Try this out on a friend.)

Another heuristic device used in decision-making is the **availability heuristic**. According to this heuristic, our estimates of frequency or probability are based on how easy it is to find examples of relevant events. Let me ask you whether there are more art majors or sociology majors at your college. Unless you are familiar with the enrollment statistics, you will probably answer on the basis of the numbers of art majors and sociology majors that you know.

The **anchoring and adjustment heuristic** suggests that there can be a good deal of inertia in our judgments. In forming opinions or making estimates, we have an initial view, or presumption. This is the anchor. As we receive additional information, we make adjustments, sometimes grudgingly. That is, if you grow up believing that one religion or one political party is the "right" one, that belief serves as a cognitive anchor. When inconsistencies show up in your religion or political party, you may adjust your views of them, but perhaps not very willingly.

Let us illustrate further with a math problem. Write each of the following multiplication problems on a separate piece of paper:

> A. 8 x 7 x 6 x 5 x 4 x 3 x 2 x 1
> B. 1 x 2 x 3 x 4 x 5 x 6 x 7 x 8

Show problem A to a few friends. Give them each five seconds to estimate the answer. Show problem B to some other friends and give them five seconds to estimate the answer.

The answers to the multiplication problems are the same because the order of quantities being multiplied does not change the outcome. When Tversky and Kahneman (1982) showed these problems to high-school students, the average estimate given by students who were shown version A was significantly higher than that given by students who were shown version B. Students who saw 8 in the first position offered an average estimate of 2,250. Students who saw 1 in the first position gave an average estimate of 512. That is, the estimate was larger when 8 served as the anchor. By the way, what is the correct answer to the multiplication problems? Can you use the anchoring and adjustment heuristic to explain why both groups were so far off?

The Framing Effect

What is the framing effect? The **framing effect** refers to the way in which wording, or the context in which information is presented, affects decision-making (Gonzalez et al., 2005; Tetlock & McGraw, 2005). Political groups, like advertisers, are aware of the *framing effect* and choose their words accordingly. For example, proponents of legalized abortion refer to themselves as "pro-choice" and opponents refer to themselves as "pro-life." Each group frames itself in a

LEFT

RIGHT

Figure 8.2

MRI Results of the Left and Right Hemispheres of the Cerebral Cortexes of a Great Ape

In their MRI study of the brains of twenty-five chimpanzees and two gorillas, Cantalupo and Hopkins found that the great majority, twenty, showed larger areas similar to Broca's area in the left hemisphere. So do most humans. Six apes showed larger areas in the right hemisphere. Only one showed no difference. It would thus appear that chimpanzees and gorillas have some rudimentary language structures in their brains, even if they are not "wired" for speech.

positive way ("pro" something) and refers to a popular value (freedom or life).

Overconfidence

Whether our decisions are correct or incorrect, most of us tend to be overconfident about them. We also tend to view our situations with twenty-twenty hindsight. When we are proven wrong, we frequently find a way to show that we "knew it all along." We also become overconfident that we would have known the actual outcome if we had had access to the information that became available after the event. For example, if we had known that a key player would pull a hamstring muscle, we would have predicted a different outcome for the football game. If we had known that it would be blustery on Election Day, we would have predicted a smaller voter turnout and a different outcome. *Why do people tend to be convinced that they are right, even when they are dead wrong?* There are several reasons for overconfidence, even when our judgments are wrong:

- We tend to be unaware of how flimsy our assumptions may be.

- We tend to focus on examples that confirm our judgments and ignore those that do not.

- Because our working memories have limited space, we tend to forget information that runs counter to our judgments.

- We work to bring about the events we believe in, so they sometimes become self-fulfilling prophecies.

LO² Language
Communication by Nonhumans

In recent years the exclusive human claim to language has been brought into question by studies of communication with various animal species. The African Grey parrot, like many other parrots, can mimic human speech, but it is also suspected of being intelligent enough to understand some of the words it imitates. It has long been suspected that spontaneous language development occurs among

many species of dolphins and whales, but we lack solid scientific evidence. Monkeys signal the peril of nearby predators with characteristic hoots. But none of these sounds contains *symbols*.

A language is a system of symbols along with rules that are used to manipulate the symbols. Symbols such as words stand for or represent other objects, events, or ideas. Because chimpanzees and gorillas have been taught to communicate by making signs with their hands, the question as to whether or not they are actually using language in the way that humans do is much more complex.

Chimpanzees are our closest genetic relatives, sharing an estimated 98.42% of their genetic code with humans (Zimmer, 2002–2003). MRI studies with chimpanzees and gorillas show that most of them, like humans, show enlargement in the left hemisphere of the cerebral cortex, in part of Broca's area (Cantalupo & Hopkins, 2001; see Figure 8.2). The differences that remain between humans and chimps are at least in part associated with capabilities such as fine control of the mouth and larynx that are not found in apes (Enard et al., 2002). The genetic codes of chimps and humans are apparently similar enough to give chimps some ability to use language, but different enough to prevent chimps from speaking.

Do Apes Really Use Language?

Although apes do not speak, they have been taught to use American Sign Language and other symbol systems. For example, a chimpanzee named Washoe, who was a pioneer in the effort to teach apes to use language, was using 181 signs by the age of thirty-two. Loulis, a baby chimp adopted by Washoe, gained the ability to use signs just by observing Washoe and some other chimps who had been trained in sign language (Fouts, 1997). Other chimps have used plastic symbols or pressed keys on a computer keyboard to communicate.

Sue Savage-Rumbaugh and her colleagues (1993; Shanker et al., 1999) believe that pygmy chimpanzees

holophrase
a single word used to express complex meanings

yellow, and blue (Regier et al., 2005). Moreover, people who use only a few words to distinguish among colors seem to perceive the same color variations as people with more words. For example, the Dani of New Guinea have just two words for colors: one that refers to yellows and reds and one that refers to greens and blues. Yet performance on matching and memory tasks shows that the Dani can discriminate the many colors of the spectrum.

Most cognitive scientists no longer accept the linguistic-relativity hypothesis (Pinker, 1990). For one thing, adults use images and abstract logical propositions, as well as words, as units of thought. Infants, moreover, display considerable intelligence before they have learned to speak. Another criticism is that a language's vocabulary suggests the range of concepts that the speakers of the language have traditionally found important, not their cognitive limits. For example, people who were magically lifted from the 19th century and placed inside an airplane probably would not think they were flying inside a bird or a large insect, even if their language lacked a word for airplane.

Language Development: The Two-Year Explosion

How does language develop? Languages around the world develop in a specific sequence of steps, beginning with the *prelinguistic* vocalizations of crying, cooing, and babbling. These sounds are not symbols. That is, they do not represent objects or events. Therefore, they are *prelinguistic*, not linguistic.

Prelinguistic Vocalizations

As parents are well aware, newborn children have one inborn, highly effective form of verbal expression: crying—and more crying. But crying does not represent language; it is a prelinguistic event. During the second month, babies begin *cooing*, another form of prelinguistic expression that appears to be linked to feelings of pleasure. By the fifth or sixth month, children begin to *babble*. Children babble sounds that occur in many languages, including the throaty German *ch,* the clicks of certain African languages, and rolling *r*'s. Babies' babbling frequently combines consonants and vowels, as in "ba," "ga," and,

Fiction

Crying does *not* represent language; it is a prelinguistic event.

sometimes, the much-valued "dada." "Dada" at first is purely coincidental (sorry, dads), despite the family's delight over its appearance.

Babbling, like crying and cooing, is inborn and prelinguistic. Deaf children babble, and children from cultures whose languages sound very different all seem to babble the same sounds (Hoff, 2005). But children single out the sounds used in the home within a few months. By the age of nine or ten months they are repeating the sounds regularly, and foreign sounds are dropping out. In fact, early experience in acquiring the phonemes native to one's own language can make it difficult to pronounce and even discriminate the phonemes used in other languages later in life (Iverson et al., 2003).

Children tend to utter their first word at about one year of age, but many parents miss it, often because it is not pronounced clearly or because pronunciation varies from one usage to the next (Nelson et al., 1993). The growth of vocabulary is slow at first. It may take children three to four months to achieve a ten-word vocabulary after they have spoken their first word. By about eighteen months, children are producing a couple of dozen words.

For both children with normal hearing and deaf children, gesturing tends to develop ahead of words (Guidetti & Nikoladis, 2008). Babies can wave bye-bye to Grandma months before they can talk, for instance, and can also be taught to use signs in the second half of the first year. The researcher of children's language development, Elizabeth Bates (2004), noted that the development of sign language "has to do with how easily one can imitate and reproduce something with a great big fat hand as opposed to the mini, delicate hundreds of muscles that control the tongue… You can also see somebody using a hand, which you can't do with a tongue." The areas in the brain that control the mouth and speech and the areas that control the hands and gestures overlap a great deal and develop together (Bates, 2001; Bernardis et al., 2008; Guidetti & Nikoladis, 2008).

Development of Grammar

The first linguistic utterances of children around the globe are single words that can express complex meanings. These initial utterances of children are called **holophrases**. For example, *mama* may be used by the child to signify meanings as varied as "There goes Mama," "Come here, Mama," and "You are my Mama." Similarly, *cat* can signify "There is a cat," "That stuffed animal looks just like my cat," or "I want you to give me my cat right now!" Most children show their parents what they intend by augmenting their holophrases with gestures and intonations. That is, they act delighted when parents do as requested and howl when they do not.

Toward the end of the second year, children begin to speak two-word sentences. These sentences are termed *telegraphic speech* because they resemble telegrams. Telegrams cut out the "unnecessary" words. "Home Tuesday" might stand for "I expect to be home on Tuesday." Two-word utterances seem to appear at about the same time in the development of all languages (Slobin, 1983). Two-word utterances are brief but grammatically correct. The child says, "Sit chair" to tell a parent to sit in a chair, not "Chair sit." The child says, "My shoe," not "Shoe my," to show possession. "Mommy go" means Mommy is leaving. "Go Mommy" expresses the wish for Mommy to go away.

There are different kinds of two-word utterances. Some, for example, contain nouns or pronouns and verbs ("Daddy sit"). Others contain verbs and objects ("Hit ball"). The sequence of emergence of the various kinds of two-word utterances is also apparently the same in all languages—languages as diverse as English, Luo (an African tongue), German, Russian, and Turkish (Slobin, 1983). The invariance of this sequence has implications for theories of language development, as we will see.

Overregularization

Overregularization is an important development for understanding the roles of nature and nurture in language development. In English, we add *d* or *ed* to make the past tense of regular verbs and *s* or *z* sounds to make regular nouns plural. Thus, *walk* becomes *walked,* and *look* becomes *looked. Cat* becomes *cats,* and *doggy* becomes *doggies.* There are also irregular verbs and nouns. For example, *see* becomes *saw, sit* becomes *sat,* and *go* becomes *went. Sheep* remains *sheep* (plural) and *child* becomes *children.*

At first children learn irregular verbs and nouns by imitating older people. Two-year-olds tend to form them correctly—at first! Then they become aware of the grammatical rules for forming the past tense and plurals. As a result, they tend to make charming errors (Pinker, 1997). A three- to five-year-old, for example, may be more likely to say "I seed it" than "I saw it," and more likely to say "Mommy sitted down" than "Mommy sat down." They are likely to talk about the "gooses" and "sheeps" they "seed" on the farm and about all the "childs" they ran into at the playground. This tendency to regularize the irregular is what is meant by overregularization.

Should parents be concerned about overregularization? Not at all. Overregularization reflects knowledge of grammar, not faulty language development. In another year or two, *mouses* will be boringly transformed into *mice,* and Mommy will no longer have *sitted* down. Parents might as well enjoy overregularization while they can.

overregularization
the application of regular grammatical rules for forming inflections (e.g., past tense and plurals) to irregular verbs and nouns

Other Developments

By the age of six, children's vocabularies have expanded to 10,000 words, give or take a few thousand. By seven to nine, most children realize that words can have more than one meaning, and they are entertained by riddles and jokes that require some sophistication with language.

Between the elementary school and high school years, language grows more complex, and children rapidly add to their vocabularies. Vocabulary, in fact, can grow for a lifetime, especially in one's fields of specialization and interest.

Truth

Young children say things like "Daddy goed away" and "Mommy sitted down" because they *do* understand rules of grammar.

Nature and Nurture in Language Development

Billions of children have acquired the languages spoken by their parents and passed them down, with minor changes, from generation to generation. Language development, like many other areas of development, apparently reflects the interactions between nature and nurture. *What are the roles of nature and nurture in language development?*

MASTERFILE (ROYALTY-FREE DIV.)

Learning Theory and Language Development

Learning theorists see language as developing according to laws of learning (Hoff, 2005). They usually refer to the concepts of imitation and reinforcement. From a social-cognitive perspective, parents serve as *models*. Children learn language, at least in part, through observation and imitation. Many words, especially nouns and verbs (including irregular verbs), are apparently learned by imitation.

Children initially repeat the irregular verb forms they have heard accurately, apparently as a result of modeling. Modeling, however, does not explain all of the events in language learning. As noted previously, children later overregularize irregular verb forms because they have developed an understanding of grammar. Nor can learning by imitation explain how children come to utter phrases and sentences they have *not* observed. Parents, for example, are unlikely to model utterances such as "Bye-bye sock" and "All gone Daddy," but children say them.

Learning theory cannot account for the unchanging sequence of language development and the spurts in children's language acquisition. Even the types of two-word utterances emerge in a consistent pattern in diverse cultures. Although timing differs from one child to another, the types of questions used, passive versus active sentences, and so on, all emerge in the same order.

The Nativist Approach to Language Development

The nativist theory of language development holds that the innate factors—which make up children's *nature*—cause children to attend to and acquire language in certain ways. From this perspective, children bring neurological "prewiring" to language learning (Newport, 1998; Pinker, 1994a, 1999).

According to psycholinguistic theory, language acquisition involves the interaction of environmental influences—such as exposure to parental speech and reinforcement—and the inborn tendency to acquire language. Noam Chomsky (1980, 1991) refers to the inborn tendency as a language acquisition device (LAD). Evidence for an LAD is found in the universality of human language abilities and in the specific sequence of language development (Baker, 2001).

The LAD prepares the nervous system to learn grammar. On the surface, languages differ a great deal. However, the LAD serves children all over the world because languages share what Chomsky refers to as a "universal grammar"—an underlying set of rules for turning ideas into sentences (Pinker, 1994a).

In the following section we see that some aspects of language development—particularly vocabulary development—are strongly related to intelligence. Numerous researchers suggest that language learning occurs during one or more *sensitive periods*, which begin at about eighteen to twenty-four months and last until puberty (Bates, 2001). During these sensitive periods, neural development (as in the differentiating of brain structures) provides plasticity that facilitates language learning (Bates, 2001). Evidence for a sensitive period is found in recovery from brain injuries in some people. Injuries to the hemisphere that controls language (usually the left hemisphere) can impair or destroy the ability to speak. But before puberty, children suffering left-hemisphere injuries frequently recover a good deal of speaking ability. Lenneberg (1967) suggested that in young children, left-hemisphere damage may encourage the development of language functions in the right hemisphere. But adaptation ability wanes in adolescence, when brain tissue has reached adult levels of differentiation.

LO^3 Intelligence

The concept of intelligence is closely related to thinking. Whereas thinking involves the understanding and manipulating of information, intelligence is the underlying ability to understand the world and cope with its challenges. Although these concepts overlap, psychologists tend to be concerned with *how* we think, but laypeople and psychologists are often concerned with *how much* intelligence we have. Although intelligence, like thinking, cannot be directly seen or touched, psychologists tie the concept to achievements such as school performance and occupational status (Pind et al., 2003; Wagner, 1997).

Theories of Intelligence

Although psychologists have engaged in thousands of studies on intelligence, they do not quite agree on what intelligence is. Psychologists have therefore developed theories to help them understand and define intelligence.

Factor Theories

Many investigators have viewed intelligence as consisting of one or more *factors*. Factor theories argue that intelligence is made up of a number of mental abilities, ranging from one kind of ability to hundreds.

In 1904, British psychologist Charles Spearman suggested that the behaviors we consider intelligent have a common underlying factor that he labeled g, for "general intelligence" or broad reasoning and problem-solving abilities. Spearman supported his view by noting that people who excel in one area (such as vocabulary) are also likely to excel in others (such as math). But he also noted that even the most capable people are relatively superior in some areas—such as music or business or poetry. For this reason, he suggested that specific, or s, factors account for specific abilities.

Contemporary psychologists continue to use the term g in research, speaking, for example, of the extent to which they believe a particular kind of test, such as the SATs, measure g (Gignac & Vernon, 2003; Rushton et al., 2003).

The American psychologist Louis Thurstone (1938) analyzed tests of specific abilities and concluded that Spearman had oversimplified intelligence. Thurstone's data suggested the presence of nine specific factors, which he labeled primary mental abilities (see Table 8.1). Thurstone's primary mental abilities contain the types of items measured on the most widely used intelligence tests today. The question remains as to whether his primary mental abilities are distinct or whether they are different ways of assessing g.

The Theory of Multiple Intelligences

Thurstone wrote about various factors or components of intelligence. Howard Gardner (1983/1993), instead, proposes that there are a number of *intelligences*, not just one. *What is meant by multiple intelligences?* Gardner refers to each kind of intelligence in his theory as "an intelligence" because they can differ so much. Two of these "intelligences" are familiar ones: language ability and logical–mathematical ability. Gardner also refers, however, to bodily–kinesthetic talents (of the sort shown by dancers and athletes), musical talent, spatial–relations skills, and two kinds of personal intelligence: awareness of one's own inner feelings and sensitivity to other people's feelings. Gardner (2001) has recently added "naturalist intelligence" and "existential intelligence." Naturalist intelligence refers to the ability to look at natural events, such as kinds of animals and plants, or the stars above, and to develop insights into their nature and the laws that govern their behavior. Existential intelligence means dealing with the larger philosophical issues of life. According to Gardner, one can compose symphonies or advance mathematical theory yet be average in, say, language and personal skills.

Critics of Gardner's view agree that people function more intelligently in some aspects of life than in others. They also agree that many people have special talents, such as bodily–kinesthetic talents, even if their overall intelligence is average. But these critics question whether such talents are best thought of as "intelligences" (Neisser et al., 1996). Language skills, reasoning ability, and ability to solve math problems seem to be more closely related than musical or gymnastic talent to what most people mean by intelligence.

The Triarchic Theory of Intelligence

Psychologist Robert Sternberg (2000; Sternberg et al., 2003) has constructed a three-pronged, or *triarchic*, theory of intelligence that resembles a view proposed by the Greek philosopher Aristotle (Tigner & Tigner, 2000). *What is Sternberg's triarchic model of intelligence?* These types of intelligence are *analytical*, *creative*, and *practical* (see Figure 8.3 on page 176).

Analytical intelligence is similar to Aristotle's "theoretical intelligence" and can be defined as academic ability. It enables us to solve problems and

g
Spearman's symbol for general intelligence, which he defined as broad reasoning and problem-solving abilities

s
Spearman's symbol for *specific* factors, or *s* factors, which he believed accounted for individual abilities

primary mental abilities
according to Thurstone, the basic abilities that make up intelligence; examples include word fluency and numerical ability

Table 8.1

Primary Mental Abilities, According to Thurstone

Ability	Definition
Visual and spatial abilities	Visualizing forms and spatial relationships
Perceptual speed	Grasping perceptual details rapidly, perceiving similarities and differences between stimuli
Numerical ability	Computing numbers
Verbal meaning	Knowing the meanings of words
Memory	Recalling information (e.g., words and sentences)
Word fluency	Thinking of words quickly (e.g., rhyming and doing crossword puzzles)
Deductive reasoning	Deriving examples from general rules
Inductive reasoning	Inferring general rules from examples

acquire new knowledge. It is the type of intelligence measured by standard intelligence tests. Problem-solving skills include encoding information, combining and comparing bits of information, and generating a solution. Consider Sternberg's analogy problem:

> *Washington* is to 1 as *Lincoln* is to
> (a) 5, (b) 10, (c) 15, (d) 50?

To solve the analogy, we must first correctly *encode* the elements—*Washington, 1,* and *Lincoln*—by identifying them and comparing them to other information. We can first encode *Washington* and *Lincoln* as the names of presidents and then try to combine *Washington* and 1 in a meaningful manner. (There are other possibilities: Both are also the names of memorials and cities, for example.) If we do encode the names as presidents, two possibilities quickly come to mind. Washington was the first president, and his picture is on the one-dollar bill. We can then generate two possible solutions and try them out. First, was Lincoln the fifth, tenth, fifteenth, or fiftieth president? Second, on what bill is Lincoln's picture found? (Do you need to consult a history book or peek into your wallet at this point?) The answer is (a) 5, because Lincoln's likeness is found on the five-dollar bill. (He was the nation's 16th president, not 15th president.)

Creative intelligence is similar to Aristotle's "productive intelligence" and is defined by the ability to cope with novel situations and generate many possible solutions to problems.

It is creative to quickly relate novel situations to familiar situations (that is, to perceive similarities and differences). Psychologists who consider creativity to be separate from analytical intelligence or academic ability note that there is only a moderate relationship between academic ability and creativity (Simonton, 2000). To Sternberg, however, creativity is a form of intelligence.

Aristotle and Sternberg both speak of practical intelligence ("street smarts"). Practical intelligence enables people to deal with other people, including difficult people, and to meet the demands of their environment. For example, keeping a job by adapting one's behavior to the employer's requirements is adaptive. But if the employer is making unreasonable demands, finding a more suitable job is also adaptive. Street smarts appear to help people get by in the real world, especially with other people, but are not particularly predictive of academic success.

Truth

It is true that street smarts are a sign of intelligence—at least according to Aristotle and Sternberg.

Emotional Intelligence

Psychologists Peter Salovey and John Mayer developed the theory of emotional intelligence, which was popularized by psychologist Daniel Goleman (1995). The theory holds that social and emotional skills, like academic skills, are a form of intelligence. *Just what is "emotional intelligence"?*

Figure 8.3

Sternberg's Theory of Intelligence

According to Robert Sternberg, there are three types of intelligence: analytical (academic ability), creative, and practical ("street smarts"). Psychologists discuss the relationships between intelligence and creativity, but within Sternberg's model, creativity is a *type* of intellectual functioning.

Analytical intelligence
(Academic ability)
Abilities to solve problems, compare and contrast, judge, evaluate, and criticize

Creative intelligence
(Creativity and insight)
Abilities to invent, discover, suppose, or theorize

Practical intelligence
("Street smarts")
Abilities to adapt to the demands of one's environment, apply knowledge in practical situations

Emotional intelligence resembles two of Gardner's "intelligences"—intrapersonal skills and interpersonal skills (including insight into the feelings of other people). It also involves self-insight and self-control—the abilities to recognize and regulate one's moods (Salovey et al., 2002).

Failure to develop emotional intelligence is connected with poor ability to cope with stress, depression, and aggressive behavior (Salovey et al., 2002; Wang, 2002).

But is emotional intelligence a form of intelligence? Psychologist Ulric Neisser (1997b) says that "the skills that Goleman describes . . . are certainly important for determining life outcomes, but nothing is to be gained by calling them forms of intelligence."

There are thus many views of intelligence—what intelligence is and how many kinds of intelligence there may be. We do not yet have the final word on the nature of intelligence, but I would like to share David Wechsler's definition. Wechsler originated the most widely used series of intelligence tests, and he defined intelligence as the "capacity of an individual to understand the world [and the] resourcefulness to cope with its challenges" (1975, p. 139).

Creativity and Intelligence

Think of artists, musicians, poets, scientists who innovate research methods, and other creative individuals. *What is creativity? How is it connected to intelligence?*

Like the concept of intelligence, the concept of creativity has been difficult to define. One issue is whether creativity is distinct from intelligence, or is, as Sternberg suggests, a type of intelligence. For example, we would not ask the question, "Do creative people tend to be intelligent?" unless we saw creativity as distinct from intelligence. If you consider creativity to be an aspect of intelligence, then the two concepts—intelligence and creativity—overlap. But if you think of intelligence as more closely related to academic ability, it is not always true that a highly intelligent person is creative or that a creative person is highly intelligent. Research findings suggest that the relationship between intelligence test scores and standard measures of creativity is only moderate (Simonton, 2000; Sternberg & Williams, 1997).

Within his triarchic theory, Sternberg defines creativity as the ability to do things that are novel and useful (Sternberg, 2001). Other psychologists note that creative people can solve problems to which there are no preexisting solutions and no proven formulas (Simonton, 2000). According to Sternberg and Lubart (1995, 1996), creative people take chances. They refuse to accept limitations. They appreciate art and music. They use common materials to make unique things. They challenge social norms and take unpopular stands. They challenge ideas that other people accept at face value.

Many psychologists see creativity as the ability to make unusual, sometimes remote, associations to the elements of a problem to generate new combinations. An essential aspect of a creative response is the leap from the elements of the problem to the novel solution.

Creative problem-solving demands divergent rather than convergent thinking. In convergent thinking, thought is limited to present facts; the problem-solver narrows his or her thinking to find the best solution. (You use convergent thinking to arrive at the right answer to a multiple-choice question.) In divergent thinking, the problem-solver associates freely to the elements of the problem, allowing "leads" to run a nearly limitless course. (You may use divergent thinking when you are trying to generate ideas to answer an essay question on a test.)

Problem-solving can involve both kinds of thinking. At first divergent thinking helps generate many possible solutions. Convergent thinking is then used to select likely solutions and reject others.

Intelligence test questions usually require analytical, convergent thinking to focus in on the one right answer. Tests of creativity determine how flexible a person's thinking is (Simonton, 2000). Here is an item from a test used by Getzels and Jackson (1962) to measure associative ability, a factor in creativity: "Write as many meanings as you can for each of the following words: (a) duck; (b) sack; (c) pitch; (d) fair." Those who write several meanings for each word, rather than only one, are rated as potentially more creative.

Now that we have begun speaking of scores on intelligence tests, let's see how psychologists go about measuring intelligence. We will also see how psychologists attempt to *validate* their measures of intelligence—that is, how they try to demonstrate that they are in fact measuring intelligence.

creativity the ability to generate novel and useful solutions to problems

convergent thinking a thought process that narrows in on the single best solution to a problem

divergent thinking a thought process that attempts to generate multiple solutions to problems

Truth/Fiction (depends)

The answer to whether an intelligent person is creative or a creative person is intelligent partly depends on definitions of the terms.

The Measurement of Intelligence

Although psychologists disagree about the nature of intelligence, laypeople and educators are concerned with "how much" intelligence people have, because the issue affects educational and occupational choices. In this section we consider two of the most widely used intelligence tests.

The Stanford–Binet Intelligence Scale

Many of the concepts of psychology have their origins in common sense. The commonsense notion that academic achievement depends on children's intelligence led Alfred Binet and Theodore Simon to invent measures of intelligence.

What is the Stanford–Binet Intelligence Scale? Early in the 20th century, the French public school system was looking for a test that could identify children who were unlikely to benefit from regular classroom instruction. If these children were identified, they could be given special attention. The first version of that test, the Binet–Simon scale, came into use in 1905. Since that time it has undergone extensive revision and refinement. The current version is the Stanford–Binet Intelligence Scale (SBIS).

Binet assumed that intelligence increases with age, so older children should get more items right than younger children. Binet therefore included a series of age-graded questions, as in Table 8.2, arranged in order of difficulty.

The Binet–Simon scale yielded a score called a mental age (MA). The MA shows the intellectual level at which a child is functioning. For example, a child with an MA of 6 is functioning intellectually like the average six-year-old. In taking the test, children earned "months" of credit for each correct answer. Their MA was determined by adding up the years and months of credit they attained.

Louis Terman adapted the Binet–Simon scale for use with American children at Stanford University. The first version of the resultant Stanford–Binet Intelligence Scale was published in 1916. The SBIS included more items than the original test and was used with children aged two to sixteen. The SBIS also yielded an intelligence quotient (IQ) rather than an MA. As a result, American educators developed interest in learning the IQs of their pupils. The SBIS is used today with children from the age of two upward and with adults.

The IQ reflects the relationship between a child's mental age and his or her actual or chronological age (CA). Use of this ratio reflects the fact that the same MA score has different implications for children of different ages. That is, an MA of 8 is an above-average score for a six-year-old but below average for a ten-year-old. In 1912 the German psychologist Wilhelm Stern suggested the IQ as a way to deal with this problem. Stern computed IQ using the formula

$$IQ = \frac{\text{Mental age (MA)}}{\text{Chronological age (CA)}} \times 100.$$

According to this formula, a child with an MA of 6 and a CA of 6 would have an IQ of 100. Children who can handle intellectual problems as well as older children do have IQs above 100. For example, an eight-year-old who does as well on the SBIS as the average ten-year-old would attain an IQ of 125. Children who do not answer as many items correctly as other children of the same age attain MAs lower than their CAs. Thus, their IQ scores are below 100.

IQ scores on the SBIS today are derived by comparing their results to those of other people of the same age. People who answer more items correctly than the average for people of the same age attain IQ scores above 100. People who answer fewer items correctly than the average for their age attain scores below 100. Therefore, two children can answer exactly the same items on an intelligence test correctly, yet one can be above average in IQ. This is because the ages of the children may differ. The more intelligent child would be the younger of the two.

Truth

Two children can answer exactly the same items on an intelligence test correctly, yet one can be above average and the other below average in IQ.

The Wechsler Scales

In contrast to the SBIS, David Wechsler developed a series of scales for use with children and adults. *What is different about the Wechsler scales of intelligence?* The Wechsler scales group test questions into a number of separate subtests (see Figure 8.4). Each subtest measures a different intellectual task. For this reason, the test shows how well a person does on one type of task (such as defining words) as compared with another (such as using blocks to construct geometric designs). In this way, the Wechsler scales highlight children's relative strengths and

Table 8.2

Items Similar to Those on the Stanford–Binet Intelligence Scale

Level (Years)	Item
2	1. Children show knowledge of basic vocabulary words by identifying parts of a doll, such as the mouth, ears, and hair.
	2. Children show counting and spatial skills along with visual–motor coordination by building a tower of four blocks to match a model.
4	1. Children show word fluency and categorical thinking by filling in the missing words when they are asked questions such as:
	"Father is a man; mother is a _____?"
	"Hamburgers are hot; ice cream is _____?"
	2. Children show comprehension by answering correctly when they are asked questions such as:
	"Why do people have automobiles?"
	"Why do people have medicine?"
9	1. Children can point out verbal absurdities, as in this question: "In an old cemetery, scientists unearthed a skull which they think was that of George Washington when he was only five years of age. What is silly about that?"
	2. Children display fluency with words, as shown by answering these questions:
	"Can you tell me a number that rhymes with snore?"
	"Can you tell me a color that rhymes with glue?"
Adult	1. Adults show knowledge of the meanings of words and conceptual thinking by correctly explaining the differences between word pairs like "sickness and misery," "house and home," and "integrity and prestige."
	2. Adults show spatial skills by correctly answering questions like: "If a car turned to the right to head north, in what direction was it heading before it turned?"

weaknesses, as well as measure overall intellectual functioning.

Wechsler described some of his scales as measuring *verbal* tasks and others as assessing *performance* tasks. In general, verbal subtests require knowledge of verbal concepts, whereas performance subtests require familiarity with spatial–relations concepts. Wechsler's scales permit the computation of verbal and performance IQs. Nontechnically oriented college students often attain higher verbal than performance IQs. Less-well-educated people often obtain higher performance than verbal IQs.

Wechsler also introduced the concept of the *deviation IQ*. Instead of dividing mental age by chronological age to compute an IQ, he based IQ scores on how a person's answers compared with those attained by people in the same age group. The average test result at any age level is defined as an IQ score of 100. Wechsler distributed IQ scores so that the middle 50% were defined as the "broad average range" of 90 to 110. As you can see in Figure 8.5, IQ scores cluster around the average. Only 4% of the population have IQ scores of above 130 or below 70.

Group Tests

The SBIS and Wechsler scales are administered to one person at a time. This one-to-one ratio is optimal because it allows the examiner to observe the test taker closely. Examiners are alerted to factors that impair performance, such as language difficulties, illness, or a noisy or poorly lit room. But large institutions with few trained examiners, such as the public schools and armed forces, require tests that can be administered simultaneously to large groups.

Group tests for children were first developed during World War I. At first these tests were hailed as remarkable instruments because they helped school administrators place children. As the years passed, however, group tests came under attack because many administrators relied on them exclusively and did not seek other sources of information about children's abilities.

At their best, intelligence tests provide only one source of information about individual children. Numbers alone, and especially IQ scores, cannot adequately define children's special abilities and talents.

Differences in Intellectual Functioning

The average IQ score in the United States is very close to 100. Yet for some socioeconomic and ethnic groups in the United States, the average is higher, and for others, it is lower. Questions have also been raised about whether males or females are more intelligent overall, and whether there are gender

Figure 8.4

Items Similar to Those on the Wechsler Adult Intelligence Scale

Picture arrangement

These pictures tell a story, but they are in the wrong order. Put them in the right order so that they tell a story.

Picture completion

What part is missing from this picture?

Block design

Put the blocks together to make this picture.

Object assembly

Put the pieces together as quickly as you can.

differences in the kinds of intellectual or cognitive skills valued in society. Tests of intellectual functioning have thus been seen as divisive and as maintaining a class system or social order that is based on prejudices and "tradition" as much as on science. In this section we discuss (1) socioeconomic and ethnic differences and (2) gender differences in cognitive skills.

Socioeconomic and Ethnic Differences

There is a body of research suggestive of differences in intelligence—or, more precisely, intelligence test scores—between socioeconomic and ethnic groups. *What are the socioeconomic and ethnic differences in intelligence?* Lower-class U.S. children obtain IQ scores some ten to fifteen points lower than those obtained by middle- and upper-class children. African American children tend to obtain IQ scores some fifteen points lower than those obtained by their European American age-mates (Neisser

et al., 1996). Latino and Latina American and Native American children also tend to score below the norms for European Americans (Neisser et al., 1996).

Many studies of IQ confuse the factors of social class and ethnicity because disproportionate numbers of African Americans, Latino and Latina Americans, and Native Americans are found among the lower socioeconomic classes (Neisser et al., 1996). When we limit our observations to particular ethnic groups, we still find an effect for social class. That is, middle-class European Americans outscore poorer European Americans. Middle-class African Americans, Latino and Latina Americans, and Native Americans outscore poorer members of their own ethnic groups.

There may also be intellectual differences between Asians and Caucasians. Asian Americans, for example, frequently outscore European Americans on the math portion of the Scholastic Aptitude Test. Students in China (Taiwan) and Japan also outscore European Americans on achievement tests in math and science (Stevenson et al., 1986). In the United States, moreover, people of Asian Indian, Korean, Japanese, Filipino, and Chinese descent are more likely than European Americans, African Americans, and Latino and Latina Americans to graduate from high school and complete college (Xie & Goyette, 2003; Yeh & Chang, 2004). They are also highly over represented in competitive colleges and universities.

Most psychologists believe that such ethnic differences reflect cultural attitudes toward education rather than inborn racial differences (Neisser et

Truth

Many psychologists and social critics argue that intelligence tests measure many things other than intelligence—including familiarity with the dominant middle-class culture in the United States and motivation to perform well.

Figure 8.5

Approximate Distribution of IQ Scores

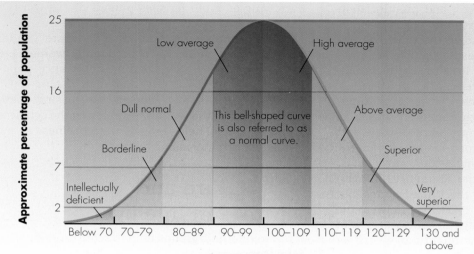

al., 1996). That is, the Asian children may be more motivated to work in school (Fuligni & Witkow, 2004; Xie & Goyette, 2003). Research shows that Chinese and Japanese students and their mothers tend to attribute academic successes to hard work (Randel et al., 2000). European Americans are more likely to attribute their children's academic successes to "natural" ability (Basic Behavioral Science Task Force, 1996b). Steinberg and his colleagues (1996) claim that parental encouragement and supervision in combination with peer support for academic achievement partially explain the superior performances of European Americans and Asian Americans as compared with African Americans and Latino and Latina Americans.

These ethnic differences lead us to ask: *Do intelligence tests contain cultural biases against ethnic minority groups and immigrants?* Are the tests valid when used with ethnic minority groups or people who are poorly educated?

Figure 8.6

Sample Items from Cattell's Culture-Fair Intelligence Test

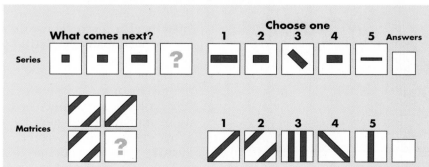

Because children reared in African American or Latino and Latina American neighborhoods may be at a cultural disadvantage in intelligence testing (Helms, 1992; Kwate, 2001), many psychologists, including Raymond B. Cattell (1949) and Florence Goodenough (Goodenough & Harris, 1950), have tried to construct culture-free intelligence tests. Cattell's Culture-Fair Intelligence Test evaluates reasoning through the child's ability to understand and use the rules that govern a progression of geometric designs (see Figure 8.6). Goodenough's Draw-A-Person test is based on the premise that children from all cultural backgrounds have had the opportunity to observe people and note the relationships between the parts and the whole. Her instructions simply require children to draw a picture of a man or woman.

Ironically, European American children outperform African American children on "culture-free" tests (Rushton et al., 2003), perhaps because they are more likely than disadvantaged children to have played with blocks (practice relevant to the Cattell test) and to have sketched animals, people, and things (practice relevant to the Goodenough test). Nor do culture-free tests predict academic success as well as other intelligence tests.

Gender Differences

It was once widely believed that males were more intelligent than females because of their greater knowledge of world affairs and their skills in science and industry. But these differences did not reflect differences in cognitive ability. Rather, they reflected exclusion of females from world affairs, science, and industry. Moreover, intelligence tests do not show overall gender differences in cognitive abilities (Halpern & LaMay, 2000).

Do males and females differ in intellectual functioning? Reviews of the research suggest that girls are somewhat superior to boys in verbal abilities, such as vocabulary, ability to generate sentences and words that are similar in meaning to other words, spelling, knowledge of foreign languages, and pronunciation (Halpern, 2003). Girls seem to acquire language somewhat faster than boys do. Also, in the United States, more boys than girls have reading problems, ranging from reading below grade level to severe disabilities (Liederman et al., 2005; Skelton, 2005).

Males seem to do somewhat better at manipulating visual images in working memory. Males as a group excel in visual–spatial abilities of the sort used in math, science, and map-reading (Collaer & Nelson, 2002; Halpern & LaMay, 2000).

There are no overall gender differences in average scores on math tests in the United States, but males are more likely than females to perform at the extremes, as in the percentage of individuals who obtain scores over 700 on the quantitative scale of the SAT (Else-Quest, N. M., Hyde, J. S., & Linn, M. C. (2010). Cross-national patterns of gender differences in mathematics: A meta-analysis. Psychological Bulletin, 136(1), 103-127).

But note that the reported gender differences are *group* differences. There is greater variation in these skills between individuals *within* the groups than between males and females (Halpern, 2003). That is, there may be a greater difference in, say, verbal skills between two women than between the typical woman and the typical man. Millions of females outdistance the "average" male in math and spatial abilities. Men have produced their verbally adept Shakespeares. Moreover, Hyde and Plant (1995) assert that in most cases, gender differences in cognitive skills are small. Differences in verbal, math, and visual–spatial abilities also appear to be narrowing as more females pursue course work in fields that had been typically populated by males.

While scholars sit around and debate gender differences in intellectual functioning, women are voting on the issue by flooding fields once populated almost exclusively by men (Cox & Alm, 2005). Figure 8.7 shows that women are tossing these stereotypes out the window by entering the sciences and professional fields ranging from business to law to medicine in increasing numbers.

LO⁴ Nature and Nurture in Intelligence

If different ethnic groups tend to score differently on intelligence tests, psychologists— like educators and other people involved in public life—want to know why. We will see that this is one debate that can make use of key empirical findings. Psychologists can point with pride to a rich mine of research on the roles of nature (genetic influences) and nurture (environmental influences) in the development of intelligence.

Genetic Influences on Intelligence

What are the genetic influences on intelligence? Research on genetic influences has employed kinship studies, twin studies, and adoptee studies (Neisser et al., 1996). Let us consider each of these to see whether heredity affects intellectual functioning.

We can examine the IQ scores of closely and distantly related people who have been reared together or apart. If heredity is involved in human intelligence, closely related people ought to have more similar IQs than distantly related or unrelated people, even when they are reared separately (Petrill & Deater-Deckard, 2004).

Figure 8.8 is a composite of the results of more than a hundred studies of IQ and heredity in human beings (Bouchard et al., 1990). The IQ scores of identical (monozygotic, or MZ)

Figure 8.7

Women Flood Professions Once Populated Almost Exclusively by Men

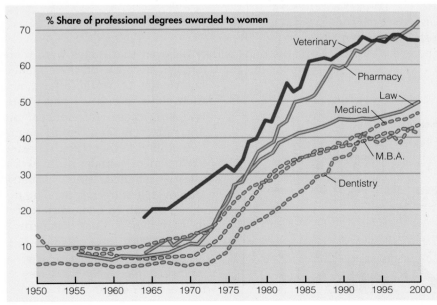

twins are more alike than scores for any other pairs, even when the twins have been reared apart. There are moderate correlations between the IQ scores of fraternal (dizygotic, or DZ) twins, between those of siblings, and between those of parents and their children. Correlations between the scores of children and their foster parents and between those of cousins are weak.

The results of large-scale twin studies are consistent with the data in Figure 8.8. A classic study of 500 pairs of MZ and DZ twins in Louisville, Kentucky (Wilson, 1983), found that the correlations in intelligence for MZ twins were higher than those for DZ twins. The correlations in intelligence between DZ twin pairs was the same as that between other siblings. The MacArthur Longitudinal Twin Study examined the intellectual abilities of 200 fourteen-month-old pairs of twins (Plomin et al., 1993). The study found that MZ twins were more similar than DZ twins in spatial memory, ability to categorize things, and word comprehension.

In sum, studies generally suggest that the heritability of intelligence is between 40% and 60% (Neisser et al., 1996). In other words, about half of the difference between your IQ score and the IQ scores of other people can be explained by heredity.

Note, too, that genetic pairs (such as MZ twins) who were reared together show higher correlations in their IQ scores than similar genetic pairs (such as other MZ twins) who were reared apart. This finding holds for DZ twins, siblings, parents and their children, and unrelated people. Being reared together is, therefore, related with similarities in IQ. *For this reason, the same group of studies used to demonstrate a role*

for the heritability of IQ scores also suggests that the environment plays a role in determining IQ scores.

Another strategy for exploring genetic influences on intelligence is to compare the correlations between the IQ scores of adopted children and those of their biological and adoptive parents. When children are separated from their biological parents at an early age, one can argue that strong relationships between their IQs and those of their natural parents reflect genetic influences. Strong relationships between the children's IQs and those of their adoptive parents might reflect environmental influences.

Several studies with one- and two-year-old children in Colorado (Baker et al., 1983), Texas (Horn, 1983), and Minnesota (Scarr & Weinberg, 1983) have found a stronger relationship between the IQ scores of adopted children and those of their biological parents than between the children's scores and those of their adoptive parents.

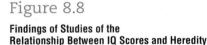

heritability
the degree to which the variations in a trait from one person to another can be attributed to, or explained by, genetic factors

Environmental Influences on Intelligence

What are the environmental influences on intelligence? To answer this question we must consider studies of environmental influences, which also employ a variety of research strategies. These include observation of the role of the home environment and evaluation of the effects of educational programs.

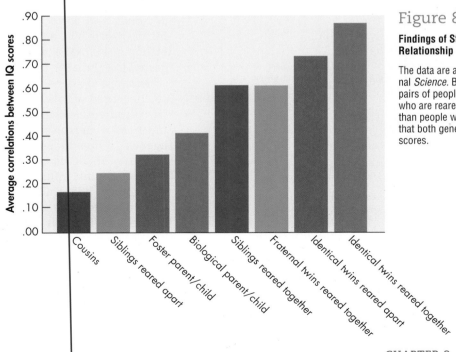

Figure 8.8

Findings of Studies of the Relationship Between IQ Scores and Heredity

The data are a composite of studies summarized in the journal *Science.* By and large, correlations are greater between pairs of people who are more closely related. Yet people who are reared together also have more similar IQ scores than people who are reared apart. Such findings suggest that both genetic and environmental factors contribute to IQ scores.

The Home Environment

The home environment and styles of parenting also affect IQ scores (Han et al., 2004; Molfese et al., 2003). Children of parents who are emotionally and verbally responsive, furnish appropriate play materials, are involved with their children, encourage independence, and provide varied daily experiences obtain higher IQ scores later on (Molfese et al., 1997). Organization and safety in the home have also been linked to higher IQs and achievement test scores (Bradley et al., 1989; Petrill et al., 2004).

Other studies support the view that children's early environment is linked to IQ scores and academic achievement. For example, Victoria Molfese and her colleagues (1997) found that the home environment was the single most important predictor of scores on IQ tests among children aged three to eight.

Education

Although intelligence is viewed as permitting people to profit from education, education also apparently contributes to intelligence. Government-funded efforts to provide preschoolers with enriched early environments have led to intellectual gains. Head Start programs, for example, enhance the IQ scores, achievement test scores, and academic skills of disadvantaged children (Stipek & Hakuta, 2007) by exposing them to materials and activities that middle-class children take for granted. These include letters and words, numbers, books, exercises in drawing, pegs and pegboards, puzzles, toy animals, and dolls. Head Start also helps poor children get medical and dental care, serves nutritious meals, and helps children develop the social skills necessary to succeed in school.

Preschool intervention programs can have long-term positive effects on children. During the elementary and high school years, graduates of preschool programs are less likely to be held back or placed in classes for slow learners. They are more likely to graduate from high school, go on to college, and earn higher incomes.

Later schooling also contributes to IQ. When children of about the same age start school a year apart because of admissions standards related to their date of birth, children who have been in school longer obtain higher IQ scores (Neisser et al., 1996). Moreover, test scores tend to decrease during the summer vacation (Neisser et al., 1996).

The findings on intelligence, the home environment, and educational experiences show that much indeed can be done to enhance intellectual functioning in children.

The Flynn Effect

Philosopher and researcher John Flynn (2003) found that IQ scores in the Western world increased substantially between 1947 and 2002, some 18 points in the United States. Psychologist Richard Nisbett (2007) argues that our genetic codes could not possibly have changed enough in half a century to account for this enormous difference and concludes that social and cultural factors such as the effects of improved educational systems and the penetration of the mass media must be among the reasons for the change.

If such environmental factors are capable of producing changes of this magnitude over time for the entire American population, they can also produce significant differences between subpopulations, such as between African Americans and European Americans. For example, the difference in IQ scores between the two racial groups has decreased from 15 points to 9.5 points over the past thirty years (Nisbett, 2007), which is again too large a difference to reflect genetic factors. Instead, it would suggest that the educational gap between the races may be narrowing.

All in all, intellectual functioning appears to reflect the interaction of a complex web of genetic, physical, personal, and sociocultural factors (Bartels et al., 2002; Bishop et al., 2003), as suggested in Figure 8.9.

Perhaps we need not be so concerned with whether we can sort out exactly how much of a person's intelligence is due to heredity and how much is due to environmental influences. Psychology has traditionally supported the dignity of the individual. It might be more appropriate for us to try to identify children of all ethnic groups who are at risk of failure and to do what we can to enrich their environments.

Genetic factors

A stimulating environment in the home and in the schools

Health
Socioeconomic status
Flexibility
Achievement motivation
Academic/educational adjustment
Belief that education and achievement are keys to self-development and fulfillment

Figure 8.9

The Complex Web of Factors That Affect Intellectual Functioning

Intellectual functioning appears to be influenced by the interaction of genetic factors, health, personality, and sociocultural factors.

Theories of Intelligence Summary Chart

Theory	Basic Information	Comments
General versus specific factors (proponent: Charles Spearman)	■ Spearman created factor analysis to study intelligence. ■ There is strong evidence for the general factor (g) in intelligence. ■ s factors are specific abilities, skills, and talents.	■ Concept of g remains in use today—a century later.
Primary mental abilities (proponent: Louis Thurstone)	■ Thurstone used factor analysis. ■ There are many "primary" abilities. ■ All abilities and factors are academically oriented.	■ Other researchers (e.g., Guilford) claim to have found hundreds of factors. ■ The more factors that are claimed, the more they overlap.
Triarchic theory (proponent: Robert Sternberg)	■ Intelligence is three-pronged—with analytical, creative, and practical components. ■ Analytical intelligence is analogous to academic ability.	■ The theory coincides with the views of Aristotle. ■ Critics do not view creativity as a component of intelligence.
Multiple intelligences (proponent: Howard Gardner)	■ Gardner theorized distinct "intelligences." ■ Intelligences include academic intelligences, personal and social intelligences, talents, and philosophical intelligences. ■ The theory posits different bases in the brain for different intelligences.	■ Proponents continue to expand the number of "intelligences." ■ Critics see little value in theorizing "intelligences" rather than aspects of intelligence. ■ Most critics consider musical and bodily skills to be special talents, not "intelligences."

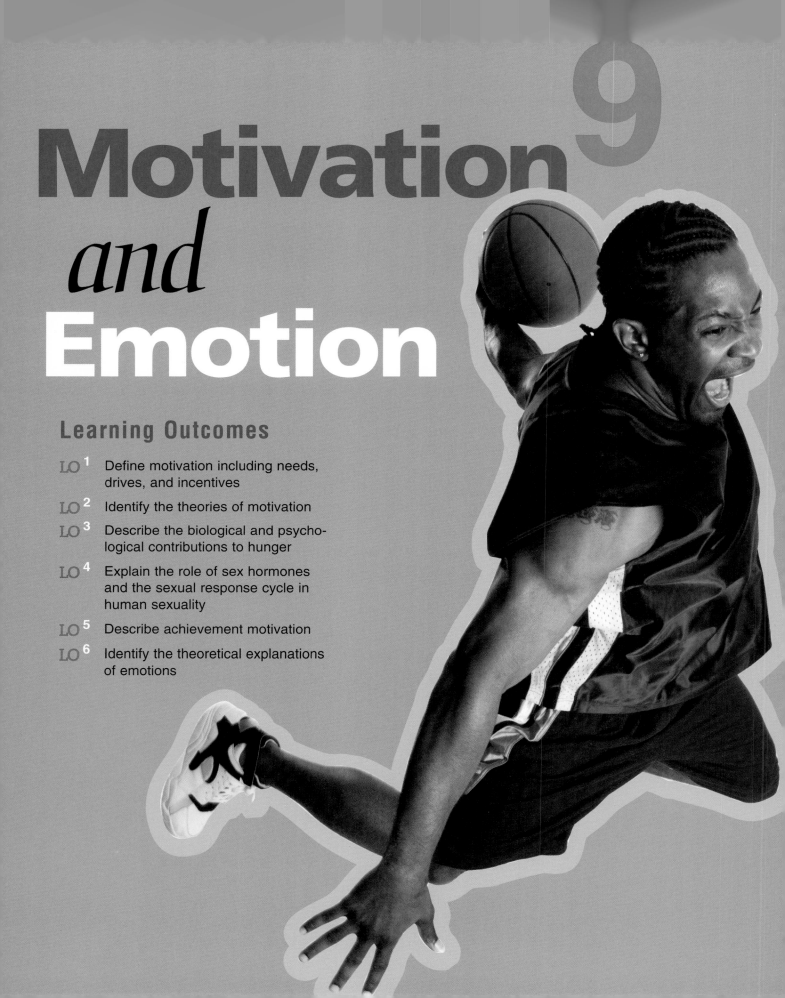

Motivation
and
Emotion

9

Learning Outcomes

LO **1**   Define motivation including needs, drives, and incentives

LO **2**   Identify the theories of motivation

LO **3**   Describe the biological and psychological contributions to hunger

LO **4**   Explain the role of sex hormones and the sexual response cycle in human sexuality

LO **5**   Describe achievement motivation

LO **6**   Identify the theoretical explanations of emotions

> ## "When a prophecy fails, how do its believers respond? Why?"

The Seekers had received word that the world was coming to an end on December 21st. A great flood would engulf their city and the rest of the Earth. Now they were gathered around their leader, Marian Keech, in her home, as she recorded messages that she said were sent to her by the Guardians from outer space. The messages were received through "automatic writing"; that is, the Guardians communicated through Ms. Keech, who wrote down their words without awareness. Another message brought good news, however. Because of their faith, the Seekers would be saved by flying saucers at the stroke of midnight on the 21st.

In their classic observational study, Leon Festinger and his colleagues (1956) described how they managed to be present in Ms. Keech's household at the fateful hour by pretending to belong to the group. Their purpose was to observe the behavior of the Seekers during and following the prophecy's failure. The cognitive theory of motivation that Festinger was working on—*cognitive-dissonance theory*—suggested that there would be a discrepancy or conflict between two key cognitions: (1) Ms. Keech is a prophet, and (2) Ms. Keech is wrong.

How might the conflict be resolved? One way would be for the Seekers to lose faith in Ms. Keech. But the researchers expected that according to their theory, the Seekers could also be motivated to resolve the conflict by going out to spread the word and find additional converts. Otherwise the group would be painfully embarrassed.

Let us return to the momentous night. Many members of the group had quit their jobs and gone on spending sprees before the anticipated end. Now, as midnight approached they fidgeted, awaiting the flying saucers. Midnight came, but there were no saucers. Anxious glances were exchanged. There was silence, and then some coughs. Minutes passed, torturously slowly. Watches were checked, more glances exchanged.

At 4:00 a.m., a bitter and frantic Ms. Keech complained that she sensed that members of the group were doubting her. At 4:45 a.m., however, she seemed suddenly relieved. Still another message was arriving, and Ms. Keech was spelling it out through automatic writing! The Seekers, it turned out, had managed to save the world through their faith. The universal powers had decided to let the world travel on along its sinful way for a while longer. Why? Because of the faith of the Seekers, there was hope!

Truth or Fiction?

What do you think?

Folklore, common sense, or nonsense? Place a T for "True" or F for "False" on the lines provided (you'll learn the answers as you read through the text).

__ Getting away from it all by going on a vacation from all sensory input for a few hours is relaxing.

__ People feel hunger due to contractions ("pangs") in the stomach.

__ Fashion magazines can contribute to eating disorders among women.

__ Money can't buy you happiness.

__ You may be able to fool a lie detector by squiggling your toes.

ERIK ISAKSON / JUPITER IMAGES

motive
a hypothetical state within an organism that propels the organism toward a goal (from the Latin *movere,* meaning "to move")

need
a state of deprivation

drive
a condition of arousal in an organism that is associated with a need

physiological drives
unlearned drives with a biological basis, such as hunger, thirst, and avoidance of pain

incentive
an object, person, or situation that can satisfy a need

instinct
an inherited disposition to activate specific behavior patterns that are designed to reach certain goals

With their faith restored, the followers called wire services and newspapers to spread the word. The three psychologists from the University of Minnesota went home, weary but enlightened. They wrote a book entitled *When Prophecy Fails,* which serves as one of the key documents of their theory.

LO¹ The Psychology of Motivation

The psychology of motivation is concerned with the *why* of behavior. Why do we eat? Why do some of us strive to get ahead? Why do some of us ride motorcycles at break-neck speeds? Why are some people aggressive? Why were the Seekers in a state of discomfort when the prophecy failed? In order to answer these questions, psychologists use concepts such as motives, needs, drives, and incentives. *What are motives, needs, drives, and incentives?* Motives are hypothetical states that activate behavior, propelling us toward goals. We call these states hypothetical because motives are not seen and measured directly. They are inferred from behavior. Motives may take the form of *needs, drives,* and *incentives,* which are also inferred from behavior.

We have physiological and psychological **needs**. We must meet physiological needs to survive—for example, the needs for oxygen, food, drink, pain avoidance, proper temperature, and elimination of waste products. Some physiological needs, such as hunger and thirst, are states of physical deprivation. When we have not eaten or drunk for a while, we develop needs for food and water. The body also needs oxygen, vitamins, and so on.

Psychological needs include needs for achievement, power, self-esteem, social approval, and belonging. Psychological needs are not necessarily based on states of deprivation. A person with a need for achievement may already have a history of successful achievements. Because people's biological makeups are similar, we share similar physiological needs. But because we are influenced by our cultural settings, our needs may be expressed in different ways. We all need food, but some prefer a vegetarian diet whereas others prefer meat. Because learning enters into psychological needs, they can differ markedly from one person to another.

Needs give rise to **drives**. Depletion of food gives rise to the hunger drive, and depletion of liquids gives rise to the thirst drive. **Physiological drives** are the counterparts of physiological needs. When we have gone without food and water, our body may *need* these substances. However, our *experience* of the drives of hunger and thirst is psychological. Drives arouse us to action and tend to be stronger when we have been deprived longer. We are hungrier when we haven't eaten for ten hours than one hour.

Psychological needs for approval, achievement, and belonging also give rise to drives. We can have a drive to get ahead in the business world just as we have a drive to eat. Psychologists are working to learn more about the origins of these drives. We do know that we can also be driven to obtain *incentives*. An **incentive** is an object, a person, or a situation that can satisfy a need or is desirable for its own sake. Money, food, a sexually attractive person, social approval, and attention can all act as incentives.

LO² Theories of Motivation

Although psychologists agree that it is important to understand why humans and lower animals do things, they do not agree about the precise nature of motivation. Let us consider various theoretical perspectives on motivation.

The Evolutionary Perspective

The evolutionary perspective notes that many animals are neurally "prewired"—that is, born with preprogrammed tendencies—to respond to certain situations in certain ways. Spiders spin webs instinctively. Bees "dance" instinctively to communicate the location of food to other bees.

These instinctive behaviors are found in particular species. They are *species-specific. What is meant by species-specific behaviors?* Species-specific behaviors are also called **instincts** and are inborn. They are genetically transmitted from generation to generation.

Psychologists have asked whether humans have instincts, and if so, how many. A century ago, psychologists William James (1890) and William McDougall (1908) argued that humans have instincts that foster survival and social behavior. James numbered love, sympathy, and modesty as social instincts. McDougall compiled twelve "basic" instincts, including hunger, sex, and self-assertion. Other psychologists have made longer lists, and still others deny that

Spiders spin webs instinctively

people have instincts. The question of whether people have instincts—and what they might be—remains unresolved.

Drive-Reductionism and Homeostasis

Sigmund Freud believed that tension motivates us to behave in ways that restore us to a resting state. His views are similar to those of the **drive-reduction theory** of learning, as set forth by psychologist Clark Hull in the 1930s. *What is drive-reduction theory?*

According to Hull, *primary drives* such as hunger, thirst, and pain trigger arousal (tension) and activate behavior. We learn to engage in behaviors that reduce the tension. We also acquire drives—called *acquired drives*—through experience. We may acquire a drive for money because money enables us to obtain food, drink, and homes, which protect us from crime and extremes of temperature. We might acquire drives for social approval and affiliation because other people, and their goodwill, help us reduce primary drives, especially as infants. In all cases, reduction of tension is the goal. Yet some people appear to acquire what could be considered excessive drives for money.

What motivates children to spend hour after hour playing video games?

They gather money long after their material needs have been met.

Primary drives like hunger are triggered when we are in a state of deprivation. Sensations of hunger motivate us to act in ways that will restore the bodily balance. This tendency to maintain a steady state is called **homeostasis**. Homeostasis works like a thermostat. When the temperature in a room drops below the set point, the furnace turns on. The furnace stays on until the set point is reached. Similarly, most animals eat until they are no longer hungry. But many people eat "recreationally"—as when they see an appealing dessert—suggesting there is more to eating than drive reduction.

The Search for Stimulation

Physical needs give rise to drives like hunger and thirst. In such cases, we are motivated to *reduce* the tension or stimulation that impinges on us. *Are all motives aimed at the reduction of tension?*

In the case of *stimulus motives,* organisms seek to *increase* stimulation. A study conducted at McGill University in Montreal during the 1950s suggests the importance of sensory stimulation and activity. Some "lucky" students were paid $20 a day (which, with inflation, would now be more like $200) for doing nothing—literally. Would you like to "work" by doing nothing for $200 a day? Don't answer too quickly. According to the results of this study you might not like it at all. In this experiment, student volunteers were placed in quiet cubicles and blindfolded (Bexton et al., 1954). Their arms were bandaged; they could hear nothing but the dull, continuous hum of air conditioning. Many slept for a while, but after a few hours of sensory-deprived wakefulness, most felt bored and irritable. As time went on, many grew more uncomfortable. Many students quit the experiment during the first day despite the financial incentive. Many of those who remained for a few

Fiction

Generally, it is not true that getting away from it all by going on a vacation from all sensory input for a few hours is relaxing.

days found it hard to concentrate on simple problems for days afterward. For many, the experiment did not provide a relaxing vacation. Instead, it produced boredom, discomfort, and disorientation.

Humans and other animals appear motivated to seek novel stimulation. Even when they have been deprived of food, rats may explore unfamiliar arms of mazes rather than head straight for the food source. Animals that have just copulated and thereby reduced their primary sex drives often show renewed interest in sex when presented with a novel sex partner. People (and nonhumans) take in more calories at buffets and smorgasbords than when fewer kinds of food are available (Raynor & Epstein, 2001). Children spend hour after hour playing video games for the pleasure of zapping virtual people or monsters. Infants play with "busy boxes"—boxes filled with objects that honk, squeak, rattle, and buzz when manipulated in certain ways. Finding ways to control the gadgets is apparently reinforcing, even though learning is not rewarded with desserts or parental hugs.

Stimulus motives provide an evolutionary advantage. Animals that are active and motivated to explore and manipulate their environment are more likely to survive. If you know where the nearest tall tree is, you're more likely to escape a leopard and transmit your genes to future generations.

Humanistic Theory

Humanistic psychologists such as Abraham Maslow (1908–1970) suggest that human behavior is more than mechanical and more than aimed toward tension-reduction and survival. *How does humanistic theory differ from other theories of motivation?* Maslow believed that people are also motivated by a conscious desire for personal growth. Humanists note that people tolerate pain, hunger, and many other kinds of tension to seek personal fulfillment.

Maslow believed that we are separated from other animals by our capacity for **self-actualization**, or self-initiated striving to become what we believe we are capable of being. Maslow considered self-actualization to be as vital a need in humans as hunger. The need for self-actualization pushes people to strive to become concert pianists, chief executive officers, or best-selling authors—even when they have plenty of money to live on.

Maslow (1970) organized human needs into a hierarchy. *What is Maslow's hierarchy of needs?* Maslow's hierarchy ranges from physiological needs such as hunger and thirst, through self-actualization (see Figure 9.1). He believed that we naturally strive to climb this hierarchy.

Critics of Maslow's theory argue that there is too much individual variation for the hierarchy of motives to apply to everyone. Some people whose physiological, safety, and love needs are met show little interest in achievement and recognition. And some artists devote themselves fully to their craft, even if they have to pass up the comforts of a warm home or alienate their families.

Cognitive Perspectives on Motivation

Cognitive theorists note that people represent their worlds mentally. As in Piaget's cognitive developmental theory, they see people as natural scientists who strive to understand the world so that they can predict and control events. Therefore, people try to eliminate inconsistencies—or, as we saw in the case of the Seekers at the beginning of the chapter—discrepancies in information so that their ability to make sense of the world remains whole.

Children also attempt to create consistency between their own gender and what experience teaches them that boys and girls are expected to do in their cultural settings. As soon as they come to understand whether they are male or female, they begin to imitate the behavior of older people of the same gender (Ruble et al., 2006). According to cognitive-dissonance theory, people are generally motivated to hold consistent beliefs and to justify their behavior. That is why we are generally more likely to appreciate what we must work to obtain.

Each theory of motivation may have something to offer. Drive-reduction theory may explain why we drink when thirsty, but stimulus motives might explain why we go clubbing and drink alcohol. Each theory might apply to certain aspects of behavior. As the chapter progresses, we will describe research that lends support to each theory. Let us first consider the hunger drive. Hunger is based on physiological needs, and drive reduction would appear to explain some—although not all—eating behavior. Then we consider two powerful motives that push us ahead in life and sometimes to the front of the line: aggression and achievement. Psychologist Henry Murray (1938) called aggression and achievement social motives. He believed that people acquired aggressive and achievement-oriented behavior patterns to meet psychological needs. But evolutionary psychologists believe that "genetic whisperings" also influence aggression, achievement, and other aspects of personality and social behavior (Buss, 2003; Plomin, 2002).

Figure 9.1

Maslow's Hierarchy of Needs

Maslow believed we progress toward higher psychological needs once basic survival needs have been met. Where do you fit in this picture?

Go to CourseMate for PSYCH at www.cengagebrain.com to access an interactive version of this figure. 🎧

- Self-actualization
- Esteem needs
- Love and belongingness
- Safety needs
- Physiological needs

LO³ Hunger

We need food to survive, but food means more than survival. Food is a symbol of family togetherness and caring. We associate food with the nurturance of the parent–child relationship, with visits home on holidays. Friends and relatives offer us food when we enter their homes, and saying no may be viewed as a personal rejection. Bacon and eggs, coffee with cream and sugar, meat and mashed potatoes—all seem to be part of sharing American values and abundance. *How is the hunger drive regulated?*

Biological Influences on Hunger

In considering the bodily mechanisms that regulate hunger, let us begin with the mouth. (After all, we are talking about eating.) After we chew and swallow a certain amount, we receive signals of satiety. We also get signals of satiety from the digestive tract, although these signals take longer to reach the brain.

To demonstrate that chewing and swallowing provide feelings of satiety, researchers conducted classic "sham feeding" experiments with dogs. They implanted a tube in the animals' throats so that any food swallowed fell out of the body. Even though no food reached the stomach, the animals stopped feeding after a while (Janowitz & Grossman, 1949). The dogs in the study, however, resumed feeding

© 2007 JUPITERIMAGES

sooner than animals whose food did reach the stomach. Let us proceed to the stomach, too, as we seek further regulatory factors in hunger.

satiety
the state of being satisfied; fullness

An empty stomach leads to stomach contractions, which we call *hunger pangs*. Classic research suggested that stomach contractions are crucial to hunger. A man (A. L. Washburn) swallowed a balloon that was inflated in his stomach. His stomach contractions squeezed the balloon, so the contractions could be recorded by observers. Washburn also pressed a key when he felt hungry, and the researchers found a correspondence between his stomach contractions and his feelings of hunger (Cannon & Washburn, 1912).

Medical observations and classic research find that humans and nonhumans whose stomachs have been removed still regulate food intake so as to maintain a normal weight (Tsang, 1938). (Food is absorbed through their intestines.) This finding led to the discovery of other mechanisms that regulate hunger, including the hypothalamus, blood sugar level, and receptors in the liver. When we are deprived of food, the level of sugar in the blood drops. The drop is communicated to the hypothalamus, which stokes the hunger drive.

Two parts of the hypothalamus have been found to be important to the hunger drive. When a

We know that pizza can taste good, but what other factors contribute to her eating?

ventromedial nucleus (VMN) a central area on the underside of the hypothalamus that appears to function as a stop-eating center

hyperphagic characterized by excessive eating

lateral hypothalamus an area at the side of the hypothalamus that appears to function as a start-eating center

aphagic characterized by undereating

researcher destroys the ventromedial nucleus (VMN) of a rat's hypothalamus during surgery, the rat will grope toward food as soon as its eyes open. Then it eats vast quantities of Purina Rat Chow or whatever. The VMN seems to be able to function like a "stop-eating center" in the rat's brain. If the VMN is electrically stimulated—that is, "switched on"—the rat stops eating until the current is turned off. When the VMN is destroyed, the rat becomes hyperphagic (see Figure 9.2). That is, it continues to eat until it has about doubled its normal weight. Then it will level off its eating rate and maintain the higher weight. It is as if the set point of the stop-eating center has been raised to a higher level. Some people develop tumors near the base of the brain that damage the VMN and apparently lead them to overeat (Miller, 1995).

The lateral hypothalamus may function like a "start-eating center" by producing hormones that signal the rat to eat (Chua, 2004). If you destroy the lateral hypothalamus, the rat may stop eating altogether—that is, become aphagic.

Psychological Influences on Hunger

Although many areas of the body work in concert to regulate the hunger drive, this is only part of the story. In human beings, the hunger drive is more complex. Psychological as well as physiological factors play an important role. How many times have you been made hungry by the sight or aroma of food? How many times have you eaten not because you were hungry but because you were at a relative's home or hanging around a cafeteria or coffee shop? Or because you felt anxious or depressed? Or simply because you were bored? One study confirmed what most of us already assumed—that watching television increases the amount of food we eat (Higgs & Woodward, 2009). One reason is that watching television can distract us from bodily changes that signal fullness and from cognitive awareness of how much we have already eaten. The same reason seems to hold true for gorging on popcorn, candy, and soft drinks at the movies. Watching television also interferes with memory formation of how much we have eaten, making us vulnerable to overeating at subsequent meals.

Obesity: A Serious and Pervasive Problem

Consider some facts about obesity:

- More than two out of three adult Americans are overweight, and one in three is obese (Flegal et al., 2010).

- Problems with unhealthy weight gain have been on the upswing in the United States; for example, 68% of Americans were overweight in 2008 as compared with 60% in 1988–1994 (Flegal et al., 2010).

- More than 78% of African American women and 81% of Latina Americans, age 40 and above, are overweight, and about half are obese (Flegal et al., 2010).

- Obesity is a risk in various chronic medical conditions including diabetes, hypertension (high blood pressure), high cholesterol levels, stroke, heart disease, some cancers, and arthritis (Flegal et al., 2010).

Figure 9.2

A Hyperphagic Rat

This rodent winner of the basketball look-alike contest went on a binge after it received a lesion in the ventromedial nucleus (VMN) of the hypothalamus. It is as if the lesion pushed the "set point" for the body weight up several notches; the rat's weight is now about five times normal. But now it eats only enough to maintain its pleasantly plump figure, so you need not be concerned that it will eventually burst. If the lesion had been made in the lateral hypothalamus, the animal might have become the Calista Flockhart of the rat world.

DR. NEAL MILLER/YALE UNIVERSITY

Table 9.1

Years of Life Lost by an Extremely Obese, Non-smoking, 40-year-old, Compared with a Normal-Weight Person of the Same Age

	European American	African American
Male	9	8
Female	7	5

Source of data: Finkelstein, E. A., Brown, D. S., Wrage, L. A., Allaire, B. T. & Hoerger, T. J. (2010). Individual and Aggregate Years-of-life-lost Associated with Overweight and Obesity. *Obesity, 18*(2), 333–339.

• Weight control is elusive for most people, who regain most of the weight they have lost, even when they have dieted "successfully" (Apovian, 2010; Heber, 2010).

American culture idealizes slender heroes and heroines. For those who want to "measure up" to TV and film idols, food may have replaced sex as the central source of guilt. Obese people encounter more than their fair share of health problems, including hypertension, heart disease, diabetes, gallbladder disease, osteoarthritis, sleep apnea and respiratory problems, and certain kinds of cancer (Centers for Disease Control and Prevention, 2005a). A study using data collected by the federal government found that severely obese young adults (those with a BMI above 45) live shorter lives than people who are normal in weight (Fontaine et al., 2003; see Table 9.1). With all the health problems connected to obesity, why are so many people obese?

Origins of Obesity

Many biological and psychological factors are involved in obesity. Overweight runs in families. Studies of monkeys (Kavanagh et al., 2007) and of human twins (Silventoinen et al., 2007) suggest there are strong roles for heredity. Efforts by overweight and obese people to maintain a slender profile may be sabotaged by an adaptive mechanism that would help preserve life in times of famine—*adaptive thermogenesis*. This mechanism causes the body to produce less energy (burn fewer calories) when someone goes on a diet (Major et al., 2007). This does not mean that overweight people will not lose weight by dieting; it means that it will take longer than expected.

Fatty tissue in the body also metabolizes (burns) food more slowly than muscle. For this reason, a person with a high fat-to-muscle ratio metabolizes food more slowly than a person of the same weight with more muscle. That is, two people of the same weight may metabolize food at different rates, depending on their distribution of muscle and fat. The average man is 40% muscle and 15% fat, whereas the average woman is 23% muscle and 25% fat. Therefore, if a typical man and woman are equal in weight, the woman has to eat less to maintain that weight.

Psychological factors, such as observational learning, stress, and emotional states also contribute to obesity. People in the United States are exposed to thousands of food commercials a year—many of them for fatty fast foods, sweetened cereals, and sugar-laden soft drinks. Situations such as family celebrations, watching TV, arguments, and tension at work can all lead to overeating or falling off a diet (Fletcher et al., 2007). Negative emotions such as depression and anxiety can trigger binge eating (Reas & Grilo, 2007).

anorexia nervosa a life-threatening eating disorder characterized by dramatic weight loss and a distorted body image

Eating Disorders

The *eating disorders* are characterized by persistent, gross disturbances in eating patterns. In this section we focus on an eating disorder in which individuals are too thin, *anorexia nervosa,* and one in which the person may be normal in weight, but certainly not in the methods used to maintain that weight—*bulimia nervosa.*

Consider some facts about eating and eating disorders in the United States, as reported by the National Eating Disorders Association (2010):

— Over half of teenage girls and nearly one-third of teenage boys use unhealthful methods to try to control their weight, including fasting, skipping meals, smoking cigarettes, vomiting, and using laxatives.

— About two out of five first to third grade girls would like to be thinner.

— More than four out of five 10-year-old girls report fear of being fat.

— Nearly half of 9- to 11-year old girls are "sometimes" or "very often" dieting.

— More than 90% of college women have dieted at some time.

Anorexia Nervosa

Anorexia nervosa is a life-threatening eating disorder characterized by extreme fear of being too heavy, dramatic weight loss, a distorted body image, and resistance to eating enough to reach or maintain a healthful weight.

Anorexia nervosa mostly afflicts women during adolescence and young adulthood. The typical person with anorexia is a young European American female of higher socioeconomic status (McLaren, 2002).

Affluent females have greater access to fitness centers and health clubs and are more likely to subscribe to the magazines that idealize slender bodies and shop in the boutiques that cater to svelte women. They are regularly confronted with unrealistic standards of slimness that make them dissatisfied with their own figures (Neumark-Sztainer et al., 2002a).

We also find eating disorders among some males, particularly among males who are compelled by their chosen activities—for example, wrestling or dancing—to keep their weight at a certain limit (Bailey, 2003a; Goode, 2000). But women with these disorders outnumber men who have them by more than six to one (Striegel-Moore & Cachelin, 2001).

Females with anorexia nervosa can drop 25% or more of their weight within a year. Severe weight loss can prevent ovulation and cause general health to deteriorate. Females with anorexia are also at risk for premature development of osteoporosis (Jacoangeli et al., 2002). Given these problems, the mortality rate for females with anorexia nervosa is approximately 5%.

In one common pattern, the girl sees that she has gained some weight after reaching puberty, and she resolves that she must lose it. But even after the weight is gone, she maintains her pattern of dieting and, in many cases, exercises at a fever pitch. This pattern continues as she plunges below her "desirable" weight. Girls with the disorder are in denial about health problems; some point to feverish exercise routines as evidence of strength. Distortion of the body image is a major feature of the disorder (Striegel-Moore et al., 2004).

Bulimia Nervosa

Bulimia nervosa entails repeated cycles of binge eating and purging. Binge eating often follows efforts to diet (Corwin, 2000). There are various methods of purging, including vomiting, strict dieting or fasting, laxatives, and prolonged exercise. Individuals

Miss America 2008 Kirsten Haglund battles anorexia. In her many interviews, she talks about the effect the disorder has had on her body.

STEVE MARCUS/REUTERS/LANDOV

with eating disorders will not settle for less than their idealized body shape and weight. Bulimia, like anorexia, triggers hormonal imbalances: One study found that nearly half of women with bulimia nervosa have irregular menstrual cycles (Gendall et al., 2000). Bulimia nervosa, like anorexia nervosa, tends to afflict mainly women during adolescence and young adulthood (Lewinsohn et al., 2000b).

Origins of the Eating Disorders

What are the origins of the eating disorders? Health professionals have done a great deal of research into the origins of eating disorders, but they admit that many questions about them remain unanswered (Striegel-Moore & Cachelin, 2001).

Many parents are obsessed with getting their children—especially their infants—to eat. Thus some psychologists suggest that children may use refusal to eat as a way of resisting or punishing parents. ("You have to eat something!" "I'm not hungry!") Parents in such families often have issues with eating and dieting themselves. They also "act out" against their daughters—letting them know that they consider them unattractive and that they should slim down (Baker et al., 2000; Cooper et al., 2001).

A particularly disturbing risk factor for eating disorders in adolescent females is a history of child abuse, particularly sexual abuse (Ackard et al., 2001; Leonard et al., 2003). One study found a history of childhood sexual abuse in about half of women with bulimia nervosa, as opposed to a rate of about 7% among women without the disorder (Deep et al., 1999).

The sociocultural climate also affects eating behavior (Williams et al., 2003). Slimness is idealized in the United States. When you check out current fashion magazines and catalogs, you are looking at models who, on average, are 9% taller and 16% thinner than the typical female—and who still manage to have ample bustlines. Miss America, the annually renewed American role model, has also been slenderizing across the years. Over the past eighty years, the winner has added only 2% in height but has lost twelve pounds in weight. In the 1920s, Miss America's weight relative to her height yielded a Body Mass Index (BMI) of 20 to 25, which is considered normal by the World Health Organization (WHO). WHO labels people as malnourished when their BMIs are lower than 18.5. Recent Miss Americas, however, come in at a BMI near 17 (Rubinstein & Caballero, 2000). So Miss America adds to the woes of "normal" young women.

As the cultural ideal slenderizes, women with average body weights according to the health charts feel overweight, and more-than-average women feel gargantuan (Utter et al., 2003; Williams et al., 2003).

Truth

It is true that fashion magazines can contribute to eating disorders among women.

LO⁴ Sexual Motivation

What triggers the sex drive? Many factors contribute to the sex drive. People vary greatly in the cues that excite them sexually and in the frequency with which they experience sexual thoughts and feelings. Sex hormones and cultural beliefs also influence sexual behavior and the pleasure people find—or do not find—in sex. Sexual motivation may be natural, but this natural function is strongly influenced by religious and moral beliefs, cultural tradition, folklore, and superstition.

Regardless of our ethnicity, our levels of education, and cultural influences, our sex drives are connected with sex hormones. *What are the effects of sex hormones on sexual motivation?*

Hormones and Sexual Motivation

Sex hormones can be said to fuel the sex drive. Research with men who produce little testosterone—due to age or health problems—shows that their sex drive increases when they receive testosterone replacement therapy (Seidman, 2003). The most common sexual problem among women is lack of sexual desire or interest, and the sex drive in women is also connected to testosterone levels (Apperloo et al., 2003). Although men produce ten to twenty times the testosterone produced by women, women produce androgens ("male" sex hormones) in the adrenal glands. Testosterone injections, patches, or pills can heighten the sex drive in women who do not produce enough of the hormone (Van Anders et al., 2005).

Sex hormones promote the development of male and female sex organs and regulate the menstrual cycle. They also have activating and organizing effects on sexual behavior. **Activating effects** involve the sex drive. Female mice, rats, cats, and dogs are receptive to males only during **estrus**, when female sex hormones are plentiful. During estrus, female rats respond to males by hopping, wiggling their ears, and arching their backs with their tails to one side, thus enabling males to penetrate them. Sex hormones also have directional or **organizing effects**. That is, they predispose lower animals toward stereotypical masculine or feminine mating patterns. Sex hormones are thus likely candidates for influencing the development of sexual orientation (Lalumière et al., 2000).

Sex hormones may further "masculinize" or "feminize" the brain by creating predispositions consistent with some gender-role tendencies (Collaer & Hines, 1995; Crews, 1994). For example, male rats are generally superior to females in maze-learning ability, a task that requires spatial skills. But female rats that are exposed to androgens in the uterus (e.g., because they have several male siblings in the uterus with them) or soon after birth learn maze routes as rapidly as males (Vandenbergh, 1993).

Sexual Response

What happens to the body when people are sexually aroused? Men show more interest in sex than women do (Peplau, 2003). Women are more likely to want to combine sex with a romantic relationship (Fisher, 2000). A survey of more than 1,000 undergraduates found that men reported being more interested than women in casual sex and multiple sex partners (Schmitt et al., 2001).

activating effect
the arousal-producing effects of sex hormones that increase the likelihood of sexual behavior

estrus
the periodic sexual excitement of many female mammals, as governed by levels of sex hormones

organizing effect
the directional effect of sex hormones—for example, along stereotypically masculine or feminine lines

sexual response cycle
Masters and Johnson's model of sexual response, which consists of four stages or phases

vasocongestion
engorgement of blood vessels with blood, which swells the genitals and breasts during sexual arousal

myotonia
muscle tension

excitement phase
the first phase of the sexual response cycle, which is characterized by muscle tension, increases in the heart rate, and erection in the male and vaginal lubrication in the female

plateau phase
the second phase of the sexual response cycle, which is characterized by increases in vasocongestion, muscle tension, heart rate, and blood pressure in preparation for orgasm

ejaculation
propulsion of seminal fluid (semen) from the penis by contraction of muscles at the base of the penis

orgasm
the height or climax of sexual excitement, involving involuntary muscle contractions, release of sexual tensions, and, usually, subjective feelings of pleasure

resolution phase
the fourth phase of the sexual response cycle, during which the body gradually returns to its prearoused state

refractory period
in the sexual response cycle, a period of time following orgasm during which an individual is not responsive to sexual stimulation

Although we may be more culturally attuned to focus on sex differences rather than similarities, William Masters and Virginia Johnson (1966) found that the biological responses of males and females to sexual stimulation are quite similar. Masters and Johnson use the term *sexual response cycle* to describe the changes that occur in the body as men and women become sexually aroused. They divide the **sexual response cycle** into four phases: *excitement, plateau, orgasm,* and *resolution*.

The cycle is characterized by *vasocongestion* and *myotonia*. **Vasocongestion** is the swelling of the genital tissues with blood, causing erection of the penis and swelling of the area surrounding the vaginal opening. The testes and the nipples swell as blood vessels dilate in these areas. **Myotonia** is muscle tension, which causes grimaces, spasms in the hands and feet, and the spasms of orgasm.

Erection, vaginal lubrication, and orgasm are all reflexes. That is, they occur automatically in response to adequate sexual stimulation.

Excitement Phase

Vasocongestion during the **excitement phase** can cause erection in young men within a few seconds after sexual stimulation begins. The scrotal skin thickens, becoming less baggy. The testes increase in size and become elevated.

In the female, excitement is characterized by vaginal lubrication, which may start 10 to 30 seconds after sexual stimulation begins. Vasocongestion swells the clitoris and flattens and spreads the vaginal lips. The inner part of the vagina expands. The breasts enlarge, and blood vessels near the surface become more prominent. The nipples

may erect in both men and women. Heart rate and blood pressure increase.

Plateau Phase

The level of sexual arousal remains somewhat stable during the **plateau phase**. Because of vasocongestion, the circumference of the head of the penis increases somewhat. The testes are elevated into position for **ejaculation** and may reach one-and-a-half times their unaroused size.

In women, vasocongestion swells the outer part of the vagina, contracting the vaginal opening in preparation for grasping the penis. The inner part of the vagina expands further. The clitoris withdraws beneath the clitoral hood and shortens.

Breathing becomes rapid, like panting. Heart rate may increase to 100 to 160 beats per minute. Blood pressure continues to rise.

Orgasmic Phase

During **orgasm** in the male, muscle contractions propel semen from the body. Sensations of pleasure tend to be related to the strength of the contractions and the amount of seminal fluid. The first three to four contractions are generally most intense and occur at 0.8-second intervals (five contractions every four seconds). Additional contractions are slower.

Orgasm in the female is manifested by three to fifteen contractions of the pelvic muscles that surround the vaginal barrel. The contractions first occur at 0.8-second intervals. Weaker and slower contractions follow.

Blood pressure and heart rate reach a peak, with the heart beating up to 180 times per minute. Respiration may increase to forty breaths per minute.

Resolution Phase

In the **resolution phase**, after orgasm, the body returns to its unaroused state. Erection and clitoral swelling subside. Blood pressure, heart rate, and breathing return to normal levels.

Unlike women, men enter a **refractory period** during which they cannot experience another orgasm or ejaculate. The refractory period of adolescent males may last only minutes, whereas that of men age fifty and above may last from hours to a day. Women do not undergo a refractory period and therefore can become quickly rearoused to the point of repeated (multiple) orgasm if they desire and receive continued sexual stimulation.

The sexual response cycle describes what happens when females and males are exposed to sexual stimulation. But what kinds of sexual experiences do people seek? How many sex partners do they have? Who are their partners? *What do we know about the sex lives of people in the United States?*

Surveys of Sexual Behavior

The well-known Kinsey reports (Kinsey et al., 1948, 1953) interviewed 5,300 males and 5,940 females in the United States between 1938 and 1949. Interviewers asked about sexual experiences including masturbation, oral sex, and premarital sex. The nation was astounded to learn that most males masturbated and had had sexual intercourse prior to marriage. Moreover, significant minorities of females reported these behaviors. But Kinsey had not obtained a random sample of the population. His samples underrepresented people of color, people in rural areas, older people, poor people, Catholics, and Jews. There is thus no way of knowing whether or not Kinsey's results accurately mirrored general American sexual behavior at the time. But the *relationships* Kinsey uncovered, such as the positive link between level of education and premarital sex, may be accurate enough.

A more recent survey—the National Health and Social Life Survey (NHSLS)—interviewed 3,432 people (Laumann et al., 1994) and may provide our most accurate information. Of this number, 3,159 were English-speaking adults aged eighteen to fifty-nine. The other 273 respondents were obtained by purposefully oversampling African American and Hispanic American households to obtain more information about these ethnic groups.

The sample probably represents the overall U.S. adult population quite well, but it may include too few Asian Americans, Native Americans, and Jews to offer much information about these groups. The NHSLS team identified households in various locales and obtained an overall participation rate of close to 80%.

The NHSLS considered the sociocultural factors of sex, level of education, religion, and race/ethnicity in many aspects of people's sexual behavior, including their number of sex partners (see Figure 9.3 on page 198). Males in the survey reported higher numbers of sex partners than females did. For example, one male in three (33%) reported having eleven or more sex partners. This compares with fewer than one woman in ten (9%). On the other hand, most Americans limit their sex partners to a handful or fewer.

Education appears to be a liberating influence on sexual behavior. People with some college, or who have completed college, report more sex partners than those who attended only grade school or high school. Conservative religious experience, on the other hand, acts as a restraint. Liberal Protestants and people who say they have no religion report higher numbers of sex partners than Catholics and more conservative Protestants.

Ethnicity is also connected with sexual behavior. The research findings in Figure 9.3 suggest that European Americans and African Americans have the highest numbers of sex partners. Asian Americans appear to be the most sexually restrained ethnic group.

Sexual Orientation

The great majority of people have a heterosexual orientation; they are sexually attracted to and interested in forming romantic relationships with people of the other sex. Some people, however, have a homosexual orientation; they are attracted to and interested in forming romantic relationships with people of their own sex. Males with a homosexual orientation are referred to as *gay males*. Homosexual females are referred to as *lesbians*. *Bisexual* people are attracted to both females and males.

Surveys find that about 3% of the males and 2% of the females in the United States identify themselves as homosexual (Mosher et al., 2005; Savin-

heterosexual referring to people who are sexually aroused by and interested in forming romantic relationships with people of the other sex

homosexual referring to people who are sexually aroused by and interested in forming romantic relationships with people of the same sex (derived from the Greek *homos*, meaning "same," not from the Latin *homo*, meaning "man")

Williams, 2006). However, it is estimated that anywhere from 2% to 10% of the population is gay male or lesbian (Martins et al., 2005). Theories of the origins of sexual orientation look both at nature and nurture— the biological makeup of the individual and environmental influences. Several theories bridge the two. *What do we know about the origins of gay male and lesbian sexual orientations?*

Learning theorists look for the roles of factors such as reinforcement and observational learning. From this perspective, reinforcement of sexual behavior with members of one's own sex—as in reaching orgasm with them when members of the other sex are unavailable—might affect one's sexual orientation. Similarly, childhood sexual abuse by someone of the same sex could lead to fantasies about sex with people of one's own sex and affect sexual orientation. Observation of others engaged in enjoyable male–male or female–female sexual encounters could also affect the development of sexual orientation. But critics point out that most individuals become aware of their sexual orientation before they have sexual contacts with other people of either sex (Laumann et al., 1994). Moreover, in a society that generally condemns homosexuality, young people are unlikely to believe that male–male or female–female contacts will have positive effects for them.

Figure 9.3

Number of Sex Partners as Found in the National Health and Social Life Survey*

	Number of Sex Partners (%)					
	0	1	2–4	5–10	11–20	21+
Gender						
Male	3	20	21	23	16	17
Female	3	32	36	20	6	3
Education						
Less than high school	4	27	36	19	9	6
High school graduate	3	30	29	20	10	7
Some college	2	24	29	23	12	9
College graduate	2	24	26	24	11	13
Advanced degree	4	25	26	23	10	13
Religion						
None	3	16	29	20	16	16
Liberal, moderate Protestant	2	23	31	23	12	8
Conservative Protestant	3	30	30	20	10	7
Catholic	4	27	29	23	8	9
Race/Ethnicity						
European American	3	26	29	22	11	9
African American	2	18	34	24	11	11
Latino and Latina American	3	36	27	17	8	9
Asian American**	6	46	25	14	6	3
Native American**	5	28	35	23	5	5

Source: From Laumann, E. O., Gagnon, J. H., Michael, R. T., & Michaels, S. (1994). The social organization of sexuality: Sexual practices in the United States. Chicago: University of Chicago Press. Copyright © 1994 by University of Chicago Press. Reprinted by permission.
*Conducted by a research team centered at the University of Chicago.
**These sample sizes are quite small.

There is evidence for genetic factors in sexual orientation (Dawood et al., 2000; Kendler et al., 2000c). One study found that 22% of the brothers of fifty-one gay men were gay or bisexual, although one would expect to find only 3% of the brothers to be gay if the relationship were coincidental (Pillard & Weinrich, 1986). Twin studies also support a role for genes. About 52% of identical (MZ) twin pairs are "concordant" (in agreement) for a gay male sexual orientation, as compared with 22% for fraternal (DZ) twins (Bailey & Pillard, 1991).

RYAN PIERSE / GETTY IMAGES

In many species, sexual motivation is governed by sex hormones. Are humans ruled by hormones or do social experiences and personal choice come into play?

In many species, there is little room for thinking about sex and deciding whether an individual will pursue sexual relationships with males or females. Sexual motivation comes under the governance of sex hormones (Hill et al., 2005; Holmes et al., 2005). And much sexual motivation is determined by whether the brains and sex organs of fetuses are bathed in large doses of testosterone in the uterus. In male fetuses, testosterone is normally produced by the developing testes. Yet female fetuses are exposed to testosterone when they share the uterus with many male siblings. Researchers have also injected male sex hormones into the uteruses of rodents. When they do, the sex organs of females become masculinized in appearance, and they show a tendency toward masculine-type behavior patterns at maturity, including mating with other females (Crews, 1994).

It has been shown, then, that sex hormones predispose nonhumans to stereotypical masculine or feminine mating patterns. Do sex hormones influence the developing human embryo and fetus as they affect rodents? We're not sure, but it is possible that the brains of some gay males were feminized in utero and that the brains of some lesbians were masculinized in utero (Collaer & Hines, 1995). We have to conclude by confessing that much about the development of sexual orientation remains speculative.

LO⁵ Achievement Motivation

Many students persist in studying despite being surrounded by distractions. Many people strive relentlessly to get ahead, to "make it," to earn large sums of money, to invent, to accomplish the impossible. *Why do some people strive to get ahead?* Psychological research suggests that these people have *achievement motivation* (Robbins et al., 2005).

Psychologist David McClelland (1958) helped pioneer the assessment of achievement motivation through evaluation of fantasies. One method involves the Thematic Apperception Test (TAT), developed by Henry Murray. The TAT contains cards with pictures and drawings that are subject to various interpretations. Individuals are shown one or more TAT cards and asked to construct stories about the pictured theme: to indicate what led up to it, what the characters are thinking and feeling, and what is likely to happen.

One TAT card is similar to the image shown below. The meaning of the card is ambiguous—unclear. Is the girl sleeping, thinking about the book, wishing she were out with friends?

Consider two stories that could be told about this card:

- *Story 1:* "She's upset that she's got to read the book because she's behind in her assignments and doesn't particularly like to work. She'd much rather be out with her friends, and she may very well sneak out to do just that."

- *Story 2:* "She's thinking, 'Someday I'll be a great scholar. I'll write books like this, and everybody will be proud of me.' She reads all the time."

The second story suggests the presence of more achievement motivation than the first. Classic studies find that people with high achievement motivation earn higher grades than people with comparable learning ability but lower

emotion
a feeling state with cognitive, physiological, and behavioral components

sympathetic nervous system
the branch of the autonomic nervous system that is most active during processes that spend body energy from stored reserves, such as in a fight-or-flight reaction to a predator or when you are anxious about a big test

achievement motivation. They are more likely to earn high salaries and be promoted than less motivated people with similar opportunities (Aronoff & Litevin, 1971; Orpen, 1995).

McClelland (1965) used the TAT to sort college students into groups—students with high achievement motivation and students with low achievement motivation. He found that 83% of college graduates with high achievement motivation found jobs in occupations characterized by risk, decision-making, and the chance for great success, such as business management, sales, or self-employment. Most (70%) of the graduates who chose non-entrepreneurial positions showed low achievement motivation. People with high achievement motivation seem to prefer challenges and are willing to take moderate risks to achieve their goals.

Extrinsic Versus Intrinsic Motives

Do you want to do well in this course? If you do, why? Carol Dweck (e.g., Molden & Dweck, 2000) finds that achievement motivation can be driven by performance or learning goals, or both. For example, are you motivated mainly by performance goals, such as your grade in the course? If so, it may be in part because your motives concern tangible rewards such as getting into graduate school, landing a good job, reaping approval from your parents or your instructor, or avoiding criticism. Performance goals are usually met through extrinsic rewards such as praise and income. Research suggests that tangible rewards, such as money, can serve as an incentive for maintaining good grades. These rewards tend to have a more lasting effect, however, when students look upon incentives as signs that they are intelligent and capable (Spencer et al., 2005).

Or is it learning goals that mainly motivate you to do well? That is, is your central motive the enhancing of your knowledge and skills—your ability to understand and master the subject matter? Learning goals usually lead to intrinsic rewards, such as self-satisfaction. Students who develop learning goals often have parents with strong achievement motivation who encourage their children to think and act independently. Parents and teachers help children develop learning goals by showing warmth and praising them for their efforts to learn, exposing them to novel and stimulating experiences, and encouraging persistence (Dweck, 2002a). Children who are stimulated in this way tend to set high standards for themselves, associate their achievements with self-worth, and attribute their achievements to their own efforts rather than to chance or to the intervention of others (Dweck, 2002b; Marshall & Brown, 2004).

Many of us strive to meet both performance and learning goals in our courses as well as in other areas of life. Grades are important because they are connected with tangible benefits, but learning for its own sake is also of value and can provide great pleasure.

LO⁶ Emotion

Emotions color our lives. We are green with envy, red with anger, blue with sorrow. Positive emotions such as love and desire can fill our days with pleasure. Negative emotions such as fear, depression, and anger can fill us with dread and make each day a chore. *Just what is an emotion?*

An emotion can be a response to a situation, in the way that fear is a response to a threat. An emotion can motivate behavior, as anger can motivate us to act aggressively. An emotion can also be a goal in itself. We may behave in ways that will lead us to experience happiness or love. Emotions are thus intertwined with motivation. We are driven by emotions, and meeting—or failing to meet—our needs can have powerful emotional results.

Emotions are defined as feeling states with physiological, cognitive, and behavioral components (Carlson & Hatfield, 1992). Strong emotions arouse the autonomic nervous system (Gomez et al., 2005; see Chapter 2). The greater the arousal, the more intense the emotion. It also appears that the type of arousal affects the emotion being experienced. Although the word *emotion* might seem to be about feeling and not about thinking, cognitions—particularly interpretations of the meanings of events—are important aspects of emotions. *Fear,* which usually occurs in response to a threat, involves cognitions that one is in danger as well as arousal of the sympathetic nervous system (e.g., rapid heartbeat and breathing, sweating, muscle tension). Emotions also involve behavioral tendencies. Fear is connected with behavioral tendencies to avoid or escape a situation (see Table 9.2). As a response to a social provocation, *anger* involves cognitions that the provocateur should be paid back, arousal of both the sympathetic and

Figure 9.4

Photographs Used in Research by Paul Ekman

Ekman's research suggests that the facial expressions connected with several important emotions such as happiness, anger, surprise, and fear are universally recognized.

© 1976 PAUL EKMAN/HUMAN INTERACTION LABORATORY

parasympathetic nervous systems, and tendencies to attack. *Depression* usually involves cognitions of helplessness and hopelessness, parasympathetic arousal, and tendencies toward inactivity—or sometimes self-destruction. *Happiness, grief, jealousy, disgust, embarrassment, liking*—all have cognitive, physiological, and behavioral components.

The Expression of Emotions

Happiness and sadness are found in all cultures, but, *How can we tell when other people are happy or sad?* It turns out that the expression of many emotions may be universal (Ekman, 2003). Smiling is apparently a universal sign of friendliness and approval. Baring the teeth, as noted by Charles Darwin (1872) in the 19th century, may be a universal sign of anger. As the originator of the theory of evolution, Darwin believed that the universal recognition of facial expressions would have survival value. In the absence of language, facial expressions could signal the approach of enemies (or friends).

Table 9.2

Components of Emotions

Emotion	Physiological	Cognitive	Behavioral
Fear	Sympathetic arousal	Belief that one is in danger	Avoidance tendencies
Anger	Sympathetic and parasympathetic arousal	Frustration or belief that one is being mistreated	Attack tendencies
Depression	Parasympathetic arousal	Thoughts of helplessness, hopelessness, worthlessness	Inactivity, possible self-destructive tendencies

Most investigators (e.g., Ekman, 2003; Izard, 1994) concur that certain facial expressions suggest the same emotions in all people. Moreover, people in diverse cultures recognize the emotions indicated by certain facial expressions. Paul Ekman (1999) describes his classic research in which he took photographs of people exhibiting anger, disgust, fear, happiness, sadness, and surprise (see Figure 9.4). He then asked people around the world to say what emotions were being depicted. Those queried ranged from European college students to members of the Fore, a tribe that dwells in the New Guinea highlands.

All groups, including the Fore, who had almost no contact with Western culture, agreed on the emotions. The Fore also displayed familiar facial expressions when asked how they would respond if they were the characters in stories that called for basic emotional responses. Ekman and his colleagues (1987) obtained similar results in a study of ten cultures. In that study, participants were allowed to identify more than one emotion in facial expressions. The participants generally agreed on which two emotions were being shown and which emotion was more intense.

On the other hand, there is no perfect one-to-one relationship between facial expressions and emotions. Facial expressions sometimes occur in the absence of the emotion they are thought to accompany (Camras, 2000). As noted by psychologist Joseph Campos (2000), the voice, posture, and gestures also provide clues to what people are feeling and are about to do.

parasympathetic nervous system the branch of the autonomic nervous system that is most active during processes that restore reserves of energy to the body, such as relaxing and eating

Positive Psychology

Ted Lewis, the Great Depression–era bandleader, used to begin his act by asking, "Is evvvvrybody happy?" Well, everybody is not happy, but surveys do suggest that most people in developed nations are satisfied with their lives (Cummins & Nistico, 2002). Many people might think that psychologists are interested only in negative emotions such as anxiety, depression, and anger. Not at all. An area of psychology called **positive psychology** deals with positive emotions such as happiness and love, optimism and hope, and joy and sensual pleasures.

What factors contribute to happiness? Are some people just "born happy" or do life experiences determine happiness? What factors interfere with happiness? Some psychologists, such as David Lykken (Lykken & Csikszentmihalyi, 2001), believe that genetic factors play a powerful role in happiness. They note that happiness tends to run in families and that we tend to have a more or less stable level of happiness throughout much of our lives. Positive events such as learning that the person we love also loves us, having a loved one support our goals, or recognition at work can certainly raise our level of happiness at the moment (Feeney, 2004). Similarly, negative life events, such as the loss of a loved one, financial reverses, or injuries can depress us—and understandably so. Yet we may tend to bounce back to a more or less characteristic level of happiness, as did the actor Christopher Reeve following the accident—being thrown from a horse—that paralyzed him.

Which life experiences contribute to happiness? U.S. surveys reveal more evidence for a role for social and socioeconomic factors in happiness. For example, European Americans tend to be happier than African Americans, and well-educated people tend to be happier than those who are not (Easterlin, 2001). The persistence of differences according to race and education suggests that socioeconomic circumstances are in fact important contributors to happiness (Easterlin, 2001). Money might not make

people happy in itself, but when we have enough money, at least we don't have to worry about money (Cummins, 2000).

People who are married (Tsou & Liu, 2001) and who have social support tend to be happier than "loners" (Feeney, 2004). Happy people also tend to be open to new experiences; they are more willing to risk becoming involved in new relationships (Rath, 2002).

Research has also suggested that religious people are happier than those who are not, as was found to be the case in studies of Americans, Chinese people, and Israelis (Francis et al., 2004; Swinyard et al., 2001). The Swinyard study found that one's inner life—one's feeling of connectedness to important things outside oneself—was found to be a greater contributor to happiness than material possessions. Chinese college students tend to think about happiness in terms of feelings of contentment, inner harmony, personal achievement, physical wellness, spiritual enrichment, hopefulness about the future, generosity, and self-development (Lu, 2001).

Then there are the attitudinal aspects of happiness (Cheng & Furnham, 2001; Cummins & Nistico, 2002). People at any income level can make themselves miserable when they compare their incomes to those who bring in more money (Stutzer, 2004). Happiness also tends to be accompanied by optimism—a cognitive bias toward assuming that things will work out (Diener et al., 2000; Keyes & Haidt, 2003). But the "bias" is not groundless, because happy people often believe in their ability to effect change. Thus, they try harder. They are also willing to pat themselves on the back for their successes and are not quick to blame themselves when things go wrong—attitudes that contribute to self-esteem, another factor in happiness.

Happy people

= believe in their ability to effect change
= are open to new experiences
= are willing to risk developing new relationships

Fiction

Despite the saying that "money can't buy you happiness," surveys in the United States, Russia, China, and Latin America suggest that people tend to be happier when they live in affluent societies or earn decent incomes (Lever, 2004; Schyns, 2001).

The Facial-Feedback Hypothesis

The face has a special place among visual stimuli. Social animals like humans need to be able to differentiate and recognize members of their group, and in people, the face is the most distinctive key to identity (Parr et al., 2000). Faces are also a key to social communication. Facial expressions reflect emotional states, and our ability to "read" these expressions enables us to interact appropriately with other people.

It is known that various emotional states give rise to certain patterns of electrical activity in the facial muscles and in the brain (Cacioppo et al., 1988). But can it work the other way around? The facial-feedback hypothesis argues that facial expressions can also affect our emotional state. *Can smiling give rise to feelings of goodwill? Can frowning produce anger?* Perhaps they can.

Psychological research has yielded some interesting findings concerning the facial feedback hypothesis. Inducing people to smile, for example, leads them to report more positive feelings and to rate cartoons as more humorous (Soussignan, 2002).

Smiling is usually a response to feeling good within, but experimental research into the facial-feedback hypothesis suggests that the act of smiling can also enhance our moods.

When induced to frown, they rate cartoons as more aggressive. When people exhibit pain through facial expressions, they rate electric shocks as more painful.

facial-feedback hypothesis the view that stereotypical facial expressions can contribute to stereotypical emotions

What are the possible links between facial feedback and emotion? One is arousal. Intense contraction of facial muscles such as those used in signifying fear heightens arousal, which, in turn, boosts emotional response. Feedback from the contraction of facial muscles may also induce emotions. Engaging in the "Duchenne smile," characterized by "crow's feet wrinkles around the eyes and a subtle drop in the eye cover fold so that the skin above the eye moves down slightly toward the eyeball" (Ekman, 2003) can induce pleasant feelings (Soussignan, 2002).

You may have heard the British expression "Keep a stiff upper lip" as a recommendation for handling stress. It might be that a "stiff" lip suppresses emotional response—as long as the lip is relaxed rather than quivering with fear or tension. But when the lip is stiffened through strong muscle tension, facial feedback may heighten emotional response.

Theories of Emotion

David, 32, is not sleeping well. He wakes before dawn and cannot get back to sleep. His appetite is off, his energy level is low, and he has started smoking again. He has a couple of drinks at lunch and muses that it's lucky that any more alcohol makes him sick to his stomach—otherwise, he'd probably be drinking too much, too. Then he thinks, "So what difference would it make?" Sometimes he is sexually frustrated; at other times he wonders whether he has any sex drive left. Although he's awake, each day it's getting harder to drag himself out of bed in the morning. This week he missed one day of work and was late twice. His supervisor has suggested in a nonthreatening way that he "do something about it." David knows that her next warning will not be nonthreatening. It's been going downhill since Sue walked out. Suicide has even crossed David's mind. He wonders if he's going crazy.

David is experiencing the emotion of depression, and seriously so. Depression is to be expected following a loss, such as the end of a relationship, but David's feelings have lingered. His friends tell him that he should get out and do things, but David is so down that he hasn't the motivation to do much at all. After much prompting by family and friends,

David consults a psychologist who ironically also pushes him to get out and do things—the things he used to enjoy. The psychologist also shows David that part of his problem is that he sees himself as a failure who cannot make meaningful changes.

How do the physiological, situational, and cognitive components of emotions interact to produce feelings and behavior? Some psychologists argue that physiological arousal is a more basic component of emotional response than cognition and that the type of arousal we experience strongly influences our cognitive appraisal and our labeling of the emotion (e.g., Izard, 1984). For these psychologists, the body takes precedence over the mind. Do David's bodily reactions—for example, his loss of appetite and energy—take precedence over his cognitions? Other psychologists argue that cognitive appraisal and physiological arousal are so strongly intertwined that cognitive processes may determine the emotional response. Are David's ideas that he is helpless to change things more at the heart of his feelings of depression?

The "commonsense theory" of emotions is that something happens (a situation) that is cognitively appraised (interpreted) by the person, and the feeling state (a combination of arousal and thoughts) follows. For example, you meet someone new, you appraise that person as delightful, and feelings of attraction follow. Or, as in the case of David, a social relationship comes to an end, you recognize your loss, feel powerless to change it, and feel down in the dumps.

However, both historic and contemporary theories of how the components of emotions interact are at variance with this commonsense view. Let us consider a number of theories and see whether we can arrive at some useful conclusions.

The James–Lange Theory

A century ago, William James suggested that our emotions follow, rather than cause, our behavioral responses to events. At about the same time this view was also proposed by the Danish physiologist Karl G. Lange. It is therefore termed the James–Lange theory of emotion.

According to James and Lange, certain external stimuli instinctively trigger specific patterns of arousal and action, such as fighting or fleeing (see Figure 9.5, part A). We then become angry *because* we are acting aggressively or become afraid *because* we are running away. Emotions are simply the cognitive representations (or by-products) of automatic physiological and behavioral responses.

The James–Lange theory is consistent with the facial-feedback hypothesis. That is, smiling apparently can induce pleasant feelings, even if the effect may not be strong enough to overcome feelings of sadness (Ekman, 1993). The theory also suggests that we may be able to change our feelings by changing our behavior. Changing one's behavior to change one's feelings is one aspect of behavior therapy. When David's psychologist urges him to get out and do things, she is assuming that by changing his behavior, David can have a positive effect on the way he feels.

Walter Cannon (1927) criticized the James–Lange assertion that each emotion has distinct physiological correlates. He argued that the physiological arousal associated with emotion A is not as distinct from the arousal associated with emotion B as the theory asserts.

Figure 9.5

Theories of Emotion

Go to CourseMate for PSYCH at www.cengagebrain.com to access an interactive version of this figure. 🔊

A. James–Lange

Events trigger specific arousal patterns and actions. Emotions result from our appraisal of our body responses.

B. Cannon–Bard

Events are first processed by the brain. Body patterns of arousal, action, and our emotional responses are then triggered simultaneously.

C. Cognitive appraisal

Events and arousal are appraised by the individual. The emotional response stems from the person's appraisal of the situation and his or her level of arousal.

The Cannon–Bard Theory

Walter Cannon (1927) and Philip Bard (1934) suggested that an event might *simultaneously* trigger bodily responses (arousal and action) and the experience of an emotion. As shown in Figure 9.5 (part B), when an event is perceived (processed by the brain), the brain stimulates autonomic and muscular activity (arousal and action) *and* cognitive activity (experience of the emotion). Thus, according to the Cannon–Bard theory, emotions *accompany* bodily responses. They are not *produced by* bodily changes, as in the James–Lange theory.

The central criticism of the Cannon–Bard theory focuses on whether bodily responses (arousal and action) and emotions are in fact stimulated simultaneously. For example, pain or the perception of danger may trigger arousal before we begin to feel distress or fear. Also, many of us have had the experience of having a "narrow escape" and becoming aroused and shaky afterward, when we have had time to consider the damage that might have occurred. What is needed is a theory that allows for an ongoing interaction of external events, physiological changes (such as autonomic arousal and muscular activity), and cognitive activities.

The Theory of Cognitive Appraisal

More recent theoretical approaches to emotion stress cognitive factors. Among those who argue that thinking comes first are Gordon Bower, Richard Lazarus, Stanley Schachter, Jerome Singer, and Robert Zajonc.

Schachter asserts that emotions are associated with similar patterns of bodily arousal that vary in strength, but that the way we label an emotion depends largely on our appraisal of the situation. Cognitive appraisal is based on many factors, including our perception of events and the ways other people respond to those events (see Figure 9.5, part C). When other people are present, we engage in social comparison to arrive at a response.

In a classic experiment, Schachter and Singer (1962) showed that arousal can be labeled quite differently, depending on the situation. The investigators told participants they wanted to determine the effects of a vitamin on vision. Half the participants received an injection of adrenaline, a hormone that stimulates the sympathetic branch of the autonomic nervous system. A control group received an injection of a placebo. Those who had been given adrenaline received one of three "cognitive manipulations." Group 1 was told nothing about possible emotional effects of the "vitamin." Group 2 was deliberately misinformed; members of this group were led to expect itching, numbness, or other irrelevant symptoms. Group 3 was informed accurately about the increased arousal they would experience. Group 4 was a control group injected with a placebo and given no information about its effects.

After receiving injections and cognitive manipulations, the participants were asked to wait in pairs while the experimental apparatus was being set up. The participants did not know that the person with whom they were waiting was a confederate of the experimenter. The confederate's purpose was to respond in a way that the participant would believe was caused by the injection.

Some participants waited with a confederate who acted happy-go-lucky. He flew paper airplanes about the room and tossed paper balls into a wastebasket. Other participants waited with a confederate who acted angry. He complained about the experiment, tore up a questionnaire, and stormed out of the room. As the confederates worked for their Oscar awards, the real participants were observed through a one-way mirror.

The people in groups 1 and 2 were likely to imitate the behavior of the confederate. Those who were exposed to the happy-go-lucky confederate acted jovial and content. Those who were exposed to the angry confederate imitated that person's complaining, aggressive behavior. But those in groups 3 and 4 were less influenced by the confederate's behavior.

Schachter and Singer concluded that participants in groups 1 and 2 were in an ambiguous situation. Members of these groups felt arousal from the adrenaline injection but couldn't label it as a specific emotion. Social comparison with a confederate led them to attribute their arousal either to happiness or to anger. Members of group 3 expected arousal from the injection, but no particular emotional consequences. These participants did not imitate the confederate's display of happiness or anger because they were not in an ambiguous situation; they knew their arousal was caused by adrenaline. Members of group 4 had no arousal for which they needed an attribution, except perhaps for some arousal induced by observing the confederate. Nor did they imitate the behavior of the confederate.

Now, happiness and anger are very different emotions. Yet Schachter and Singer suggest that the bodily differences between these two emotions are slight enough that different views of the situation can lead one person to label arousal as happiness and another person to label it as anger. The Schachter–Singer view could not be further removed from the James–Lange theory, which holds that each emotion is associated with specific and readily recognized body sensations. The truth, it happens, may lie somewhere in between.

In science, it must be possible to replicate experiments and attain identical or similar results; otherwise, a theory cannot be considered valid. The Schachter and Singer study has been replicated, but with *different* results (Ekman, 1993). For example, some studies found that participants were less likely to imitate the behavior of the confederate and were likely to perceive unexplained arousal negatively, attributing it to nervousness or anger (Zimbardo et al., 1993).

The connections between arousal and emotions have led to the development of many kinds of lie detection, as we see in the following section.

The Polygraph: Just What Do Lie Detectors Detect?

Lying—for better or worse—is a part of life. A *New York Times* poll found that 60% of American adults believe that it is sometimes necessary to lie, especially to protect people's feelings (Smiley, 2000). Political leaders lie to get elected. Many people lie to get dates or initiate sexual relations—for example, about other relationships, making professions of love, or in the case of the Internet, about one's appearance or age (Suler, 2005). People also lie about their qualifications to get jobs, and, of course, some people lie in denying guilt for crimes. Although we are unlikely

to subject political leaders and lovers to lie-detector tests, such tests are frequently used in hiring and in criminal investigations.

Facial expressions often offer clues to deceit, but some people can lie with a straight face—or a smile. As Shakespeare pointed out in *Hamlet,* "One may smile, and smile, and be a villain." The use of devices to detect lies has a long, if not laudable, history:

> The Bedouins of Arabia . . . until quite recently required conflicting witnesses to lick a hot iron; the one whose tongue was burned was thought to be lying. The Chinese, it is said, had a similar method for detecting lying: Suspects were forced to chew rice powder and spit it out; if the powder was dry, the suspect was guilty. (Kleinmuntz & Szucko, 1984, pp. 766–767)

These methods may sound primitive, even bizarre, but they are broadly consistent with modern psychological knowledge. Anxiety about being caught in a lie is linked to arousal of the sympathetic division of the autonomic nervous system. One sign of sympathetic arousal is lack of saliva, or dryness in the mouth. The emotions of fear and guilt are also linked to sympathetic arousal and hence to dryness in the mouth.

How do lie detectors work? How reliable are they? Modern polygraphs monitor indicators of sympathetic arousal during an interrogation: heart rate, blood pressure, respiration rate, and electrodermal response (sweating). But questions have been raised about the validity of assessing truth or fiction by means of polygraphs (Branaman & Gallagher, 2005).

The American Polygraph Association claims that use of the polygraph is 85% to 95%

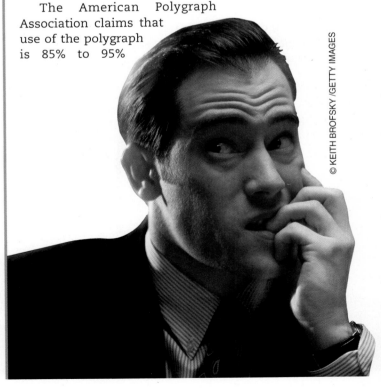

accurate. Critics find polygraph testing to be less accurate and claim that it is sensitive to more than lies (Saxe & Ben-Shakhar, 1999). Tense muscles, drugs, and previous experience with polygraph tests can significantly reduce their accuracy rate. In one experiment, people were able to reduce the accuracy of polygraph-based judgments to about 50% by biting their tongue (to produce pain) or pressing their toes against the floor (to tense muscles) while being interrogated (Honts et al., 1985). You might thus give the examiner the impression that you are lying even when you are telling the truth, throwing off the test's results.

It appears that no specific pattern of bodily responses pinpoints lying (*Nature* editorial, 2004). Because of validity problems, results of polygraph examinations are no longer admitted as evidence in many courts. But the lure of technology to determine lying remains strong. Research is under way in the development of techniques that measure brain waves, heat patterns in the face, and other biological events (*Nature* editorial, 2004).

Truth

It is true that you might be able to fool a lie detector by wiggling your toes.

Evaluation

What can we make of all this? First of all, stronger emotions are connected with higher levels of arousal (Gomez et al., 2005), but research by Paul Ekman (1993) suggests that the patterns of arousal connected with various emotions are more specific than suggested by Schachter and Singer. They are, however, apparently less specific than suggested by James and Lange. Brain imaging suggests that different emotions, such as happiness and sadness, involve different structures within the brain (Goleman, 1995). Moreover, lack of control over our emotions and lack of understanding of what is happening to us are disturbing experiences (Zimbardo et al., 1993). Thus our cognitive appraisals of situations affect our emotional responses, even if not quite in the way envisioned by Schachter.

In sum, various components of an experience—cognitive, physiological, and behavioral—contribute to our emotional responses. Our bodies may become aroused in a given situation, but as we saw in the classic research of Schachter and Singer, people also appraise those situations so that arousal alone does not appear to directly cause one emotion or another. The fact that none of the theories of emotion we have discussed applies to all people in all situations is comforting. Apparently our emotions are not quite as easily understood, manipulated, or—as in the case of the polygraph—even detected as some theorists have suggested.

3/10 < fraction that represents the number of obese American adults

total number of additional calories Americans consume than needed to maintain their weights each day > **200 billion**

total number of daily calories needed to feed a nation of 80 million people > **200 billion**

percent muscle of the average man > **40**

23 < percent muscle of the average woman

6:1 < ratio of women with an eating disorder, compared to men

3 and 2 < percent of U.S. males and females, respectively, that identify themselves as homosexual

60 < percent of Americans that believe it is sometimes necessary to lie

percent of APA respondents who believe that polygraph results should not be admitted as evidence in courts of law > **74**

Personality:
Theory and
Measurement

Learning Outcomes

LO **1**   Describe the psychoanalytical perspective and
how it contributed to the study of personality

LO **2**   Explain the trait perspective and the
"Big Five" trait model

LO **3**   Identify the contributions of learning
theory to understanding personality

LO **4**   Describe the humanistic perspective
on personality

LO **5**   Describe the sociocultural perspective on
personality

LO **6**   Describe the different kinds of tests
psychologists use to measure personality

"Can there ever be one true portrait of human personality?"

Nearly 1,000 years ago, an Islamic theologian told his pupils the fable of *The Blind Men and the Elephant:*

Once upon a time, a group of blind men heard that an unusual animal called an elephant had come to their country. Since they had no idea what an elephant looked like and had never even heard its name, they resolved that they would obtain a "picture" of sorts, and the knowledge they sought, by feeling the animal. After all, that was the only possibility available to them. They sought out the elephant, and its handler kindly permitted them to touch the beast. One blind man stroked its leg, the other a tusk, the third an ear, and believing that they now had knowledge of the elephant, they returned home satisfied. But when they were questioned by others, they provided very different descriptions. The one who had felt the leg said that the elephant was firm, strong, and upright, like a pillar. The one who had felt the tusk disagreed. He described the elephant as hard and smooth, clearly not as stout as a pillar, and sharp at the end. Now spoke the third blind man, who had held the ear of the elephant. "By my faith," he asserted, "the elephant is soft and rough." It was neither pillar-like nor hard and smooth. It was broad, thick, and leathery. And so the three argued about the true nature of the beast. Each was right in part, but none grasped the real nature of the elephant. Yet each was fervent in his belief that he knew the animal.

Each of the blind men had come to know the elephant from a different angle. Each was bound by his first experience and blind to the beliefs of his fellows and to the real nature of the beast—not just because of his physical limitations, but also because his initial encounter led him to think of the elephant in a certain way.

Truth or Fiction?

What do you think?

Folklore, common sense, or nonsense? Place a T for "True" or F for "False" on the lines provided (you'll learn the answers as you read through the text).

___ Biting one's fingernails or smoking cigarettes is a sign of conflict experienced during early childhood.

___ Twenty-five hundred years ago, a Greek physician devised a way of looking at personality that—with a little "tweaking"—remains in use today.

___ Bloodletting and vomiting were once recommended as ways of coping with depression.

___ Actually, there are no basic personality traits. We are all conditioned by society to behave in certain ways.

___ The most well-adjusted immigrants are those who abandon the language and customs of their country of origin and become like members of the dominant culture in their new host country.

___ Psychologists can determine whether a person has told the truth on a personality test.

___ There is a psychological test made up of inkblots, and test-takers are asked to say what the blots look like to them.

Our own conceptions about people, and about ourselves, may be similarly bound up with our own perspectives and initial beliefs. Some think of personality as consisting of the person's most striking traits, as in "This person has an outgoing personality" or "That person has an agreeable personality." But many psychological theorists look deeper. Those schooled in the Freudian tradition look at personality as consisting of underlying mental structures that jockey for supremacy outside the range of our ordinary awarenss. Other theorists focus on how personality is shaped by learning. And to the humanistic theorists, personality is not something people *have* but rather something they *create*, to give meaning and direction to their lives. Then, too, sociocultural theorists remind us that we must always consider the influences of culture, race, and ethnicity on personality.

Sometimes even psychologists prefer the first theory of personality they learn about. The Islamic theologian taught his pupils the legend of the blind men and the elephant to illustrate that no person can have a complete view of religious truths; we must therefore remain flexible in our thinking and open to new ideas. It may also be that none of the views of personality presented in this chapter will offer the one true portrait of human personality, but each may have something to contribute to our understanding of personality. So let us approach our study with an open mind, because years from now psychologists may well be teaching new ideas about personality.

While the blind men could touch the elephant, researchers cannot touch a personality; therefore, personality is even harder to describe and understand. Before we discuss psychologists' various approaches to personality, let us define our subject matter: personality refers to the reasonably stable patterns of emotions, motives, and behavior that distinguish one person from another.

LO¹ The Psychoanalytic Perspective

Where do we get the idea that there is something like an unconscious mind that can exert control over our behavior? One source is psychoanalytic theory.

There are several psychoanalytic theories of personality, each of which owes its origin to Sigmund Freud. Each teaches that personality is characterized by conflict. At first the conflict is external: Drives like sex, aggression, and the need for superiority come into conflict with laws, social rules, and moral codes. But at some point laws and social rules are brought inward—that is, *internalized*. The conflict is then between opposing *inner* forces.

At any given moment our behavior, our thoughts, and our emotions represent the outcome of these inner contests. *What is Freud's psychoanalytic theory?*

Sigmund Freud's Theory of Psychosexual Development

Sigmund Freud (1856–1939) was a mass of contradictions. Some have lauded him as one of the greatest thinkers of the 20th century. Others have criticized him as overrated. He preached liberal views on sexuality but was himself a model of sexual restraint. He invented a popular form of psychotherapy but experienced lifelong psychologically related problems such as migraine headaches, fainting under stress, hatred of the telephone, and an addiction to cigars. He smoked 20 cigars a day and could not break the habit even after he developed cancer of the jaw.

Freud was trained as a physician. Early in his practice, he was surprised to find that some people apparently experienced loss of feeling in a hand or paralysis of the legs even though they have no medical disorder. These odd symptoms often disappeared once the person recalled and discussed stressful events and feelings of guilt or anxiety that seemed to be related to the symptoms. Although these events and feelings lay hidden beneath the surface of awareness, they could influence behavior.

From this sort of clinical evidence, Freud concluded that the mind is like an iceberg. Only the tip of an iceberg rises above the surface of the water; the great mass of it lies hidden in the deep (see Figure 10.1). Freud came to believe that people, similarly, are aware of only a small part of the ideas and impulses that dwell within their minds. He thought that a larger portion of the mind—one that contained our deepest images, thoughts, fears, and urges—lies beneath the surface of awareness, where little light illumines them.

Figure 10.1

The Human Iceberg According to Freud

According to psychoanalytic theory, only the tip of human personality rises above the surface of the mind into conscious awareness. Material in the preconscious can become conscious if we direct our attention to it. Unconscious material tends to remain shrouded in mystery.

Go to Coursemate for PSYCH at www.cengagebrain.com to access an interactive version of this figure.

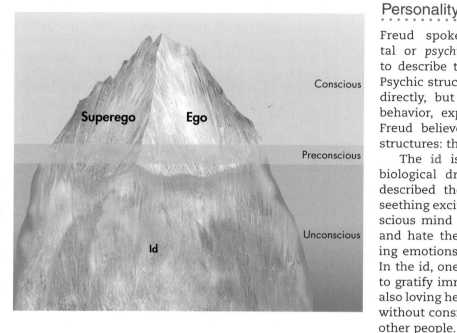

Freud labeled the region that pokes into the light of awareness the conscious part of the mind. He called the regions below the surface the *preconscious* and the *unconscious*. The preconscious mind contains ideas that are out of awareness but can be made conscious by focusing on them. The unconscious mind contains primitive instincts such as sex and aggression. Some unconscious urges cannot be experienced consciously because mental images and words cannot portray them in all their color and fury. Other unconscious urges may be kept below the surface by repression because they would create anxiety. *Repression* is defined as the automatic ejection of anxiety-evoking ideas from awareness. People forget many ugly experiences, and some research evidence suggests that people *might* repress them (Furnham et al., 2003; Myers & Brewin, 1994). Other investigators allow that forgetting and distortion of memory occurs, but view the concept of repression as nothing but a myth (Kihlstrom, 2002).

In the unconscious mind, primitive drives seek expression, while learned values try to keep them in check. The conflict can arouse emotional outbursts and psychological problems. To explore the unconscious mind, Freud used a form of mental detective work called *psychoanalysis*. In psychoanalysis, people are encouraged to talk about anything that pops into their mind while they remain comfortable and relaxed.

The Structure of Personality

Freud spoke of mental or *psychic structures* to describe the clashing forces of personality. Psychic structures cannot be seen or measured directly, but their presence is suggested by behavior, expressed thoughts, and emotions. Freud believed that there are three psychic structures: the id, the ego, and the superego.

The **id** is present at birth. It represents biological drives and is unconscious. Freud described the id as "a chaos, a cauldron of seething excitations" (1927/1964, p. 73). The conscious mind might find it inconsistent to love and hate the same person, but such conflicting emotions can dwell side by side in the id. In the id, one can hate one's mother for failing to gratify immediately all of one's needs, while also loving her. The id seeks instant gratification without consideration for law, social custom, or other people.

The **ego** begins to develop during the first year of life, largely because a child's demands for gratification cannot all be met immediately. The ego stands for reason and good sense, for rational ways of coping with frustration. It curbs the appetites of the id and seeks ways to find gratification yet avoid social disapproval. The id informs you that you are hungry, but the ego decides to microwave enchiladas. The ego takes into

id
the psychic structure, present at birth, that represents physiological drives and is fully unconscious

ego
the second psychic structure to develop, characterized by self-awareness, planning, and delay of gratification

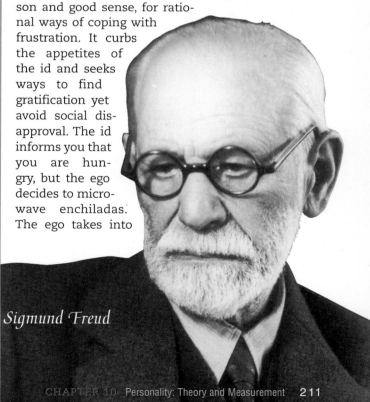

Sigmund Freud

superego
the third psychic structure, which functions as a moral guardian and sets forth high standards for behavior

identification
in psychoanalytic theory, the unconscious adoption of another person's behavior

psychosexual development
in psychoanalytic theory, the process by which libidinal energy is expressed through different erogenous zones during different stages of development

oral stage
the first stage of psychosexual development, during which gratification is hypothesized to be attained primarily through oral activities

anal stage
the second stage of psychosexual development, when gratification is attained through anal activities

account what is practical along with what is urged by the id. The ego also provides the conscious sense of self.

Although most of the ego is conscious, some of its business is carried out unconsciously. For example, the ego also acts as a censor that screens the impulses of the id. When the ego senses that improper impulses are rising into awareness, it may use psychological defenses to prevent them from surfacing. Repression is one such psychological defense, or *defense mechanism.*

The **superego** develops as the child incorporates the moral standards and values of parents and other members of the community. The child does so through **identification**, by trying to become like these people. The superego holds up shining models of an ideal self and monitors the intentions of the ego, handing out judgments of right and wrong. It floods the ego with feelings of guilt and shame when the verdict is negative.

Freud believed that a healthy personality has found ways to gratify most of the id's demands without seriously offending the superego. Most of these demands are contained or repressed. If the ego is not a good problem solver, or if the superego is too stern, the ego will have a hard time of it.

Stages of Psychosexual Development

Freud stirred controversy by arguing that sexual impulses are a central factor in personality development, even among children. Freud believed that sexual feelings are closely linked to children's basic ways of relating to the world, such as nursing and moving their bowels.

Freud believed that a major instinct, *eros,* aims to preserve and perpetuate life. Eros is fueled by psychological, or psychic, energy, which Freud labeled *libido.* Libidinal energy involves sexual impulses, so Freud considered it to be *psychosexual.* As the child develops, this energy is expressed through sexual feelings in different parts of the body, or *erogenous zones.* To Freud, human development involves the transfer of libidinal energy from one erogenous zone to another. He hypothesized five periods of **psychosexual development:** oral, anal, phallic, latency, and genital.

During the first year of life a child experiences much of her or his world through the mouth. If it fits, into the mouth it goes. This is the **oral stage.** Freud argued that oral activities such as sucking and biting give the child sexual gratification as well as nourishment.

Freud believed that children encounter conflict during each stage of psychosexual development. During the oral stage, conflict centers on the nature and extent of oral gratification. Early weaning (cessation of breastfeeding) can lead to frustration. Excessive gratification, on the other hand, can lead an infant to expect that it will routinely get anything it wants. Insufficient or excessive gratification in any stage could lead to *fixation* in that stage and to the development of traits that are characteristic of the stage. Oral traits include dependency, gullibility, and excessive optimism or pessimism (depending on the child's experiences with gratification).

Freud theorized that adults with an *oral fixation* could experience exaggerated desires for "oral activities," such as smoking, overeating, alcohol abuse, and nail biting. Like the infant whose survival depends on the mercy of an adult, adults with oral fixations may desire clinging, dependent relationships.

The anal stage begins in the second year. During the **anal stage**, gratification is attained through contraction and relaxation of the muscles that control elimination of waste products. Elimination, which is reflexive during most of the first year, comes under voluntary muscular control, even if such control is

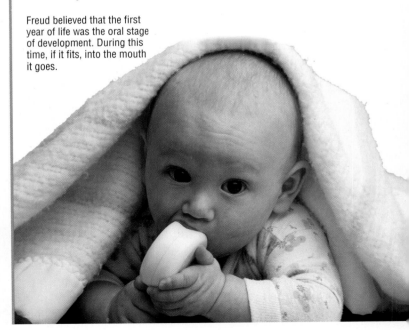

Freud believed that the first year of life was the oral stage of development. During this time, if it fits, into the mouth it goes.

not reliable at first. During the anal stage children learn to delay the gratification that comes from eliminating whenever they feel the urge. The general issue of self-control may bring conflict between parent and child. *Anal fixations* may stem from this conflict and lead to either of two sets of traits in adulthood. *Anal-retentive* traits involve excessive use of self-control: perfectionism, a strong need for order, and exaggerated neatness and cleanliness. *Anal-expulsive* traits, on the other hand, "let it all hang out": carelessness, messiness, even sadism.

Children enter the phallic stage during the third year. The major erogenous zone is the penis in boys and the clitoris in girls. Parent–child conflict is likely to develop over masturbation, to which parents may respond with threats or punishment. During this stage children may develop strong sexual attachments to the parent of the other sex and begin to view the parent of the same sex as a rival for the other parent's affections. Thus boys may want to marry their mothers, and girls may want to marry their fathers.

Children have difficulty dealing with feelings of lust and jealousy. These feelings, therefore, remain unconscious, but their influence is felt through fantasies about marriage with the parent of the other sex and hostility toward the parent of the same sex. In boys, this conflict is labeled the Oedipus complex, after the legendary Greek king who unwittingly killed his father and married his mother. Similar feelings in girls give rise to the Electra complex. According to Greek legend, Electra was the daughter of the king Agamemnon. She longed for him after his death and sought revenge against his slayers— her mother and her mother's lover.

The Oedipus and Electra complexes are resolved by about the ages of five or six. Children repress their hostilities toward the parent of the same sex and begin to identify with her or him. In psychoanalytic theory, identification is the key to gender-typing: It leads children to play the gender roles of the parent of the same sex and to internalize his or her values.

Sexual feelings toward the parent of the other sex are repressed for several years. When the feelings reemerge during adolescence, they are displaced, or transferred, to socially appropriate members of the other sex.

Freud believed that by the age of five or six, children have been in conflict with their parents over sexual feelings for several years. The pressures of the Oedipus and Electra complexes cause them to repress all sexual urges. In so doing, they enter a period of latency, during which their sexual feelings remain unconscious, they prefer playmates of their own sex, and they focus on schoolwork.

Freud believed that we enter the final stage of psychosexual development, the genital stage, at puberty. Adolescent males again experience sexual urges toward their mother, and adolescent females experience such urges toward their father. But the *incest taboo* causes them to repress these impulses and displace them onto other adults or adolescents of the other sex. Boys might seek girls "just like the girl that married dear old Dad." Girls might be attracted to boys who resemble their fathers.

People in the genital stage prefer to find sexual gratification through intercourse with a member of the other sex. In Freud's view, oral or anal stimulation, masturbation, and sexual activity with people of the same sex all represent *pregenital* fixations and immature forms of sexual conduct.

Other Psychoanalytic Theorists

Freud had several intellectual heirs. Their theories, like his, include conflict and defense mechanisms. In other respects, they differ considerably. *Who are some other psychoanalytic theorists? What are their views on personality?*

Carl Jung

Carl Jung (1875–1961) was a Swiss psychiatrist who had been a member of Freud's inner circle. He fell into disfavor with Freud when he developed his own psychoanalytic theory—analytical psychology. Jung downplayed the importance of sex, which he saw as one of several important instincts.

Jung, like Freud, was intrigued by unconscious processes. He believed that we not only have a *personal* unconscious that contains repressed memories and impulses, but also a collective unconscious containing primitive images, or archetypes, that

phallic stage
the third stage of psychosexual development, characterized by a shift of libido to the phallic region (from the Greek *phallos*, referring to an image of the penis; however, Freud used the term *phallic* to refer both to boys and girls)

Oedipus complex
a conflict of the phallic stage in which the boy wishes to possess his mother sexually and perceives his father as a rival in love

Electra complex
a conflict of the phallic stage in which the girl longs for her father and resents her mother

latency
a phase of psychosexual development characterized by repression of sexual impulses

genital stage
the mature stage of psychosexual development, characterized by preferred expression of libido through intercourse with an adult of the other gender

analytical psychology
Jung's psychoanalytic theory, which emphasizes the collective unconscious and archetypes

collective unconscious
Jung's hypothesized store of vague memories that represent the history of humankind

inferiority complex feelings of inferiority hypothesized by Adler to serve as a central motivating force

creative self according to Adler, the self-aware aspect of personality that strives to achieve its full potential

individual psychology Adler's psychoanalytic theory, which emphasizes feelings of inferiority and the creative self

reflect the history of our species. Examples of archetypes are the all-powerful God, the young hero, the fertile and nurturing mother, the wise old man, the hostile brother—even fairy godmothers, wicked witches, and themes of rebirth or resurrection. Archetypes themselves remain unconscious, but Jung believed they affect our thoughts and feelings and cause us to respond to cultural themes in the media.

Alfred Adler

Alfred Adler (1870–1937), another follower of Freud, also felt that Freud had placed too much emphasis on sex. Adler believed that people are basically motivated by an individual inferiority complex. In some people, feelings of inferiority may be based on physical problems and the need to compensate for them. Adler believed, however, that all of us encounter some feelings of inferiority because of our small size as children, and that these feelings give rise to a drive for superiority. As a child, Adler was crippled by rickets and suffered from pneumonia, and it may

be that his theory developed in part from his own striving to overcome bouts of illness.

Adler believed that self-awareness plays a major role in the formation of personality. He spoke of a creative self, a self-aware aspect of personality that strives to overcome obstacles and develop the person's potential. Because each person's potential is unique, Adler's views have been termed individual psychology.

Karen Horney

Karen Horney (1885–1952) was criticized by the New York Psychoanalytic Institute because she took issue with the way in which psychoanalytic theory portrayed women. Early in the century, psychoanalytic theory taught that a woman's place was in the home. Women who sought to compete with men in the business world were assumed to be suffering from unconscious penis envy. Psychoanalytic theory taught that little girls feel inferior to boys when they learn that boys have a penis and they do not. But Horney argued that little girls do *not* feel inferior to boys and that these views were founded on Western cultural prejudice, not scientific evidence.

Horney agreed with Freud that childhood experiences are important in psychological development. Like other neoanalysts, however, she asserted that unconscious sexual and aggressive impulses are less important than social relationships. She also

{Why Do We Need to Have Sports Heroes?}

What have psychologists learned about the appeal of celebrities, and especially sports celebrities? Many people form deep and enduring bonds of attachment with athletes and sports teams. Once they identify with a team, their self-esteem rises and falls with the team's wins and losses (Wann et al., 2000). Wins lead to a surge of testosterone in males (Bernhardt et al., 1998), which is connected with aggressiveness and self-confidence. Wins increase the optimism of both males and females.

Psychoanalytic theory suggests that children identify with parents and other "big" people in their lives because big people seem to hold the keys to the resources they need for sustenance and stimulation or

excitement. Athletes and entertainers—the rich and famous—have their fan clubs, filled with people who tie their own lights to the brilliant suns of their stars.

Teams and sports heroes provide both entertainment and the kind of gutsy competition that evolutionary psychologists believe whispers to us from our genes, pushing us toward aggression and dominance. If we can't do it on our own, we can do it *through* someone else. In some kind of psychological sense, we can *be* someone who is more effective at climbing the heap of humankind into the sun.

VISIONS OF AMERICA/JOE SOHM/GETTY IMAGES

Karen Horney
Horney, like many of Freud's intellectual descendants, took issue with Freud on many issues. For one thing, Horney did not believe that little girls had penis envy or felt inferior to boys in any other way. She also believed that children's social relationships are more important in their development than unconscious sexual and aggressive impulses.

believed that genuine and consistent love can alleviate the effects of a traumatic childhood.

Erik Erikson

Like many other modern psychoanalysts, Erik Erikson (1902–1994) believed that Freud had placed undue emphasis on sex. Like Horney, he believed that social relationships are more important than sex. Erikson also believed that to a large extent we are the conscious architects of our own personalities.

Erikson, like Freud, is known for devising a comprehensive theory of personality development. But whereas Freud proposed stages of psycho*sexual* development, Erikson proposed stages of psycho*social* development. The first stage of psychosocial development is labeled the stage of trust versus mistrust because two outcomes are possible: (1) a warm, loving relationship with the mother and others during infancy might lead to a sense of basic trust in people and the world; or (2) a cold, ungratifying relationship with the mother and others might generate a general sense of mistrust. For Erikson, the goal of adolescence is the attainment of ego identity, not genital sexuality. The focus is on who we see ourselves as being and what we stand for, not on sexual interests.

Evaluation of the Psychoanalytic Perspective

Psychoanalysis has tremendous appeal. It is rich in concepts and seems to explain many human traits. *What are the strengths and weaknesses of the psychoanalytic perspective?*

On the positive side, Freud fought for the idea that personality is subject to scientific analysis. He developed his theory at a time when many people viewed psychological problems as signs of possession by the devil or evil spirits. Freud argued that psychological

disorders stem from psychological problems—not spirits. His views contributed to the development of compassion for people with psychological disorders and to methods of psychotherapy.

Psychoanalytic theory also focused attention on the far-reaching effects of childhood events and suggested that parents respond to the emotional needs of their children.

Freud taught us that sexual and aggressive urges are common, and that recognizing them is not the same as acting on them. As W. Bertram Wolfe put it, "Freud found sex an outcast in the outhouse, and left it in the living room an honored guest."

Critics note that "psychic structures"—id, ego, and superego—are too vague to measure scientifically (Hergenhahn, 2009). Nor can they be used to predict behavior. Nor have the stages of psychosexual development escaped criticism. Children begin to masturbate as early as the first year, not in the phallic stage. As parents know from discovering their children playing "doctor," the latency stage is not as sexually latent as Freud believed.

The evidence for Erikson's developmental views seems sturdier. For example, people who fail to develop ego identity in adolescence seem to have problems with intimate relationships later on.

Freud's clinical method of gathering evidence is also suspect (Hergenhahn, 2009). Therapists may subtly guide clients into producing memories and

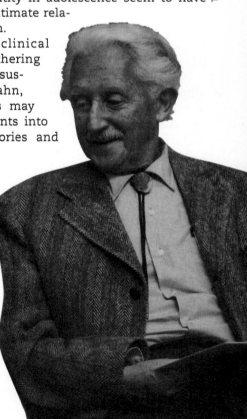

Erik Erikson
Like other modern-day analysts, Erikson believed that Freud had placed too much emphasis on sex and unconscious conflict. Erikson believed that social relationships were the key to healthful development.

> **psychosocial development**
> Erikson's theory of personality and development, which emphasizes social relationships and eight stages of growth
>
> **ego identity**
> a firm sense of who one is and what one stands for

trait
a relatively stable aspect of personality that is inferred from behavior and assumed to give rise to consistent behavior

introversion
a trait characterized by intense imagination and the tendency to inhibit impulses

extraversion
a trait characterized by tendencies to be socially outgoing and to express feelings and impulses freely

feelings they expect to find. Also, most psychoanalytic theorists restricted their evidence gathering to case studies with individuals who sought help, particularly people from the middle and upper classes. People who seek therapy differ from the general population.

Psychoanalytic theory focused on reasons that people develop certain traits. We next discuss trait theory, which is not so much concerned with the origins of traits as with their description and categorization.

LO² The Trait Perspective

The notion of traits is familiar enough. If I asked you to describe yourself, you would probably do so in terms of traits such as bright, sophisticated, and witty. (That is you, is it not?) We also describe other people in terms of traits. *What are traits?*

Traits are reasonably stable elements of personality that are inferred from behavior. If you describe a friend as "shy," it may be because you have observed anxiety or withdrawal in that person's social encounters. Traits are assumed to account for consistent behavior in different situations. You probably expect your "shy" friend to be retiring in most social confrontations.

From Hippocrates to the Present

What is the history of the trait perspective? The trait perspective dates at least to the Greek physician Hippocrates (ca. 460–377 BCE). It has generally been assumed that traits are embedded in people's bodies. Hippocrates believed they were embedded in bodily fluids. In his view, a person's personality depends on the balance of four basic fluids, or "humors," in the body. Yellow bile is associated with a choleric (quick-tempered) disposition; blood with a sanguine (warm, cheerful) one; phlegm with a phlegmatic

> In most of us by the age of thirty, the character has set like plaster, and will never soften again.
> —William James

(sluggish, calm, cool) disposition; and black bile with a melancholic (gloomy, pensive) temperament. Disease was believed to reflect an imbalance among the humors. Depression, for example, represented an excess of black bile. Although Hippocrates' theory was speculative, the terms *choleric*, *sanguine*, and so on remain in use.

More contemporary trait theories assume that traits are heritable and are embedded in the nervous system. These theories rely on the mathematical technique of factor analysis to determine which traits are basic to others.

Early in the 20th century, Gordon Allport and a colleague (Allport & Oddbert, 1936) catalogued some 18,000 human traits from a search through word lists like dictionaries. Some were physical traits such as *short*, *weak*, and *brunette*. Others were behavioral traits such as *shy* and *emotional*. This exhaustive list has served as the basis for personality research by many other psychologists. *How have psychologists reduced Allport's traits to more manageable lists?*

Hans Eysenck's Trait Theory

British psychologist Hans J. Eysenck (1916–1997) focused much of his research on the relationships between two personality traits: introversion–extraversion and emotional stability–instability (Eysenck & Eysenck, 1985). (Emotional *instability* is also called *neuroticism*). Carl Jung was the first to distinguish between introverts and extraverts. Eysenck added the dimension of emotional stability–instability to introversion–extraversion. He catalogued various personality traits according to where they are situated along these dimensions (see Figure 10.2). For example, an anxious person would be high in both introversion and neuroticism—that is, preoccupied with his or her own thoughts and emotionally unstable.

Eysenck acknowledged that his scheme is similar to Hippocrates'. According to Eysenck's dimensions, the choleric type would be extraverted and unstable; the sanguine type, extraverted and stable; the phlegmatic type, introverted and stable; and the melancholic type, introverted and unstable.

The "Big Five": The Five-Factor Model

More recent research suggests that there may be five basic personality factors, not two. These include the two found by Eysenck—extraversion and neuroticism—along with conscientiousness, agreeableness, and openness to experience (see Table 10.1).

Many personality theorists, especially Robert McCrae and Paul T. Costa, Jr., have developed the five-factor model. Cross-cultural research has found that these five factors appear to define the personality

Figure 10.2

Eysenck's Personality Dimensions and Hippocrates' Personality Types

Various personality traits shown in the outer ring fall within the two major dimensions of personality suggested by Hans Eysenck. The inner circle shows how Hippocrates' four major personality types—choleric, sanguine, phlegmatic, and melancholic—fit within Eysenck's dimensions.

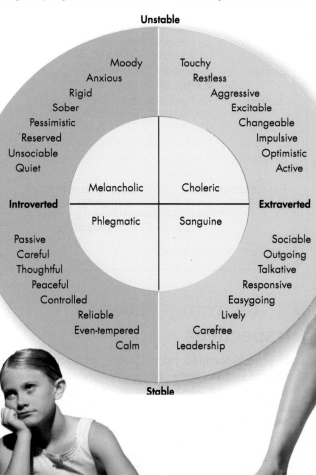

structure of American, German, Portuguese, Israeli, Chinese, Korean, Japanese, and Philippine people (Katigbak et al., 2002; McCrae & Costa, 1997). A study of more than 5,000 German, British, Spanish, Czech, and Turkish people suggests that the factors are related to people's basic temperaments, which are considered to be largely inborn (McCrae et al., 2000). The researchers interpreted the results to suggest that our personalities tend to mature over time rather than be shaped by environmental conditions, although the expression of personality traits is certainly affected by culture.

The five-factor model—also known as the "Big Five" model—is quite popular. There are hundreds of studies correlating scores on the five factors, according to a psychological test constructed by Costa and McCrae (the *NEO Five-Factor Inventory*), with various behavior patterns, psychological disorders, and kinds of "personalities." Consider driving. Significant negative correlations have been found between the numbers of traffic citations people receive and the accidents they get into, on the one hand, and the factor of agreeableness on the other (Cellar et al., 2000). In other words, it's safer to share the freeway with agreeable people. People who are

Table 10.1

The "Big Five": The Five-Factor Model

Factor	Name	Traits
I	Extraversion	Contrasts talkativeness, assertiveness, and activity with silence, passivity, and reserve
II	Agreeableness	Contrasts kindness, trust, and warmth with hostility, selfishness, and distrust
III	Conscientiousness	Contrasts organization, thoroughness, and reliability with carelessness, negligence, and unreliability
IV	Neuroticism	Contrasts nervousness, moodiness, and sensitivity to negative stimuli with coping ability
V	Openness to experience	Contrasts imagination, curiosity, and creativity with shallowness and lack of perceptiveness

not judgmental—who will put up with your every whim—tend to score low on conscientiousness (they don't examine you closely) and high on agreeableness (you can be yourself) (Bernardin et al., 2000). Despite the stereotype that older people, especially men, are "crotchety," assessment of sixty-five- to one-hundred-year-olds using the *NEO Five-Factor Inventory* suggests that people, especially men, become more agreeable as they grow older (Weiss et al., 2005). People who are anxious or depressed tend to score higher on the trait of neuroticism (Bienvenu et al., 2005). Introverts are more likely than extraverts to fear public gatherings and public speaking (Bienvenu et al., 2005).

Evaluation of the Trait Perspective

What are the strengths and weaknesses of trait theory? Trait theorists have focused much attention on the development of personality tests. They have also given rise to theories about the fit between personality and certain kinds of jobs (Holland, 1996). The qualities that suit a person for various kinds of work can be expressed in terms of abilities, personality traits, and interests. By using interviews and tests to learn about an individual's abilities and traits, testing and counseling centers can make helpful predictions about that person's chances of success and personal fulfillment in certain kinds of jobs.

One limitation of trait theory is that it has tended to be more descriptive than explanatory. It has historically focused on describing traits rather than on tracing their origins or seeking ways to modify maladaptive personality traits and behavior.

{ **Virtuous Traits: Positive Psychology and Trait Theory** }

Trait theory has applications within positive psychology, a field that studies character strengths and virtues, such as those in the table below—how they come into being and how they are related to life satisfaction. Christopher Peterson and Martin E. P. Seligman (2004) summarized many of the research findings in their book, *Character Strengths and Virtues: A Handbook and Classification* (the *CSV*). The handbook lists six major virtuous traits found in 40 different countries as different as Azerbaijan and Venezuela, along with the United States and other developed nations. These virtues were widely recognized and valued, despite cultural and religious differences (Park et al., 2005).

The *CSV* was partly developed as a counterpoint to the *DSM*, which is the *Diagnostic and Statistical Manual of the Mental Disorders* of the American Psychiatric Association (2000). Whereas the *DSM* is a catalogue of (nearly) everything that can go wrong with people, the *CSV* is a catalogue of things that go right. Fortunately, there are many of them.

Virtue	Corresponding Character Strengths
Wisdom and knowledge	Creativity, curiosity, open-mindedness, love of learning, perspective (ability to provide other people with sound advice)
Courage	Authenticity (speaking one's mind), bravery, persistence, zest
Humanity	Kindness, love, social intelligence (see emotional intelligence, discussed in Chapter 8)
Justice	Fairness, leadership, teamwork
Temperance	Forgiveness, modesty, prudence, self-regulation
Transcendence	Appreciation of beauty and excellence, gratitude (when appropriate), hope, humor, religiousness (having a belief system about the meaning of life)

Source: Peterson & Seligman, 2004.

LO³ Learning-Theory Perspectives

Trait theory focused on enduring personality characteristics that were generally presumed to be embedded in the nervous system. Learning theorists tend not to theorize in terms of traits. They focus instead on behaviors and presume that those behaviors are largely learned.

That which is learned is also, in principle, capable of being unlearned. As a result, learning theory and personality theory may not be a perfect fit. Nevertheless, learning theorists—both behaviorists and social cognitive theorists—have contributed to the discussion of personality. *What does behaviorism contribute to our understanding of personality?*

Behaviorism

At Johns Hopkins University in 1924, John B. Watson sounded the battle cry of the behaviorist movement:

Give me a dozen healthy infants, well-formed, and my own specified world to bring them up in, and I'll guarantee to take any one at random and train him to become any type of specialist I might suggest—doctor, lawyer, merchant-chief and, yes, even beggar-man and thief, regardless of his talents, penchants, tendencies, abilities, vocations, and the race of his ancestors. (p. 82)

This proclamation underscores the behaviorist view that personality is plastic—that situational or environmental influences, not internal, individual variables, are the key shapers of personality. In contrast to the psychoanalysts and structuralists of his day, Watson argued that unseen, undetectable mental structures must be rejected in favor of that which can be seen and measured. In the 1930s Watson's flag was carried onward by B. F. Skinner, who agreed that psychologists should avoid trying to see into the "black box" of the organism and instead emphasize the effects of reinforcements on behavior.

The views of Watson and Skinner largely ignored the notions of personal freedom, choice, and self-direction. Most of us assume that our wants originate within us. Watson and Skinner suggested that environmental influences such as parental approval and social custom shape us into *wanting* certain things and *not wanting* others.

In his novel *Walden Two*, Skinner (1948) described a Utopian society in which people are happy and content because they are allowed to do as they please. From early childhood, however, they have been trained or conditioned to be cooperative. Because of their reinforcement histories, they *want* to behave in decent, kind, and unselfish ways. They see themselves as free because society makes no effort to force them to behave in particular ways. The American poet Robert Frost wrote, "You have freedom when you're easy in your harness." Society in Skinner's *Walden Two* made children "easy" in their "harnesses," but the harnesses were very real.

Some object to behaviorist notions because they play down the importance of consciousness and choice. Others argue that humans are not blindly ruled by pleasure and pain. In some circumstances people have rebelled against the so-called necessity of survival by choosing pain and hardship over pleasure, or suicide. Many people have sacrificed their own lives to save those of others; and some commit suicide as a weapon. The behaviorist "defense" might be that the apparent choice of pain or death is forced on some just as conformity to social custom is forced on others.

Social Cognitive Theory

Social cognitive theory was developed by Albert Bandura (1986, 1999, 2002) and other psychologists (e.g., Mischel & Shoda, 1995). *How does social cognitive theory differ from the behaviorist view?* In contrast to behaviorism, which focuses on observable behavior and the situations in which behavior occurs, social cognitive theory focuses on learning by observation and on the cognitive processes that underlie personal differences. Social cognitive theorists see people as influencing their environment just as their environment affects them. Social cognitive theorists agree with behaviorists that discussions of human nature should be tied to observable behavior, but they assert that variables within people—*person variables*—must also be considered if we are to understand people. *Situational variables* include rewards and punishments. Person variables include knowledge and skills, ways of interpreting experience, expectancies, emotions, and self-regulatory systems and plans (Bandura & Locke, 2003; Mischel & Shoda, 1995; see Figure 10.3).

Figure 10.3

Situational and Personal Variables

Neither situational variables nor personal variables enable us to fully understand people and predict behavior. Social cognitive theorists look to their interaction to tell the tale.

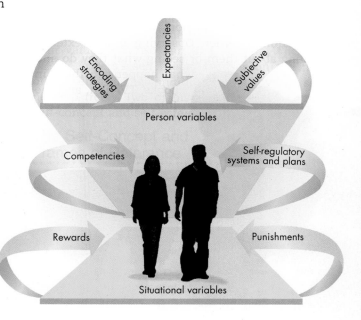

unconditional positive regard a persistent expression of esteem for the value of a person, but not necessarily an unqualified acceptance of all of the person's behaviors

conditional positive regard judgment of another person's value on the basis of the acceptability of that person's behaviors

conditions of worth standards by which the value of a person is judged

that we judge ourselves according to different sets of values. To one person, achievement–failure may be the most important dimension. To another person, the most important dimension may be decency–indecency. A third person may not even think in these terms.

Self-Esteem and Positive Regard

Rogers assumed that we all develop a need for self-regard, or self-esteem. At first, self-esteem reflects the esteem in which others hold us. Parents help children develop self-esteem when they show them unconditional positive regard—that is, when they accept them as having intrinsic merit regardless of their behavior at the moment. But when parents show children conditional positive regard—that is, when they accept them only when they behave in a desired manner—children may develop conditions of worth. Therefore, children may come to think that they have merit only if they behave as their parents wish them to behave.

Because each individual has a unique potential, children who develop conditions of worth must be somewhat disappointed in themselves. They cannot fully live up to the wishes of others and be true to themselves. This does not mean that the expression of the self inevitably leads to conflict. Rogers believed that we hurt others or act in antisocial ways only when we are frustrated in our efforts to develop our potential. When parents and others are loving and tolerant of our differentness, we, too, are loving—even if our preferences, abilities, and values differ from those of our parents.

Children in some families, however, learn that it is bad to have ideas of their own, especially about sexual, political, or religious matters. When they perceive their caregivers' disapproval, they may come to see themselves as rebels and label their feelings as selfish, wrong, or evil. If they wish to retain a consistent self-concept and self-esteem, they may have to deny their feelings or disown parts of themselves. In this way their self-concept becomes distorted. According to Rogers, anxiety often stems from recognition that people have feelings and desires that are inconsistent with their distorted self-concept. Because anxiety is unpleasant, people may deny the existence of their genuine feelings and desires.

Rogers believed that the path to self-actualization requires getting in touch with our genuine feelings, accepting them, and acting on them. This is the goal of Rogers's method of psychotherapy, *client-centered therapy*. Rogers also believed that we have mental images of what we are capable of becoming. These are termed self-ideals. We are motivated to reduce the difference between our self-concepts and our self-ideals.

Evaluation of the Humanistic Perspective

What are the strengths and weaknesses of humanistic theory? The humanistic perspective has tremendous appeal for college students because of its focus on the importance of personal experience. We tend to treasure our conscious experiences (our "selves"). For most nonhumans, to live is to move, to process food, to exchange oxygen and carbon dioxide, and to reproduce. But for humans, an essential aspect of life is conscious experience—the sense of oneself as progressing through space and time.

Ironically, the primary strength of the humanistic approach—its focus on conscious experience—is also its main weakness. Conscious experience is private and subjective. Therefore, the validity of formulating theories in terms of consciousness has been questioned.

Humanistic theories, like learning theories, have little to say about the development of traits and personality types. They assume that we are all unique, but they do not predict the sorts of traits, abilities, and interests we will develop.

You are unique, and if that is not fulfilled, then something has been lost.
—Martha Graham

LO⁵ The Sociocultural Perspective

Thirteen-year-old Hannah brought her lunch tray to the table in the cafeteria. Her mother, Julie, eyed with horror the french fries, the plate of mashed potatoes in gravy, the bag of potato chips, and the large paper cup brimming with soda. "You can't eat that!" she said. "It's garbage!"

"Oh come on, Mom! Chill, okay?" Hannah rejoined before taking her tray to sit with some friends rather than with us.

This scene occurred one Saturday at the Manhattan School of Music. I was sitting with other parents whose children studied piano, voice, or another instrument.

Julie and Hannah are Korean Americans. Flustered, Julie shook her head and said, "I've now been in the United States longer than I was in Korea, and I still can't get used to the way children act here." Dimitri, a Russian American parent, chimed in, "I never would have spoken to my parents the way Michael speaks to me. I would have been . . . whipped or beaten."

"I try to tell Hannah she is part of the family," Julie continued. "She should think of other people. When she talks that way, it's embarrassing."

"Over here children are not part of the family," said Ken, an African American parent. "They are either part of their own crowd or they are 'individuals.'"

"Being an individual does not mean you have to talk back to your mother," Julie said.

Why is the sociocultural perspective important to the understanding of personality? In our multicultural society, personality cannot be understood without reference to the sociocultural perspective. According to a *New York Times* poll, 91% of people in the United States agree that "being an American is a big part" of who they are (Powers, 2000). Seventy-nine percent say that their religion has played a big role or some role in making them who they are, and 54% say that their race has played either a big role or some role (Powers, 2000). Different cultural groups within the United States have different attitudes, beliefs, norms, self-definitions, and values (Phinney, 2000, 2005).

Hannah's traits included exceptional academic ability and musical talent, which were at least partly determined by her heredity. Clearly, she was consciously striving to become a great violinist. We could also detail the ways in which she had learned to play the violin. But we could not fully understand her personality without also considering the sociocultural influences acting on her.

Hannah, a teenager, was strongly influenced by her peers—she was completely at home with blue jeans and french fries. She was also a daughter in an Asian American immigrant group that views education as the key to success in our culture (Leppel, 2002). Belonging to this ethnic group had probably contributed to her ambition. But being a Korean American had not prevented her from becoming an outspoken American teenager. Her outspoken behavior had struck her mother as brazen and inappropriate.

Let us consider how sociocultural factors can affect one's sense of self.

> **sociocultural perspective**
> the view that focuses on the roles of ethnicity, gender, culture, and socioeconomic status in personality formation, behavior, and mental processes
>
> **individualist**
> a person who defines herself or himself in terms of personal traits and gives priority to her or his own goals
>
> **collectivist**
> a person who defines herself or himself in terms of relationships to other people and groups and gives priority to group goals

Individualism Versus Collectivism: Who Am I (in This Cultural Setting)?

One could say that Julie's complaint was that Hannah saw herself as an individual and an artist to a greater extent than as a family member and a Korean girl. *What is meant by individualism and collectivism?* Cross-cultural research reveals that people in the United States and many northern European nations tend to be individualistic. Individualists tend to define themselves in terms of their personal identities and to give priority to their personal goals (Triandis, 2005). When asked to complete the statement "I am. . . ," they are likely to respond in terms of their personality traits ("I am outgoing," "I am artistic") or their occupations ("I am a nurse," "I am a systems analyst") (Triandis & Suh, 2005). In contrast, many people from cultures in Africa, Asia, and Central and South America tend to be collectivistic. Collectivists tend to define themselves in terms of the groups to which they belong and to give priority to the group's goals (Bandura, 2003; Triandis, 2005). They feel complete in terms of their relationships with others (see Figure 10.4 on page 224). They are more likely than individualists to conform to group norms and judgments. When asked to complete the statement "I am. . . ," collectivists are more likely to respond in terms of their families, gender, or nation ("I am a father," "I am a Buddhist," "I am a Japanese") (Triandis, 2005).

The seeds of individualism and collectivism are found in the culture in which a person grows up. The capitalist system fosters individualism to some degree. It assumes that individuals are entitled to amass personal fortunes and that the process of

acculturation
the process of adaptation in which immigrants and native groups identify with a new, dominant culture by learning about that culture and making behavioral and attitudinal changes

doing so creates jobs and wealth for large numbers of people. The individualist perspective is found in the self-reliant heroes and antiheroes of Western literature and mass media—from Homer's Odysseus to James Bond. The traditional writings of the East have exalted people who resist personal temptations to do their duty and promote the welfare of the group.

Another issue from the sociocultural perspective is *acculturation*. Just how much acculturation is good for you? *How does acculturation affect the psychological well-being of immigrants and their families?*

Acculturation, Adjustment, and Self-Esteem

Should Hindu women who emigrate to the United States surrender the sari in favor of California Casuals? Should Russian immigrants try to teach their children English at home? Should African American children be acquainted with the music and art of African peoples or those of Europe? Such activities are examples of acculturation, the process by which immigrants become acclimated to the customs and behavior patterns of their new host culture.

Self-esteem has been shown to be connected with patterns of acculturation among immigrants (Berry et al., 2006; Phinney, 2005). Those patterns take various forms. Some immigrants are completely assimilated by the dominant culture. They lose the language and customs of their country of origin and identify with the dominant culture in the new host country. Others maintain almost complete separation. They retain the language and customs of their country of origin and never acclimate to those of the new country. Still others become bicultural. They remain fluent in the language of their country of origin but also become conversant in the language of their new country. They blend the customs and values of both cultures. They can switch "mental gears"; they apply the values of one culture under some circumstances and apply the values of the other culture under others. Perhaps they relate to other people in one way at work or in school, and in another way at home or in the neighborhood.

Research evidence suggests that people who do not surrender their traditional backgrounds have relatively higher self-esteem than those who do. African American and Mexican Americans who are bicultural are less likely to be anxious and depressed than their peers who identify fully either with the majority culture or their subculture (Kim et al., 2003; Phinney & Devich-Navarro, 1997).

Fiction

Actually, research evidence suggests that people who do not fully surrender their traditional backgrounds have higher self-esteem than those who do.

Figure 10.4

The Self in Relation to Others from the Individualist and Collectivist Perspectives

To an individualist, the self is separate from other people (part A). To a collectivist, the self is complete only in terms of relationships to other people (part B). (Based on Markus & Kitayama, 1991).

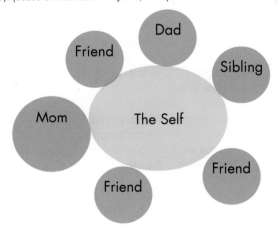

A. Independent view of the self

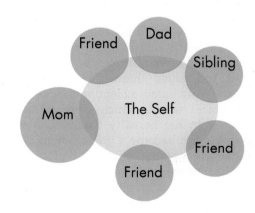

B. Interdependent view of the self

Evaluation of the Sociocultural Perspective

The sociocultural perspective provides valuable insights into the roles of ethnicity, gender, culture, and socioeconomic status in personality formation. It enhances our sensitivity to cultural differences and expectations and allows us to appreciate the richness of human behavior and mental processes.

LO⁶ Measurement of Personality

Physicians have an easy time of it measuring heart rate and blood pressure. Psychologists, biologists, and neuroscientists find it easier to measure electricity in the brain or substances in the blood than to measure psychological concepts such as intelligence, depression, extraversion, or emotional stability. It may take time, money, and expertise to develop and operate the proper instruments, but once you have them, the measurements tend to be accurate enough.

In Chapter 8 we saw that many critics argue that "intelligence tests" measure many things other than intelligence, including motivation and familiarity with European American middle-class culture. In Chapter 9 we saw that "lie detectors" measure four physiological variables and detect much more than lies. The reliability and validity of intelligence tests and lie detectors have been brought into question. So too have the reliability and validity of personality tests.

The **validity** of a test is the extent to which it measures what it is supposed to measure. We usually assess the validity of personality tests by comparing test results to external criteria or standards. For example, a test of hyperactivity might be compared with teachers' reports about whether or not children in their classes are hyperactive. The **reliability** of a test is the stability of one's test results from one testing to another. We usually determine the reliability of tests by comparing testing results on different occasions or at different ages. A reliable IQ test should provide scores during childhood that remain reasonably similar in adolescence and adulthood. Test **standardization** is a process that checks out the scores, validity, and reliability of a test with people of various ages and from various groups. We cannot assess the intellectual

functioning of an individual without relating it to other people in the same age group. Such information is made available when tests are professionally developed and scored.

Behavior-rating scales assess behavior in settings such as classrooms or mental hospitals. With behavior-rating scales, trained observers usually check off each occurrence of a specific behavior within a certain time frame—say, fifteen minutes. Standardized objective and projective tests, however, are used more frequently, and we focus on them in this section.

How are personality measures used? Measures of personality are used to make important decisions, such as whether a person is suited for a certain type of work, a particular class in school, or a drug to reduce agitation. As part of their admissions process, graduate schools often ask professors to rate prospective students on scales that assess traits such as intelligence, emotional stability, and cooperation. Students may take tests to measure their *aptitudes* and interests to gain insight into whether they are suited for certain occupations. It is assumed that students who share the aptitudes and interests of people who function well in certain positions are also likely to function well in those positions.

Let us consider the two most widely used types of personality tests: objective tests and projective tests.

Objective Tests

What are objective personality tests? **Objective tests** present respondents with a standardized group of test items in the form of a questionnaire. Respondents are limited to a specific range of answers. One test might ask respondents to indicate whether items are true or false for them. Another might ask respondents to select the preferred activity from groups of three.

validity in psychological testing, the degree to which a test measures what it is supposed to measure

reliability in psychological testing, the consistency or stability of test scores from one testing to another

standardization in psychological testing, the process by which one obtains and organizes test scores from various population groups, so that the results of a person's completing a test can be compared to those of others of his or her sex, in his or her age group, and so on

objective tests tests whose items must be answered in a specified, limited manner; tests whose items have concrete answers that are considered correct

PHOTODISC/GETTY IMAGES

response set
a tendency to answer test items according to a bias—for example, to make oneself seem perfect or bizarre

Some tests have a *forced-choice format*, in which respondents are asked to indicate which of two or more statements is more true for them or which of several activities they prefer. The respondents are not usually given the option of answering "none of the above." Forced-choice formats are frequently used in interest inventories, which help predict whether the person would function well in a certain occupation. They are typically the only means of responding to online assessments because the test-taker is usually required to "click" the chosen answer. The following item is similar to those found in occupational interest inventories:

I would rather
a. be a forest ranger.
b. work in a busy office.
c. play a musical instrument.

The Minnesota Multiphasic Personality Inventory (MMPI[3]) contains hundreds of items presented in a true–false format. The MMPI is designed to be used by clinical and counseling psychologists to help diagnose psychological disorders. Accurate measurement of an individual's problems should point to appropriate treatment. The MMPI is the most widely used psychological test in clinical work and is widely used in psychological research.

The MMPI is usually scored for the four *validity scales* and ten *clinical scales* described in Table 10.2. The validity scales suggest whether answers actually represent the person's thoughts, emotions, and behaviors.

The validity scales in Table 10.2 assess different response sets, or biases, in answering the questions. People with high L scores, for example, may be attempting to present themselves as excessively moral and well-behaved individuals. People with high F scores may be trying to seem bizarre or are answering haphazardly. Many personality measures have some kind of validity scale. The clinical scales of the MMPI assess the problems shown in Table 10.2, as well as stereotypical masculine or feminine interests and introversion.

The MMPI scales were constructed and validated *empirically*—that is, on the basis of actual clinical data rather than psychological theory. A test-item bank of several hundred items was derived from questions that are often asked in clinical interviews. Here are some examples of the kinds of items that were used:

Table 10.2

Minnesota Multiphasic Personality Inventory (MMPI) Scales

Scale	Abbreviation	Possible Interpretations
Validity scales		
Question	?	Corresponds to number of items left unanswered
Lie	L	Lies or is highly conventional
Frequency	F	Exaggerates complaints or answers items haphazardly; may have bizarre ideas
Correction	K	Denies problems
Clinical scales		
Hypochondriasis	Hs	Has bodily concerns and complaints
Depression	D	Is depressed; has feelings of guilt and helplessness
Hysteria	Hy	Reacts to stress by developing physical symptoms; lacks insight
Psychopathic deviate	Pd	Is immoral, in conflict with the law; has stormy relationships
Masculinity/femininity	Mf	High scores suggest interests and behavior considered stereotypical of the other gender
Paranoia	Pa	Is suspicious and resentful, highly cynical about human nature
Psychasthenia	Pt	Is anxious, worried, high-strung
Schizophrenia	Sc	Is confused, disorganized, disoriented; has bizarre ideas
Hypomania	Ma	Is energetic, restless, active, easily bored
Social introversion	Si	Is introverted, timid, shy; lacks self-confidence

PHOTODISC/GETTY IMAGES

My father was a good man.	T	F
I am very seldom troubled by headaches.	T	F
My hands and feet are usually warm enough.	T	F
I have never done anything dangerous for the thrill of it.	T	F
I work under a great deal of tension.	T	F

The items were administered to people with previously identified symptoms, such as depressive or schizophrenic symptoms. Items that successfully set these people apart were included.

Projective Tests

How do projective tests differ from objective tests? In **projective tests** there are no clear, specified answers. People are shown ambiguous stimuli such as inkblots or ambiguous drawings and asked to say what they look like or to tell stories about them. There is no one correct response. It is assumed that people *project* their own personalities into their responses. The meanings they attribute to these stimuli are assumed to reflect their personalities as well as the drawings or blots themselves.

The Rorschach Inkblot Test

There are a number of psychological tests made up of inkblots, and test-takers are asked to say what the blots look like to them. The best known of these is the Rorschach inkblot test, named after its originator, Hermann Rorschach.

People are handed the inkblots, one by one, and are asked what they look like or what they could be. A response that reflects the shape of the blot is considered a sign of adequate *reality testing*. A response that richly integrates several features of the blot is considered a sign of high intellectual functioning. Supporters of the Rorschach believe that it provides insight into a person's intelligence, interests, cultural background, personality traits, psychological disorders, and many other variables. Critics argue that there is little empirical evidence to support the test's validity (Garb et al., 2005).

MASTERFILE (ROYALTY-FREE DIV.)

Although there is no single "correct" response to the inkblot shown in Figure 10.5, some responses are not in keeping with the features of the blots and reveal to the examiner that the test-taker is projecting his or her personality onto the test stimuli. The shape of the inkblot in Figure 10.5 might commonly suggest a butterfly or a flower, or many other things. A test-taker who makes unusual or uncommon responses to the features of the blot may be revealing personality problems.

projective test
a psychological test that presents ambiguous stimuli onto which the test taker projects his or her own personality in making a response

The Thematic Apperception Test

The Thematic Apperception Test (TAT) was developed in the 1930s by Henry Murray and Christiana Morgan. It consists of drawings, like the one shown on page 199, that are open to various interpretations. Individuals are given the cards one at a time and asked to make up stories about them.

The TAT is widely used in research on motivation and in clinical practice. The assumption is that we are likely to project our own needs into our responses to ambiguous situations, even if we are unaware of them or reluctant to talk about them. The TAT is also widely used to assess attitudes toward other people, especially parents and intimate partners.

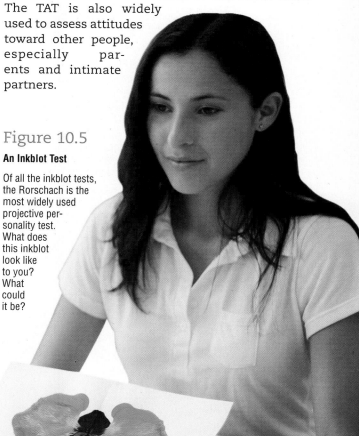

Figure 10.5

An Inkblot Test

Of all the inkblot tests, the Rorschach is the most widely used projective personality test. What does this inkblot look like to you? What could it be?

Stress, Health, and Adjustment

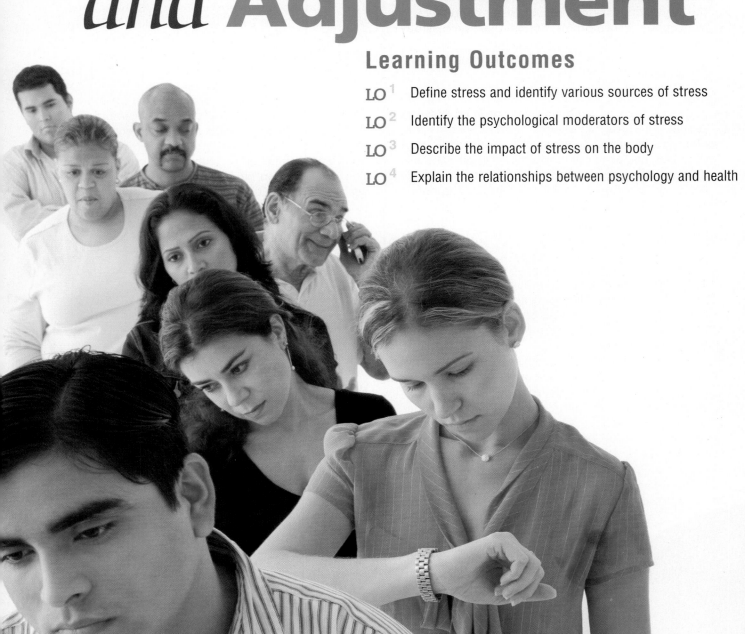

Learning Outcomes

LO ^{1} Define stress and identify various sources of stress

LO ^{2} Identify the psychological moderators of stress

LO ^{3} Describe the impact of stress on the body

LO ^{4} Explain the relationships between psychology and health

> ## "Then it dawned on them that people around them were screaming for help."

Katrina came through the door of a home in a New Orleans suburb at ten o'clock on Monday morning. She didn't knock. She flowed underneath the door, and then she began to come in through the windows, the rising waters of a tempest whose winds had tossed torrents against the shore at close to 150 miles per hour.

Gail, a nurse, and her husband Earl, a machinist, had socked away some money for the future and nearly owned their one-story brick home free and clear. They had been looking forward to spending more time with their grandchildren.

But in minutes Katrina changed their lives forever. Before they fully comprehended what was happening, water was sloshing up against their waists.

The front door normally opened out, but Katrina held it shut. Gail and Earl managed to climb out a window against Katrina's onrushing fury.

Gail and Earl, like many of their neighbors, owned a boat—a seventeen-foot Sunbird. They slogged to the boat through the sudden river and the pouring rain, to where it was parked under the roof of the carport. They pulled themselves up onto it, and then they realized that the keys to the engine were still in the house.

Truth or Fiction?

What do you think?

Folklore, common sense, or nonsense? Place a T for "True" or F for "False" on the lines provided (you'll learn the answers as you read through the text).

__ Some stress is good for us.

__ Vacations can be stressful.

__ Searching for social approval or perfection is an excellent way of making yourself miserable.

__ Type A people achieve more than Type B people, but they are less satisfied with themselves.

__ Humor helps us cope with stress.

__ At any given moment, countless microscopic warriors within our bodies are carrying out search-and-destroy missions against foreign agents.

__ If you have a family history of heart disease or cancer, there is little or nothing you can do to prevent developing the illness yourself.

Gail and Earl looked at each other. Earl knew what he had to do. He slid back into the water. There was no more reaching the ground to walk through it. He swam back to the house. Once he was in the house, the water continued to rise.

"The boat was just about touching the roof of the carport," Gail said. "I'm screaming for him to hurry up. Because if we got stuck under there, you know, we would have died" (Herbert, 2005).

Somehow Earl found the keys and worked his way back to the boat and they got the engine going. By the time they left the carport, the water was up to the roof of the house. They could barely see through the rain, much less maneuver, but they managed to move the boat two blocks to the shelter of the roof of the drive-through lane of a bank. But about an hour later they had to return to the storm because the boat was bouncing up against the roof of the drive-through.

Fortunately, the rain eased and Gail and Earl piloted the Sunbird out across the alien waterscape. There was no refilling the engine with gasoline. The gas stations were underwater. Even locating themselves had turned eerie, with the street signs underwater. Cars and trucks bobbed by like strange logs in a stream.

Then it dawned on them that people around them were screaming for help. Drenched people stood on rooftops or leaned out of upper-story windows, waving and yelling. Gail and Earl took as many as they could in the Sunbird and found their way to a shelter in a local high school.

Then they turned about and went out for more people. Others—police, firefighters, civilians—were also out in boats doing their part. Local officials managed to find them gasoline. They rode the waters and ferried people to the shelter for two days, bringing in 150. Hungry, unwashed despite the flooding, and exhausted, Gail and Earl were then evacuated themselves to Baton Rouge, where they rested for a couple of days and then made their way to relatives in Florida. It never occurred to them that they were heroes.

Their home is gone. So, too, are their jobs. They lost a car and a truck. Yet they were lucky. "If we did not have family," Gail said, "we'd be living under a bridge." When asked how the ordeal had affected her psychologically, Gail said, "Don't ask me now. It's too early." Later she added, "Listen, everybody's depressed and kind of still in shock. Everybody who's been through this thing. It's hard to believe it happened" (Herbert, 2005).

Disasters like Katrina have their emotional toll as well as their physical toll (Carey, 2005; Leitch, 2005). Studies of communities devastated by hurricanes, oil spills, earthquakes, tsunamis, fires, and other disasters suggest that most survivors eventually come to live with their memories and their grief. But many have lingering nightmares, flashbacks, depression, and irritability that suggest deeper effects of stress.

This chapter is about stress—its origins, its psychological and physical effects, and ways of coping. *What is stress?*

LO¹ Stress: What It Is, Where It Comes From

In physics, stress is defined as a pressure or force exerted on a body. Tons of rock pressing on the earth, one car smashing into another, a rubber band stretching—all are types of physical stress. Psychological forces, or stresses, also press, push, or pull. We may feel "crushed" by the weight of a big decision, "smashed" by adversity, or "stretched" to the point of snapping. In the case of the victims of Katrina, physical events had psychological as well as physical consequences. As we will see throughout the chapter, those psychological consequences can also affect our health.

Psychologists define stress as the demand made on an organism to adapt, cope, or adjust. Some stress is healthful and necessary to keep us alert and occupied. Stress researcher Hans Selye (1980) referred to such healthful stress as eustress. We may experience eustress when we begin a sought-after job or are trying to choose the color of an iPod. But intense or prolonged stress, such as that caused by Hurricane Katrina or social or financial problems, can overtax our adjustive capacity, affect our moods, impair our ability to experience pleasure, and harm the body (Kiecolt-Glaser et al., 2002a, 2002b; Schneiderman et al., 2005).

Stress is one of the key topics in health psychology. Health psychology

AP PHOTO/ERIC GAY

studies the relationships between psychological factors and the prevention and treatment of physical health problems. Health psychologists investigate how

- psychological factors such as stress, behavior patterns, and attitudes can lead to or aggravate illness;

- people can cope with stress;

- stress and pathogens (disease-causing organisms such as bacteria and viruses) interact to influence the immune system;

- people decide whether or not to seek health care; and

- psychological interventions such as health education (for example, concerning nutrition, smoking, and exercise) and behavior modification can contribute to physical health.

Daily Hassles and Life Changes

What are daily hassles? Daily *hassles* are the stresses of everyday life, which can pile up until we can no longer deal with them. Lazarus and his colleagues (1985) analyzed a scale that measures daily hassles and their opposites—termed *uplifts*—and found that hassles could be grouped as follows:

- *Household hassles:* preparing meals, shopping, and home maintenance

- *Health hassles:* physical illness, concern about medical treatment, side effects of medication

- *Time-pressure hassles:* having too many things to do and not enough time

- *Inner concern hassles:* being socially isolated, lonely

- *Environmental hassles:* crime, neighborhood deterioration, noise, pollution

- *Financial responsibility hassles:* concern about owing money, such as mortgage payments and loans

- *Work hassles:* job dissatisfaction

- *Security hassles:* concerns about job security, terrorism, investments, retirement

pathogen
a microscopic organism (e.g., bacterium or virus) that can cause disease

What are life changes? **Life changes differ from daily hassles in two ways:**

- Many life changes are positive, whereas all hassles are negative.

- Hassles occur regularly, whereas life changes occur at irregular intervals.

Peggy Blake and her colleagues (1984) constructed a scale of "life-change units" to measure the impact of life changes among college students. Surveys with students revealed that death of a spouse or parent were considered the most stressful life changes (94 and 88 life-change units, respectively). Academic failure (77 units) and graduation from college (68 units) were also considered highly stressful, even though graduation from college is a positive event—considering the alternative. Positive life changes such as an outstanding personal achievement (49 units) and going on vacation (30 units) also made the list.

A worker tries to capture some of the oil washing on to a beach in the Gulf of Mexico following the Deepwater Horizon oil spill of 2010. The oil spill killed rig workers, decimated animal life in and around the Gulf, and financially devastated communities whose livelihoods depended on fishing and tourism.

JOE RAEDLE/GETTY IMAGES

Hassles, Life Changes, and Health Problems

Hassles and life changes—especially negative life changes—can cause us to worry and can affect our moods (Lavee & Ben-Ari, 2003). Stressors such as hassles and life changes also predict physical health problems such as heart disease and athletic injuries (Schneiderman et al., 2005). Holmes and Rahe (1967) found that people who "earned" 300 or more life-change units within a year, according to their scale, were at greater risk for health problems. Eight of ten developed health problems, compared with only one of three people whose totals of life-change units for the year were below 150.

Stress in America: The American Psychological Association Survey

Each year the American Psychological Association (2009) has been commissioning surveys of stress in America. In 2009, Harris Interactive conducted an online survey of a nationally representative sample of Americans. The figures for sex, age, race and ethnicity, level of education, region, and household income were adjusted as necessary so that they were brought into line with their actual percentages of the American population at large.

As you see in Figure 11.1, the respondents overwhelmingly reported that money and work were their major sources of stress. We will see later that "job strain" is a key contributor to heart disease. When we add in the costs of housing, which are mentioned by nearly half the sample, we find another area in which finances contribute to stress. Health is another major area of concern, mentioned in various ways by more than half of the sample. Finally, Figure 11.1 shows that intimate relationships are also a source of stress for half (51%) of the sample. One might think that intimate relationships would serve as a buffer against external sources of stress for people, *and perhaps they do*. (Life is complex.) However, these relationships can also contribute to stress.

Respondents reported many symptoms of stress, both physical and psychological. As shown in Figure 11.2, nearly half the respondents (45%) reported that stress made them irritable or angry. Stress made more than two in five respondents (43%) tired, and about one-third (34%) reported having them headaches. More than one in four (27%) had indigestion, and about one in four (24%) felt tense. Two in five lacked interest in things, and about one-third felt depressed (34%) or as though they could cry (32%).

Figure 11.3 shows that the most commonly reported methods of coping with stress were listening to music (49%), exercising or going for walks (44%0, and reading (41%). Watching TV or movies was tied (36%) with spending time with friends or family. About one-third (32%) reported napping or praying. One in seven (14%) smoke or drank.

Figure 11.1

Significant Sources of Stress

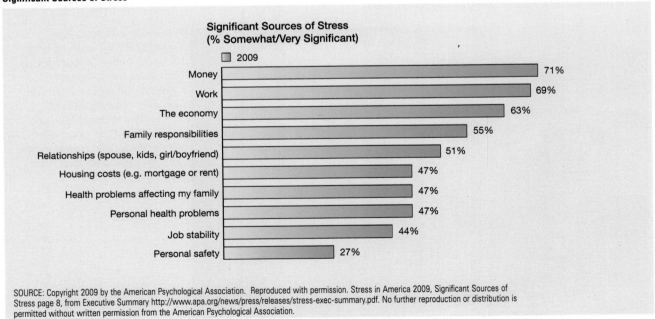

SOURCE: Copyright 2009 by the American Psychological Association. Reproduced with permission. Stress in America 2009, Significant Sources of Stress page 8, from Executive Summary http://www.apa.org/news/press/releases/stress-exec-summary.pdf. No further reproduction or distribution is permitted without written permission from the American Psychological Association.

Figure 11.2

Symptoms of Stress

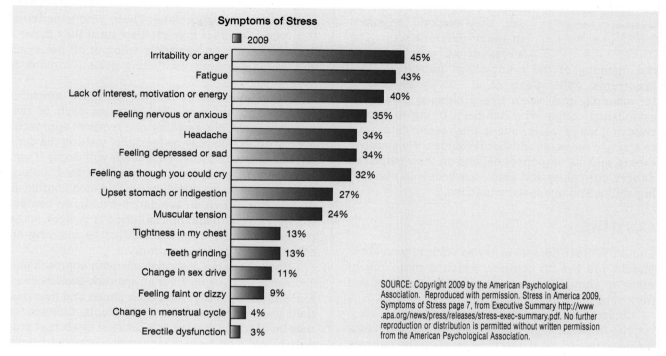

Symptoms of Stress

■ 2009

Irritability or anger	45%
Fatigue	43%
Lack of interest, motivation or energy	40%
Feeling nervous or anxious	35%
Headache	34%
Feeling depressed or sad	34%
Feeling as though you could cry	32%
Upset stomach or indigestion	27%
Muscular tension	24%
Tightness in my chest	13%
Teeth grinding	13%
Change in sex drive	11%
Feeling faint or dizzy	9%
Change in menstrual cycle	4%
Erectile dysfunction	3%

SOURCE: Copyright 2009 by the American Psychological Association. Reproduced with permission. Stress in America 2009, Symptoms of Stress page 7, from Executive Summary http://www.apa.org/news/press/releases/stress-exec-summary.pdf. No further reproduction or distribution is permitted without written permission from the American Psychological Association.

Figure 11.3

Stress Management Techniques Used by Americans

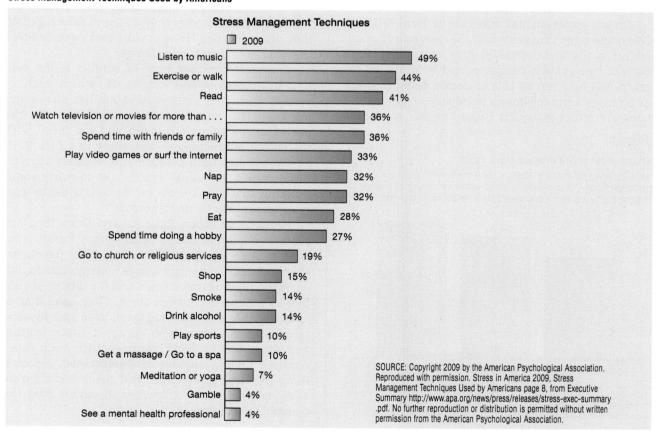

Stress Management Techniques

■ 2009

Listen to music	49%
Exercise or walk	44%
Read	41%
Watch television or movies for more than . . .	36%
Spend time with friends or family	36%
Play video games or surf the internet	33%
Nap	32%
Pray	32%
Eat	28%
Spend time doing a hobby	27%
Go to church or religious services	19%
Shop	15%
Smoke	14%
Drink alcohol	14%
Play sports	10%
Get a massage / Go to a spa	10%
Meditation or yoga	7%
Gamble	4%
See a mental health professional	4%

SOURCE: Copyright 2009 by the American Psychological Association. Reproduced with permission. Stress in America 2009, Stress Management Techniques Used by Americans page 8, from Executive Summary http://www.apa.org/news/press/releases/stress-exec-summary.pdf. No further reproduction or distribution is permitted without written permission from the American Psychological Association.

conflict being torn in different directions by opposing motives; feelings produced by being in conflict

Not all people report that the same events cause them stress, or course. And, as we see, they respond to stress in many different ways. The stress of an event reflects the meaning of the event to an individual (CNS Spectrums, 2005; Gaab et al., 2005). Pregnancy, for example, may seem like a blessing to a well-established couple who has been trying to have a child for many years, but it may seem disastrous to a single teenager without resources. We appraise events, and our responses depend on their perceived danger, our values and goals, our beliefs in our coping ability, and our social situations.

Conflict

Should you eat dessert or try to stick to your diet? Should you live on campus, which is more convenient, or should you rent an apartment, where you may have more independence?

Choices like these can place us in conflict. *What is conflict?* In psychology, conflict is the feeling of being pulled in two or more directions by opposing motives. Conflict is frustrating and stressful. Psychologists often classify conflicts into four types: approach–approach, avoidance–avoidance, approach–avoidance, and multiple approach–avoidance.

Classic experimental research by Neal E. Miller (1944) and others suggests that the *approach–approach conflict* is the least stressful type of conflict. Here each of two goals is desirable, and both are within reach. You may not be able to decide between pizza or tacos, or a trip to Nassau or Hawaii. I recently had such a conflict in which I was "forced" to choose

between triple-chocolate fat-free frozen yogurt and coffee chocolate-chip fat-free frozen yogurt. Such conflicts are usually resolved by making a decision (I took the triple chocolate). Those who experience this type of conflict may vacillate until they make a decision, as shown by people who put off decisions and ruminate about conflicting goals (Emmons & King, 1988).

Avoidance–avoidance conflict is more stressful because you are motivated to avoid each of two negative goals. But avoiding one requires approaching the other. You may be fearful of visiting the dentist but also afraid that your teeth will decay if you do not make an appointment and go. Each potential outcome in an avoidance–avoidance conflict is undesirable. When an avoidance–avoidance conflict is highly stressful and no resolution is in sight, some people withdraw from the conflict by focusing on other matters or doing nothing.

When the same goal produces both approach and avoidance motives, we have an *approach–avoidance conflict*. People and things have their pluses and minuses, their good points and their bad points. Cheesecake may be delicious, but oh, the calories! Goals that produce mixed motives may seem more attractive from a distance but undesirable from up close (Miller, 1944). Many couples who repeatedly break up and reunite recall each other fondly when apart and swear that they could make the relationship work if they got together again. But after they do spend time together, they again wonder, "How could I ever have believed that this so-and-so would change?"

The most complex form of conflict is the *multiple approach–avoidance conflict*, in which each of several alternative courses of action has pluses and minuses. This sort of conflict might arise on the eve of an examination, when you are faced with the choice of studying or, say, going to a film. Each alternative has both positive and negative aspects: "Studying's a bore, but I won't have to worry about flunking. I'd love to see the movie, but I'd just be worrying about how I'll do tomorrow."

Research by Robert Emmons and Laura King has connected internal conflict with various health problems. In one study (Emmons & King, 1988), the researchers enlisted eighty-eight college undergraduates and surveyed their personal goals and the degree of conflict experienced between them. They used diaries to assess the students' emotional lives and physical symptoms. Students who reported more conflict and more ambivalence about conflict more often reported feeling anxious and depressed, reported more physical complaints, and made significantly more visits to the college health center over the course of two years.

Figure 11.4

Impact of Stress on Eating and Sleep Habits

In their survey on stress in America, the American Psychological Association found that respondents reported that stress caused them to disrupt their usual eating and sleep habits, as shown in this figure.

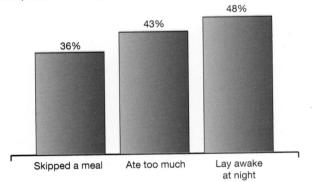

Table 11.1

Irrational Beliefs: Cognitive Doorways to Distress

Irrational Belief 1:	You must have sincere love and approval almost all the time from the people who are important to you.
Irrational Belief 2:	You must prove yourself to be thoroughly competent, adequate, and achieving at something important.
Irrational Belief 3:	Things must go the way you want them to go. Life is awful when you don't get your first choice in everything.
Irrational Belief 4:	Other people must treat everyone fairly and justly. When people act unfairly or unethically, they are rotten.
Irrational Belief 5:	When there is danger or fear in your world, you must be preoccupied with and upset by it.
Irrational Belief 6:	People and things should turn out better than they do. It's awful and horrible when you don't find quick solutions to life's hassles.
Irrational Belief 7:	Your emotional misery stems from external pressures that you have little or no ability to control. Unless these external pressures change, you must remain miserable.
Irrational Belief 8:	It is easier to evade life's responsibilities and problems than to face them and undertake more rewarding forms of self-discipline.
Irrational Belief 9:	Your past influenced you immensely and must therefore continue to determine your feelings and behavior today.
Irrational Belief 10:	You can achieve happiness by inertia and inaction, or by just enjoying yourself from day to day.

catastrophize
to interpret negative events as being disastrous; to "blow out of proportion"

JUPITERIMAGES / GETTY IMAGES

Irrational Beliefs

Psychologist Albert Ellis noted that our beliefs about events, as well as the events themselves, can be stressors (Ellis, 2002, 2004a, 2004b). Consider a case in which a person is fired from a job and is anxious and depressed about it. It may seem logical that losing the job is responsible for the misery, but Ellis pointed out how the individual's beliefs about the loss compounded his or her misery.

How do irrational beliefs create or compound stress? Let us examine this situation according to Ellis's A→B→C approach: Losing the job is an *activating event* (A). The eventual outcome, or *consequence* (C), is misery. Between the activating event (A) and the consequence (C), however, lie *beliefs* (B), such as these: "This job was the most important thing in my life," "What a no-good failure I am," "My family will starve," "I'll never find a job as good," "There's nothing I can do about it." Beliefs such as these compound misery, foster helplessness, and divert us from planning and deciding what to do next. The belief that "There's nothing I can do about it" fosters helplessness. The belief that "I am a no-good failure" internalizes the blame and may be an exaggeration. The belief that "My family will starve" may also be an exaggeration.

Let's diagram the situation:

> Activating events →Beliefs →Consequences
> or A→B→C

Anxieties about the future and depression over a loss are normal and to be expected. The beliefs of the person who lost the job, however, tend to catastrophize the extent of the loss and contribute to anxiety and depression—and thus raise the person's blood pressure (Dunkley et al., 2003; Melmed, 2003). By heightening the individual's emotional reaction to the loss and fostering feelings of helplessness, these beliefs also impair coping ability. They lower the person's self-efficacy expectations.

Ellis proposed that many of us carry with us the irrational beliefs shown in Table 11.1. They are our personal doorways to distress. In fact, they can give rise to problems in themselves. When problems assault us from other sources, these beliefs can magnify their effect.

Truth

Research findings confirm the connections between irrational beliefs (e.g., excessive dependence on social approval and perfectionism) and feelings of anxiety and depression (Ciarrochi, 2004; Rice & Dellwo, 2001; Wiebe & McCabe, 2002).

Ellis found it understandable that we would want the approval of others but irrational to believe that we cannot survive without it. It would be nice to be competent in everything we do, but it's unreasonable to *expect* it. Sure, it would be nice to be able to serve and volley like a tennis pro, but most of us haven't the time or natural ability to perfect the game. Demanding perfection prevents us from going out on the court on weekends and batting the ball back and forth just for fun (Ciarrochi, 2004). The belief that one must be preoccupied by threats is a prescription for perpetual emotional upheaval. Believing that we cannot overcome the influences of the past leads to feelings of helplessness and demoralization. Sure, Ellis might say, childhood experiences can explain the origins of irrational beliefs, but it is our own cognitive appraisal—here and now—that causes us to be miserable.

The Type A Behavior Pattern

Some people create stress for themselves through the Type A behavior pattern. *What is Type A behavior?* Type A people are highly driven, competitive, impatient, hostile, and aggressive—so much so that they are prone to getting into auto accidents (Ben-Zur, 2002; Karlberg et al., 1998; Magnavita et al., 1997). They feel rushed and pressured and keep one eye glued to the clock (Conte et al., 2001). They are not only prompt for appointments but often early. They eat, walk, and talk rapidly. They grow restless when others work slowly. They attempt to dominate group discussions. Type A people find it difficult to surrender control or share power. They are reluctant to delegate authority in the workplace and thus increase their own workloads. They watch their form, perfect their strokes, and strive for continual self-improvement. They require

Truth

It is true that Type A people achieve more than Type B people but are less satisfied with themselves.

themselves to achieve in everything they do.

Type B people relax more readily than Type A people and focus more on the quality of life. They are less ambitious and less impatient, and they pace themselves. Type A people earn higher grades and more money than Type B's who are equal in intelligence, but Type A people are more likely to continue to strive for more and more.

LO² Psychological Moderators of Stress

Five out of six respondents to the *Stress in America* survey reported that stress caused some physical symptom or some psychological symptom, but there is no one-to-one relationship between stress and physical or psychological health problems. Some people inherit predispositions to specific health problems. Psychological factors can also play a role (Melmed, 2003). In the next section we discuss several psychological factors that can influence, or *moderate*, the effects of stress.

Self-Efficacy Expectations: "The Little Engine That Could"

Our self-efficacy expectations affect our abilities to withstand stress and make things happen.

JOSE LUIS PELAEZ INC/BLEND IMAGES/JUPITER IMAGES

Self-efficacy is the ability to make things happen. Our self-efficacy expectations affect our ability to withstand stress (Basic Behavioral Science Task Force, 1996a; Maciejewski et al., 2000). *How do our self-efficacy expectations affect our ability to withstand stress?*

A classic experiment by Albert Bandura and his colleagues (1985) shows that high self-efficacy expectations are accompanied by relatively *lower* levels of adrenaline and noradrenaline in the bloodstream when we are faced with fear-inducing objects. The Bandura group assessed subjects' self-efficacy, exposed them to fearful stimuli, and monitored the levels of adrenaline and noradrenaline in their bloodstreams as they did so. Adrenaline and noradrenaline are secreted when we are under stress. They arouse the body in several ways, such as accelerating the heart rate and releasing glucose from the liver. As a result, we may have "butterflies in the stomach" and feel nervous. Excessive arousal can also distract us from coping with the tasks at hand.

People who are self-confident are less prone to be disturbed by adverse events (Kaslow et al., 2002; Lang & Heckhausen, 2001). People with higher self-efficacy expectations are more likely to lose weight or quit smoking and less likely to relapse afterward (E. S. Anderson et al., 2000, 2001; Shiffman et al., 2000). They are better able to function in spite of pain (Lackner et al., 1996). A study of Native Americans found that alcohol abuse was correlated with self-efficacy expectations (Walle, A. H., 2004). That is, individuals with feelings of powerlessness were more likely to abuse alcohol, perhaps as a way of lessening stress.

People are more likely to comply with medical advice when they believe that it will work (Schwartzer & Renner, 2000). Women, for example, are more likely to engage in breast self-examination when they believe that they will really be able to detect abnormal growths (Miller et al., 1996). People are more likely to try to quit smoking when they believe that they can do so successfully (Segan et al., 2002).

Psychological Hardiness

Psychological hardiness also helps people resist stress (Kaddour, 2003; Richardson, 2002). Our understanding of hardiness is derived largely from the pioneering work of Suzanne Kobasa and her colleagues (1994). They studied business executives who seemed able to resist illness despite stress. In one phase of the research, executives completed a battery of psychological tests. Kobasa (1990) found that the psychologically hardy executives had three key characteristics. *What characteristics are connected with psychological hardiness?* The characteristics

include commitment, challenge, and control.

- Kobasa found that psychologically hardy executives were high in *commitment*. They tended to involve themselves in, rather than feel alienated from, whatever they were doing or encountering. A Slovakian study found that psychologically hardy secondary school students try to actively solve problems rather than avoid them (Baumgartner, 2002).

- They were also high in *challenge*. They believed that change, rather than stability, is normal in life. They appraised change as an interesting incentive to personal growth, not as a threat to security.

- They were high in perceived *control* over their lives. A sense of control is one of the keys to psychological hardiness (Folkman & Moskowitz, 2000b; Tennen & Affleck, 2000). Hardy participants felt and behaved as though they were influential, rather than helpless, in facing the various rewards and punishments of life. Psychologically hardy people tend to have what Julian B. Rotter (1990) terms an internal **locus of control**.

Hardy people may be more resistant to stress because they *choose* to face it (Baumgartner, 2002; Kobasa, 1990). They also interpret stress as making life more interesting. For example, they see a conference with a supervisor as an opportunity to persuade the supervisor rather than as a risk to their position.

psychological hardiness a cluster of traits that buffer stress and are characterized by commitment, challenge, and control

locus of control the place (locus) to which an individual attributes control over the receiving of reinforcers—either inside or outside the self

Sense of Humor

The idea that humor lightens the burdens of life and helps people cope with stress has been with us for millennia. Consider the biblical maxim, "A merry heart doeth good like a medicine" (Proverbs 17: 22). *Is there any evidence that humor helps us cope with stress?* Research suggests that humor can moderate the effects of stress (Godfrey, 2004). In one classic study, for example, students completed a checklist of negative life events and a measure of mood disturbance (Martin &

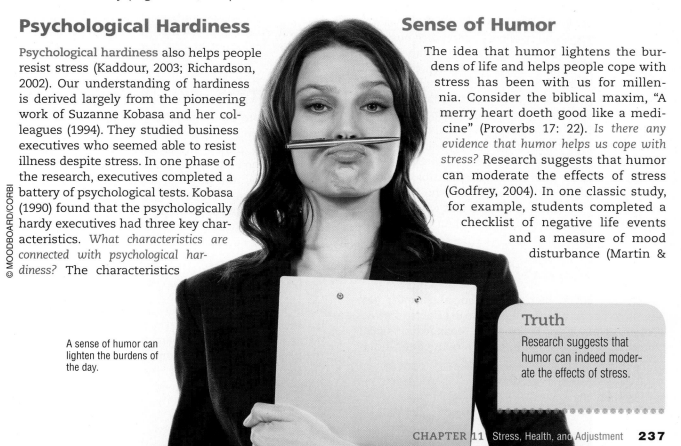

A sense of humor can lighten the burdens of the day.

Truth

Research suggests that humor can indeed moderate the effects of stress.

Lefcourt, 1983). The measure of mood disturbance yielded a stress score. The students also rated their sense of humor. Students were asked to try to produce humor in an experimental stressful situation, and their ability to do so was rated by the researchers. Students who had a greater sense of humor and were capable of producing humor in the stressful experimental condition were less affected by the stress than other students. In other experiments, Lefcourt (1997) found that exposing students to humorous videotapes raised the level of immunoglobin A (a measure of the functioning of the immune system) in their saliva.

How does humor help people cope with stress? We are uncertain, but there are many possibilities. One is that laughter stimulates the output of endorphins, which might enhance the functioning of the immune system. Another is that the benefits of humor may be explained in terms of the positive cognitive shifts they entail and the positive emotions that accompany them.

Predictability and Control

The ability to predict a stressor apparently moderates its impact. *How do predictability and control help us cope with stress?* Predictability allows us to brace ourselves for the inevitable and, in many cases, plan ways of coping with it. Control—even the illusion of being in control—allows us to feel that we are not at the mercy of the fates (Folkman & Moskowitz, 2000b; Tennen & Affleck, 2000). There is also a relationship between the desire to assume control over one's situation and the usefulness of information about impending stressors. Predictability is of greater benefit to internals—that is, to people who wish to exercise control over their situations—than to externals. People who want information about medical procedures and what they will experience cope better with pain when they undergo those procedures (Ludwick-Rosenthal & Neufeld, 1993).

Social Support

People are social beings, and social support also seems to act as a buffer against the effects of stress (Cohen et al., 2003; Folkman & Moskowitz, 2000a). The concept of social support has many definitions:

- *Emotional concern:* listening to people's problems and expressing feelings of sympathy, caring, understanding, and reassurance.

- *Instrumental aid:* the material supports and services that facilitate adaptive behavior. For example, after a disaster the government may arrange for low-interest loans so that survivors can rebuild. Relief organizations may provide food, medicines, and temporary living quarters.

- *Information:* guidance and advice that enhance people's ability to cope.

- *Appraisal:* feedback from others about how one is doing. This kind of support involves helping people interpret, or "make sense of," what has happened to them.

- *Socializing:* conversation, recreation, going shopping with someone. Socializing is beneficial even when it is not oriented toward solving problems.

Does social support help people cope with stress? Yes, research does support the value of social support. Introverts, people who lack social skills, and people who live by themselves seem more prone to developing infectious diseases such as colds under stress (Cohen et al., 2003). Social support helps Mexican Americans and other immigrants to cope with the stresses of acculturation (Hovey, 2000). Social support helped children cope with the stresses of Hurricane Andrew (Vernberg et al., 1996) and Chinese villagers cope with an earthquake (X. Wang et al., 2000). Stress is less likely to lead to high blood pressure or alcohol abuse in people who have social support (Linden et al., 1993). Even online social support helps people cope with the stresses of cancer and other health problems (Broom, 2005; Hoybye et al., 2005).

How does stress contribute to the development of physical health problems? In the next section, we consider the effects of stress on the body.

LO³ Stress and the Body

Stress is more than a psychological event. It is more than "knowing" it is there; it is more than "feeling" pushed and pulled. Stress also has very definite effects on the body which, as we will see, can lead to psychological and physical health problems. Stress researcher Hans Selye outlined a number of the bodily effects in his concept of the general adaptation syndrome (GAS).

The General Adaptation Syndrome

Hans Selye suggested that under stress the body is like a clock with an alarm that does not shut off until the clock shakes apart or its energy has been depleted. The body's response to different stressors shows certain similarities whether the stressor is a bacterial invasion, perceived danger, or a major life change (Selye, 1976). For this reason, Selye labeled this response the general adaptation syndrome (GAS). *What is the general adaptation syndrome?* The GAS is a group of bodily changes that occur in three stages: an alarm reaction, a resistance stage, and an exhaustion stage. These changes mobilize the body for action and—like that alarm that goes on ringing—can eventually wear out the body.

The Alarm Reaction

The alarm reaction is triggered by perception of a stressor. This reaction mobilizes or arouses the body, biologically speaking. Early in the 20th century, physiologist Walter B. Cannon (1932) argued that this mobilization was the basis for an instinctive fight-or-flight reaction. The fight-or-flight response kicks the endocrine, cardiovascular, and musculoskeletal systems into action to enable survival. Short-term stress can enhance the functioning of the immune system as well, thus helping prevent infection from wounds, but chronic or long-term stress can impair the functioning of the immune system (Dhabhar, 2009).

Stress has a domino effect on the endocrine system (Bauer et al., 2003; Melmed, 2003; see Figure 11.5). The hypothalamus secretes corticotrophin-releasing hormone (CRH). CRH causes the pituitary gland to secrete adrenocorticotrophic hormone (ACTH). ACTH then causes the adrenal cortex to secrete cortisol and other corticosteroids (steroidal hormones produced by the adrenal cortex). Corticosteroids help protect the body by combating allergic reactions (such as difficulty in breathing) and producing inflammation (Leonard, 2005). (However, corticosteroids can be harmful to the cardiovascular system, which is one reason that chronic stress can impair one's health and why athletes who use steroids to build the muscle mass can experience cardiovascular problems.) Inflammation increases circulation to parts of the body that are injured. It ferries in hordes of white blood cells to fend off invading pathogens.

Two other hormones that play a major role in the alarm reaction are secreted by the adrenal medulla. The sympathetic division of the ANS activates the adrenal medulla, causing it to release a mixture of adrenaline and noradrenaline. This mixture arouses the body by accelerating the heart rate and causing the liver to release glucose (sugar). This provides the energy that fuels the fight-or-flight reaction, which activates the body so that it is prepared to fight or flee from a predator.

The fight-or-flight reaction stems from a period in human prehistory when many stressors were life

general adaptation syndrome (GAS) Selye's term for a hypothesized three-stage response to stress

alarm reaction the first stage of the GAS, which is triggered by the impact of a stressor and characterized by sympathetic activity

fight-or-flight reaction an innate adaptive response to the perception of danger

Figure 11.5

Stress and the Endocrine System

Stress has a domino effect on the endocrine system, leading to the release of corticosteroids and a mixture of adrenaline and noradrenaline. Corticosteroids combat allergic reactions (such as difficulty in breathing) and cause inflammation. Adrenaline and noradrenaline arouse the body to cope by accelerating the heart rate and providing energy for the fight-or-flight reaction.

Go to CourseMate for PSYCH to access an interactive version of this figure.

© SIRI STAFFORD/GETTY IMAGES

Hypothalamus

Pituitary

Adrenal cortex

Adrenal medulla

The hypothalamus secretes corticotrophin-releasing hormone (CRH)

CRH causes the pituitary gland to secrete adrenocorticotrophic hormone (ACTH)

Stressor

ACTH then causes the adrenal cortex to secrete corticosteroids

The adrenal medulla releases a mixture of adrenaline and noradrenaline threatening. It was triggered by the sight of a predator at the edge of a thicket or by a sudden rustling in the undergrowth. Today it may be aroused when you are caught in stop-and-go traffic or learn that your mortgage payments are going to increase. Once the threat is removed, the body returns to a lower state of arousal. Many of the bodily changes that occur in the alarm reaction are outlined in Table 11.2.

Many contemporary theorists do not believe that the fight-or-flight reaction is universal. Shelley Taylor and her colleagues (2000) report evidence that many women engage in a tend-and-befriend response to threats, rather than a fight-or-flight response. Margaret Kemeny and her colleagues (e.g., Updegraff et al., 2002) also observe that some people attempt to respond productively to stress by pulling back from the situation to better appraise it and conserve their resources while they are doing so. This response pattern to stress is described by two theories that are currently under development: cognitive adaptation theory and conservation of resources theory.

The Resistance Stage

According to Selye's theory, if the alarm reaction mobilizes the body and the stressor is not removed, we enter the adaptation or resistance stage of the GAS. Levels of endocrine and sympathetic activity are lower than in the alarm reaction but still higher than normal. (It's as if the alarm is still on, but a bit softer.) But make no mistake: The person feels tense, and the body remains under a heavy burden.

The Exhaustion Stage

If the stressor is still not dealt with adequately, we may enter the exhaustion stage of the GAS. Individual capacities for resisting stress vary, but anyone will eventually become exhausted when stress continues indefinitely. The muscles become fatigued. The body is depleted of the resources required for combating stress. With exhaustion, the parasympathetic division of the ANS may predominate. As a result, our heartbeat and respiration rate slow down, and many aspects of sympathetic activity are reversed. It might sound as if we would profit from the respite, but remember that we are still under stress—possibly an external threat. Continued stress in the exhaustion stage may lead to what Selye terms "diseases of adaptation." These are connected with constriction of blood vessels and

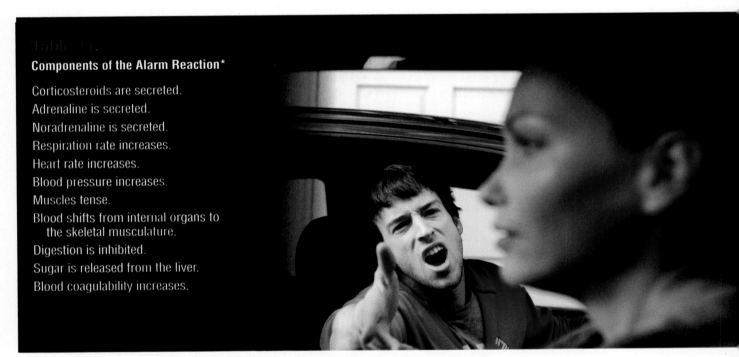

Table 11.2

Components of the Alarm Reaction*

Corticosteroids are secreted.

Adrenaline is secreted.

Noradrenaline is secreted.

Respiration rate increases.

Heart rate increases.

Blood pressure increases.

Muscles tense.

Blood shifts from internal organs to the skeletal musculature.

Digestion is inhibited.

Sugar is released from the liver.

Blood coagulability increases.

COCOON/PHOTODISC/JUPITER IMAGES

*The alarm reaction is triggered by stressors. It is defined by the release of corticosteroids and adrenaline and by activity of the sympathetic branch of the autonomic nervous system.

alternation of the heart rhythm, and can range from allergies to hives and coronary heart disease (CHD)—and, ultimately, death.

Discussion of the effects of stress on the immune system paves the way for understanding the links between psychological factors and physical illness.

Effects of Stress on the Immune System

Research shows that stress suppresses the immune system, as measured by the presence of various substances in the blood that make up the immune system (Antoni et al., 2005; Hawkley & Cacioppo, 2004). Psychological factors such as feelings of control and social support moderate these effects (Cohen et al., 2001a).

The Immune System

Given the complexity of the human body and the fast pace of scientific change, we often feel that we are dependent on trained professionals to cope with illness. Yet we actually do most of this coping by ourselves, by means of the immune system. *How does the immune system work?*

The immune system combats disease in several ways (Delves & Roitt, 2000; Leonard, 2005). One way is the production of white blood cells, which engulf and kill pathogens such as bacteria, fungi, and viruses, and worn-out and cancerous body cells. The technical term for white blood cells is leukocytes. They engage in search-and-destroy missions in which they "recognize" and eradicate foreign agents and unhealthy cells.

Leukocytes recognize foreign substances, or antigens, by their shapes. The body reacts to antigens by generating specialized proteins, or antibodies. Antibodies attach themselves to the antigens, deactivating them and marking them for destruction. The immune system "remembers" how to battle antigens by maintaining their

immune system the system of the body that recognizes and destroys foreign agents (antigens) that invade the body

leukocytes white blood cells (derived from the Greek words *leukos*, meaning "white," and *kytos*, literally meaning "a hollow" but used to refer to cells)

antigen a substance that stimulates the body to mount an immune system response to it (short for *anti*body *gen*erator)

antibodies substances formed by white blood cells that recognize and destroy antigens

Truth
Leukocytes carry on microscopic warfare.

{ Are There Gender Differences in Response to Stress? }

For a century, it has been widely believed that humans are prewired to experience what biologist Walter Cannon labeled a "fight-or-flight" reaction to stress. Cannon believed we are instinctively pumped up to fight like demons or, when advisable, to beat a hasty retreat.

Or are we? Not all of us, according to UCLA psychologist Shelley E. Taylor and her colleagues (2000b). Taylor found that women under stress are more likely to tend to the kids or "interface" with family and friends than either fight or flee. The "woman's response" to stress, the "tend-and-befriend" response, involves nurturing and seeking social support rather than fighting or fleeing. When females face a threat, a disaster, or even an especially bad day at the office, they often respond by caring for their children and seeking social contact and support from others, especially other women.

This response may be prewired in female humans and in females of other mammalian species. Evolutionary psychologists suggest that the tend-and-befriend response might have become sealed in human genes because it promotes the survival of females who are tending their young. Females who choose to fight might die or be separated from their young—no evolutionary brass ring there.

Males may be more aggressive than females under stress because of the balance of hormones in their bodies. Due to such differences, women tend to outlive men. "Men are more likely than women to respond to stressful experiences by developing certain stress-related disorders, including hypertension, aggressive behavior, or abuse of alcohol or hard drugs," Taylor added in a press release (May 2000).

PLAINPICTURE/CORBIS

inflammation increased blood flow to an injured area of the body, resulting in redness, warmth, and an increased supply of white blood cells

biopsychosocial having to do with the interactions of biological, psychological, and sociocultural factors

antibodies in the bloodstream, often for years.[1]

Inflammation is another function of the immune system. When injury occurs, blood vessels in the area first contract (to stem bleeding) and then dilate. Dilation increases the flow of blood, cells, and natural chemicals to the damaged area, causing the redness, swelling, and warmth that characterize inflammation (Leonard, 2005). The increased blood supply also floods the region with white blood cells to combat invading microscopic life-forms such as bacteria, which otherwise might use the local damage as a port of entry into the body.

Stress and the Immune System

One of the reasons that stress eventually exhausts us is that it stimulates the production of steroids. Steroids suppress the functioning of the immune system. Suppression has negligible effects when steroids are secreted occasionally. But persistent secretion of steroids decreases inflammation and interferes with the formation of antibodies. As a consequence, we become more vulnerable to infections, including the common cold (Barnard et al., 2005; Cohen et al., 2001b, 2003).

In one study, dental students showed lower immune system functioning, as measured by lower levels of antibodies in their saliva, during stressful periods of the school year than immediately following vacations (Jemmott et al., 1983). In contrast, social support buffers the effects of stress and enhances the functioning of the immune system (Cohen et al., 2001a, 2001b). In the Jemmott study, students who had many friends showed less suppression of immune system functioning than students with few friends.

Other studies with students show that the stress of exams depresses the immune system's response to the Epstein-Barr virus, which causes fatigue and other problems (Glaser et al., 1993). Here, too, lonely students showed greater suppression of the immune system than students who had social support. All in all, however, there is only modest evidence that psychological interventions enhance the functioning of the immune system. A review of the research found that hypnosis (intended to help people relax), stress management methods, and conditioning methods were of some use, but less than reliable (Miller & Cohen, 2001).

⁂

[1] A vaccination introduces a weakened form of an antigen (usually a bacteria or a virus) into the body to stimulate the production of antibodies. Antibodies can confer immunity for many years, in some cases for a lifetime.

LO⁴ Psychology and Chronic Health Problems

Why do people become ill? Why do some people develop cancer? Why do others have heart attacks? Why do still others seem to be immune to these illnesses? *What is the biopsychosocial approach to health?* The biopsychosocial approach recognizes that there is no single, simple answer to these questions. The likelihood of contracting an illness—be it a case of the flu or cancer—can reflect the interaction of many factors, including biological, psychological, and sociocultural factors (Schneiderman et al., 2005).

Biological factors such as pathogens, inoculations, injuries, age, gender, and a family history of disease may strike us as the most obvious causes of illness. Genetics, in particular, tempts some people to assume that there is little they can do about their health. Some cases of health problems are unavoidable for people with certain genes. However, if you have a family history of heart disease or cancer, it is *not* true that there is little or nothing you can do to prevent developing the disease. In many cases, especially with heart problems and cancer, genes only create *predispositions* toward the health problem. The life choices we make—the behaviors we select—also affect our likelihood of becoming ill (Hoover, 2000).

Genetic predispositions interact with the environment to express themselves (Kéri, 2003). For example, genetic factors are involved in breast cancer. However, rates of breast cancer among women who have recently emigrated to the United States from rural Asia are similar to those in their countries of origin and nearly 80% lower than the rates among third-generation Asian American women, whose rates are similar to those of European American

Fiction

It is *not* true that if you have a family history of heart disease or cancer, there is little or nothing you can do to prevent developing the illness yourself.

women (Hoover, 2000). Thus, factors related to one's lifestyle are also intimately connected with the risk of breast cancer—and most other kinds of cancer.

Biological, psychological (behavior and personality), sociocultural factors, and stressors all play roles in health and illness. Many health problems are affected by psychological factors, such as attitudes, emotions, and behavior (Kiecolt-Glaser et al., 2002b; Salovey et al., 2000). Table 11.3 reveals that nearly one million deaths each year in the United States are preventable (Health, United States, 2002). Stopping smoking, eating right, exercising, and controlling alcohol use would prevent nearly 80% of these. Psychological states such as anxiety and depression can impair the functioning of the immune system, rendering us more vulnerable to physical disorders ranging from viral infections to cancer (McGuire et al., 2002; Salovey et al., 2000).

Let us now discuss the chronic health problems of heart disease and cancer. Each involves biological, psychological, and environmental factors—including the social and technological environments. Although these are medical problems, we also explore ways in which psychologists have contributed to their prevention and treatment.

Coronary Heart Disease

Coronary heart disease (CHD) is the leading cause of death in the United States, most often from heart attacks (American Heart Association, 2005b). *What are the major risk factors for coronary heart disease?* Let us begin by considering the risk factors for CHD. (American Heart Association, 2008):

- *Family history:* People with a family history of CHD are more likely to develop the disease themselves.

- *Physiological conditions:* Obesity, high *serum cholesterol* levels, and *high blood pressure* are risk factors for CHD. About one American in five has hypertension, or abnormally high blood pressure, which can lead to CHD. When high blood pressure has no identifiable cause, it is referred to as *essential hypertension.* This condition has a genetic component. Blood pressure is also, however, connected with emotions like depression and anxiety. It also rises when we inhibit the expression of strong feelings or are angry or on guard against threats. When we are under stress, we may believe that we can feel our blood pressure "pounding through the roof," but this notion is usually false. Most people cannot recognize hypertension. Therefore, it is important to check the blood pressure regularly.

- *Patterns of consumption:* Patterns include heavy drinking, smoking, and overeating. On the other hand, a little alcohol seems to be good for the heart.

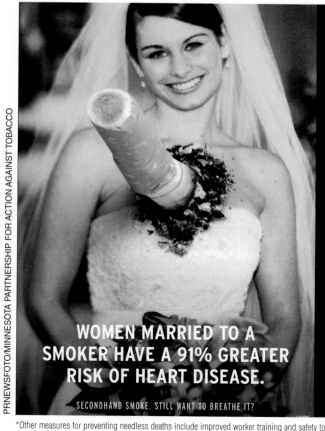

WOMEN MARRIED TO A SMOKER HAVE A 91% GREATER RISK OF HEART DISEASE.

SECONDHAND SMOKE. STILL WANT TO BREATHE IT?

Table 11.3

Annual Preventable Deaths in the United States*

- Elimination of tobacco use could prevent 400,000 deaths each year from cancer, heart and lung diseases, and stroke.

- Improved diet and exercise could prevent 300,000 deaths from conditions like heart disease, stroke, diabetes, and cancer.

- Control of underage and excess drinking of alcohol could prevent 100,000 deaths from motor vehicle accidents, falls, drownings, and other alcohol-related injuries.

- Immunizations for infectious diseases could prevent up to 100,000 deaths.

- Safer sex or sexual abstinence could prevent 10,000–20,000 deaths from sexually transmitted infections (STIs).

*Other measures for preventing needless deaths include improved worker training and safety to prevent accidents in the workplace, wider screening for breast and cervical cancer, and control of high blood pressure and elevated blood cholesterol levels.

- *Type A behavior:* Most studies suggest that there is at least a modest relationship between Type A behavior and CHD. Research suggests that alleviating Type A behavior may reduce the risk of *recurrent* heart attacks.

- *Hostility and holding in feelings of anger:* Hostility seems to be the component of the Type A behavior pattern that is most harmful to physical health. People who are highly prone to anger are about three times as likely as other people to have heart attacks (Williams et al., 2000). The stress hormones connected with anger can constrict blood vessels to the heart, leading to a heart attack. Highly hostile young adults—as young as 18 to 30—are already at greater risk for hardening of the arteries, which increases the risk of heart attacks (Iribarren et al., 2000).

- *Job strain:* Overtime work, assembly line labor, and exposure to conflicting demands can all contribute to CHD. High-strain work, which makes heavy demands on workers but gives them little personal control, puts workers at the highest risk (Bishop et al., 2003; Krantz et al., 1988; Smith & Ruiz, 2002).

- *Chronic fatigue, stress, anxiety, depression, and emotional strain*

- *Sudden stressors:* After the 1994 Los Angeles earthquake there was an increased incidence of death from heart attacks in people with heart disease (Leor et al., 1996).

- *A physically inactive lifestyle.*

African Americans are more likely than any other ethnic group in the United States to have heart attacks and to die from them (National Center for Health Statistics, 2009). Figure 11.6 compares the death rates from heart disease of American men and women of various ethnic backgrounds. Asian Americans, Native Americans, and Latina and Latino Americans are less likely than Europeans or African Americans to die from heart disease. Early diagnosis and treatment might help decrease the racial gap.

Measures such as the following may help reduce the risk of coronary heart disease: stopping smoking; eating fewer saturated fats and more fruits, vegetables, and whole grains; reducing hypertension and lowering LDL (harmful) serum cholesterol, through medicine if necessary; modifying Type A behavior; managing feelings of anger; and exercising regularly (get a medical checkup first).

Figure 11.6

Deaths from Heart Disease per 100,000 People, All Ages

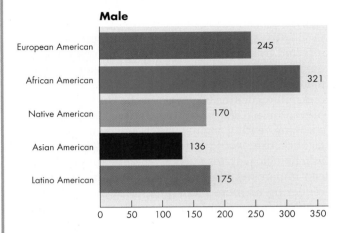

Male

European American	245
African American	321
Native American	170
Asian American	136
Latino American	175

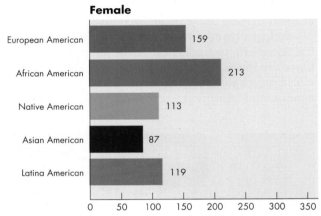

Female

European American	159
African American	213
Native American	113
Asian American	87
Latina American	119

Cancer

According to the National Vital Statistics Reports, cancer is the second-leading cause of death in the United States (Minino et al., 2007). Cancer is characterized by the development of abnormal, or mutant, cells that may take root anywhere in the body: in the blood, bones, digestive tract, lungs, and sex organs. If their spread is not controlled early, the cancerous cells may *metastasize*—that is, establish colonies elsewhere in the body. It appears that our bodies develop cancerous cells frequently. However, these are normally destroyed by the immune system. People whose immune system is damaged by physical or psychological factors may be more likely to develop tumors (Antoni, 2003, 2009).

Risk Factors

What are the major risk factors for cancer? As with many other disorders, people can inherit a disposition toward cancer (American Cancer Society, 2005a; Hoover, 2000). Carcinogenic genes may remove the brakes from cell division, allowing cells to multiply wildly. Or they may allow mutations to accumulate unchecked. Many behavior patterns, however, markedly heighten the risk for cancer. These include smoking, drinking alcohol (especially in women), and sunbathing (which may cause skin cancer due to exposure to ultraviolet light). Prolonged psychological conditions such as depression or stress may heighten the risk of some kinds of cancer by depressing the functioning of the immune system (Bauer et al., 2003; McGuire et al., 2002; Salovey et al., 2000).

African Americans are more likely than European Americans to contract most forms of cancer (American Cancer Society, 2005b). Possibly because of genetic factors, the incidence of lung cancer is significantly higher among African Americans than European Americans (American Cancer Society, 2005b). Once they contract cancer, African Americans are more likely than European Americans to die from it (American Cancer Society, 2005b). The results for African Americans are connected with their lower socioeconomic status and relative lack of access to health care (Altman, 2005; Whitfield et al., 2002).

Also consider cultural differences in health. Death rates from cancer are higher in such nations as the Netherlands, Denmark, England, Canada, and—yes—the United States, where average rates of animal fat intake are high (Bray & Atkin, 2004). Death rates from cancer are lower in such nations as Thailand, the Philippines, and Japan, where fat intake is lower and people eat more fruits and vegetables. However, studies in the United States have brought into question the usefulness of eating fruits and vegetables in preventing cancer.

For example, Karin Michels and her colleagues (2000) followed some 80,000 women and 40,000 men over several years and found little connection between eating fruits and vegetables and the risk of colon and rectal cancers. Arthur Schatzkin and his colleagues (2000) studied some 2,000 women and men who had had precancerous growths removed from their colons. The subjects were randomly assigned to eat low-fat diets that were high in fiber, fruits, and vegetables and were assessed four years later. There were no differences in the incidence of new precancerous growths in the colons of the two groups.

Researchers have also suggested possible links between stress and cancer (Salovey et al., 2000). For example, Rachel Yehuda (2003) suggests that stress sometimes lowers levels of cortisol and impairs the ability of the immune system to destroy cancer cells. But here, too, the research evidence calls these theoretical links into question.

For example, Polly Newcomb (2005), head of a Seattle cancer prevention program, interviewed nearly 1,000 women, some of whom had developed breast cancer and others who had not. The women were asked about the incidence of major life changes over a five-year period. There were no differences in the incidence of these life events between the cancer patients and the other women.

Does stress cause cancer, then? "I have no idea, and nobody else does, either," replies Ohio State psychologist Barbara Andersen (2005), who researches stress reduction in cancer patients. "If somebody suggested that they know, I would question them."

Measures such as the following may help reduce the risk of developing or dying from cancer: getting regular medical checkups to detect cancer early; stopping smoking; eating fewer saturated fats and more fruits, vegetables, and whole grains; and exercising regularly (get a medical checkup first). Cancer is most curable when it is detected early, before it metastasizes.

51 < percent of people report being stressed by their children

percent of people report being stressed out by money > 71

percent of people report having stress-related headaches > 34

percent of people report having stress-related upset stomachs or indigestion > 27

47 < percent of people report being stressed about their health

28 < percent of people killed by heart disease

24 < percent of people killed by cancer

Psychological
Disorders

Learning Outcomes

LO¹ Define psychological disorders and describe their prevalence

LO² Describe the symptoms, types, and possible origins of schizophrenia

LO³ Describe the symptoms and possible origins of mood disorders

LO⁴ Describe the symptoms and possible origins of anxiety disorders

LO⁵ Describe the symptoms and possible origins of somatoform disorders

LO⁶ Describe the symptoms and possible origins of dissociative disorders

LO⁷ Describe the symptoms and possible origins of personality disorders

" *The devil made me do it.* "

Let's listen in on part of an interview with Etta:

Etta: Well . . . ah . . . Jesus was giving me all these cracks, window cracks, and screen crack sounds telling me that they was going to break into the house. So I put the camera stereo in the room where they jiggled the window off to come through the window. And the camera stereo, the security guards picked that up, the message by putting that camera in that room.
Interviewer: Were you in danger?
Etta: Well, if anyone gets into the house they said I'd get shot.
Interviewer: Who said?
Etta: That's The Eagle.
Interviewer: Can you say a little something about The Eagle?
Etta: The Eagle works through General Motors. It has something to do with my General Motors check I get every month.
Interviewer: And you get that check because it's part of your husband's work with GM?
Etta: Yes.
Interviewer: Say something about the relationship between GM and The Eagle.
Etta: Well . . . ah . . . when you do the twenty-five of the clock it means that you leave the house after one to mail letters so that they can check on you what how you're mailing the mail and they know when you're at that time.
Interviewer: And who's "they"?
Etta: That's The Eagle.

If you have the feeling that Etta is not making sense, you are quite correct. Etta has been diagnosed with the psychological disorder termed schizophrenia. Schizophrenia is a thought disorder—meaning that Etta's thoughts are not coherent. Normally our thoughts are rather tightly knit, having a beginning, a middle, and an end. Etta's thoughts—the way things are associated with one another—have come loose. She jumps from Jesus to cracks in the window to her "camera stereo" to "The Eagle" to General Motors to twenty-five o'clock (which does not exist) and the mail.

Etta also sees herself as being under attack. "They" are trying to break into the house. There's some kind of plot afoot having to do with The Eagle and General Motors. "They" are checking on her. Etta

schizophrenia
a psychotic disorder characterized by loss of control of thought processes and inappropriate emotional responses

KATRINA WITTKAMP/TAXI/GETTY IMAGES

delusions
false, persistent beliefs that are unsubstantiated by sensory or objective evidence

affect (AFF-ekt)
feeling or emotional response, particularly as suggested by facial expression and body language

psychological disorders
patterns of behavior or mental processes that are connected with emotional distress or significant impairment in functioning

has false beliefs, or delusions, that she is being observed and persecuted. Yet for someone who believes she is being persecuted, Etta doesn't appear to be all that upset. Her affect—that is, her emotional response—is "flat" and inappropriate to the situation.

Schizophrenia is a psychological disorder, perhaps the most severe of psychological disorders. Fortunately—or unfortunately—it affects only about 1% of the population.

If Etta had lived in Salem, Massachusetts, in 1692, just 200 years after Columbus set foot in the New World, she might have been hanged as a witch. At that time, most people assumed that the strange behaviors that we associate with psychological disorders were caused by possession by the devil. A score of people were executed in Salem that year for allegedly practicing the arts of Satan.

Possession could stem from retribution, in which God allowed the devil to possess a person's soul as punishment for committing certain kinds of sins. Agitation and confusion were ascribed to such retribution. Possession was also believed to result from deals with the devil, in which people traded their souls for earthly gains. Such individuals were called witches. Witches were held responsible for unfortunate events ranging from a neighbor's infertility to a poor harvest. During the Middle Ages in Europe, as many as 500,000 accused witches were killed (Hergenhahn, 2009). The goings on at Salem were trivial by comparison.

A document authorized by Pope Innocent VIII, *The Hammer of Witches,* proposed ingenious "diagnostic" tests, such as the water-float test, to identify those who were possessed. The water-float test was based on the principle that pure metals sink to the bottom during smelting. Impurities float to the surface. Suspects were thus placed in deep water. Those who sank to the bottom (and drowned) were judged to be pure. Those who managed to keep their heads above water were assumed to be "impure" and in league with the devil. Then they were in real trouble. This ordeal is the origin of the phrase, "Damned if you do, and damned if you don't."

Exorcism
This medieval woodcut represents the practice of exorcism, in which a demon is expelled from a person who has been "possessed."

© 2010 THE GRANGER COLLECTION, NEW YORK

Few people in the United States today would claim that unusual or unacceptable behavior is caused by demons. Still, we continue to use "demonic" language. How many times have you heard the expressions "Something got into me" or "The devil made me do it"?

Sometimes unusual and unacceptable behavior is a result of a psychological disorder. *What exactly are psychological disorders?*

LO¹ What Are Psychological Disorders?

Psychology is the study of behavior and mental processes. Psychological disorders are behaviors or mental processes that are connected with distress or disability. They are not predictable responses to specific events.

Some psychological disorders are characterized by anxiety, but many people are anxious now and then without being considered disordered. It is appropriate to be anxious before an important date or on the eve of a midterm exam. When then are feelings like anxiety deemed to be abnormal or signs of a psychological disorder?

For one thing, anxiety may suggest a disorder when it does not fit the situation. For example, there is (usually) little or no reason to be anxious when entering an elevator or looking out of a fourth-story window. The magnitude of the problem may also suggest disorder. Some anxiety can be expected before a job interview. However, feeling that your heart is pounding so intensely that it might leap out of your chest—and then avoiding the interview—are not.

Truth

A document authorized by Pope Innocent VIII proposed tests, such as the water-float test, to identify those who were possessed.

248 LO1 What Are Psychological Disorders?

Behaviors or mental processes are suggestive of psychological disorders when they meet some combination of the following standards:

- *Is the behavior unusual?* Etta's thoughts and her speech patterns were quite unusual, found only among a small minority of the population. Yet uncommon behavior or mental processes are not necessarily abnormal in themselves. Only one person holds the record for running or swimming the fastest mile. That person is different from you and me but is not abnormal. Thus, rarity or statistical deviance is not sufficient for behavior or mental processes to be labeled abnormal. We must also consider the situation. Although many of us feel "panicked" when we realize that a term paper or report is due the next day, most of us do not have panic attacks "out of the blue." Unpredictable panic attacks are thus a psychological disorder.

- *Does the behavior suggest faulty perception or interpretation of reality?* Etta's beliefs about The Eagle and General Motors suggested faulty interpretation of reality. Hearing voices and seeing things that are not there are considered **hallucinations**. **Ideas of persecution**, such as believing that the Mafia or the FBI is "out to get you," are also considered signs of disorder. (Unless, of course, they *are* out to get you.)

- *Is the person's emotional response appropriate to the situation?* Irrational fears, such as intense fear of injections and depression among people with "good lives," may be considered inappropriate and thus abnormal. Etta, on the other hand, showed **flat affect**—too little emotional response—when she reported imaginary events that should have been frightening.

- *Is the behavior self-defeating?* Behavior or mental processes that cause misery rather than happiness and fulfillment may suggest psychological disorder. Chronic drinking impairs one's health and may therefore be deemed abnormal. Fear of needles is more likely to be considered abnormal if it prevents one from receiving necessary medical treatment.

- *Is the behavior dangerous?* Behavior or mental processes that are hazardous to the self or others may be considered suggestive of psychological disorders. People who threaten or attempt suicide may be considered abnormal, as may people who threaten or attack others. But aggressive behavior in athletics—within certain limits, as in contact sports—is not considered disordered.

- *Is the behavior socially unacceptable?* We must consider the cultural context of a behavior pattern in judging whether or not it is normal.

Classifying Psychological Disorders

Classification is at the heart of science. Without classifying psychological disorders, investigators would not be able to communicate with each other and scientific progress would come to a halt. The most widely used classification scheme for psychological disorders is the *Diagnostic and Statistical Manual of Mental Disorders (DSM–IV–TR)* of the American Psychiatric Association (2000). *How are psychological disorders classified?*

Classification is at the heart of science.

The current edition of the *DSM* is the *DSM-IV-TR* (fourth edition, text revision), and it provides information about a person's overall functioning as well as a diagnosis. People may receive diagnoses for clinical syndromes or personality disorders, or for both. It also includes information about people's medical conditions, psychosocial problems, and a global assessment of functioning. Medical conditions include physical disorders or problems that may affect people's response to psychotherapy or drug treatment. Psychosocial and environmental problems include difficulties that may affect the diagnosis, treatment, or outcome of a psychological disorder. The global assessment of functioning allows the clinician to compare the client's current level of functioning with her or his highest previous level of functioning to help set goals for restoring functioning.

Although the *DSM* is widely used, researchers have some concerns about it. Two of them concern the *reliability* and *validity* of the diagnostic standards. The *DSM* might be considered *reliable* if different interviewers or raters would make the same diagnosis when they evaluate the same people. The *DSM* might be considered *valid* if the diagnoses described in the manual correspond to clusters of behaviors observed in the real world. In the case of Etta, the *DSM* might be considered reliable if various evaluators who were using the manual arrived at the same diagnosis—schizophrenia. Referring once more to Etta, the *DSM* might be considered valid if the diagnosis of schizophrenia, described in the manual, fits Etta's actual behavior. A specific type of validity, called predictive validity, means that if a diagnosis is valid, we should be able to predict what will happen to the person over time (that is, the *course* of the disorder) and what type of treatment may be of help.

Prevalence of Psychological Disorders

At first glance, psychological disorders might seem to affect only a few of us. Relatively few people are admitted to psychiatric hospitals. Most people will never seek the help of a psychologist or psychiatrist.

hallucination a perception in the absence of sensory stimulation that is confused with reality

ideas of persecution erroneous beliefs that one is being victimized or persecuted

flat affect a severe reduction in emotional expressiveness, found among many people with schizophrenia or serious depression

predictive validity in this usage, the extent to which a diagnosis permits one to predict the course of a disorder and the type of treatment that may be of help

Table 12.1

Past-Year and Lifetime Prevalences of Psychological Disorders

	Anxiety Disorders	Mood Disorders	Bipolar Disorders	Substance Use Disorders	Any Disorders
Prevalence during past year	18.1%	9.5%	2.8%	3.8%	26.2%
Lifetime prevalence	28.8%	20.8%	4.4%	14.6%	46.4%
Median age of onset	11 years	30 years	21 years	20 years	14 years

Sources: Kessler et al., 2005, Merikangas, K. R., et al. (2007).

Note: The data in this table are based on a nationally representative sample of 9,282 English-speaking U.S. residents aged 18 and above. Respondents could report symptoms of more than one type of disorder. For example, anxiety and mood disorders are often "comorbid"—that is, go together. Anxiety and mood disorders are discussed in this chapter. Substance use disorders include abuse of or dependence on alcohol or other drugs, as described in Chapter 5.

And the insanity plea—though well publicized—is a rarity in the criminal justice system. Many of us have "eccentric" relatives or friends, but most of them are not considered to be literally "crazy." Nonetheless, psychological disorders affect us all in one way or another.

About half of us will meet the criteria for a *DSM-IV* disorder at some time or another in our lives, with the disorder most often first beginning in childhood or adolescence (Kessler et al., 2005a; see Table 12.1). Slightly more than one-quarter of us will experience a psychological disorder in any given year (Kessler et al., 2005c); (see Table 12.1). But if we include the problems of family members, friends, and coworkers, add in the number of those who foot the bill in terms of health insurance and taxes, and factor in increased product costs due to lost productivity, perhaps everyone is affected.

Let us now consider the various kinds of psychological disorders. We begin with schizophrenia, the disorder with which Etta was diagnosed.

LO² Schizophrenia

When interviewers listened to Etta's incoherent story about Jesus and cracks in the window and her "camera stereo," they suspected that she could be diagnosed with schizophrenia. *What is schizophrenia?* Schizophrenia is a severe psychological disorder that touches every aspect of a person's life. It is characterized by disturbances in thought and language, perception and attention, motor activity, and mood, and by social withdrawal and absorption in daydreams or fantasy (Heinrichs, 2005).

Schizophrenia has been referred to as the worst disorder affecting people. It afflicts nearly 1% of the population worldwide. Its onset occurs relatively early in life, and it tends to endure.

People with schizophrenia have problems in memory, attention, and communication. Their thinking and communication ability becomes unraveled (Kerns & Berenbaum, 2002). Unless we allow our thoughts to wander, our thinking is normally tightly knit. We start at a certain point, and thoughts are logically connected. But people with schizophrenia often think illogically. As with Etta, their speech may be jumbled. They may combine parts of words into new words or make meaningless rhymes. They may jump from topic to topic, conveying little useful information. They usually do not recognize that their thoughts and behavior are abnormal.

Many people with schizophrenia, like Etta, have delusions—for example, delusions of grandeur, persecution, or reference. In the case of delusions of grandeur, a person may believe that he is a famous historical figure such as Jesus, or a person on a special mission. He may have grand, illogical plans for saving the world. Delusions tend to be unshakable even in the face of evidence that they are not true. People with delusions of persecution, like Etta, may believe that they are sought by the Mafia, CIA, FBI, or some other group. A woman with delusions of reference said that news stories contained coded information about her. A man with such delusions complained that neighbors had "bugged" his walls with "radios." Other people with schizophrenia have had delusions that they have committed unpardonable sins, that they were rotting away from disease, or that they or the world did not exist.

People with schizophrenia may see or hear things that are not really there. Their perceptions often include hallucinations—imagery in the absence of external stimulation that the person cannot distinguish from reality. Other people who experience hallucinations may see colors or even obscene words spelled out in midair. Auditory hallucinations are most common.

In individuals with schizophrenia, motor activity may become wild or so slowed that the person is said to be in a stupor—that is, a condition in which the senses, thought, and movement are inhibited. There may be strange gestures and grimaces. The person's emotional responses may be flat or blunted, or inappropriate—as in giggling upon hearing bad news. People with schizophrenia tend to withdraw from social contacts, and become wrapped up in their own thoughts and fantasies.

Positive Versus Negative Symptoms

Many investigators find it useful to distinguish between positive and negative symptoms of schizophrenia. *What are the positive and negative symptoms of schizophrenia?* The positive symptoms are the excessive and sometimes bizarre symptoms, including hallucinations, delusions, and looseness of associations. The negative symptoms are the deficiencies we find among people with schizophrenia, such as lack of emotional expression and motivation, loss of pleasure in activities, social withdrawal, and poverty of speech.

Etta showed an abundance of positive symptoms, including delusions, along with negative symptoms, such as flat affect. The distinction is useful not only in terms of description, but also in terms of development of the disorder and likely outcome. For example, people with mainly positive symptoms are more likely to experience an abrupt onset of the disorder and tend to preserve their intellectual abilities. The positive symptoms also respond more favorably to antipsychotic medication (Roth et al., 2004; Walker et al., 2004). People with mainly negative symptoms tend to experience a more gradual development of the disorder and severe intellectual impairments in attention, memory, and so on. The negative symptoms also respond more poorly to antipsychotic drugs.

It may be that positive and negative symptoms represent different but related biological processes. Positive symptoms may involve deficiency in the brain mechanisms that normally inhibit excessive or bizarre behaviors. They may reflect a disturbance in regulation of dopamine in the brain, because drugs

stupor
a condition in which the senses, thought, and movement are dulled

positive symptoms
the excessive and sometimes bizarre symptoms of schizophrenia, including hallucinations, delusions, and loose associations

negative symptoms
the deficiencies among people with schizophrenia, such as flat affect, lack of motivation, loss of pleasure, and social withdrawal

{ The Insanity Plea }

In 1982, John Hinckley, Jr., was found not guilty of the assassination attempt on President Reagan's life, even though the shooting was witnessed by millions on television. Expert witnesses testified that he should be diagnosed with schizophrenia. Hinckley was found not guilty by reason of insanity and committed to a psychiatric institution, where he remains to this day. What does it mean to be "insane"? What is the "insanity plea"?

In pleading insanity, lawyers use the M'Naghten rule, named after Daniel M'Naghten, who tried to assassinate the British prime minister, Sir Robert Peel, in 1843. He killed Peel's secretary in the attempt. M'Naghten had delusions that Peel was persecuting him. The court found M'Naghten not guilty by reason of insanity. The M'Naghten rule states that the accused did not understand what she or he was doing at the time of the act or did not realize it was wrong. (Follingstad & McCormick, 2002; McSherry, 2005; Nagtegaal, 2004).

Many people would like to ban the insanity plea because they equate it with people's "getting away with murder." But there may not be all that much cause for concern. The insanity defense is raised in only about 1% of cases (Silver, 1994). Moreover, people found to be not guilty by reason of insanity are institutionalized for indefinite terms—supposedly until they are no longer insane.

While on trial, John Hinckley, Jr., looks on while his father cries and claims responsibility for "John's tragedy" because he prevented his son from coming home when he desperately needed help.

(AP PHOTO/JUDY LINEBERGER)

paranoid schizophrenia a type of schizophrenia characterized primarily by delusions—commonly of persecution—and vivid hallucinations

disorganized schizophrenia a type of schizophrenia characterized by disorganized delusions, vivid hallucinations, and inappropriate affect

catatonic schizophrenia a type of schizophrenia characterized by striking motor impairment

waxy flexibility a feature of catatonic schizophrenia in which people can be molded into postures that they maintain for quite some time

mutism refusal to talk

Truth

It is true that people with schizophrenia may see and hear things that are not really there.

that regulate dopamine levels generally reduce bizarre behavior. Negative symptoms may reflect structural damage to the brain. Even so, positive and negative symptoms can coexist in the same person. Thus, these groups of symptoms have descriptive value but do not appear to represent distinct types of schizophrenia. *What types of schizophrenia are there?*

All types of schizophrenia involve a thought disorder. There are, however, various "types" with different emphases on positive and negative symptoms, including paranoid, disorganized, and catatonic schizophrenia.

Paranoid Schizophrenia

People with paranoid schizophrenia, such as Etta, have systematized delusions and, frequently, related auditory hallucinations. They usually have delusions of grandeur and persecution, but they may also have delusions of jealousy, in which they believe that a spouse or lover has been unfaithful. They may show agitation, confusion, and fear, and may experience vivid hallucinations that are consistent with their delusions. People with paranoid schizophrenia often construct complex or systematized delusions involving themes of wrongdoing or persecution. John Nash, whose life was depicted in the movie *A Beautiful Mind,* believed that the government was recruiting him to decipher coded messages by our Cold War enemies.

Disorganized Schizophrenia

People with disorganized schizophrenia show incoherence, loosening of associations, disorganized behavior, disorganized delusions, fragmentary delusions or hallucinations, and flat or highly inappropriate emotional responses. Extreme social impairment is common. People with this type of schizophrenia may also exhibit silliness and giddiness of mood,

giggling, and nonsensical speech. They may neglect their appearance and personal hygiene and lose control of their bladder and bowels.

Catatonic Schizophrenia

People with catatonic schizophrenia show striking impairment in motor activity. It is characterized by a slowing of activity into a stupor that may suddenly change into an agitated phase. Catatonic people may maintain unusual and even difficult postures for hours, even as their limbs grow swollen or stiff. A striking feature of this condition is waxy flexibility, in which the person maintains positions into which he or she has been manipulated by others. Catatonic individuals may also show mutism, but afterward they usually report that they heard what others were saying at the time.

Schizophrenia is thus characterized by extremely unusual behavior. *What is known about the origins of schizophrenia?*

Explaining Schizophrenia

Biological, psychological, and sociocultural factors may all contribute to schizophrenia.

Biological Perspectives

Schizophrenia appears to be a brain disorder (Heinrichs, 2005). Many studies have been done to determine how the brains of schizophrenic people may differ from those of others. Studies have

Catatonic Schizophrenia People with catatonic schizophrenia show striking motor impairment and may hold unusual positions for hours.

focused on the amount of gray matter in the brain, the size of ventricles (hollow spaces), activity levels in the brain, and brain chemistry.

One avenue of brain research connects the major deficits we find in schizophrenia—problems in attention, working memory, abstract thinking, and language—with dysfunction in the prefrontal cortex of the brain (Heinrichs, 2005). Brain imaging has shown that some but not all people with schizophrenia have less gray matter than other people (Heinrichs, 2005; Kasai et al., 2003; Thompson et al., 2001; see Figure 12.1). Many have smaller brains and, in particular, a smaller prefrontal region of the cortex (Heinrichs, 2005; Selemon et al., 2003). They also tend to have larger ventricles in the brain than other people (Keller et al., 2003). Brain scans suggest that people with schizophrenia also tend to have a lower level of activity in the frontal region of the brain (Lahti, et al., 2001; Meyer-Lindenberg et al., 2001). Still other research connects the lower activity levels with a loss in synapses in the region (Glantz & Lewis, 2000; Selemon et al., 2003; Wolkin et al., 2003).

What might account for differences in brain structure and functioning? Heredity, complications during pregnancy and birth, and birth during winter are all risk factors for schizophrenia. Schizophrenia, like many other psychological disorders, runs in families (Conklin & Iacono, 2002; Hwu et al., 2003). People with schizophrenia make up about 1% of the population. Yet children with one parent who has been diagnosed with schizophrenia have about a 10% chance of being diagnosed with schizophrenia themselves. Children with two such parents have about a 35% to 40% chance of being so diagnosed (Gottesman, 1991; Straube & Oades, 1992). Twin studies also find about a 45% matching rate for the diagnosis among pairs of identical (MZ) twins, whose genetic codes are the same, compared with a 17% rate among pairs of fraternal (DZ) twins, who share half their genetic code (Plomin & Crabbe, 2000). Moreover, adoptee studies find that the biological parent typically places the child at greater risk for schizophrenia than the adoptive parent—even though the child has been reared by the adoptive parent (Gottesman, 1991). Sharing genes with relatives who have schizophrenia apparently places a person at risk of developing the disorder. Many studies have been carried out to try to isolate the gene or genes involved in schizophrenia. Some studies find locations for multiple genes on several chromosomes.

Many people with schizophrenia have undergone complications during pregnancy and birth (Heinrichs, 2005). For example, the mothers of many people with schizophrenia had the flu during the sixth or seventh month of pregnancy (Brown & Susser, 2002). An interaction between biology and the sociocultural setting is found in the link between poor maternal nutrition and schizophrenia (Hulshoff et al., 2000; Pol et al., 2000). Complications during childbirth, especially prolonged labor, seem to be connected with the larger ventricles we find among people with schizophrenia (McNeil et al., 2000). People with schizophrenia are also somewhat more likely to have been born during winter than would be predicted by chance (Pol et al., 2000; Suvisaari et al., 2002). Alcohol abuse may also lead to differences in brain structures among people with schizophrenia (E. V. Sullivan et al., 2000). On the

Rate of gray matter loss

Normal adolescents

Schizophrenic subjects

Average annual loss

0%

-1%

-2%

-3%

-4%

-5%

Source: Thompson et al., 2001.

Figure 12.1

Average Rates of Loss of Gray Matter Among Normal Adolescents and Adolescents Diagnosed with Schizophrenia

High-resolution MRI scans show rates of gray matter loss in normal thirteen- to eighteen-year-olds and among adolescents of the same age diagnosed with schizophrenia. Maps of brain changes reveal profound, progressive loss in schizophrenia (right). Loss also occurs in normal adolescents (left), but at a slower rate.

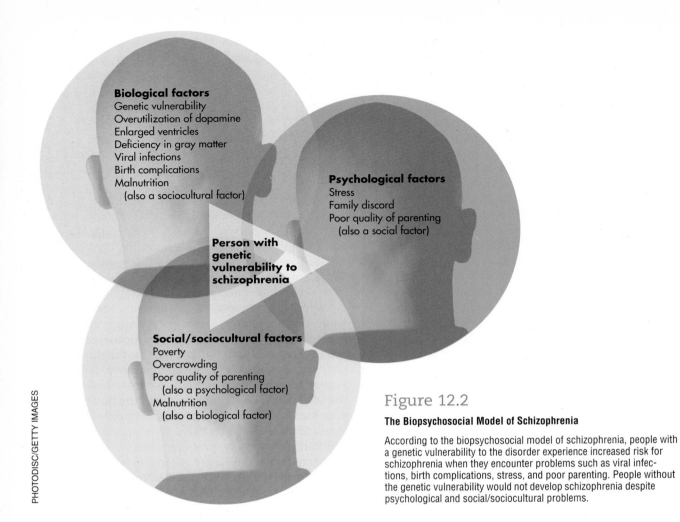

Biological factors
Genetic vulnerability
Overutilization of dopamine
Enlarged ventricles
Deficiency in gray matter
Viral infections
Birth complications
Malnutrition
    (also a sociocultural factor)

Psychological factors
Stress
Family discord
Poor quality of parenting
    (also a social factor)

Person with
genetic
vulnerability to
schizophrenia

Social/sociocultural factors
Poverty
Overcrowding
Poor quality of parenting
    (also a psychological factor)
Malnutrition
    (also a biological factor)

PHOTODISC/GETTY IMAGES

Figure 12.2

The Biopsychosocial Model of Schizophrenia

According to the biopsychosocial model of schizophrenia, people with a genetic vulnerability to the disorder experience increased risk for schizophrenia when they encounter problems such as viral infections, birth complications, stress, and poor parenting. People without the genetic vulnerability would not develop schizophrenia despite psychological and social/sociocultural problems.

other hand, research evidence is mixed about whether viral infections in childhood are connected with schizophrenia (Suvisaari et al., 2003). But taken together, these risk factors suggest that schizophrenia involves faulty development of the central nervous system.

Problems in the nervous system may involve brain chemistry as well as brain structures, and research along these lines has led to the dopamine theory of schizophrenia. According to the dopamine theory, people with schizophrenia overutilize dopamine (use more of it than other people do) although they may not produce more of it (Gijsman et al., 2002; Tsai & Coyle, 2002). Why? Research suggests that people with schizophrenia have increased concentrations of dopamine at the synapses in the brain and also larger numbers of dopamine receptors (Butcher, 2000). It's a sort of "double hit" of neural transmission that may be connected with the confusion that characterizes schizophrenia.

Sociocultural Perspectives

Many investigators have considered whether and how social and cultural factors such as poverty, discrimination, and overcrowding contribute to schizophrenia—especially among people with a genetic vulnerability. Classic research in New Haven, Connecticut, showed that the rate of schizophrenia was twice as high in the lowest socioeconomic class as in the next-higher class on the socioeconomic ladder (Hollingshead & Redlich, 1958). Poor-quality housing may contribute to schizophrenia (Mueser & McGurk, 2004). Some sociocultural theorists therefore suggest that "treatment" of schizophrenia requires alleviation of poverty and other social ills.

Critics of this view suggest that low socioeconomic status may be a result, rather than a cause, of schizophrenia. People with schizophrenia may drift toward low social status because they lack the social skills and cognitive abilities to function at higher social-class levels. Thus, they may wind up in poor neighborhoods or among the homeless in disproportionately high numbers.

Evidence for the hypothesis that people with schizophrenia drift downward in socioeconomic status is mixed. Many people with schizophrenia do drift downward occupationally in comparison with their fathers' occupations. Many others, however, were reared in families in which the father came from the lowest socioeconomic class. Because poverty may play a role in the development of schizophrenia, many researchers are interested in the possible interactions between biological and psychosocial factors (Buckley et al., 2000; Sawa & Snyder, 2002).

Quality of parenting is also connected with the development of schizophrenia (Buckley et al., 2000), but critics note that many people who are reared in socially punitive settings are apparently immune to the extinction of socially appropriate behavior. Other people develop schizophrenic behavior without having had opportunities to observe other people with schizophrenia.

The Biopsychosocial Perspective

Because biological, psychological, and sociocultural factors are implicated in schizophrenia, most investigators today favor the biopsychosocial model. According to this model, genetic factors create a predisposition toward or vulnerability to schizophrenia (see Figure 12.2). Genetic vulnerability to the disorder interacts with other factors, such as complications of pregnancy and birth, stress, quality of parenting, and social conditions to give rise to the disorder (Buckley et al., 2000; Sawa & Snyder, 2002).

LO³ Mood Disorders

Mood disorders are characterized by disturbance in expressed emotions. The disruption generally involves sadness or elation. Most instances of sadness are normal, or "run-of-the-mill." If you have failed an important test, if you have lost money in a business venture, or if your closest friend becomes ill, it is understandable and fitting for you to be sad about it. It would be odd, in fact, if you were *not* affected by adversity.

What kinds of mood disorders are there? In this section we discuss two mood disorders: major depression and bipolar disorder.

ROMAN MAKHMUTOV/GETTY IMAGES

Major Depression

People with run-of-the-mill depression may feel sad, blue, or "down in the dumps." They may complain of lack of energy, loss of self-esteem, difficulty concentrating, loss of interest in activities and other people (Nezlek et al., 2000), pessimism, crying, and thoughts of suicide.

These feelings are more intense in people with major depressive disorder (MDD). According to a nationally representative sample of 9,000 English-speaking adults in the United States, MDD affects 6% to 7% of men and about 12% of women within any given year, and one person in five to six over the course of a lifetime (Kessler et al., 2005a, 2005c). About half of those with MDD experience severe symptoms such as poor appetite, serious weight loss, and agitation or psychomotor retardation. They may be unable to concentrate and make decisions. They may say that they "don't care" anymore and in some cases attempt suicide. A minority may display faulty perception of reality—so-called psychotic behaviors. These include delusions of unworthiness, guilt for imagined wrongdoings, even the notion that one is rotting from disease. There may also be delusions, as of the devil administering deserved punishment, or hallucinations, as of strange bodily sensations.

Bipolar Disorder

People with bipolar disorder, formerly known as *manic–depressive disorder,* have mood swings from ecstatic elation to deep depression. The cycles seem to be unrelated to external events. The manic person may also be argumentative. The manic person may show excessive energy, lessened need for sleep, and inflated self-esteem. He or she may also be argumentative, show poor judgment, destroy property, make huge contributions to charity,

major depressive disorder (MDD) a serious to severe depressive disorder in which the person may show loss of appetite, psychomotor retardation, and impaired reality testing

psychomotor retardation slowness in motor activity and (apparently) in thought

bipolar disorder a disorder in which the mood alternates between two extreme poles (elation and depression); also referred to as *manic depression*

manic elated, showing excessive excitement

Truth

In the case of bipolar disorder, feeling elated is not a good thing because in the elated, or manic phase, the person may show excessive excitement or silliness, carrying jokes too far.

or give away expensive possessions. People often find manic individuals abrasive and avoid them. They are often oversexed and too restless to sit still or sleep restfully. They often speak rapidly (showing "pressured speech") and jump from topic to topic (showing rapid flight of ideas). It can be hard to get a word in edgewise.

Depression is the other side of the coin. People with bipolar depression often sleep more than usual and are lethargic. People with major (or unipolar) depression are more likely to have insomnia and agitation. Those with bipolar depression also exhibit social withdrawal and irritability. Some people with bipolar disorder attempt suicide when the mood shifts from the elated phase toward depression (Jamison, 2000). They will do almost anything to escape the depths of depression that lie ahead.

Explaining Mood Disorders

What is known about the origins of mood disorders?

Biological Perspectives

Researchers are searching for biological factors in mood disorders. Depression, for example, is often associated with the trait of neuroticism, which is heritable (Chioqueta & Stiles, 2005; Khan et al., 2005). Anxiety is also connected with neuroticism, and mood and anxiety disorders are frequently found in the same person (Khan et al., 2005). Genetic factors appear to be involved in major depression and bipolar disorder, as suggested by twin and adoption studies (Evans et al., 2005; Farmer et al., 2005).

Psychological Perspectives

Many learning theorists suggest that depressed people behave as though they cannot obtain reinforcement. For example, they appear to be inactive and apathetic. Many people with depressive disorders have an *external locus of control*. That is, they do not believe they can control events so as to achieve reinforcements (Tong, 2001; Weinmann et al., 2001). Research conducted by learning theorists has also found links between depression and learned

helplessness. In classic research, psychologist Martin Seligman taught dogs that they were helpless to escape an electric shock. The dogs were prevented from leaving a cage in which they received repeated shocks. Later, a barrier to a safe compartment was removed, offering the animals a way out. When they were shocked again, however, the dogs made no effort to escape. They had apparently learned that they were helpless. Seligman's dogs were also, in a sense, reinforced for doing nothing. That is, the shock *eventually* stopped when the dogs were showing helpless behavior—inactivity and withdrawal. "Reinforcement" might have increased the likelihood of repeating the "successful behavior"—that is, doing nothing—in a similar situation. This helpless behavior resembles that of people who are depressed.

Other cognitive factors contribute to depression. For example, perfectionists set themselves up for depression by making irrational demands on themselves. They are likely to fall short of their (unrealistic) expectations and to feel depressed as a result (Flett & Hewitt, 2002).

Cognitive psychologists also note that people who ruminate about feelings of depression are more likely to prolong the feelings (Spasojevic & Alloy, 2001). Women are more likely than men to ruminate about feelings of depression (Nolen-Hoeksema, 2001). Men are more likely than women to fight negative feelings by distracting themselves or turning to alcohol (Nolen-Hoeksema, 2001). They thus expose themselves and their families to further problems.

Still other cognitions involve the ways in which people explain their failures and shortcomings to themselves (Hankin et al., 2005). Seligman (1996) suggests that when things go wrong we may think of the causes of failure as either *internal* or *external, stable* or *unstable, global* or *specific*. These various attributional styles can be illustrated using the example of having a date that does not work out. An internal attribution involves self-blame, as in "I really loused it up." An external attribution places the blame elsewhere (as in "Some couples just don't take to each other," or, "She was the wrong person for me"). A stable attribution ("It's my personality") suggests a problem that cannot be changed. An unstable attribution ("It was because I had a head cold") suggests a temporary condition. A global attribution of failure ("I have no idea what to do when I'm with people") suggests that the problem is quite large. A specific attribution ("I have problems making small talk at the beginning of a relationship") chops the problem down to a manageable size. Research has shown that people who are depressed are more likely to attribute the causes of their failures to internal, stable, and global factors—factors that they are relatively powerless to change (Riso et al., 2003).

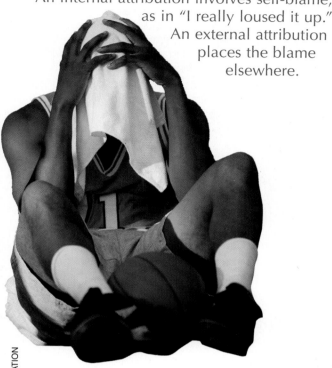

An internal attribution involves self-blame, as in "I really loused it up." An external attribution places the blame elsewhere.

Let's add one remarkable note about attributional styles and the mind–body connection. Shelley Taylor and her colleagues (2000a) found that self-blame for negative events is connected with poorer functioning of the immune system. Too much self-blame, in other words, is not only depressing; it may also be able to make us physically ill.

The Biopsychosocial Perspective

Relationships between mood disorders and biological factors are complex and under intense study. Even if people are biologically predisposed toward depression, self-efficacy expectations and attitudes—particularly attitudes about whether one can change things for the better—may also play a role.

Although the mood disorders are connected with processes within the individual, many kinds of situations are also connected with depression. For example, depression may be a reaction to loss or stress (Cowen, 2002). Sources of chronic strain such as marital discord, physical discomfort, incompetence, and failure or pressure at work all contribute to depression. We tend to be more depressed by things we bring on ourselves, such as academic problems, financial problems, unwanted pregnancy, conflict with the law, arguments, and fights. Some people recover from depression less readily than others, however. People who remain depressed have lower self-esteem, are less likely to be able to solve social problems, and have less social support.

Suicide

Why do people commit suicide? We will deal with suicide terrorism in Chapter 14. Here let us talk about people who choose to take their lives to escape feelings of depression, hopelessness, and helplessness. We may think many of these people have "so much to live for." Apparently, they disagree. So do the thousands of others who take their own lives each year.

In any given year, about 3% of the American population considers suicide (Nock et al., 2008). About 31,000 Americans commit suicide each year (Nock et al., 2008). Suicide is the third- or fourth-leading cause of death among older teenagers (Nock et al., 2008). Who is most at risk of attempting or committing suicide?

Risk Factors in Suicide

Most suicides are linked to feelings of depression and hopelessness (Beautrais, 2003). Jill Rathus and her colleagues (Miller et al., 2000) found that suicidal adolescents experience four areas of psychological problems: (1) confusion about the self, (2) impulsiveness, (3) emotional instability, and (4) interpersonal problems. Some suicidal teenagers, like suicidal adults, are highly achieving, rigid perfectionists who have set impossibly high expectations for themselves (Miller et al., 2000). Many people throw themselves into feelings of depression and hopelessness by comparing themselves negatively with others, even when the comparisons are inappropriate (Barber, 2001). For example, some people criticize themselves for being hired at a lower salary than others were, even though the financial climate of a company has changed.

Suicide attempts are more common following stressful life events, especially "exit events" (Beautrais, 2003). Exit events entail loss of social support, as in the death of a parent or friend, divorce, or a family member's leaving home. These exit events result in what Shneidman (2001) refers to as psychological pain, or "psychache." Other contributors to suicidal behavior among adolescents include concerns over sexuality, grades in school, problems at home, and substance abuse (Cuellar & Curry, 2007). It is not always a stressful event itself that precipitates suicide but can also be the individual's anxiety or fear of being "found out" about something, such as failing a course or getting arrested (Marttunen, 1998).

There is a tendency for suicide to run in families (Miller et al., 2007). Many suicide attempters have family members with serious psychological problems, and about 25% have family members who have taken their lives (Segal & Roy, 2001; Sorenson

& Rutter, 1991). The causal connections are unclear, however. Do people who attempt suicide inherit disorders that can lead to suicide? Does the family environment subject family members to feelings of hopelessness? Does the suicide of a family member give a person the idea of committing suicide, or create the impression that he or she is destined to commit suicide? These possibilities and others—such as poor problem-solving ability—form a complex web of contributors.

Sociocultural Factors in Suicide

Suicide is connected not only with feelings of depression and stressful events, but also with age, educational status, ethnicity, and gender.

> Although teenage suicides loom large in the media spotlight, older people are actually more likely to commit suicide.

Consider some facts about suicide:

• Suicide is the third-leading cause of death among young people aged fifteen to twenty-four (Miller et al., 2007). More teenagers and young adults die from suicide than from cancer, heart disease, AIDS, birth defects, stroke, pneumonia and influenza, and chronic lung disease combined (National Center for Health Statistics, 2005).

• Suicide is more common among college students than among people of the same age who do not attend college.

• Although teenage suicides loom large in the media spotlight, older people are actually more likely to commit suicide (National Center for Health Statistics, 2005). The suicide rate among older people who are single is twice that of older people who are married (National Center for Injury Prevention and Control, 2005).

Rates of suicide and suicide attempts also vary among different ethnic groups and according to gender. For example, about one in six Native Americans (17%) has attempted suicide—

{ Women and Depression }

Women are nearly twice as likely to be diagnosed with depression as men (Keyes & Goodman, 2006). This sex difference begins to emerge during adolescence, at about the age of thirteen. In any given year, about 12% of women and 7% of men in the United States are diagnosed with depression. It was once assumed that depression was most likely to accompany menopause in women, because women could no longer carry out their "natural" function of childbearing. However, women are more likely to encounter depression during the childbearing years (Deecher et al., 2008; Keyes & Goodman, 2006).

Many people assume that biological sex differences largely explain why women are more likely to become depressed (Deecher et al., 2008). Low levels of estrogen are widely seen as the culprit. Estrogen levels plummet prior to menstruation, and the deficit may trigger psychological changes. How often do we hear degrading remarks such as "It must be that time of the month" when a woman expresses feelings of anger or irritation? Some theorists suggest that women may also have a "cognitive vulnerability" to depression, connected with greater tendencies than men to ruminate about stresses and other negative events (Hankin & Abramson, 2001).

Some of the sex difference may also reflect the greater stresses placed on women, which tend to be maximized when they are working a triple shift—one in the workforce and the others meeting the demands of homemaking, child rearing, and aging parents (Plaisier et al., 2008; Rathus, 2009-2010). Women are more likely to experience physical and sexual abuse, poverty, single parenthood, and sexism. Single mothers, in particular, have lower socioeconomic status than men, and depression and other psychological disorders are more common among poor people (Nicholson et al., 2008). A part of treatment for depressed women, then, is to modify the demands on women. The pain may lie in the individual, but the cause often lies in society.

a rate higher than that of other Americans (Blum et al., 1992). About one in eight Latino and Latina Americans has attempted suicide and three in ten have considered it (National Center for Health Statistics, 2005). European Americans are next, with 8% attempting and 28% contemplating suicide. African Americans are least likely to attempt suicide (6.5%) or to consider it (20%). The suicide rates for African Americans are only about two-thirds of those for European Americans, even though African Americans are more likely to live in poverty and suffer discrimination (National Center for Health Statistics, 2005).

About three times as many females as males attempt suicide, but about four times as many males "succeed," in part because males are likely to choose more deadly methods (National Center for Injury Prevention and Control, 2005). Males are more likely to shoot or hang themselves; females more often use drugs, such as overdoses of tranquilizers or sleeping pills, or poisons. Females often do not take enough of these chemicals. It also takes awhile for the chemicals to work, giving others the opportunity to find the person and intervene.

Myths About Suicide

Some believe that those who fail at suicide attempts are only seeking attention. But many people who commit suicide have made prior attempts (Jackson & Nuttall, 2001; Waters, 2000). Contrary to widespread belief, discussing suicide with a person who is depressed does not prompt the person to attempt suicide (National Center for Injury Prevention and Control, 2005). Extracting a promise not to commit suicide before calling or visiting a helping professional seems to prevent some suicides.

Some believe that only "insane" people (meaning people who are out of touch with reality) would take their own lives. However, suicidal thinking is not necessarily a sign of bizarre thinking. Instead, people may consider suicide when they think they have run out of options (Nock & Kazdin, 2002; Townsend et al., 2001).

LO⁴ Anxiety Disorders

Anxiety has psychological and physical symptoms. Psychological symptoms include worrying, fear of the worst things happening, fear of losing control, nervousness, and inability to relax. Physical symptoms reflect arousal of the sympathetic branch of the autonomic nervous system. They include trembling, sweating, a pounding or racing heart, elevated blood pressure (a flushed face), and faintness. Anxiety is an appropriate response to a real threat. It can be abnormal, however, when it is excessive or when it comes out of nowhere—that is, when events do not seem to warrant it. *What kinds of anxiety disorders are there?*

There are different kinds of anxiety disorders, but all of them are characterized by excessive or unwarranted anxiety. The anxiety disorders include phobias, panic disorder, generalized anxiety, obsessive–compulsive disorder, and stress disorders.

Phobias

Phobias include specific phobias, social phobia, and agoraphobia. They can be detrimental to one's quality of life. Specific phobias are irrational fears of specific objects or situations, such as spiders, snakes, or heights. One specific phobia is fear of elevators. Some people will not enter elevators despite the hardships they incur as a result (such as walking up ten flights of steps). Yes, the cable *could* break. The ventilation *could* fail. One *could* be stuck in midair waiting for repairs. But these problems are uncommon, and it affects one's quality of life to walk up and down several flights of stairs to elude them. Similarly, some people with a specific phobia for hypodermic needles will not have injections, even to treat serious illness. Injections can be painful, but most people with a phobia for needles would gladly suffer an even more painful pinch if it would help them fight illness. Other specific phobias include claustrophobia (fear of tight or enclosed places), acrophobia (fear of heights), and fear of mice, snakes, and other creepy crawlies. Social phobias are persistent fears of scrutiny by others or of doing something that will be humiliating or embarrassing. Fear of public speaking is a common social phobia.

Agoraphobia is also widespread among adults.

specific phobia
persistent fear of a specific object or situation

claustrophobia
fear of tight, small places

acrophobia
fear of high places

social phobia
an irrational, excessive fear of public scrutiny

agoraphobia
fear of open, crowded places

© GOODSHOOT/JUPITERIMAGES

Agoraphobia is derived from the Greek words meaning "fear of the marketplace," or fear of being out in open, busy areas. Persons with agoraphobia fear being in places from which it might be difficult to escape or in which help might not be available if they get upset. In practice, people who receive this diagnosis often refuse to venture out of their homes, especially by themselves. They find it difficult to hold a job or to maintain an ordinary social life.

Panic Disorder

Panic disorder is an abrupt attack of acute anxiety that is not necessarily triggered by a specific object or situation. People with panic disorder have strong physical symptoms such as shortness of breath, heavy sweating, tremors, and pounding of the heart. They are particularly aware of cardiac sensations. It is not unusual for them to think they are having a heart attack. People with the disorder may also experience choking sensations, nausea, numbness or tingling, flushes or chills, and fear of going crazy or losing control. Panic attacks may last minutes or hours. Afterward, the person usually feels drained.

Many people panic now and then. The diagnosis of panic disorder is reserved for those who undergo a series of attacks or live in fear of attacks.

Panic attacks seem to come from nowhere. Thus, some people who have had them stay home for fear of having an attack in public. They are diagnosed as having panic disorder with agoraphobia.

Generalized Anxiety Disorder

The central feature of generalized anxiety disorder is persistent anxiety. As with panic disorder, the anxiety cannot be attributed to a phobic object, situation, or activity. Rather, it seems to be free floating. The core of the disorder appears to be pervasive worrying about numerous problems. Features of the disorder include motor tension (shakiness, inability to relax, furrowed brow, fidgeting); autonomic overarousal (sweating, dry mouth, racing heart, light-headedness, frequent urinating, diarrhea); and excessive vigilance, as shown by irritability, insomnia, and a tendency to be easily distracted.

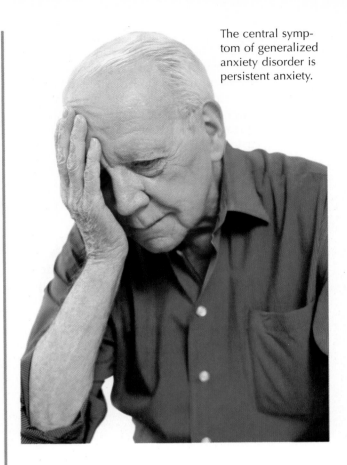

The central symptom of generalized anxiety disorder is persistent anxiety.

Obsessive–Compulsive Disorder

Obsessions are recurrent, anxiety-provoking thoughts or images that seem irrational and beyond control. They are so compelling and recurrent that they disrupt daily life. They may include doubts about whether one has locked the doors and shut the windows, or images such as one mother's repeated fantasy that her children had been run over on the way home from school. One woman became obsessed with the idea that she had contaminated her hands with Sani-Flush and that the chemicals were spreading to everything she touched. A sixteen-year-old boy complained that he was distracted by "numbers in my head" when he was about to study or take a test. The more he tried to ignore them, the louder they became.

© 2010 GEORGE DOYLE/ JUPITERIMAGES CORPORATION

125   10,789
3.14159265...
21 21 21!

Compulsions are thoughts or behaviors that tend to reduce the anxiety connected with obsessions. They are seemingly irresistible urges to engage in specific acts, often repeatedly, such as elaborate washing after using the bathroom or repeatedly checking that one has locked the door or turned off the gas burners before leaving home. The impulse is recurrent and forceful, interfering with daily life.

Stress Disorders

Sharia dreamed of a man assaulting her in the night at the Superdome in New Orleans, after she had been moved to this "refuge" following Hurricane Katrina in the summer of 2005. Darla, who lives in Oregon, dreamed that she was trapped in a World Trade Center tower when it was hit by an airplane on September 11, 2001. About one in six Iraq or Afghanistan veterans has nightmares and flashbacks to buddies being killed by snipers or explosive devices (Hoge et al., 2004). These all-too-real nightmarish events have caused many bad dreams. Such dreams are part of the experience of posttraumatic stress disorder.

Post-traumatic stress disorder (PTSD) is characterized by a rapid heart rate and feelings of anxiety and helplessness that are caused by a traumatic experience. Such experiences may include a natural or human-made disaster, a threat or assault, or witnessing a death. PTSD may occur months or years after the event. It frequently occurs among firefighters, combat veterans, and people whose homes and communities have been swept away by natural disasters or who have been victims of accidents or violence (DeAngelis, 2008).

The traumatic event is revisited in the form of intrusive memories, recurrent dreams, and flashbacks— the sudden feeling that the event is recurring. People with PTSD typically try to avoid thoughts and activities connected to the traumatic event. They may find it more difficult to enjoy life and have sleep problems, irritable outbursts, difficulty concentrating, extreme vigilance, and an intensified "startle" response (Griffin, 2008). The attacks of September 11, 2001, took their toll on sleep. According to a poll taken by the National Sleep Foundation (2001) two months afterward, nearly half of Americans had difficulty falling asleep, as compared with about one-quarter of Americans before the attacks (see Figure 12.3).

Acute stress disorder, like PTSD, is characterized by feelings of anxiety and helplessness that are caused by a traumatic event. PTSD, however, can occur six months or more after the traumatic event and tends to persist. Acute stress disorder occurs within a month of the event and lasts from two days to four weeks. Women who have been raped, for example, experience acute distress that tends to peak in severity a few weeks after the assault. Yet the same women often go on to experience PTSD (Koss et al., 2002).

compulsion
an irresistible urge to repeat an act or engage in ritualistic behavior such as hand washing

post-traumatic stress disorder (PTSD)
a disorder that follows a distressing event outside the range of normal human experience and that is characterized by features such as intense fear, avoidance of stimuli associated with the event, and reliving of the event

acute stress disorder
a disorder, like PTSD, that is characterized by feelings of anxiety and helplessness and caused by a traumatic event; acute stress disorder occurs within a month of the event and lasts from two days to four weeks

Figure 12.3

Sleep Problems Among Americans Before and After September 11, 2001

Insomnia is one of the symptoms of stress disorders. A poll by the National Sleep Foundation found that Americans had a greater frequency of sleep problems after the terrorist attacks of September 11, 2001.

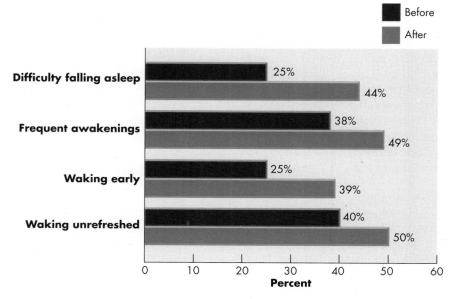

- Before
- After

Difficulty falling asleep: 25% / 44%
Frequent awakenings: 38% / 49%
Waking early: 25% / 39%
Waking unrefreshed: 40% / 50%

Percent (0 10 20 30 40 50 60)

somatoform disorders disorders in which people complain of physical (somatic) problems even though no physical abnormality can be found

conversion disorder a somatoform disorder in which anxiety or unconscious conflicts are "converted" into physical symptoms that often have the effect of helping the person cope with anxiety or conflict

Explaining Anxiety Disorders

What is known about the origins of anxiety disorders?

Biological Perspectives

Biological factors play a role in anxiety disorders. Genetic factors are implicated in most psychological disorders, including anxiety disorders (Low et al., 2008). Anxiety disorders tend to run in families. Twin studies find a higher rate of match for anxiety disorders among identical twins than among fraternal twins (Kendler et al., 2001). Studies of adoptees who are anxious similarly show that the biological parent places the child at risk for anxiety and related traits.

Perhaps a predisposition toward anxiety—in the form of a highly reactive autonomic nervous system—can be inherited. What might make a nervous system "highly reactive"?

In the case of panic disorder, faulty regulation of levels of serotonin and norepinephrine may be involved. Other anxiety disorders may involve the neurotransmitter glutamate, and receptor sites in the brain may not be sensitive enough to gamma-aminobutyric acid (GABA), a neurotransmitter that may counteract glutamate (Kalin, 2003). The benzodiazepines, a class of drugs that reduce anxiety, may work by increasing the sensitivity of receptor sites to GABA.

Psychological and Social Perspectives

Some learning theorists—particularly behaviorists—consider phobias to be conditioned fears that were acquired in early childhood. Therefore, their origins are beyond memory. Avoidance of feared stimuli is reinforced by the reduction of anxiety.

Other learning theorists—social cognitive theorists—dwell on the social aspects of developing phobias (Basic Behavioral Science Task Force, 1996b). If parents squirm, grimace, and shudder at the sight of mice, blood, or dirt on the kitchen floor, children might assume that these stimuli are awful and imitate their parents' behavior.

Cognitive theorists note that people's appraisals of the magnitude of threats help determine whether they are traumatic and can lead to PTSD (Folkman & Moskowitz, 2000a; Koss et al., 2002). People with panic attacks tend to overreact to physical sensations. Obsessions and compulsions may serve to divert attention from more frightening issues, such as "What am I going to do with my life?" When anxieties are acquired at a young age, we may later interpret them as enduring traits and label ourselves as "people who fear _____" (you fill it in). We then live up to the labels. We also entertain thoughts that heighten and perpetuate anxiety such as "I've got to get out of here," or "My heart is going to leap out of my chest." Such ideas intensify physical features of anxiety, disrupt planning, make stimuli seem worse than they are, motivate avoidance, and lower self-efficacy expectations. The belief that we will not be able to handle a threat heightens anxiety. The belief that we are in control reduces anxiety (Bandura et al., 1985).

The Biopsychosocial Perspective

Many cases of anxiety disorders reflect the interaction of biological, psychological, and social factors. In panic disorder, biological imbalances may initially trigger attacks. However, subsequent fear of attacks—and of the bodily cues that signal their onset—may heighten discomfort and give one the idea that nothing can be done about them (Craske & Zucker, 2001). Moreover, panic attacks are likely to occur in social situations, especially in crowds. Feelings of helplessness increase fear. People with panic disorder can be helped by methods that reduce physical discomfort—including regular breathing—and show them that there are ways to cope with attacks (Craske & Zucker, 2001). They are also sometimes taken into social settings, such as crowded streets or stores, by psychologists who offer them social support and show them that they can tolerate such situations.

LO⁵ Somatoform Disorders

People with **somatoform disorders** complain of physical problems such as paralysis, pain, or a persistent belief that they have a serious disease. But health professionals can find no evidence of a physical abnormality. *What kinds of somatoform disorders are there?* In this section we discuss three somatoform disorders: conversion disorder, hypochondriasis, and body dysmorphic disorder.

Conversion Disorder

Conversion disorder is characterized by a major change in or loss of physical functioning, although there are no medical findings to explain the loss of functioning. The behaviors are not intentionally produced. That is, the person is not faking. Conversion disorder is so named because it appears to "convert" a source of stress into a physical difficulty.

If you lost the ability to see at night, or if your legs became paralyzed, you would understandably show concern. But some people with conversion disorder show indifference to their symptoms, a remarkable feature referred to as la belle indifférence.

During World War II, some bomber pilots developed night blindness. They could not carry out their nighttime missions, although no damage to the optic nerves was found. In rare cases, women with large families have been reported to become paralyzed in the legs, again with no medical findings. More recently, a Cambodian woman who had witnessed atrocities became blind as a result.

Hypochondriasis

Another more common type of somatoform disorder is hypochondriasis (also called *hypochondria*). People with this disorder insist that they are suffering from a serious physical illness, even though no medical evidence of illness can be found. They become preoccupied with minor physical sensations and continue to believe that they are ill despite the reassurance of physicians that they are healthy. They may run from doctor to doctor, seeking the one who will find the causes of the sensations. Fear of illness may disrupt their work or home life.

Body Dysmorphic Disorder

People with body dysmorphic disorder are preoccupied with a fantasized or exaggerated physical defect in their appearance. They may spend hours examining themselves in the mirror and go to extreme lengths to correct the "problem," including cosmetic surgery. Others remove all mirrors from their homes so as not to be reminded of the "flaw." People with the disorder may assume that others see them as deformed. They may compulsively groom themselves or pay close attention to styling every strand of hair.

Explaining Somatoform Disorders

What is known about the origins of somatoform disorders? The somatoform disorders offer a fascinating study in the biopsychosocial perspective. Psychologically speaking, the somatoform disorders have much

to do with what one focuses on— actual social and financial problems, for example, or one's body. Some investigators consider conversion disorder to be a form of self-hypnosis (Roelofs et al., 2002), and they note that there is research evidence that people with conversion disorder are highly susceptible to being hypnotized. The idea here would be that people with conversion disorder focus on an imaginary physical problem to the point where they exclude conflicting information.

In the case of hypochondriasis, people may misinterpret run-of-the-mill physical sensations— or symptoms—as signifying deadly illness. There is research evidence that people who develop hypochondriasis are particularly sensitive to bodily sensations and tend to ruminate about them (Lecci & Cohen, 2002). Moreover, enacting the role of a sick person has the "benefits" of relieving one of ordinary responsibilities and concerns. For example, how can one focus on work or family life when one believes he or she is rotting away with disease?

Certainly the social value of personal attractiveness can contribute to dissatisfaction with one's body. But people with body dysmorphic disorder may focus irrationally on an exaggerated blemish or other minor feature, suggestive of perfectionistic and ruminative tendencies.

Biologically speaking, tendencies toward perfectionism and rumination, which are found among many people with somatoform disorders, are thought to be at least partly heritable. Squeamishness about one's body may be too much of a good thing from the evolutionary perspective. That is, concern about bodily harm will presumably encourage one to avoid danger and provide advantages in survival and reproduction. But too much concern may lead to useless preoccupations.

LO⁶ Dissociative Disorders

During one long fall semester, the Ohio State University campus lived in terror. Four college women were kidnapped, forced to take out cash from ATMs,

la belle indifférence
a French term descriptive of the lack of concern for their (imagined) medical problem sometimes shown by people with conversion disorders

hypochondriasis
a somatoform disorder characterized by persistent belief that one is ill despite lack of medical findings

body dysmorphic disorder
a somatoform disorder characterized by preoccupation with an imagined or exaggerated physical defect in one's appearance

dissociative disorders
disorders in which there are sudden, temporary changes in consciousness or self-identity

dissociative amnesia
a dissociative disorder marked by loss of memory or self-identity; skills and general knowledge are usually retained

dissociative fugue
a dissociative disorder in which one experiences amnesia and then flees to a new location

dissociative identity disorder
a disorder in which a person appears to have two or more distinct identities or personalities that may alternately emerge

multiple personality disorder
the previous term for *dissociative identity disorder*

and raped. A mysterious phone call led to the arrest of a twenty-three-year-old drifter—let's call him "William"—who had been dismissed from the Navy.

William was not the boy next door.

Psychologists and psychiatrists who interviewed William concluded that ten personalities—eight male and two female—dwelled in him (Keyes, 1995). His personality had been "fractured" by an abusive childhood. His several personalities displayed distinct facial expressions, speech patterns, and memories. They performed differently on psychological tests.

Arthur, the most rational personality, spoke with a British accent. Danny and Christopher were quiet adolescents. Christine was a three-year-old girl. Tommy, a sixteen-year-old, had enlisted in the Navy. Allen was eighteen and smoked. Adelena, a nineteen-year-old lesbian personality, had committed the rapes. Who had placed the mysterious phone call? Probably David, nine, an anxious child.

The defense claimed that William's behavior was caused by *dissociative identity disorder*. Of the identities or personalities dwelling within him, some were aware of the others. Some believed they were unique. As a child, Billy, the core identity, had learned to sleep to avoid his father's abuse. A psychiatrist asserted that Billy had also been "asleep," or in a "psychological coma," during the abductions. Billy should therefore be found not guilty by reason of insanity.

William was found not guilty. He was committed to a psychiatric institution and released six years later.

Dissociative identity disorder is one of the **dissociative disorders**. In dissociative disorders, there is a splitting of psychological processes such as thoughts, emotions, identity, memory, or consciousness—the processes that make the person feel whole. *What kinds of dissociative disorders are there?* The dissociative disorders include dissociative amnesia, dissociative fugue, and William's disorder: dissociative identity disorder (also termed *multiple personality disorder*).

Dissociative Amnesia

In **dissociative amnesia**, the person is suddenly unable to recall important personal information (that is, explicit episodic memories). The loss of memory cannot be attributed to biological problems such as a blow to the head or excessive drinking. It is thus a psychological disorder and not an organic one. In the most common example, the person cannot recall events for a number of hours after a stressful incident, as in warfare or in the case of an uninjured survivor of an accident. In generalized amnesia, people forget their entire lives. Amnesia may last for hours or years.

Dissociative Fugue

In **dissociative fugue**, the person abruptly leaves his or her home or place of work and travels to another place, having lost all memory of his or her past life. While at the new location, the person either does not think about the past or reports a past filled with invented memories. The new personality is often more outgoing and less inhibited than the "real" identity. Following recovery, the events that occurred during the fugue are not recalled.

Dissociative Identity Disorder

In **dissociative identity disorder** (formerly termed **multiple personality disorder**), two or more identities or personalities, each with distinct traits and memories, "occupy" the same person. Each identity may or may not be aware of the others or of events experienced by the others.

The different personalities might have different eyeglass prescriptions (Braun, 1988). Braun reports cases in which assorted identities showed different allergic responses. In one person, an identity named Timmy was not sensitive to orange juice. But when another identity drank orange juice, he would break out with hives. Hives would also erupt if another identity emerged while the juice was being digested. If Timmy reappeared when the allergic reaction was present, the itching of the hives would cease and the blisters would start to subide. In other cases reported by Braun, different identities within a person might show various responses to the same medicine. Or one identity might exhibit color blindness while others have normal color vision.

Explaining Dissociative Disorders

The dissociative disorders are some of the odder psychological disorders. *What is known about the origins of dissociative disorders?* Biopsychosocial factors may well be involved in dissociative disorders. According to learning and cognitive psychologists, people with dissociative disorders may have learned *not to think* about bad memories or disturbing impulses in an effort to avoid feelings of anxiety, guilt, and shame. Dissociative disorders may help people keep disturbing ideas out of mind.

What might such memories contain? The answer is painful interpersonal— or social—information. Research suggests that many cases of dissociative disorders involve memories of sexual or physical abuse during childhood, usually by a relative or caretaker (Martinez-Taboas & Bernal, 2000; Migdow, 2003).

Truth

The personalities of people with dissociative identity disorder can be very different from one another.

On a biological level, research with abused children and adolescents suggests that the trauma-related dissociation observed in dissociative disorders may have a neurological basis (Diseth, 2005). Child abuse may lead to some permanent neurochemical and structural abnormalities in parts of the brain involved in cognition and memory. Although it seems that the nature of the trauma in such cases is interpersonal, it need not necessarily be sexual in nature. In any event, one might expect resultant impairments in the recall of personal information.

personality disorders
enduring patterns of maladaptive behavior that are sources of distress to the individual or others

paranoid personality disorder
a personality disorder characterized by persistent suspiciousness, but not involving the disorganization of paranoid schizophrenia

schizotypal personality disorder
a personality disorder characterized by oddities of thought and behavior, but not involving bizarre psychotic behaviors

LO⁷ Personality Disorders

Personality disorders, like personality traits, are characterized by enduring patterns of behavior. Personality disorders, however, are inflexible and maladaptive. They impair personal or social functioning and are a source of distress to the individual or to other people. *What kinds of personality disorders are there?* There are a number of personality disorders. They include the paranoid, schizotypal, schizoid, antisocial, and avoidant personality disorders.

Paranoid Personality Disorder

The defining trait of the paranoid personality disorder is a tendency to interpret other people's behavior as threatening or demeaning. People with the disorder do not show the grossly disorganized thinking of paranoid schizophrenia. They are mistrustful of others, however, and their relationships suffer for it. They may be suspicious of coworkers and supervisors, but they can generally hold a job.

Schizotypal and Schizoid Personality Disorders

Schizotypal personality disorder is characterized by peculiarities of thought, perception, or behavior, such as excessive fantasy and suspiciousness, feelings of being unreal, or odd usage of words. The bizarre

© 2010 JOHN LUND / JUPITERIMAGES CORPORATION

PRNEWSFOTO/GENTEX CORPORATION

behaviors that characterize schizophrenia are absent, so this disorder is schizotypal, not schizophrenic.

The schizoid personality is defined by indifference to relationships and flat emotional response. People with this disorder are "loners." They do not develop warm, tender feelings for others. They have few friends and rarely maintain long-term relationships. Some people with schizoid personality disorder do very well on the job, provided that continuous social interaction is not required. They do not have hallucinations or delusions.

Borderline Personality Disorder

People with borderline personality disorder show instability in their relationships, self-image, and mood, and lack of control over impulses. They tend to be uncertain of their values, goals, loyalties, careers, choices of friends, sometimes even their sexual orientations. Instability in self-image or identity may leave them with feelings of emptiness and boredom. Many cannot tolerate being alone and make desperate attempts to avoid feelings of abandonment. They may be clinging and demanding in social relationships, but clinging often pushes away the people on whom they depend. They alternate between extremes of adulation in their relationships (when their needs are met) and loathing (when they feel scorned). They tend to view other people as all good or all bad, shifting abruptly from one extreme to the other. As a result, they may flit from partner to partner in brief and stormy relationships. People whom they had idealized are treated with contempt when they feel the other person has failed them.

Instability of moods is a central characteristic of borderline personality disorder. Moods run the gamut from anger and irritability to depression and anxiety, with each lasting from a few hours to a few days. People with the disorder have difficulty controlling anger and are prone to fights or smashing things. They often act on impulse, such as eloping with someone they have just met. This impulsive and unpredictable behavior is often self-destructive and linked to a risk of suicidal attempts and gestures. It may involve spending sprees, gambling, drug abuse, engaging in unsafe sexual activity, reckless driving, binge eating, or shoplifting. People with the disorder may also engage in self-mutilation, such as scratching their wrists or burning cigarettes on their arms. Self-mutilation is sometimes a means of manipulating others, particularly in times of stress. Frequent self-mutilation is also associated with suicide attempts.

Antisocial Personality Disorder

People with antisocial personality disorder often show a superficial charm and are at least average in intelligence. They fail to learn to improve their behavior from punishment, and they do not form meaningful bonds with other people. Though they are often heavily punished by their parents and rejected by peers, they continue in their impulsive, careless styles of life. While women are more likely than men to have anxiety and depressive disorders, men are more likely than women to have antisocial personality disorder.

Table 12.2

Characteristics of People Diagnosed with Antisocial Personality Disorder

Key Characteristics
History of delinquency and truancy
Persistent violation of the rights of others
Impulsiveness
Poor self-control
Lack of remorse for misdeeds
Lack of empathy
Deceitfulness and manipulativeness
Irresponsibility
Glibness; superficial charm
Exaggerated sense of self-worth

Other Common Characteristics
Lack of loyalty or of formation of enduring relationships
Failure to maintain good job performance over the years
Failure to develop or adhere to a life plan
Sexual promiscuity
Substance abuse
Inability to tolerate boredom
Low tolerance for frustration
Irritability

Sources: Levenston et al., 2000; Romero et al., 2001.

Avoidant Personality Disorder

People with avoidant personality disorder are generally unwilling to enter a relationship without some assurance of acceptance because they fear rejection and criticism. As a result, they may have few close relationships outside their immediate families. Unlike people with schizoid personality disorder, however, they have some interest in, and feelings of warmth toward, other people.

Explaining Personality Disorders

What is known about the origins of personality disorders? Numerous biological, psychological, and sociocultural factors have been implicated in the personality disorders.

Biological Factors

Genetic factors are apparently involved in some personality disorders (Rutter & Silberg, 2002). Personality traits are to some degree heritable (Plomin, 2000), and many personality disorders seem to be extreme variations of normal personality traits. An analysis of fifty-one twin and adoption studies estimated that genetic factors were the greatest influences on antisocial behavior (Rhee & Waldman, 2002). Referring to the five-factor model of personality, people with schizoid personalities tend to be highly introverted (Ross et al., 2002; Widiger & Costa, 1994). People with avoidant personalities tend to be both introverted and emotionally unstable (Ross et al., 2002; Widiger & Costa, 1994).

Perhaps the genetics of antisocial personality involve the prefrontal cortex of the brain, a part of the brain connected with emotional responses.

There is some evidence that people with antisocial personality, as a group, have less gray matter (associative neurons) in the prefrontal cortex of the brain than other people do (Damasio, 2000; Yang et al., 2005). The lesser amount of gray matter could lessen the level of arousal of the nervous system. As a result, it could be more difficult to condition fear responses (Blair & James, 2003). People with the disorder would then be unlikely to show guilt for their misdeeds and would seem to be unafraid of punishment. But a biological factor such as a lower-than-normal level of arousal might not in itself cause the development of an antisocial personality (Rutter & Silberg, 2002). Perhaps a person must also be reared under conditions that do not foster the self-concept of a law-abiding citizen.

Psychological Factors

Learning theorists suggest that childhood experiences can contribute to maladaptive ways of relating to others in adulthood—that is, can lead to personality disorders. Cognitive psychologists find that antisocial adolescents encode social information in ways that bolster their misdeeds. For example, they tend to interpret other people's behavior as threatening, even when it is not (Crick & Dodge, 1994). Aggressive individuals often find it difficult to solve social problems in useful ways (McMurran et al., 2002). Cognitive therapists have encouraged some antisocial male adolescents to view social provocations as problems to be solved rather than as threats to their "manhood," with some favorable initial results (Lochman & Dodge, 1994).

Sociocultural Factors

The label of borderline personality has been applied to people as diverse as Marilyn Monroe and Lawrence of Arabia. Some theorists believe we live in fragmented and alienating times that tend to create problems in forming a stable identity and stable relationships. "Living on the edge," or border, can be seen as a metaphor for an unstable society.

Although the causes of many psychological disorders remain in dispute, various methods of therapy have been devised to deal with them. Those methods are the focus of Chapter 13.

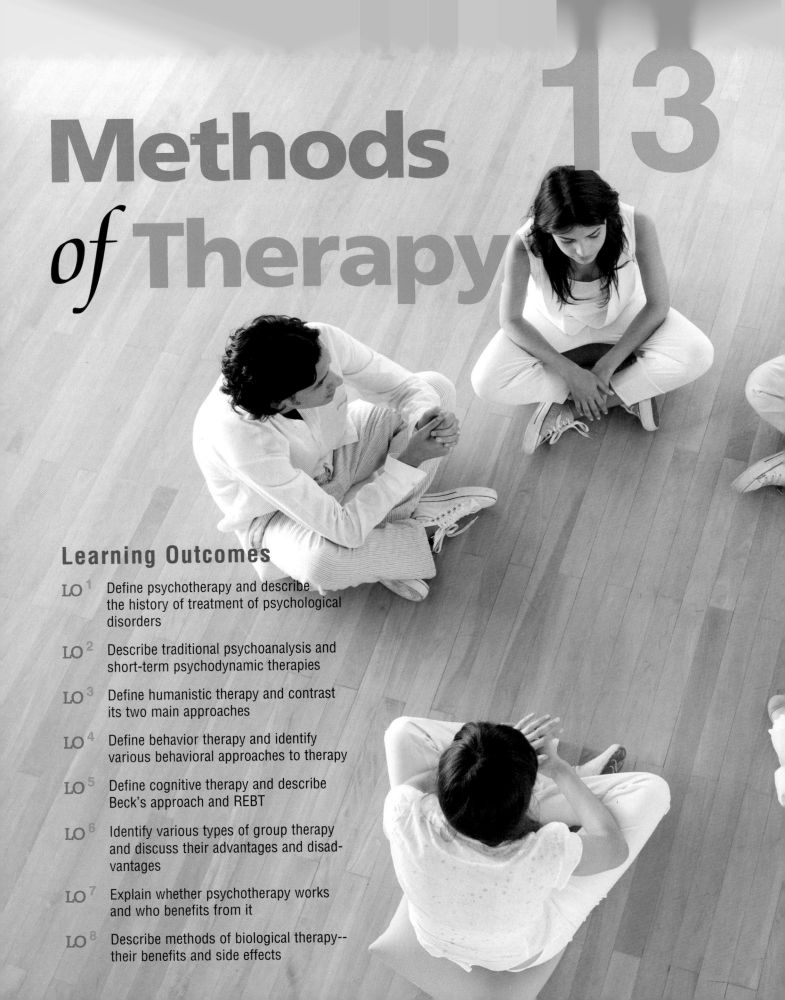

Methods of Therapy

13

Learning Outcomes

LO 1   Define psychotherapy and describe the history of treatment of psychological disorders

LO 2   Describe traditional psychoanalysis and short-term psychodynamic therapies

LO 3   Define humanistic therapy and contrast its two main approaches

LO 4   Define behavior therapy and identify various behavioral approaches to therapy

LO 5   Define cognitive therapy and describe Beck's approach and REBT

LO 6   Identify various types of group therapy and discuss their advantages and disadvantages

LO 7   Explain whether psychotherapy works and who benefits from it

LO 8   Describe methods of biological therapy-- their benefits and side effects

> **"** *Had she broken her leg, her treatment would have followed a fairly standard course.* **"**

Jasmine, a nineteen-year-old college sophomore, has been crying almost without letup for several days. She feels that her life is falling apart. Her college aspirations lie in shambles. She believes that she has brought shame upon her family. Thoughts of suicide have crossed her mind. She can barely drag herself out of bed in the morning. She is avoiding friends. She can pinpoint some sources of stress in her life: a couple of less-than-shining grades, an argument with a boyfriend, friction with roommates. Still, her misery seemed to descend on her from nowhere.

Jasmine is depressed—she feels so down that family and friends have finally prevailed upon her to seek professional help. Had she broken her leg, her treatment would have followed a fairly standard course. Yet treatment of psychological problems and disorders like depression is sometimes approached from different perspectives. Depending on the therapist Jasmine sees, she may be

Truth or Fiction?

What do you think?

Folklore, common sense, or nonsense? Place a T for "True" or F for "False" on the lines provided (you'll learn the answers as you read through the text).

__ Residents of London used to visit the local insane asylum for a fun night out on the town.

__ Some psychotherapists let their clients take the lead in psychotherapy.

__ Some psychotherapists tell their clients exactly what to do.

__ Lying in a reclining chair and fantasizing can be an effective way of confronting fears.

__ Smoking cigarettes can be an effective method for helping people stop smoking cigarettes.

__ There is no scientific evidence that psychotherapy helps people with psychological disorders.

__ The originator of a surgical technique to reduce violence learned that it was not always successful when one of his patients shot him.

- Lying on a couch, talking about anything that pops into awareness, and exploring the possible meaning of her recurrent dreams;

- Sitting face to face with a warm, gentle therapist who expresses faith in Jasmine's ability to manage her problems;

- Listening to a frank, straightforward therapist assert that Jasmine's problems stem from self-defeating attitudes and perfectionistic beliefs;

- Taking medication; or

- Participating in some combination of these approaches.

These methods, although very different, all represent methods of therapy. In this chapter we explore various methods of psychotherapy and biological therapy. *What is psychotherapy?*

ZENSHU/ALIX MINDE/PHOTOALTO AGENCY RF COLLECTIONS/GETTY IMAGES

psychotherapy
a systematic interaction between a therapist and a client that brings psychological principles to bear on influencing the client's thoughts, feelings, or behavior to help the client overcome abnormal behavior or adjust to problems in living

asylum
an institution for the care of the mentally ill

LO¹ What Is Psychotherapy?

There are many kinds of psychotherapy, but they all have certain common characteristics.

Psychotherapy is a systematic interaction between a therapist and a client that applies psychological principles to affect the client's thoughts, feelings, or behavior in an effort to help the client overcome psychological disorders, adjust to problems in living, or develop as an individual.

Quite a mouthful? True. But note the essentials:

✔ *Systematic interaction*
Psychotherapy is a systematic interaction between a client and a therapist. The therapist's theoretical point of view interacts with the client's to determine how the therapist and client relate to each other.

✔ *Psychological principles*
Psychotherapy is based on psychological theory and research in areas such as personality, learning, motivation, and emotion.

✔ *Thoughts, feelings, and behavior*
Psychotherapy influences clients' thoughts, feelings, and behavior. It can be aimed at any or all of these aspects of human psychology.

✔ *Psychological disorders, adjustment problems, and personal growth*
Psychotherapy is often used with people who have psychological disorders. Other people seek help in adjusting to problems such as shyness, weight problems, or loss of a life partner. Still other clients want to learn more about themselves and to reach their full potential as individuals, parents, or creative artists.

The History of Therapies

Historically speaking, "treatments" of psychological disorders often reflected the assumption that people who behaved in strange ways were possessed by demons. *How have people with psychological problems and disorders been treated throughout the ages?* Because of this belief, treatment tended to involve cruel practices such as exorcism and execution. Some people who could not meet the demands of everyday life were tossed into prisons. Others begged in the streets, stole food, or became prostitutes. A few found their way to monasteries or other retreats that offered a kind word and some support. Generally speaking, they died early.

Asylums

Asylums originated in European monasteries. They were the first institutions meant primarily for people with psychological disorders. But their function was warehousing, not treatment. Their inmate populations mushroomed until the stresses created by noise, overcrowding, and disease aggravated the problems they were meant to ease. Inmates were frequently chained and beaten.

The word *bedlam* derives from St. Mary's of *Bethlehem*, the London asylum that opened its gates in 1547. Here unfortunate people with psychological disorders were chained, whipped, and allowed to lie in their own waste.

Humanitarian reform movements began in the 18th century. In Paris, the physician Philippe Pinel unchained the patients at La Salpêtrière. Rather than run amok, as had been feared, most patients profited from kindness and freedom. Many eventually reentered society. Later movements to reform institutions were led by William Tuke in England and Dorothea Dix in America.

Truth

The ladies and gentlemen of the British upper class might stroll by on a lazy afternoon to be amused by asylum inmates' antics. The price of admission was one penny.

Mental Hospitals

In the United States mental hospitals gradually replaced asylums. In the mid-1950s more than a million people resided in state, county, Veterans Administration, or private facilities. The mental hospital's function is treatment, not warehousing.

Still, because of high patient populations and understaffing, many patients received little attention. Even today, with somewhat improved conditions, one psychiatrist may be responsible for the welfare of several hundred residents on the weekend when other staff are absent.

The Community Mental Health Movement

Since the 1960s, efforts have been made to maintain people with serious psychological disorders in their communities. Community mental health centers attempt to maintain new patients as outpatients and to serve patients who have been released from mental hospitals. Today most people with chronic psychological disorders live in the community, not in the hospital. Social critics note that many people who had resided in hospitals for decades were suddenly discharged to "home" communities that seemed foreign and forbidding to them. Many do not receive adequate follow-up care. Many join the ranks of the homeless.

LO² Psychoanalytic Therapies

Psychoanalytic therapies are based on the thinking of Sigmund Freud, the founder of psychoanalytic theory. These therapies assume that psychological problems reflect early childhood experiences and internal conflicts. According to Freud, these conflicts involve the shifting of psychic energy among the id, ego, and superego. These shifts of psychic energy determine our behavior. When primitive urges threaten to break through from the id or when the superego floods us with excessive guilt, defenses are established and distress is created. Freud's therapy method—psychoanalysis—aims to bulwark the ego against the torrents of energy loosed by the id and the superego. With impulses and feelings of guilt and shame placed under greater control, clients are freer to develop adaptive behavior.

How do psychoanalysts conduct a traditional Freudian psychoanalysis?

Traditional Psychoanalysis

Imagine your therapist asking you to lie on a couch in a slightly darkened room. She or he would sit behind you and encourage you to talk about anything that comes to mind, no matter how trivial, no matter how personal. To avoid interfering with your self-exploration, she or he might say little or nothing for session after session. That would be par for the course. A traditional **psychoanalysis** can extend for months, even years.

Psychoanalysis is the clinical method devised by Sigmund Freud. It aims to provide *insight* into the conflicts that are presumed to lie at the roots of a person's problems. Insight means many things, including knowledge of the experiences that lead to conflicts and maladaptive behavior, recognition of unconscious feelings and conflicts, and conscious evaluation of one's thoughts, feelings, and behavior.

Psychoanalysis also aims to help the client express feelings and urges that have been repressed.

psychoanalysis
Freud's method of psychotherapy; (also the name of Freud's theory of personality)

ROBERT-FLEURY, TONY (1837-1912) (AFTER) / BIBLIOTHEQUE DES ARTS DECORATIFS, PARIS, FRANCE / ARCHIVES CHARMET / THE BRIDGEMAN ART LIBRARY INTERNATIONAL

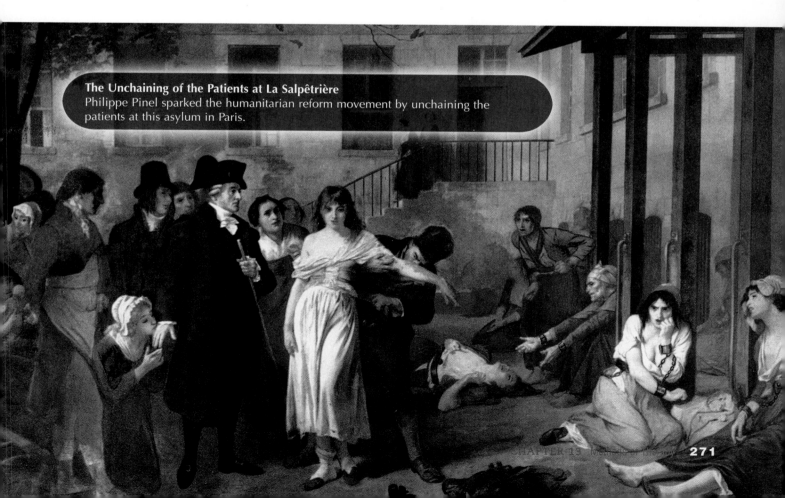

The Unchaining of the Patients at La Salpêtrière
Philippe Pinel sparked the humanitarian reform movement by unchaining the patients at this asylum in Paris.

catharsis
release of emotional tension, as after a traumatic experience, that has the effect of restoring one's psychological well-being

free association
in psychoanalysis, the uncensored uttering of all thoughts that come to mind

resistance
the tendency to block the free expression of impulses and primitive ideas—a reflection of the defense mechanism of repression

transference
responding to one person (such as a spouse or the psychoanalyst) in a way that is similar to the way one responded to another person (such as a parent) in childhood

wish fulfillment
a primitive method used by the id to attempt to gratify basic instincts

A View of Freud's Consulting Room
Freud would sit in a chair by the head of the couch while a client free-associated. The basic rule of free association is that no thought is censored. Freud did not believe that free association was really "free"; he assumed that significant feelings would rise to the surface and demand expression.

FREUD MUSEUM, LONDON

By so doing, Freud believed that the client spilled forth the psychic energy that had been repressed by conflicts and guilt. He called this "spilling forth" catharsis. Catharsis would provide relief by alleviating some of the forces assaulting the ego. Freud also sought to replace impulsive and defensive behavior with coping behavior. In this way, for example, a man with a phobia for knives might discover that he had been repressing the urge to harm someone who had taken advantage of him. He might also find ways to confront the person verbally.

Early in his career as a therapist, Freud found that hypnosis allowed his clients to focus on repressed conflicts and talk about them. He also found, however, that some clients denied the accuracy of this material once they were out of the trance. Others found the memories to be brought out into the open prematurely and painfully. Freud therefore turned to free association, a more gradual method of breaking through the walls of defense that block a client's insight into unconscious processes. In free association, the client is made comfortable—for example, by lying on a couch—and asked to talk about any topic that comes to mind. No thought is to be censored—that is the basic rule. Psychoanalysts ask their clients to wander "freely" from topic to topic, but they do not believe that the process occurring *within* the client is fully free. Repressed impulses clamor for release.

The ego persists in trying to repress unacceptable impulses and threatening conflicts. As a result, clients might show resistance to recalling and discussing threatening ideas. The therapist observes the dynamic struggle between the compulsion to talk about disturbing ideas and resistance. Through discreet comments and questions, the analyst hopes to encourage the client to discuss his or her problems. Talking helps the client gain insight into his or her true wishes and explore ways of fulfilling them.

Transference

Freud believed that clients not only responded to him as an individual but also in ways that reflected their attitudes and feelings toward other people in their lives. He labeled this process transference. For example, a young woman client might respond to him as a father figure and displace her feelings toward her father onto Freud, perhaps seeking affection and wisdom.

> Analyzing and working through transference has been considered a key aspect of psychoanalysis.

Analyzing and working through transference has been considered a key aspect of psychoanalysis. Freud believed that clients reenact their childhood conflicts with their parents when they are in therapy.

Dream Analysis

Freud often asked clients to jot down their dreams upon waking so they could discuss them in therapy. Freud considered dreams the "royal road to the unconscious." He believed that the content of dreams is determined by unconscious processes as well as by the events of the day. Unconscious impulses were expressed in dreams as wish fulfillment.

Short-Term Dynamic Therapies

How do modern psychoanalytic approaches differ from traditional psychoanalysis? Although some psychoanalysts still adhere to Freud's techniques, shorter-term dynamic therapies have been devised. Modern psychoanalytic therapy is briefer and less intense and makes treatment available to clients who do not have the time or money to make therapy part of their lifestyle.

Some modern psychoanalysts continue to focus on revealing unconscious material and breaking through psychological defenses. Nevertheless, they differ from traditional psychoanalysis in several ways (Prochaska & Norcross, 2007). One is that the client and therapist usually sit face to face (i.e., the client does not lie on a couch). The therapist may be directive. That is, modern therapists often suggest helpful behavior instead of focusing on insight alone. Finally, there is more focus on the ego as the "executive" of personality and less emphasis on the id. For this reason, many modern psychoanalysts are called ego analysts.

Interpersonal Psychotherapy

One contemporary dynamic therapy, interpersonal psychotherapy (ITP), focuses on clients' current relationships rather than their childhoods and usually lasts no longer than 9 to 12 months. Developers of ITP view problems such as anxiety and depression as often occurring within social relationships. They therefore focus on clients' relationships and also try to directly alleviate feelings of anxiety and depression (de Mello et al., 2005; Kirschenbaum & Jourdan, 2005).

LO³ Humanistic Therapies

Psychoanalytic therapies focus on internal conflicts and unconscious processes. Humanistic therapies focus on the quality of the client's subjective, conscious experience. Traditional psychoanalysis focuses on early childhood experiences. Humanistic therapies are more likely to focus on what clients are experiencing here and now.

Carl Rogers believed that our psychological well-being is connected with our freedom to develop our unique frames of reference and potentials. Do you think you can separate your "real self" from your sociocultural experiences and religious training?

Client-Centered Therapy

What is Carl Rogers's method of client-centered therapy? Rogers believed that we are free to make choices and control our destinies, despite the burdens of the past. He also believed that we have natural tendencies toward health, growth, and fulfillment. Psychological problems arise from roadblocks placed in the path of self-actualization—that is, what Rogers believed was an inborn tendency to strive to realize one's potential. If, when we are young, other people approve of us only when we are doing what they want us to do, we may learn to disown the parts of ourselves to which they object. We may learn to be seen but not heard—not even by ourselves. As a result, we may experience stress and discomfort and the feeling that we—or the world—are not real.

Client-centered therapy aims to provide insight into the parts of us that we have disowned so that we can feel whole. It creates a warm, therapeutic atmosphere that encourages self-exploration and self-expression. The therapist's acceptance of the client is thought to foster self-acceptance and self-esteem. Self-acceptance frees the client to make choices that develop his or her unique potential.

Client-centered therapy is nondirective. An effective client-centered therapist has several qualities:

1 *Unconditional positive regard:* respect for clients as human beings with unique values and goals.

2 *Empathy:* recognition of the client's experiences and feelings. Therapists view the world through the client's *frame of reference* by setting aside their own values and listening closely.

3 *Genuineness:* Openness and honesty in responding to the client. Client-centered therapists must be able to tolerate differentness because they believe that every client is different in important ways.

The following excerpt from a therapy session shows how Carl Rogers uses empathetic understanding and paraphrases a client's (Jill's) feelings. His goal is to help her recognize feelings that she has partially disowned:

Jill: I'm having a lot of problems dealing with my daughter. She's twenty years old; she's in

Glossary

ego analyst
a psychoanalyst therapist who focuses on the conscious, coping behavior of the ego instead of the hypothesized, unconscious functioning of the id

interpersonal psychotherapy (ITP)
a short-term dynamic therapy that focuses on clients' relationships and direct alleviation of negative emotions such as anxiety and depression

client-centered therapy
Carl Rogers's method of psychotherapy, which emphasizes the creation of a warm, therapeutic atmosphere that frees clients to engage in self-exploration and self-expression

Truth

It is true that in client-centered therapy, the client takes the lead, stating and exploring problems.

college; I'm having a lot of trouble letting her go.... And I have a lot of guilt feelings about her; I have a real need to hang on to her.

C. R.: A need to hang on so you can kind of make up for the things you feel guilty about. Is that part of it?

Jill: There's a lot of that.... Also, she's been a real friend to me, and filled my life. . . . And it's very hard. . . . a lot of empty places now that she's not with me.

C. R.: The old vacuum, sort of, when she's not there.

Jill: Yes. Yes. I also would like to be the kind of mother that could be strong and say, you know, "Go and have a good life," and this is really hard for me, to do that.

C. R.: It's very hard to give up something that's been so precious in your life, but also something that I guess has caused you pain when you mentioned guilt.

Jill: Yeah. And I'm aware that I have some anger toward her that I don't always get what I want. I have needs that are not met. And, uh, I don't feel I have a right to those needs. You know . . . she's a daughter; she's not my mother. Though sometimes I feel as if I'd like her to mother me . . . it's very difficult for me to ask for that and have a right to it.

C. R.: So, it may be unreasonable, but still, when she doesn't meet your needs, it makes you mad.

Jill: Yeah, I get very angry, very angry with her.

C. R.: (*Pauses*) You're also feeling a little tension at this point, I guess.

Jill: Yeah. Yeah. A lot of conflict.... (C. R.: M-hm.) A lot of pain.

C. R.: A lot of pain. Can you say anything more about what that's about? (Farber et al., 1996, pp. 74–75)

Client-centered therapy is practiced widely in college and university counseling centers, not just to help students experiencing, say, anxieties or depression but also to help them make decisions. Many

By showing the qualities of unconditional positive regard, empathic understanding, and genuineness, client-centered therapists create an atmosphere in which clients can explore their feelings.

college students have not yet made career choices, or wonder whether they should become involved with particular people or in sexual activity. Client-centered therapists do not tell clients what to do. Instead, they help clients arrive at their own decisions.

Gestalt Therapy

Gestalt therapy was originated by Fritz Perls (1893–1970). *What is Fritz Perls's method of Gestalt therapy?* Like client-centered therapy, Gestalt therapy assumes that people disown parts of themselves that might meet with social disapproval or rejection. People also don social masks, pretending to be things that they are not. Therapy aims to help individuals integrate conflicting parts of their personality. Perls used the term *Gestalt* to signify his. The German word *Gestalt* means "unified whole." Perls adopted the term because he wanted to help clients integrate conflicting parts of their personalities.

Although Perls's ideas about conflicting personality elements owe much to psychoanalytic theory, his form of therapy, unlike psychoanalysis, focuses on the here and now. Exercises heighten clients' awareness of their current feelings and behavior. Perls also believed, along with Rogers, that people are free to make choices and to direct their personal growth. But the charismatic and forceful Perls was unlike the gentle and accepting Rogers in temperament (Prochaska & Norcross, 2007). Thus, unlike client-centered therapy, Gestalt therapy is directive. The therapist leads the client through planned experiences.

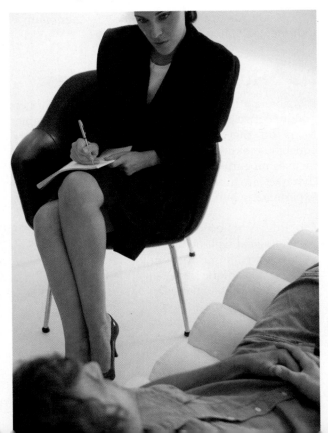

© ANGELO CAVALLI/CORBIS

LO⁴ Behavior Therapy

Psychoanalytic and humanistic forms of therapy tend to focus on what people think and feel. Behavior therapists tend to focus on what people *do*. *What is behavior therapy?* Behavior therapy—also called *behavior modification*—applies principles of learning to directly promote desired behavioral changes. Behavior therapists rely heavily on principles of conditioning and observational learning. They help clients discontinue self-defeating behavior patterns such as overeating, smoking, and phobic avoidance of harmless stimuli. They help clients acquire adaptive behavior patterns such as the social skills required to start social relationships or say no to insistent salespeople.

Behavior therapists may help clients gain "insight" into maladaptive behaviors such as feelings of anxiety by helping the person become aware of the circumstances in which the behaviors occur. They do not help unearth the childhood origins of problems and the symbolic meanings of maladaptive behaviors as psychoanalysts do. Behavior therapists, like other therapists, may also build warm, therapeutic relationships with clients, but they see the effectiveness of behavior therapy as deriving from specific, learning-based procedures (Rachman, 2000). They insist that their methods be established by experimentation and that results be assessed in terms of measurable behavior. In this section we consider some frequently used behavior-therapy techniques.

> **Truth**
>
> Gestalt therapists and behavior therapists may use specific procedures—telling their clients what to do.

Fear-Reduction Methods

Many people seek therapy because of fears and phobias that interfere with their functioning. This is one of the areas in which behavior therapy has made great inroads. *What are some behavior-therapy methods for reducing fears?* These include flooding (see Chapter 6), systematic desensitization, virtual therapy, and modeling.

Systematic Desensitization

Adam has a phobia for receiving injections. His behavior therapist treats him as he reclines in a comfortable padded chair. In a state of deep muscle relaxation, Adam observes slides projected on a screen. A slide of a nurse holding a needle has just been shown three times, thirty seconds at a time. Each time

Adam has shown no anxiety. So now a slightly more discomforting slide is shown: one of the nurse aiming the needle toward someone's bare arm. After fifteen seconds, our armchair adventurer notices twinges of discomfort and raises a finger as a signal (speaking might disturb his relaxation). The projector operator turns off the light, and Adam spends 2 minutes imagining his "safe scene"— lying on a beach beneath the tropical sun. Then the slide is shown again. This time Adam views it for thirty seconds before feeling anxiety.

Adam is undergoing systematic desensitization, a method for reducing phobic responses originated by psychiatrist Joseph Wolpe (1915–1997). Systematic desensitization is a gradual process in which the client learns to handle increasingly disturbing stimuli while anxiety to each one is being counter-conditioned. About ten to twenty stimuli such as slides are arranged in a sequence, or hierarchy, according to their "fear factor"—their capacity to trigger anxiety. In imagination or by being shown photos, the client travels gradually up through this hierarchy, approaching the target behavior. In Adam's case, the target behavior was the ability to receive an injection without undue anxiety.

behavior therapy systematic application of the principles of learning to the direct modification of a client's problem behaviors

systematic desensitization Wolpe's method for reducing fears by associating a hierarchy of images of fear-evoking stimuli with deep muscle relaxation

hierarchy an arrangement of stimuli according to the amount of fear they evoke

> **Truth**
>
> Using systematic desensitization, Adam is in effect confronting his fear while lying in a recliner and relaxing.

Virtual Therapy

Virtual therapy may use more elaborate equipment than slides, but the principle is desensitization. New York Fire Chief Stephen King was in the north tower at the World Trade Center on September 11, 2001, which was hit first by the airplanes. The experience led him to retire from the department, avoid bridges and tunnels, and stay out of Manhattan (King, 2005). "Where I was and what I saw that day—the many people that jumped, the magnitude of it—was just overwhelming."

But virtual therapy has helped King face the past—and his future. Using the technology we find in video games, programs mimic traumatic settings and events—public speaking in an auditorium, flying in an airplane, spiders, or, in King's case, images of the World Trade Center. "The idea behind the treatment,"

modeling
a behavior-therapy technique in which a client observes and imitates a person who approaches and copes with feared objects or situations

Figure 13.1

A Program Containing Images of the World Trade Center Intended to Help People with Post-Traumatic Stress Disorder

Virtual therapy clients are exposed to virtual stimuli that represent their source of anxiety and stress to help them gradually confront their fears.

explains Dr. JoAnn Difede (2005), "is to systematically expose the patient to aspects of their experience in a graded fashion so they can confront their fear of the trauma" (see Figure 13.1). Psychologist Albert Rizzo has developed scenes from classrooms and parties to help people overcome social anxieties. "To help people deal with their problems, you must get them exposed to what they fear most," Rizzo (2004) notes.

Atlanta-based company Virtually Better focuses on creating virtual environments that therapists can use to treat phobias, substance abuse, and post-traumatic stress disorder (Virtually Better, 2010). Virtually Better has developed scenes of a bridge and a glass elevator to desensitize patients to fear of heights, a virtual airplane cabin for people who fear flying, and a virtual thunderstorm to help people lessen fear of tempestuous weather. "Virtual Iraq" is available to help therapists teach veterans how to cope with the stresses of wartime Iraq. Virtual exposure to alcohol, drugs, and cigarettes can evoke cravings that patients can learn to resist. Virtually Better's contributions include scenes of a virtual crack house and a virtual bar.

Psychologist Hunter Hoffman (2004) describes a virtual environment, *SpiderWorld*, that helps people with spider phobias overcome their aversion by gradually approaching virtual spiders and reaching out to touch them. A toy spider and a device that tracks the patient's hand movements provide tactile sensations akin to touching a real spider (see Figure 13.2).

Modeling

Modeling relies on observational learning. In this method clients observe and then imitate people who approach and cope with the objects or situations that the clients fear. Bandura and his colleagues (1969) found that modeling worked as well as systematic desensitization—and more rapidly—in reducing fear of snakes. Clients observed models handling snakes. In the same session, they were able to touch the snakes, pick them up, and let them crawl on their bodies. Like systematic desensitization, modeling is likely to increase self-efficacy expectations in coping with feared stimuli.

Aversive Conditioning

Many people also seek behavior therapy because they want to break bad habits, such as smoking, excessive drinking, nail-biting, and the like. One

Figure 13.2

Dr. Hunter Hoffman of the University of Washington Uses Virtual Therapy to Treat "Miss Muffet"

Miss Muffet is the name playfully given by Hoffman to a woman with a phobia for spiders. She is wearing virtual-reality headgear and sees the scene displayed on the monitor, which shows a large and hairy—but virtual—tarantula.

behavior-therapy approach to helping people do so is **aversive conditioning**. *How do behavior therapists use aversive conditioning to help people break bad habits?* Aversive conditioning is a controversial procedure in which painful or aversive stimuli are paired with unwanted impulses, such as desire for a cigarette or desire to engage in antisocial behavior, in an effort to make the impulse less appealing. For example, to help people control alcohol intake, tastes of different alcoholic beverages can be paired with drug-induced nausea and vomiting or with electric shock.

Aversive conditioning has been used with problems as diverse as cigarette smoking, sexual abuse, and retarded children's self-injurious behavior. Rapid smoking is an aversive conditioning method designed to help smokers quit. In this method, the

{ Eye-Movement Desensitization and Reprocessing }

Helping professionals are often inspired to develop therapy methods based on their personal experiences. Such was the case with Francine Shapiro. As she paints it, Shapiro (1989) had troubling thoughts on her mind when she strolled into a park one day. But as her eyes darted about, taking in the scene, she found her troubled thoughts disappearing. Thus she developed a therapy method called **eye-movement desensitization and reprocessing (EMDR)**, which has joined the arsenal of therapeutic weapons against stress disorders. In this method, the client is asked to imagine a traumatic scene while the therapist moves a finger rapidly back and forth before his or her eyes for about twenty to thirty seconds. The client follows the finger while keeping the troubling scene in mind. Evidence from a number of studies suggests that EMDR helps decrease the anxiety associated with traumatic events.

Devilly (2002) allows that EMDR is often effective, but his review finds other exposure therapies to be more effective. Research even challenges the idea that eye movements are a necessary part of therapy (May, 2005; Devilly, 2002). Skeptics have tried EMDR—or a cousin of it—using finger tapping rather than finger wagging, or instructing clients to keep their eyes straight ahead, and the results have remained the same.

Clients receiving EMDR may profit from a "therapeutic alliance" with the helping professional and from expectations of success. Moreover, the client *is* to some degree being exposed to the trauma that haunts him or her, and under circumstances in which the client believes he or she will be able to manage the trauma.

Conclusion? Exposure helps people cope with trauma. Eye movements may not be needed.

would-be quitter inhales every six seconds. In another method the hose of a hair dryer is hooked up to a chamber containing several lit cigarettes. Smoke is blown into the quitter's face as he or she also smokes a cigarette. A third method uses branching pipes so that the smoker draws in smoke from several cigarettes at the same time. In these methods, overexposure makes once-desirable cigarette smoke aversive. The quitter becomes motivated to avoid, rather than seek, cigarettes. Interest in aversive conditioning for quitting smoking has waned, however, because of side effects such as raising blood pressure and the availability of nicotine-replacement techniques.

Operant Conditioning Procedures

We tend to repeat behavior that is reinforced. Behavior that is not reinforced tends to become extinguished. Behavior therapists have used these principles of operant conditioning with psychotic patients as well as with clients with milder problems. *How do behavior therapists apply principles of operant conditioning in behavior modification?*

The staff at one mental hospital was at a loss about how to encourage withdrawn schizophrenic patients to eat regularly. Ayllon and Haughton (1962) observed that staff members were making the problem worse by coaxing patients into the dining room and even feeding them. Staff attention apparently reinforced the patients' lack of cooperation. Some rules were changed. Patients who did not arrive at the dining hall within thirty minutes after serving were locked out. Staff could not interact with patients at mealtime. With uncooperative behavior no longer reinforced, patients quickly changed their eating habits. Then patients were required to pay one penny

aversive conditioning
a behavior therapy technique in which undesired responses are inhibited by pairing repugnant or offensive stimuli with them

rapid smoking
an aversive conditioning method for quitting smoking in which the smoker inhales rapidly, thus rendering once-desirable cigarette smoke aversive

eye-movement desensitization and reprocessing (EMDR)
a method of treating stress disorders by having clients visually follow a rapidly oscillating finger while they think of the traumatic events connected with the disorders

Truth

In the method of rapid smoking, behavior therapists use smoking as a way of making cigarette smoke unappealing to smokers, helping them to stop smoking.

to enter the dining hall. Pennies were earned by interacting with other patients and showing other socially appropriate behaviors. These target behaviors also became more frequent.

Health professionals are concerned about whether people who are, or have been, dependent on alcohol can exercise control over their drinking. One study showed that rewards for remaining abstinent from alcohol can exert a powerful effect (Petry et al., 2000). In the study, one group of alcohol-dependent veterans was given a standard treatment while another group received the treatment *plus* the chance to win prizes for remaining alcohol-free, as measured by a Breathalyzer test. By the end of the eight-week treatment period, 84% of the veterans who could win prizes remained in the program, as compared with 22% of the standard treatment group. The prizes had an average value of $200, far less than what alcohol-related absenteeism from work and other responsibilities can cost.

The Token Economy

Many psychiatric wards and hospitals use token economies in which patients need tokens such as poker chips to purchase TV viewing time, extra visits to the canteen, or a private room (Comaty et al., 2001). The tokens are dispensed as reinforcers for productive activities such as making beds, brushing teeth, and socializing. Token economies have not eliminated all symptoms of schizophrenia but have increased patients' activity and cooperation. Tokens have also been used to modify the behavior of children with conduct disorders.

Successive Approximations

The operant conditioning method of successive approximations is often used to help clients build good habits. For example: You want to study three hours each evening but can concentrate for only half an hour. Rather than attempting to increase your study time all at once, you could do so gradually by adding, say, five minutes each evening. After every

hour or so of studying, you could reinforce yourself with five minutes of people-watching in a busy section of the library.

Biofeedback Training

Through biofeedback training (BFT), therapists help clients become more aware of, and gain control over, various bodily functions. Therapists attach clients to devices that measure bodily functions such as heart rate. "Bleeps" or other electronic signals are used to indicate (and thereby reinforce) changes ("operants") in the desired direction—for example, a slower heart rate. (Knowledge of results is a powerful reinforcer.) One device, the electromyograph (EMG), monitors muscle tension. It has been used to increase control over muscle tension in the forehead and elsewhere, thereby alleviating anxiety, stress, and headaches (Nestoriuc et al., 2008).

BFT also helps clients voluntarily regulate functions once thought to be beyond conscious control, such as heart rate and blood pressure. Hypertensive clients use a blood-pressure cuff and electronic signals to gain control over their blood pressure. The electroencephalograph (EEG) monitors brain waves and can be used to teach people how to produce alpha waves, which are associated with relaxation. Some people have overcome insomnia by learning to produce the kinds of brain waves associated with sleep.

Social Skills Training

In social skills training, behavior therapists decrease social anxiety and build social skills through operant-conditioning procedures that employ self-monitoring, coaching, modeling, role-playing, behavior rehearsal, and feedback. Social skills training has been used to help formerly hospitalized mental patients maintain jobs and apartments in the community.

For example, a worker can rehearse politely asking a supervisor for assistance or asking a landlord to fix the plumbing in an apartment. Social skills training is effective in groups. Group members can role-play important people—such as parents, spouses, or potential dates—in the lives of other members.

LO⁵ Cognitive Therapies

What thoughts do you have when things go wrong at school or on the job? Do you tell yourself that you're facing a problem that needs a solution? That you've successfully solved problems before and will be able to create a solution this time? Or do you think, "Oh no! This is awful! It's going to get worse, and I'm going to flunk (or get fired)!" If you go the "This is awful" route, you are probably heightening your discomfort and impairing your coping ability. Cognitive therapy focuses directly on your thoughts and encourages ideas that will help you solve problems rather than blow them out of proportion and magnify your discomfort.

What is cognitive therapy? **Cognitive therapy** focuses on changing the beliefs, attitudes, and automatic types of thinking that create and compound people's problems. Cognitive therapists, like psychoanalytic and humanistic therapists, aim to foster self-insight, but they mainly aim to help make people more aware of their *current cognitions*. Cognitive therapists also aim to directly change maladaptive thoughts in an effort to reduce negative feelings and help clients solve problems.

Many behavior therapists incorporate cognitive procedures in their methods. For example, techniques such as systematic desensitization, covert sensitization, and covert reinforcement ask clients to focus on visual imagery. Behavioral methods for treating bulimia nervosa focus on clients' irrational attitudes toward their weight and body shape as well as foster good eating habits. Let us look at the approaches and methods of the cognitive therapists Aaron Beck and Albert Ellis.

Aaron Beck's Cognitive Therapy

Psychiatrist Aaron Beck began his professional life as a psychoanalyst. He became impatient, however, with analysis's lengthy methods and reluctance to offer specific advice. In his own life he had successfully defeated his fear of blood by assisting in surgical operations and argued himself out of irrational fear of driving through tunnels. Similarly, his methods of cognitive therapy focus on arguing clients out of beliefs that are making them miserable and exposing them to situations they avoid because of irrational fear (Berk et al.,

2004; Warman et al., 2005). *What is Aaron Beck's method of cognitive therapy?* Beck encourages clients to become their own personal scientists and challenge feelings and beliefs that make no sense.

Beck encourages clients to see the irrationality of their ways of thinking. For example, depressed people tend to minimize their accomplishments and to assume that the worst will happen. Minimizing accomplishments and expecting the worst are (usually) distortions of reality that lead to feelings of depression. Cognitive distortions can be fleeting and automatic, difficult to detect. Beck's methods help clients become aware of such distortions and challenge them.

Beck notes a number of "cognitive errors" that contribute to clients' miseries:

1 Clients may *selectively perceive* the world as a harmful place and ignore evidence to the contrary.

2 Clients may *overgeneralize* on the basis of a few examples. For example, they may perceive themselves as worthless because they were laid off at work or as unattractive because they were refused a date.

3 Clients may *magnify*, or blow out of proportion, the importance of negative events. They may catastrophize failing a test by assuming they will flunk out of college or catastrophize losing a job by believing that they will never find another one and that serious harm will befall their family as a result.

4 Clients may engage in *absolutist thinking*, or looking at the world in black and white rather than in shades of gray. In doing so, a rejection on a date takes on the meaning of a lifetime of loneliness; an uncomfortable illness takes on life-threatening proportions.

Becoming aware of cognitive errors and modifying catastrophizing thoughts help us cope with stress. Internal, stable, and global attributions of failure lead to depression and feelings of helplessness. Cognitive therapists also alert clients to cognitive errors or irrational thoughts so that the clients can change their attitudes and pave the way for more effective overt behavior.

cognitive therapy a form of therapy that focuses on how clients' cognitions (e.g., expectations, attitudes, beliefs) lead to distress and may be modified to relieve distress and promote adaptive behavior

Aaron Beck (left) and Albert Ellis (right)

Rational Emotive Behavior Therapy

What is Albert Ellis's method of rational emotive behavior therapy (REBT)? In rational emotive behavior therapy (REBT), Albert Ellis (1913–2007) pointed out that our beliefs *about* events, not only the events themselves, shape our responses to them. Moreover, many of us harbor a number of irrational beliefs that can give rise to problems or magnify their impact. Two of the most important ones are the belief that we must have the love and approval of people who are important to us and the belief that we must prove ourselves to be thoroughly competent, adequate, and achieving.

Albert Ellis, like Aaron Beck, began his career as a psychoanalyst. And, also like Beck, he became disturbed by the passive role of the analyst and by the slow rate of obtaining results—if they were obtained at all. Ellis's REBT methods are active and directive. He did not sit back like the traditional psychoanalyst and occasionally offer an interpretation. Instead, he urged clients to seek out their irrational beliefs, which can be unconscious, though not as deeply buried as Freud believed. Nevertheless, they can be hard to pinpoint without some direction. Ellis showed clients how those beliefs lead to misery and challenged clients to change them. When Ellis saw clients behaving according to irrational beliefs, he refuted the beliefs by asking "Where is it written that you must . . . ?" or "What evidence do you have that . . . ?" According to Ellis, we need less misery and less blaming in our lives, and more action.

Toward a Cognitive-Behavioral Therapy

Many theorists consider cognitive therapy to be a collection of techniques that are a part of behavior therapy. Aaron Beck himself appears to be comfortable referring to his approach as *cognitive* in one article and *cognitive-behavioral* in another (Berk et al., 2005; Warman & Beck, 2003). We are apparently headed toward an integration of the two approaches that is termed cognitive-behavioral therapy (CBT).

Ellis straddled behavioral and cognitive therapies. He originally dubbed his method of therapy *rational-emotive therapy,* because his focus was on the cognitive—irrational beliefs and how to change them. However, Ellis also always promoted behavioral changes to cement cognitive changes. In keeping with his broad philosophy, he recently changed the name of rational-emotive therapy to rational-emotive *behavior* therapy.

LO⁶ Group Therapies

When a psychotherapist has several clients with similar problems—anxiety, depression, adjustment to divorce, lack of social skills—it often makes sense to treat them in a group rather than in individual sessions. The methods and characteristics of the group reflect the needs of the members and the theoretical orientation of the leader. In group psychoanalysis, clients might interpret one another's dreams. In a client-centered group, they might provide an accepting atmosphere for self-exploration. Members of behavior therapy groups might be jointly desensitized to anxiety-evoking stimuli or might practice social skills together. *What are the advantages and disadvantages of group therapy?*

Group therapy has the following advantages:

1 It is economical. It allows the therapist to work with several clients at once.

2 Compared with one-to-one therapy, group therapy provides more information and life experience for clients to draw on.

3 Appropriate behavior receives group support. Clients usually appreciate an outpouring of peer approval.

4 When we run into troubles, it is easy to imagine that we are different from other people or inferior to them. Affiliating with people with similar problems is reassuring.

5 Group members who show improvement provide hope for other members.

6 Many individuals seek therapy because of problems in relating to other people. People who seek therapy for other reasons also may be socially inhibited. Members of groups have the opportunity to practice social skills in a relatively nonthreatening atmosphere. In a group consisting of men and women of different ages, group members can role-play one another's employers, employees, spouses, parents, children, and friends. Members can role-play asking one another out on dates, saying no (or yes), and so on.

But group therapy is not for everyone. Some clients fare better with individual treatment. Many prefer not to disclose their problems to a group. They may be overly shy or want individual attention. It is the responsibility of the therapist to insist that group disclosures be kept confidential, to establish a supportive atmosphere, and to ensure that group members obtain the attention they need.

Many types of therapy can be conducted either individually or in groups. Couple therapy and family therapy are conducted only with groups.

Couple Therapy

Couple therapy helps couples enhance their relationship by improving their communication skills and helping them manage conflict (Prochaska & Norcross, 2007). There are often power imbalances in relationships, and couple therapy helps individuals find "full membership" in the couple. Correcting power imbalances increases happiness and can decrease the incidence of domestic violence. Ironically, in situations of domestic violence, the partner with *less* power in the relationship is usually the violent one. Violence sometimes appears to be a way of compensating for inability to share power in other aspects of the relationship (Rathus & Sanderson, 1999).

Today the main approach to couple therapy is cognitive-behavioral (Rathus & Sanderson, 1999). It teaches couples communications skills (such as how to listen and how to express feelings), ways of handling feelings like depression and anger, and ways of solving problems.

Family Therapy

What is family therapy? Family therapy is a form of group therapy in which one or more families constitute the group. Family therapy may be undertaken from various theoretical viewpoints. One is the systems approach, in which family interaction is studied and modified to enhance the growth of individual family members and of the family unit as a whole (Prochaska & Norcross, 2007).

Family members with low self-esteem often cannot tolerate different attitudes and behaviors in other family members. Faulty communication within the family also creates problems. In addition, it is not uncommon for the family to present an "identified patient"—that is, the family member who has *the* problem and is *causing* all the trouble. Yet family therapists usually assume that the identified patient is a scapegoat for other problems within and among family members. It is a sort of myth: Change

the "bad apple," or identified patient, and the "barrel," or family, will be functional once more. The family therapist—often a specialist in this field—attempts to teach the family to communicate more effectively and encourage growth and autonomy in each family member.

LO⁷ Does Psychotherapy Work?

In 1952, the British psychologist Hans Eysenck published a review of psychotherapy research—"The Effects of Psychotherapy"—that sent shock waves through the psychotherapy community. On the basis of his review of the research, Eysenck concluded that the rate of improvement among people in psychotherapy was no greater than the rate of "spontaneous remission"—that is, the rate of improvement that would be shown by people with psychological disorders who received no treatment at all. Eysenck was not addressing people with schizophrenia, who typically profit from biological forms of therapy, but he argued that whether or not people with problems such as anxiety and depression received therapy, two of three reported substantial improvement within two years.

That was half a century ago. There is now quite a bit of research evidence—with many studies employing a sophisticated statistical averaging method called meta-analysis—that show that psychotherapy is effective (Luborsky et al., 2002; Shadish et al., 2000). *What, then, has research shown about the effectiveness of psychotherapy?*

> **Fiction**
>
> Actually, there is now quite a bit of research evidence that shows that psychotherapy is effective.

It is a sort of myth: Change the "bad apple," or identified patient, and the "barrel," or family, will be functional once more.

In their classic early use of meta-analysis, Mary Lee Smith and Gene Glass (1977) analyzed the results of dozens of outcome studies of various types of therapies. They concluded that people who obtained psychoanalytic therapy showed greater well-being, on the average, than 70% to 75% of those who did not obtain treatment. Similarly, nearly 75% of the clients who obtained client-centered therapy were better off than people who did not obtain treatment. Psychoanalytic and client-centered therapies appear to be most effective with well-educated, verbal, strongly motivated clients who report problems with anxiety, depression (of light to moderate proportions), and interpersonal relationships. Neither form of therapy appears to be effective with people with psychotic disorders such as major depression, bipolar disorder, and schizophrenia. Smith and Glass (1977) found that people who obtained Gestalt therapy showed greater well-being than about 60% of those who did not obtain treatment. The effectiveness of psychoanalysis and client-centered therapy thus was reasonably comparable. Gestalt therapy fell behind.

Smith and Glass (1977) did not include cognitive therapies in their meta-analysis because at the time of their study many cognitive approaches were relatively new. Because behavior therapists also incorporate many cognitive techniques, it can be difficult to sort out which aspects—cognitive or otherwise—of behavioral treatments are most effective. Many meta-analyses of cognitive–behavioral therapy have been conducted since the early work of Smith and Glass, however. Their results are encouraging (e.g., DeRubeis et al., 2005; Hollon et al., 2005). A meta-analysis of ninety studies by William R. Shadish and his colleagues (2000) concurred that psychotherapy is generally effective. Generally speaking, the more therapy, the better; that is, people who have more psychotherapy tend to fare better than people who have less of it. Therapy also appears to be more effective when the outcome measures reflect the treatment (e.g., when the effects of treatment aimed at fear-reduction are measured in terms of people's ability to approach fear-inducing objects and situations).

Studies of cognitive therapy have shown that modifying irrational beliefs of the type described by Albert Ellis helps people with problems such as anxiety and depression (Engels et al., 1993; Haaga & Davison, 1993). Modifying self-defeating beliefs of the sort outlined by Aaron Beck also frequently alleviates anxiety and depression (Butler & Beck, 2001). Cognitive therapy has also helped people with personality disorders (Beck et al., 2001; Trull et al., 2003).

Behavioral and cognitive therapies have provided strategies for treating anxiety disorders, social-skills deficits, and problems in self-control. These therapies—which are often integrated as cognitive-behavioral therapy (CBT)—have also provided empirically supported methods for helping couples and families in distress (Baucom et al., 1998), and for modifying behaviors related to health problems such as headaches, smoking, chronic pain, and bulimia nervosa (Agras et al., 2000). Cognitive-behavioral therapists have also innovated treatments for sexual dysfunctions for which there were no effective treatments.

Cognitive-behavioral therapy has been used to help anorexic and bulimic individuals challenge their perfectionism and their attitudes toward their bodies. It has also been used to systematically reinforce appropriate eating behavior. Studies that compare the effectiveness of CBT and antidepressants find them to be comparably effective, with CBT sometimes showing a slight advantage (e.g., De Maat et al., 2006). Drugs, after all, do not directly "attack" people's perfectionist attitudes and their distorted body images. They ease the presence of negative feelings and may help individuals enlist their own psychological resources, but pills do not offer advice or even a sympathetic ear.

The combination of cognitive therapy or CBT and drug therapy has helped many people with schizophrenia modify their delusional beliefs and behave in more socially acceptable ways (Turkington et al., 2004; Warman et al., 2005). But psychological therapy alone is apparently inadequate to treat the quirks of thought exhibited in people with severe psychotic disorders.

Thus, it is not enough to ask which type of therapy is most effective. We must ask which type is most effective for a particular problem and a particular patient. What are its advantages? Its limitations? Clients may successfully use systematic desensitization or virtual therapy to overcome stage fright, but if they also want to know *why* they have stage fright, behavior therapy alone will not provide the answer. But, then again, insight-oriented forms of therapy might also be unable to provide the answer.

All in all, despite Han Eysenck's skepticism noted at the beginning of the section, research suggests that psychotherapy appears to be effective more often than not. But, we might wonder, does psychotherapy help

> It is not enough to ask which type of therapy is most effective. We must ask which type is most effective for a particular problem and a particular patient.

because of specific factors and treatment methods or because a client is receiving the support of an educated and trained helping professional?

So-called nonspecific factors in therapy, such as the formation of the client-therapist "alliance," are connected with better therapeutic results (Scaturo, 2005). However, specific techniques—such as specific cognitive and behavioral methods—appear to be much more effective than the therapist-client relationship in bringing about helpful changes (Stevens et al., 2000).

Psychotherapy and Race/Ethnicity

Multiculturalism raises other issues concerning the effectiveness of psychotherapy. Most of the "prescriptions" for psychotherapy discussed in this chapter were originated by, and intended for use with, European Americans. Let us note that people from different racial or ethnic backgrounds are less likely than European Americans to seek therapy for psychological problems for reasons such as the following:

- lack of awareness that therapy would help

- lack of information about the availability of professional services, or inability to pay for them

- distrust of professionals, particularly European American professionals and (for women) male professionals

- language barriers

- reluctance to open up about personal matters to strangers—especially strangers who are not members of one's own ethnic group

- cultural inclinations toward other approaches to problem solving, such as religious approaches and psychic healers

- negative experiences with professionals and authority figures

> CLINICIANS NEED TO BE SENSITIVE TO THE CULTURAL HERITAGE, LANGUAGE, AND VALUES OF THE PEOPLE THEY SEE IN THERAPY.

Clinicians need to be sensitive to the cultural heritage, language, and values of the people they see in therapy (Chen & Davenport, 2005). Let us consider some of the issues involved in conducting psychotherapy with African Americans, Asian Americans, Latino and Latina Americans, and Native Americans.

African Americans

In addition to addressing the psychological problems of African American clients, therapists often need to help them cope with the effects of prejudice and discrimination. Some African Americans develop low self-esteem because they internalize negative stereotypes (Boyd-Franklin, 2001).

African Americans often are reluctant to seek psychological help because of cultural assumptions that people should manage their own problems and because of mistrust of the therapy process. They tend to assume that people are supposed to solve their own problems. Signs of emotional weakness such as tension, anxiety, and depression are stigmatized (Ivey & Brooks-Harris, 2005).

Many African Americans are also suspicious of their therapists—especially when the therapist is a European American. They may withhold personal information because of the society's history of racial discrimination.

Asian Americans

Asian Americans tend to stigmatize people with psychological disorders. As a result, they may deny problems and refuse to seek help for them (Chen & Davenport, 2005). Asian Americans, especially recent immigrants, also may not understand or believe in Western approaches to psychotherapy. For example, Western psychotherapy typically encourages people to express their feelings openly. This mode of behavior may conflict with the Asian tradition of restraint in public. Many Asians prefer to receive concrete advice rather than Western-style encouragement

specific factors
those factors in psychotherapy that are specific to a given approach, such as free association in psychoanalysis or systematic desensitization in behavior therapy

nonspecific factors
those factors in psychotherapy that are common to many approaches, such as the "therapeutic alliance" with the client

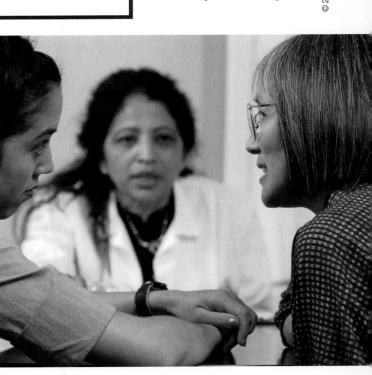

rebound anxiety anxiety that can occur when one discontinues use of a tranquilizer

to develop their own solutions (Chen & Davenport, 2005).

Because of a cultural tendency to deny painful thoughts, many Asians experience and express psychological problems as physical symptoms (Chen & Davenport, 2005). Rather than thinking of themselves as being anxious, they may focus on physical features of anxiety such as a pounding heart and heavy sweating. Rather than thinking of themselves as depressed, they may focus on fatigue and low energy levels.

Latino and Latina Americans

Therapists need to be aware of potential conflicts between the traditional Latino and Latina American value of interdependency in the family and the typical European American belief in independence and self-reliance (Anger-Díaz et al., 2004). Measures like the following may help bridge the gaps between psychotherapists and Latino and Latina American clients:

- Interacting with clients in the language requested by them or, if this is not possible, referring them to professionals who can do so.
- Using methods that are consistent with the client's values and levels of acculturation, as suggested by fluency in English and level of education.
- Developing therapy methods that incorporate clients' cultural values (Cervantes & Parham, 2005). Malgady and his colleagues (1990), for example, use *cuento therapy* with Puerto Ricans. *Cuento therapy* uses Latino and Latina folktales (*cuentos*) with characters who serve as models for adaptive behavior.

Native Americans

Many psychological disorders experienced by Native Americans involve the disruption of their traditional culture caused by European colonization (Walle, 2004). Native Americans have also been denied full access to key institutions in Western culture. Loss of cultural identity and social disorganization have set the stage for problems such as alcoholism, substance abuse, and depression (Walle, 2004). If psychologists are to help Native Americans cope with psychological disorders, they need to do so in a way that is sensitive to their culture, customs, and values. Efforts to prevent such disorders should focus on strengthening Native American cultural identity, pride, and cohesion.

LO⁸ Biological Therapies

The kinds of therapy we have discussed are psychological in nature—forms of *psycho*therapy. Psychotherapies apply *psychological* principles to treatment, principles based on psychological

knowledge of matters such as learning and motivation. People with psychological disorders are also often treated with biological therapies. Biological therapies apply what is known of people's *biological* structures and processes to the amelioration of psychological disorders. For example, they may work by altering events in the nervous system, as by changing the action of neurotransmitters. In this section, we discuss three biological, or medical, approaches to treating people with psychological disorders: drug therapy, electroconvulsive therapy, and psychosurgery. *What kinds of drug therapy are available for psychological disorders?*

Drug Therapy

In the 1950s Fats Domino popularized the song "My Blue Heaven." Fats was singing about the sky and happiness. Today "blue heavens" is one of the street names for the 10-milligram dose of the antianxiety drug Valium. Clinicians prescribe Valium and other drugs for people with various psychological disorders.

Antianxiety Drugs

Most antianxiety drugs, such as Valium and Serax, belong to the chemical class known as *benzodiazepines*. Antianxiety drugs are usually prescribed for outpatients who complain of generalized anxiety or panic attacks, although many people also use them as sleeping pills. Valium and other antianxiety drugs depress the activity of the central nervous system (CNS). The CNS, in turn, decreases sympathetic activity, reducing the heart rate, respiration rate, and nervousness and tension.

Many people come to tolerate antianxiety drugs very quickly. When tolerance occurs, dosages must be increased for the drug to remain effective.

Sedation (feeling of being tired or drowsy) is the most common side effect of antianxiety drugs. Problems associated with withdrawal from these drugs include **rebound anxiety**. That is, some people who have been using these drugs regularly report that their anxiety becomes worse than before once they discontinue them. Antianxiety drugs can induce physical dependence, as evidenced by withdrawal symptoms such as tremors, sweating, insomnia, and rapid heartbeat.

Antipsychotic Drugs

People with schizophrenia are often given antipsychotic drugs (also called *major tranquilizers*). In most cases these drugs reduce agitation, delusions, and hallucinations. Many antipsychotic drugs, including phenothiazines (e.g., Thorazine) and clozapine

(Clozaril) are thought to act by blocking dopamine receptors in the brain. Research along these lines supports the theory that schizophrenia is connected with overactivity of the neurotransmitter dopamine.

Antidepressants

People with major depression often take so-called antidepressant drugs. These drugs are also helpful for some people with eating disorders, panic disorder, obsessive–compulsive disorder, and social phobia. Problems in the regulation of noradrenaline and serotonin may be involved in eating and panic disorders as well as in depression. Antidepressants are believed to work by increasing levels of these neurotransmitters, which can affect both depression and the appetite. As noted in the section on the effectiveness of psychotherapy, however, cognitive therapy addresses irrational attitudes concerning weight and body shape, fosters normal eating habits, and helps people resist the urges to binge and purge, often making therapy more effective than drugs for people with bulimia. But when cognitive therapy does not help people with bulimia nervosa, drug therapy may do so.

There are various antidepressants. Each increases the concentration of noradrenaline or serotonin in the brain. **Selective serotonin-reuptake inhibitors (SSRIs)** such as Prozac and Zoloft block the reuptake of serotonin by presynaptic neurons. As a result, serotonin remains in the synaptic cleft longer, influencing receiving neurons.

Antidepressant drugs must usually build up to a therapeutic level over several weeks. Because overdoses can be lethal, some people stay in a hospital during the buildup to prevent suicide attempts. There are also side effects such as nausea, agitation, and weight gain. The nausea and agitation tend to dissipate after patients have been using the drugs for a day or two.

Lithium

The ancient Greeks and Romans were among the first to use the metal lithium as a psychoactive drug. They prescribed mineral water—which contains lithium—for people with bipolar disorder. They had no inkling as to why this treatment sometimes helped. A salt of the metal lithium (lithium carbonate), in tablet form, flattens out cycles of manic behavior and depression in most people. It is not known exactly how lithium works, although it affects the functioning of neurotransmitters.

People with bipolar disorder may have to use lithium indefinitely, as a person with diabetes must use insulin to control the illness. Lithium also has been shown to have side effects such as hand tremors, memory impairment, and excessive thirst and urination. Memory impairment is reported as the main reason why people discontinue lithium.

Does Drug Therapy Work?

There are thus a number of drugs available to treat psychological disorders. There is little question that drug therapy has helped many people with severe psychological disorders. For example, antipsychotic drugs largely account for the reduced need for the use of restraint and supervision (e.g., padded cells, straitjackets,

antidepressant acting to relieve depression

selective serotonin-reuptake inhibitors (SSRIs) antidepressant drugs that work by blocking the reuptake of serotonin by presynaptic neurons hospitalization, and so on) with people diagnosed with schizophrenia. Antipsychotic drugs have allowed hundreds of thousands of former mental hospital residents to lead largely normal lives in the community, hold jobs, and maintain family lives. Most of the problems related to these drugs concern their side effects.

But many comparisons of psychotherapy (in the form of cognitive therapy) and drug therapy for depression suggest that cognitive therapy is as effective as or more effective than antidepressants (DeRubeis et al., 2005; De Maat et al., 2006). Cognitive therapy appears to provide coping skills that reduce the risk of recurrence of depression once treatment ends (Hollon et al., 2005).

Many psychologists and psychiatrists are comfortable with the short-term use of antianxiety drugs in helping clients manage periods of unusual anxiety or tension. Many people, however, use antianxiety drugs routinely to dull the arousal stemming from anxiety-producing lifestyles or interpersonal problems. Rather than make the often painful decisions required to confront their problems and change their lives, they prefer to take a pill.

One study found that both tranquilizers and CBT (stress management training plus imagined exposure to the fearful stimuli) helped phobic people get through a dental session. However, 70% of those who received cognitive-behavioral therapy continued to go for dental treatment, as compared with only 20% of those who took the tranquilizer (Thom et al., 2000). CBT apparently taught people in the study coping skills, whereas the tranquilizers afforded only temporary relief.

In sum, drug therapy is effective for some disorders that do not respond to psychotherapy alone. Yet common sense and research evidence suggest that psychotherapy is preferable for problems such as anxiety and mild depression. No chemical can show a person how to change an idea or solve an interpersonal problem.

Electroconvulsive Therapy

What is electroconvulsive therapy? **Electroconvulsive therapy (ECT)** is a biological form of therapy for psychological disorders that was introduced by the Italian psychiatrist Ugo Cerletti in 1939. Cerletti had noted that some slaughterhouses used electric shock to render animals unconscious. The shocks also produced convulsions. Along with other European researchers of the period, Cerletti erroneously believed that convulsions were incompatible with schizophrenia and other major psychological disorders.

ECT was originally used for a variety of psychological disorders. Because of the advent of antipsychotic drugs, however, it is now used mainly for people with major depression who do not respond to antidepressants.

People typically obtain one ECT treatment three times a week for up to ten sessions. Electrodes are attached to the temples and an electrical current strong enough to produce a convulsion is induced. The shock causes unconsciousness, so the patient does not recall it. Nevertheless, patients are given a **sedative** so that they are asleep during the treatment.

ECT is controversial for many reasons, such as the fact that many professionals are distressed by the thought of passing an electric shock through a patient's head and producing convulsions. There are also side effects, including memory problems.

Psychosurgery

Psychosurgery is more controversial than ECT. *What is psychosurgery? How is it used to treat psychological disorders?* The best-known modern technique, **prefrontal lobotomy**, has been used with people with severe disorders. In this method, a pick-like instrument severs the nerve pathways that link the prefrontal lobes of the brain to the thalamus. It is intended to sever thought from emotion and enable severely disturbed patients to regain control.

The method was pioneered by the Portuguese neurologist Antonio Egas Moniz and was brought to the United States in the 1930s. The theoretical rationale for the operation was vague and misguided, and Moniz's reports of success were exaggerated. Nevertheless, by 1950 prefrontal lobotomies had been performed on thousands of people in an effort to reduce violence and agitation. Anecdotal evidence of the method's unreliable outcomes is found in an ironic footnote to history: one of Dr. Moniz's patients returned to shoot him.

Truth

One of Dr. Moniz's "failures" did indeed shoot him, leaving a bullet lodged in his spine and paralyzing his legs.

NAJILAH FEANNY/STOCK BOSTON, LLC

Electroconvulsive Therapy
In ECT, electrodes are placed on each side of the patient's head and a current is passed between them, inducing a seizure. ECT is used mainly in cases of major depression when antidepressant drugs and psychotherapy are not sufficient.

Prefrontal lobotomy also has side effects, including hyperactivity and distractibility, impaired learning ability, overeating, apathy and withdrawal, epileptic-type seizures, reduced creativity, and, now and then, death. Because of these side effects, and because of the advent of antipsychotic drugs, this method has been largely discontinued in the United States.

Social Psychology

14

Learning Outcomes

LO 1 Define social psychology

LO 2 Define attitude and discuss factors that shape it

LO 3 Define social perception and describe the factors that contribute to it

LO 4 Explain why people obey authority figures and conform to social norms

LO 5 Describe how and why people behave differently as group members than as individuals

> **❝** *People can be goaded by social influences into doing things that are not necessarily consistent with their personalities.* **❞**

Consider some news from the early years of the 21st century. On December 27, 2007, Benazir Bhutto, the two-time prime minister of Pakistan, was killed by a suicide bomber during a political rally as she was campaigning to hold that post for a third time. On July 7, 2005, four suicide bombers blew themselves up aboard three London commuter trains and a bus, killing more than fifty people and wounding 700. And, of course, in the United States there were the nineteen suicide terrorists who used fully fueled airplanes as bombs on September 11, 2001, and flew them into the World Trade Center and the Pentagon, killing 3,000.

Although you might think of suicide terrorism as a recent phenomenon, it dates back thousands of years (Pastor, 2004). But we have become most recently aware of suicide terrorism by strikes throughout the Muslim world, in Israel, and—with the attacks on New York, Washington, D.C., Madrid, and London—in the Western world. The word "suicide" in the phrase "suicide bomber" leads people to turn to psychologists for understanding, with the idea that something must be very wrong psychologically with these terrorists (Pastor, 2004). But many social scientists assert that suicide terrorists have no telltale psychological profile (Consortium of Social Science Associations, 2003; Lester et al., 2004). Social psychologist Philip Zimbardo (2008) argues that we must look to social influence to understand suicide terrorism.

One area of social psychology studies the ways in which people can be goaded by social influences into doing things that are not necessarily consistent with their personalities. In particular, Zimbardo (2004) has investigated the relative ease with which "ordinary" men and women can be incited to behave in evil ways.

Truth or Fiction?

What do you think?

Folklore, common sense, or nonsense? Place a T for "True" or F for "False" on the lines provided (you'll learn the answers as you read through the text).

__ People act in accord with their consciences.

__ We appreciate things more when we have to work for them.

__ Beauty is in the eye of the beholder.

__ Opposites attract.

__ We tend to hold others responsible for their misdeeds but to see ourselves as victims of circumstances when we misbehave.

__ Most people will torture an innocent person if they are ordered to do so.

__ Seeing is believing.

__ Nearly forty people stood by and did nothing while a woman was being stabbed to death.

LO¹ What Is Social Psychology?

The situationist perspective is part of the field of social psychology. *What is social psychology?* Social psychology studies the nature and causes of behavior and mental processes in social situations. The

social psychology
the field of psychology that studies the nature and causes of people's thoughts and behavior in social situations

attitude
an enduring mental representation of a person, place, or thing that evokes an emotional response and related behavior

A–B problem
the issue of how well we can predict behavior on the basis of attitudes

social psychological topics we discuss in this chapter include attitudes, social perception, social influence, and group behavior. As we explore each of these, we will ask what they might offer to those of us who have difficulty imagining why people would surrender their own lives to take the lives of others.

Suicide Bombers: Evil? Ordinary?

Why did these nineteen men fly into the World Trade Center and the Pentagon? Was it a matter of personality and personal choice? Was it a web of situational factors? Were they evil? Social psychologists who have studied the nature of evil find that many, perhaps most, perpetrators of evil are "ordinary people" (Baumeister, 1996; Berkowitz, 2004b). How can this be true? As you'll read later in this chapter, when we seek to "profile" someone, we might be making a fundamental attribution error—that is, we attribute too much of other people's behavior to internal factors such as attitude and choice (Gilovich & Eibach, 2001; Reeder, 2001.) Indeed, in 2003, the Consortium of Social Science Associations (COSSA) testified to Congress that they had to conclude there was no clear profile of the suicide terrorist.

GETTY IMAGES

LO² Attitudes

How do you feel about abortion, stem cell research, and exhibiting the Ten Commandments in courthouses? These are hot-button topics because people have strong attitudes toward them. They each give rise to cognitive evaluations (such as approval or disapproval), feelings (such as liking, disliking, or something stronger), and behavioral tendencies (such as approach or avoidance). Although I asked you how you "feel," attitudes are not just feelings or emotions. Many psychologists view thinking—or judgment—as more basic. Feelings and behavior follow. *What are attitudes?* Attitudes are behavioral and cognitive tendencies that are expressed by evaluating particular people, places, or things with favor or disfavor.

Attitudes are largely learned, and they affect behavior. They can foster love or hate. They can give rise to helping behavior or to mass destruction. They can lead to social conflict or to the resolution of conflicts. Attitudes can change, but not easily. Most people do not change their religion or political affiliation without serious reflection or coercion.

The A–B Problem

Is our behavior consistent with our attitudes—that is, with our beliefs and feelings? *Do people do as they think? (For example, do people really vote their consciences?)* When we are free to do as we wish, the answer is often yes. But, as indicated by the term **A–B problem**, there are exceptions. For example, research reveals that attitudes toward health-related behaviors such as excessive drinking, smoking, and drunken driving do not necessarily predict these behaviors (Stacy et al., 1994).

Several factors affect the likelihood that we can predict behavior from attitudes:

1 *Specificity.* We can better predict specific behavior from specific attitudes than from global attitudes. For example, we can better predict church attendance by knowing people's attitudes toward church attendance than by knowing whether they are Christian.

2 *Strength of attitudes.* Strong attitudes are more likely

Fiction

Actually, people do not always act in accord with their consciences. The links between attitudes (A) and behaviors (B) tend to be weak to moderate.

to determine behavior than weak attitudes (Huskinson & Haddock, 2004; Petty et al., 1997). A person who believes that the nation's destiny depends on Democrats taking control of Congress is more likely to vote than a person who leans toward that party but does not believe that elections make much difference.

3 *Vested interest.* People are more likely to act on their attitudes when they have a vested interest in the outcome. People are more likely to vote for (or against) unionization of their workplace when they believe that their job security depends on it (Lehman & Crano, 2002).

4 *Accessibility.* People are more likely to behave in accord with their attitudes when they are accessible—that is, when they are brought to mind (Kallgren et al., 2000; Petty et al., 1997). This is why politicians attempt to "get out the vote" by means of media blitzes just prior to an election. It does little good to have supporters who forget them on Election Day. Attitudes with a strong emotional impact are more accessible, which is one reason that politicians strive to get their supporters "worked up" over issues.

Attitude Formation

You were not born a Republican or a Democrat. You were not born a Catholic, Jew, or Muslim—although your parents may have prac-

ticed one of these religions when you came along. *Where do attitudes come from?* Political, religious, and other attitudes are learned or derived from cognitive processes.

Conditioning may play a role in attitude formation (Walther et al., 2005). Laboratory experiments have shown that attitudes toward national groups can be influenced by associating them with positive words (such as *gift* or *happy*) or negative words (such as *ugly* or *failure*) (De Houwer et al., 2001). Parents often reward children for saying and doing things that agree with their own attitudes. Patriotism is encouraged by showing children approval when they sing the national anthem or wave the flag.

Attitudes formed through direct experience may be stronger and easier to recall, but we also acquire attitudes by observing, listening to, or reading the works of other people. The approval or disapproval of peers leads adolescents to prefer short or long hair, baggy jeans, or preppy sweaters. How do the things you read in newspapers or hear on the radio influence your attitudes?

Cognitive Appraisal

Nevertheless, attitude formation is not fully mechanical. People are also motivated to understand the environment so that they can make predictions and exercise some control over it (Bizer et al.,

Politicians participate in media blitzes just prior to an election so that they will be "accessible" to their voters on election day.

2004; Wood, 2000). People also sometimes form or change attitudes on the basis of new information (Dovidio et al., 2004; Petty et al., 1999; Walther et al., 2005). For example, we may believe that a car is more reliable than we had thought if a survey by *Consumer Reports* finds that it has an excellent repair record. Even so, initial attitudes act as cognitive anchors (Wegener et al., 2001; Wood, 2000). We often judge new ideas in terms of how much they deviate from our existing attitudes. Accepting larger deviations requires more information processing—in other words, more intellectual work (Petty et al., 1999; Tormala & Petty, 2004). For this reason, perhaps, great deviations—such as changes from liberal to conservative attitudes, or vice versa—are apt to be resisted.

Changing Attitudes Through Persuasion

Will Rogers's comment below sounds on the mark, but he was probably wrong. It does little good to have a wonderful product if it remains a secret. *Can you really change people's attitudes and behavior?*

The **elaboration likelihood model** describes the ways in which people respond to persuasive messages (Crano, 2000; Salovey & Wegener, 2003). Consider two routes to persuading others to change attitudes. The first, or central, route inspires thoughtful consideration of arguments and evidence. The second, or peripheral, route associates objects with positive or negative cues. When politicians avow, "This bill is supported by liberals (or conservatives)," they are seeking predictable, knee-jerk reactions rather than careful consideration of a bill's merits. Other cues are rewards (such as a smile or a hug), punishments (such as parental disapproval), and such factors as the trustworthiness and attractiveness of the communicator.

Advertisements, which are a form of persuasive communication, also rely on central and peripheral routes. Some ads focus on the quality of the product (central route). Others attempt to associate the product with appealing images (peripheral route). Ads for Total cereal, which highlight its nutritional benefits, provide information about the quality of the product. So, too, did the "Pepsi Challenge" taste-

test ads, which claimed that Pepsi tastes better than Coca-Cola. Ads that show football players heading for Disney World or choosing a brand of beer offer no information about the product itself.

In this section we look at one central factor in persuasion—the nature of the message—and three peripheral factors: the messenger, the context of the message, and the audience.

The Persuasive Message

How do we respond when TV commercials are repeated until we have memorized the dimples on the actors' faces? Research suggests that familiarity breeds content, not contempt (Zajonc, 2001; Zizak & Reber, 2004). It appears that repeated exposure to people and things as diverse as the following enhances their appeal:

- political candidates (who are seen in repeated TV commercials)
- photos of African Americans
- photos of college students
- abstract art
- classical music

When trying to persuade someone, is it helpful or self-defeating to alert them to the arguments presented by the opposition? In two-sided arguments, the communicator recounts the arguments of the opposition in an effort to refute them. In research concerning a mock trial, college undergraduates were presented with two-sided arguments—those of the prosecution and those of the defendant (McKenzie et al., 2002). When one argument was weak, the college "jurors" expressed more confidence in their decision than when they did not hear the other side at all. Theologians and politicians sometimes forewarn their followers about the arguments of the opposition and then refute each one. Forewarning creates a kind of psychological immunity to them (Jacks & Devine, 2000).

It would be nice to think that people are too sophisticated to be persuaded by emotional factors in attitude formation, but they usually aren't (DeSteno et al., 2004). Consider the **fear appeal**: Women who are warned of the dire risk they run if they fail to be screened for breast cancer are more likely to obtain mammograms than women who are informed of the *benefits* of mammography (Ruiter et al., 2001). Interestingly, although sun tanning has been shown to increase the likelihood of skin cancer, warnings against sun tanning were shown to be more effective when students were warned of risks

> *Let advertisers spend the same amount of money improving their product that they do on advertising and they wouldn't have to advertise it.*
> —Will Rogers

to their *appearance* (e.g., premature aging, wrinkling, and scarring of the skin) than when the warning dealt with the risk to their health. That is, students informed of tanning's cosmetic effects were more likely to say they would protect themselves from the sun than were students informed about the risk of cancer. Fear appeals are most effective when the audience believes that the risks are serious—as in causing wrinkles!—and that the audience members can change their behavior to avert the risks—as in preventing cancer or wrinkling.

Audiences also tend to believe arguments that appear to run counter to the vested interests of the communicator (Lehman & Crano, 2002). If the president of Ford or General Motors said that Toyotas and Hondas were superior, you can bet that we would prick up our ears.

The Persuasive Communicator

Would you go to a doctor who admitted that he or she was behind the times? Would you buy a used car from a person who had been convicted of larceny? Research shows that persuasive communicators are characterized by expertise, trustworthiness, attractiveness, or similarity to their audiences (Petty et al., 1997). Because of the adoration of their fans, sports superstars such as Peyton Manning are the most valuable endorsers. Some companies who had used Tiger Woods as a spokesperson dropped him when news of his infidelities emerged. He was no longer as much of a role model.

People find it painful when they are confronted with information that counters their own views (Foerster et al., 2000). Therefore, they often show selective avoidance and selective exposure (Lavine et al., 2005). That is, they tend to watch news channels that endorse their own views and switch channels when the news coverage counters their own attitudes. They also seek communicators who share their views.

The Context of the Message

You are too shrewd to let someone persuade you by buttering you up, but perhaps someone you know would be influenced by a sip of wine, a bite of cheese,

We often selectively expose ourselves to opinions with which we agree—and vice versa.

and a sincere compliment. Aspects of the immediate environment, such as music, increase the likelihood of persuasion. When we are in a good mood, we apparently are less likely to evaluate the situation carefully (Petty et al., 1997).

It is also counterproductive to call your friends foolish when they differ with you—even though their ideas are bound to be "foolish" if they do not agree with yours. Agreement and praise are more effective ways to encourage others to embrace your views.

The Persuaded Audience

Why can some people say no to salespeople? Why do others enrich the lives of every door-to-door salesperson? It may be that people with high self-esteem and low social anxiety are more likely to resist social pressure (Ellickson et al., 2001).

A classic study by Schwartz and Gottman (1976) describes the cognitive nature of the social anxiety that can make it difficult to refuse requests. They found that people who comply with unreasonable requests are more apt to report thoughts such as:

- "I was worried about what the other person would think of me if I refused."
- "It is better to help others than to be self-centered."
- "The other person might be hurt or insulted if I refused."

People who refuse unreasonable requests reported thoughts like these:

- "It doesn't matter what the other person thinks of me."
- "I am perfectly free to say no."
- "This request is unreasonable."

Changing Attitudes and Behavior by Means of Cognitive Dissonance

What is cognitive-dissonance theory? According to **cognitive-dissonance theory**, people are thinking creatures who seek consistency in their behaviors and their attitudes—that is, their views of the world. People must apparently mentally represent the world accurately to predict and control events. Consistency in beliefs, attitudes, and behavior helps make the world seem like a predictable place. Therefore, if we

selective avoidance diverting one's attention from information that is inconsistent with one's attitudes

selective exposure deliberately seeking and attending to information that is consistent with one's attitudes

cognitive-dissonance theory the view that we are motivated to make our cognitions or beliefs consistent find ourselves in the uncomfortable spot where two cherished ideas conflict, we are motivated to reduce the discrepancy.

In the first and still one of the best-known studies on cognitive dissonance, one group of participants received one dollar (worth about ten dollars today) for telling someone else that a boring task was interesting (Festinger & Carlsmith, 1959). Members of a second group received twenty dollars (worth about $200 today) to describe the chore positively. Both groups were paid to engage in attitude-discrepant behavior—that is, behavior that ran counter to what they actually thought. After presenting their fake enthusiasm for the boring task, the participants were asked to rate their own liking for it. Ironically, those who were paid *less* rated the task as actually more interesting than their better-paid colleagues reported. Similarly, being compelled by the law to recycle can lead to people's supporting recycling as opposed to throwing out all trash and garbage in a bundle.

Learning theorists (see Chapter 6) might predict a different outcome—that the more we are reinforced for doing something (given more money, for example), the more we should like it (not find the task quite as boring, that is). But that is not what happened here. Cognitive-dissonance theorists rightly predicted that because the ideas (cognitions) of (a) "I was paid very little" and (b) "I told someone that this assignment was interesting" are dissonant, people will tend to engage in effort justification. The discomfort of cognitive dissonance motivates people to explain their behavior to themselves in such a way that unpleasant undertakings seem worth it. Participants who were paid only a dollar may have justified their lie by concluding that they may not have been lying in the first place.

Prejudice and Discrimination

Prejudice is an attitude toward a group that leads people to evaluate members of that group negatively—even though they have never met them. On a cognitive level, prejudice is linked to expectations that members of the target group will behave poorly, say, in the workplace, or engage in criminal behavior or terrorism. On an emotional level, prejudice is associated with negative feelings such as fear, dislike, or hatred (No, 2004).

Truth

We do tend to appreciate things more when we have to work for them. This is an example of effort justification.

In behavioral terms, prejudice is connected with avoidance, aggression, and discrimination. Prejudice is the most troubling kind of attitude. It is connected with the genocide of millions of people. One form of behavior that results from prejudice is discrimination. Discrimination takes many forms, including denial of access to jobs, housing, and the voting booth.

Stereotypes

Are Jewish Americans shrewd and ambitious? Are African Americans superstitious and musical? Are gay men and lesbians unfit for military service? Such ideas are stereotypes—fixed, conventional attitudes toward certain groups that lead people to view members of those groups in a biased fashion.

Some stereotypes are positive rather than negative, such as the cultural stereotypes about physically attractive people. By and large, we assume that "good things come in pretty packages." Attractive children and adults are judged and treated more positively than their unattractive peers (Langlois et al., 2000). We expect attractive people to be poised, sociable, popular, intelligent, mentally healthy, fulfilled, persuasive, and successful in their jobs.

> By and large, we assume that "good things come in pretty packages."

Sources of Prejudice

The sources of prejudice are many and varied:

1 *Dissimilarity.* We are apt to like people who share our attitudes. In forming impressions of others, we are influenced by attitudinal similarity and dissimilarity (Duckitt et al., 2002). People of different religions and races often have different backgrounds, however, giving rise to dissimilar attitudes. Even when people of different races share important values, they may assume that they do not.

2 *Social conflict.* There is often social and economic conflict between people of different races and religions (Duckitt & Fisher, 2003).

3 *Social learning.* Children acquire some attitudes from other people, especially their parents. Children tend to imitate their parents, and parents reinforce their children for doing so (Duckitt et al., 2002). In this way prejudices can be transmitted from generation to generation.

4 *Information processing.* Prejudices act as cognitive filters through which we view the social world. We tend to think of people as "familiar" or "foreign," or "good" or "bad." Our feelings and reactions toward others may be biased by these perceptions (Crisp & Nicel, 2004).

5 *Social categorization.* We also tend to divide our social world into "us" and "them." People usually view those who belong to their own groups—the "in-group"—more favorably than those who do not—the "out-group" (Förster et al., 2004; Smith & Weber, 2005). Isolation from the out-group makes it easier to maintain our stereotypes.

Interpersonal Attraction

Attitudes of liking and loving can lead to important, lasting relationships. They are the flip side of the coin of prejudice—positive attitudes that are associated with interpersonal attraction rather than avoidance. *What factors contribute to attraction in our culture?* Among the factors contributing to attraction are physical appearance, similarity, and reciprocity (Smith & Weber, 2005).

Physical Appearance

Physical appearance is a key factor in attraction and in the consideration of romantic partners (Langlois et al., 2000). What determines physical allure? Are our standards subjective—that is, "in the eye of the beholder"? Or is there general agreement on what is appealing?

Many standards for beauty appear to be cross-cultural (Langlois et al., 2000; Little & Perrett, 2002). For example, a study of people in England and Japan found that both British and Japanese men consider

Figure 14.1

What Features Contribute to Facial Attractiveness?

In both England and Japan, features such as large eyes, high cheekbones, and narrow jaws contribute to perceptions of the attractiveness of women. Part A shows a composite of the faces of fifteen women rated as the most attractive of a group of sixty. Part B is a composite in which the features of these fifteen women are exaggerated—that is, developed further in the direction that separates them from the average of the entire sixty.

A.

B.

women with large eyes, high cheekbones, and narrow jaws to be most attractive (Perrett, 1994). In his research, Perrett created computer composites of the faces of sixty women and, as shown in part A of Figure 14.1, of the fifteen women who were rated the most attractive. He then used computer enhancement to exaggerate the differences between the composite of the sixty and the composite of the fifteen most attractive women. He arrived at the image shown in part B of Figure 14.1. Part B, which shows higher cheekbones and a narrower jaw than Part A, was rated as the most attractive image. Similar results were found for the image of a Japanese woman. Works of art suggest that the ancient Greeks and Egyptians favored similar facial features.

Gender Differences in Selection of a Partner

Physical appearance may be a major factor in the selection of a romantic partner, but cross-cultural studies on mate selection find that women tend to place greater emphasis on traits such as professional status, consideration, dependability, kindness, and fondness for children. Men tend to place relatively greater emphasis on physical allure, cooking ability, even thrift (Buss, 1994).

Susan Sprecher and her colleagues (1994) surveyed more than 13,000 Americans, attempting to represent the ethnic diversity we

Fiction

Although there may be individual preferences, it does not seem that standards for beauty are so flexible that they are fully "in the eye of the beholder."

find in the United States. They found that women were more willing than men to marry someone who was not good-looking, but less willing to marry someone who did not hold a steady job (see Figure 14.2).

Why do males tend to place relatively more emphasis than females on physical appearance in mate selection? Why do females tend to place relatively more emphasis on personal factors such as financial status and reliability? Evolutionary psychologists believe that evolutionary forces favor the survival of women who desire status in their mates and men who emphasize physical allure because these preferences provide reproductive advantages. According to the "parental investment model," a woman's appeal is more strongly connected with her age and health, both of which are markers of reproductive capacity. The value of men as reproducers, however, is more intertwined with factors that contribute to a stable environment for child rearing—such as social standing and reliability (Schmitt, 2003).

The Attraction–Similarity Hypothesis

The *attraction–similarity hypothesis* holds that people tend to develop romantic relationships with people who are similar to themselves in physical attractiveness and other traits (Morry & Gaines, 2005). Researchers have found that people who are involved in committed relationships are most likely to be similar to their partners in their attitudes and cultural attributes (Amodio & Showers, 2005).

Our partners tend to be like us in race and ethnicity, age, level of education, and religion. Note some facts and trends:

- Ninety-five percent of marriages and nearly 90% of cohabiting unions were between partners of the same race at the time of the most recent census (Batson et al., 2006).
- Even so, highly educated people are more likely than poorly educated people to marry people of other races (Batson et al., 2006).
- African Americans are less likely than Native Americans, Asian Americans and Latino and Latina Americans to marry European Americans (Batson et al., 2006)
- As non-European immigrants become assimilated over the generations, they become more likely to intermarry with people of other races. For example, third-generation Asian Americans are more likely than recent Asian immigrants to marry or cohabit with European Americans (Brown et al., 2008).
- Puerto Rican men and women have the highest percentage of intermarriage with European Americans (Batson et al., 2006).

Figure 14.2

Gender Differences in Preferences for Mates

The study by Sprecher and her colleagues found that women are more likely than men to be willing to marry someone who is older, makes more money, is better educated, but not good-looking. Men, on the other hand, are less willing to marry someone who is not good-looking. Men are also more willing to have partners who are younger, earn less, and are less well-educated. How would you interpret these findings?

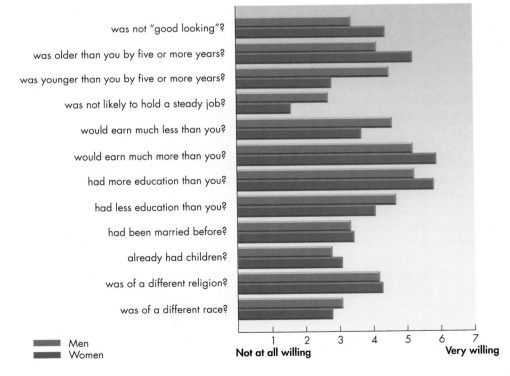

How willing would you be to marry someone who . . .

- was not "good looking"?
- was older than you by five or more years?
- was younger than you by five or more years?
- was not likely to hold a steady job?
- would earn much less than you?
- would earn much more than you?
- had more education than you?
- had less education than you?
- had been married before?
- already had children?
- was of a different religion?
- was of a different race?

Men
Women

1   2   3   4   5   6   7
Not at all willing   **Very willing**

Liking = Intimacy alone (true friendships without passion or long-term commitment)

Intimacy

Romantic love = Intimacy + Passion (lovers physically and emotionally attracted to each other but without commitment, as in a summer romance)

Companionate love = Intimacy + Commitment (long-term committed friendship such as a marriage in which the passion has faded)

Consummate love = Intimacy + Passion + Commitment (a complete love consisting of all three components— an ideal difficult to attain)

Passion

Commitment

Infatuation = Passion alone (passionate, obsessive love at first sight without intimacy or commitment)

Fatuous love = Passion + Commitment (commitment based on passion but without time for intimacy to develop— shallow relationship such as a whirlwind courtship)

Empty love = Commitment alone (commitment to remain together without intimacy or passion)

triangular model of love Sternberg's view that love involves combinations of three components: intimacy, passion, and commitment

intimacy close acquaintance and familiarity; a characteristic of a relationship in which partners share their inmost feelings

passion strong romantic and sexual feelings

commitment the decision to maintain a relationship

Figure 14.3

The Triangular Model of Love

According to this model, love has three components: intimacy, passion, and commitment. The ideal of consummate love consists of romantic love plus commitment.

Source: From *The Psychology of Love* by R. J. Sternberg. Copyright 1988 Yale University Press. Reprinted by permission of the publisher.

Similarity in Attitudes

We are actually less apt to be attracted to people who disagree with our views and tastes than to people who share them (Singh et al., 2007).

Why do the great majority of us have partners from our own backgrounds? One reason is *propinquity*, or nearness. Although mobility has increased in Western societies in recent decades, we tend to live among people who are reasonably similar to us in background and thus come into contact with them. Another is that we are drawn to people who are similar in their attitudes. People similar in background are more likely to be similar in their attitudes. Similarity in attitudes and tastes is a key contributor to attraction, friendships, and love relationships (Morry & Gaines, 2005).

Let us also note a sex difference. Evidence shows that women place greater weight on attitude

similarity as a determinant of attraction to a stranger of the other sex than do men, whereas men place more value on physical attractiveness (Laumann et al., 1994). We also tend to assume that people we find attractive share our attitudes (Morry, 2005). Although similarity may be important in determining initial attraction, compatibility appears to be a stronger predictor of maintaining an intimate relationship (Amodio & Showers, 2005).

Love

Just what is love? Love is a strong positive emotion. We had a look at love between children and parents in Chapter 3. Here we will focus on that most dramatic, heated, passionate love we label *romantic love*.

There are a number of theories about romantic love. One theory is Robert Sternberg's (1988) triangular model of love, which can be thought of as a love triangle. This love triangle does not refer to two men wooing the same woman. It refers to Sternberg's view that love involves three components: intimacy, passion, and commitment (see Figure 14.3).

Intimacy refers to a couple's closeness, to their mutual concern and sharing of feelings and resources. Passion means romance and sexual feelings. Commitment is the decision to maintain a relationship. Passion is most crucial in short-term relationships. Intimacy and commitment are more important

Fiction

Actually, it is not true that "opposites attract." People who share attitudes are more likely to be attracted to one another.

consummate love
the ideal form of love within Sternberg's model, which combines passion, intimacy, and commitment

romantic love
an intense, positive emotion that involves sexual attraction, feelings of caring, and the belief that one is in love

social perception
a subfield of social psychology that studies the ways in which we form and modify impressions of others

primacy effect
the tendency to evaluate others in terms of first impressions

recency effect
the tendency to evaluate others in terms of the most recent impression

attribution
a belief concerning why people behave in a certain way

dispositional attribution
an assumption that a person's behavior is determined by internal causes such as personal attitudes or goals

situational attribution
an assumption that a person's behavior is determined by external circumstances such as the social pressure found in a situation

in enduring relationships. The ideal form of love—consummate love—combines all three. Consummate love is made up of romantic love plus commitment.

Romantic love, in Sternberg's scheme, is characterized by passion and intimacy. Passion involves fascination (preoccupation with the loved one), sexual craving, and the desire for exclusiveness (a special relationship with the loved one). Intimacy involves caring—championing the interests of the loved one, even if it entails sacrificing one's own. People are cognitively biased toward evaluating their partners positively (Loving & Agnew, 2001). That is, we idealize those we love.

LO³ Social Perception

An important area of social psychology concerns the ways in which we perceive other people—for example, the importance of the first impressions they make on us. Next we explore some factors that contribute to social perception: the primacy and recency effects, attribution theory, and body language.

Primacy and Recency Effects

Why do you wear a suit to a job interview? Why do defense attorneys make sure that their clients dress neatly and get their hair cut before they are seen by the jury? *Do first impressions really matter?* Apparently first impressions do matter—a great deal.

What are the primacy and recency effects? Whether we are talking about the business or social worlds, or even the relationship between a therapist and a client, first impressions are important (Bidell et al., 2002). First impressions are an example of the primacy effect.

Subjects in a classic experiment on the primacy effect read different stories about "Jim" (Luchins, 1957). The stories consisted of one or two paragraphs. The one-paragraph stories portrayed Jim as either friendly or unfriendly. These paragraphs were also used in the two-paragraph stories, but in this case the paragraphs were read in the reverse order. Of those reading only the "friendly" paragraph, 95% rated Jim as friendly. Of those who read just the "unfriendly" paragraph, 3% rated him as friendly. Seventy-eight percent of those who read two-paragraph stories in the "friendly-unfriendly" order labeled Jim as friendly. When they read the paragraphs in the reverse order, only 18% rated Jim as friendly.

How can we encourage people to pay more attention to impressions occurring after the first encounter? Abraham Luchins accomplished this by allowing time to pass between the presentations of the two paragraphs. In this way, fading memories allowed more recent information to take precedence. This is known as the recency effect. Luchins also found a second way to counter first impressions: He simply asked subjects to avoid making snap judgments and to weigh all the evidence.

Attribution Theory

What is attribution theory? Why do we assume that other people intend the mischief that they do? An attribution is an assumption about why people do things. When you assume that one child is mistreating another child because she is "mean," you are making an attribution. This section focuses on *attribution theory*, or the processes by which people draw conclusions about the factors that influence one another's behavior. Attribution theory is important because attributions lead us to perceive others either as purposeful actors or as victims of circumstances.

Dispositional and Situational Attributions

Social psychologists describe two types of attributions. Dispositional attributions ascribe a person's behavior to internal factors such as personality traits and free will. Situational attributions attribute a person's actions to external factors such as social influence or socialization. If you assume that one child is mistreating the other because her parents have given her certain attitudes toward the other child, you are making a situational attribution.

The Actor–Observer Effect

When we see people (including ourselves) doing things that we do not like, we tend to see the others as willful actors but to see ourselves as victims of circumstances (Baron et al., 2006; Stewart, 2005). The

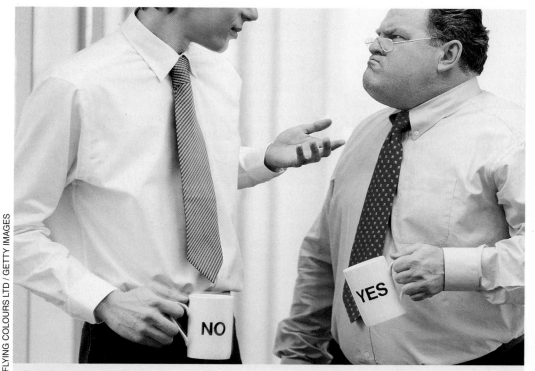

FLYING COLOURS LTD / GETTY IMAGES

The Actor-Observer Effect
Who is at fault here? People tend to make dispositional attributions for other people's behavior, but they tend to see their own behavior as motivated by situational factors. Thus, people are aware of the external forces acting on themselves when they behave, but tend to attribute other people's behavior to choice and will.

actor–observer effect the tendency to attribute our own behavior to situational factors but to attribute the behavior of others to dispositional factors

fundamental attribution error the assumption that others act predominantly on the basis of their dispositions, even when there is evidence suggesting the importance of their situations

self-serving bias the tendency to view one's successes as stemming from internal factors and one's failures as stemming from external factors

tendency to attribute other people's behavior to dispositional factors and our own behavior to situational influences is called the actor–observer effect.

Parents and teenagers often argue about the teen's choice of friends or partners. When they do, the parents tend to infer traits from behavior and to see the teens as stubborn and resistant. The teenagers also infer traits from behavior. Thus, they may see their parents as bossy and controlling. Parents and teens alike attribute the others' behavior to internal causes. That is, both make dispositional attributions about other people's behavior.

How do the parents and teenagers perceive themselves? The parents probably see themselves as being forced into combat by their children's foolishness. If they become insistent, it is in response to the teens' stubbornness. The teenagers probably see themselves as responding to peer pressures. Both parents and children make situational attributions for their own behavior.

The Fundamental Attribution Error

In cultures that view the self as independent, such as ours, people tend to attribute other people's behavior primarily to internal factors such as personality, attitudes, and free will (Gilovich & Eibach, 2001; Reeder, 2001). This bias is known as the fundamental attribution error. If a teenager gets into trouble with the law, individualistic societies are more likely to blame the teenager than the social environment in which the teenager lives.

One reason for the fundamental attribution error is that we tend to infer traits from behavior. But in collectivist cultures that stress interdependence, such as Asian cultures, people are more likely to attribute other people's behavior to that person's social roles and obligations (Basic Behavioral Science Task Force, 1996c). For example, Japanese people might be more likely to attribute a businessperson's extreme competitiveness to the "culture of business" rather than to his or her personality.

> **Truth**
>
> We do tend to hold others responsible for their misdeeds and to see ourselves as victims of circumstances when we misbehave.

The Self-Serving Bias

There is also a self-serving bias in the attribution process. We are likely to ascribe our successes to internal, dispositional factors but our failures to external, situational influences (Smith & Weber, 2005).

social influence
the area of social psychology that studies the ways in which people influence the thoughts, feelings, and behavior of others

A study with twenty-seven college wrestlers found that they tended to attribute their wins to stable and internal conditions such as their abilities, but their losses to unstable and external conditions such as an error by a referee (De Michele et al., 1998). Sports fans fall into the same trap. They tend to attribute their team's victories to internal conditions and their losses to external conditions (Wann & Shrader, 2000).

Another interesting attribution bias is a gender difference in attributions for friendly behavior. Men are more likely than women to interpret a woman's smile or friendliness toward a man as flirting (Abbey, 1987).

Body Language

Body language is important in social perception. *What is body language?* Body language is nonverbal language; it refers to the meanings we infer from the ways in which people carry themselves and the gestures they make. The way people carry themselves provides cues to how they feel and are likely to behave. When people are emotionally "uptight," they may also be rigid and straight-backed. People who are relaxed are more likely to "hang loose." Factors such as eye contact, posture, and the distance between two people provide cues to their moods and their feelings toward one another. When people face us and lean toward us, we may assume that they like us or are interested in what we are saying.

Touching

Women are more likely than men to touch other people when they are interacting with them (Stier & Hall, 1984). In one "touching" experiment, Kleinke (1977) showed that appeals for help can be more effective when the distressed person makes physical contact with people who are asked for aid. A woman obtained more coins for phone calls when she touched the arm of the person she was asking for money. In another experiment, waitresses obtained higher tips when they touched patrons on the hand or the shoulder while making change (Crusco & Wetzel, 1984).

Gazing and Staring

When other people "look us squarely in the eye," we may assume that they are being assertive or open with us. Avoidance of eye contact may suggest deception or depres-

sion. Gazing is interpreted as a sign of liking or friendliness (Kleinke, 1986). In one study, men and women were asked to gaze into each other's eyes for two minutes (Kellerman et al., 1989). After doing so, they reported having passionate feelings toward one another.

A gaze is not the same thing as a persistent hard stare. A hard stare is interpreted as a provocation or a sign of anger. Adolescent males sometimes engage in staring contests as an assertion of dominance. The male who looks away first loses the contest. In a classic series of field experiments, Phoebe Ellsworth and her colleagues (1972) subjected drivers stopped at red lights to hard stares by riders of motor scooters (see Figure 14.4). When the light changed, people who were stared at crossed the intersection more rapidly than people who were not. People who are stared at experience higher levels of physiological arousal than people who are not (Strom & Buck, 1979).

LO⁴ Social Influence

Other people and groups can exert enormous pressure on us to behave according to their norms. **Social influence** is the area of social psychology that studies the ways in which people alter the thoughts, feelings, and behavior of others. Let us describe a couple of

Figure 14.4

Diagram of an Experiment in Hard Staring and Avoidance

A 1978 study by Greenbaum and Rosenfeld found that the confederate of the experimenter stared at some drivers and not at others. Recipients of the stares drove across the intersection more rapidly once the light turned green. Why?

classic experiments that demonstrate how people influence others to engage in destructive obedience or conform to social norms.

Obedience to Authority

Throughout history soldiers have followed orders—even when it comes to slaughtering innocent civilians. The Turkish slaughter of Armenians, the Nazi slaughter of Jews, the mutual slaughter of Hutus and Tutsis in Rwanda—these are all examples of the tragedies that can arise from simply following orders. We may say we are horrified by such crimes, and we cannot imagine why people engage in them. But how many of us would refuse to follow orders issued by authority figures? *Why will so many people commit crimes against humanity if they are ordered to do so? (Why don't they refuse?)*

The Milgram Studies

Yale University psychologist Stanley Milgram also wondered how many people would resist immoral requests made by authority figures. To find out, he undertook a series of classic experiments at the university that have become known as the Milgram studies on obedience.

In an early phase of his work, Milgram (1963) placed ads in local newspapers for people who would be willing to participate in studies on learning and memory. He enlisted forty people ranging in age from twenty to fifty—teachers, engineers, laborers, salespeople, people who had not completed elementary school, and people with graduate degrees.

Let's suppose that you have answered the ad. You show up at the university in exchange for a reasonable fee ($4.50, which in the early 1960s might easily fill your gas tank) and to satisfy your own curiosity. You might be impressed. After all, Yale is a venerable institution that dominates the city. You are no less impressed by the elegant labs, where you meet a distinguished behavioral scientist dressed in a white coat and another person who has responded to the ad. The scientist explains that the purpose of the experiment is to study the *effects of punishment on learning*. The experiment requires a "teacher" and a "learner." By chance, you are appointed the teacher and the other recruit, the learner.

You, the scientist, and the learner enter a laboratory room containing a threatening chair with dangling straps. The scientist straps the learner in. The learner expresses some concern, but this is, after all, for the sake of science. And this is Yale, isn't it? What could happen to a person at Yale?

You follow the scientist to an adjacent room, from which you are to do your "teaching." This teaching promises to have an impact. You are to punish the learner's errors by pressing levers marked from fifteen to 450 volts on a fearsome-looking console. Labels describe twenty-eight of the thirty levers as running the gamut from "Slight Shock" to "Danger: Severe Shock." The last two levers are simply labeled "XXX." Just in case you have no idea what electric shock feels like, the scientist gives you a sample forty-five-volt shock. It stings. You pity the person who might receive more.

Your learner is expected to learn pairs of words, which are to be read from a list. After hearing the list once, the learner is to produce the word that pairs with the stimulus word from a list of four alternatives. This is done by pressing a switch that lights one of four panels in your room. If it is the correct panel, you proceed to the next stimulus word. If not, you are to deliver an electric shock. With each error, you are to increase the voltage of the shock (see Figure 14.5).

You probably have some misgivings. Electrodes

Overbearing experimenter

"Teacher" with "aggression" machine

"Learner" who appears to be receiving shocks

Figure 14.5

The Experimental Setup in the Milgram Studies

When the "learner" makes an error, the experimenter prods the "teacher" to deliver a painful electric shock.

have been strapped to the learner's wrists, and the scientist has applied electrode paste "to avoid blisters and burns." You have also been told that the shocks will cause "no permanent tissue damage," although they might be painful. Still, the learner is going along. And after all, this is Yale.

The learner answers some items correctly and then makes some errors. With mild concern you press the levers up through forty-five volts. You've tolerated that much yourself. Then a few more mistakes are made. You press the sixty-volt lever, then seventy-five. The learner makes another mistake. You pause and look at the scientist, who is reassuring: "Although the shocks may be painful, there is no permanent tissue damage, so please go on." The learner makes more errors, and soon you are up to a shock of 300 volts. But now the learner is pounding on the other side of the wall! Your chest tightens, and you begin to perspire. "Damn science and the $4.50!" you think. You hesitate and the scientist says, "The experiment requires that you continue." After the delivery of the next stimulus word, the learner chooses no answer at all. What are you to do? "Wait for five to ten seconds," the scientist instructs, "and then treat no answer as a wrong answer." But after the next shock the pounding on the wall resumes! Now your heart is racing, and you are convinced you are causing extreme pain and discomfort. Is it possible that no lasting damage is being done? Is the experiment that important, after all? What to do? You hesitate again, and the scientist says, "It is absolutely essential that you continue." His voice is very convincing. "You have no other choice," he says, "you *must* go on." You can barely think straight, and for some unaccountable reason you feel laughter rising in your throat. Your finger shakes above the lever. *What are you to do?*

Milgram had foreseen that some "teachers" in his experiment would hesitate. He had therefore conceived standardized statements that his assistants would use when subjects balked—for example: "Although the shocks may be painful, there is no permanent tissue damage, so please go on." "The experiment requires that you continue." "It is absolutely essential that you continue." "You have no other choice: you *must* go on."

To repeat: If you are a teacher in the Milgram study, what do you do? Milgram (1963, 1974) found out what most people in his sample would do. The sample was a cross-section of the male population of New Haven. Of the forty men in this phase of his research, only five refused to go beyond the 300-volt level, the level at which the learner first pounded the wall. Nine other "teachers" defied the scientist within the 300-volt range. But 65% of the subjects complied with the scientist throughout the series, believing they were delivering 450-volt, XXX-rated shocks.

Were these subjects unfeeling? Not at all. Milgram was impressed by their signs of stress. They trembled, they stuttered, they bit their lips. They groaned, they sweated, they dug their fingernails into their flesh. Some had fits of laughter, although laughter was inappropriate. One salesperson's laughter was so convulsive that he could not continue with the experiment.

Milgram's initial research on obedience was limited to a sample of New Haven men.

Could he generalize his findings to other men or to women? Would college students, who are considered to be independent thinkers, show more defiance? A replication of Milgram's study with a sample of Yale men yielded similar results. What about women, who are supposedly less aggressive than men? In subsequent research, women, too, administered shocks to the learners. All this took place in a nation that values independence and free will.

On Deception and Truth

I have said that the "teachers" in the Milgram studies *believed* that they were shocking other people when they pressed the levers on the console. They weren't. The only real shock in this experiment was the forty-five-volt sample given to the teachers. Its purpose was to make the procedure believable.

The learners in the experiment were actually confederates of the experimenter. They had not answered the newspaper ads but were in on the truth from the start. The "teachers" were the only real subjects. They were led to believe they had been chosen at random for the teacher role, but the choice was rigged so that newspaper recruits would always become teachers.

Milgram debriefed his subjects after the experiment was complete. He explained the purpose and methods of his research in detail. He emphasized the fact that they had not actually harmed anyone. But of course the subjects did believe that they were hurting other people as the experiment was being carried out. As you can imagine, the ethics of the Milgram studies have been debated by psychologists for decades. College and university review committees might prevent them from being conducted today.

Truth

It appears to be true that most people will torture an innocent person, just because they are ordered to do so.

Why Did People in the Milgram Studies Obey the Experimenters?

Many people obey the commands of others even when they are required to perform immoral tasks. But *why?* Why did Germans "just follow orders" during the Holocaust? Why did "teachers" obey the experimenter in Milgram's study? We do not have all the answers, but we can offer a number of hypotheses:

1 *Socialization.* Despite the expressed American ideal of independence, we are socialized from early childhood to obey authority figures such as parents and teachers (Blass, 1999).

2 *Lack of social comparison.* In Milgram's experimental settings, experimenters displayed command of the situation, but teachers (subjects), did not have the opportunity to compare their ideas and feelings with those of other people in the same situation.

3 *Perception of legitimate authority.* An experimenter at Yale might have appeared to be a highly legitimate authority figure—as might a government official or a high-ranking officer in the military (Blass & Schmitt, 2001). Yet further research showed that the university setting contributed to compliance but was not fully responsible for it. The percentage of individuals who complied with the experimenter's demands dropped from 65% to 48% when Milgram (1974) replicated the study in a dingy storefront in a nearby town. At first glance, this finding might seem encouraging. But the main point of the Milgram studies is that most people are willing to engage in morally reprehensible acts at the behest of a legitimate-looking authority figure. Hitler and his henchmen were authority figures in Nazi Germany. "Science" and Yale University legitimized the authority of the experimenters in the Milgram studies.

4 *Foot-in-the-door.* In the **foot-in-the-door technique,** social pressure is gradually increased so that the recipient complies with small requests before complying with large requests. Once teachers had begun to deliver shocks to learners, they might have conceptualized themselves as people who help researchers and found it progressively more difficult to extricate themselves from the situation (Rodafinos et al., 2005).

5 *Inaccessibility of values.* Most people believe that it is wrong to harm innocent people. But strong emotions interfere with clear thinking. As the teachers in the Milgram experiments became more aroused, their values might thus have become less "accessible."

6 *Buffers.* Several buffers decreased the effect of the learners' pain on the teachers. For example, the "learners" were in another room. When they were in the same room with the teachers, the teachers' compliance rate dropped from 65% to 40%. Moreover, when the teacher held the learner's hand on the shock plate, the compliance rate dropped to 30%.

> **foot-in-the-door technique**
> a method for inducing compliance in which a small request is followed by a larger request

Conformity

We are said to *conform* when we change our behavior to adhere to *social norms.* Explicit social norms are often made into rules and laws such as those that require us to whisper in libraries and to slow down when driving past a school. There are also unspoken or implicit social norms, such as those that cause us to face the front in an elevator or to be "fashionably late" for social gatherings. Can you think of some instances in which you have conformed to social pressure?

The tendency to conform to social norms is often good. Many norms have evolved because they promote comfort and survival. Group pressure can also promote maladaptive behavior, as when people engage in risky behavior because "everyone is doing it." *Why do so many people tend to follow the crowd?* To answer this question, let us look at a classic experiment on conformity conducted by Solomon Asch in the early 1950s.

The Asch Study

Can you believe what you see with your own eyes? Seeing is believing, isn't it? Not if you were a subject in Asch's (1952) study.

Let's say you entered a laboratory room with seven other subjects, supposedly taking part in an experiment on visual discrimination. At the front of the room stood a man holding cards with lines drawn on them.

The eight of you were seated in a series. You were given the seventh seat, a minor fact at the time. The man explained the task. There was a single line on the card on the left. Three lines were drawn on the card at the right (see Figure 14.6). One line on the right card

A. Standard line

B. Comparison lines

Figure 14.6

Cards Used in the Asch Study on Conformity

Which line on card B (1, 2, or 3) is the same length as the line on card A? Line 2, right? But would you say "2" if you were a member of a group and six people answering ahead of you all said "3"? Are you sure?

social facilitation
the process by which a person's performance is increased when other members of a group engage in similar behavior

was the same length as the line on the left card. You and the other subjects were to call out, one at a time, which of the three lines—1, 2, or 3—was the same length as the one on the card on the left. Simple.

The subjects to your right spoke out in order: "3," "3," "3," "3," "3," "3." Now it was your turn. Line 3 was clearly the same length as the line on the first card, so you said "3." The fellow after you then chimed in: "3." That's all there was to it. Then two other cards were set up at the front of the room. This time line 2 was clearly the same length as the line on the first card. The answers were "2," "2," "2," "2," "2," "2." Again it was your turn. You said "2," and perhaps your mind began to wander. Your stomach was gurgling a bit. The fellow after you said "2." Another pair of cards was held up. Line 3 was clearly the correct answer. The six people on your right spoke in turn: "1," "1 . . ." Wait a second! ". . . 1," "1." You forgot about dinner and studied the lines briefly. No, line 1 was too short by a good half-inch. But the next two subjects said "1" and suddenly it was your turn. Your hands had become sweaty, and there was a lump in your throat. You wanted to say "3," but was it right? There was really no time, and you had already paused noticeably. You said "1," and so did the last fellow.

Now your attention was riveted on the task. Much of the time you agreed with the other seven judges, but sometimes you did not. And for some reason beyond your understanding, they were in perfect agreement even when they were wrong—assuming you could trust your eyes. The experiment was becoming an uncomfortable experience, and you began to doubt your judgment.

The discomfort in the Asch study was caused by the pressure to conform. Actually, the other seven recruits were confederates of the experimenter. They prearranged a number of incorrect responses. The sole purpose of the study was to see whether you would conform to the erroneous group judgments.

How many people in Asch's study caved in? How many went along with the crowd rather than give what they thought to be the right answer? Seventy-five percent. *Three out of four agreed with the majority's wrong answer at least once.*

Fiction

Seeing is not always believing—especially when the group sees things differently.

Factors That Influence Conformity

Several factors increase the tendency to conform, including belonging to a collectivist rather than an individualistic society, the desire to be liked by other members of the group (but valuing being right over being liked decreases the tendency to conform), low self-esteem, social shyness, and lack of familiarity with the task (Phalet & Schoenpflug, 2001; Santee & Maslach, 1982). Other factors in conformity include group size and social support. The likelihood of conformity, even to incorrect group judgments, increases rapidly as group size grows to five members, then rises more slowly as the group grows to about eight members. At about that point the maximum chance of conformity is reached. Yet finding one other person who supports your minority opinion is apparently enough to encourage you to stick to your guns (Morris et al., 1977).

LO⁵ Group Behavior

To be human is to belong to groups. Groups have much to offer us. They help us satisfy our needs for affection, attention, and belonging. They empower us to do things we could not manage by ourselves. But groups can also pressure us into doing things we might not do if we were acting alone, such as taking great risks or attacking other people.

This section considers ways in which people behave differently as group members than they would as individuals. We begin with social facilitation.

Social Facilitation

When you are given a group assignment, do you work harder or less hard than you would alone? Why? One effect of groups on individual behavior is social facilitation. Runners and bicycle riders tend to move faster when they are members of a group. Research suggests that the presence of other people

JULIAN FINNEY/GETTY IMAGES

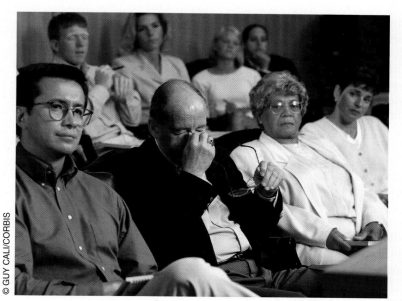
© GUY CALI/CORBIS

Group Decision Making

Organizations use groups such as committees or juries to make decisions in the belief that group decisions are more accurate than individual decisions (Gigone & Hastie, 1997). *How do groups make decisions?* Social psychologists have discovered a number of "rules," or social decision schemes, that govern much of group decision making (Stasser, 1999). Here are some examples:

1 *The majority-wins scheme.* In this commonly used scheme, the group arrives at the decision that was initially supported by the majority. This scheme appears to guide decision making most often when there is no single objectively correct decision. An example is a decision about which car models to build when their popularity has not been tested in the court of public opinion.

2 *The truth-wins scheme.* In this scheme, as more information is provided and opinions are discussed, the group comes to recognize that one approach is objectively correct. For example, a group deciding whether to use SAT scores in admitting students to college would profit from information about whether the scores do predict college success.

3 *The two-thirds majority scheme.* Juries tend to convict defendants when two-thirds of the jury initially favors conviction.

4 *The first-shift rule.* In this scheme, the group tends to adopt the decision that reflects the first shift in opinion expressed by any group member. If a jury is deadlocked, the members may eventually follow the lead of the first juror to switch his position.

Polarization and the "Risky Shift"

Are group decisions more risky or more conservative than those of the individual members of the group? We might think that a group decision would be more conservative than an individual decision. After all, shouldn't there be an effort to compromise, to "split the difference"? We might also expect that a few mature individuals would be able to balance the opinions of daredevils.

Groups do not always appear to work as we

increases our levels of arousal, or motivation (Platania & Moran, 2001; Thomas et al., 2002). At high levels of arousal, our performance of simple tasks is facilitated. Our performance of complex responses may be impaired, however. For this reason, a well-rehearsed speech may be delivered masterfully before a larger audience, while an impromptu speech may be hampered by a large audience.

+ = −

Social facilitation may be influenced by evaluation apprehension as well as arousal—that is, by concern that they are evaluating us (Platania & Moran, 2001; Thomas et al., 2002). When giving a speech, we may "lose our thread" if we are distracted by the audience and focus too much on its apparent reaction. If we believe that we have begun to flounder, evaluation apprehension may skyrocket. As a result, our performance may falter even more.

The presence of others can also impair performance—not when we are acting *before* a group but when we are anonymous members *of* a group (Guerin, 1999). Workers, for example, may "goof off" or engage in *social loafing*—that is failure to make a significant effort because others have made or are making such an effort—when they believe they will not be found out and held accountable. Under these group conditions there is no evaluation apprehension, but rather there may be diffusion of responsibility in groups. Each person may feel less obligation to help because others are present, especially if the others are perceived as being capable of doing the job (Hart et al., 2001). Group members may also reduce their efforts if an apparently capable member makes no contribution but "rides free" on the efforts of others.

> "Smart people working collectively can be dumber than the sum of their brains."
> —Schwartz & Wald, 2003

might expect, however. Consider the *polarization* effect. As an individual, you might recommend that your company risk an investment of $500,000 to develop or market a new product. Other company executives, polled individually, might risk similar amounts. If you were gathered together to make a group decision, however, you would probably recommend either an amount well above this figure or nothing at all (Kamalanabhan et al., 2000). This group effect is called *polarization,* or the taking of an extreme position. If you had to gamble on which way the decision would go, however, you would do better to place your money on movement toward the higher sum—that is, to bet on a *risky shift.* Why?

One possibility is that one member of the group may reveal information that the others were not aware of. This information may clearly point in one direction or the other. With doubts removed, the group moves decisively in the appropriate direction. It is also possible that social facilitation occurs in the group setting and that the resulting greater motivation prompts more extreme decisions.

Why, however, do groups tend to take *greater* risks than those their members would take as individuals? One answer is diffusion of responsibility (Kamalanabhan et al., 2000). If the venture flops, the blame will not be placed on you alone.

Groupthink

Groupthink, a concept originated by Irving Janis (1982), is a problem that sometimes arises in group decision making. *What is groupthink?* In **groupthink**, group members tend to be more influenced by group cohesiveness and a dynamic leader than by the realities of the situation (Turner et al., 2007). Group problem solving may degenerate into groupthink when a group senses an external threat (Underhill, 2008). Groupthink is usually fueled by a dynamic group leader. The threat heightens the cohesiveness of the group and is a source of stress. Under stress, group members tend not to consider all their options carefully and frequently make flawed decisions.

Groupthink has been connected with fiascos such as the Bay of Pigs invasion of Cuba, the escalation of the Vietnam War, the Watergate scandal, and NASA's decision to launch the *Challenger* and *Columbia* space shuttles despite engineers' warnings about the dangers created by cold weather and falling foam (Brownstein, 2003; Schwartz & Wald, 2003). Janis (1982) and other researchers (Pratkanis, 2007) note several characteristics of groupthink that contribute to flawed group decisions:

1 *Feelings of invulnerability.* Each decision-making group might have believed that it was beyond the reach of critics or the law.

2 *The group's belief in its rightness.* These groups apparently believed in the rightness of what they were doing.

3 *Discrediting of information contrary to the group's decision.* The government group involved in the Iran-Contra affair knowingly broke the law. Its members apparently discredited the law by (a) deciding that it was inconsistent with the best interests of the United States, and (b) enlisting private citizens to do the dirty work so that the government was not directly involved.

4 *Pressures on group members to conform.* Striving for unanimity overrides the quest for realism, and authority can trump expertise.

5 *Stereotyping of members of the out-group.* Members of the group that broke the law in the Iran-Contra affair reportedly stereotyped people who would oppose them as "communist sympathizers" and "knee-jerk liberals."

Groupthink can be averted if group leaders encourage members to remain skeptical about options and to feel free to ask probing questions and disagree with one another.

{ **Strength in Numbers? Maybe Not.** }

In their classic experiment, Darley and Latané (1968) had male subjects perform meaningless tasks in cubicles. Then, while they were working they heard a (convincing) recording of a person apparently having an epileptic seizure. When the men thought that four other persons were immediately available, only 31% tried to help the victim. When they thought that no one else was available, however, 85% of them tried to help.

As in other areas of group behavior, it seems that diffusion of responsibility inhibits helping behavior in groups or crowds. When we are in a group, we are often willing to let George (or Georgette) do it. When George isn't around, we are more willing to help others ourselves.

© 2010 DIGITAL VISION / PHOTO LIBRARY

Mob Behavior and Deindividuation

Have you ever done something as a member of a group that you would not have done as an individual? What was it? What motivated you? How do you feel about it?

The Frenchman Gustave Le Bon (1895–1960) branded mobs and crowds as irrational, resembling a "beast with many heads." Mob actions such as race riots and lynchings sometimes seem to operate on a psychology of their own. *How is it that mild-mannered people commit mayhem when they are part of a mob?*

Deindividuation

When people act as individuals, fear of consequences and self-evaluation tend to prevent them from engaging in antisocial behavior. But in a mob, they may experience deindividuation, a state of reduced self-awareness and lowered concern for social evaluation. Many factors lead to deindividuation, including anonymity, diffusion of responsibility, arousal due to noise and crowding, and a focus on emerging group norms rather than on one's own values (Baron et al., 2006). Under these circumstances crowd members behave more aggressively than they would as individuals.

Altruism and the Bystander Effect

Altruism—selfless concern for the welfare of others—is connected with some heroic behavior. Humans have sacrificed themselves to ensure the survival of their children or of comrades in battle. So how, one might ask, could the murder of twenty-eight-year-old Kitty Genovese have happened? It took place in New York City more than forty years ago (Rasenberger, 2004). Murder was not unheard of in the Big Apple, but Kitty had screamed for help as her killer stalked her for more than half an hour and stabbed her in three separate attacks. Thirty-eight neighbors heard the commotion. Twice, the assault was interrupted by their voices and bedroom lights. Each time the attacker returned. Yet nobody came to the victim's aid. No one even called the police.

Why? Some witnesses said matter-of-factly that they did not want to get involved. One said that he was tired. Still others said, "I don't know." As a nation,

Truth

It is true that nearly forty people stood by and did nothing while a woman was being stabbed to death.

are we a callous bunch who would rather watch than help when others are in trouble?

The Helper

Why do people come to the aid of others, or ignore them? It turns out that many factors are involved in helping behavior:

1 Observers are more likely to help when they are in a good mood (Baron et al., 2006; Sprecher et al., 2007). Perhaps good moods impart a sense of personal power—the feeling that we can handle the situation.

2 People who are empathic are more likely to help people in need (Decety & Batson, 2009). Women are more likely than men to be empathic and thus more likely to help people in need (Trobst et al., 1994).

3 Bystanders may not help unless they believe that an emergency exists (Baron et al., 2006).

4 Observers must assume the responsibility to act (Baron et al., 2006). A lone person may have been more likely to try to help Kitty Genovese. *Diffusion of responsibility* may inhibit helping behavior in crowds.

5 Observers must know what to do. Observers who are not sure that they can take charge of the situation may stay on the sidelines for fear of making a social blunder or of getting hurt themselves.

6 Observers are more likely to help people they know (Hopkins & Powers, 2009). Evolutionary psychologists suggest that altruism is selfish from an evolutionary point of view when it helps close relatives or others who are similar to us to survive (Bruene & Ribbert, 2002). It helps us perpetuate a genetic code similar to our own. This view suggests that we are more likely to be altruistic with our relatives rather than strangers, however.

7 Observers are more likely to help people who are similar to themselves. Being able to identify with the person in need promotes helping behavior (Cialdini et al., 1997).

Ordinary People in Extraordinary Times

But let us not end this chapter and this book on a negative note. Let us think, instead, about the altruism of the firefighters, police officers, and ordinary people who came to the aid of the victims of the suicide terrorism of September 11, 2001. Following the attacks, thousands evacuated lower Manhattan by ferry to New Jersey. Residents of New Jersey drove up and down the streets near the ferry, asking if they could give evacuees rides or help in any other way. And people heading away from the devastation in Manhattan were happy to share their taxicabs, even with strangers. If you know a little about New York City, you know that's rather special—but it's also something done by ordinary people in extraordinary times.

deindividuation the process by which group members may discontinue self-evaluation and adopt group norms and attitudes

altruism unselfish concern for the welfare of others

Statistics

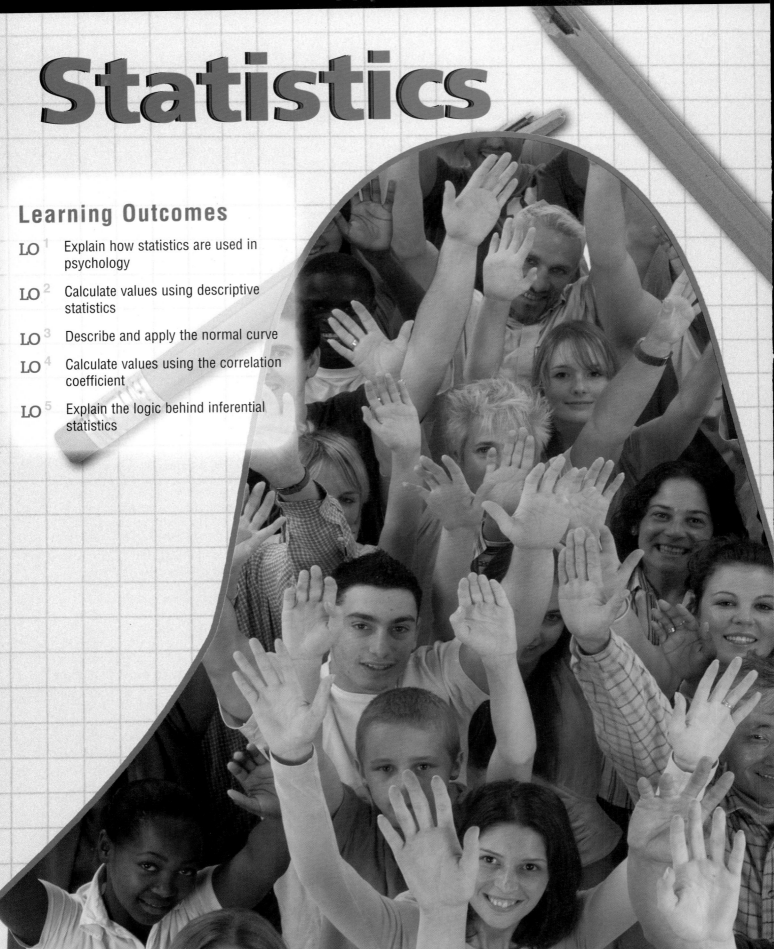

Learning Outcomes

LO ^{1} Explain how statistics are used in psychology

LO ^{2} Calculate values using descriptive statistics

LO ^{3} Describe and apply the normal curve

LO ^{4} Calculate values using the correlation coefficient

LO ^{5} Explain the logic behind inferential statistics

> **To what degree do you think the people in your school represent the population of the United States? North America? The world?**

LO¹ Statistics

Imagine that some visitors from outer space arrive outside Madison Square Garden in New York City. Their goal this dark and numbing winter evening is to learn all they can about planet Earth. They are drawn inside the Garden by lights, shouts, and warmth. The spotlighting inside rivets their attention to a wood-floored arena where the New York Big Apples are hosting the California Quakes in a briskly contested basketball game.

Our visitors use their sophisticated instruments to take some measurements of the players. Some interesting statistics are sent back to their planet of origin: It appears that (1) 100% of Earthlings are male and (2) the height of Earthlings ranges from 6'1" to 7'2".

Truth or Fiction?

What do you think?

Folklore, common sense, or nonsense? Place a T for "True" or F for "False" on the lines provided (you'll learn the answers as you read through the text).

__ Basketball players could be said to be abnormal.

__ Being a "ten" is not always a good thing.

__ You should not assume that you can walk across a river with an average depth of four feet.

__ Adding people's incomes and then dividing them by the number of people can be an awful way of showing the average income.

__ Psychologists express your IQ score in terms of how deviant you are.

__ An IQ score of 130 is more impressive than an SAT score of 500.

These measurements are called **statistics**. *What is statistics?* Statistics is the name given the science concerned with obtaining and organizing numerical information or measurements. Our imagined visitors have sent home statistics about the gender and size of human beings that are at once accurate and misleading. Although they accurately measured the basketball players (we have translated their units of measurement into feet and inches for readers' convenience), their small **sample** of Earth's **population** was, shall we say, distorted.

What are samples and populations? A population is a complete group of people, other animals, or measures from which a sample is drawn. For example, all people on Earth could be defined as the population of interest. So could all women, or all women in the United States. A sample is a group of measures drawn from a population. Fortunately for us Earthlings, about half of the world's population is female. And the **range** of heights observed by the aliens, of 6'1" to 7'2", is both restricted and too high— much too high. People vary in height by more than 1 foot and

statistics
numerical facts assembled in such a manner that they provide useful information about measures or scores; (from the Latin *status*, meaning "standing" or "position")

sample
part of a population

population
a complete group from which a sample is selected

range
a measure of variability defined as the high score in a distribution minus the low score

average
the central tendency of a group of measures, expressed either as the mean, median, or mode of a distribution

descriptive statistics
the branch of statistics that is concerned with providing descriptive information about a distribution of scores

1 inch. And our average height is not between 6'1" and 7'2"; rather, it is a number of inches below.

Psychologists, like our imagined visitors, are vitally concerned with measuring human as well as animal characteristics and traits—not just physical characteristics as height, but also psychological traits such as intelligence, sociability, aggressiveness, neatness, anxiety, and depression. By observing the central tendencies (averages) and variations in measurement from person to person, psychologists can say that one person is average or above average in intelligence, or that someone else is less anxious than, say, 60% of the population.

But psychologists, unlike our aliens, attempt to select a sample that accurately represents the entire population. Professional basketball players do not represent the entire human species. Their "abnormalities" are assets to them, of course, not deficits.

In this appendix we survey some of the statistical methods used by psychologists to draw conclusions about the measurements they take in research. First we discuss *descriptive statistics* and learn what types of statements we can make about height and other human traits. Then we discuss the *normal curve* and learn why basketball players are abnormal—at least in terms of height. We explain *correlation coefficients* and provide you with some less-than-shocking news: As a group, students who study obtain higher grades than students who do not study. Finally, we have a look at *inferential statistics,* and we see why we can be bold enough to say that the difference in height between basketball players and other people

is not a chance fluctuation or fluke. Basketball players are in fact *statistically significantly* taller than the general population.

LO^2 Descriptive Statistics

Being told that someone is a ten may sound great at first. However, it is not very descriptive unless you know something about how the scores on the scale are distributed and how frequently one finds a ten. Fortunately—for tens, if not for the rest of us—one usually means that the person is a ten on a scale of from one to ten, and that ten is the highest possible score on the scale. If this is not sufficient, one will also be told that tens are few and far between—rather unusual statistical events.

The idea of the scale from one to ten may not be very scientific, but it does suggest something about **descriptive statistics.** *What is descriptive statistics?* (Why isn't it always good to be a ten?) Descriptive statistics is the branch of statistics that provides information about distributions of scores. We can use descriptive statistics to clarify our understanding of a distribution of scores such as heights, test grades, IQs, or even

© IMAGE SOURCE BLACK/JUPITERIMAGES

Table A.1

Roster of Quakes Versus Big Apples at New York

A glance at the rosters for a recent basketball game in which the New York Big Apples "entertained" the California Quakes shows that the heights of the team members, combined, ranged from 6'1" to 7'2". Do the heights of the team members represent those of the general male population? What do you think?

CALIFORNIA QUAKES		NEW YORK BIG APPLES	
2 Callahan	6'7"	3 Roosevelt	6'1"
5 Daly	6'11"	12 Chaffee	6'5"
6 Chico	6'2"	13 Baldwin	6'9"
12 Capistrano	6'3"	25 Delmar	6'6"
21 Brentwood	6'5"	27 Merrick	6'8"
25 Van Nuys	6'3"	28 Hewlett	6'6"
31 Clemente	6'9"	33 Hollis	6'9"
32 Whittier	6'8"	42 Bedford	6'5"
41 Fernando	7'2"	43 Coram	6'2"
43 Watts	6'9"	45 Hampton	6'10"
53 Huntington	6'6"	53 Ardsley	6'10"

increases or decreases in measures of aggressive behavior following the drinking of alcohol. For example, descriptive statistics can help us determine measures of central tendency (averages) and to determine how much fluctuation or variability there is in the scores. Being a ten loses much of its charm if the average score is an eleven. Being a 10 is more remarkable in a distribution whose scores range from 1 to 10 than it is in a distribution whose scores range from 9 to 11.

Let us now consider some of the concerns of descriptive statistics: the frequency distribution, measures of central tendency (types of averages), and measures of variability.

Table A.2

Frequency Distribution of Basketball Players (Quakes and Big Apples Combined), with a One-Inch Class Interval

CLASS INTERVAL	NUMBER OF PLAYERS IN CLASS
6'1"–6'1.9"	1
6'2"–6'2.9"	2
6'3"–6'3.9"	2
6'4"–6'4.9"	0
6'5"–6'5.9"	3
6'6"–6'6.9"	3
6'7"–6'7.9"	1
6'8"–6'8.9"	2
6'9"–6'9.9"	4
6'10"–6'10.9"	2
6'11"–6'11.9"	1
7'0"–7'0.9"	0
7'1"–7'1.9"	0
7'2"–7'2.9"	1

The Frequency Distribution

What is a frequency distribution? A frequency distribution takes scores or items of raw data, puts them into order from the lowest to the highest, and indicates how often a score appears. A frequency distribution groups data according to class intervals, although the class may be a single unit (one), as in Table A.2. Table A.1 shows the rosters for a

> **frequency distribution**
> an ordered set of data that indicates the frequency (how often) with which scores appear

frequency histogram
a graphic representation of a frequency distribution that uses rectangular solids (bars) to represent the frequency with which scores appear

frequency polygon
a graphic representation of a frequency distribution that connects the points that show the frequencies with which scores appear, thereby creating a multisided geometric figure

recent basketball game between the California Quakes and the New York Big Apples. The players are listed according to the numbers on their uniforms. Table A.2 shows a frequency distribution of the heights of the players, with the two teams combined. The class interval in Table A.2 is 1 inch.

It would also be possible to use other class intervals, such as 3 inches, as shown in Table A.3. In determining the size of a class interval, the researcher tries to collapse the data into a small enough number of classes to ensure that they will be meaningful at a glance. But the researcher also tries to keep a large enough number of categories (classes) to ensure that important differences are not obscured.

Table A.3 obscures the fact that no players are 6'4" tall. If the researcher believes that this information is extremely important, a class interval of 1 inch may be maintained.

Figure A.1 shows two methods of graphing the information in Table A.3: the frequency histogram and the frequency polygon. Students sometimes have difficulty interpreting graphs, but the purpose of graphs is to reveal key information about frequency distributions at a glance. Note that in both kinds of graph, the frequency histogram and the frequency polygon, the class intervals are usually

drawn along the horizontal line. The horizontal line is also known as the x-axis. The numbers of cases (scores, persons, or events) in each class interval are shown along the vertical line, which is also known as the y-axis. In the histogram, the number of scores in each class interval is represented by a bar—a rectangular solid—so that the graph looks like a series of steps. In the polygon, the number of scores in each class interval is plotted as a point. The points are connected to form a many-sided geometric figure (polygon). Note that empty class intervals were added at each end of the frequency polygon so that the sides of the figure could be brought down to the x-axis to close the geometric figure.

Table A.3

Frequency Distribution of Heights of Basketball Players, Using a Three-Inch Class Interval

CLASS INTERVAL	NUMBER OF PLAYERS IN CLASS
6'1"–6'3.9"	5
6'4"–6'6.9"	6
6'7"–6'9.9"	7
6'10"–7'0.9"	3
7'1"–7'3.9"	1

Measures of Central Tendency

What are measures of central tendency? Measures of central tendency are "averages" that show the center or balancing points of a frequency distribution. There are three commonly used types of measures of central tendency: the *mean*, the *median*, and the *mode*. Each attempts to describe something about

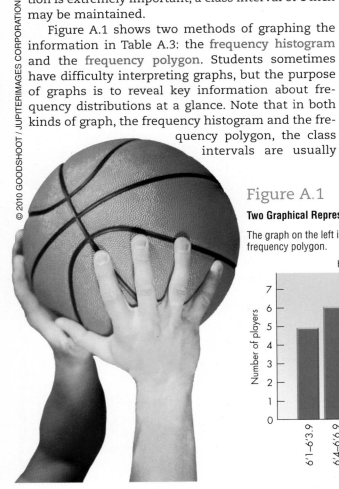

Figure A.1

Two Graphical Representations of the Data in Table A.3

The graph on the left is called a frequency histogram, or bar graph. The graph on the right is called a frequency polygon.

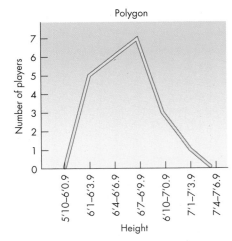

the scores in a frequency distribution through the use of a typical or representative number.

The **mean** is what most people think of as "the average." We obtain the mean of a distribution by adding up the scores and then dividing the sum by the number of scores. In the case of the basketball players, it would be advisable to first convert the heights into a single unit, such as inches (6'1" becomes 73", and so on). If we add all the heights in inches and then divide by the number of players (22), we obtain a mean height of 78.73". If we convert that number back into units of feet and inches, we obtain 6'6.73".

The **median** is the score of the middle case in a distribution. It is the score beneath which 50% of the cases fall. In a distribution with an even number of cases, such as the distribution of the heights of the 22 basketball players as shown in Table A.2, we obtain the median by finding the mean of the two middle cases. When we list the 22 cases in ascending order (moving from lowest to highest), the 11th case is 6'6" and the 12th case is 6'7". Therefore, the median of the distribution is (6'6" + 6'7") /2, or 6'6.5".

When we analyze the heights of the basketball players, we find that the mean and the median are similar. Either one serves as a useful indicator of the central tendency of the data. But suppose we are trying to find the average savings of 30 families living on a suburban block. Let us assume that 29 of the 30 families have savings between $8,000 and $12,000, adding up to $294,000. But the 30th family has savings of $1,400,000! The mean savings for a family on this block would thus be $56,467. The mean can be greatly distorted by one or two extreme scores. An IQ score of 145 would similarly distort the mean of the IQ scores of a class of 20 students, among whom the other 19 IQ scores ranged from 93 to 112. Then, too, if a few basketball players signed up for one

Never try to walk across a river just because it has an average depth of four feet.
—Martin Friedman

of your classes, the mean of the students' heights would be distorted in an upward direction.

When there are a few extreme scores in a distribution, the median is a better indicator of central tendency. The median savings on our hypothetical block would lie between $8,000 and $12,000. Thus it would be more representative of the central tendency of savings. Studies of the incomes of families in the United States usually report median rather than mean incomes just to avoid the distortion of findings that would occur if the incomes of a handful of billionaires were treated in the same way as more common incomes. On the other hand, one could argue that choosing the median as the average obscures or hides the extreme scores, which are just as "real" as the other scores. Perhaps it is best to use the median and a footnote—a rather big footnote.

The **mode** is simply the most frequently occurring score or measure in a distribution. The mode of the data in Table A.1 is 6'9" because this height occurs most often among the players on the two teams. The median class interval for the data shown in Table A.3 is 6'6.5" to 6'9.5". With this particular distribution, the mode is somewhat higher than the mean or the median.

In some cases the mode is a more appropriate description of the central tendency of a distribution than the mean or the median. Figure A.2 shows a **bimodal** distribution—that is, a distribution with two modes. This is a hypothetical distribution of test scores obtained by a class. The mode at the left indicates the most common class interval (45 to 49) for students who did not study, and the mode to the right shows the most common class interval (65 to 69) for students who did study. (Don't be alarmed. I'm sure that the professor, who is extremely fair, will be delighted to curve the grades so that the interval of 75 to 79 is an A+ and the interval of 65 to 69 is at least a B.) The mean and median test scores would probably lie within the 55 to 59 class interval, yet use of that interval as the measure of central tendency could obscure rather than reveal the important aspects of this distribution of test scores. It might suggest that the test was too hard, not that a number of students chose not to study. Similarly, one of the distribution's modes might be a bit larger than the other, so one

mean
a type of average that is calculated by adding all the scores and then dividing by the number of scores

median
the central score in a frequency distribution; the score beneath which 50% of the cases fall

mode
the most frequently occurring number or score in a distribution

bimodal
having two modes

standard deviation
a measure of the variability of a distribution, obtained by the formula

$$S.D. = \sqrt{\frac{\text{Sum of } d^2}{N}}$$

could follow the exact rule for finding the mode and report just one of them. But this approach would also hide the meaning of this particular distribution of scores. All in all, it is clearly best to visualize this distribution of scores as bimodal. Even when the modes are not exactly equal, it is often most accurate to report distributions as bimodal, or, when there are three or more modes, as multimodal. One chooses one's measure or measures of central tendency to describe the essential features of a frequency distribution, not to hide them.

Figure A.2

A Bimodal Distribution

This hypothetical distribution represents students' scores on a test. The mode at the left represents the central tendency of the test scores of students who did not study. The mode at the right represents the mode of the test scores of students who did study.

Measures of Variability

Our hypothetical class obtained test scores ranging from class intervals of 35 to 39 to class intervals of 75 to 79. That is, the scores *varied* from the lower class interval to the higher class interval. Now, if all the students had obtained scores from 55 to 59 or from to 65 to 69, the scores would not have varied as much; that is, they would have clustered closer to one another and would have had lower variability.

What are measures of variability? The measures of the variability of a distribution inform us about the spread of scores—that is, about the typical distances of scores from the average score. Two commonly used measures of variability are the *range* of scores and the *standard deviation* of scores.

The range of scores in a distribution is defined as the difference between the highest score and the lowest score. The range is obtained by subtracting the lowest score from the highest score. The range of heights in Table A.2 is obtained by subtracting 6'1" from 7'2", or 1'1". It is useful to know the range of temperatures when we move to an area with a different climate so that we may anticipate the weather and dress for it appropriately. A teacher must have some understanding of the range of abilities or skills in a class in order to teach effectively. An understanding of the range of human heights can be used to design doorways, beds, and headroom in automobiles. Even so, the typical doorway is 6'8" high; and, as we saw with the California Quakes and New York Big Apples, some people will have to duck to get through.

The range is an imperfect measure of variability because of the manner in which it is influenced by extreme scores. The range of savings of the 30 families on our suburban block is $1,400,000 minus $8,000, or $1,392,000. This is a large number, and it is certainly true. However, it tells us little about the *typical* variation of savings accounts, which lie within a more restricted range of $8,000 to $12,000.

The **standard deviation** is a statistic that does a better job of showing how the scores in a distribution are distributed (spread) about the mean. It is usually better than the range because it considers every score in the distribution, not just the extreme (highest and lowest) scores. Consider Figure A.3. Each distribution in the figure has the same number of scores, the same mean, and the same range of scores. However, the scores in the distribution on the right side cluster more closely about the mean. Therefore, the standard deviation of the distribution on the right is smaller. That is, the typical score deviates less from the mean score.

Figure A.3

Hypothetical Distributions of Student Test Scores

Each distribution has the same number of scores, the same mean, even the same range, but the standard deviation (a measure of variability) is greater for the distribution on the left because the scores tend to be farther from the mean.

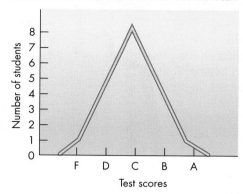

The standard deviation is usually abbreviated as S.D. It is calculated by the formula

$$\text{S.D.} = \sqrt{\frac{\text{Sum of } d^2}{N}}$$

where d equals the deviation of each score from the mean of the distribution and N equals the number of scores in the distribution.

Let us find the mean and standard deviation of the IQ scores listed in column 1 of Table A.4. To obtain the mean we add all the scores, attain 1,500, and then divide by the number of scores (15) to obtain a mean of 100. We obtain the deviation score (d) for each IQ score by subtracting the score from 100. The d for an IQ score of 85 equals 100 minus 85, or 15, and so on. Then we square each d and add the squares. The S.D. equals the square root of the sum of squares (1,426) divided by the number of scores (15), or 9.75.

As an additional exercise, we can show that the S.D. of the test scores on the left (in Figure A.3) is greater than that for the scores on the right. First we assign the grades a number according to a 4.0 system. Let A = 4, B = 3, C = 2, D = 1, and F = 0. The S.D. for each distribution is computed in Table A.5. The larger S.D. for the

Table A.4

Hypothetical Scores Obtained from an IQ Testing

IQ SCORE	d (DEVIATION SCORE)	d^2 (DEVIATION SCORE SQUARED)
85	15	225
87	13	169
89	11	121
90	10	100
93	7	49
97	3	9
97	3	9
100	0	0
101	−1	1
104	−4	16
105	−5	25
110	−10	100
112	−12	144
113	−13	169
117	−17	289
Sum of IQ scores = 1,500		Sum of d^2 scores = 1,426

Mean = $\dfrac{\text{Sum of scores}}{\text{Number of scores}} = \dfrac{1,500}{15} = 100$

Standard Deviation (S.D.) = $\sqrt{\dfrac{\text{Sum of } d^2}{N}} = \sqrt{\dfrac{1,426}{15}} = \sqrt{95.07} = 9.75$

Table A.5

Computation of Standard Deviations for Test-Score Distributions in Figure A.3

DISTRIBUTION AT LEFT			DISTRIBUTION TO THE RIGHT		
GRADE	d	d^2	GRADE	d	d^2
A (4)	2	4	A (4)	2	4
A (4)	2	4	B (3)	1	1
A (4)	2	4	B (3)	1	1
B (3)	1	1	B (3)	1	1
B (3)	1	1	B (3)	1	1
B (3)	1	1	C (2)	0	0
B (3)	1	1	C (2)	0	0
C (2)	0	0	C (2)	0	0
C (2)	0	0	C (2)	0	0
C (2)	0	0	C (2)	0	0
C (2)	0	0	C (2)	0	0
D (1)	−1	1	C (2)	0	0
D (1)	−1	1	C (2)	0	0
D (1)	−1	1	D (1)	−1	1
D (1)	−1	1	D (1)	−1	1
F (0)	−2	4	D (1)	−1	1
F (0)	−2	4	D (1)	−1	1
F (0)	−2	4	F (0)	−2	4
Sum of grades = 36			Sum of grades = 36		
Mean grade = 36/18 = 2			Mean grade = 36/18 = 2		
Sum of d^2 = 32			Sum of d^2 = 16		
Sum of grades = 36			Sum of grades = 36		
Mean grade = 36/18 = 2			Mean grade = 36/18 = 2		
Sum of d^2 = 32			Sum of d^2 = 16		
S.D. = $\sqrt{32/18}$ = 1.33			S.D. = $\sqrt{16/18}$ = 0.94		

Truth

Psychologists may express your IQ score in terms of how deviant you are from the average or mean score.

distribution on the left indicates that the scores in that distribution are more variable, or tend to be farther from the mean.

LO³ The Normal Curve

Many human traits and characteristics including height and intelligence seem to be distributed in a pattern known as a normal distribution. *What is a normal distribution?* In a **normal distribution**, the mean, the median, and the mode all fall at the same data point or score. Scores cluster most heavily about the mean, fall off rapidly in either direction at first (as shown in Figure A.4), and then taper off more gradually.

The curve in Figure A.4 is bell-shaped. This type of distribution is also called a **normal curve** or bell-shaped curve. This curve is hypothesized as the distribution of variables in which different scores are determined by chance variation. Height is thought to be largely determined by chance combinations of genetic material. A distribution of the heights of a random sample of the population approximates normal distributions for men and women, with the mean of the distribution for men a few inches higher than the mean for women.

Test developers traditionally assumed that intelligence was also randomly or normally distributed among the population. For that reason, they constructed intelligence tests so that scores would be distributed as close to "normal" as possible. In actuality, IQ scores are also influenced by environmental factors and chromosomal abnormalities, so that the resultant curves are not perfectly normal. The means of most IQ tests are defined as scores of 100 points. The Wechsler scales are constructed to have standard deviations of 15 points, as shown in Figure A.4. A standard deviation of 15 points causes 50% of the Wechsler scores to fall between 90 and 110, which is called the "broad average" range. About 68% of scores (two out of three) fall between 85 and 115 (within a standard deviation of the mean), and more than 95% fall between 70 and 130—that is, within two standard deviations of the mean. The more extreme high (and low) IQ scores deviate more from the mean score.

The Scholastic Assessment Tests (SATs) were constructed so that the mean scores would be 500 points and the S.D. would be 100 points. Thus a score of 600 would equal or excel that of some 84% to 85% of the test takers. Because of the complex interaction of variables that determine SAT scores, their distribution is not exactly normal either. Moreover, the actual mean scores and standard deviations tend to vary from year to year, and, in the case of the SAT IIs, from test to test. The normal curve is an idealized curve.

MIKE DUNNING / GETTY IMAGES

Figure A.4

A Bell-Shaped or Normal Curve

In a normal curve, approximately two out of three cases (68%) lie within a standard deviation (S.D.) from the mean. The mean, median, and mode all lie at the same score. IQ tests and the Scholastic Assessment Tests (SATs) are constructed so that their distributions approximate the normal curve.

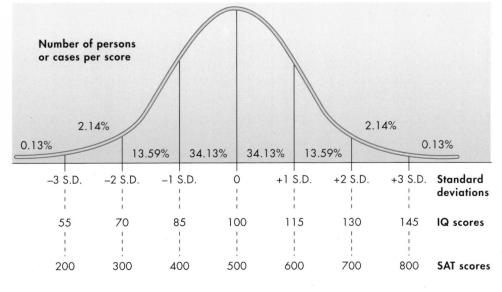

Number of persons or cases per score

0.13%	2.14%	13.59%	34.13%	34.13%	13.59%	2.14%	0.13%
−3 S.D.	−2 S.D.	−1 S.D.	0	+1 S.D.	+2 S.D.	+3 S.D.	**Standard deviations**
55	70	85	100	115	130	145	**IQ scores**
200	300	400	500	600	700	800	**SAT scores**

The IQ score of 130 is two standard deviations above the mean and exceeds that of more than 97% of the population. An SAT score of 500 is the mean SAT score and thus equals or excels that of about 50% of the population.

> ### Truth
>
> An IQ score of 130 is more impressive than an SAT score of 500. The IQ score is two standard deviations above the mean, and the SAT score is the mean for that test.

LO⁴ The Correlation Coefficient

What is the relationship between intelligence and educational achievement? Between cigarette smoking and lung cancer among humans? Between the personality trait of introversion and numbers of dates among college students? We cannot run experiments to determine whether the relationships between these variables are causal, because we cannot manipulate the independent variable. That is, we cannot assign high or low intelligence at random. Nor can we (ethically) assign some people to smoke cigarettes and others not to smoke. People must be allowed to make their own decisions, so it is possible that the same factors that lead some people to smoke—or to continue to smoke after they have experimented with cigarettes—also lead to lung cancer. (Even if we were to assign a group of people to a nonsmoking condition, could we monitor them continuously to make sure that they weren't sneaking puffs?) Nor can we designate who will be introverted and who will be extraverted. True, we could encourage people to act as if they are introverted or extraverted, but behavior is not the same thing as a personality trait. We cannot run true experiments to answer any of these questions, but the **correlation coefficient** can be used to reveal whether there is a relationship between intelligence and achievement,

a relationship between smoking and cancer, or a relationship between personality and dating. Correlational research shows that smoking and cancer are related but does not reveal cause and effect. However, experimental research with animals does strongly suggest that smoking will cause cancer in humans.

What is the correlation coefficient? The correlation coefficient is a statistic that describes the relationship between two variables. A correlation coefficient can vary from +1.00 to −1.00. A correlation coefficient of +1.00 is called a perfect positive correlation, and it describes the relationship between temperatures as measured by the Fahrenheit and Centigrade scales. A correlation coefficient of −1.00 is a perfect negative correlation, and a correlation of 0 (zero) reveals no relationship between variables.

As suggested by Figures A.5 and A.6, most correlation coefficients in psychological research are less than perfect. The left graph in Figure A.5 reveals a positive relationship between time spent studying and grade point averages. Because there is a positive correlation between the variables but the relationship is not perfect, the correlation coefficient will lie between 0.00 and +1.00. Perhaps it is about +0.60 or +0.70. However, we cannot absolutely predict what

> **correlation coefficient**
> a number between −1.00 and +1.00 that indicates the direction (negative or positive) and extent (from none to perfect) of the relationship between two variables

Figure A.5

Positive and Negative Correlations

When there is a positive correlation between variables, as there is between intelligence and achievement, one increases as the other increases. By and large, the more time students spend studying, the better their grades are likely to be, as suggested in the diagram to the left. (Each dot represents the amount of time a student spends studying each week and his or her grade point average.) But there is a negative correlation between grades and juvenile delinquency. As the number of delinquent acts per year increases, one's grade point average tends to decline. Correlational research may suggest but does not demonstrate cause and effect.

Positive correlation, as found between intelligence and academic achievement

Negative correlation, as found between delinquency and academic achievement

Figure A.6

Correlational Relationships, Cause and Effect

Correlational relationships may suggest but do not demonstrate cause and effect. In part A, there is a correlation between variables X and Y. Does this mean that either variable X causes variable Y or that variable Y causes variable X? Not necessarily. Other factors could affect both variables X and Y. Consider the examples of academic grades (variable X) and time spent studying (variable Y) in part B. There is a positive correlation between the two. Does this mean that studying contributes to good grades? Perhaps. Does it mean that good grades encourage studying? Again, perhaps. But there could also be other variables—such as cultural belief in the value of education, enjoyment of learning, even parental pressure to do well—that contribute both to time spent studying and good grades.

a person's GPA will be if we know the hours per week that he or she spends studying (nor can we predict exactly how much time the person spends studying on the basis of his or her GPA). Nevertheless, it would seem advisable to place oneself among those who spend a good deal of time studying if one wishes to achieve a good GPA.

The right drawing in Figure A.5 reveals a negative relationship between number of delinquent acts committed per year and GPA. The causal connection is less than perfectly clear. Does delinquency interfere with studying and academic achievement? Does poor achievement weaken a student's commitment to trying to get ahead through work? Do feelings of distance from "the system" contribute both to delinquent behavior and a low GPA? The answers are not to be found in Figure A.5, but the negative correlation between delinquent behavior and GPA does suggest that it is worthwhile to study the issues involved and—for a student—to distance himself or herself from delinquent behavior if he or she wishes to achieve in the academic world.

LO⁵ Inferential Statistics

Head Start programs have apparently raised children's intellectual functioning, as reflected in their grades and IQ scores. In one such study, children enrolled in a Head Start program obtained a mean IQ score of 99, whereas children similar in background who were not enrolled in Head Start obtained a mean IQ score of 93. Is this difference of six points in IQ *significant,* or does it represent a chance fluctuation in scores? In a study reported in Chapter 1, college students were provoked by people in league with the researchers. Some of the students believed they had drunk alcohol (in a cocktail with tonic water); others believed they had drunk tonic water only. The students were then given the opportunity to shock the individuals who had provoked them. Students who believed they had drunk alcohol chose higher levels of shock than students who believed they had drunk tonic water only. Did the mean difference in shock level chosen by the two groups of students represent actual differences between the groups, or might it have been a chance fluctuation? The individuals in the Head Start study were a sample of young children. The individuals in the alcohol study were a sample of college students. Inferential statistics help us determine whether we can conclude that the differences between such samples reflect real differences that are found in the populations that they represent.

Figure A.7

Distribution of Heights for Random Samples of Men and Women

Note that the mean height of the men is greater than that of the women. Is the group mean difference in height statistically significant? Researchers use a tool called inferential statistics to determine the answer.

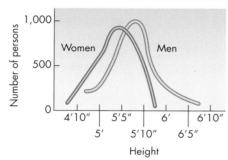

Descriptive statistics enables us to provide descriptive information about samples of scores. *What are inferential statistics?* **Inferential statistics** assist us in determining whether we can generalize differences among samples to the populations that they represent.

Figure A.7 shows the distribution of heights of 1,000 men and 1,000 women who were selected at random from the general U.S. population. The mean height for men is greater than the mean height for women. Can we conclude, or **infer**, that this difference in height is not just a chance fluctuation but represents an actual difference between the general populations of men and women? Or must we avoid such an inference and summarize our results by stating only that the mean height of the sample of men in the study was greater than the mean height of the sample of women in the study?

If we could not draw inferences about populations from studies of samples, our research findings would be limited indeed. We could speak only about the specific individuals studied. There would be no point to learning about any study in which you did not participate because it would not apply to you! Fortunately, that is not the case. Inferential statistics permits us to extend findings with samples to the populations from which they were drawn.

Statistically Significant Differences

We asked whether the differences in height between our samples of men and women were simply a chance fluctuation or whether they represented actual differences between the heights of men and women. Researchers tend not to talk about "real

> "Statistically significant differences are differences that are unlikely to be due to chance fluctuation."

differences" or "actual differences" between groups, however. Instead, they speak of statistically significant differences. Similarly, researchers asked whether differences in IQ scores between children in Head Start programs and other children from similar backgrounds were chance fluctuations or statistically significant differences. *What are "statistically significant" differences?* Statistically significant differences are differences that are unlikely to be due to chance fluctuation. Psychologists usually do not accept a difference as being statistically significant unless the probability (*p*) that it is due to chance fluctuation is less than 1 in 20 (i.e., $p < .05$). They are more comfortable labeling a difference as statistically significant when the probability (*p*) that it is due to chance fluctuation is less than 1 in 100 (i.e., $p < .01$).

Psychologists use formulas involving the means (e.g., mean IQ scores of 93 versus 99) and the standard deviations of sample groups to determine whether differences in means are statistically significant. As you can see in Figure A.8, the farther apart group means are, the more likely it is that they are statistically significant. In other words, if the men are on the average five inches taller than the women, it is more likely that the difference is statistically significant than if the men are only one-quarter of an inch taller on average. *Principle 1: Everything else being equal, the greater the difference between means, the greater the probability that the difference is statistically significant.* This makes common sense. After all, if you were told that your neighbor's car had gotten one-tenth of a mile more per gallon of gas than your car in the past year, you would probably attribute the difference to chance fluctuation. But if the difference were greater, say fourteen miles per gallon, you would probably assume that the difference reflected an actual difference in driving habits or the efficiency of the automobile.

As you can see in Figure A.9, the smaller the standard deviations (a measure of variability) of the groups, the more likely it is that the difference between means is statistically significant. Consider the extreme example in which there is *no* variability within each group. That is, imagine that every woman in the randomly selected sample of 1,000 women is exactly 5'5" tall. Similarly, imagine that every man in the randomly selected sample of 1,000

inferential statistics
the branch of statistics that is concerned with confidence with which conclusions drawn about samples can be extended to the populations from which the samples were drawn

infer
to go from the particular to the general; to draw a conclusion

Figure A.8

Decreasing and Increasing the Mean Group Difference in Heights

Everything else being equal, the greater the difference in group means, the greater the probability that the difference is statistically significant. The distribution on the right shows a greater difference in group means; therefore, there is a greater probability that the difference is statistically significant.

 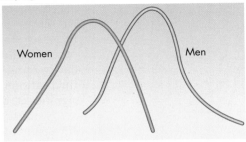

men is exactly 5'10" tall. In such a case the heights of the men and women would not overlap at all, and it would appear that the differences were statistically significant. Consider the other extreme—one with unnaturally large variability. Imagine that the heights of the women vary from 2' to 14' and that the heights of the men vary from 2'1" to 14'3". In such a case we might be more likely to assume that the difference in group means of 5" was a chance fluctuation. *Principle 2: Everything else being equal, the smaller the variability of the distributions of scores, the greater the probability that the difference in group means is statistically significant.*

Therefore, we cannot conclude that men are taller than women unless we know the average heights of men and women and how much the heights within each group vary. We must know both the central tendencies (means) and variability of the two distributions of heights in order to infer that the mean heights are statistically significantly different.

> It is often the case that eyeballing real data does not yield clear results or even good guesses.

We have been "eyeballing" the data and making assumptions. We have been relying on what one professor of mine called the "Wow!" effect. As noted, psychologists and other researchers actually use mathematical techniques that take group means and standard deviations into account to determine whether group differences are statistically significant. It is often the case that eyeballing real data does not yield clear results or even good guesses.

Samples and Populations

Inferential statistics are mathematical tools that psychologists apply to samples of scores to determine whether they can generalize or extend their findings to populations of scores. They must, therefore, be quite certain that the samples involved actually represent the populations from which they were drawn. Sampling techniques are crucial. Random sampling is the best method, and sampling is random only if every member of the target population has an equal chance of being selected.

It matters little how sophisticated our statistical methods are if the samples studied do not represent the target populations. We could use a variety of sophisticated statistical techniques to analyze the heights of the New York Big Apples and the California Quakes, but none of these methods would tell us much about the height of the general population. Or about the height of women. (Or about the height of people who can't pass the ball, shoot, or play defense.)

Figure A.9

Decreasing and Increasing the Variability of the Distributions of Scores

Everything else being equal, the smaller the variability in group scores, the greater the probability that the difference in groups means is statistically significant. The distribution on the right shows a greater difference in the variability of the groups; therefore, there is a *lower* probability that the difference in group means is statistically significant.

References

A

Abbey, A. (1987). Misperceptions of friendly behavior as sexual interest. *Psychology of Women Quarterly, 11,* 173–194.

Abraham, H. D.,& Duffy, F.H. (2001). EEG coherence in post-LSD visual hallucinations. *Psychiatry Research: Neuroimaging, 107*(3), 151–163.

Ackard, D. M., Neumark-Sztainer, D., Hannan, P. J., French, S., & Story, M. (2001). Binge and purge behavior among adolescents: Associations with sexual and physical abuse in a nationally representative sample: The Commonwealth Fund survey. *Child Abuse & Neglect, 25*(6), 771–785.

Agras, W. S., Walsh, T., Fairburn, C. G., Wilson, G. T., & Kraemer, H. C. (2000). A multicenter comparison of cognitive-behavioral therapy and interpersonal psychotherapy for bulimia nervosa.

Ainsworth, M. D. S., & Bowlby, J. (1991). An ethological approach to personality development. *American Psychologist, 46,* 333–341.

Ainsworth, M. D. S., Blehar, M. C., Waters, E., & Wall, S. (1978). *Patterns of attachment: A psychological study of the strange situation.* Hillsdale, NJ: Erlbaum.

Alexander, C. N., et al. (1996). Trial of stress reduction for hypertension in older African Americans: II. Sex and risk subgroup analysis. *Hypertension, 28,* 228–237.

Allport, G. W., & Oddbert, H. S. (1936). Trait names: A psycho-lexical study. *Psychological Monographs, 47,* 1–36.

Altman, L. K. (2005, May 16). Studies find disparity in U.S. cancer care. *The New York Times online.*

Altran, S. (Accessed 2005, May). Genesis and future of suicide terrorism. http://www.interdisci plines.org/terrorism /papers/1.

American Cancer Society. (2005a). Cancer facts & figures 2005. http://www.cancer.org.

American Cancer Society. (2005c; accessed 2005, September 23). Alcohol increases breast cancer risk. http://www.cancer.org/docroot/NWS/content/NWS_1_1x_Alcohol_Increases_Breast_Cancer_Risk.asp.

American Heart Association. (2005b). Leading causes of death—Statistics. http://www.americanheart.org/presenter.jhtml?identifier_30009 63.

American Heart Association. (2008). www.americanheart.org

American Lung Association (2008). http://www.lungusa.org.

American Psychological Association (2002). Ethical principles of psychologists and code of conduct. *American Psychologist, 57*(12), 1060–1073.

American Psychologist, 47(4), 559–569.

Amodio, D. M., & Showers, C. J. (2005). "Similarity breeds liking" revisited: The moderating role of commitment. *Journal of Social and Personal Relationships, 22*(6), 817–836.

Andersen, B. L. (2002). Biobehavioral outcomes following psychological interventions for cancer patients. *Journal of Consulting & Clinical Psychology, 70*(3), 590–610.

Andersen, B. L., Kiecolt-Glaser, J. K., & Glaser, R. (1994). A biobehavioral model of cancer stress and disease course. *American Psychologist, 49,* 389–404.

Anderson, C. A. (2004). An update on the effects of violent video games. *Journal of Adolescence, 27,* 113–122.

Anderson, C. A., & Dill, K. E. (2000). Video games and aggressive thoughts, feelings, and behavior in the laboratory and in life. *Journal of Personality and Social Psychology, 78*(4), 772–790.

Anderson, C. A., Berkowitz, L., Donnerstein, E., Huesmann, R. L., Johnson, J., Linz, D., Malamuth, N., & Wartella, E. (2003). The influence of media violence on youth. *Psychological Science in the Public Interest, 4,* 81–110.

Anderson, C. A., et al. (2004). Violent video games: Specific effects of violent content on aggressive thoughts and behavior. *Advances in Experimental Social Psychology, 36,* 199–249.

Anderson, C., & Horne, J. A. (2004). Presleep relaxed 7–8 Hz EEG from left frontal region: Marker of localised neuropsychological performance? *Physiology & Behavior, 81*(4), 657–664.

Anderson, E. S., Winett, R. A., & Wojcik, J. R. (2000). Social-cognitive determinants of nutrition behavior among supermarket food shoppers: A structural equation analysis. *Health Psychology, 19*(5), 479–486.

Anderson, E. S., Winett, R. A., Wojcik, J. R., Winett, S. G., & Bowden, T. (2001). A computerized social cognitive intervention for nutrition behavior: Direct and mediated effects on fat, fiber, fruits and vegetables, self-efficacy and outcome expectations among food shoppers. *Annals of*

Behavioral Medicine, 23(2), 88–100.

Anderson, K. P., LaPorte, D. J., & Crawford, S. (2000). Child abuse and bulimic symptomology: Review of specific abuse variables. *Child Abuse and Neglect 24*(11), 1495–1502.

Anderson, O. (1995). The buzz on exercise. *Men's Health, 10,* 88–89. This article discusses the Runner's High, what contributes to it and how a person might experience it.

Andreasen, N. C. (2003). From molecule to mind: Genetics, genomics, and psychiatry. *American Journal of Psychiatry, 160,* 613.

Andreou, G., et al. (2002). Handedness, asthma, and allergic disorders: Is there an association? *Psychology, Health & Medicine, 7*(1), 53–60.

Anger-Diáz, B., Schlanger, K., Rincon, C., & Abbey, A. (1987). Misperceptions of friendly behavior as sexual interest. *Psychology of Women Quarterly, 11,* 173–194.

Ansburg, P. I. (2000). Individual differences in problem solving via insight. *Current Psychology, 19,* 143. This article describes insight and the differences seen in individuals.

Antoni, M. H., et al. (2005). Increases in a marker of immune system reconstitution are predated by decreases in 24-h urinary cortisol output and depressed mood during a 10-week stress management intervention in symptomatic HIV-infected men. *Journal of Psychosomatic Research, 58*(1), 3–13.

Antoni, M. H. (2009). Stress management effects on biobehavioral processes in breast cancer. *Brain, Behavior, and Immunity, 23*(Suppl. 2), S26.

Apovian, C. M. (2010). The causes, prevalence, and treatment of obesity revisited in 2009: What have we learned so far? *American Journal of Clinical Nutrition 91*(1), 277S–279S.

Apperloo, M. J. A., Van Der Stege, J. G., Hoek, A., & Weijmar Schultz, W. C. M. (2003). In the mood for sex: The value of androgens. *Journal of Sex & Marital Therapy, 29*(2), 87–102.

Arendt, J. (2000). Melatonin, circadian rhythms, and sleep. *The New England Journal of Medicine online, 343*(15).

Arnett, J. J. (1999). Adolescent storm and stress, reconsidered. *American Psychologist, 54*(5), 317–326.

Aronoff, J., & Litevin, G. H. (1971). Achievement motivation training and executive advancement. *Journal of Applied Behavioral Science, 7*(2), 215–229. *Psychological Bulletin, 131*(3), 410–411.

Asch, S. E. (1952). *Social psychology.* Englewood Cliffs, NJ: Prentice-Hall.

Ashtari, M., et al. (2009). Diffusion abnormalities in adolescents and young adults with a history of heavy cannabis use. *Journal of Psychiatric Research, 43*(3), 189-204.

Atkins, M. S., et al. (2002). Suspensions and detention in an urban, low-income school: Punishment or reward? *Journal of Abnormal Child Psychology, 30*(4), 361–371.

Atkinson, R. C., & Shiffrin, R. M. (1968). Human memory: A proposed system and its control processes. In K. Spence (Ed.), *The psychology of learning and motivation* (Vol. 2). New York: Academic Press.

Ayllon, T., & Haughton, E. (1962). Control of the behavior of schizophrenic patients by food. *Journal of the Experimental Analysis of Behavior, 5,* 343–352.

B

Baddeley, A. (1982). *Your memory: A user's guide.* New York: Macmillan.

Bahrick, H. P., Bahrick, P. O., & Wittlinger, R. P. (1975). Fifty years of memory for names and faces. *Journal of Experimental Psychology: General, 104,* 54–75.

Bailey, J. M. (2003a). Personal communication.

Bailey, J. M., & Pillard, R. C. (1991). A genetic study of male sexual orientation. *Archives of general psychiatry 48,* 1089–1096.

Baker, C. W., Whisman, M. A., & Brownell, K. D. (2000). Studying intergenerational transmission of eating attitudes and behaviors: Methodological and conceptual questions. *Health Psychology, 19*(4), 376–381.

Baker, L. A., DeFries, J. C., & Fulker, D. W. (1983). Longitudinal stability of cognitive ability in the Colorado adoption project. *Child Development, 54,* 290–297.

Baker, M. C. (2001). *The atoms of language: The mind's hidden rules of grammar.* New York: Basic Books.

Baldo, J. V., Delis, D. C., Wilkins, D. P., & Shimamura, A. P. (2004). Is it bigger than a breadbox? Performance of patients with prefrontal lesions on a new executive function test. *Archives of Clinical Neuropsychology, 19*(3), 407–419.

Baltes, P. B., & Staudinger, U. M. (2000). Wisdom: A meta-heuristic (pragmatic) to orchestrate mind and virtue toward excellence. *American Psychologist, 55,* 122–136.

Bandura, A. (1986). *Social foundations of thought and action: A social-cognitive theory.* Englewood Cliffs, NJ: Prentice-Hall.

Bandura, A. (1999). Social cognitive theory: An agentic perspective. *Asian Journal of Social Psychology, 2*(1), 21–41.

Bandura, A. (2002). Social cognitive theory in cultural context. *Applied Psychology: An International Review, 51*(2), 269–290.

Bandura, A., & Locke, E. A. (2003). Negative selfefficacy and goal effects revisited. *Journal of Applied Psychology, 88*(1), 87–99.

Bandura, A., Barbaranelli, C., Vittorio Caprara, G., & Pastorelli, C. (2001). Self-efficacy beliefs as shapers of children's aspirations and career trajectories. *Child Development, 72*(1), 187–206.

Bandura, A., Blanchard, E. B., & Ritter, B. (1969). The relative efficacy of desensitization and modeling approaches for inducing behavioral, affective, and cognitive changes.

Journal of Personality and Social Psychology, 13, 173–199. 274–281.

Bandura, A., Pastorelli, C., Barbaranelli, C., & Caprara, G. V. (1999). Self-efficacy pathways to childhood depression. *Journal of Personality & Social Psychology, 76*(2), 258–269.

Bandura, A., Ross, S. A., & Ross, D. (1963). Imitation of film-mediated aggressive models. *Journal of Abnormal and Social Psychology, 66,* 3–11.

Bandura, A., Taylor, C. B., Williams, S. L., Medford, I. N., & Barchas, J. D. (1985). Catecholamine secretion as a function of perceived coping self-efficacy. *Journal of Consulting and Clinical Psychology, 53,* 406–414.

Banks, M. S., & Shannon, E. (1993). Spatial and chromatic visual efficiency in human neonates. In C. E. Granrud (Ed.), *Visual perception and cognition in infancy.* Hillsdale, NJ: Erlbaum.

Barber, J. G. (2001). Relative misery and youth suicide. *Australian & New Zealand Journal of Psychiatry, 35*(1), 49–57.

Barber, T. X. (2000). A deeper understanding of hypnosis: Its secrets, its nature, its essence. *American Journal of Clinical Hypnosis, 42*(3–4), 208–272.

Barbor, C. (2001). The science of meditation. *Psychology Today, 34,* 54. This article discusses research efforts at Harvard Medical School using MRI to investigate brain processing changes that occur while meditating.

Bard, P. (1934). The neurohumoral basis of emotional reactions. In C. A. Murchison (Ed.), *Handbook of general experimental psychology.* Worcester, MA: Clark University Press.

Barnard, C. J., Collins, S. A., Daisley, J. N., & Behnke, J. M. (2005). Maze performance and immunity costs in mice. *Behaviour, 142*(2), 241–263.

Baron, R. A., Byrne, D., & Branscombe, N. R. (2006). *Social psychology* (11th ed.). Boston: Allyn & Bacon.

Barringer, F. (1993, April 1). Some traps of surveys. *The New York Times,* pp. A1, B9.

Barrios, A. A. (2001). A theory of hypnosis based on principles of conditioning and inhibition. *Contemporary Hypnosis, 18*(4), 163–203.

Bartels, M., Rietveld, M. J. H., Van Baal, G. C. M., & Boomsma, D. I. (2002). Genetic and environmental influences on the development of intelligence. *Behavior Genetics, 32*(4), 237–249.

Bartholow, B. D., & Anderson, C. A. (2002). Effects of violent video games on aggressive behavior: Potential sex differences. *Journal of Experimental Social Psychology, 38,* 283–290.

Bartoshuk, L. M. (2000). Psychophysical advances aid the study of genetic variation in taste. *Appetite, 34*(1), 105.

Basic Behavioral Science Task Force of the National Advisory Mental Health Council. (1996b). Basic behavioral science research for mental health: Perception, attention, learning and memory. *American Psychologist, 51,*133–142.

Basic Behavioral Science Task Force of the National Advisory Mental Health Council. (1996c). Basic behavioral science research for mental health: Sociocultural and environmental practices. *American Psychologist, 51,* 722–731.

Bassetti, C., Vella, S., Donati, F., Wielepp, P., & Weder, B. (2000). SPECT during sleepwalking. *Lancet, 356,* 484–485.

Bates, E. (2001) Plasticity, localization and language development. In S. T. Parker, J. Langer & C. Milbrath (Eds.), *Biology and knowledge revisited* (pp. 205-254). London: Routledge.

Bates, E. (2004). In J. Berck, Before baby talk, signs and signals. *The New York Times online.*

Batson, C. D., Qian, Z., & Lichter, D. T. (2006). Interracial and intraracial patterns of mate selection among America's diverse black populations. *Journal of Marriage and the Family, 68,* 658-672.

Battaglia, F. P., Sutherland, G. R., & McNaughton, B. L. (2004). Local sensory cues and place cell directionality: Additional evidence of prospective coding in the hippocampus. *Journal of Neuroscience, 24*(19), 4541–4550.

Baucom, D. H., Shoham, V., Mueser, K. T., Daiuto, A. D., & Stickle, T. R. (1998). Empirically supported couple and family interventions for marital distress and adult mental health problems. *Journal of Consulting and Clinical Psychology, 66,* 53–88.

Bauer, M. E., et al. (2003). Altered glucocorticoid immunoregulation in treatment resistant depression. *Psychoneuroendocrinology, 28*(1), 49–65.

Baumeister, R. F. (1996). *Evil: Inside human cruelty and violence.* New York: W. H. Freeman /Times Books/ Henry Holt & Co.

Baumgartner, F. (2002). The effect of hardiness in the choice of coping strategies in stressful situations. *Studia Psychologica, 44*(1), 69–75.

Beautrais, A. L. (2003). Suicide and serious suicide attempts in youth: A multiple-group comparison study. *American Journal of Psychiatry, 160,* 1093–1099.

Beck, A. T., et al. (2001). Dysfunctional beliefs discriminate personality disorders. *Behaviour Research & Therapy, 39*(10), 1213–1225.

Bekoff, M. (2002). *Minding animals: Awareness, emotions, and heart.* New York: Oxford University Press.

Belsky, J., Weinraub, M., Owen, M., & Kelly, J. (2001, April). Quantity of child care and problem behavior. In J. Belsky (Chair), *Early childcare and children's development prior to school entry.* Symposium conducted at the 2001 Biennial Meetings of the Society for Research in Child Development, Minneapolis, MN.

Bem, D. J., & Honorton, C. (1994). Does Psi exist? Replicable evidence for an anomalous process of information transfer. *Psychological Bulletin, 115,* 4–18.

Bem, D. J., Palmer, J., & Broughton, R. S. (2001).Updating the ganzfeld database: A victim of its own success? *Journal of Parapsychology, 65*(3), 207–218.

Benson, H. (1975). *The relaxation response.* New York: Morrow.

Ben-Zur, H. (2002). Associations of type A behavior with the emotional traits of anger and curiosity. *Anxiety, Stress & Coping: An International Journal, 15*(1), 95–104.

Bergen, A. W., et al. (2003). Candidate genes for anorexia nervosa in the 1p33–36 linkage region: Serotonin 1D and delta opioid receptor loci exhibit significant association to anorexia nervosa.

Berk, M. S., Henriques, G. R., Warman, D. M., Brown, G. K., & Beck, A. T. (2004). A cognitive therapy intervention for suicide attempters: An overview. *Cognitive and Behavioral Practice. 11*(3), 265–277.

Berkowitz, L. (2004b). Two views of evil: Evil is not only banal. *PsycCRITIQUES.*

Bernardin, H. J., Cooke, D. K., & Villanova, P. (2000). Conscientiousness and agreeableness as predictors of rating leniency. *Journal of Applied Psychology, 85*(2), 232–236.

Bernardis, P. et al. (2008). Manual actions affect vocalizations of infants. *Experimental Brain Research 184*(4), 599-603.

Bernhardt, P. C., Dabbs, J. M., Jr., Fielden, J. A., & Lutter, C. D. (1998). Testosterone changes during vicarious experiences of winning and losing among fans at sporting events. *Physiology & Behavior, 65*(1), 59–62.

Berry, J. W., Phinney, J. S., Sam, D. L., & Vedder, P. (Eds.) (2006). *Immigrant youth in cultural transition.* Mahwah, NJ: Erlbaum.

Bexton, W. H., Heron, W., & Scott, T. H. (1954). Effects of decreased variation in the sensory environment. *Canadian Journal of Psychology, 8,* 70–76.

Bidell, M. P., Turner, J. A., & Casas, J. M. (2002). First impressions count: Ethnic/racial and lesbian /gay/ bisexual content of professional psychology application materials. *Professional Psychology: Research & Practice, 33*(1), 97–103.

Bienvenu, O. J., et al. (2005). Anxiety and depressive disorders and the five-factor model of personality: A higher- and lower-order personality trait investigation in a community sample. *Depression & Anxiety, 20*(2), 92–97.

Bilkey, D. K. (2004). Neuroscience: In the place space. *Science, 305,* 1245–1246.

Birch, C. D., Stewart, S. H., & Brown, C. G. (2007). Exploring differential patterns of situational risk for binge eating and heavy drinking. *Addictive Behaviors, 32*(3), 433.

Bishop, G. D., et al. (2003). Job demands, decisional control, and cardiovascular responses. *Journal of Occupational Health Psychology, 8*(2), 146–156.

Bizer, G. Y., et al. (2004). The impact of personality on cognitive, behavioral, and affective political processes: The effects of need to evaluate. *Journal of Personality, 72*(5), 995–1027.

Bjorklund, D. F. (2000). *Children's thinking* (3rd ed). Pacific Grove, CA: Brooks/Cole.

Blagrove, M., Farmer, L., & Williams, E. (2004). The relationship of nightmare frequency and nightmare distress to well-being. *Journal of Sleep Research, 13*(2), 129–136.

Blair, R. , & James, R. (2003). Neurobiological basis of psychopathy. *British Journal of Psychiatry, 182,* 5–7.

Blanchard, E. B., et al. (2003). A controlled evaluation of cognitive behavioral therapy for posttraumatic stress in motor vehicle accident survivors. *Behaviour Research & Therapy, 41*(1), 79–96.

Blass, T. (1999). The Milgram paradigm after 35 years: Some things we now know about obedience to authority. *Journal of Applied Social Psychology, 29*(5), 955–978.

Blass, T., & Schmitt, C. (2001). The nature of perceived authority in the Milgram paradigm: Two replications. *Current Psychology: Developmental, Learning, Personality, Social, 20*(2), 115–121.

Blum, R. W., Harmon, B., Harris, L., & Bergeisen, L (1992). American Indian–Alaska Native youth health. Journal of the American Medical Association, *268*(7), 874.

Blumenthal, J. A., et al. (2005). Effects of exercise and stress management training on markers of cardiovascular risk in patients with ischemic heart disease: A randomized controlled trial. *Journal of the American Medical Association, 293*(13), 1626–1634.

Bogen, J. E. (1969). The other side of the brain II: An appositional mind. *Bulletin of the Los Angeles Neurological Society, 34,* 135–162.

Bogen, J. E. (1998). My developing understanding of Roger Wolcott Sperry's philosophy. *Neuropsychologia, 36*(10), 1089–1096.

Bogen, J. E. (2000). Split-brain basics: Relevance for the concept of one's other mind. *Journal of the American Academy of Psychoanalysis, 28*(2), 341–369.

Bohlin, G., Hagekull, B., & Rydell, A. (2000). Attachment and social functioning: A longitudinal study from infancy to middle childhood. *Social Development, 9*(1), 24–39.

Bonds-Raacke, J. M., Fryer, L. S., Nicks, S. D., and Durr, R. T. (2001). Hindsight bias demonstrated in the prediction of a sporting event. *The Journal of Social Psychology, 141,* 349. This article describes a research study in which students predict a sporting event outcome to illustrate the hindsight bias.

Bonin, M. F., McCreary, D. R., & Sadava, S. W. (2000). Problem drinking behavior in two community- based samples of adults: Influence of gender, coping, loneliness, and depression. *Psychology of Addictive Behaviors, 14*(2), 151–161.

Bonn-Miller, M. O., Zvolensky, M. J., & Bernstein, A. (2007). Marijuana use motives: Concurrent relations to frequency of past 30-day use and anxiety sensitivity among young adult marijuana smokers. *Addictive Behaviors, 32*(1) 49–62.

Boom, J., Wouters, H., & Keller, M. (2007). A cross cultural validation of stage development. A Rasch re-analysis of longitudinal socio-moral reasoning data. *Cognitive Development, 22*(2), 213–229.

Both, L., Needham, D., & Wood, E. (2004). Examining tasks that facilitate the experience of incubation while problem-solving. *Alberta Journal of Educational Research, 50*(1), 57–67.

Bouchard, T. J., Jr., & Loehlin, J. C. (2001). Genes, evolution, and personality. *Behavior Genetics, 31*(3), 243–273.

Bouchard, T. J., Jr., Lykken, D. T., McGue, M., Segal, N. L., & Tellegen, A. (1990). Sources of human psychological differences: The Minnesota study of twins reared apart. *Science, 250,* 223–228.

Bouchard, T. J., Jr., Lykken, D. T., McGue, M., Segal, N. L., & Tellegen, A. (1990). Sources of human psychological differences: The Minnesota study of twins reared apart. *Science, 250,* 223–228.

Bower, B. (2000). Certain mental ills may be tied to violence. *Science News, 158,* 279. This article discusses mental disorders that are tied to violence.

Boyd-Franklin, N. (2001). Using the multisystems model with an African American family: Crossracial therapy and supervision. In S. H. McDaniel, et al. (Eds.), *Casebook for integrating family therapy: An ecosystemic approach* (pp. 395–400). Washington, DC: American Psychological Association.

Bradley, R. H., et al. (1989). Home environment and cognitive development in the first 3 years of life. *Developmental Psychology, 25,* 217–235.

Branaman, T. F., & Gallagher, S. N. (2005). Polygraph testing in sex offender treatment: A review of limitations. American *Journal of Forensic Psychology, 23*(1), 45–64.

Brand, J. (2000). Cited in McFarling, U. L. (2000, August 27). Sniffing out genes' role in our senses of taste and smell. *The Los Angeles Times online.*

Braun, B. G. (1988). *Treatment of multiple personality disorder.* Washington, DC: American Psychiatric Press.

Bray, F., & Atkin, W. (2004). International cancer patterns in men: Geographical and temporal variations in cancer risk and the role of gender. *Journal of Men's Health & Gender, 1*(1), 38–46.

Brigman, S., & Cherry, K. E. (2002). Age and skilled performance: Contributions of working memory and processing speed. *Brain & Cognition, 50*(2), 242–256.

Brissette, I., Scheier, M. F., & Carver, C. S. (2002). The role of optimism in social network development, coping, and psychological adjustment during a life transition. *Journal of Personality & Social Psychology, 82*(1), 102–111.

Brody, J. E. (2000, April 25). Memories of things that never were. *The New York Times,* p. F8.

Brody, J. E. (2008, May 20). Trying to break nicotine's grip. *The New York Times online.*

Brook, J. S., Zheng, L., Whiteman, M., & Brook, D. W. (2001). Aggression in toddlers: Associations with parenting and marital relations. *Journal of Genetic Psychology, 162*(2), 228–241.

Broom, A. (2005). The eMale: Prostate cancer, masculinity and online support as a challenge to medical expertise. *Journal of Sociology, 41*(1), 87–104.

Brown, A. S., & Susser, E. S. (2002). In utero infection and adult schizophrenia. *Mental Retardation & Developmental Disabilities Research Reviews, 8*(1), 51–57.

Brown, R., & McNeill, D. (1966). The tip-of-the tongue phenomenon. *Journal of Verbal Learning and Verbal Behavior, 5,* 325–337.

Brown, S. L., Van Hook, J., & Glick, J. E. (2008). Generational differences in cohabitation and marriage in the U.S. *Population Research and Policy Review, 27*(5), 531-550.

Brownstein, A. L. (2003). Biased predecision processing. *Psychological Bulletin, 129*(4), 545–568.

Bruene, M., & Ribbert, H. (2002). Grundsaetzliches zur Konzeption einer evolutionaeren Psychiatrie. *Schweizer Archiv für Neurologie und Psychiatrie, 153*(1), 4–11.

Buchanan, R. W., Pearlson, G., & Tamminga, C. A. (2004). Prefrontal cortex, structural analysis: Segmenting the prefrontal cortex. *American Journal of Psychiatry, 161*(11), 1978.

Buckley, P. F., Buchanan, R. W., Tamminga, C. A., & Schulz, S. C. (2000). Schizophrenia research. *Schizophrenia Bulletin, 26*(2), 411–419.

Buckner, R. L., Wheeler, M. E., & Sheridan, M. A. (2001). Encoding processes during retrieval tasks. *Journal of Cognitive Neuroscience, 13*(3), 406–415.

Budney, A. J., Vandrey, R. G., Hughes, J. R., Moore, B. A., & Bahrenburg, B. (2007). Oral delta-9-tetrahydrocannabinol suppresses cannabis withdrawal symptoms. *Drug and Alcohol Dependence, 86*(1), 22–29.

Bull, N. J., Hunter, M., & Finlay, D. C. (2003). Cue gradient and cue density interact in the detection and recognition of objects defined by motion, contrast, or texture. *Perception, 32*(1), 29–39.

Bullough, V. L. (1998). Alfred Kinsey and the Kinsey Report: Historical overview and lasting contributions. *The Journal of Sex Research, 35,* 127–131. This article summarizes the contributions that Kinsey made to the field of sex research.

Buss, D. M. (1994). *The evolution of desire.* New York: Basic Books.

Buss, D. M. (2000). The evolution of happiness. *American Psychologist, 55,* 15–23.

Buss, D. M. (2003). Sexual strategies: A journey into controversy. *Psychological Inquiry, 14*(3–4), 219–226.

Butcher, J. (2000). Dopamine hypothesis gains further support. *The Lancet, 356,* 139–146.

Butler, A. C., & Beck, J. S. (2001). Cognitive therapy outcomes. A review of meta-analyses. *Tidsskrift for Norsk Psykologforening, 38*(8), 698–706.

C

Cacioppo, J. T., Martzke, J. S., Petty, R. E., & Tassinary, L. G. (1988). Specific forms of facial EMG response index emotions during an interview.

Caffray, C. M., & Schneider, S. L. (2000). Why do they do it? Affective motivators in adolescents' decisions to participate in risk behaviours. *Cogintion & Emotion, 14*(4), 543–576.

Cailhol, S., & Mormede, P. (2002). Conditioned taste aversion and alcohol drinking: Strain and gender differences. *Journal of Studies on Alcohol, 63,* 91–99. This article discusses research conducted with rats to determine etiological basis for alcohol abuse.

Campos, J. J., Hiatt, S., Ramsey, D., Henderson, C., & Svejda, M. (1978). The emergence of fear on the visual cliff. In M. Lewis & L. Rosenblum (Eds.), *The origins of affect.* New York: Plenum.

Camras, L. (2000). Cited in Azar, B. (2000). What's in a face? *Monitor on Psychology, 31*(1), 44–45.

Canalis, R. F., & Lambert, P. R. (2000). *The ear: Comprehensive otology.* Philadelphia: Lippincott Williams & Wilkins.

Cannon, W. B. (1927). The James-Lange theory of emotions: A critical examination and an alternative theory. *American Journal of Psychology, 39,* 106–124.

Cannon, W. B. (1932). *The wisdom of the body.* New York: Norton.

Cannon, W. B., & Washburn, A. (1912). An explanation of hunger. *American Journal of Physiology, 29,* 441–454.

Cantalupo, C., & Hopkins, W. D. (2001). Asymmetric Broca's area in great apes: A region of the ape brain is uncannily similar to one linked with speech in humans. *Nature, 414*(6863), 505.

Carey, B. (2005, January 4). After food and shelter, help in coping with unbearable loss. *The New York Times online.*

Carlson, J. G., & Hatfield, E. (1992). *Psychology of emotion.* Fort Worth: Harcourt Brace Jovanovich.

Carpenter, S. (2001, March). Everyday fantasia: The world of synesthesia. *Monitor on Psychology, 32.* Retrieved May 22, 2003, from the World Wide Web: http://www.apa.org/monitor.mar01/synesthesia.html This article discusses the interesting condition known as synesthesia.

Carroll, D. (2004). *Psychology of language* (4th ed.). Belmont, CA: Wadsworth Publishing Company.

Cassaday, H. J., et al. (2003). Intraventricular 5,7- dihydroxytryptamine lesions disrupt acquisition of working memory task rules but not performance once learned. *Progress in Neuro-Psychopharmacology & Biological Psychiatry, 27*(1), 147–156.

Castillo-Richmond, A., et al. (2000). Effects of stress reduction on carotid atherosclerosis in hypertensive African Americans. *Stroke, 31,* 568.

Cattell, R. B. (1949). *The culture-free intelligence test.* Champaign, IL: Institute for Personality and Ability Testing.

Ceci, S. J., & Bruck, M. (1993). Suggestibility of the child witness. *Psychological Bulletin, 113,* 403–439.

Cellar, D. F., Nelson, Z. C., & Yorke, C. M. (2000). The five-factor model and driving behavior: Personality and involvement in vehicular accidents. *Psychological Reports, 86*(2), 454–456.

Centers for Disease Control and Prevention. (2000b). Suicide in the United States. Page updated January 28, 2000.

http://www.cdc.gov/ ncipc/factsheets/suifacts.htm.

Centers for Disease Control and Prevention. (2005). National Center for Health Statistics. *America's children, 2005. America's children: Key national indicators of well-being 2005.* Childstats.gov.

Centers for Disease Control and Prevention. (2005a, April 21). Overweight and obesity: Health consequences. http://www.cdc.gov/nccd php/dnpa/obesity/consequences.htm.

Cervantes, J. M., & Parham, T. A. (2005). Toward a meaningful spirituality for people of color: Lessons for the counseling practitioner. *Cultural Diversity & Ethnic Minority Psychology, 11*(1), 69–81.

Cervilla, J. A., et al. (2000). Long-term predictors of cognitive outcome in a cohort of older people with hypertension. *British Journal of Psychiatry, 177,* 66–71.

Chafee, M. V., & Goldman-Rakic, P. S. (2000). Inactivation of parietal and prefrontal cortex reveals interdependence of neural activity during memory-guided saccades. *Journal of Neurophysiology, 83*(3), 1550–1566.

Chang, D. F., & Sue, S. (2003). The effects of race and problem type on teachers' assessments of student behavior. *Journal of Consulting & Clinical Psychology, 71*(2), 235–242.

Chen, C., et al. (2004). Association analysis of dopamine D2-like receptor genes and methamphetamine abuse. *Psychiatric Genetics, 14*(4), 223–226.

Chen, S. W., & Davenport, D. S. (2005). Cognitive behavioral therapy with Chinese American clients: Cautions and modifications. *Psychotherapy: Theory, Research, Practice, Training, 42*(1), 101–110.

Cheng, H., & Furnham, A. (2001). Attributional style and personality as predictors of happiness and mental health. *Journal of Happiness Studies, 2*(3), 307–327.

Chioqueta, A. P., & Stiles, T. C. (2005). Personality traits and the development of depression, hopelessness, and suicide ideation. *Personality & Individual Differences, 38*(6), 1283–1291.

Chomsky, N. (1980). Rules and representations. *Behavioral and Brain Sciences, 3,* 1–16.

Chomsky, N. (1991). Linguistics and cognitive science. In A. Kasher (Ed.), *The Chomskyan turn.* Cambridge, MA: Blackwell.

Chu, L., Ma, E. S. K., Lam, K. K. Y., Chan, M. F., & Lee, D. H. S. (2005). Increased alpha 7 nicotinic acetylcholine receptor protein levels in Alzheimer's disease patients. *Dementia & Geriatric Cognitive Disorders, 19*(2–3), 106–112.

Chua, S. C., Jr. (2004). Molecular and cellular correlates of the developmental acquisition of mechanisms modulating ingestive behavior. *Physiology & Behavior, 82*(1), 145–147.

Cialdini, R. B. (2000). Cited in McKinley, J. C., Jr. (2000, August 11). It isn't just a game: Clues to avid rooting. *The New York Times online.*

Cialdini, R. B., & Goldstein, N. J. (2004). Social influence: Compliance and conformity. *Annual Review of Psychology, 55,* 591–621.

Cialdini, R. B., et al. (1997). Reinterpreting the empathy-altruism relationship: When one into one equals oneness. *Journal of Personality & Social Psychology, 73*(3), 481–494.

Ciarrochi, J. (2004). Relationships between dysfunctional beliefs and positive and negative indices of well-being: A critical evaluation of the common beliefs survey–III. *Journal of Rational- Emotive & Cognitive Behavior Therapy, 22*(3), 171–188.

Clark, S. E., & Loftus, E. F. (1996). The construction of space alien abduction memories. *Psychological Inquiry, 7*(2), 140–143.

Clark, S. E., & Loftus, E. F. (2004). The psychological pay dirt of space alien abduction memories.

Clarke-Stewart, K. A., & Beck, R. J. (1999). Maternal scaffolding and children's narrative retelling of a movie story. *Early Childhood Research Quarterly, 14*(3), 409–434.

Clayton, E. C., & Williams, C. L. (2000). Adrenergic activation of the nucleus tractus solitarius potentiates amygdala norepinephrine release and enhances retention performance in emotionally arousing and spatial memory tasks. *Behavioural Brain Research. 112*(1–2), 151–158.

Clènet, F., Hascoët, M., Fillion, G., Galons, H., & Bourin, M. (2005). Role of GABA-ergic and serotonergic systems in the anxiolytic-like mechanism of action of a 5-HT-moduline antagonist in the mouse elevated plus maze. *Behavioural Brain Research, 158*(2), 339–348.

Cohen, L. L. (2002). Reducing infant immunization distress through distraction. *Health Psychology, 21*(2), 207–211.

Cohen, S., Doyle, W. J., Turner, R., Alper, C. M., & Skoner, D. P. (2003). Sociability and susceptibility to the common cold. *Psychological Science, 14*(5), 389–395.

Cohen, S., Gottlieb, B. H., & Underwood, L. G. (2001a). Social relationships and health: Challenges for measurement and intervention. *Advances in Mind-Body Medicine, 17*(2), 129–141.

Cohen, S., Miller, G. E., & Rabin, B. S. (2001b). Psychological stress and antibody response to immunization: A critical review of the human literature. *Psychosomatic Medicine, 63*(1), 7–18.

Cohn, L. D., Macfarlane, S., Yanez, C., & Imai, W. K. (1995). Risk-perception: Differences between adolescents and adults. *Health Psychology, 14,*217–222.

Collaer, M. L., & Hines, M. (1995). Human behavioral sex differences: A role for gonadal hormones during early development? *Psychological Bulletin, 118,* 55–107.

Collaer, M. L., & Nelson, J. D. (2002). Large visuospatial sex difference in line judgment: Possible role of attentional factors. *Brain & Cognition, 49*(1), 1–12.

Coltraine, S., & Messineo, M. (2000). The perpetuation of subtle prejudice: Race and gender imagery in 1990s television advertising. *Sex Roles, 42*(5–6), 363–389.

Colvin, M. K., Funnell, M. G., & Gazzaniga, M. S. (2005). Numerical processing in the two hemispheres: Studies of a split-brain patient. *Brain & Cognition, 57*(1), 43–52.

Comas-Díaz, L. (2003). The Black Madonna: The psychospiritual feminism of Guadeloupe, Kali, and Monserrat. In L. B. Silverstein & T. J. Goodrich (Eds.), *Feminist family therapy: Empowerment in social context* (pp. 147–160).

Comaty, J. E., Stasio, M., & Advokat, C. (2001). Analysis of outcome variables of a token economy system in a state psychiatric hospital: A program evaluation. *Research in Developmental Disabilities, 22*(3), 233–253.

Concar, D. (2002, April 20). Ecstasy on the brain. http://www.NewScientist.com.

Conklin, H. M., & Iacono, W. G. (2002). Schizophrenia: A neurodevelopmental perspective. *Current Directions in Psychological Science, 11*(1), 33–37.

Conrad, P. J., Peterson, J. B., & Pihl, R. O. (2001). Reliability and validity of alcohol-induced heart rate increase as a measure of sensitivity to the stimulant properties of alcohol. *Psychopharmacology, 157*(1), 20–30.

Consortium of Social Science Associations. (2003, May 23). McQueary testifies to Homeland Security Science Subcommittee. *Washington Update, 22*(10), 1–7.

Constantinidis, C., Franowicz, M. N., & Goldman- Rakic, P. S. (2001). Coding specificity in cortical microcircuits: A multiple-electrode analysis of primate prefontal cortex. *Journal of Neuroscience, 21*(10), 3646–3655.

Conte, J., M., Schwenneker, H. H., Dew, A. F., & Romano, D. M. (2001). Incremental validity of time urgency and other Type A subcomponents in predicting behavioral and health criteria. *Journal of Applied Social Psychology, 31*(8), 1727–1748.

Cooper, M., Galbraith, M., & Drinkwater, J. (2001). Assumptions and beliefs in adolescents with anorexia nervosa and their mothers. *Eating Disorders: The Journal of Treatment & Prevention, 9*(3), 217–223.

Cooper, Z., & Fairburn, C. G. (2001). A new cognitive behavioural approach to the treatment of obesity. *Behaviour Research & Therapy, 39*(5), 499–511.

Corballis, P. M., Funnell, M. G., & Gazzaniga, M. S. (2002). Hemispheric asymmetries for simple visual judgments in the split brain. *Neuropsychologia, 40*(4), 401–410.

Corwin, R. L. (2000). Biological and behavioral consequences of food restriction. *Appetite, 34*(1), 112.

Cory, G. A. (2002). MacLean's evolutionary neuroscience, the CSN model and Hamilton's rule: Some developmental, clinical, and social policy implications. *Brain & Mind, 3*(1), 151–181.

Courtenay, W. H. (2000). Engendering health: A social constructionist examination of men's health beliefs and behaviors. *Psychology of Men & Masculinity, 1*(1), 4–15.

Cowen, P. J. (2002). Cortisol, serotonin and depression: All stressed out? *British Journal of Psychiatry, 180*(2), 99–100.

Cox, W. M., & Alm, R. (2005, February 25). Scientists are made, not born. *The New York Times online.*

Craig, J. C., & Rollman, G. B. (1999, Annual). Somesthesis.

Annual Review of Psychology, p. 305. This article is an in-depth article focusing on the skin senses (Somesthesis).

Craik, F. I. M., & Lockhart, R. S. (1972). Levels of processing. *Journal of Verbal Learning and Verbal Behavior, 11,* 671–684.

Crano, W. D. (2000) Milestones in the psychological analysis of social influence. *Group Dynamics, 4*(1), 68–80.

Craske, M. G., & Zucker, B. G. (2001). Consideration of the APA practice guideline for the treatment of patients with panic disorder: Strengths and limitations for behavior therapy. *Behavior Therapy, 32*(2), 259–281.

Crews, D. (1994). Animal sexuality. *Scientific American, 270*(1), 108–114.

Crick, N. R., & Dodge, K. A. (1994). A review and reformulation of social information-processing mechanisms in children's social adjustment. *Psychological Bulletin, 115,* 74–101.

Crisp, R. J., & Nicel, J. K. (2004). Disconfirming intergroup evaluations: Asymmetric effects for ingroups and outgroups. *Journal of Social Psychology, 144*(3), 247–271.

Crusco, A. H., & Wetzel, C. G. (1984). The Midas touch: The effects of interpersonal touch on restaurant tipping. *Personality and Social Psychology Bulletin, 10,* 512–517.

Cuellar, J. C., & Curry, T. R. (2007). The prevalence and comorbidity between delinquency, drug abuse, suicide attempts, physical and sexual abuse, and self-mutilation among delinquent Hispanic females. *Hispanic Journal of Behavioral Sciences, 29*(1), 68-82.

Cummins, R. A., & Nistico, H. (2002). Maintaining life satisfaction: The role of positive cognitive bias. *Journal of Happiness Studies, 3*(1), 37–69.

Cumsille, P. E., Sayer, A. G., & Graham, J. W. (2000). Perceived exposure to peer and adult drinking as predictors of growth in positive alcohol expectancies during adolescence. *Journal of Consulting and Clinical Psychology, 68*(3), 531–536.

Curry, K. (1993, October 22). Male menopause: Is it myth, or a reality of aging. *Knight Ridder/Tribune News Service.* This article discusses the possibility of male menopause and provides expert opinion.

D

d'Ydewalle, G., Luwel, K., & Brunfaut, E. (1999). The importance of on-going concurrent activities as a function of age in time- and event-based prospective memory. *European Journal of Cognitive Psychology, 11*(2), 219–237.

Dabbs, J. M., Jr., Chang, E-L., Strong, R. A., & Milun, R. (1998). Spatial ability, navigation strategy, and geographic knowledge among men and women. *Evolution & Human Behavior, 19*(2), 89–98.

Dalkvist, J. (2001). The ganzfeld method: Its current status. *European Journal of Parapsychology, 16,* 19–22.

Damasio, A. R. (2000). A neural basis for sociopathy. *Archives of General Psychiatry online, 57*(2).

Darley, J. M., & Latané, B. (1968). Bystander intervention in emergencies: Diffusion of responsibility. *Journal of Personality and Social Psychology, 8,* 377–383.

Darwin, C. A. (1872). *The expression of the emotions in man and animals.* London: J. Murray.

Davis, C., Strachan, S., & Berkson, M. (2004). Sensitivity to reward: Implications for overeating and overweight. *Appetite, 42*(2), 131–138.

Davis, S. (2000). Testosterone and sexual desire in women. *Journal of Sex Education & Therapy, 25*(1), 25–32.

Dawood, K., Pillard, R. C., Horvath, C., Revelle, W., & Bailey, J. M. (2000). Familial aspects of male homosexuality. *Archives of Sexual Behavior, 29*(2), 155–163.

Dawson, T. L. (2002). New tools, new insights: Kohlberg's moral judgement stages revisited. *International Journal of Behavioral Development,* 26(2), 154–166.

De Houwer, J., Thomas, S., & Baeyens, F. (2001). Associative learning of likes and dislikes: A review of 25 years of research on human evaluative conditioning. *Psychological Bulletin, 127*(6), 853–869.

De Maat, S., Dekker, J., Schoevers, R., & De Jonghe, F. (2006). Relative efficacy of psychotherapy and pharmacotherapy in the treatment of depression: A meta-analysis. *Psychotherapy Research, 16*(5), 562-572.

de Mello, M. F., et al. (2005). A systematic review of research findings on the efficacy of interpersonal therapy for depressive disorders. *European Archives of Psychiatry & Clinical Neuroscience, 255*(2), 75–82.

De Michele, P. E., Gansneder, B., & Solomon, G. B. (1998). Success and failure attributions of wrestlers: Further evidence of the self-serving bias. *Journal of Sport Behavior, 21*(3), 242–255.

DeAngelis, T. (2002). A genetic link to anorexia. *APA Monitor, 33*(3), 34–36.

DeAngelis, T. (2008). PTSD treatments grow in evidence, effectiveness. *Monitor on Psychology, 39*(1). Also delete references: Blanchard 2003 and Vasterling 2002.

DeCasper, A. J., & Prescott, P. A. (1984). Human newborns' perception of male voices. *Developmental Psychobiology, 17,* 481–491.

Decety, J., & Batson, C. D. (2009). Empathy and morality: Integrating social and neuroscience approaches. In J. Verplaetse et al. (Eds.). *The moral brain.* (pp. 109-127). New York: Springer.

Deecher, D., Andree, T. H., Sloan, D., & Schechter, L. E. (2008). From menarche to menopause: Exploring the underlying biology of depression in women experiencing hormonal changes. *Psychoneuroendocrinology,* 33(1), 3–17.

Deep, A. L., et al. (1999). Sexual abuse in eating disorder subtypes and control women: The role of comorbid substance dependence in bulimia nervosa. Activating the ZPD: Mutual scaffolding in L2 peer revision. *Modern Language Journal, 84*(1), 51–68.

Dehghani, M., Sharpe, L., & Nicholas, M. K. (2004). Modification of attentional biases in chronic pain patients: A preliminary study. *European Journal of Pain, 8*(6), 585–594.

Delgado, J. M. R. (1969). *Physical control of the mind.* New York: Harper & Row.

Delves, P. J., & Roitt, I. M. (2000). Advances in immunology: The immune system. *The New England Journal of Medicine online, 343*(1).

Dennerstein, L. L. (2003). The sexual impact of menopause. In S. B. Levine, et al. (Eds.), *Handbook of clinical sexuality for mental health professionals* (pp. 187–198). New York: Brunner- Routledge.

DeRubeis, R. J., et al. (2005). Cognitive therapy vs. medications in the treatment of moderate to severe depression. *Archives of General Psychiatry, 62*(4), 409–416.

DeSteno, D., Petty, R. E., Rucker, D. D., Wegener, D. T., & Braverman, J. (2004). Discrete emotions and persuasion: The role of emotion induced expectancies. *Journal of Personality & Social Psychology, 86*(1), 43–56.

Devilly, G. J. (2002). Eye movement desensitization and reprocessing: A chronology of its development and scientific standing. *Scientific Review of Mental Health Practice, 1*(2), 113–138.

DeVries, R. (2000). Vygotsky, Piaget, and education: A reciprocal assimilation of theories and educational practices. *New Ideas in Psychology, 18*(2–3), 187–213.

Dhabhar, F. S. (2009). A hassle a day may keep the pathogens away: The fight-or-flight stress response and the augmentation of immune function. *Integrative and Comparative Biology, 49*(3), 215-236.

Dickson, N., Paul, C., Herbison, P., & Silva, P. (1998). First sexual intercourse: age, coercion, and later regrets reported by a birth cohort. *British Medical Journal, 316,* 29–33.

Diener, E., Napa Scollon, C. K., Oishi, S., Dzokoto, V., Suh, E. M. (2000). Positivity and the construction of life satisfaction judgments: Global happiness is not the sum of its parts. *Journal of Happiness Studies, 1*(2), 159–176.

Dierker, L. C., et al. (2001). Association between psychiatric disorders and the progression of tobacco use behaviors. *Journal of the American Academy of Child & Adolescent Psychiatry, 40*(10), 1159–1167.

Dietrich, A. (2004). Neurocognitive mechanisms underlying the experience of flow. *Consciousness & Cognition: An International Journal, 13*(4), 746–761.

DiLalla, D. L., Carey, G., Gottesman, I. I., & Bouchard, T. J., Jr. (1996). Heritability of MMPI personality indicators of psychopathology in twins reared apart. *Journal of Abnormal Psychology, 105,* 491–499.

Diseth, T. H. (2005). Dissociation in children and adolescents as reaction to trauma—An overview of conceptual issues and neurobiological factors. *Nordic Journal of Psychiatry, 59*(2), 79–91.

Dobbins, I. G., Simons, J. S., & Schacter, D. L. (2004). fMRI evidence for separable and lateralized prefrontal memory monitoring processes. *Journal of Cognitive Neuroscience, 16*(6), 908–920.

Doblin, R. (2002). A clinical plan for MDMA (ecstasy) in the treatment of posttraumatic stress disorder (PTSD): Partnering with the FDA. *Journal of Psychoactive Drugs, 34*(2), 185–194.

Dogil, G., et al. (2002). The speaking brain: A tutorial introduction to fMRI experiments in the production of speech, prosody and syntax. *Journal of Neurolinguistics, 15*(1), 59–90.

Dollard, J., Doob, L. W., Miller, N. E., Mowrer, O. H., & Sears, R. R. (1939). *Frustration and aggression.* New Haven, CT: Yale University Press.

Domhoff, G. W. (2001). A new neurocognitive theory of dreams. *Dreaming: Journal of the Association for the Study of Dreams, 11*(1), 13–33.

Domhoff, G. W. (2003). *The scientific study of dreams: Neural networks, cognitive development, and content analysis.* Washington, DC: American Psychological Association.

Donohue, K. F., Curtin, J. J., Patrick, C. J., & Lang, A. R. (2007). Intoxication level and emotional response. *Emotion, 7*(1), 103–112.

Donovan, C.A., & Smolkin, L. B. (2002). Children's genre knowledge: An examination of K-5 student's performance on multiple tasks providing differing levels of scaffolding. *Reading Research Quarterly, 37,* 428–466. This article discusses cognitive scaffolding in K-5 age children.

Dovidio, J. F., et al. (2004). Perspective and prejudice: Antecedents and mediating mechanisms. *Personality & Social Psychology Bulletin, 30*(12), 1537–1549.

Duckitt, J., & Fisher, K. (2003). The impact of social threat on world view and ideological attitudes. *Political Psychology, 24*(1), 199–222.

Duckworth, A. L., & Seligman, M. E. P. (2005). Self-discipline outdoes IQ in predicting academic performance of adolescents. *Psychological Science, 16*(12), 939-944.

Duffy, V. B., Peterson, J. M., & Bartoshuk, L. M. (2004). Associations between taste genetics, oral sensation and alcohol intake. *Physiology & Behavior, 82*(2–3), 435–445.

Dunkley, D. M., Zuroff, D. C., & Blankstein, K. R. (2003). Self-critical perfectionism and daily affect: Dispositional and situational influences on stress and coping. *Journal of Personality & Social Psychology, 84*(1), 234–252.

Durbin, D. L., Darling, N., Steinberg, L., & Brown, B. B. (1993). Parenting style and peer group membership among European American adolescents. *Journal of Research on Adolescence, 3*(1), 87–100.

Dweck, C. S. (2002a). Messages that motivate: How praise molds students' beliefs, motivation, and performance (in surprising ways). In J. Aronson, (Ed.), *Improving academic achievement: Impact of psychological factors on education* (pp. 37–60). San Diego: Academic Press.

Dweck, C. S. (2002b). The development of ability conceptions. In A. Wigfield & J. S. Eccles (Eds.), *Development of achievement motivation* (pp. 57–88). San Diego: Academic Press.

Dweck, C. S. (2002b). The development of ability conceptions. In A. Wigfield & J. S. Eccles (Eds.), *Development of achievement motivation* (pp. 57–88). San Diego: Academic Press.

E

Eagle, M. (2000). Repression, part I of II. *Psychoanalytic Review, 87*(1), 1–38.

Easterlin, R. A. (2002). Is reported happiness five years ago comparable to present happiness? A cautionary note. *Journal of Happiness Studies, 3*(2), 193–198.

Ebbinghaus, H. (1913). *Memory: A contribution to experimental psychology.* (H. A. Roger & C. E. Bussenius, Trans.). New York: Columbia University Press. (Original work published 1885).

Eberly, M. B., & Montemayor, R. (1999). Adolescent affection and helpfulness toward parents: A 2–year follow-up. *Journal of Early Adolescence, 19*(2), 226–248.

Egawa, T., et al. (2002). Impairment of spatial memory in kaolin-induced hydrocephalic rats is associated with changes in the hippocampal cholinergic and noradrenergic contents. *Behavioural Brain Research, 129*(1–2), 31–39.

Egerton, A., Allison, C., Brett, R. R., & Pratt, J. A. (2006). Cannabinoids and prefrontal cortical function: Insights from preclinical studies. *Neuroscience & Biobehavioral Reviews, 30*(5), 680–695.

Eichenbaum, H., & Fortin, N. (2003). Episodic memory and the hippocampus: It's about time. *Current Directions in Psychological Science, 12*(2), 53–57.

Ekman, P. (1999). Facial expressions. In T. Dalgleish & M. J. Power (Eds.), *Handbook of cognition and emotion* (pp. 301–320). New York: John Wiley & Sons.

Ekman, P. (2003). Cited in Foreman, J. (2003, August 5). A conversation with: Paul Ekman: The 43 facial muscles that reveal even the most fleeting emotions. *The New York Times online.*

Ekman, P., et al. (1987). Universals and cultural differences in the judgments of facial expressions of emotion. *Journal of Personality and Social Psychology, 53,* 712–717.

Elkind, D. (1967). Egocentrism in adolescence. *Child Development, 38,* 1025–1034.

Elkind, D. (1985). Egocentrism redux. *Developmental Review, 5,* 218–226.

Elkind, D., & Bowen, R. (1979). Imaginary audience behavior in children and adolescents. *Developmental Psychology, 15*(1), 38–44.

Ellickson, P. L., Tucker, J. S., Klein, D. J., & McGuigan, K. A. (2001). Prospective risk factors for alcohol misuse in late adolescence. *Journal of Studies on Alcohol, 62*(6), 773–782.

Ellis, A. (2004a). How my theory and practice of psychotherapy has influenced and changed other psychotherapies. *Journal of Rational-Emotive & Cognitive Behavior Therapy, 22*(2), 79–83.

Ellis, A. (2004b). Why rational emotive behavior therapy is the most comprehensive and effective form of behavior therapy. *Journal of Rational- Emotive & Cognitive Behavior Therapy, 22*(2), 85–92.

Ellsworth, P. C., Carlsmith, J. M., & Henson, A. (1972). The stare as a stimulus to flight in human subjects. *Journal of Personality and Social Psychology, 21,* 302–311.

Emmons, R. A., & King, L. A. (1988). Conflict among personal strivings: Immediate and longterm implications for psychological and physical well-being. *Journal of Personality & Social Psychology, 54*(6), 1040–1048.

Enard, W., et al. (2002). Molecular evolution of FOXP2, a gene involved in speech and language. *Nature, 418*(6900), 869–872.

Engels, G. I., Garnefski, N., & Diekstra, R. F. W. (1993). Efficacy of rational-emotive therapy. *Journal of Consulting and Clinical Psychology, 61,* 1083–1090.

Erikson, E. H. (1963). *Childhood and society.* New York: W. W. Norton.

Eron, L. D. (1982). Parent–child interaction, television violence, and aggression of children. *American Psychologist, 37,* 197–211.

Eron, L. D. (2000). A psychological perspective. In V. B. Van Hasselt & M. Hersen, (Eds.), *Aggression and violence: An introductory text* (pp. 23–39). Needham Heights, MA: Allyn & Bacon.

Erskine, A., Markham, R., & Howie, P. (2001). Children's script-based inferences: Implications for eyewitness testimony. *Cognitive Development, 16*(4), 871–887.

Eslinger, P. J., Flaherty-Craig, C. V., & Benton, A. L. (2004). Developmental outcomes after early prefrontal cortex damage. *Brain & Cognition, 55*(1), 84–403.

Evans, L., et al. (2005). Familiality of temperament in bipolar disorder: Support for a genetic spectrum. *Journal of Affective Disorders, 85*(1–2), 153–168.

Evans, S. W., et al. (2001). Dose-response effects of methylphenidate on ecologically valid measures of academic performance and classroom behavior in adolescents with ADHD. *Experimental & Clinical Psychopharmacology, 9*(2), 163–175.

Eysenck, H. J., & Eysenck, M. W. (1985). *Personality and individual differences.* New York: Plenum.

F

Fairburn, C. G., & Harrison, P. J. (2003). Eating disorders. *The Lancet, 361,* 407. This article is an in-depth look at anorexia and bulimia including diagnostic criteria and treatment options.

Fantz, R. L. (1961). The origin of form perception. *Scientific American, 204*(5), 66–72.

Farber, B. A., Brink, D. C., & Raskin, P. M. (1996). *The psychotherapy of Carl Rogers: Cases and commentary* (pp. 74–75). New York: Guilford Press.

Farmer, A., Eley, T. C., & McGuffin, P. (2005). Current strategies for investigating the genetic and environmental risk factors for affective disorders. *British Journal of Psychiatry, 186*(3), 179–181.

Farooqi, I. S., et al. (2003). Clinical spectrum of obesity and mutations in the melanocortin 4 receptor gene. *New England Journal of Medicine, 348*(12), 1085–1095.

Favaro, A. (2005). The relationship between temperament and impulsive behaviors in eating disordered subjects. *Eating Disorders: The Journal of Treatment & Prevention, 13*(1), 61–70.

Feeney, B. C. (2004). A secure base: Responsive support of goal strivings and exploration in adult intimate relationships. *Journal of Personality & Social Psychology, 87*(5), 631–648. Lever, J. P. (2004). Poverty and subjective well-being in Mexico. *Social Indicators Research, 68*(1), 1–33.

Feingold, A. (1992a). Gender differences in mate selection preferences. *Psychological Bulletin, 112,*

Festinger, L., & Carlsmith, J. M. (1959). Cognitive consequences of forced compliance. *Journal of Abnormal and Social Psychology, 58,* 203–210.

Fields, R. D. (2005, February). Making memories stick. *Scientific American,* 75–81.

Fifer, W. P., & Moon, C. (2003). Prenatal development. In A. Slater & G. Bremner (Eds.), *An introduction to developmental psychology* (pp. 95–114). Malden, MA: Blackwell Publishers.

Finkenauer, C., et al. (1998). Flashbulb memories and the underlying mechanisms of their formation: Toward an emotional-integrative model. *Memory & Cognition, 26*(3), 516–531.

Fisher, H. E. (2000). Brains do it: Lust, attraction and attachment. *Cerebrum, 2,* 23–42.

Flavell, J. H. (2000). Development of children's knowledge about the mental world. *International Journal of Behavioral Development, 24*(1), 15–23.

Flegal, K. M., Carroll, M. D., Ogden, C. L., & Curtin, L. R. (2010). Prevalence and trends in obesity among U.S. adults, 1999-2008. *Journal of the American Medical Association, 303*(3), 235-241.

Flegal, K. M., Carroll, M. D., Ogden, C. L., & Johnson, C. L. (2002). Prevalence and trends in obesity among U.S. adults, 1999–2000. *Journal of the American Medical Association, 288*(14), 1723–1727.

Fletcher, B., Pine, K. J., Woodbridge, Z., & Nash, A. (2007). How visual images of chocolate affect the craving and guilt of female dieters. *Appetite, 48*(2), 211–217.

Flett, G. L., Madorsky, D., Hewitt, P. L., & Heisel, M. J. (2002). Perfectionism cognitions, rumination, and psychological distress. *Journal of Rational-Emotive & Cognitive Behavior Therapy, 20*(1), 33–47.

Flouri, E., & Buchanan, A. (2003). The role of father involvement and mother involvement in adolescents' psychological well-being. *British Journal of Social Work, 33*(3), 399–406.

Foerster, J., Higgins, E. T., & Strack, F. (2000). When stereotype disconfirmation is a personal threat: How prejudice and prevention focus moderate incongruency effects. *Social Cognition, 18*(2), 178–197.

Folkman, S., & Moskowitz, T. (2000). Positive affect and the other side of coping. *American Psychologist, 55*(6), 647–654.

Follingstad, D., & McCormick, M. (2002). *Law and mental health professionals.* Washington, DC: American Psychological Association.

Fontaine, K. R., Redden, D. T., Wang, C., Westfall, A. O., & Allison, D. B. (2003). Years of life lost due to obesity. *Journal of the American Medical Association, 289*(2), 187–193.

Förster, J., Higgins, E. T., & Werth, L. (2004). How threat from stereotype disconfirmation triggers self-defense. *Social Cognition, 22*(1), 54–74.

Fortin, S., Godbout, L., & Braun, C. M. J. (2002). Strategic sequence planning and prospective memory impairments in frontally lesioned head trauma patients performing activities of daily living. *Brain & Cognition, 48*(2–3), 361–365.

Fouts, R. S. (1997). *Next of kin: What chimpanzees have taught me about who we are.* New York: Morrow.

Francis, L. J., Katz, Y. J., Yablon, Y., & Robbins, M. (2004). Religiosity, personality, and happiness: A study among Israeli male undergraduates. *Journal of Happiness Studies, 5(4),* 315–333.

Freeman, M. S., Spence, M. J., & Oliphant, C. M. (1993, June). *Newborns prefer their mothers' lowpass filtered voices over other female filtered voices.* Paper presented at the annual convention of the American Psychological Society, Chicago.

Freese, T. E., Miotto, K., & Reback, C. J. (2002). The effects and consequences of selected club drugs. *Journal of Substance Abuse Treatment, 23*(2), 151–156.

Freud, S. (1998). The baby and the bathwater: Some thoughts on Freud as a postmodernist. *Families in Society: The Journal of Contemporary Human Services, 79,* 455–464. This article suggests that there are aspects of Freud's theory that continue to have relevance today.

Freud, S. (1927). A religious experience. In *Standard edition of the complete psychological works of Sigmund Freud* (Vol. 21). London: Hogarth Press, 1964.

Friedman, M., & Ulmer, D. (1984). *Treating Type A behavior and your heart.* New York: Fawcett Crest.

Frisch, R. (1997). Cited in Angier, N. (1997). Chemical tied to fat control could help trigger puberty. *The New York Times,* pp. C1, C3.

Fritsch, G., & Hitzig, E. (1960). On the electrical excitability of the cerebrum. In G. von Bonin (Ed.), *Some papers on the cerebral cortex.* Springfield, IL: Charles C. Thomas. (Original work published 1870)

Fromme, K., et al. (2004). Biological and behavioral markers of alcohol sensitivity. *Alcoholism: Clinical & Experimental Research, 28*(2), 247–256.

Fuertes, A., et al. (2002). Factores asociados a las conductas sexuales de reigso en la adolencia. *Infancia y Aprendizaje, 25*(3), 347–361.

Fuligni, A. J., & Witkow, M. (2004). The postsecondary educational progress of youth from immigrant families. *Journal of Research on Adolescence, 14*(2), 159–183.

Furnham, A., Petrides, K. V., Sisterson, G., & Baluch, B. (2003). Repressive coping style and positive self-presentation. *British Journal of Health Psychology, 8*(2), 223–249.

Fuster, J. M. (2000). The prefrontal cortex of the primate: A synopsis. *Psychobiology, 28*(2), 125–131.

G

Gaab, J., Rohleder, N., Nater, U. M., & Ehlert, U. (2005). Psychological determinants of the cortisol stress response: The role of anticipatory cognitive appraisal. *Psychoneuroendocrinology,* 30(6), 599–610.

Gais, S., & Born, J. (2004). Declarative memory consolidation: Mechanisms acting during human sleep. *Learning & Memory, 11*(6), 679–685.

Galambos, N. L., Barker, E. T., & Almeida, D. M. (2003). Parents do matter: Trajectories of change in externalizing and internalizing problems in early adolescence. *Child Development, 74*(2), 578–594.

Garb, H. N., Wood, J. M., Lilienfeld, S. O., & Nezworski, M. T. (2005). Roots of the Rorschach controversy. *Clinical Psychology Review, 25*(1), 97–118.

Garcia, J., & Koelling, R. A. (1966). Relation of cue to consequences in avoidance learning. *Psychonomic Science 4,* 123–124.

Gould, S. J. (2002). *The structure of evolutionary theory.* Cambridge, MA: Belknap Press /Harvard University Press.

Garcia, J., Brett, L. P., & Rusiniak, K. W. (1989). Limits of Darwinian conditioning. In S. B. Klein & R. R. Mowrer (Eds.), *Contemporary learning theories: Instrumental conditioning theory and the impact of biological constraints on learning.* Hillsdale, NJ: Erlbaum.

Gardner, H. (1983/1993). *Frames of mind.* New York: Basic Books.

Gardner, H. (2001, April 5). Multiple intelligence. *The New York Times,* p. A20.

Gay, M., Philippot, P., & Luminet, O. (2002). Differential effectiveness of psychological interventions for reducing osteoarthritis pain: A comparison of Erickson hypnosis and Jacobson relaxation. *European Journal of Pain, 6*(1), 1–16.

Gay, P. (1999). Psychoanalyst: Sigmund Freud. *Time, 153,* 66. This article summarizes the work of Sigmund Freud and the contributions he made to psychology and the world.

Geers, A., Spehar, B., & Sedey, A. (2002). Use of speech by children from total communication programs who wear cochlear implants. *American Journal of Speech-Language Pathology, 11*(1), 50–58.

Gegenfurtner, K. R., & Kiper, D. C. (2003). Color vision. *Annual Review of Neuroscience, 26,* 181–206.

Gendall, K. A., Bulik, C. M., Joyce, P. R., McIntosh, V. V., &

Carter, F. A. (2000). Menstrual cycle irregularity in bulimia nervosa: Associated factors and changes with treatment. *Journal of Psychosomatic Research, 49*(6), 409–415.

Gentry, M. V., et al. (2000). Nicotine patches improve mood and response speed in a lexical decision task. *Addictive Behaviors,* 25(4), 549–557.

Gershoff, E. T. (2002). Corporal punishment by parents and associated child behaviors and experiences: A meta-analytic and theoretical review. *Psychological Bulletin, 128*(4), 539–579.

Gershon, J., Zimand, E., Pickering, M., Rothbaum, B. O., & Hodges, L. (2004). A pilot and feasibility study of virtual reality as a distraction for children with cancer. *Journal of the American Academy of Child & Adolescent Psychiatry, 43*(10), 1243–1249. Video games calm kids before surgery. (2004, December 10). Associated Press.

Geschwind, N., & Galaburda, A. M. (1987). *Cerebral lateralization: Biological mechanisms, associations, and pathology.* Cambridge, MA: Harvard University Press.

Getzels, J. W., & Jackson, P. W. (1962). *Creativity and intelligence.* New York: Wiley.

Gignac, G., & Vernon, P. A. (2003). Digit symbol rotation: A more g-loaded version of the traditional digit symbol subtest. *Intelligence, 31*(1), 1–8.

Gigone, D., & Hastie, R. (1997). Proper analysis of the accuracy of group judgments. *Psychological Bulletin,* 121, 149–167.

Gijsman, H. J., et al. (2002). A dose-finding study on the effects of branch chain amino acids on surrogate markers of brain dopamine function. *Psychopharmacology, 160*(2), 192–197.

Gill, T. M., DiPietro, L., & Krumholz, H. M. (2000). Role of exercise stress testing and safety monitoring for older persons starting an exercise person. *Journal of the American Medical Association, 284,* 342–349.

Gilligan, C. (1982). *In a different voice.* Cambridge, MA: Harvard University Press.

Gilligan, C., Ward, J. V., & Taylor, J. M. (1989). *Mapping the moral domain: A contribution of women's thinking to psychological theory and education.* Cambridge, MA: Harvard University Press.

Gilovich, T., & Eibach, R. (2001). The fundamental attribution error where it really counts. *Psychological Inquiry, 12*(1), 23–26.

Gilovich, T., et al. (Eds.). (2002). *Heuristics and biases: The psychology of intuitive judgment* (pp. 348–366). New York: Cambridge University Press.

Glantz, L. A., & Lewis, D. A. (2000). Decreased dendritic spine density on prefrontal cortical pyramidal neurons in schizophrenia. *Archives of General Psychiatry, 57*(1), 65–73.

Glaser, R., et al. (1993). Stress and the memory Tcell response to the Epstein-Barr virus. *Health Psychology, 12,* 435–442.

Godfrey, J. R. (2004). Toward optimal health: The experts discuss therapeutic humor. *Journal of Women's Health, 13*(5), 474–479.

Goldman-Rakic, P. S. (1995). Cited in Goleman, D. (1995, May 2). Biologists find site of working memory. *The New York Times,* pp. C1, C9.

Goldman-Rakic, P. S., et al. (2000b). Memory. In M. S. Gazzaniga (Ed.), *The new cognitive neurosciences* (2nd ed., pp. 733–840). Cambridge, MA: MIT Press.

Goldman-Rakic, P. S., Muly, E. C., III, & Williams, G. V. (2000a). D-sub-1 receptors in prefrontal cells and circuits. *Brain Research Reviews, 31*(2–3), 295–301.

Goldstein, E. B. (2004). *Sensation and perception, media edition.* (6th ed.). Belmont, CA: Wadsworth Publishing Company.

Goleman, D. J. (1995). *Emotional intelligence.* New York: Bantam Books.

Gomez, P., Zimmermann, P., Guttormsen-Schär, S., & Danuser, B. (2005). Respiratory responses associated with affective processing of film stimuli. *Biological Psychology, 68*(3), 223–235.

Gonzalez, C., Dana, J., Koshino, H., & Just, M. (2005). The framing effect and risky decisions: Examining cognitive functions with fMRI. *Journal of Economic Psychology, 26*(1), 1–20.

Goode, E. (2000, June 25). Thinner: The male battle with anorexia. *The New York Times,* p. MH8.

Goodenough, F. L., & Harris, D. B. (1950). Studies in the psychology of children's drawings: II 1928–1949. *Psychological Bulletin, 47,* 369–433.

Goodwin, P. J., et al. (2001). The effect of group psychosocial support on survival in metastatic breast cancer. *New England Journal of Medicine, 345*(24), 1719–1726.

Gordon, B. N., Baker-Ward, L., & Ornstein, P. A. (2001). Children's testimony: A review of research on memory for past experiences. *Clinical Child & Family Psychology Review, 4*(2), 157–181.

Gorman, J. M. (2001). A call to action: Overcoming anxiety through active coping. *American Journal of Psychiatry, 158*(12), 1953–1955.

Gorodetsky, M., & Klavir, R. (2003). What can we learn from how gifted /average pupils describe their processes of problem solving? *Learning & Instruction, 13*(3), 305–325.

Gottesman, I. I. (1991). *Schizophrenia genesis.* New York: Freeman.

Grady, C. L., McIntosh, A. R., Rajah, M. N., Beig, S., & Craik, F. I. M. (1999). The effects of age on the neural correlates of episodic encoding. *Cerebral Cortex, 9*(8), 805–814.

Granot, D., & Mayseless, O. (2001). Attachment security and adjustment to school in middle childhood. *International Journal of Behavioral Development, 25*(6), 530–541.

Greenberg, J. (1985). Small family size has a number of apparently positive effects on a child's intellectual development. *Science News, 127(22),* 340–341.

Greenberger, E., Chen, C., Tally, S. R., & Dong, Q. (200). Family, peer, and individual correlates of depressive symptomology among U.S. and Chinese adolescents. *Journal of Consulting and Clinical Psychology, 68,* 209–219.

Griffin, C. (2001). Imagining new narratives of youth. *Childhood: A Global Journal of Child Research,* 8(2), 147–166.

Griffin, K. W., Botvin, G. J., Nichols, T. R., & Scheier, L. M. (2004). Low perceived chances for success in life and binge drinking among inner-city minority youth. *Journal of Adolescent Health, 34*(6), 501–507.

Griffin, M. G. (2008). A prospective assessment of auditory startle alterations in rape and physical assault survivors. *Journal of Traumatic Stress, 21*(1), 91–99.

Gross, R. (2002). The prison simulation experiment. *Psychology Review, 8,* 15–17. This article summarizes the classic prison simulation study conducted by Zimbardo.

Grusec, J. E. (2002). Parenting socialization and children's acquisition of values. In M. H. Bornstein (Ed.), *Handbook of parenting: Vol. 5: Practical issues in parenting* (2nd ed., pp. 143–167).

Guerin, B. (1999). Social behaviors as determined by different arrangements of social consequences: Social loafing, social facilitation, deindividuation, and a modified social loafing. *Psychological Record, 49*(4), 565–578.

Guidetti, M. & Nikoladis, E. (2008). Gestures and communication development. *First Language, 28*(2), 107-115.

Gupta, V. B., Nwosa, N. M., Nadel, T. A., & Inamdar, S. (2001). Externalizing behaviors and television viewing in children of low-income minority parents. *Clinical Pediatrics, 40*(6), 337–341.

H

Haaga, D. A. F., & Davison, G. C. (1993). An appraisal of rational-emotive therapy. *Journal of Consulting and Clinical Psychology, 61,* 215–220.

Habib, M., & Robichon, F. (2003). Structural correlates of brain asymmetry: Studies in left-handed and dyslexic individuals. In K. Hugdahl & R. J. Davidson (Eds.), *The asymmetrical brain* (pp. 681–716). Cambridge, MA: MIT Press.

Haenen, J. (2001). Outlining the teaching–learning process: Piotr Gal'perin's contribution. *Learning & Instruction, 11*(2), 157–170.

Hakim, A. A., et al. (1998). Effects of walking on mortality among nonsmoking retired men. *New England Journal of Medicine, 338,* 94–99.

Hall, Calvin S. *The Meaning of Dreams.* New York: Harper & Brothers, 1953

Halpern, D. F. (2003). Sex differences in cognitive abilities. *Applied Cognitive Psychology, 17*(3), 375–376

Halpern, D. F., & LaMay, M. L. (2000). The smarter sex: A critical review of sex differences in intelligence. *Educational Psychology Review, 12*(2), 229–246.

Halpern, D. F., Hansen, C., & Riefer, D. (1990). Analogies as an aid to understanding and memory. *Journal of Educational Psychology, 82,* 298–305.

Hamilton, N. A., Karoly, P., & Kitzman, H. (2004). Self-regulation and chronic pain: The role of emotion. *Cognitive Therapy & Research, 28*(5), 559–576.

Han, W., Leventhal, T., & Linver, M. R. (2004). The Home Observation for Measurement of the Environment (HOME) in middle childhood: A study of three large-scale data sets. *Parenting: Science & Practice, 4*(2–3), 189–210.

Hankin, B. L., & Abramson, L. Y. (2001). Development of gender differences in depression: An elaborated cognitive vulnerability-transactional stress theory. *Psychological Bulletin, 127*(6), 773–796.

Hankin, B. L., Fraley, R. C., & Abela, J. R. Z. (2005). Daily depression and cognitions about cognitive style and the prediction of depressive symptoms in a prospective daily diary study. *Journal of Personality and Social Psychology, 88*(4), 673–685.

Hansell, N. K., et al. (2001). Genetic influence on ERP slow wave measures of working memory. *Behavior Genetics, 31*(6), 603–614.

Haridakis, P. M. (2002). Viewer characteristics, exposure to television violence, and aggression. *Media Psychology, 4*(4), 323–352.

Harker, L., & Keltner, D. (2001). Expressions of positive emotion in women's college yearbook pictures and their relationship to personality and life outcomes across adulthood. *Journal of Personality and Social Psychology, 80*(1), 112–124.

Harley, K., & Reese, E. (1999). Origins of autobiographical memory. *Developmental Psychology, 35*(5), 1338–1348.

Harlow, H. F. (1959). Love in infant monkeys. *Scientific American, 200,* 68–86.

Harlow, J. M. (1868). Recovery from the passage of an iron bar through the head. *Publication of the Massachusetts Medical Society, 2,* 327.

Hart, J. W., Bridgett, D. J., & Karau, S. J. (2001). Coworker ability and effort as determinants of individual effort on a collective task. *Group Dynamics, 5*(3), 181–190.

Hawkley, L. C., & Cacioppo, J. T. (2004). Stress and the aging immune system. *Brain, Behavior & Immunity, 18*(2), 114–119.

Health, United States (2002). http:/www.cdc.gov/ nchs (National Center for Health Statistics).

Heber, D. (2010). An integrative view of obesity. *American Journal of Clinical Nutrition 91*(1), 280S-283S.

Heidenreich, P. A. (2003). Understanding and modifying physician behavior for prevention and management of cardiovascular disease. *Journal of General Internal Medicine, 18*(12), 1060–1061.

Heidenreich, T., & Michalak, J. (2003). Mindfulness as a treatment principle in behavior therapy. *Verhaltenstherapie, 13(4),* 264–274.

Heimpel, S. A., Wood, J. V., Marshall, M. A., & Brown, J. D. (2002). Do people with low self-esteem really want to feel better? Self-esteem differences in motivation to repair negative moods. *Journal of Personality & Social Psychology, 82*(1), 128–147.

Heinrichs, R. W. (2005). The primacy of cognition in schizophrenia. *American Psychologist, 60*(3), 229–242.

Heinz, A. (2004). Reward and dependence—A psychological and neurobiological analysis of reward mechanisms and of their role in dependence (European University Studies, Vol. 685). *Addiction, 99*(11), 1482.

Helms, J. E. (1992). Why is there no study of cultural equivalence of standardized cognitive ability testing? *American Psychologist, 47,* 1083–1101.

Hensley, W. E. (1981). The effects of attire, location, and sex on aiding behavior. *Journal of Nonverbal Behavior, 6,* 3–11.

Herbert, B. (2005, September 26). A waking nightmare. *The New York Times online.*

Hergenhahn, B. R. (2009). *History of psychology* (6th ed.). Belmont, CA: Wadsworth Publishing Company.

Hertz-Pannier, L., et al. (2002). Late plasticity for language in a child's non-dominant hemisphere: A pre- and post-surgery fMRI study. *Brain, 125*(2), 361–372.

Hill, W. L., Ballard, S., Coyer, M. J., & Rowley, T. (2005). The interaction of testosterone and breeding phase on the reproductive behavior and use of space of male zebra finches. *Hormones & Behavior, 47*(4), 452–458.

Hingson, R., et al. (2002). A call to action: Changing the culture of drinking at U.S. colleges. National Institutes of Health: National Institute of Alcohol Abuse and Alcoholism. Washington, DC.

Hobson, J. A. (2003). *Dreaming: An introduction to the science of sleep.* New York: Oxford University Press.

Hoff, E. (2005). *Language development* (3rd ed.). Belmont, CA: Wadsworth Publishing Company.

Hoge, C. W., et al. (2004). Combat duty in Iraq and Afghanistan, mental health problems, and barriers to care. *New England Journal of Medicine, 351*(1), 13–22.

Hohwy, J., & Frith, C. (2004). Can neuroscience explain consciousness? *Journal of Consciousness Studies, 11*(7–8), 180–198.

Holland, J. L. (1996). Exploring careers with a typology. *American Psychologist, 51,* 397–406.

Hollinger, L. M., & Buschmann, M. B. (1993).Factors influencing the perception of touch by elderly nursing home residents and their health caregivers. *International Journal of Nursing Studies, 30,* 445–461.

Hollingshead, A. B., & Redlich, F. C. (1958). *Social class and mental illness.* New York: Wiley.

Hollon, S. D., et al. (2005). Prevention of relapse following cognitive therapy vs. medications in moderate to severe depression. *Archives of General Psychiatry, 62*(4), 417–422.

Holmes, M. M., Putz, O., Crews, D., & Wade, J. (2005). Normally occurring intersexuality and testosterone induced plasticity in the copulatory system of adult leopard geckos. *Hormones & Behavior, 47*(4), 439–445.

Holmes, T. H., & Rahe, R. H. (1967). The social readjustment rating scale. *Journal of Psychosomatic Research, 11,* 213–218.

Honorton, C. (1985). Meta-analysis of psi Ganzfeld research.

Journal of Parapsychology, 49, 51–91.

Honorton, C., et al. (1990). Psi communication in the Ganzfeld. *Journal of Parapsychology, 54,* 99–139.

Honts, C. R., Hodes, R. L., & Raskin, D. C. (1985). Effects of physical countermeasures on the physiological detection of deception. *Journal of Applied Psychology, 70*(1), 177–187.

Hoover, R. N. (2000). Cancer: Nature, nurture, or both. *New England Journal of Medicine, 343,* 135–136.

Hopkins, R. A., & Powers, T. L. (2009). Development and test of new dimensions of altruistic buying behavior. *Journal of Consumer Marketing, 26*(3), 185-199.

Horgan, O., & MacLachlan, M. (2004). Psychosocial adjustment to lower-limb amputation: A review. *Disability & Rehabilitation: An International Multidisciplinary Journal, 26*(14–15), 837–850.

Horn, J. M. (1983). The Texas adoption project. *Child Development, 54,* 268–275.

Hornstein, E. P., Verweij, J., & Schnapf, J. L. (2004). Electrical coupling between red and green cones in primate retina. *Nature Neuroscience, 7*(7), 745–750.

Horowitz, T. S., Cade, B. E., Wolfe, J. M., & Czeisler, C. A. (2003). Searching night and day: A dissociation of effects of circadian phase and time awake on visual selective attention and vigilance. *Psychological Science, 14*(6), 549–557.

Hoybye, M. T., Johansen, C., & Tjornhoj-Thomsen, T. (2005). Online interaction. Effects of storytelling in an Internet breast cancer support group. *Psycho-Oncology, 14*(3), 211–220.

Huesmann, L. R., Moise-Titus, J., Podolski, C., & Eron, L. D. (2003). Longitudinal relations between children's exposure to TV violence and their aggressive and violent behavior in young adulthood: 1977–1992. *Developmental Psychology, 39*(2), 201–221.

Hulshoff, P., et al. (2000). Prenatal exposure to famine and brain morphology in schizophrenia. *American Journal of Psychiatry, 157*(7), 1170–1172.

Human Genome Sequencing Consortium. (2004, October 29). Cited in "Number of genes in human genome lower than previously estimated." News Office, Massachusetts Institute of Technology. http://web.mit.edu /newsoffice/ 2004/ humangenome.html.

Hunter, B.T. (2002). How food communicates with your taste buds: The chemistry of perception. *Consumers' Research Magazine, 85,* 26–28. This article describes the complex interaction of taste and smell. The article also discusses taste modifiers and blockers.

Huskinson, T. L. H., & Haddock, G. (2004). Individual differences in attitude structure: Variance in the chronic reliance on affective and cognitive information. *Journal of Experimental Social Psychology, 40*(1), 82–90.

Hvas, L., Reventlow, S., & Malterud, K. (2004). Women's needs and wants when seeing the GP in relation to menopausal issues. *Scandinavian Journal of Primary Health Care, 22*(2), 118–121.

Hwu, H., Liu, C., Fann, C. S., Ou-Yang, W., & Lee, S. F. (2003). Linkage of schizophrenia with chromosome 1q loci in Taiwanese families. *Molecular Psychiatry, 8*(4), 445–452.

Hyde, J. S., & Plant, E. A. (1995). Magnitude of psychological gender differences. *American Psychologist, 50,* 159–161.

Hypnosis: Theory and application Part I. (2002, May). *Harvard Mental Health Letter, 18,* NA. This article discusses the theoretical component to hypnosis including subject experience and hypnotizability.

Hypnosis: Theory and application Part II. (2002, June). *Harvard Mental Health Letter, 18,* NA. This article continues the series on hypnosis and discusses hypnotherapy, hypnosis used to control pain and hypnosis and memory.

I

Iacono, W. G., & Lykken, D. T. (1997). The validity of the lie detector: Two surveys of scientific opinion. *Journal of Applied Psychology, 82*(3), 426–433.

Iidaka, T., Anderson, N. D., Kapur, S., Cabeza, R., & Craik, F. I. M. (2000). The effect of divided attention on encoding and retrieval in episodic memory revealed by positron emission tomography. *Journal of Cognitive Neuroscience, 12*(2), 267–280.

Inhelder, B., & Piaget, J. (1958). *The growth of logical thinking from childhood to adolescence.* Chicago: University of Chicago Press.

Insel, T. R. (2000). Toward a neurobiology of attachment. *Review of General Psychology, 4*(2), 176–185.

Iribarren, C., et al. (2000). Association of hostility with coronary artery calcification in young adults: The CARDIA study. *Journal of the American Medical Association, 283,* 2546–2551.

Isabella, R. A. (1998). Origins of attachment: The role of context, duration, frequency of observation, and infant age in measuring maternal behavior. *Journal of Social & Personal Relationships, 15*(4), 538–554.

Isarida, T., & Isarida, T. (1999). Effects of contextual changes between class and intermission on episodic memory. *Japanese Journal of Psychology, 69*(6), 478–485.

Iverson, P., et al. (2003). A perceptual interference account of acquisition difficulties for non-native phonemes. *Cognition, 87*(1), B47–B57.

Ivey, A. E., & Brooks-Harris, J. E. (2005). Integrative psychotherapy with culturally diverse clients. In J. C. Norcross & M. R. Goldfried (Eds.), *Handbook of psychotherapy integration* (2nd ed., pp. 321–339). London: Oxford University Press.

Izard, C. E. (1984). Emotion-cognition relationships and human development. In C. E. Izard, J.

Izard, C. E. (1994). Basic emotions, relations among emotions, and emotion-cognition relations. *Psychological Bulletin, 115,* 561–565.

J

Jacks, J. Z., & Devine, P. G. (2000). Attitude importance, forewarning of message content, and resistance to persuasion.

Basic & Applied Social Psychology, 22(1), 19–29.

Jackson, H., & Nuttall, R. L. (2001). Risk for preadolescent suicidal behavior: An ecological model. *Child & Adolescent Social Work Journal, 18*(3), 189–203.

Jacoangeli, F., et al. (2002). Osteoporosis and anorexia nervosa: Relative role of endocrine alterations and malnutrition. *Eating & Weight Disorders, 7*(3), 190–195.

Jaffee, S., & Hyde, J. S. (2000). Gender differences in moral orientation. *Psychological Bulletin, 126*(5), 703–726.

James, L. E., & Burke, D. M. (2000). Phonological priming effects on word retrieval and tip-of-the tongue experiences in young and older adults. *Journal of Experimental Psychology—Learning, Memory, and Cognition, 26*(6), 1378–1391.

James, W. (1890). *The principles of psychology*. New York: Henry Holt.

Jamison, K. R. (2000). Suicide and bipolar disorder. *Journal of Clinical Psychiatry, 61*(Suppl. 9), 47–51.

Janis, I. L. (1982). *Groupthink* (2nd ed.). Boston: Houghton Mifflin.

Janowitz, H. D., & Grossman, M. I. (1949). Effects of variations in nutritive density on intake of food in dogs and cats. *American Journal of Physiology, 158,* 184–193. 1400–1402.

Janowsky, J. S., Chavez, B., & Orwoll, E. (2000). Sex steroids modify working memory. *Journal of Cognitive Neuroscience, 12,* 407–414.

Jemmott, J. B., et al. (1983). Academic stress, power motivation, and decrease in secretion rate of salivary secretory immunoglobin A. *Lancet, 1,* 1400–1402.

Jensen, M. P., et al. (2005). Hypnotic analgesia for chronic pain in persons with disabilities: A case series. *International Journal of Clinical & Experimental Hypnosis, 53*(2), 198–228.

Johnson, W., & Krueger, R. F. (2006). How money buys happiness: Genetic and environmental processes linking finances and life satisfaction. *Journal of Personality and Social Psychology, 90*(4) 680–691.

Johnston, L. D., O'Malley, P. M., Bachman, J. G. & Schulenberg, J. E. (2009). *Monitoring the future national results on adolescent drug use: Overview of key findings, 2008* (NIH Publication No. 09-7401). Bethesda, MD: National Institute on Drug Abuse

Jonsdottir, I. H., Hellstrand, K., Thoren, P., & Hoffman, P. (2000). Enhancement of natural immunity seen after voluntary exercise in rats. Role of central opioid receptors. *Life Sciences, 66*(13), 1231–1239.

Jorgensen, R. S., Johnson, B. T., Kolodziej, M. E., & Schreer, G. E. (1996). Elevated blood pressure and personality. *Psychological Bulletin, 120,* 293–320.

Journal of Happiness Studies, 2(2), 173–204.

K

Kaddour, J. (2003). Psychological endurance (hardiness): Definitional, nomological, and critical aspects. *European Review of Applied Psychology, 53*(3–4), 227–

237.

Kagan, & R. B. Zajonc (Eds.), *Emotions, cognition, and behavior.* New York: Cambridge University Press.

Kahneman, D., & Frederick, S. (2002). Representativeness revisited: Attribute substitution in intuitive judgment. In T. Gilovich, et al. (Eds.), *Heuristics and biases: The psychology of intuitive judgment* (pp. 49–81). New York: Cambridge University Press.

Kainz, K. (2002). A behavioral conditioning program for treatment of nocturnal enuresis. *Behavior Therapist, 25*(10), 185–187.

Kalin, N. H. (2003). Nonhuman primate studies of fear, anxiety, and temperament and the role of benzodiazepine receptors and GABA systems. *Journal of Clinical Psychiatry, 64*(Suppl. 3), 41–44.

Kallgren, C. A., Reno, R. R., & Cialdini, R. B. (2000). A focus theory of normative conduct: When norms do and do not affect behavior. *Personality & Social Psychology Bulletin, 26*(8), 1002–1012.

Kamalanabhan, T. J., Sunder, D. L., & Vasanthi, M. (2000). An evaluation of the Choice Dilemma Questionnaire as a measure of risk-taking propensity. *Social Behavior & Personality, 28*(2), 149–156.

Kandel, E. R. (2001). The molecular biology of memory storage: A dialogue between genes and synapses. *Science, 294,* 1030–1038.

Kapur, S. (2003). Psychosis as a state of aberrant salience: A framework linking biology, phenomenology, and pharmacology in schizophrenia. *American Journal of Psychiatry, 160*(1), 13–23.

Karlberg, L., et al. (1998). Is there a connection between car accidents, near accidents, and Type A drivers? *Behavioral Medicine, 24*(3), 99–106.

Karon, B. P., & Widener, A. (1998). Repressed memories: The real story. *Professional Psychology: Research & Practice, 29*(5), 482–487.

Karwautz, A., et al. (2001). Individual-specific risk factors for anorexia nervosa: A pilot study using a discordant sister-pair design. *Psychological Medicine, 31*(2), 317–329.

Kasai, K., et al. (2003). Progressive decrease of left Heschl gyrus and planum temporale gray matter volume in first-episode schizophrenia: A longitudinal magnetic resonance imaging study. *Archives of General Psychiatry, 60*(8), 766–775.

Kashima, Y. (2000). Maintaining cultural stereotypes in the serial reproduction of narratives. *Personality & Social Psychology Bulletin, 26*(5), 594–604.

Kaslow, N. J., et al., (2002). Risk and protective factors for suicidal behavior in abused African American women. *Journal of Consulting & Clinical Psychology, 70*(2), 311–319.

Kataria, S. (2004). A clinical guide to pediatric sleep: Diagnosis and management of sleep problems. *Journal of Developmental & Behavioral Pediatrics, 25*(2), 132–133.

Katigbak, M. S., Church, A. T., Guanzon- Lapena, M. A., Carlota, A. J., & del Pilar, G. H. (2002). Are indigenous personality dimensions culture specific? Philippine inventories and the five-factor model. *Journal of Personality & Social Psychology, 82*(1), 89–101.

Kauff, N. D., & Offit, K. (2007). Modeling genetic risk of breast cancer. *Journal of the American Medical Association, 297,* 2637–2639.

Kavanagh, K., et al. (2007). Characterization and heritability of obesity and associated risk factors in vervet monkeys. *Obesity, 15*(7), 1666–1674.

Kaye, W. H., et al. (2004). Genetic analysis of bulimia nervosa: Methods and sample description. *International Journal of Eating Disorders, 35*(4), 556–570.

Kazuomi Kario, J. E., et al. (2001). Gender differences in associations of diurnal blood pressure variation, awake physical activity, and sleep quality with negative affect: The Work Site Blood Pressure Study. *Hypertension, 38,* 997–1002.

Kéri, S. (2003). Genetics, psychology, and determinism. *American Psychologist, 58*(4), 319.

Keller, A., et al. (2003). Progressive loss of cerebellar volume in childhood-onset schizophrenia. *American Journal of Psychiatry, 160,* 128–133.

Keller, S., Maddock, J. E., Laforge, R. G., Velicer, W. F., & Basler, H-D. (2007). Binge drinking and health behavior in medical students. *Addictive Behaviors, 32*(3), 505–515.

Kellerman, J., Lewis, J., & Laird, J. D. (1989). Looking and loving: The effects of mutual gaze on feelings of romantic love. *Journal of Research in Personality, 23,* 145–161.

Kellman, P. J., & von Hofsten, C. (1992). The world of the moving infant. In C. Rovee-Collier & L. P. Lipsitt (Eds.), *Advances in Infancy Research* (Vol. 7). Norwood, NJ: Ablex.

Kendler, K. S., et al. (2000a). Illicit psychoactive substance use, heavy use, abuse, and dependence in a U.S. population-based sample of male twins. *Archives of General Psychiatry, 57,* 261–269.

Kendler, K. S., Myers, J., Prescott, C. A., & Neale, M. C. (2001). The genetic epidemiology of irrational fears and phobias in men. *Archives of General Psychiatry, 58*(3), 257–265.

Kendler, K. S., Thornton, L. M., Gilman, S. E., & Kessler, R. C. (2000c). Sexual orientation in a U.S. national sample of twin and nontwin sibling pairs. *American Journal of Psychiatry, 157,* 1843–1846.

Kennedy, C. H. (2002). Effects of REM sleep deprivation on a multiple schedule of appetitive reinforcement. *Behavioural Brain Research, 128*(2), 205–214.

Kerns, J. G., & Berenbaum, H. (2002). Cognitive impairments associated with formal thought disorder in people with schizophrenia. *Journal of Abnormal Psychology, 111*(2), 211–224.

Kessler, R. C., Berglund, P., Borges, G., Nock, M., & Wang, P. S. (2005b). Trends in suicide ideation, plans, gestures, and attempts in the United States, 1990–1992 to 2001–2003. *Journal of the American Medical Association, 293,* 2487–2495.

Kessler, R. C., Chiu, W. T., Demler, O., & Walters, E. E. (2005c).

Prevalence, severity, and comorbidity of 12-month *DSM–IV* disorders in the National Comorbidity Survey Replication. *Archives of General Psychiatry, 62*(6), 617–627.

Kessler, R. C., et al. (2005a) Lifetime prevalence and age-of-onset distributions of DSM–IV disorders in the National Comorbidity Survey Replication. *Archives of General Psychiatry, 62*(6), 593–602.

Keyes, C. L. M., & Goodman, S. H. (Eds.). (2006). *Women and depression: A handbook for the social, behavioral, and bio-medical sciences.* New York: Cambridge University Press.

Keyes, C. L. M., & Haidt, J. (2003). *Flourishing: Positive psychology and the life well-lived.* Washington, DC: American Psychological Association.

Keyes, D. (1995). *The minds of Billy Milligan.* New York: Bantam Books.

Khan, A. A., Jacobson, K. C., Gardner, C. O., Prescott, C. A., & Kendler, K. S. (2005). Personality and comorbidity of common psychiatric disorders. *British Journal of Psychiatry, 186*(3), 190–196.

Kiecolt-Glaser, J. K., Marucha, P. T., Atkinson, C., & Glaser, R. (2001). Hypnosis as a modulator of cellular immune dysregulation during acute stress. *Journal of Consulting & Clinical Psychology, 69*(4), 674–682. *Annual Review of Psychology, 53*(1), 83–107.

Kiecolt-Glaser, J. K., McGuire, L., Robles, T. F., & Glaser, R. (2002a). Psychoneuroimmunology and psychosomatic medicine: Back to the future.

Kiecolt-Glaser, J. K., McGuire, L., Robles, T. F., & Glaser, R. (2002b). Emotions, morbidity, and mortality: New perspectives from psychoneuroimmunology.

Kihlstrom, J. F. (2002). No need for repression. *Trends in Cognitive Sciences, 6*(12), 502.

Kilshaw, D., & Annett, M. (1983). Right- and lefthand skill: Effects of age, sex, and hand preferences showing superior in left-handers. *British Journal of Psychology, 74,* 253–268.

Kim, B. S. K., Brenner, B. R., Liang, C. T. H., & Asay, P. A. (2003). A qualitative study of adaptation experiences of 1.5-generation Asian Americans. *Cultural Diversity & Ethnic Minority Psychology, 9*(2), 156–170.

Kim, K., & Rohner, R. P. (2002). Parental warmth, control, and involvement in schooling: Predicting academic achievement among Korean American adolescents. *Journal of Cross-Cultural Psychology, 33*(2), 127–140.

King, S. (2005). In Lake, M. (2005, May 2). Virtual reality heals 9/11 wounds. http://www.cnn.com/ 2005/TECH/04/29/spark.virtual /index.html.

Kingsbury, S.J. (1997). What is solution-focused therapy? *Harvard Mental Health Letter, 13,* 8. This article describes solution-focused therapy.

Kinsey, A. C., Pomeroy, W. B., & Martin, C. E. (1948). *Sexual behavior in the human male.* Philadelphia: W. B. Saunders.

Kinsey, A. C., Pomeroy, W. B., Martin, C. E., & Gebhard, P. H. (1953). *Sexual behavior in the human female.* Philadelphia:

W. B. Saunders.

Kirsch, I. (2000). The response set theory of hypnosis. *American Journal of Clinical Hypnosis, 42*(3–4), 274–292.

Kirsch, I., Lynn, S. J., Vigorito, M., & Miller, R. R. (2004). The role of cognition in classical and operant conditioning. *Journal of Clinical Psychology, 60*(4), 369–392.

Kirschenbaum, H., & Jourdan, A. (2005). The current status of Carl Rogers and the person-centered approach. *Psychotherapy: Theory, Research, Practice, Training, 42*(1), 37–51.

Klaczynski, P. A. (2001). Framing effects on adolescent task representations, analytic and heuristic processing and decision making. Implications for the normative /descriptive gap. *Journal of Applied Developmental Psychology, 22*(3), 289–309.

Kleinke, C. L. (1977). Compliance to requests made by gazing and touching experimenters in field settings. *Journal of Experimental Social Psychology, 13,* 218–223.

Kleinke, C. L. (1986). Gaze and eye contact. *Psychological Review, 100,* 78–100.

Kleinmuntz, B., & Szucko, J. J. (1984). Lie detection in ancient and modern times. *American Psychologist, 39,* 766–776.

Knafo, A., Iervolino, A. C., & Plomin, R. (2005). Masculine girls and feminine boys: Genetic and environmental contributions to atypical gender development in early childhood. *Journal of Personality & Social Psychology, 88*(2), 400–412.

Kobasa, S. C. O. (1990). Stress-resistant personality. In R. E. Ornstein & C. Swencionis (Eds.), *The healing brain* (pp. 219–230). New York: Guilford Press.

Kobasa, S. C. O., Maddi, S. R., Puccetti, M. C., & Zola, M. A. (1994). Effectiveness of hardiness, exercise, and social support as resources against illness. In A. Steptoe & J. Wardle (Eds.), *Psychosocial processes and health* (pp. 247–260).

Kohlberg, L. (1969). *Stages in the development of moral thought and action.* New York: Holt, Rinehart and Winston.

Kohlberg, L. (1981). *The philosophy of moral development.* San Francisco: Harper & Row.

Kooijman, C. M., et al. (2000). Phantom pain and phantom sensations in upper limb amputees: An epidemiological study. *Pain, 87*(1), 33–41.

Kopelman, M. D. (2002). Disorders of memory. *Brain, 125*(10), 2152–2190.

Koss, M. P., Figueredo, A. J., & Prince, R. J. (2002). Cognitive mediation of rape's mental, physical and social health impact: Tests of four models in cross-sectional data. *Journal of Consulting & Clinical Psychology, 70*(4), 926–941.

Kramer, P. D. (2003, June 22). Your Zoloft might prevent a heart attack. *The New York Times,* p. WK3.

Krantz, D. S., Contrada, R. J., Hill, D. R., & Friedler, E. (1988). Environmental stress and biobehavioral antecedents of coronary heart disease. *Journal of Consulting and Clinical Psychology, 56,* 333–341.

Krcmar, M., & Cooke, M. C. (2001). Children's moral reasoning and their perceptions of television violence. *Journal of Communication, 51*(2), 300–316.

Kroger, J. K., et al. (2002). Recruitment of anterior dorsolateral prefrontal cortex in human reasoning: A parametric study of relational complexity. *Cerebral Cortex, 12*(5), 477–485.

Kuczmarski, R. J., et al. (2000, December 4). CDC Growth charts: United States. Advance data from vital and health statistics, no. 314. Hyattsville, MD: National Center for Health Statistics.

Kwate, N. O. A. (2001). Intelligence or misorientation? Eurocentrism in the WICS-III. *Journal of Black Psychology, 27*(2), 221–238. Washington, DC: American Psychological Association.

L

Labiano, L. M., & Brusasca, C. (2002). Psychological treatments in arterial hypertension. *Interdisciplinaria, 19*(1), 85–97.

Lackner, J. M., Carosella, A. M., & Feuerstein, M. (1996). Pain expectancies, pain, and functional self-efficacy expectancies as determinants of disability in patients with chronic low back disorders. *Journal of Consulting and Clinical Psychology, 64,* 212–220.

Lahti, A. C., et al. (2001). Abnormal patterns of regional cerebral blood flow in schizophrenia with primary negative symptoms during an effortful auditory recognition task. *American Journal of Psychiatry, 158,* 1797–1808.

Lalumére, M. L., Blanchard, R., & Zucker, K. J. (2000). Sexual orientation and handedness in men and women: A meta-analysis. *Psychological Bulletin, 126*(4), 575–592.

Lam, A. G., & Sue, S. (2001). Client diversity. *Psychotherapy: Theory, Research, Practice, Training, 38*(4), 479–486.

Lang, A. R., Goeckner, D. J., Adesso, V. J., & Marlatt, G. A. (1975). Effects of alcohol on aggression in male social drinkers. *Journal of Abnormal Psychology, 84,* 508–518.

Lang, E. V., et al. (2000). Adjunctive non-pharmacological analgesia for invasive medical procedures: a randomised trial. *The Lancet, 355,* 1486–1490.

Lang, F. R., & Heckhausen, J. (2001). Perceived control over development and subjective wellbeing: Differential benefits across adulthood. *Journal of Personality & Social Psychology, 81*(3), 509–523.

Langlois, J. H., et al. (2000). Maxims or myths of beauty? A meta-analytic and theoretical review. *Psychological Bulletin, 126*(3), 390–423.

Lanier, S. A., Hayes, J. E., & Duffy, V. B. (2005). Sweet and bitter tastes of alcoholic beverages mediate alcohol intake in of-age undergraduates. *Physiology & Behavior, 83*(5), 821–831.

Larkin, M. (2000). Can lost hearing be restored? *The Lancet, 356,* 741–748.

Lashley, K. S. (1950). In search of the engram. In *Symposium of the Society for Experimental Biology* (Vol. 4). New York: Cambridge University Press.

Laumann, E. O., Gagnon, J. H., Michael, R. T., & Michaels,

S. (1994). *The social organization of sexuality.* Chicago: University of Chicago Press.

Lavee, Y., & Ben-Ari, A. (2003). Daily stress and uplifts during times of political tension: Jews and Arabs in Israel. *American Journal of Orthopsychiatry, 73*(1), 65–73.

Lavine, H., Lodge, M., & Freitas, K. (2005). Threat, authoritarianism, and selective exposure to information. *Political Psychology, 26*(2), 219–244.

Lawson, T. J., & Reardon, M. (1997). A humorous demonstration of in vivo systematic desensitization: The case of eraser phobia. *Teaching of Psychology, 24,* 270–271. This article describes a humorous teaching demonstration to aid students in their understanding of systematic desensitization.

Lazar, S. W., et al. (2000). Functional brain mapping of the relaxation response and meditation. *Neuroreport: For Rapid Communication of Neuroscience Research, 11*(7), 1581–1585.

Lazarus, R. S., DeLongis, A., Folkman, S., & Gruen, R. (1985). Stress and adaptational outcomes. *American Psychologist, 40,* 770–779.

Le Bon, G. (1960). *The crowd.* New York: Viking. (Original work published 1895)

Leahey, E., & Guo, G. (2001). Gender differences in mathematical trajectories. *Social Forces, 80*(2), 713–732.

Lecci, L., & Cohen, D. J. (2002). Perceptual consequences of an illness-concern induction and its relation to hypochondriacal tendencies. *Health Psychology, 21*(2), 147–156.

LeDoux, J. E. (1998). Fear and the brain: Where have we been, and where are we going? *Biological Psychiatry, 44*(12), 1229–1238.

LeDoux, J. E. (1998). Fear and the brain: Where have we been, and where are we going? *Biological Psychiatry, 44*(12), 1229–1238.

Lefcourt, H. M. (1997). Cited in Clay, R. A. (1997). Researchers harness the power of humor. *APA Monitor, 28*(9), 1, 18.

Lenneberg, E. H. (1967). *Biological foundations of language.* New York: Wiley.

Liebman, B., & Schardt, D. (2002). Tangled memories: Alzheimer's disease: The story so far. *Nutrition Action Healthletter, 29,* 1–8. This article discusses Alzheimer's disease including symptoms, possible causes and possible preventative measures.

Leitch, M. L. (2005, May 31). Just like bodies, psyches can drown in disasters. *The New York Times online.*

Lehman, B. J., & Crano, W. D. (2002). The pervasive effects of vested interest on attitude-criterion consistency in political judgment. *Journal of Experimental Social Psychology, 38*(2), 101–112.

Lensvelt-Mulders, G., & Hettema, J. (2001). Genetic analysis of autonomic reactivity to psychologically stressful situations. *Biological Psychology, 58*(1), 25–40.

Leonard, B. E. (2005). Mind over matter: Regulation of peripheral inflammation by the CNS. *Human Psychopharmacology: Clinical & Experimental, 20*(1), 71–72.

Leonard, S., Steiger, H., & Kao, A. (2003). Childhood and adulthood abuse in bulimic and nonbulimic women: Prevalences and psychological correlates. *International Journal of Eating Disorders, 33*(4), 397–405.

Leonardo, E. D., & Hen, R. (2006). Genetics of affective and anxiety disorders. *Annual Review of Psychology, 57,* 117–137.

Leor, J., Poole, K., & Kloner, R. A. (1996). Sudden cardiac death triggered by an earthquake. *New England Journal of Medicine, 334,* 413–419.

Leppel, K. (2002). Similarities and differences in the college persistence of men and women. *Review of Higher Education: Journal of the Association for the Study of Higher Education, 25*(4), 433–450.

Less sex, more protection, fewer pregnancies. (2004, March 7). *The New York Times,* p. 36N.

Lester, D., Yang, B., & Lindsay, M. (2004). Suicide bombers: Are psychological profiles possible?

Lever, J. P. (2004). Poverty and subjective well-being in Mexico. *Social Indicators Research, 68*(1), 1–33.

Levin, R., & Fireman, G. (2002). Nightmare prevalence, nightmare distress, and self-reported psychological disturbance. *Sleep: Journal of Sleep & Sleep Disorders Research, 25*(2), 205–212.

Levinson, D. J. (1996). *The seasons of a woman's life.* New York: Knopf.

Levinson, D. J., Darrow, C. N., Klein, E. B., Levinson, M. H., & McKee, B. (1978). *The seasons of a man's life.* New York: Knopf.

Levy, D., et al. (2000). Evidence for a gene influencing blood pressure on chromosome 17: Genome scan linkage results for longitudinal blood pressure phenotypes in subjects from the Framingham Heart Study. *Hypertension, 36,* 477–483.

Lewinsohn, P. M., Brown, R. A., Seeley, J. R., & Ramsey, S. E. (2000a). Psychological correlates of cigarette smoking abstinence, experimentation, persistence, and frequency during adolescence. *Nicotine & Tobacco Research, 2*(2), 121–131.

Li, G., Baker, S. P., Smialek, J. E., & Soderstrom, C. A. (2001). Use of alcohol as a risk factor for bicycling injury. *Journal of the American Medical Association, 284,* 893–896.

Li, W., & DeVries, S. H. (2004). Separate blue and green cone networks in the mammalian retina.

Lidow, M. S., et al. (2001). Antipsychotic treatment induces alterations in dendrite- and spine-associated proteins in dopamine-rich areas of the primate cerebral cortex. *Biological Psychiatry, 49*(1), 1–12.

Lieber, C. S. (1990). Cited in Barroom biology: How alcohol goes to a woman's head (January 14). *The New York Times,* p. E24.

Liebman, B., & Schardt, D. (2002). Tangled memories: Alzheimer's disease: The story so far. *Nutrition Action Healthletter, 29,* 1–8. This article discusses Alzheimer's disease including symptoms, possible causes and possible preventative measures.

Liederman, J., Kantrowitz, L., & Flannery, K. (2005). Male vulnerability to reading disability is not likely to be a myth: A call for new data. *Journal of Learning Disabilities, 38*(2), 109–129.

Linden, W., Chambers, L., Maurice, J., & Lenz, J. W. (1993). Sex differences in social support, selfdeception, hostility, and ambulatory cardiovascular activity. *Health Psychology, 12,* 376–380.

Little, A. C., & Perrett, D. I. (2002). Putting beauty back in the eye of the beholder. *Psychologist, 15*(1), 28–32.

Lochman, J. E., & Dodge, K. A. (1994). Social-cognitive processes of severely violent, moderately aggressive, and nonaggressive boys. *Journal of Consulting and Clinical Psychology, 62,* 366–374.

Loftus, E. F. (1983). Silence is not golden. *American Psychologist, 38,* 564–572.

Loftus, E. F. (2001). Imagining the past. *Psychologist, 14*(11), 584–587.

Loftus, E. F. (2004). Memories of things unseen. *Current Directions in Psychological Science, 13*(4), 145–147.

Loftus, E. F., & Bernstein, D. M. (2005). Rich false memories: The royal road to success. In A. F. Healy (Ed.), *Experimental cognitive psychology and its applications* (pp. 101–113). Washington, DC: American Psychological Association.

Loftus, G. R. (1983). The continuing persistence of the icon. *Behavioral and Brain Sciences, 6,* 28.

Loftus, G. R., & Loftus, E. F. (1976). *Human memory.*

Loop, M. S., Shows, J. F., Mangel, S. C., & Kuyk, T. K. (2003). Colour thresholds in dichromats and normals. *Vision Research, 43*(9), 983–992.

Lorenz, K. Z. (1981). *The foundations of ethology.* New York: Springer-Verlag.

Los Angeles Unified School District. (2000). Youth Suicide Prevention Information. http://www.sanpedro.com /spyc/ suicide.htm.

Louie, K., & Wilson, M. A. (2001). Temporally structured replay of awake hippocampal ensemble activity during rapid eye movement sleep. *Neuron, 29*(1), 145–156.

Loving, T. J., & Agnew, C. R. (2001). Socially desirable responding in close relationships: A dualcomponent approach and measure. *Journal of Social & Personal Relationships, 18*(4), 551–573.

Low, N. C. P., Cui, L., & Merikangas, K. R. (2008). Specificity of familial transmission of anxiety and comorbid disorders. *Journal of Psychiatric Research. 42*(7), 596-604.

Lu, L. (2001). Understanding happiness: A look into the Chinese folk psychology. *Journal of Happiness Studies, 2*(4), 407–432.

Luborsky, L., et al. (2002). The dodo bird verdict is alive and well—mostly. *Clinical Psychology: Science & Practice, 9*(1), 2–12.

Luchins, A. S. (1957). Primacy-recency in impression formation. In C. I. Hovland (Ed.), *The order of presentation in persuasion.* New Haven, CT: Yale University Press.

Ludwick-Rosenthal, R., & Neufeld, R. W. J. (1993). Preparation for undergoing an invasive medical procedure. *Journal of Consulting and Clinical Psychology, 61,* 156–164.

Lupton, D. (2002). Road rage: Driver's understandings and experiences. *Journal of Sociology, 38,* 275–291. This article discusses a qualitative research study designed to explore the phenomenon of road rage.

Lykken, D. T., & Csikszentmihalyi, M. (2001). Happiness—stuck with what you've got? *Psychologist, 14*(9), 470–472.

Lykken, D. T., McGue, M., Tellegen, A., & Bouchard, T. J., Jr. (1992). Emergenesis: Genetic traits that may not run in families. *American Psychologist, 47,* 1565–1577.

Lynn, S. J., Shindler, K., & Meyer, E. (2003). Hypnotic suggestibility, psychopathology, and treatment outcome. *Sleep & Hypnosis, 5*(1), 2–10.

M

Maccoby, E. E. (1992). The role of parents in the socialization of children: An historical overview. *Developmental Psychology, 28,* 1006–1017.

MacGregor, J. (2005). *Sunday money.* New York: HarperCollins.

Maciejewski, P. K., Prigerson, H. G., & Mazure, C. M. (2000). Self-efficacy as a mediator between stressful life events and depressive symptoms: Differences based on history of prior depression. *British Journal of Psychiatry, 176,* 373–378.

Mackert, B., et al. (2003). The eloquence of silent cortex: Analysis of afferent input to deafferented cortex in arm amputees. *Neuroreport: For Rapid Communication of Neuroscience Research, 14*(3), 409–412.

MacNeill, I. (2003). Stressed: Warning signs that you could be hitting the danger zone. *BC Business, 31,* 60–63. This article presents physiological warning signs of stress and negative side effects of stress.

Magnavita, N., et al. (1997). Type A behaviour pattern and traffic accidents. *British Journal of Medical Psychology, 70*(1), 103–107.

Maher, B. A., & Maher, W. B. (1994). Personality and psychopathology. *Journal of Abnormal Psychology, 103,* 72–77.

Mahmud, A., & Feely, F. (2003). Effect of smoking on arterial stiffness and pulse pressure amplification. *Hypertension, 41,* 183–187.

Maier, N. R. F., & Schneirla, T. C. (1935). *Principles of animal psychology.* New York: McGraw-Hill.

Major, G. C., etal. (2007). Clinical significance of adaptive thermogenesis. *International Journal of Obesity, 31*(2), 204–212.

Malgady, R. G., Rogler, L. H., & Costantino, G. (1990). Hero/heroine modeling for Puerto Rican adolescents. *Journal of Consulting and Clinical Psychology, 58,* 469–474.

Malkin, E. (2004, November 11). In health care, gap between rich and poor persists, W.H.O. says. *The New York Times online.*

Maltby, J., & Day, L. (2001). The relationship between exercise motives and psychological well-being. *The Journal of Psychology, 135,* 651–660. This article describes research in an attempt to identify the motivations for exercise. The article focuses on both intrinsic and extrinsic motivation.

Mamtani, R., & Cimino, A. (2002). A primer of complementary and alternative medicine and its relevance in the treatment of mental health problems. *Psychiatric Quarterly, 73*(4), 367–381.

Marian, V., & Neisser, U. (2000). Language-dependent recall of autobiographical memories. *Journal of Experimental Psychology: General, 129*(3), 361–368.

Markon, K. E., Krueger, R. F., Bouchard, T. J., Jr., & Gottesman, I. I. (2002). Normal and abnormal personality traits: Evidence for genetic and environmental relationships in the Minnesota Study of Twins Reared Apart. *Journal of Personality, 70*(5), 661–693.

Marks, I. M., & Dar, R. (2000). Fear reduction by psychotherapies: Recent findings, future directions. *The British Journal of Psychiatry, 176,* 507–511.

Markus, H., & Kitayama, S. (1991). Culture and the self. *Psychological Review, 98*(2), 224–253.

Marsh, R. L., Hicks, J. L., & Cook, G. I. (2005). On the relationship between effort toward an ongoing task and cue detection in event-based prospective memory. *Journal of Experimental Psychology: Learning, Memory & Cognition, 31*(1), 68–75.

Marshall, M. A., & Brown, J. D. (2004). Expectations and realizations: The role of expectancies in achievement settings. *Motivation & Emotion, 28*(4), 347–361.

Martin, C. L., & Ruble, D. (2004). Children's search for gender cues: Cognitive perspectives on gender development. *Current Directions in Psychological Science, 13*(2), 67–70.

Martin, S. (2002). Easing migraine pain. *Monitor on Psychology, 33*(4), 71.

Martinez-Taboas, A., & Bernal, G. (2000). Dissociation, psychopathology, and abusive experiences in a nonclinical Latino university student group. *Cultural Diversity & Ethnic Minority Psychology, 6*(1), 32–41.

Martins, Y., et al. (2005). Preference for human body odors is influenced by gender and sexual orientation. *Psychological Science, 16*(9), 694-701.

Marttunen, M. J., et al. (1998). Completed suicide among adolescents with no diagnosable psychiatric disorder. *Adolescence, 33*(131), 669–681.

Maslow, A. H. (1970). *Motivation and personality* (2nd ed.). New York: Harper & Row.

Mason II, T. & Pack, A. (2005). Sleep terrors in childhood. *The Journal of Pediatrics, 147*(3), 388-392.

Masters, W. H., & Johnson, V. E. (1966). *Human sexual response.* Boston: Little, Brown.

May, R. (2005). How do we know what works? *Journal of College Student Psychotherapy, 19*(3), 69–73.

Mayes, S. D., & Calhoun, S. L. Wechsler Intelligence Scale for Children-Third and -Fourth Edition predictors of academic achievement in children with attention-deficit/hyperactivity disorder. *School Psychology Quarterly, 22*(2), 234-249.

McAndrew, F. T. (2002). New evolutionary perspectives on altruism: Multilevel-selection and costly-signaling theories. *Current Directions in Psychological Science, 11*(2), 79–82.

McCormick, M. J. (2001). Self-efficacy and leadership effectiveness: Applying social cognitive theory to leadership. *Journal of Leadership Studies, 8,* 22–33. This article describes a model of effective leadership utilizing social cognitive theory.

McCourt, K., et al. (1999). Authoritarianism revisited: Genetic and environmental influences examined in twins reared apart and together. *Personality & Individual Differences, 27*(5), 985–1014.

McCrae, R. R., & Costa, P. T., Jr. (1997). Personality trait structure as a human universal. *American Psychologist, 52,* 509–516.

McCrae, R. R., et al. (2000). Nature over nurture: Temperament, personality, and life span development. *Journal of Personality & Social Psychology, 78*(1), 173–186.

McDaniel, M. A., Glisky, E. L., Guynn, M. J., & Routhieaux, B. C. (1999). Prospective memory: A neuropsychological study. *Neuropsychology, 13*(1), 103–110.

McDougall, W. (1904). The sensations excited by a single momentary stimulation of the eye. *British Journal of Psychology, 1,* 78–113.

McDougall, W. (1908). *An introduction to social psychology.* London: Methuen.

McGaugh, J. L., McIntyre, C. K., & Power, A. E. (2002). Amygdala modulation of memory consolidation: Interaction with other brain systems. *Neurobiology of Learning & Memory. 78*(3), 539–552.

McGovern, C. M. (1993). Asylum: The complex and controversial story of mental institutions in the U.S.A. *Journal of Social History, 26,* 668–669. This article is a review of a movie that focuses on the history of mental institutions and the controversy surrounding them.

McGrath, P. (2004). Psychological methods of pain control: Basic science and clinical perspectives. *Pain Research & Management, 9*(4), 217–217.

McGraw, A. P., Mellers, B. A., & Ritov, I. (2004). The affective costs of overconfidence. *Journal of Behavioral Decision Making, 17*(4), 281–295.

McGue, M., Pickens, R. W., & Svikis, D. S. (1992). Sex and age effects on the inheritance of alcohol problems: A twin study. *Journal of Abnormal Psychology, 101,* 3–17.

McKee, P., & Barber, C. E. (2001). Plato's theory of aging. *Journal of Aging & Identity, 6*(2), 93–104.

McKenzie, C. R. M., Lee, S. M., & Chen, K. K. (2002). When negative evidence increases confidence: Changes in belief after hearing two sides of a dispute. *Journal of Behavioral Decision Making, 15*(1), 1–18.

McLaren, L. (2002). Cited in Wealthy women most troubled by poor body image. (2002, February 11). Reuters online.

McMurran, M., Blair, M., & Egan, V. (2002). An investigation of the correlations between aggression, impulsiveness, social problem-solving, and alcohol use. *Aggressive Behavior, 28,* 439–445.

McNally, R. J., & Clancy, S. A. (2005). Sleep paralysis, sexual abuse, and space alien abduction. *Transcultural Psychiatry, 42*(1), 113–122.

McNeil, T. F., Cantor-Graae, E., & Weinberger, D. R. (2000). Relationship of obstetric complications and differences in size of brain structures in monozygotic twin pairs discordant for schizophrenia. *American Journal of Psychiatry, 157,* 203–212.

McSherry, B. (2005). Men behaving badly: Current issues in provocation, automatism, mental impairment and criminal responsibility. *Psychiatry, Psychology and Law, 12*(1), 15–22.

Meijer, J., & Elshout, J. J. (2001). The predictive and discriminant validity of the zone of proximal development. *British Journal of Educational Psychology, 71*(1), 93–113.

Mellon, M. W., & McGrath, M. L. (2000). Empirically supported treatments in pediatric psychology: Nocturnal enuresis. *Journal of Pediatric Psychology, 25*(4), 193–214.

Melmed, R. N. (2003). Mind, body, and medicine: An integrative text. *American Journal of Psychiatry, 160*(3), 605–606.

Meltzoff, A. N., & Gopnik, A. (1997). *Words, thoughts, and theories.* Cambridge, MA: MIT Press.

Melzack, R. (1999, August). From the gate to the neuromatrix. *Pain* (Suppl. 6), S121–S126.

Merikangas, K. R., et al. (2007). Lifetime and 12-month prevalence of bipolar spectrum disorder in the national comorbidity survey replication. *Archives of General Psychiatry, 64*(5), 432-552.

Metcalfe, J. (1986). Premonitions of insight predict impending error. *Journal of Experimental Psychology: Learning, Memory, and Cognition, 12,* 623–634.

Metz, R. (2005, March 10). Think of a number . . .Come on, think! *The New York Times online.*

Metzger, B. L. (2003). The effect of a genetic variant for obesity and type 2 diabetes on the therapeutic potential of exercise and calorie restrictive diets in Zucker rats. *Research and Theory for Nursing Practice: An International Journal, 17*(4) 321–333.

Meyer-Lindenberg, A., et al. (2001). Evidence for abnormal cortical functional connectivity during working memory in schizophrenia. *American Journal of Psychiatry, 158,* 1809–1817.

Michael, R. T., Gagnon, J. H., Laumann, E. O., & Kolata, G. (1994). *Sex in America: A definitive survey.* Boston: Little, Brown.

Michels, K. B., et al. (2000). Prospective study of fruit and vegetable consumption and incidence of colon and rectal cancers. *Journal of the National Cancer Institute, 92*(21), 1740–1752.

Migdow, J. (2003). The problem with pleasure. *Journal of Trauma & Dissociation, 4*(1), 5–25.

Miles, J. (2005, May 22). Nascar nation. *The New York Times Book Review,* pp. 1, 10–11.

Milgram, S. (1963). Behavioral study of obedience. *Journal of Abnormal and Social Psychology, 67,* 371–378.

Milgram, S. (1974). *Obedience to authority.* New York: Harper & Row.

Milius, S. (2002). Rescue Rat: Could wired rodents save the day? *Science News Online.* http://www .phschool.com /science /science_news/articles / rescue_rat.html.

Miller, A. L., Rathus, J. H., & Linehan, M. M. (2007). *Dialectical behavior therapy with suicidal adolescents.* New York: Guilford Press.

Miller, A. L., Wyman, S. E., Huppert, J. D., Glassman, S. L., & Rathus, J. H. (2000). Analysis of behavioral skills utilized by suicidal adolescents receiving dialectical behavior therapy. *Cognitive & Behavioral Practice, 7*(2), 183–187.

Miller, G. A. (1956). The magical number seven, plus or minus two: Some limits on our capacity for processing information. *Psychological Review, 63,* 81–97.

Miller, N. E. (1969). Learning of visceral and glandular responses. *Science, 163,* 434–445.

Miller, N. E. (1995). Clinical-experimental interactions in the development of neuroscience. *American Psychologist, 50,* 901–911.

Milne, R. D., Syngeniotis, A., Jackson, G., & Corballis, M. C. (2002). Mixed lateralization of phonological assembly in developmental dyslexia. *Neurocase, 8*(3), 205–209.

Milner, B. R. (1966). Amnesia following operation on temporal lobes. In C. W. M. Whitty & O. L.

Milstead, M., Lapsley, D., & Hale, C. (1993, March). *A new look at imaginary audience and personal fable.* Paper presented at the meeting of the Society for Research in Child Development, New Orleans, LA.

Milton, J., & Wiseman, R. (1999). Does psi exist? Lack of replication of an anomalous process of information transfer. *Psychological Bulletin, 125*(4), 387–391.

The mind and the immune system-part I. (2002). *Harvard Mental Health Letter, 18,* NA. This article discusses the immune system and how the immune system can learn. Also discussed are hormonal effects on stress.

Minino, A. M., Heron, M. P., Murphy, S. L., & Kochanek, K. D. (2007, October 10). Deaths: Final data for 2004. National vital statistics reports, 55(19). http://www.cdc.gov/nchs/data/nvsr/nvsr55/nvsr55_19.pdf.

Mischel, W., & Shoda, Y. (1995). A cognitive-affective system theory of personality. *Psychological Review, 102,* 246–268.

MIT researchers ID gene involved in memory retrieval. (2002, June 21). *Genomics & Genetics Weekly,* p. 4. This article discusses comparative research conducted with mice that implicates the hippocampus in memory retrieval.

Mitchell, A. L. (2006). Medical consequences of cocaine. *Journal of Addictions Nursing, 17*(4), 249.

Mittal, M., & Wieling, E. (2004). The influence of therapists' ethnicity on the practice of feminist family therapy: A pilot study. *Journal of Feminist Family Therapy, 16*(2), 25–42.

Molden, D. C., & Dweck, C. S. (2000). Meaning and motivation. In C. Sansone & J. M. Harackiewicz (Eds.), *Intrinsic and extrinsic motivation: The search for optimal motivation and performance*, (pp. 131–159). San Diego: Academic Press.

Molfese, V. J., DiLalla, L. F., & Bunce, D. (1997). Prediction of the intelligence test scores of 3–to 8–year-old children by home environment, socioeconomic status, and biomedical risks. *Merrill- Palmer Quarterly, 43*(2), 219–234.

Molfese, V. J., Modglin, A., & Molfese, D. L. (2003). The role of environment in the development of reading skills: A longitudinal study of preschool and school-age measures. *Journal of Learning Disabilities, 36*(1), 59–67.

Montgomery, G. H., DuHamel, K. N., & Redd, W. H. (2000). A meta-analysis of hypnotically induced analgesia: How effective is hypnosis? *International Journal of Clinical & Experimental Hypnosis, 48(2),* 138–153.

Moore, C. C., Romney, A. K., & Hsia, T. (2002). Cultural, gender, and individual differences in perceptual and semantic structures of basic colors in Chinese and English. *Journal of Cognition & Culture, 2*(1), 1–28.

Moro, C., & Rodriguez, C. (2000). La creation des representations chez l'enfant au travers des processus de semiosis. *Enfance, 52*(3), 287–294.

Morris, E. J. (1991). Classroom demonstration of behavioral effects of the split-brain operation. *Teaching of Psychology, 18 (4),* 226–228. This article discusses a fun activity to demonstrate what it must be like for those who undergo brain surgery that results in a split brain.

Morris, W. N., Miller, R. S., & Spangenberg, S. (1977). The effects of dissenter position and task difficulty on conformity and response conflict. *Journal of Personality, 45,* 251–256.

Morry, M. M. (2005). Relationship satisfaction as a predictor of similarity ratings: A test of the attraction-similarity hypothesis. *Journal of Social and Personal Relationships, 22*(4), 561–584.

Mosher, W. D., Chandra, A., & Jones, J. (2005, September 15). Sexual behavior and selected health measures: Men and women 15–44 years of age in the U.S., 2002. Advance Data Number 362. Hyattsville, MD: National Center for Health Statistics.

Moss, D. P. (2002). Cited in Clay, R. A. (2002). A renaissance for humanistic psychology. *Monitor on Psychology, 33*(8), 42–43.

Moss, E., & St-Laurent, D. (2001). Attachment at school age and academic performance. *Developmental Psychology, 37*(6), 863–874.

Moyà-Solà, S., Köhler, M., Alba, D. M., Casanovas-Vilar, I., & Galindo, J. (2004). Pierolapithecus catalaunicus, a new middle Miocene great ape from Spain. *Science, 19,* 1339–1344.

Mozaffarian, D., et al. (2003). Cereal, fruit, and vegetable fiber intake and the risk of cardiovascular disease in elderly individuals. *Journal of the American Medical Association, 289,* 1659–1666.

Mueser, K. T., & McGurk, S. R. (2004). Schizophrenia. *Lancet, 363*(9426), 2063–2072.

Muir, G. D. (2000). Early ontogeny of locomotor behaviour: A comparison between altricial and precocial animals. *Brain Research Bulletin, 53*(5), 719–726.

Mukamal, K. J., Maclure, M., Muller, J. E., Sherwood, J. B., & Mittleman, M. A. (2001). Prior alcohol consumption and mortality following acute myocardial infarction. *Journal of the American Medical Association, 285*(15), 1965–1970.

Murray, H. A. (1938). *Explorations in personality.* New York: Oxford University Press.

Muscari, M. (2002). Media violence: Advice for parents. *Pediatric Nursing, 28,* 585–591. This article provides suggestions for parents to help in mediating the effects that media violence can have on children.

Myers, L. B., & Brewin, C. R. (1994). Recall of early experience and the repressive coping style. *Journal of Abnormal Psychology, 103,* 288–292.

N

Nader, K., Schafe, G. E., & Le Doux, J. E. (2000). Fear memories require protein synthesis in the amygdala for reconsolidation after retrieval. *Nature, 406*(6797), 722–726.

Nagourney, E. (2002, April 2). Neal E. Miller is dead at 92; studied brain and behavior. *The New York Times,* p. A21.

Nagtegaal, J. E., et al. (2000). Effects of melatonin on the quality of life in patients with delayed sleep phase syndrome. *Journal of Psychosomatic Research, 48*(1), 45–50.

Naimi, T. S., et al. (2003b). Definitions of binge drinking. *Journal of the American Medical Association, 289*(13), 1636.

National Center for Health Statistics. *Health, United States, 2009: With Special Feature on Medical Technology.* Hyattsville, MD. 2010. Table 32. (Accessed March 15, 2010). http://www.cdc.gov/nchs/data/hus/hus09.pdf#032.

National Center for Health Statistics. (2005, June 19). Self-inflicted injury/suicide. Atlanta: Centers for Disease Control and Prevention. http://www.cdc.gov/nchs/fastats/suicide.htm.

National Center for Injury Prevention and Control. (2005, June 19). Suicide: Fact sheet. http://www.cdc.gov/ncipc/factsheets/suifacts.htm.

National Eating Disorders Associations (2010). (Accessed 3 March 2010). http://www.nationaleatingdisorders.org/information-resources/general-information.php

National Science Foundation (2002). Science and technology: Public attitudes and public understanding. http://www.nsf.gov/sbe/srs/seind02/c7/c7h.htm.

National Sleep Foundation (2001, November 19). Events of 9–11 took their toll on Americans' sleep, particularly for women, according to new National Sleep Foundation poll.

http://www.sleepfoundation.org/whatsnew/crisis_poll.html.

National Sleep Foundation (2008). *2005 Sleep in America Poll.* Washington, DC: National Sleep Foundation. http://www.sleepfoundation.org.

Nature editorial. (2004). *True lies. Nature, 428*(6984), 679.

Nature Neuroscience, 7(7), 751–756.

Navarro, J. F., & Maldonado, E. (2002). Acute and subchronic effects of MDMA ("ecstasy") on anxiety in male mice tested in the elevated plus-maze. *Progress in Neuro-Psychopharmacology & Biological Psychiatry, 26*(6), 1151–1154.

Neisser, U. (1993). Cited in Goleman, D. J. (1993, April 6). Studying the secrets of childhood memory. *The New York Times,* pp. C1, C11.

Neisser, U., et al. (1996). Intelligence: Knowns and unknowns. *American Psychologist, 51*(2), 77–101.

Neisser, U. (1997a). Never a dull moment. *American Psychologist, 52,* 79–81.

Neisser, U. (1997b). Cited in Sleek, S. (1997). Can "emotional intelligence" be taught in today's schools? *APA Monitor, 28*(6), 25.

Nelson, K., Hampson, J., & Shaw, L. K. (1993). Nouns in early lexicons: Evidence, explanations, and implications. *Journal of Child Language, 20,* 228.

Nestoriuc, Y., Rief, W., & Martin, A. (2008). Meta-analysis of biofeedback for tension-type headache: Efficacy, specificity, and treatment moderators. *Journal of Consulting and Clinical Psychology, 76*(3), 379–396.

Neumark-Sztainer, D., et al. (2002a). Ethnic/ racial differences in weight-related concerns and behaviors among adolescent girls and boys: Findings from Project EAT. *Journal of Psychosomatic Research, 53*(5), 963–974.

Neumark-Sztainer, D., et al. (2002a). Ethnic/ racial differences in weight-related concerns and behaviors among adolescent girls and boys: Findings from Project EAT. *Journal of Psychosomatic Research, 53*(5), 963–974.

Neveus, T., Cnattingius, S., Olsson, U., & Hetta, J. (2002). Sleep habits and sleep problems among a community sample of schoolchildren. *Journal of the American Academy of Child & Adolescent Psychiatry, 41*(7), 828.

Newman, L. S., & Baumeister, R. F. (1998). Abducted by aliens: Spurious memories of interplanetary masochism. In S. J. Lynn & K. M. Mc- Conkey (Eds), *Truth in memory* (pp. 284–303).

Newport, E. L. (1998). Cited in Azar, B. (1998). Acquiring sign language may be more innate than learned. *APA Monitor, 29*(4), 12.

Nezlek, J. B., Hampton, C. P., & Shean, G. D. (2000). Clinical depression and day-to-day social interaction in a community sample. *Journal of Abnormal Psychology, 109*(1), 11–19.

Nicholson, A. (2008). Socio-economic status over the life-course and depressive symptoms in men and women in Eastern Europe. *Journal of Affective Disorders, 105*(1-3), 125–136.

Nickell, J. (2001). Exorcism! Driving out the nonsense. *Skeptical Inquirer, 25,* 20. This article describes that one reason attributed to psychological disorders was demon possession. Exorcism was an attempt to help people possessed. This article describes this historical perspective.

No, S. (2004). From prejudice to intergroup emotions: Differentiated reactions to social groups. *Asian Journal of Social Psychology, 7*(1), 119–122.

Nock, M. K., et al. (2008). Suicide and suicidal behavior. *Epidemiologic Reviews, 30*(1), 133-154.

Nock, M. K., & Kazdin, A. E. (2002). Examination of affective, cognitive, and behavioral factors and suicide-related outcomes in children and young adolescents. *Journal of Community Psychology, 31*(1), 48–58.

Nolen-Hoeksema, S. (2001). Gender differences in depression. *Current Directions in Psychological Science, 10*(5), 173–176.

Norton, A. (2000, July 21). A drink a day keeps brain in tip-top shape. Reuters News Agency online.

Novick, L. R., & Coté, N. (1992). The nature of expertise in anagram solution. In *Proceedings of the Fourteenth Annual Conference of the Cognitive Science Society.* Hillsdale, NJ: Erlbaum.

Nowakowska, C., Strong, C. M., Santosa, C. M., Wang, P. W., & Ketter, T. A. (2005). Temperamental commonalities and differences in euthymic mood disorder patients, creative controls, and healthy controls. *Journal of Affective Disorders, 85*(1–2), 207–215.

Nuland, S. (2005, February). Do you want to live forever? *MIT Technology Review, 108*(2), 36–45.

Nurnberger, J. I., Jr., et al. (2004). A family study of alcohol dependence: Coaggregation of multiple disorders in relatives of alcohol-dependent probands. *Archives of General Psychiatry, 61*(12), 1246–1256.

Nyberg, L., et al. (2000). Large scale neurocognitive networks underlying episodic memory. *Journal of Cognitive Neuroscience, 12*(1), 163–173.

O

O'Dell, C. D., & Hoyert, M. D. (2002). Active and passive touch: A research methodology project. *Teaching of Psychology, 29*(4), 292–294.

Ogawa, K., Nittono, H., & Hori, T. (2002). Brain potential associated with the onset and offset of rapid eye movement (REM) during REM sleep. *Psychiatry & Clinical Neurosciences, 56*(3), 259–260.

Ohayon, M. M., Guilleminault, C., & Priest, R.G. (1999). Night terrors, sleepwalking, and confusional arousals in the general population: Their frequency and relationship to other sleep and mental disorders. *Journal of Clinical Psychiatry, 60*(4), 268–276.

Ohno, H., Urushihara, R., Sei, H., & Morita, Y. (2002). REM sleep deprivation suppresses acquisition of classical eye-blink conditioning. *Sleep: Journal of Sleep Research & Sleep Medicine, 25*(8), 877–881.

Oktedalen, O., Solberg, E. E., Haugen, A. H., & Opstad, P. K. (2001). The influence of physical and mental training on plasma beta-endorphin level and pain perception after intensive physical exercise. *Stress & Health: Journal of the International Society for the Investigation of Stress, 17*(2), 121–127.

Olanow, W. M. (2000, July). Clinical and pathological perspective on Parkinsonism. Paper presented to the World Alzheimer Congress 2000, Washington, DC.

Olds, J., & Milner, P. (1954). Positive reinforcement produced by electrical stimulation of the septal area and other regions of the rat brain. *Journal of Comparative and Physiological Psychology, 47,* 419–427.

Omer, H., & Elitzur, A. C. (2001). What would you say to the person on the roof ? A suicide prevention text. *Suicide & Life-Threatening Behavior, 31*(2), 129–139.

Orpen, C. (1995). The Multifactorial Achievement Scale as a predictor of salary growth and motivation among middle-managers. *Social Behavior & Personality, 23*(2), 159–162.

Ostatníková, D., et al. (2002). Biological aspects of intellectual giftedness. *Studia Psychologica, 44*(1), 3–13.

Otani, H., et al. (2005). Remembering a nuclear accident in Japan: Did it trigger flashbulb memories? *Memory, 13*(1), 6–20.

P

Pappas, G., Queen, S., Hadden, W., & Fisher, G. (1993). The increasing disparity of mortality between socioeconomic groups in the United States, 1960 and 1986. *New England Journal of Medicine, 329,* 103–109.

Park, N., Peterson, C., & Seligman, M. E. P. (2005). *Character strengths in forty nations and fifty states.* Unpublished manuscript, University of Rhode Island.

Parker, A. (2001). The ganzfeld: Suggested improvements of an apparently successful method for psi research. *European Journal of Parapsychology, 16,* 23–29.

Parr, L. A., Winslow, J. T., Hopkins, W. D., & de Waal, F. B. M. (2000). Recognizing facial cues: Individual discrimination by chimpanzees (*Pan troglodytes*) and Rhesus monkeys (Macaca mulatta).

Parrott, A. (Ed.) (2003). Cognitive deficits and cognitive normality in recreational cannabis and ecstasy/MDMA users. *Human Psychopharmacology: Clinical & Experimental, 18*(2), 89–90.

Pastor, L. H. (2004). Countering the psychological consequences of suicide terrorism. *Psychiatric Annals, 34*(9), 701–707.

Patenaude, J., Niyonsenga, T., & Fafard, D. (2003). Changes in students' moral development during medical school: A cohort study. *Canadian Medical Association Journal, 168*(7), 840–844.

Patry, A. L., & Pelletier, L. G. (2001). Extraterrestrial beliefs and experiences: An application of the theory of reasoned action. *Journal of Social Psychology, 141*(2), 199–217.

Patterson, D. R. (2004). Treating pain with hypnosis. *Current Directions in Psychological Science, 13*(6), 252–255.

Patterson, G. R., Dishion, T. J., & Yoerger, K. (2000). Adolescent growth in new forms of problem behavior: Macro- and micro-peer dynamics.

Pavlov, I. (1927). *Conditioned reflexes.* London: Oxford University Press.

Pelham, W. E., et al. (2002). Effects of methyphenidate and expectancy on children with ADHD: Behavior, academic performance, and attributions in a summer treatment program and regular classroom settings. *Journal of Consulting & Clinical Psychology, 70*(2), 320–335.

Penfield, W. (1969). Consciousness, memory, and man's conditioned reflexes. In K. H. Pribram (Ed.), *On the biology of learning.* New York: Harcourt Brace Jovanovich.

Pentney, A. R. (2001). An exploration of the history and controversies surrounding MDMA and MDA. *Journal of Psychoactive Drugs, 33*(3), 213–221.

Peplau, L. A. (2003). Human sexuality: How do men and women differ? *Current Directions in Psychological Science, 12*(2), 37–40.

Peters, M., et al. (2004). Migraine and chronic daily headache management: A qualitative study of patients' perceptions. *Scandinavian Journal of Caring Sciences, 18*(3), 294–303.

Peterson, C. (2002). Children's long-term memory for autobiographical events. *Developmental Review, 22*(3), 370–402.

Peterson, L. R., & Peterson, M. J. (1959). Shortterm retention of individual verbal items. *Journal of Experimental Psychology, 58,* 193–198.

Petrill, S. A., & Deater-Deckard, K. (2004). The heritability of general cognitive ability: A withinfamily adoption design. *Intelligence, 32*(4), 403–409.

Petrill, S. A., Pike, A., Price, T., & Plomin, R. (2004). Chaos in the home and socioeconomic status are associated with cognitive development in early childhood: Environmental mediators identified in a genetic design. *Intelligence, 32*(5), 445–460.

Petry, N. M., Martin, B., Cooney, J. L., & Kranzler, H. R. (2000). Give them prizes and they will come: Contingency management for treatment of alcohol dependence. *Journal of Consulting and Clinical Psychology, 68,* 250–257.

Petty, R. E., Fleming, M. A., & White, P. H. (1999). Stigmatized sources and persuasion: Prejudice as a determinant of argument scrutiny. *Journal of Personality & Social Psychology, 76*(1), 19–34.

Petty, R. E., Wegener, D. T., & Fabrigar, L. R. (1997). Attitudes and attitude change. *Annual Review of Psychology, 48,* 609–647.

Phalet, K., & Schoenpflug, U. (2001). Intergenerational transmission of collectivism and achievement values in two acculturation contexts: The case of Turkish families in Germany and Turkish and Moroccan families in the Netherlands. *Journal of Cross-Cultural Psychology, 32*(2), 186–201.

Phinney, J. S. (2000). Identity formation across cultures: The interaction of personal, societal, and historical change. *Human Development, 43*(1), 27–31.

Phinney, J. S. (2005). Ethnic identity in late modern times. *Identity, 5*(2), 187–194.

Phinney, J. S., Cantu, C. L., & Kurtz, D. A. (1997). Ethnic and American identity as predictors of self-esteem among African American, Latino, and White adolescents. *Journal of Youth & Adolescence, 26*(2), 165–185.

Phinney, J. S., & Devich-Navarro, M. (1997). Variations in bicultural identification among African American and Mexican American adolescents. *Journal of Research on Adolescence, 7*(1), 3–32.

Piaget, J. (1963). *The origins of intelligence in children.* New York: W. W. Norton.

Piaget, J., & Smith, L. (Trans). (2000). Commentary on Vygotsky's criticisms of language and thought of the child and judgment and reasoning in the child. *New Ideas in Psychology, 18*(2–3), 241–259.

Pickens, C. L., & Holland, P. C. (2004). Conditioning and cognition. *Neuroscience & Biobehavioral Reviews, 28*(7), 651–661.

Pihl, R. O., Peterson, J. B., & Finn, P. (1990). Inherited predisposition to alcoholism. *Journal of Abnormal Psychology, 99*, 291–301.

Pillard, R. C., & Weinrich, J. D. (1986). Evidence of familial nature of male homosexuality. *Archives of General Psychiatry, 43*(8), 808–812.

Pind, J., Gunnarsdottir, E. K., & Johannesson, H. S. (2003). Raven's Standard Progressive Matrices: New school age norms and a study of the test's validity. *Personality and Individual Differences, 34*(3), 375–386.

Pinel, J. P. J., Assanand, S., & Lehman, D. R. (2000). Hunger, eating, and ill health. *American Psychologist, 55*(10), 1105–1116.

Pinker, S. (1990). Language acquisition. In D. N. Osherson & H. Lasnik (Eds.), *An invitation to cognitive science: Language* (Vol. 1). Cambridge, MA: MIT Press, a Bradford Book.

Pinker, S. (1994a). *The language instinct.* New York: William Morrow.

Pinker, S. (1997). Words and rules in the human brain. *Nature, 387*(6633), 547–548.

Pinker, S. (1999). Out of the minds of babes. *Science, 283*(5398), 40–41

Pinnell, C. M., & Covino, N. A. (2000). Empirical findings on the use of hypnosis in medicine: A critical review. *International Journal of Clinical & Experimental Hypnosis, 48*(2), 170–194.

Plaisier, I., et al. (2008). Work and family roles and the association with depressive and anxiety disorders: Differences between men and women. *Journal of Affective Disorders, 105*(1-3), 63–72.

Platania, J., & Moran, G. P. (2001). Social facilitation as a function of mere presence of others. *Journal of Social Psychology, 141*(2), 190–197.

Plomin, R. (2000). Behavioural genetics in the 21st century. *International Journal of Behavioral Development, 24*(1), 30–34.

Plomin, R. (Ed.). (2002). *Behavioral genetics in the postgenomic era.* Washington, DC: American Psychological Association.

Plomin, R. (Ed.). (2002). *Behavioral genetics in the postgenomic era.* Washington, DC: American Psychological Association.

Plomin, R., & Crabbe, J. (2000). DNA. *Psychological Bulletin, 126*(6), 806–828.

Plomin, R., Emde, R., Braungart, J. M., & Campos. (1993). Genetic change and continuity from fourteen to twenty months: The MacArthur Longitudinal Twin Study. *Child Development, 64*(5), 1354–1376.

Pointer, S. C., & Bond, N. W. (1998). Context-dependent memory: Colour versus odor. *Chemical Senses, 23*(3), 359–362.

Pol, H. E. H., et al. (2000). Prenatal exposure to famine and brain morphology in schizophrenia. *American Journal of Psychiatry, 157*, 1170–1172.

Porter, R. (1997). Bethlem/Bedlam: Methods of madness? *History Today, 47*, 41–46. This article is an excellent history of perhaps the most famous mental institution in psychology.

Posada, G., et al. (2002). Maternal caregiving and infant security in two cultures. *Developmental Psychology, 38*(1), 67–78.

Power, T. G., Stewart, C. D., Hughes, S. O., & Arbona, C. (2005). Predicting patterns of adolescent alcohol use: A longitudinal study. *Journal of Studies on Alcohol, 66*(1), 74–81.

Powers, R. (2000, May 7). American dreaming. *The New York Times Magazine*, pp. 66–67.

Prevention Science, 1(1), 3–13.

Pratkanis, A. R. (Ed.). (2007). *The science of social influence: Advances and future progress.* New York: Psychology Press.

Prior, S. M., & Welling, K. A. (2001). "Read in your head": A Vygotskian analysis of the transition from oral to silent reading. *Reading Psychology, 22*(1), 1–15.

Prochaska, J. O., & Norcross, J. C. (2007). *Systems of psychotherapy* (6th ed.). Belmont, CA: Wadsworth.

Pryce, C. R., Bettschen, D., Bahr, N. I., & Feldon, J. (2001). Comparison of the effects of infant handling, isolation, and nonhandling on acoustic startle, prepulse inhibition, locomotion, and HPA activity in the adult rat. *Behavioral Neuroscience, 115*(1), 71–83.

Psychodynamic perspective. (1999). *Psychology Review, 6*, 32. This article provides a succinct summary of the psychodynamic perspective.

Psychology & Health, 17(5), 611–627.

Psychosomatic Medicine, 64(1), 15–28.

Pulley, B. (1998, June 16). Those seductive snake eyes: Tales of growing up gambling. *The New York Times,* A1, A28.

R

Rachman, S. (2000). Joseph Wolpe (1915–1997): Obituary. *American Psychologist, 55*(4), 431–432.

Radel, M., et al. (2005). Haplotype-based localization of an alcohol dependence gene to the 5q34 γ-aminobutyric acid type A gene cluster. *Archives of General Psychiatry, 62*(1), 47–55.

Rainville, P., et al. (2002). Hypnosis modulates activity in brain structures involved in the regulation of consciousness. *Journal of Cognitive Neuroscience, 14*(6), 887–901.

Ramel, W., Goldin, P. R. Carmona, P. E., & Mc- Quaid, J. R. (2004). The effects of mindfulness meditation on cognitive processes and affect in patients with past depression. *Cognitive Therapy & Research, 28*(4), 433–455.

Ramsey, J. L., & Langlois, J. H. (2002). Effects of the "beauty is good" stereotype on children's information processing. *Journal of Experimental Child Psychology, 81*(3), 320–340.

Ramsey, J. L., et al. (2004). Origins of a stereotype: Categorization of facial attractiveness by 6–month-old infants. *Developmental Science, 7*(2), 201–211.

Randel, B., Stevenson, H. W., & Witruk, E. (2000). Attitudes, beliefs, and mathematics achievement of German and Japanese high school students. *International Journal of Behavioral Development, 24*(2), 190–198.

Rasenberger, J. (2004, February 8). Kitty, 40 years later. *The New York Times online.*

Rath, N. (2002). The power to feel fear and the one to feel happiness are the same. *Journal of Happiness Studies, 3*(1), 1–21.

Rathus, J. H., & Sanderson, W. C. (1999). *Marital distress: Cognitive behavioral interventions for couples.* Northvale, NJ: Jason Aronson.

Rathus, S. A. (2008-2009). *HDEV.* Mason, OH: 4LTR Press/ Cengage Learning.

Raynor, H., A., & Epstein, L. H. (2001). Dietary variety, energy regulation, and obesity. *Psychological Bulletin, 127*(3), 325–341.

Ready, T. (2000, June 7). Meditation apparently good for the heart as well as the mind. Healtheon /WebMD.

Reas, D. L., & Grilo, C. M. (2007). Timing and sequence of the onset of overweight, dieting, and binge eating in overweight patients with binge eating disorder. International *Journal of Eating Disorders, 40*(2), 165-170.

Reed, J. M., & Squire, L. R. (1997). Impaired recognition memory in patients with lesions limited to the hippocampal formation. *Behavioral Neuroscience, 111*(4), 667–675.

Reeder, G. D. (2001). On perceiving multiple causes and inferring multiple internal attributes. *Psychological Inquiry, 12*(1), 34–36.

Reese, C. M., & Cherry, K. E. (2002). The effects of age, ability, and memory monitoring on prospective memory task performance.

Aging, Neuropsychology & Cognition, 9(2), 98–113.

Reeve, C. L. (2002). Race and intelligence: Separating science from myth. (Book Review). *Personnel Psychology, 55,* 778–781. This article presents an attempt at uncovering the myths surrounding race and intelligence and includes such topics as defining race and the bell curve.

Regier, T., Kay, P., & Cook, R. S. (2005). Focal colors are universal after all. *Proceedings of the National Academy of Sciences, 102*(23), 8386–8391.

The relation of child care to cognitive and language development. (2000). *Child Development, 71,* 960. This article discusses the contributors to children's language and cognitive development and the differences seen with children who experience various types of care.

Rescorla, R. A. (1967). Inhibition of delay in Pavlovian fear conditioning. *Journal of Comparative & Physiological Psychology, 64*(1), 114–120.

Rescorla, R. A. (1988). Pavlovian conditioning: It's not what you think it is. *American Psychologist, 43,* 151–160.

Rescorla, R. A. (1999). Partial reinforcement reduces the associative change produced by nonreinforcement.

Rezvani, A. H., & Levin, E. D. (2001). Cognitive effects of nicotine. *Biological Psychiatry, 49*(3), 258–267.

Rhee, S. H., & Waldman, I. D. (2002). Genetic and environmental influences on antisocial behavior: A meta-analysis of twin and adoption studies. *Psychological Bulletin, 128*(3), 490–529.

Ribeiro, S., & Nicolelis, M. A. L. (2004). Reverberation, storage, and postsynaptic propagation of memories during sleep. *Learning & Memory, 11*(6), 686–696.

Ricciardelli, L. A., & McCabe, M. P. (2001, February). Self-esteem and negative affect as moderators of sociocultural influences on body dissatisfaction, strategies to decrease weight, and strategies to increase muscles among adolescent boys and girls. *Sex Roles: A Journal of Research,* 189. This article discusses the complex interactions of self-esteem, sociocultural influences and body image.

Rice, K. G., & Dellwo, J. P. (2001). Within-semester stability and adjustment correlates of the Multidimensional Perfectionism Scale. *Measurement & Evaluation in Counseling & Development, 34*(3), 146–156.

Richards, J. C., Hof, A., & Alvarenga, M. (2000). Serum lipids and their relationships with hostility and angry affect and behaviors in men. *Health Psychology, 19*(4), 393–398.

Richardson, G. E. (2002). The metatheory of resilience and resiliency. *Journal of Clinical Psychology, 58*(3), 307–321.

Rickard, T. C., et al. (2000). The calculating brain: An fMRI study. *Neuropsychologia, 38*(3), 325–335. Riley & Kendler, 2005.

Riley, B., & Kendler, K. S. (2005). Genetics of Schizophrenia: Linkage and Association Studies. In K. S. Kendler, & L. J. Eaves (Eds.). *Psychiatric genetics.* (pp. 95-140). *Review of psychiatry series, 24*(1). Washington, DC: American Psychiatric Publishing, Inc.

Riniolo, T. C., Koledin, M., Drakulic, G. M., & Payne, R. A. (2003).

An archival study of eyewitness memory of the Titanic's final plunge. *The Journal of General Psychology, 130,* 89–95. This article presents a study which examined the eyewitness accounts of the Titanic disaster to determine the veracity of eyewitness testimony in traumatic events.

Riso, L. P., et al. (2003). Cognitive aspects of chronic depression. *Journal of Abnormal Psychology, 112*(1), 72–80.

Robbins, S. B., Le, H., & Lauver, K. (2005). Promoting successful college outcomes for all students.

Roberson, D., Davidoff, J., & Shapiro, L. (2002). Squaring the circle: The cultural relativity of good shape. *Journal of Cognition & Culture, 2*(1), 29–51.

Robins, R. W., Gosling, S. D., & Craik, K. H. (1999). An empirical analysis of trends in psychology. *American Psychologist, 54*(2), 117–128.

Rodafinos, A., Vucevic, A., & Sideridis, G. D. (2005). The effectiveness of compliance techniques: Foot in the door versus door in the face. *Journal of Social Psychology, 145*(2), 237–239.

Roelofs, K., et al. (2002). Hypnotic susceptibility in patients with conversion disorder. *Journal of Abnormal Psychology, 111*(2), 390–395.

Romero, E., Luengo, M. A., & Sobral, J. (2001). Personality and antisocial behaviour: Study of temperamental dimensions. *Personality & Individual Differences, 31*(3), 329–348.

Roncesvalles, M. N. C., Woollacott, M. H., & Jensen, J. L. (2001). Development of lower extremity kinetics for balance control in infants and young children. *Journal of Motor Behavior, 33*(2), 180–192.

Rosenbaum, M. (2002). Ecstasy: America's new "reefer madness." *Journal of Psychoactive Drugs, 34*(2), 137–142.

Rosenthal, E. (1993, July 20). Listening to the emotional needs of cancer patients. *The New York Times,* pp. C1, C7.

Roser, M., & Gazzaniga, M. S. (2004). Automatic brains— Interpretive minds. *Current Directions in Psychological Science, 13*(2), 56–59.

Reeve, C. L. (2002). Race and intelligence: Separating science from myth. (Book Review). *Personnel Psychology, 55,* 778–781. This article presents an attempt at uncovering the myths surrounding race and intelligence and includes such topics as defining race and the bell curve.

Ross, S. E., Niebling, B. C., & Heckert, T. M. (1999). Sources of stress among college students. *College Student Journal, 33,* 312. This article presents the results of a study conducted to determine stressful life events college students experience.

Ross, S. R., Lutz, C. J., & Bailley, S. E. (2002). Positive and negative symptoms of schizotypy and the Five-Factor Model: A domain and facet level analysis. *Journal of Personality Assessment, 79*(1), 53–72.

Roth, B. L., Hanizavareh, S. M., & Blum, A. E. (2004). Serotonin receptors represent highly favorable molecular targets for cognitive enhancement in schizophrenia and other disorders. *Psychopharmacology, 174*(1), 17–24.

Roth, G. (2000). The evolution and ontogeny of consciousness. *Neural correlates of consciousness: Empirical and conceptual questions.* Cambridge, MA: MIT Press.

Rothbaum, F., Rosen, K., Ujiie, T., & Uchida, N. (2002). Family systems theory, attachment theory, and culture. *Family Process, 41,* 328–350. This article compares and contrasts family systems theory and attachment theory. These theories are discusses in the context of non-western cultures.

Rotter, J. B. (1990). Internal versus external control of reinforcement. *American Psychologist, 45,* 489–493.

Rovee-Collier, C. (1999). The development of infant memory. *Current Directions in Psychological Science, 8*(3), 80–85.

Rowe, J. B., Owen, A. M., Johnsrude, I. S., & Passingham, R. E. (2001). Imaging the mental components of a planning task. *Neuropsychologia, 39*(3), 315–327.

Rubinstein, S., & Caballero, B. (2000). Is Miss America an undernourished role model? *Journal of the American Medical Association online, 283*(12).

Rude, S. S., Hertel, P. T., Jarrold, W., Covich, J., & Hedlund, S. (1999). Depression-related impairments in prospective memory. *Cognition & Emotion, 13*(3), 267–276.

Rudy, D., & Grusec, J. E. (2001). Correlates of authoritarian parenting in individualist and collectivist cultures and implications for understanding the transmission of values. *Journal of Cross-Cultural Psychology, 32*(2), 202–212.

Ruff, S., et al. (2003). Neural substrates of impaired categorical perception of phonemes in adult dyslexics: An fMRI study. *Brain & Cognition, 53*(2) 331–334.

Ruiter, R. A. C., Abraham, C., & Kok, G. (2001). Scary warnings and rational precautions: A review of the psychology of fear appeals. *Psychology & Health, 16*(6), 613–630.

Rushton, J. P., Skuy, M., & Fridjhon, P. (2003). Performance on Raven's Advanced Progressive Matrices by African, East Indian, and White engineering students in South Africa. *Intelligence, 31*(2), 123–137.

Rutkowski, G. K., Gruder, C. L., & Romer, D. (1983). Group cohesiveness, social norms, and bystander intervention. *Journal of Personality and Social Psychology, 44,* 545–552.

Rutter, M., & Silberg, J. (2002). Gene-environment interplay in relation to emotional and behavioral disturbance. *Annual Review of Psychology, 53*(1), 463–490.

S

Sacks, F. M., et al. (2001). Effects on blood pressure of reduced dietary sodium and the Dietary Approaches to Stop Hypertension (DASH) Diet. *The New England Journal of Medicine, 344*(1), 3–10.

Sagrestano, L. M., McCormick, S. H., Paikoff, R. L., & Holmbeck, G. N. (1999). Pubertal development and parent-child conflict in low-income, urban, African American adolescents. *Journal of Research on Adolescence, 9*(1), 85–107.

Salmon, P., et al. (2004). Mindfulness meditation in clinical practice. *Cognitive & Behavioral Practice, 11*(4), 434–446.

Salovey, P., & Wegener, D. T. (2003). Communicating about health: Message framing, persuasion and health behavior. In J. Suls & K. A. Wallston (Eds.), *Social psychological foundations of health and illness* (pp. 54–81). Malden, MA: Blackwell Publishers.

Salovey, P., Stroud, L. R., Woolery, A., & Epel, E. S. (2002). Perceived emotional intelligence, stress reactivity, and symptom reports: Further explorations using the trait meta-mood scale.

Sanders, G. S. (1984). Effects of context cues on eyewitness identification responses. *Journal of Applied Social Psychology, 14,* 386–397.

Sanna, L. J., & Meier, S. (2000). Looking for clouds in a silver lining: Self-esteem, mental simulations, and temporal confidence changes. *Journal of Research in Personality, 34*(2), 236–251.

Santee, R. T., & Maslach, C. (1982). To agree or not to agree: Personal dissent amid social pressure to conform. *Journal of Personality and Social Psychology, 42*(4), 690–700.

Sarbin, T. R., & Coe, W. C. (1972). *Hypnosis.* New York: Holt, Rinehart and Winston.

Saunders, K. W. (2003). Regulating youth access to violent video games: Three responses to First Amendment concerns. http://www.law.msu.edu/lawrev/2003–1/2–Saunders.pdf.

Savage, C. R., et al. (2001). Prefrontal regions supporting spontaneous and directed application of verbal learning strategies. Evidence from PET. *Brain, 124*(1), 219–231.

Savage-Rumbaugh, E. S., & Fields, W. M. (2000). Linguistic, cultural and cognitive capacities of bonobos (Pan paniscus). *Culture & Psychology, 6*(2), 131–153.

Savage-Rumbaugh, E. S., et al. (1993). *Monographs of the Society for Research in Child Development, 58*(3–4), v–221.

Sawa, A., & Snyder, S. H. (2002, April 26). Schizophrenia: Diverse approaches to a complex disease. *Science,* pp. 692–695.

Saxe, L., & Ben-Shakhar, G. (1999). Admissibility of polygraph tests: The application of scientific standards post-Daubert. *Psychology, Public Policy & Law, 5*(1), 203–223.

Scarr, S., & Weinberg, R. A. (1976). IQ test performance of Black children adopted by White families.

Schachter, S., & Singer, J. E. (1962). Cognitive, social, and physiological determinants of emotional state. *Psychological Review, 69,* 379–399.

Schacter, D. L. (1992). Understanding implicit memory: A cognitive neuroscience approach.

Schacter, D. L. (1999). The seven sins of memory: Insights from psychology and cognitive neuroscience. *American Psychologist, 54*(3), 182–203.

Schacter, D. L. (2000). Memory: Memory systems. In A. E. Kazdin (Ed.), *Encyclopedia of psychology* (Vol. 5, pp.

169–172). Washington, DC: American Psychological Association.

Schacter, D. L., Cooper, L. A., & Treadwell, J. (1993). Preserved priming of novel objects across size transformation in amnesic patients. *Psychological Science, 4*(5), 331–335.

Schacter, D. L., Dobbins, I. G., & Schnyer, D. M. (2004). Specificity of priming: A cognitive neuroscience perspective. *Nature Reviews Neuroscience, 5*(11), 853–862.

Schaie, K. W., Willis, S. L., & Caskie, G. I. L. (2004). The Seattle longitudinal study: Relationship between personality and cognition. *Aging, Neuropsychology & Cognition, 11*(2–3), 304–324.

Schiffman, S. S. (2000). Taste quality and neural coding: Implications from psychophysics and neurophysiology. *Physiology and Behavior, 69*(1–2), 147–159.

Schiffman, S. S., et al. (2003). Effect of repeated presentation on sweetness intensity of binary and ternary mixtures of sweeteners. *Chemical Senses, 28*(3), 219–229.

Schmitt, D. P. (2003). Universal sex differences in the desire for sexual variety: Tests from 52 nations, 6 continents, and 13 islands. *Journal of Personality and Social Psychology, 85*(1), 85–104.

Schmitt, D. P., Shackelford, T. K., Duntley, J., Tooke, W., & Buss, D. M. (2001). The desire for sexual variety as a key to understanding basic human mating strategies. *Personal Relationships, 8*(4), 425–455.

Schneider, K. J., Bugental, J. F. T., & Pierson, J. F. (Eds). (2003). The handbook of humanistic psychology: Leading edges in theory, research, and practice. *Psychotherapy Research, 13*(1), 119–121.

Schneider, R. H., et al. (1995). A randomized controlled trial of stress reduction for hypertension in older African Americans. *Hypertension, 26,* 820.

Schneiderman, N., Ironson, G., & Siegel, S. D. (2005). Stress and health: Psychological, behavioral, and biological determinants. *Annual Review of Clinical Psychology, 1*(1), 607–628

Schredl, M., Ciric, P., Go¨tz, S., & Wittmann, L. (2004). Typical dreams: Stability and gender differences. *Journal of Psychology: Interdisciplinary & Applied, 138*(6), 485–494.

Schupf, N. (2000, July). Epidemiology of dementia in Down syndrome. Paper presented to the World Alzheimer Congress 2000, Washington, DC.

Schultz, D. P., & Schultz, S. E. (2008). *A history of modern psychology,* 9th Edition. Belmont, CA: Cengage.

Schuster, M. A., et al. (2001). A national survey of stress reactions after the September 11, 2001, terrorist attacks. *New England Journal of Medicine, 345*(20), 1507–1512.

Schwartz, J. R. L. (2004). Pharmacologic management of daytime sleepiness. *Journal of Clinical Psychiatry, 65*(Suppl. 16), 46–49.

Schwartz, J., & Wald, M. L. (2003, March 9). NASA's curse? "Groupthink" is 30 years old, and still going strong. *The New York Times online.*

Schwartz, R. M., & Gottman, J. M. (1976). Toward a task analysis of assertive behavior. *Journal of Consulting and Clinical Psychology, 44,* 910–920.

Schwartzer, R., & Renner, B. (2000). Social-cognitive predictors of health behavior: Action selfefficacy and coping self-efficacy. *Health Psychology, 19*(5), 487–495.

Schyns, P. (2001). Income and satisfaction in Russia. *Journal of Happiness Studies, 2*(2), 173–204.

Scott, T. R. (2001). The role of taste in feeding. *Appetite, 37*(2), 111–113.

Scruggs, T. E., & Mastropieri, M. A. (1992). Remembering the forgotten art of memory. *American Educator, 16*(4), 31–37.

Second thoughts. (1989). *The Economist, 313,* 69. This article focuses on the remarkable comeback of asylums in Britain.

Segal, E. (2004). Incubation in insight problem solving. *Creativity Research Journal, 16*(1), 141–148.

Segal, N. L., & Roy, A. (2001). Suicidal attempts and ideation in twins whose co-twins' deaths were non-suicides: Replication and elaboration. *Personality & Individual Differences, 31*(3), 445–452.

Segan, C. J., Borland, R., & Greenwood, K. M. (2002). Do transtheoretical model measures predict the transition from preparation to action in smoking cessation? *Psychology & Health, 17*(4), 417–435.

Seidman, S. M. (2003). The aging male: Androgens, erectile dysfunction, and depression. *Journal of Clinical Psychiatry, 64*(Suppl. 10), 31–37.

Selemon, L. D., Mrzljak, J., Kleinman, J. E., Herman, M. M., & Goldman-Rakic, P. S. (2003). Regional specificity in the neuropathologic substrates of schizophrenia: A morphometric analysis of Broca's area 44 and area 9. *Archives of General Psychiatry, 60*(1), 69–77.

Seligman, M. E. P. (1996, August). Predicting and preventing depression. Master lecture presented to the meeting of the American Psychological Association, Toronto.

Selye, H. (1976). *The stress of life* (Rev. ed.). New York: McGraw-Hill. Kutash, et al. (Eds.), *Handbook on stress and anxiety.* San Francisco: Jossey-Bass.

Selye, H. (1980). The stress concept today. In I. L. *Sex & Marital Therapy, 31*(3), 173–185.

Shadish, W. R., Matt, G. E., Navarro, A. M., & Phillips, G. (2000). The effects of psychological therapies under clinically representative conditions: A meta-analysis. *Psychological Bulletin, 126*(4), 512–529.

Shafran, R., Cooper, Z., & Fairburn, C. (2002). Clinical perfectionism: A cognitive–behavioural analysis. *Behaviour Research and Therapy, 40*(7), 773–791.

Shanker, S. G., Savage-Rumbaugh, E. S., & Taylor, T. J. (1999). Kanzi: A new beginning. *Animal Learning & Behavior, 27*(1), 24–25.

Shapiro, F. (1989). Efficacy of the eye movement desensitization procedure in the treatment of traumatic memories. *Journal of Traumatic Stress, 2,* 199–223.

Shapley, R., & Hawken, M. (2002). Neural mechanisms for color perception in the primary visual cortex. *Current Opinion in Neurobiology, 12*(4), 426–432.

Shen, R-Y, Choong, K-C, & Thompson, A. C. (2007). Long-term reduction in ventral tegmental area dopamine neuron population activity following repeated stimulant or ethanol treatment. *Biological Psychiatry, 61*(1), 93–100.

Shenal, B. V., & Harrison, D. W. (2003). Investigation of the laterality of hostility, cardiovascular regulation, and auditory recognition. *International Journal of Neuroscience, 113*(2), 205–222.

Shenefelt, P. D. (2003). Hypnosis-facilitated relaxation using self-guided imagery during dermatologic procedures. *American Journal of Clinical Hypnosis, 45*(3), 225–232.

Shepperd, J. A., & Koch, E. J. (2005). Pitfalls in teaching judgment heuristics. *Teaching of Psychology, 32*(1), 43–46.

Sherrington, J. M., Hawton, K. E., Fagg, J., Andrews, B., & Shiffman, S., et al. (2000). Dynamic effects of self-efficacy on smoking lapse and relapse. *Health Psychology, 19*(4), 315–323.

Shimamura, A. P. (2002). Memory retrieval and executive control processes. In D. T. Stuss & R. T. Knight (Eds.), *Principles of frontal lobe function* (pp. 210–220). London: Oxford University Press.

Shneidman, E. S. (2001). *Comprehending suicide.* Washington, DC: American Psychological Association.

Sieber, J. E. (2004). Using our best judgment in conducting human research. *Ethics & Behavior, 14*(4), 297–304.

Siegel, J. M. (2002). The REM sleep–memory consolidation hypothesis. *Science, 294*(5544), 1058–1063.

Siesta time; Power napping. (2002, June 1). *The Economist.* This article discusses a research study where subjects took afternoon naps and were subsequently tested on a visual perception task.

Silventoinen, K., et al. (2007). Genetic and environmental factors in relative weight from birth to age 18: The Swedish young male twins study. *International Journal of Obesity, 31*(4), 615-621.

Silver, E. (1994). Cited in DeAngelis, T. (1994). Experts see little impact from insanity plea ruling. *APA Monitor, 25*(6), 28.

Simonton, D. K. (2000). Creativity: Cognitive, personal, developmental, and social aspects. *American Psychologist, 55,* 151–158

Simpson, M. L., Olejnik, S., Tam, A. Y., & Supattathum, S. (1994). Elaborative verbal rehearsals and college students' cognitive performance. *Journal of Educational Psychology, 86,* 267–278.

Singareddy, R. K., & Balon, R. (2002). Sleep in posttraumatic stress disorder. *Annals of Clinical Psychiatry, 14*(3), 183–190.

Singh, R., Yeo, S. E-L., Lin, P. K. F., & Tan, L. (2007). Multiple mediators of the attitude similarity-attraction relationship: Dominance of inferred attraction and subtlety of affect. *Basic and Applied Social Psychology, 29*(1), 61–74.

Singletary, K. W., & Gapstur, S. M. (2001). Alcohol and breast cancer: Review of epidemiologic and experimental evidence and potential mechanisms. *Journal of the American Medical Association, 286*(17), 2143–2151.

Skelton, C. (2005). Boys and schooling in the early years. *International Journal of Early Years Education, 13*(1), 83–84

Skinner, B. F. (1938). *The behavior of organisms: An experimental analysis.* New York: Appleton.

Skinner, B. F. (1948). *Walden Two.* New York: Macmillan.

Sleep and dreams. (2002). *Science Weekly, 19,* 1–12. This article is geared towards helping children understand the various aspects of sleep.

Slobin, D. I. (1983). Crosslinguistic evidence for basic child grammar. Paper presented to the biennial meeting of the Society for Research in Child Development, Detroit.

Sloman, S. A., Harrison, M. C., & Malt, B. C. (2002). Recent exposure affects artifact naming. *Memory & Cognition, 30*(5), 687–695.

Smetana, J. G., Daddis, C., & Chuang, S. S. (2003). "Clean your room!" A longitudinal investigation of adolescent–parent conflict and conflict resolution in middle-class African American families. *Journal of Adolescent Research, 18*(6), 631–650.

Smiley, J. (2000, May 7). The good life. *The New York Times magazine,* pp. 58–59.

Smith, D. (2001). Outcome of women admitted to hospital for depressive illness: Factors in the prognosis of severe depression. *Psychological Medicine, 31*(1), 115–125.

Smith, D. (2003b). Five principles for research ethics. *Monitor on Psychology, 34*(1), 56–60.

Smith, D. (2003c). What you need to know about the new code: The chair of APA's Ethics Code Task Force highlights changes to the 2002 Ethics Code. *Monitor on Psychology online, 34*(1).

Smith, J. F. (2001). Biological evidence for evolution. *Journal of the Idaho Academy of Science, 37,* 102–104. This article discusses considerations for the biological evidence for evolution.

Smith, M. L., & Glass, G. V. (1977). Meta-analysis of psychotherapy outcome studies. *American Psychologist, 32,* 752–760.

Smith, R. A., & Weber, A. L. (2005). Applying social psychology in everyday life. In F. W. Schneider, et al. (Eds.), *Applied social psychology: Understanding and addressing social and practical problems* (pp. 75–99). Thousand Oaks, CA: Sage Publications.

Smith, T. W., & Ruiz, J. M. (2002). Course of coronary heart disease: Current status and implications for research and practice. *Journal of Consulting and Clinical Psychology, 70*(3), 548–568.

Smith, V. (2000, February 16). Female heart, geography link shown. The Associated Press.

Smits, T., Storms, G., Rosseel, Y., & De Boeck, P. (2002). Fruits and vegetables categorized: An application of the generalized context model. *Psychonomic Bulletin & Review, 9*(4), 836–844.

Soll, J. B., & Klayman, J. (2004). Overconfidence in interval estimates. *Journal of Experimental Psychology: Learning, Memory & Cognition, 30*(2), 299–314.

Sorenson, S. B., & Rutter, C. M. (1991). Transgenerational patterns of suicide attempt. *Journal of Consulting and Clinical Psychology, 59,* 861–866.

Soussignan, R. (2002). Duchenne smile, emotional experience, and autonomic reactivity: A test of the facial feedback hypotheses. *Emotion, 2*(1), 52–74.

Spasojevic, J., & Alloy, L. B. (2001). Rumination as a common mechanism relating depressive risk factors to depression. *Emotion, 1*(1), 25–37.

Spencer, M. B., Noll, E., & Cassidy, E. (2005). Monetary incentives in support of academic achievement: Results of a randomized field trial involving high-achieving, low-resource, ethnically diverse urban adolescents. *Evaluation Review, 29*(3), 199–222.

Speranza, M., et al. (2001). Obsessive compulsive disorders in eating disorders. *Eating Behaviors, 2*(3), 193–207.

Sperling, G. (1960). The information available in brief visual presentations. *Psychological Monographs, 74,* 1–29.

Sperry, R. W. (1982). Some effects of disconnecting the cerebral hemispheres. *Science, 217*(4566), 1223–1226.

Spiers, H. J., Maguire, E. A., & Burgess, N. (2001). Hippocampal amnesia. *Neurocase, 7*(5), 357–382.

Sprecher, S., Fehr, B., & Zimmerman, C. (2007). Expectation for mood enhancement as a result of helping: The effects of gender and compassionate love. *Sex Roles, 56*(7-8), 543-549.

Sprecher, S., Sullivan, Q., & Hatfield, E. (1994). Mate selection preferences. *Journal of Personality and Social Psychology, 66*(6), 1074–1080.

Squire, L. R. (2004). Memory systems of the brain: A brief history and current perspective. *Neurobiology of Learning & Memory, 82*(3), 171–177.

Squire, L. R. (2004). Memory systems of the brain: A brief history and current perspective. *Neurobiology of Learning & Memory, 82*(3), 171–177.

Stacy, A. W., Bentler, P. M., & Flay, B. R. (1994). Attitudes and health behavior in diverse populations. *Health Psychology, 13,* 73–85.

Stampfer, M. J., Kang, J. H., Chen, J., Cherry, R., & Grodstein, F. (2005). Effects of moderate alcohol consumption on cognitive function in women. *New England Journal of Medicine, 352*(3), 245–253.

Stasser, G. (1999). A primer of social decision scheme theory: Models of group influence, competitive model-testing, and prospective modeling. *Organizational Behavior & Human Decision Processes, 80*(1), 3–20.

Steenari, R., Vuontela, V., Paavonen, E. J., Carlson, S., Fjallberg, M., & Aronen, E.T. (2003). Working memory and sleep in

6 to 13-year old schoolchildren. *Journal of the American Academy of Child and Adolescent Psychiatry, 42,* 85–92. This article reports the results of a study showing that lack of sleep can impair memory performance.

Steinberg, L. (1996). *Beyond the classroom.* New York: Simon & Schuster.

Steinberg, L. (2001). We know some things: Parent–adolescent relationships in retrospect and prospect. *Journal of Research on Adolescence, 11*(1), 1–19.

Sternberg, R. J. (1988). Triangulating love. In R. J.Sternberg & M. J. Barnes (Eds.), *The psychology of love.* New Haven, CT: Yale University Press.

Sternberg, R. J. (2000). Wisdom as a form of giftedness. *Gifted Child Quarterly, 44*(4), 252–260.

Sternberg, R. J. (2001). What is the common thread of creativity? *American Psychologist, 56*(4), 360–362.

Sternberg, R. J., & Lubart, T. I. (1996). Investing in creativity. *American Psychologist, 51,* 677–688.

Sternberg, R. J., & Williams, W. M. (1997). Does the Graduate Record Examination predict meaningful success in the graduate training of psychologists?

Sternberg, R. J., Lautrey, J., & Lubart, T. I. (2003). *Models of intelligence: International perspectives.*

Stevens, S. E., Hynan, M. T., & Allen, M. (2000). A meta-analysis of common factor and specific treatment effects across the outcome domains of the phase model of psychotherapy. *Clinical Psychology: Science and Practice, 7,* 273–290.

Stevenson, H. W., Lee, S. Y., & Stigler, J. W. (1986). Mathematics achievement of Chinese, Japanese, and American children. *Science, 231,* 693–699.

Stewart, A. E. (2005). Attributions of responsibility for motor vehicle crashes. *Accident Analysis & Prevention. 37*(4), 681–688.

Stickgold, R., Hobson, J. A., Fosse, R., & Fosse, M. (2001). Sleep, learning, and dreams: Off-line memory reprocessing. *Science, 294*(5544), 1052–1057.

Stier, D. S., & Hall, J. A. (1984). Gender differences in touch. *Journal of Personality and Social Psychology, 47,* 440–459.

Stipek, D., & Hakuta, K. (2007). Strategies to ensure that no child starts from behind. In Aber, J. L., et al. (Eds.). *Child development and social policy: Knowledge for action, APA Decade of Behavior volumes.* (pp. 129–145). Washington, DC: American Psychological Association.

Stocker, S. (1994). Stop a headache in 5 minutes. *Prevention, 46,* 65–72. This article discusses the importance of relaxation when faced with a tension headache and suggests that if a person relaxes for five minutes in the early stages of the headache, that it will go away.

Storm, L., & Ertel, S. (2001). Does psi exist? Comments on Milton and Wiseman's (1999) metaanalysis of Ganzfeld research. *Psychological Bulletin, 127*(3), 424–433.

Storm, L., & Ertle, S. (2002). The Ganzfeld debate continued: A response to Milton & Wiseman (2001). *Journal of Parapsychology, 66*(1), 73–82.

Straube, E. R., & Oades, R. D. (1992). *Schizophrenia.* San Diego: Academic Press.

Strickland, T. L., & Gray, G. (2000). Neurobehavioral disorders and pharmacologic intervention: The significance of ethnobiological variation in drug responsivity. In E. Fletcher-Janzen, et al. (Eds.), Handbook of cross-cultural neuropsychology (pp. 361–369). Dordrecht, Netherlands: Kluwer Academic Publishers.

Striegel-Moore, R. H., & Cachelin, F. M. (2001). Etiology of eating disorders in women. *Counseling Psychologist, 29*(5), 635–661.

Striegel-Moore, R. H., et al. (2003). Eating disorders in White and Black women. *American Journal of Psychiatry, 160,* 1326–1331.

Striegel-Moore, R. H., et al. (2004). Changes in weight and body image over time in women with eating disorders. *International Journal of Eating Disorders, 36*(3), 315–327.

Stroele, A., et al. (2002). GABA-sub(A) receptormodulating neuroactive steroid composition in patients with panic disorder before and during paroxetine treatment. *American Journal of Psychiatry, 159*(1), 145–147.

Strom, J. C., & Buck, R. W. (1979). Staring and participants' sex. *Personality and Social Psychology Bulletin, 5,* 114–117.

Strote, J., Lee, J. E., & Wechsler, H. (2002). Increasing MDMA use among college students: Results of a national survey. *Journal of the American Academy of Child & Adolescent Psychiatry, 41*(10), 1215.

Stroud, M. W., Thorn, B. E., Jensen, M. P., & Boothby, J. L. (2000). The relation between pain beliefs, negative thoughts, and psychosocial functioning in chronic pain patients. *Pain, 84*(2–3), 347–352.

Studies in Conflict & Terrorism, 27(4), 283–295.

Stutts, J. C., Wilkins, J. W., Osberg, J. S., & Vaughn, B. V. (2003). Driver risk factors for sleep-related crashes. *Accident Analysis & Prevention, 35*(3), 321–331.

Stutzer, A. (2004). The role of income aspirations in individual happiness. *Journal of Economic Behavior & Organization, 54*(1), 89–109.

Sufka, K. J., & Price, D. D. (2002). Gate control theory reconsidered. *Brain & Mind, 3*(2), 277–290.

Suler, J. (2005, March 29). Psychological qualities of cyberspace. http://www.rider.edu/suler/psycyber/netself.html.

Suttle, C. M., Banks, M. S., & Graf, E. W. (2002). FPL and sweep VEP to tritan stimuli in young human infants. *Vision Research, 42*(26), 2879–2891.

Suvisaari, J., Mautemps, N., Haukka, J., Hovi, T., & Löönnqvist, J. (2003). Childhood central nervous system viral infections and adult schizophrenia. *American Journal of Psychiatry, 160,* 1183–1185.

Swendsen, J. D., et al. (2000). Mood and alcohol consumption: An experience sampling test of the self-medication hypothesis. *Journal of Abnormal Psychology, 109*(2), 198–204.

Swerdlow, N. R., et al. (2003). Prestimulus modification of the startle reflex: Relationship to personality and psychological markers of dopamine function. *Biological Psychology, 62*(1), 17–26.

Swinyard, W. R., Kau, A., & Phua, H. (2001). Happiness, materialism, and religious experience in the U.S. and Singapore. *Journal of Happiness Studies, 2*(1), 13–32.

Szala, M. (2002). Two-level pattern recognition in a class of knowledge-based systems. *Knowledge-Based Systems, 15*(1–2), 95–101.

T

Taffe, M. A., et al. (2002). Cognitive performance of MDMA-treated rhesus monkeys: Sensitivity to serotonergic challenge. *Neuropsychopharmacology, 27*(6), 993–1005.

Tait, R. C. (2005). Mind matters: Psychological interventions for chronic pain. *Clinical Journal of Pain, 21*(1), 106–107.

Takahashi, T., et al. (2002). Melatonin alleviates jet lag symptoms caused by an 11-hour eastward flight. *Psychiatry & Clinical Neurosciences, 56*(3), 301–302.

Takemura, K. (1994). Influence of Elaboration on the Framing of Decision. *The Journal of Psychology, 128,* 33–39. This article presents a demonstration of the framing effect.

Tanasescu, M., et al. (2002). Exercise type and intensity in relation to coronary heart disease in men. *Journal of the American Medical Association, 288,* 1994–2000.

Taylor, D. J., & McFatter, R. M. (2003). Cognitive performance after sleep deprivation: Does personality make a difference? *Personality & Individual Differences, 34*(7), 1179–1193.

Taylor, S. E. (2000). Cited in Goode, E. (2000, May 19). Response to stress found that's particularly female. *The New York Times,* p. A20.

Taylor, S. E., et al. (2000b). Biobehavioral responses to stress in females: Tend-and-befriend, not fight-or-flight. *Psychological Review, 107*(3), 411–429.

Teachout, T. (2000, April 2). For more artists, a fine old age. *The New York Times online.*

Teller, D. Y. (1998). Spatial and temporal aspects of infant color vision. *Vision Research, 38*(21), 3275–3282.

Tenenbaum, H. R., & Leaper, C. (2002). Are parents' gender schemas related to their children's gender-related cognitions? A meta-analysis. *Developmental Psychology, 38*(4), 615–630.

Tennen, H., & Affleck, G. (2000). The perception of personal control: Sufficiently important to warrant careful scrutiny. *Personality & Social Psychology Bulletin, 26*(2), 152–156.

Terrace, H. S. (1979, November). How Nim Chimpsy changed my mind. *Psychology Today,* pp. 65–76.

Tetlock, P. E., & McGraw, A. P. (2005). Theoretically framing relational framing. *Journal of Consumer Psychology, 15*(1), 35–37.

Thom, A., Sartory, G., & Jo¨hren, P. (2000). Comparison between one-session psychological treatment and benzodiazepine in dental phobia. *Journal of Consulting and Clinical Psychology, 68*(3), 378–387.

Thomas, A. K., & Loftus, E. F. (2002). Creating bizarre false memories through imagination. *Memory & Cognition, 30*(3), 423–431.

Thompson, B. R., & Thornton, H. J. (2002). The transition from extrinsic to intrinsic motivation in the college classroom: A first year experience. *Education, 122,* 785–782. This article describes the difficulties some college students have as they move from an extrinsically based high school motivation to an intrinsically based college experience.

Thompson, P. M., et al. (2001). Mapping adolescent brain change reveals dynamic wave of accelerated gray matter loss in very early-onset schizophrenia.

Thurstone, L. L. (1938). Primary mental abilities. *Psychometric Monographs, 1.*

Tigner, R. B., & Tigner, S. S. (2000). Triarchic theories of intelligence: Aristotle and Sternberg. *History of Psychology, 3*(2), 168–176.

Tkachuk, G. A., & Martin, G. L. (1999). Exercise therapy for patients with psychiatric disorders: Research and clinical implications. *Professional Psychology: Research and Practice, 30*(3), 275–282.

Tolman, E. C., & Honzik, C. H. (1930). Introduction and removal of reward, and maze performance in rats. *University of California Publications in Psychology, 4,* 257–275.

Tong, H. (2001). Loneliness, depression, anxiety, and the locus of control. *Chinese Journal of Clinical Psychology, 9*(3), 196–197.

Tormala, Z. L., & Petty, R. E. (2004). Source credibility and attitude certainty: A metacognitive analysis of resistance to persuasion. *Journal of Consumer Psychology, 14*(4), 427–442.

Townsend, E., et al. (2001). The efficacy of problem-solving treatments after deliberate selfharm. Meta-analysis of randomizes controlled trials with respect to depression, hopelessness and improvement in problems. *Psychological Medicine,* 31(6), 979-988.

Triandis, H. C. (2005). Issues in individualism and collectivism research. In R. M. Sorrentino, et al. (Eds.). *Cultural and social behavior: The Ontario Symposium, 10.* (pp. 207–225). Mahwah, NJ: Erlbaum.

Triandis, H. C., & Suh, E. M. (2002). Cultural influences on personality. *Annual Review of Psychology, 53*(1), 133–160.

Trobst, K. K., Collins, R. L., & Embree, J. M. (1994). The role of emotion in social support provision. *Journal of Social and Personal Relationships, 11,* 45–62.

Trull, T. J., Stepp, S. D., & Durrett, C. A. (2003). Research on borderline personality disorder: An update. *Current Opinion in Psychiatry, 16*(1), 77–82.

Tsai, G., & Coyle, J. T. (2002). Glutamatergic mechanisms in schizophrenia. *Annual Review of Pharmacology & Toxicology, 42,* 165–179.

Tsang, Y. C. (1938). Hunger motivation in gastrectomized rats. *Journal of Comparative Psychology, 26,* 1–17.

Tsou, M., & Liu, J. (2001). Happiness and domain satisfaction in Taiwan. *Journal of Happiness Studies, 2*(3), 269–288.

Tulving, E. (1985). How many memory systems are there? *American Psychologist, 40,* 385–398.

Turk, D. C., & Okifuji, A. (2002). Psychological factors in chronic pain: Evolution and revolution. *Journal of Consulting and Clinical Psychology, 70*(3), 678–690.

Turkington, D., Dudley, R., Warman, D. M., & Beck, A. T. (2004). Cognitive-behavioral therapy for schizophrenia: A review. *Journal of Psychiatric Practice, 10*(1), 5–16.

Turner, M. E., Pratkanis, A. R., & Struckman, C. K. (2007). Groupthink as social identity maintenance. In A. R. Pratkanis (Ed.). *The science of social influence: Advances and future progress.* (pp. 223-246). New York: Psychology Press.

Tversky, A., & Kahneman, D. (1982). Judgment under uncertainty. In D. Kahneman, P. Slovic, & A. Tversky (Eds.), *Judgment under uncertainty: Heuristics and biases.* New York: Cambridge University Press.

Tyrka, A. R., Waldron, I., Graber, J. A., & Brooks-Gunn, J. (2002). Prospective predictors of the onset of anorexic and bulimic syndromes. *International Journal of the Eating Disorders, 32*(3), 282–290.

U

U.S. Department of Education, NCES. (2004).

Ulett, G. A., & Wedding, D. (2003). Electrical stimulation, endorphins, and the practice of clinical psychology. *Journal of Clinical Psychology in Medical Settings, 10*(2), 129–131.

Underhill, J. B. (2008). The politics of crisis management: Public leadership under pressure and Lessons on leadership by terror: Finding Shaka Zulu in the attic. *Political Psychology, 29*(1), 139-143.

Updegraff, J. A., Taylor, S. E., Kemeny, M. E., & Wyatt, G. E. (2002). Positive and negative effects of HIV infection in women with low socioeconomic resources. *Personality & Social Psychology Bulletin, 28*(3), 382–394.

Utter, J., Neumark-Sztainer, D., Wall, M., & Story, M. (2003). Reading magazine articles about dieting and associated weight control behaviors among adolescents. *Journal of Adolescent Health, 32*(1), 78–82.

Uzakov, S., Frey, J. U., & Korz, V. (2005). Reinforcement of rat hippocampal LTP by holeboard training. *Learning & Memory, 12,* 165–171.

V

Van Anders, S. M., Chernick, A. B., Chernick, B. A., Hampson, E., & Fisher, W. A. (2005). Preliminary clinical experience with androgen administration for pre- and postmenopausal women with hypoactive sexual desire. *Journal of Sex & Marital Therapy, 31*(3), 173–185.

van de Wetering, S., Bernstein, D. M., & Loftus, E. F. (2002). Public education against false memories: A modest proposal. *International Journal of Cognitive Technology, 7*(2), 4–7.

Vandenbergh, J. G. (1993). Cited in Angier, N. (1993, August 24). Female gerbil born with males is found to be begetter of sons. *The New York Times,* p. C4.

Vasterling, J. J., et al. (2002). Attention, learning, and memory performances and intellectual resources in Vietnam veterans: PTSD and no disorder comparisons. *Neuropsychology, 16*(1), 5–14.

Veenstra-Vanderweele, J., & Cook, E. H. (2003). Genetics of childhood disorders: XLVI. Autism, part 5: Genetics of autism. *Journal of the American Academy of Child and Adolescent Psychiatry, 42*(1), 116–118.

Velting, D. M., Rathus, J. H., & Miller, A. L. (2000). MACI personality scale profiles of depressed adolescent suicide attempters: A pilot study. *Journal of Clinical Psychology, 56*(10), 1381–1385.

Vernon, D., et al. (2003). The effect of training distinct neurofeedback protocols on aspects of cognitive performance. *International Journal of Psychophysiology, 47*(1), 75–85.

Villa, K. K., & Abeles, N. (2000). Broad spectrum intervention and the remediation of prospective memory declines in the able elderly. *Aging & Mental Health, 4*(1), 21–29.

Virtually Better. (2010, January 13). *Splash page.* (Accessed March 15, 2010). http://www.virtuallybetter.com/

Vorobyev, V. A., et al. (2004). Linguistic processing in visual and modality-nonspecific brain areas: PET recordings during selective attention. *Cognitive Brain Research, 20*(2), 309–322.

Vygotsky, L. (1978). *Mind in society: The development of higher psychological processes.* Cambridge, MA: Harvard University Press.

Vygotsky, L. S. (1962). *Thought and language.* Cambridge, MA: MIT Press.

W

Wagar, B. M., & Thagard, P. (2004). Spiking Phineas Gage: A neurocomputational theory of cognitive-affective integration in decision making. *Psychological Review, 111*(1), 67–79.

Wagner, R. K. (1997). Intelligence, training, and employment. *American Psychologist, 52*(10), 1059–1069.

Walker, E., Kestler, L., Bollini, A., & Hochman, K. M. (2004). Schizophrenia: Etiology and course. *Annual Review of Psychology, 55,* 401–430.

Walle, A. H. (2004). Native Americans and alcoholism therapy: The example of Handsome Lake as a tool of recovery. *Journal of Ethnicity in Substance Abuse, 3*(2), 55–79.

Walther, E., Nagengast, B., & Trasselli, C. (2005). Evaluative conditioning in social psychology: Facts and speculations. *Cognition & Emotion, 19*(2), 175–196.

Wang, C. (2002). Emotional intelligence, general self-efficacy, and coping style of juvenile delinquents.

Wang, J., Lin, W., & Chen, Z. (2002). The effects of psychological intervention on chemotherapy of cancer patients. *Psychological Science* (China), *25*(5), 517–519.

Wang, Q. (2003). Infantile amnesia reconsidered: A cross-cultural analysis. *Memory, 11*(1), 65–80.

Wang, X., et al. (2000). Longitudinal study of earthquake-related PTSD in a randomly selected community sample in North China. *American Journal of Psychiatry, 157,* 1260–1266.

Wann, D. L., & Schrader, M. P. (2000). Controllability and stability in the self-serving attributions of sport spectators. *Journal of Social Psychology, 140*(2), 160–168.

Wann, D. L., Royalty, J., & Roberts, A. (2000). The self-presentation of sports fans: Investigating the importance of team identification and self-esteem. *Journal of Sport Behavior, 23*(2), 198–206.

Warman, D. M., & Beck, A. T. (2003). Cognitive behavioral therapy for schizophrenia: An overview of treatment. *Cognitive & Behavioral Practice, 10*(3), 248–254.

Warman, D. M., & Cohen, R. (2000). Stability of aggressive behaviors and children's peer relationships. *Aggressive Behavior, 26*(4), 277–290.

Warman, D. M., Grant, P., Sullivan, K., Caroff, S., & Beck, A. T. (2005). Individual and group cognitive-behavioral therapy for psychotic disorders: A pilot investigation. *Journal of Psychiatric Practice, 11*(1), 27–34.

Washington, DC: American Psychological Association.

Waters, M. (2000). Psychologists spotlight growing concern of higher suicide rates among adolescents. *Monitor on Psychology, 31*(6), 41.

Watson, J. B. (1913). Psychology as the behaviorist views it. *Psychological Review, 20,* 158–177.

Weaver, C. A., III, & Krug, K. S. (2004). Consolidation- like effects in flashbulb memories: Evidence from September 11, 2001. *American Journal of Psychology, 117*(4), 517–530.

Webster, J. D. (2003). An exploratory analysis of a self-assessed wisdom scale. *Journal of Adult Development, 10*(1), 13–22.

Wechsler, D. (1975). Intelligence defined and undefined. *American Psychologist, 30,* 135–139.

Wegener, D. T., Petty, R. E., Detweiler-Bedell, B. T., & Jarvis, W. B. G. (2001). Implications of attitude change theories for numerical anchoring: Anchor plausibility and the limits of anchor effectiveness. *Journal of Experimental Social Psychology, 37*(1), 62–69.

Weinmann, M., Bader, J., Endrass, J., & Hell, D. (2001). Sind Kompetenz- und Kontrollueberzeugungen depressionsabhaengig? Eine Verlaufsuntersuchung. *Zeitschrift fuer Klinische Psychologie und Psychotherapie,* 30(3), 153–158.

Weiss, A., et al. (2005). Cross-sectional age differences in personality among Medicare patients aged 65 to 100. *Psychology and Aging, 20*(1), 182–185.

Wells, G. L., & Olsen, E. A. (2003). Eyewitness testimony. *Annual Review of Psychology, 54,* 277–295.

West, R., & Craik, F. I. M. (1999). Age-related decline in pro-spective memory: The roles of cue accessibility and cue sensitivity. *Psychology & Aging, 14*(2), 264–272.

Wetzler, S. E., & Sweeney, J. A. (1986). Childhood amnesia. In D. C. Rubin (Ed.), *Autobiographical memory.* New York: Cambridge University Press.

Wheeler, M. A., & McMillan, C. T. (2001). Focal retrograde amnesia and the episodic-semantic distinction. *Cognitive, Affective & Behavioral Neuroscience, 1*(1), 22–36.

Wheeler, M. E., & Treisman, A. M. (2002). Binding in short-term visual memory. *Journal of Experimental Psychology: General, 131*(1), 48–64.

Whitfield, K. E., Weidner, G., Clark, R., & Anderson, N. B. (2002). Sociodemographic diversity and behavioral medicine. *Journal of Consulting and Clinical Psychology, 70*(3), 463–481.

Whorf, B. (1956). *Language, thought, and reality.* New York: Wiley.

Widiger, T. A., & Costa, P. T., Jr. (1994). Personality and personality disorders. *Journal of Abnormal Psychology, 103,* 78–91.

Wiebe, R. E., & McCabe, S. B. (2002). Relationship perfectionism, dysphoria, and hostile interpersonal behaviors. *Journal of Social & Clinical Psychology, 21*(1), 67–91.

Wilkinson, D., & Abraham, C. (2004). Constructing an integrated model of the antecedents of adolescent smoking. *British Journal of Health Psychology, 9*(3), 315–333.

Willett, W. C. (2002). Balancing lifestyle and genomics research for disease prevention. *Science, 296*(5568), 695–698.

Williams, J. E., et al. (2000). Anger proneness predicts coronary heart disease risk : Prospective analysis from the Atherosclerosis Risk In Communities (ARIC) study. *Circulation, 101*(17), 2034–2039.

Williams, M. S., Thomsen, S. R., & McCoy, J. K. (2003). Looking for an accurate mirror: A model for the relationship between media use and anorexia. *Eating Behaviors, 4*(2), 127–134.

Williams, S. M., et al. (2000). Combinations of variations in multiple genes are associated with hypertension. *Hypertension, 36,* 2–6.

Wilson, K. D., & Farah, M. J. (2003). When does the visual system use viewpoint-invariant representations during recognition? *Cognitive Brain Research, 16*(3), 399–415.

Wilson, R. S. (1983). The Louisville twin study: Developmental synchronies in behavior. *Child Development, 54,* 298–316.

Winocur, G., et al. (2000). Cognitive rehabilitation in clinical neuropsychology. *Brain & Cognition, 42*(1), 120–123. *American Journal of Psychiatry, 160,* 572–574.

Wolkin, A., et al. (2003). Inferior frontal white matter anisotropy and negative symptoms of schizophrenia: A diffusion tensor imaging study.

Woloshyn, V. E., Paivio, A., & Pressley, M. (1994). Use of elaborative interrogation to help students acquire information consistent with prior knowledge and information inconsistent with prior knowledge. *Journal of Educational Psychology, 86,* 79–89.

Wood, W. (2000). Attitude change: Persuasion and social influence. *Annual Review of Psychology, 51,* 539–570.

Wooten, P. (1996). Humor: An antidote for stress. *Holistic Nursing Practice, 10,* 49–56. This article describes how stress can impact occupational functioning and suggests ways of dealing with stress including humor and laughter.

X

Xie, Y., & Goyette, K. (2003). Social mobility and the educational choices of Asian Americans. *Social Science Research, 32*(3), 467–498.

Y

Yacoubian, G. S. (2003). Correlates of ecstasy use among high school seniors surveyed through Monitoring the Future. *Drugs: Education, Prevention & Policy, 10*(1), 65–72.

Yang, Y., et al. (2005). Volume reduction in prefrontal gray matter in unsuccessful criminal psychopaths. *Biological Psychiatry, 57*(10), 1103–1108.

Yatham, L. N., et al. (2000). Brain serotonin2 receptors in major depression: A positron emission tomography study. *Archives of General Psychiatry, 57,* 850–858.

Ybarra, G. J., Passman, R. H., & Eisenberg, C. S. L. (2000). The presence of security blankets or mothers (or both) affects distress during pediatric examinations. *Journal of Consulting and Clinical Psychology, 68,* 322–330.

Yeh, C., & Chang, T. (2004). Understanding the multidimensionality and heterogeneity of the Asian American experience. *PsycCRITIQUES.*

Yesavage, J. A., et al. (2002). Modeling the prevalence and incidence of Alzheimer's disease and mild cognitive impair-ment. *Journal of Psychiatric Research, 36*(5), 281–286.

Yokota, F., & Thompson, K. M. (2000). Violence in G-rated animated films. *Journal of the American Medical Association, 283,* 2716–2720.

Young, E. A., et al. (2003). Mineralocorticoid receptor function in major depression. *Archives of General Psychiatry, 60,* 24–28.

Z

Zahavi, A. (2003). Anniversary essay: Indirect selection and individual selection in sociobiology: My personal views on theories of social behavior. *Animal Behaviour, 65*(5), 859–863.

Zajonc, R. B. (2001). Mere exposure: A gateway to the subliminal. *Current Directions in Psychological Science, 10*(6), 224–228.

Zangwill (Eds.), *Amnesia.* London: Butterworth.

Zimbardo, P. G. (2004). A situationist perspective on the psychology of evil: Understanding how good people are transformed into perpetrators.

Zimbardo, P. G. (2008). The journey from the Bronx to Stanford to Abu Ghraib. In R. Levine, A. Rodrigues & L. Zelezny. (Eds.). *Journeys in social psychology: Looking back to inspire the future.* (pp. 85-104). New York: Psychology Press.

Zimbardo, P. G., LaBerge, S., & Butler, L. D. (1993). Psychophysiological consequences of unexplained arousal. *Journal of Abnormal Psychology, 102,* 466–473.

Zimmer, C. (2002–2003). Searching for your inner chimp. *Natural History, 112*(December, 2002–January, 2003).

Zimprich, D., & Martin, M. (2002). Can longitudinal changes in processing speed explain longitudinal age changes in fluid intelligence? *Psychology & Aging, 17*(4), 690–695.

Zizak, D. M., & Reber, A. S. (2004). Implicit preferences: The role(s) of familiarity in the structural mere exposure effect. *Consciousness & Cognition: An International Journal, 13*(2), 336–362.

Zucker, A. N., Ostrove, J. M., & Stewart, A. J. (2002). College-educated women's personality development in adulthood: Perceptions and age differences. *Psychology & Aging, 17*(2), 236–244.

Name Index

Hall, J. A., 300
Hall, G. Stanley, 67
Halpern, D. F., 166, 181, 182
Han, W., 184
Hankin, B. L., 256, 258
Hansell, N. K., 48
Haridakis, P. M., 138
Harlow, Harry F., 62
Harris, D. B., 181
Harrison, D. W., 40
Hart, J. W., 305
Hastie, R., 305
Hatfield, E., 200
Haughton, E., 277
Hawken, M., 81
Hawkley, L. C., 241
Heber, D., 193
Heckhausen, J., 237
Heidenreich, P. T., 108
Heimpel, S. A., 220
Heinrichs, R. W., 250, 252, 253
Heinz, A., 30
Helms, J. E., 181
Hen, R., 45
Herbert, B., 229, 230
Hergenhahn, B. R., 17, 215, 248
Hering, Ewald, 81
Heron, M. P., 244
Hertz-Pannier, L., 39
Hettema, J., 48
Hewitt, P. L., 256
Hill, W. L., 45, 199
Hines, M., 195, 199
Hingson, R., 111
Hippocrates, 216
Hitzig, E., 39
Hobson, J. A., 103
Hoff, E., 171, 172, 174
Hoffman, Hunger, 276
Hoge, C. W., 261
Hohwy, J., 33
Holland, J. L., 218
Holland, P. C., 121
Hollingshead, A. B., 254
Hollon, S. D., 282, 286
Holmes, T. C., 232
Holmes, M. M., 199
Honorton, C., 94, 95
Hoover, R. N., 242, 243
Hopkins, R. A., 307
Hopkins, W. D., 169
Horn, J. M., 183
Horne, J. A., 104
Horney, Karen, 12, 214, 215
Hornstein, E. P., 81
Horowitz, T. S., 102
Hoybye, M. T., 238
Hoyert, M. D., 92
Hoznik, C. H., 136
Hubel, David, 76

Huesmann, L. R., 137, 138
Hull, Clark, 189
Hulshoff, P., 253
Huskinson, T. L. H., 290
Hvas, L., 68
Hwu, H., 253
Hyde, J. S., 67, 182

I

Iacono, W. G., 207, 253
Inhelder, B., 171
Insel, T. R., 42
Iribarren, C., 244
Isabella, R. A., 62
Isarida, T., 153
Iverson, P., 172
Ivey, A. E., 283
Izard, C. E., 201, 204

J

Jacks, J. Z., 292
Jackson, H., 259
Jackson, P. W., 177
Jacoangeli, F., 194
Jaffee, S., 67
James, L. E., 153
James, R., 267
James, William, 8, 97, 145, 188, 204, 207
Jamison, K. R., 256
Janis, Irving, 306
Janowitz, H. D., 191
Janowsky, J. S., 43
Jemmott, J. B., 242
Jenkins, Richard Suinn, 13
Jensen, M. P., 106
Johnson, W., 45
Johnson, Virginia, 196
Johnston, L. D., 109, 112, 113
Jones, Constance, 70
Jones, Mary Cover, 127
Jonsdottir, I. H., 31
Jourdan, A., 273
Jung, Carl, 213, 216

K

Kabat-Zinn, Jon, 108
Kaddour, J., 237
Kahneman, D., 168
Kainz, K., 105
Kalin, N. H., 262
Kallgren, C. A., 291
Kamalanabhan, T. J., 306
Kandel, E. R., 159
Kapur, S., 30
Karlberg, L., 236
Karon, B. P., 156

Kasai, K., 253
Kaslow, N. J., 217
Kataria, S., 105
Katigbak, M. S., 217
Kavanagh, K., 193
Kazdin, A. E., 259
Keller, A., 253
Keller, S., 111
Kellerman, J., 300
Kellman, P. J., 54
Kendler, K. S., 45, 198, 262
Kennedy, C. H., 102
Kéri, S., 242
Kerns, J. G., 250
Kessler, R. C., 250, 255
Keyes, C. L. M., 202, 258
Keyes, D., 264
Khan, A. A., 256
Kiecolt-Glaser, J. K., 106, 230, 243
Kihlstrom, J. F., 211
Kilshaw, D., 41
Kim, B. S. K., 224
Kim, K., 64
King, S., 275
King, Laura, 234
Kinsey, Alfred, 17, 197
Kiper, D. C., 81
Kirsch, I., 3, 107
Kirschenbaum, H., 273
Klaczynski, P. A., 165
Klavir, R., 166
Kleinke, C. L., 300
Kleinmuntz, B., 206
Klemfuss, J. Z., 160
Klüver, Heinrich, 38
Knafo, A., 45
Kobasa, Suzanne, 237
Koch, E. J., 168
Kochanek, K. D., 244
Koelling, R. A., 123
Koffka, Kurt, 9
Kohlberg, Lawrence, 55, 60, 61, 66, 67
Köhler, Wolfgang, 9, 10
Kooijman, C. M., 93
Kopelman, M. D., 157
Koss, M. P., 261, 262
Kovera, M. B., 160
Krähenbühl, S., 160
Krantz, D. S., 244
Krcmar, M., 137
Kroger, J. K., 36
Krueger, R. F., 45
Kuczmarski, R. J., 53
Kulkofsky, S., 160
Kwate, N. O. A., 181

L

Lackner, J. M., 237

Lahti, A. C., 253
LaMay, M. L., 181, 182
Lambert, P. R., 90
Lang, Alan, 21, 22
Lang, E. V., 106
Lang, F. R., 237
Lange, Karl G., 204, 207
Langlois, J. H., 294
Lanier, S. A., 91
Larkin, M., 90
Lashley, Karl, 158
Latané, B., 306
Laumann, E. O., 197, 198, 297
Lavee, Y., 232
Lavine, H., 293
Lazar, S. W., 108
Lazarus, Richard, 205, 231
Leaper, C., 220, 221
Le Bon, Gustave, 307
Lecci, L., 263
LeDoux, J. E., 38
Lefcourt, H. M., 238
Lehman, B. J., 291, 293
Leitch, M. L., 230
Lenneberg, E. H., 174
Lensvelt-Mulders, G., 48
Leonard, B. E., 239, 242
Leonard, S., 194
Leonardo, E. D., 45
Leor, J., 244
Leppel, K., 223
Lester, D., 289
Lever, J. P., 202
Levin, E. D., 114
Levin, R., 103
Levinson, Daniel J., 70, 71
Lewinsohn, P. M., 110, 194
Li, G., 111
Li, W., 81
Lidow, M. S., 30
Lieber, C. S., 111
Liederman, J., 182
Lief, Harold, 156
Linden, W., 238
Linn, M. C., 182
Litevin, G. H., 200
Little, A. C., 295
Liu, J., 202
Lochman, J. E., 267
Locke, E. A., 219, 220
Lockhart, Robert, 151
Loehlin, J. C., 45
Loftus, Elizabeth F., 4, 13, 17, 150, 156, 160
Loftus, G. R., 147, 150
Loop, M. S., 82
Lorenz, Konrad, 62, 63
Louie, K., 30
Loving, T. J., 298
Low, N. C. P., 262

Subject Index

bottom-up processing, **84,** 84
brain, 33–41, *36*
    features detectors in, 76
    memory, structures connected
        with, 159–161, *161*
brain-imaging techniques,
    35–36, *35*
brightness constancy, **86,**
    86–87, *86*
Broca's aphasia, 40, **40**
Broca's area, 39–40, *40, 169*
bulimia nervosa, **194,** 194
bystander effect, 307

C

cancer, 244–245
Cannon-Bard Theory, 205, *204*
case study, 17, **17**
catastrophize, **235**
catatonic schizophrenia, **252,** 252
catharsis, **272,** 272
CAT scans, **35,** 35, *35*
Cattell's Culture-Fair Intelligence
    Test, *181*
cause and effect, 317, *318*
central nervous system, **32,** 32–33
cerebellum, **36,** *36*
cerebral cortex, **38,** 38, *38*
cerebrum, *36,* **38,** 38
childhood, 53
    attachment, 61–63
    cognitive development, 55–61
    emotional development, 61
    parenting styles, 63–64
    physical development, 53–55
    repressed memories of, 156
    social development, 61
chimpanzees and language,
    169–170
chromosomes, **46,** *46,* 46–47
chunk, **149**
chunking, 149
circadian rhythms, 99–100, **100**
clairvoyance, 94–95
classical conditioning, **120,**
    120–127
classroom behavior modification,
    134–135
claustrophobia, **259**
client-centered therapy, 222, **273,**
    273–274
clinical psychologists, 5
closure, **82**
cocaine, 113, *114, 117*
cochlea, **89,** 89
cochlear implants, 90
cognitive, **11**
cognitive appraisal theory,
    205–206, *204*
cognitive-behavior therapy (CBT),

280, 280
cognitive development
    adolescence, 65–66
    adulthood, 69–70
    childhood, 55–61
cognitive-dissonance theory, **293,**
    293–294
cognitive maps, 135–136, *167*
cognitive perspective, 11
cognitive perspectives on motiva-
    tion, 190
cognitive therapies, 278–279, **279**
    Beck's cognitive therapy, 279
    cognitive-behavior therapy, 280
    rational emotive behavior
        therapy, 280
collective unconscious, **213,**
    213–214
collectivism *versus* individualism,
    223–224
collectivist, **223**
color blindness, 82
color constancy, **86,** 86–87
color vision, 79–81, *81*
color wheel, *80*
commitment, **297**
common fate, **84**
community mental health move-
    ment, 270–271
complementary, **80**
complementary colors, 80
compulsion, **261**
computerized axial tomography
    (CAT or CT scan), **35,** 35, *35*
concepts, **164,** 164–165
concrete-operational stage, **58,**
    58–59
concrete operations, **58**
conditional positive regard,
    222, 222
conditioned reinforcer, **130**
conditioned response (CR),
    122, 122
conditioned stimulus (CS), **122,** 122
conditioning
    aversive, 276–277
    classical, 120–127
    operant. *See* Operant condition-
        ing
conditions of worth, **222**
conductive deafness, 90
cones, **79**
conflict, **234**
conflict and stress, 234–235
conformity, 303–304
consciousness, 97
    altering, 105–116
    as awareness, 98
    as personal unity, 99
    as the waking state, 99
conservation, **57**

consumer psychologists, 6
consummate love, **298**
contact comfort, **62**
context, importance of, *9*
context-dependent memory, **153,**
    153–154
contingency theory, **136,** 136
continuity, **84**
continuous reinforcement, **132**
control and stress, 238
control groups, **20,** 20–21
controlled substances. *See* Drugs
conventional level, **61**
convergence, **86**
convergent thinking, **177,** 177
conversion disorder, **262,** 262–263
cool colors, 80
cornea, **78**
coronary heart disease,
    243–244, *244*
corpus callosum, *36,* **38**
correlation coefficient, **18, 317,**
    317–318
correlations, **15,** 18–20
    versus cause and effect, *318*
    positive and negative, *317*
corticosteroids, 43
counseling psychologists, 5
counterconditioning, **127,** 127
couple therapy, 281
creative self, **214**
creativity, **177**
    and intelligence, 177
cretinism, 43
critical period, **63**
critical thinking, 14
crystallized intelligence, **70**
CT scans, **35,** 35, *35*

D

daily hassles, 231–234
dark adaptation, **79**
Darwin's evolutionary theory, 44
deafness, 90
debrief, **22**
decentration, **58**
deception and truth, 302–303
decibel (dB), **88**
    familiar sounds, rating of, *88*
decision making
    group, 305
    judgment and, 167–169
deindividuation, **307,** 307
delayed *versus* immediate rein-
    forcers, 130
delta waves, **101**
delusions, **248**
dendrites, **27**
dependent variables, 20, **20**
depolarize, **28**
depressants, **109,** 111–112, *117*

depression, *201*
    antidepressants, 285
    major, 255
    manic, 255–256
    women and, 258
depth perception, 84–86
descriptive statistics, **310,**
    310–316
desensitization, **76**
developmental psychologists, 5,
    51. *See also* Human develop-
    ment
dichromat, **82**
difference threshold, 74–75, **75**
diffusion of responsibility, **305**
direct inner awareness, **98**
discrimination, **125**
    in classical conditioning,
        125–126
    prejudice and, 294–295
discriminative stimuli, **131,**
    131–132
disorders
    eating, 193–195
    psychological. *See* Psychologi-
        cal disorders
disorganized schizophrenia,
    252, 252
displace, **150**
displacement, **171,** 171
dispositional attribution, **298**
dissociative amnesia,
    156, 264, 264
dissociative disorders,
    263–265, **264**
dissociative fugue, **264,** 264
dissociative identity disorder, **264,**
    264–265
divergent thinking, **177,** 177
dizygotic (DZ) twins, **47**
DNA, *46,* **46**
dopamine, **30**
double-blind study, 21, **21**
down syndrome, **47**
dream analysis, 272
The Dream, **70,** 103–104
drive, **188**
drive-reduction theory, **189,** 189
drugs
    alcohol, 111–112, *117*
    altering consciousness through,
        109–116
    depressants, 109,
        111–112, *117*
    hallucinogens, 115–116, *117*
    stimulants, 109, 112–115, *117*
    substance abuse, 109–111
    substance dependence,
        109–111
drug therapy, 284

health psychology, **230**
hearing, 88–90
heredity, **45**, 45–46
    and intelligence, 182–183, *183*
    and stress, 242–243
Hering-Helmholtz illusion, 87, *87*
heritability, **183**
heroin, 112, *117*
hertz (Hz), **88**
heterosexual, **197**
heuristics, **165**
    in decision making, 168
    devices, use of, 165–166
hierarchical structure of long-term
    memory, *152*
hierarchy, **275**
higher-order conditioning,
    126, 126
hippocampus, **30, 157**
    and memory, *158,* 159–161
Hippocrates, 234
historical overview, 7–10
holophrase, **172,** 172–173
home environment and intelligence,
    184
homeostasis, **189,** 189
homosexual, **197**
hormones, **42**
    adrenocorticotrophic
        hormone, 43
    and sexual motivation, 195
Horney's psychoanalytic theory,
    214–215
hue, **77**
human development
    adolescence. *See* Adolescence
    adulthood. *See* Adulthood
    childhood. *See* Childhood
    prenatal development,
        52–53, *52*
human ear, 89, *89*
human eye, 78–79, *78*
human factors psychologists, 6
humanism, **221**
humanistic-existential
    perspective, 11
humanistic perspective of personal-
    ity, 221–222
humanistic theory of
    motivation, 190
humanistic therapies, 273
    client-centered therapy,
        273–274
    Gestalt therapy, 274
human research, 22–23
humor, 237–238
hunger, 191–192
hydrocarbons, **115**
hyperphagic, **192**
hypnosis, **105,** 105–107

hypnotic suggestibility, 106
hypnotic trance, 106
hypochondriasis, **263,** 263
hypothalamus, **36, 37,** 37, 42
hypothesis, **15**
    testing, 15
hypothyroidism, 43

I
icon, **147**
iconic memory, **147,** 147
    and saccadic eye movements,
        147
id, **211,** 211
ideas of persecution, **249**
identification, **212**
identity disorder, 264–265
illusions, **84,** 87, *87*
imaginary audience, **66,** 66
immediate *versus* delayed rein-
    forcers, 130
immune system, **241**
    stress and, 241, 242
implicit memory, **142,** 142–143
imprinting, **63**
incentive, **188**
incubation, **167,** 167
independence from parents, 67
independent variables, 20, **20**
individualism *versus* collectivism,
    223–224
individualist, **223**
individual psychology, **214**
industrial psychologists, 6
infantile amnesia, **157,** 157
infer, **319**
inferential statistics, 318–320, **319**
inferiority complex, **214,** 214
infinite creativity, **171,** 171
inflammation, **242**
informed consent, **22**
inkblot test, 227, *227*
insanity plea, *251*
insight, 10, *10,* **166,** 166–167
insomnia, 104
instinct, **45, 188**
instinctive behavior, 45
intelligence, **174,** 174
    creativity and, 177
    environmental influences on,
        183–184
    ethnic differences, 180
    factors influencing,
        182–184, *183*
    gender differences in, 181–182
    genetic influences on, 182–183
    measurement of, 178–179
    socioeconomic
        differences, 180
    theories of, 174–177, 185

intelligence quotient (IQ),
    178, 178
    distribution of scores, *181*
    heredity and, *183*
interference in short-term memory,
    149–150, *150*
interference theory, **155,**
    155–156
internals, **238**
interpersonal attraction, 295–298
interpersonal psychotherapy (ITP),
    273, 273
interval schedules of reinforcement,
    132–133, *133*
intimacy, **297**
    versus isolation, **71,** 71
intrinsic motives, 200
introspection, **7**
introversion, **216**
iris, **78**
irrational beliefs and stress,
    235–236, *236*

J
James-Lange Theory,
    204, *204*
judgment and decision making,
    167–169
Jungian psychoanalytic theory,
    213–214
just noticeable difference
    (jnd), **75**

K
kinesthesis, **93,** 93–94
kinship studies, 47–48
Kohlberg's theory of moral develop-
    ment, 60–61

L
la belle indifférence, **263**
Lang study, *21,* 22
language, **170**
    and the cerebral cortex, 39
    and cognition, 171
    and culture, 171–172
    functions of, 39–40
    in nonhuman communications,
        169–170
    what is, 170–171
language acquisition device (LAD),
    174, 174
language development, 172
    grammar development, 172–173
    learning theory and, 174
    nativist approach to, 174
    overregularization of, 173
    prelinguistic vocalizations, 172
late adulthood, 69, *69,* 71
latency, **213**

latent, **136**
latent learning, 135–136
lateral hypothalamus, **192,** 192
learned helplessness, **256**
learning, 119–120, *120. See also*
    Conditioning
    cognitive factors in, 135–136
    contingency theory, 136
    latent, 135–136
    observational. *See* Observa-
        tional learning
    perspectives on, 12
    programmed, 135
    relearning, 155
    and sleep, 102
learning curves, *124*
learning theory
    and language development, 174
    and personality development,
        218–219
"left-brained," 40
left-handedness, 40–41
lens, **78**
lesbians, 197–199
leukocytes, **241**
levels-of-processing model of
    memory, 151
libido, 212
lie detectors, 206–207
life changes and stress, 231–232
light, 76–77, *77*
light adaptation, 79
limbic system, **37,** 37, *37*
linguistic-relativity hypothesis,
    171, 171–172
lithium, 285
locus of control, **237**
long-term memory, **150,** 150–154
long-term potentiation, **159,**
    159, *159*
loudness, 88–89
    perception of, 90
love, 297–298
LSD, **116,** 116, *117*

M
magnetic resonance imaging (MRI),
    35, 35–36, *35, 169*
maintenance rehearsal, **144**
major depressive disorder (MDD),
    255, 255
mammal sleep times, *100*
manic, **255**
manic depression, 255–256
marijuana, **115,** 115–116, *117*
Maslow's hierarchy of needs,
    190, *191*
Maslow's self-actualization theory,
    221
MDMA, *117*

secondary reinforcers, **130,** 130
secondary sex characteristics, 43, **64**
secondhand smoke, **115**
sedative, **286**
selection factor, **15**
selective attention, **98**
selective avoidance, **293**
selective exposure, **293**
selective serotonin-reuptake inhibitors (SSRIS), **285**
self-actualization, **190,** 190, **221,** 221
self-concept, 221
self-efficacy expectations, **236,** 236–237
self-esteem, 222
   acculturation and adjustment, 224
self-ideals, 222
self-monitoring, **278**
self-serving bias, **299,** 299–300
semanticity, **171,** 171
semantic memory, **142**
sensation, 73–76, **74**
sensitive periods, 174
sensitization, **76**
sensorimotor stage, 56–57, **57**
sensorineural deafness, 90
sensory adaptation, **76,** 76
sensory memory, **145,** 145–147
serial-position effect, **148,** 148–149
serotonin, **31**
sex characteristics, 43
sex chromosomes, **47**
sex organs, 43
sex partners, 197, *198, 199*
sexuality in adolescence, 68
sexual motivation, 195–199
sexual orientation, 197–199, **198**
sexual response cycle, 195–197, **196**
s factors, 175
shape constancy, **87,** 87
shaping, **133,** 133–134
short-term dynamic therapies, 273
short-term memory, **147,** 147–150
signal-detection theory, **75,** 75–76
similarity, **84**
situational attribution, **298**
size constancy, **86,** 86
skill memories, 143
skin sense, 91–93
sleep, 99–104
   and stress, 232, *234*
sleep apnea, 105
sleep disorders, 104–105
   9/11/2001, before and after, *261*
sleep terrors, **105,** 105

sleepwalking, 105
smell, 91
smoking. *See* Nicotine
social-cognitive theory, **12, 219**
   and gender-typing, 220–221
   and personality, 219–220, *219*
social decision schemes, **305**
social development
   adolescence, 67–68
   adulthood, 70–71
   childhood, 61
social facilitation, **304,** 304–305
social influence, **300,** 300–304
social perception, **298,** 298–300
social phobia, **259**
social psychologists, 5
social psychology, **289,** 289
   attitudes. *See* Attitudes
   group behavior, 304–308
   what is, 289–290
social skills training, 278
social support, 238
sociocultural factors
   personality disorders, 267
   suicide, 258–259
sociocultural perspective, **12,** 12–13, **223**
   of anxiety disorders, 262
   of personality, 223–225
   of schizophrenia, 254–255
sociocultural theory, 59–60
socioeconomic differences in intelligence, 180
somatic nervous system, **32**
somatoform disorders, **262,** 262
   body dysmorphic disorder, 263
   conversion disorder, 262–263
   hypochondriasis, 263
somatosensory cortex, **39,** 39
sounds, locating, 89–90
sound waves, *88*
species, **45**
specific factors, **283**
specific phobia, **259**
spinal cord, **32**
spinal reflex, **33**
split-brain experiments, 41, *41*
spontaneous recovery, **125**
   classical conditioning, 125
   operant conditioning, 131
sport psychologists, 6
sports heroes, need for, 214
s (Spearman's symbol for specific factors), **175**
stages of sleep, 100–101, *101*
standard deviation, **314,** 314–316
standardization, **225**
Stanford-Binet Intelligence Scale, 178, *179*
staring, 300, *300*

state-dependent memory, **154,** 154
statistically significant differences, 319–320
statistics, **309,** 309–320
   central tendency measures, 312–314
   correlation coefficient, 18, 317–318
   descriptive, 310–316
   frequency distribution, 311–312, *312*
   inferential, 318–320
   normal curve, 316–317, *316*
   samples and populations, 15–17, 309–310, 320
   variability measures, 314–315
stereotypes, **294,** 294–295
Sternberg's triarchic model of intelligence, 175–176, *176*
steroids and mental processes, 43
stimulants, **109,** 112–115, *117*
stimulus, **121**
stimulus motives, 189–190
storage in memory, **144,** 144
   long-term memory, 150–151
stratified sample, **16,** 16–17
stress, 229–230, **230**
   in America, 232–234
   conflict and, 234
   coping with, 212, *213*
   irrational beliefs and, 235–236, *235*
   physical symptoms of, *213, 233,* 238–242
   psychological moderators of, 236–238, 242–245
   sources of, 231–236, *232*
   what is, 230
stress disorders, 261–262
stroboscopic motion, **84,** 84
structuralism, 8, **8**
study methods, 14–23
stupor, **251**
subjective moral judgment, **58**
substance abuse, **109,** 109–111
substance dependence, **109,** 109–111
successive approximations, **133,** 133, **278,** 278
suicide, 257
   myths about, 259
   risk factors, 257–258
   sociocultural factors, 258–259
superego, **212,** 212
suppression, **99**
surveys, **17,** 17–18
   of sexual behavior, 197, *198, 199*
sympathetic, **32**

sympathetic nervous system, 32, *33,* **200**
synapse, **29**
systematic desensitization, **127,** 127, **275,** 275
systematic random search, **165**

T

taste, 91
taste aversion, 122–124
taste buds, **91**
taste cells, **91**
telepathy, 94–95
temperature, sensation of, 92
testes, 43
testosterone, 43
texture gradient, **85**
thalamus, *36, 37,* 37
   and memory, *158,* 161
Thematic Apperception Test (TAT), 199–200, 245
theory, **4**
therapies. *See* Psychotherapy
theta waves, **101**
thinking, **163,** 163–169
   and the cerebral cortex, 39
   convergent, 177
   critical, 14
   divergent, 177
thyroid gland, 43
thyroxin, 43
thyroxin deficiency, 42
tip-of-the-tongue (TOT) phenomenon, **153,** 153
token economy, **278,** 278
tolerance, **109**
top-down processing, **84,** 84
touch, sense of, 91–92
touching, 300
trait, **216**
trait perspective of personality, 216–218
transcendental meditation (TM), **107,** 107–108
transference, **272,** 272
triangular model of love, **297,** 297, *297*
triarchic theory of intelligence, 175–176, *176,* 185
trichromat, **82**
trichromatic theory, **81,** 81, *81*
trust *versus* mistrust, **61**
twin studies, 47–48
type A behavior, **236,** 236
type B behavior, 236

U

UFO memories, 3–4
umbilical cord, **53**
unconditional positive regard, **222,**

Chapter 1:

- "Participants" now used instead of "subjects"
- New figure providing information on demographics of new doctorates in psychology
- Revised section on The Biological and Evolutionary Perspectives
- New statistic at end of chapter to indicate the percent of new doctorate degrees earned by women

Chapter 2

- New definition provided for "neuron"
- New figure of the Parasympathetic and Sympathetic Branches of the Automatic Nervous System
- New figure of Broca's and Wernicke's Areas of the Cerebral Cortex
- New figure of the Endocrine Glands
- New figure of Cells, Chromosomes, and DNA

Chapter 3

- Updated example for *animism*
- New photo of Mary D. Salter Ainsworth
- New photo of Frank Lloyd Wright

Chapter 4

- Revised section on top-down and bottom-up processing

Chapter 5

- New definition of activation-synthesis model
- Updated table providing information about the gender, level of education, and percentage of those Americans who smoke
- New statistics about the number of Americans who regularly use heroin and the number of alcoholics in the U.S.

Chapter 6

- Updated definition of unconditioned stimulus (UCS)
- Updated definition of unconditioned response (UCR)
- Updated definition of conditioned stimulus (CS)
- Updated definition of conditioned response (CR)
- New section on Teaching Children *Not* to Imitate Media Violence

Chapter 7

- New box feature on trusting eyewitness testimony

Chapter 8

- New information about *sensitive periods*
- New Theories of Intelligence Summary Chart

Chapter 9

- Updated facts about obesity
- New photo of hyperphagic rats
- Updated table providing information on the number of years lost by an extremely obese person compared to a normal-weight person

© BEAU LARK/CORBIS

IMAGES.COM/CORBIS

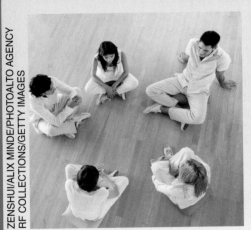

ZENSHUI/ALIX MINDE/PHOTOALTO AGENCY
RF COLLECTIONS/GETTY IMAGES

Chapter 10

- Formerly Chapter 11 (in the previous edition)
- Revised section/definition of personality
- Addition of *gender-typing* to running glossary

Chapter 11

- Formerly Chapter 10 (in previous edition)
- Revised section on Stress in America
- Updated figure on the number of deaths from heart disease

Chapter 12

- Bipolar Disorder added to Table 12.1 (prevalence of psychological disorders)

Chapter 13

- New information about Virtually Better

Chapter 14

- Deleted situationist perspective as a key term
- Updated facts about people choosing partners that are like them in race, ethnicity, age, level of education, and religion

Chapter in Review

1

LO¹ **psychology**
the science that studies behavior and mental processes

theory
a formulation of relationships underlying observed events

LO² **pure research**
research conducted without concern for immediate applications

applied research
research conducted in an effort to find solutions to particular problems

LO³ **introspection**
deliberate looking into one's own cognitive processes to examine one's thoughts and feelings

structuralism
the school of psychology that argues that the mind consists of ___ sations, feelings, ___ to form experienc___

functionalism
the school of psy___ uses or functions of the mind rather than the elements of experience

behaviorism
the school of psychology that defines psychology as the study of observable behavior and studies relationships between stimuli and responses

reinforcement
a stimulus that follows a response and increases the frequency of the response

Gestalt psychology
the school of psychology that emphasizes the tendency to organize perceptions into wholes and to integrate separate stimuli into meaningful patterns

psychoanalysis
the school of psychology that emphasizes the importance of unconscious motives and conflicts as dete___

> **How to Use the Card:**
>
> 1. Look over the card to preview the new concepts you'll be introduced to in the chapter.
>
> 2. Read your chapter to fully understand the material.
>
> 3. Go to class (and pay attention).
>
> 4. Review the card one more time to make sure you've registered the key concepts.
>
> 5. Don't forget, this card is only one of many PSYCH learning tools available to help you succeed in your psychology course.

LO⁴ **cog___**
hav___ such as sens___ intelligence, l___ solving

social-cogr___
a school of p___ tradition that ___ the explanati___ formerly term___

sociocultu___
the view that ___ gender, cultu___ behavior and ___

gender
the culturally ___ and *feminit___*

LO¹ Define psychology. Psychology is the scientific study of behavior and mental processes. Topics of interest to psychologists include the nervous system, sensation and perception, learning and memory, intelligence, language, thought, growth and development, personality, stress and health, psychological disorders, ways of treating those disorders, sexual behavior, and the behavior of people in social settings such as gro___ of the psychologist, like other scientists, is to describe, explain, pr___ or she studies—in this case, behavior and mental processes.

> In this column, you'll find summary points supported by exhibits from the chapters.

> Here, you'll find the key terms and definitions in the order they appear in the chapter.

LO² Describe the various fields and subfields of psychology. Psychologists are found in a number of different specialties:

Clinical psychologists help people with psychological disorders adjust to the demands of life.

Counseling psychologists typically see clients with adjustment problems but not serious psychological disorders.

School psychologists help school systems identify and assist students who have problems that interfere with learning.

Educational psychologists research theoretical issues related to learning, measurement, and child development.

Developmental psychologists study the changes—physical, cognitive, social, and personality—that occur throughout the life span.

Personality psychologists identify and measure human traits and determine influences on human thought processes, feelings, and behavior.

Social psychologists are concerned with the nature and causes of individuals' thoughts, feelings, and behavior in social situations.

Environmental psychologists study the ways in which people and the environment influence one another.

Experimental psychologists specialize in basic processes such as the nervous system, sensation and perception, learning and memory, thought, motivation, and emotion.

Industrial psychologists focus on the relationships between people and work.

Organizational psychologists study the behavior of people in organizations such as businesses.

Human factors psychologists make technical systems more user-friendly.

Consumer psychologists study the behavior of shoppers in an effort to predict and influence their behavior.

Health psychologists examine the ways in which behavior and attitudes are related to physical health.

Sport psychologists help people improve their performance in sports.

Forensic psychologists apply principles of psychology to the criminal justice system.

LO³ Describe the origins of psychology and identify those who made significant contributions to the field. An ancient contributor to the modern field of psychology, Aristotle argued that human behavior, like the movements of the stars and the seas, is subject to rules and laws. Today, as then, the subject matter of the study of human behavior includes the study of personality, sensation and perception, thought, intelligence, needs and motives, feelings and emotion, and memory. The following is a list of the historic schools of psychology and the major proponent(s) of each: *Structuralism:* Wilhelm Wundt; *Functionalism:* William James; *Behaviorism:* John B. Watson and B. F. Skinner; *Gestalt Psychology:* Max Wertheimer, Kurt Koffka, and Wolfgang Köhler; and *Psychoanalysis:* Sigmund Freud, Carl Jung, Alfred Adler, Karen Horney, and Erik Erikson.

LO⁴ Identify theoretical perspectives of modern psychologists toward behavior and mental processes. There are several influential perspectives in contemporary psychology: biological and evolutionary, cognitive, humanistic–existential, psychodynamic, learning, and sociocultural.

- *Evolutionary psychologists* focus on the evolution of behavior and mental processes.

> When it's time to prepare for exams, use the Card and the technique to the left to ensure successful study sessions.

studentresources

PSYCH was designed for students just like you—busy people who want choices, flexibility, and multiple learning options.

PSYCH delivers concise, focused information in a fresh and contemporary way. In addition to your tear-out review cards, PSYCH offers a variety of learning materials designed with you in mind. Visit CourseMate for PSYCH at www.cengagebrain.com to access multiple PSYCH resources to help you succeed.

- *Printable Flash Cards* Our extensive research shows that almost all students use flash cards to reinforce their understanding of core psychology concepts. To help you prepare flash cards that fit your specific study needs, the website provides three varieties of downloadable flash cards: 1) term only, 2) definition only, or 3) term and definition. Each set of cards is formatted to fit the standard Avery business card template.
- *Interactive Flashcards* Key terms are also available as interactive flash cards that allow you to shuffle the deck, remove a card, view the term first, or view the definition first.
- *PowerVisuals* Important concepts covered in images and graphs from PSYCH are provided as interactive visuals.
- *Learning Outcomes* Downloadable learning outcomes from PSYCH.
- *Build a Summary* You can select a chapter and check your understanding of text concepts by filling in the blanks of these paragraphs.
- *Glossary* Select a chapter to view glossary terms and definitions.
- *Tutorial Quizzes* You can practice before chapter tests, midterms, and finals by taking these interactive quizzes.
- *Web Links* Select a chapter to view web links that reinforce or extend concepts from the text.
- *Study Games* Fun study practice with Sort-It-Out and Crossword puzzles.

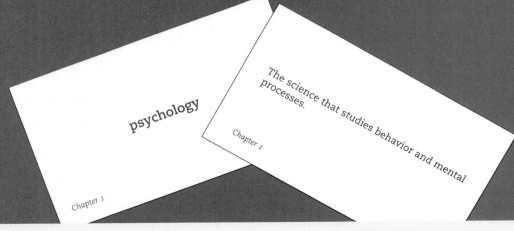

psychology

Chapter 1

The science that studies behavior and mental processes.

Chapter 1

YOU TOLD US HOW YOU LIKE TO STUDY, AND

WE LISTENED.

Chapter in Review

LO¹ psychology
the science that studies behavior and mental processes

theory
a formulation of relationships underlying observed events

LO² pure research
research conducted without concern for immediate applications

applied research
research conducted in an effort to find solutions to particular problems

LO³ introspection
deliberate looking into one's own cognitive processes to examine one's thoughts and feelings

structuralism
the school of psychology that argues that the mind consists of three basic elements—sensations, feelings, and images—that combine to form experience

functionalism
the school of psychology that emphasizes the uses or functions of the mind rather than the elements of experience

behaviorism
the school of psychology that defines psychology as the study of observable behavior and studies relationships between stimuli and responses

reinforcement
a stimulus that follows a response and increases the frequency of the response

Gestalt psychology
the school of psychology that emphasizes the tendency to organize perceptions into wholes and to integrate separate stimuli into meaningful patterns

psychoanalysis
the school of psychology that emphasizes the importance of unconscious motives and conflicts as determinants of human behavior

LO⁴ cognitive
having to do with mental processes such as sensation and perception, memory, intelligence, language, thought, and problem solving

social-cognitive theory
a school of psychology in the behaviorist tradition that includes cognitive factors in the explanation and prediction of behavior; formerly termed *social learning theory*

sociocultural perspective
the view that focuses on the roles of ethnicity, gender, culture, and socioeconomic status in behavior and mental processes

gender
the culturally defined concepts of *masculinity* and *femininity*

LO¹ Define psychology.
Psychology is the scientific study of behavior and mental processes. Topics of interest to psychologists include the nervous system, sensation and perception, learning and memory, intelligence, language, thought, growth and development, personality, stress and health, psychological disorders, ways of treating those disorders, sexual behavior, and the behavior of people in social settings such as groups and organizations. The goal of the psychologist, like other scientists, is to describe, explain, predict, and control the events he or she studies—in this case, behavior and mental processes.

LO² Describe the various fields and subfields of psychology.
Psychologists are found in a number of different specialties:

Clinical psychologists help people with psychological disorders adjust to the demands of life.

Counseling psychologists typically see clients with adjustment problems but not serious psychological disorders.

School psychologists help school systems identify and assist students who have problems that interfere with learning.

Educational psychologists research theoretical issues related to learning, measurement, and child development.

Developmental psychologists study the changes—physical, cognitive, social, and personality—that occur throughout the life span.

Personality psychologists identify and measure human traits and determine influences on human thought processes, feelings, and behavior.

Social psychologists are concerned with the nature and causes of individuals' thoughts, feelings, and behavior in social situations.

Environmental psychologists study the ways in which people and the environment influence one another.

Experimental psychologists specialize in basic processes such as the nervous system, sensation and perception, learning and memory, thought, motivation, and emotion.

Industrial psychologists focus on the relationships between people and work.

Organizational psychologists study the behavior of people in organizations such as businesses.

Human factors psychologists make technical systems more user-friendly.

Consumer psychologists study the behavior of shoppers in an effort to predict and influence their behavior.

Health psychologists examine the ways in which behavior and attitudes are related to physical health.

Sport psychologists help people improve their performance in sports.

Forensic psychologists apply principles of psychology to the criminal justice system.

LO³ Describe the origins of psychology and identify those who made significant contributions to the field.
An ancient contributor to the modern field of psychology, Aristotle argued that human behavior, like the movements of the stars and the seas, is subject to rules and laws. Today, as then, the subject matter of the study of human behavior includes the study of personality, sensation and perception, thought, intelligence, needs and motives, feelings and emotion, and memory. The following is a list of the historic schools of psychology and the major proponent(s) of each: *Structuralism:* Wilhelm Wundt; *Functionalism:* William James; *Behaviorism:* John B. Watson and B. F. Skinner; *Gestalt Psychology:* Max Wertheimer, Kurt Koffka, and Wolfgang Köhler; and *Psychoanalysis:* Sigmund Freud, Carl Jung, Alfred Adler, Karen Horney, and Erik Erikson.

LO⁴ Identify theoretical perspectives of modern psychologists toward behavior and mental processes.
There are several influential perspectives in contemporary psychology: biological and evolutionary, cognitive, humanistic–existential, psychodynamic, learning, and sociocultural.

- *Evolutionary psychologists* focus on the evolution of behavior and mental processes.

LO⁵ hypothesis
in psychology, a specific statement about behavior or mental processes that is tested through research

correlation
an association or relationship among variables, as we might find between height and weight or between study habits and school grades

selection factor
a source of bias that may occur in research findings when subjects are allowed to choose for themselves a certain treatment in a scientific study

sample
part of a population

population
a complete group of organisms or events

random sample
a sample drawn so that each member of a population has an equal chance of being selected to participate

stratified sample
a sample drawn so that identified subgroups in the population are represented proportionately in the sample

volunteer bias
a source of bias or error in research reflecting the prospect that people who offer to participate in research studies differ systematically from people who do not

case study
a carefully drawn biography that may be obtained through interviews, questionnaires, and psychological tests

survey
a method of scientific investigation in which a large sample of people answer questions about their attitudes or behavior

naturalistic observation
a scientific method in which organisms are observed in their natural environments

correlation coefficient
a number between +1.00 and −1.00 that expresses the strength and direction (positive or negative) of the relationship between two variables

experiment
a scientific method that seeks to confirm cause-and-effect relationships by introducing independent variables and observing their effects on dependent variables

independent variable
a condition in a scientific study that is manipulated so that its effects may be observed

dependent variable
a measure of an assumed effect of an independent variable

experimental groups
in experiments, groups whose members obtain the treatment

control groups
in experiments, groups whose members do not obtain the treatment, while other conditions are held constant

placebo
a bogus treatment that has the appearance of being genuine

- Psychologists with a *cognitive perspective* investigate the ways in which we perceive and mentally represent the world by learning, memory, planning, problem solving, decision making, and language.

- *The humanistic–existential perspective* is cognitive in flavor, yet emphasizes more the role of subjective (personal) experience.

- Neoanalysts with a *psychodynamic perspective* focus less on the unconscious—as was done in Freud's day—and more on conscious choice and self-direction.

- The first of two learning perspectives, *behaviorists* emphasize environmental influences and the learning of habits through repetition and reinforcement. *Social-cognitive theorists,* in contrast, suggest that people can modify and create their environments, and engage in intentional learning by observing others.

- A psychologist with a *sociocultural perspective* studies the influences of ethnicity, gender, culture, and socioeconomic status on behavior and mental processes.

LO⁵ Describe modern approaches to research and practice—critical thinking, the scientific method, and ethical considerations. Psychologists, like other scientists, must use careful means to observe and measure behavior and the factors that influence behavior. Psychologists use evidence and critical thinking—the process of thoughtfully analyzing and probing the questions, statements, and arguments of others. The scientific method is a systematic way of organizing and expanding scientific knowledge. Daily experiences, common beliefs, and scientific observations all contribute to the development of theories. Psychological theories explain observations and lead to hypotheses about behavior and mental processes. Observations can then confirm the theory or lead to its refinement or abandonment. Many factors—such as the nature of the research sample—must be considered in interpreting the accuracy of the results of scientific research. Psychologists must also adhere to a number of ethical standards that are intended to promote individual dignity, human welfare, and scientific integrity. The standards are also intended to ensure that psychologists do not engage in harmful research methods or treatments.

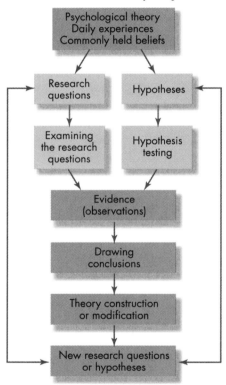

blind
in experimental terminology, unaware of whether or not one has received a treatment

double-blind study
a study in which neither the subjects nor the observers know who has received the treatment

informed consent
a subject's agreement to participate in research after receiving information about the purposes of the study and the nature of the treatments

debrief
to explain the purposes and methods of a completed procedure to a participant

Chapter in Review

2

LO¹ neuron
a specialized cell of the nervous system that transmits messages

glial cells
cells that nourish and insulate neurons, direct their growth, and remove waste products from the nervous system

dendrites
rootlike structures, attached to the cell body of a neuron, that receive impulses from other neurons

axon
a long, thin part of a neuron that transmits impulses to other neurons from branching structures called *terminal buttons*

myelin
a fatty substance that encases and insulates axons, facilitating transmission of neural impulses

afferent neurons
neurons that transmit messages from sensory receptors to the spinal cord and brain. Also called *sensory neurons*

efferent neurons
neurons that transmit messages from the brain or spinal cord to muscles and glands. Also called *motor neurons*

neural impulse
the electrochemical discharge of a nerve cell, or neuron

polarize
to ready a neuron for firing by creating an internal negative charge in relation to the body fluid outside the cell membrane

resting potential
the electrical potential across the neural membrane when it is not responding to other neurons

depolarize
to reduce the resting potential of a cell membrane from about 70 millivolts toward zero

action potential
the electrical impulse that provides the basis for the conduction of a neural impulse along an axon of a neuron

all-or-none principle
the fact that a neuron fires an impulse of the same strength whenever its action potential is triggered

refractory period
a phase following firing during which a neuron is less sensitive to messages from other neurons and will not fire

synapse
a junction between the axon terminals of one neuron and the dendrites or cell body of another neuron

neurotransmitters
chemical substances involved in the transmission of neural impulses from one neuron to another

receptor site
a location on a dendrite of a receiving neuron tailored to receive a neurotransmitter

LO¹ Describe the nervous system, including neurons, neural impulses, and neurotransmitters.
The nervous system regulates the body and is involved in thought processes, emotional responses, heartbeat, and motor activity. The central nervous system contains the brain and the spinal cord. The somatic system transmits sensory information about skeletal muscles, skin, and joints and controls skeletal muscular activity. The autonomic system regulates glands and activities like digestion. Neurons transmit information through electrochemical neural impulses. Their dendrites receive messages and their axons conduct messages, transmitting them to other cells via neurotransmitters.

The Anatomy of a Neuron. "Messages" enter neurons through dendrites, are transmitted along the trunk-like axon, and then are sent from axon terminal buttons to muscles, glands, and other neurons. Axon terminal buttons contain sacs of chemicals called *neurotransmitters*. Neurotransmitters are released into the synaptic cleft, where many of them bind to receptor sites on the dendrites of the receiving neuron.

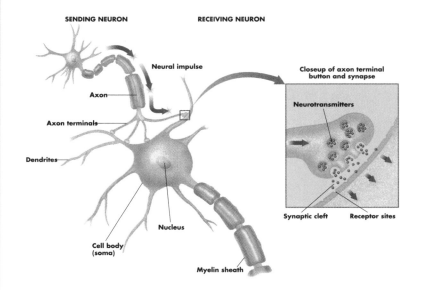

acetylcholine (ACh)
a neurotransmitter that controls muscle contractions

hippocampus
a part of the limbic system of the brain that is involved in memory formation

dopamine
a neurotransmitter that is involved in Parkinson's disease and that appears to play a role in schizophrenia

norepinephrine
a neurotransmitter whose action is similar to that of the hormone epinephrine and that may play a role in depression

serotonin
a neurotransmitter, deficiencies of which have been linked to affective disorders, anxiety, and insomnia

gamma-aminobutyric acid (GABA)
an inhibitory neurotransmitter that apparently helps calm anxiety

endorphins
neurotransmitters that are composed of amino acids and that are functionally similar to morphine

nerve
a bundle of axons from many neurons

central nervous system
the brain and spinal cord

peripheral nervous system
the part of the nervous system consisting of the somatic nervous system and the autonomic nervous system

somatic nervous system
the division of the peripheral nervous system that connects the central nervous system with sensory receptors, skeletal muscles, and the surface of the body

autonomic nervous system (ANS)
the division of the peripheral nervous system that regulates glands and activities such as heartbeat, respiration, digestion, and dilation of the pupils

sympathetic
the branch of the ANS that is most active during emotional responses, such as fear and anxiety, that spend the body's reserves of energy

parasympathetic
the branch of the ANS that is most active during processes (such as digestion) that restore the body's reserves of energy

spinal cord
a column of nerves within the spine that transmits messages from sensory receptors to the brain and from the brain to muscles and glands throughout the body

spinal reflex
a simple, unlearned response to a stimulus that may involve only two neurons

gray matter
in the spinal cord, the grayish neurons and neural segments that are involved in spinal reflexes

white matter
in the spinal cord, axon bundles that carry messages from and to the brain

The Parasympathetic and Sympathetic Branches of the Autonomic Nervous System (ANS). The parasympathetic branch of the ANS generally acts to replenish stores of energy in the body. The sympathetic branch is most active during activities that expend energy. The two branches of the ANS frequently have antagonistic effects on the organs they service.

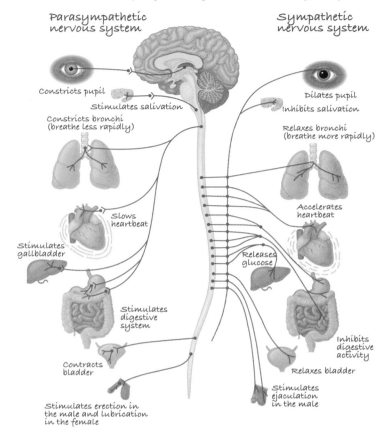

LO² List the structures of the brain and their functions. The hindbrain includes the medulla, the pons, and the cerebellum. The reticular activating system begins in the hindbrain and continues into the forebrain. Important structures of the forebrain include the thalamus, which serves as a relay station for sensory stimulation; the hypothalamus, which regulates body temperature and influences motivation and emotion; the limbic system, which is involved in memory, emotion, and motivation; and the cerebrum, which handles thinking and language. The outer fringe of the cerebrum is the cerebral cortex, which is divided into four lobes: frontal, parietal, temporal, and occipital.

The Parts of the Human Brain
The view of the brain, split top to bottom, shows some of the most important structures. The "valleys" in the cerebrum are called fissures.

Chapter in Review

2

LO^2 electroencephalo-graph (EEG)
a method of detecting brain waves by means of measuring the current between electrodes placed on the scalp

computerized axial tomography (CAT scan)
a method of brain imaging that passes a narrow X-ray beam through the head and measures structures that reflect the rays from various angles, enabling a computer to generate a three-dimensional image

positron emission tomography (PET scan)
a method of brain imaging that injects a radioactive tracer into the bloodstream and assesses activity of parts of the brain according to the amount of glucose they metabolize

magnetic resonance imaging (MRI)
a method of brain imaging that places a person in a magnetic field and uses radio waves to cause the brain to emit signals that reveal shifts in the flow of blood which, in turn, indicate brain activity

functional MRI (fMRI)
a form of MRI that enables researchers to observe the brain "while it works" by taking repeated scans

medulla
a oblong area of the hindbrain involved in regulation of heartbeat and respiration

pons
a structure of the hindbrain involved in respiration, attention, and sleep and dreaming

cerebellum
a part of the hindbrain involved in muscle coordination and balance

reticular activating system (RAS)
a part of the brain involved in attention, sleep, and arousal

thalamus
an area near the center of the brain involved in the relay of sensory information to the cortex and in the functions of sleep and attention

hypothalamus
a bundle of nuclei below the thalamus involved in body temperature, motivation, and emotion

limbic system
a group of structures involved in memory, motivation, and emotion that forms a fringe along the inner edge of the cerebrum

amygdala
a part of the limbic system that apparently facilitates stereotypical aggressive responses

cerebrum
the large mass of the forebrain, which consists of two hemispheres

cerebral cortex
the wrinkled surface area (gray matter) of the cerebrum

corpus callosum
a thick fiber bundle that connects the hemispheres of the cortex

The geography of the cerebral cortex. The cortex has four lobes: frontal, parietal, temporal, and occipital. The visual area of the cortex is in the occipital lobe. The hearing or auditory cortex lies in the temporal lobe. The motor and somatosensory areas—shown below—face each other across the central fissure. Note that the face and the hands are "super-sized" in the motor and somatosensory areas. Why do you think this is so?

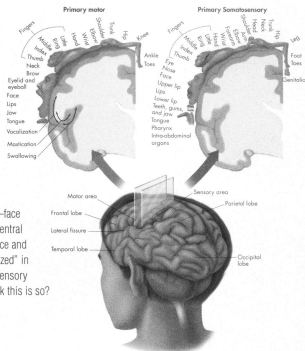

LO^3 Explain the role of the endocrine system and list the endocrine glands. The glands of the endocrine system secrete hormones regulating development and activity. The pituitary gland secretes growth hormone, prolactin, and oxytocin. The thyroid regulates metabolism. The adrenal cortex produces steroids. The adrenal medulla secretes epinephrine, which increases the metabolic rate and stimulates general emotional arousal. The sex hormones are responsible for sexual differentiation and regulate the menstrual cycle in females.

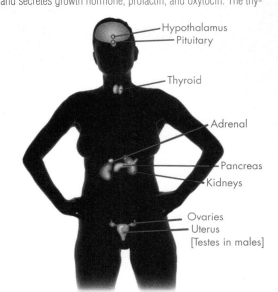

somatosensory cortex
the section of cortex in which sensory stimulation is projected. It lies just behind the central fissure in the parietal lobe

motor cortex
the section of cortex that lies in the frontal lobe, just across the central fissure from the sensory cortex. Neural impulses in the motor cortex are linked to muscular responses throughout the body

aphasia
a disruption in the ability to understand or produce language

Wernicke's aphasia
a language disorder characterized by difficulty comprehending the meaning of spoken language

Broca's aphasia
a language disorder characterized by slow, laborious speech

epilepsy
temporary disturbances of brain functions that involve sudden neural discharges

LO³ gland
an organ that secretes one or more chemical substances such as hormones, saliva, or milk

endocrine system
the body's system of ductless glands that secrete hormones and release them directly into the bloodstream

hormone
a substance secreted by an endocrine gland that regulates various body functions

pituitary gland
the gland that secretes growth hormone, prolactin, antidiuretic hormone, and other hormones

LO⁴ Describe evolutionary psychology and the connections between heredity, behavior, and mental processes. Evolutionary psychology studies the way natural selection influences mental processes and behavior. Evolutionary psychologists suggest that behavior evolves as it is transmitted from generation to generation. Evolutionarily advantageous behaviors like aggression, strategic mate selection, and familial altruism are often influenced by heredity.

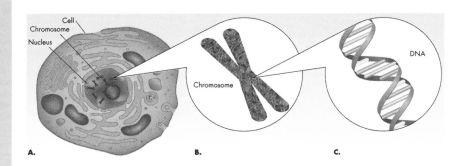

LO⁴ natural selection
a core concept of the theory of evolution that holds that adaptive genetic variations among members of a species enable individuals with those variations to survive and reproduce

mutation
a sudden variation in an inheritable characteristic, as distinguished from a variation that results from generations of gradual selection

evolutionary psychology
the branch of psychology that studies the ways in which adaptation and natural selection are connected with mental processes and behavior

species
a category of biological classification consisting of related organisms who are capable of interbreeding. *Homo sapiens*—humans—make up one species

instinct
a stereotyped pattern of behavior that is triggered by a particular stimulus and nearly identical among members of a species, even when they are reared in isolation

heredity
the transmission of traits from parent to offspring by means of genes

genetics
the area of biology that focuses on heredity

gene
a basic unit of heredity, which is found at a specific point on a chromosome

chromosome
a microscopic rod-shaped body in the cell nucleus carrying genes that transmit hereditary traits from generation to generation. Humans normally have 46 chromosomes

DNA
acronym for deoxyribonucleic acid, the substance that forms the basic material of chromosomes. It takes the form of a double helix and contains the genetic code

polygenic
referring to traits that are influenced by combinations of genes. Genotype One's genetic makeup, based on the sequencing of the nucleotides we term A, C, G, and T

phenotype
one's actual development and appearance, as based on one's genotype and environmental influences

nature
the inborn, innate character of an organism

nurture
the sum total of the environmental factors that affect an organism from conception onward

sex chromosomes
the 23rd pair of chromosomes, whose genetic material determines the sex of the individual

Down syndrome
a condition caused by an extra chromosome on the 21st pair and characterized by mental deficiency, a broad face, and slanting eyes

monozygotic (MZ) twins
twins that develop from a single fertilized ovum that divides in two early in prenatal development. MZ twins thus share the same genetic code. Also called *identical twins*

dizygotic (DZ) twins
twins that develop from two fertilized ova and who are thus as closely related as brothers and sisters in general. Also called *fraternal twins*

Chapter in Review

3

LO¹ zygote
a fertilized ovum
(egg cell)

germinal stage
the first stage of prenatal development, during
which the dividing mass of cells has not become
implanted in the uterine wall

amniotic sac
a sac within the uterus that contains the embryo
or fetus

placenta
a membrane that permits the exchange of nutrients
and waste products between the mother and her
developing child but does not allow the maternal
and fetal bloodstreams to mix

umbilical cord
a tube between the mother and her developing
child through which nutrients and waste products
are conducted

LO² reflex
a simple unlearned response to a stimulus

rooting
the turning of an infant's head toward a touch,
such as by the mother's nipple

fixation time
the amount of time spent looking at a visual stimulus

assimilation
according to Piaget, the inclusion of a new event
into an existing schema

schema
according to Piaget, a hypothetical mental structure that permits the classification and organization of new information

accommodation
according to Piaget, the modification of schemas so
that information inconsistent with existing schemas
can be integrated or understood

object permanence
recognition that objects removed from sight still
exist, as demonstrated in young children by continued pursuit

sensorimotor stage
the first of Piaget's stages of cognitive development, characterized by coordination of sensory
information and motor activity, early exploration of
the environment, and lack of language

preoperational stage
the second of Piaget's stages, characterized by
illogical use of words and symbols, spotty logic,
and egocentrism

egocentrism
according to Piaget, the assumption that others
view the world as one does oneself

conservation
according to Piaget, recognition that basic properties of substances such as weight and mass
remain the same when superficial features change

objective responsibility
according to Piaget, the assignment of blame
according to the amount of damage done rather
than the motives of the actor

LO¹ Explain prenatal development and the role that sex hormones play.
The fetal stage lasts from the beginning of the third month until birth. By the end of
the third month, the major organ systems and the fingers and toes have formed. In the middle of
the fourth month, the mother usually detects the first fetal movements. By the end of the sixth
month, the fetus moves its limbs so vigorously that mothers often feel that they are being kicked.
The fetus opens and shuts its eyes, sucks its thumb, alternates between periods of being awake
and sleeping, and responds to light. It also turns somersaults, which can be perceived by the
mother. During the three months prior to birth, the organ systems of the fetus continue to
mature. The heart and lungs become increasingly capable of sustaining independent life. The
fetus gains about five-and-a-half pounds and doubles in length. Newborn boys average about
seven-and-a-half pounds and newborn girls about seven pounds.

LO² Explain the physi-
cal, cognitive,
moral, social, and emotional
development of children.
Childhood begins with birth. During
infancy—the first two years of
childhood—dramatic gains in
height and weight continue. Babies
usually double their birth weight in
about five months and triple it by
their first birthday. Their height
increases by about ten inches in the
first year. Children grow another
four to six inches during the second
year and gain some four to seven
pounds. After that, they gain about
two to three inches a year until they
reach the adolescent growth spurt.
Other aspects of physical develop-

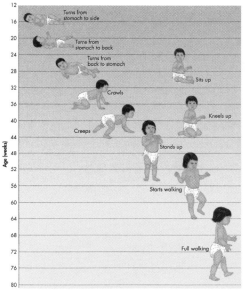

ment in childhood include reflexes and perceptual development. Theories in cognitive development include Piaget's stage theory, Vygotsky's sociocultural theory, and Kohlberg's
theory of moral development. Erikson's theory of psychosocial development and Ainsworth's
attachment studies explore critical aspects of social and emotional development in childhood.

LO³ Explain the physical, cognitive, moral, social, and emotional devel-
opment of adolescents. Adolescence is bounded by the onset of puberty—the
period during which the body becomes sexually mature—and the assumption of adult
responsibilities. Except for infancy, more changes occur during adolescence than during any
other time. One of the most noticeable physical developments of adolescence is a growth spurt
that lasts two to three years and ends the gradual changes in height and weight that characterize most of childhood. Within this short span of years, adolescents grow some eight to twelve
inches. According to Piaget, children undergo three stages of cognitive development prior to
adolescence: sensorimotor, preoperational, and concrete operational. The stage of formal operations is the final stage in Piaget's theory, and it represents cognitive maturity. Formal operational thought generally begins at about the beginning of adolescence. The major achievements
of the stage of formal operations involve classification, logical thought, and the ability to
hypothesize. Central features are the ability to think about ideas as well as objects and to group
and classify ideas, such as symbols and statements. Kohlberg's research around the levels of
moral reasoning found postconventional moral judgments were absent until about age sixteen,
when stage 5 reasoning is shown by about 20% of adolescents. According to Erik Erikson's
eight stages of psychosocial development, the fifth stage—ego identity versus role diffusion—
occurs in adolescence.

concrete operational stage
Piaget's third stage, characterized by logical thought concerning tangible objects, conservation, and subjective morality

decentration
simultaneous focusing on more than one dimension of a problem, so that flexible, reversible thought becomes possible

subjective moral judgment
according to Piaget, moral judgment that is based on the motives of the perpetrator

zone of proximal development (ZPD)
Vygotsky's term for the situation in which a child carries out tasks with the help of someone who is more skilled, frequently an adult who represents the culture in which the child develops

scaffolding
Vygotsky's term for temporary cognitive structures or methods of solving problems that help the child as he or she learns to function independently

preconventional level
according to Kohlberg, a period during which moral judgments are based largely on expectation of rewards or punishments

conventional level
according to Kohlberg, a period during which moral judgments largely reflect social conventions; a "law and order" approach to morality

trust versus mistrust
Erikson's first stage of psychosocial development, during which children do—or do not—come to trust that primary caregivers and the environment will meet their needs

attachment
the enduring affectional tie that binds one person to another

contact comfort
a hypothesized primary drive to seek physical comfort through contact with another

ethologist
a scientist who studies the characteristic behavior patterns of species of animals

critical period
a period of time when an instinctive response can be elicited by a particular stimulus

imprinting
a process occurring during a critical period in the development of an organism, in which that organism responds to a stimulus in a manner that will afterward be difficult to modify

authoritative parents
parents who are strict and warm; authoritative parents demand mature behavior but use reason rather than force in discipline

authoritarian parents
parents who are rigid in their rules and who demand obedience for the sake of obedience

permissive parents
parents who impose few, if any, rules and who do not supervise their children closely

uninvolved parents
parents who generally leave their children to themselves

LO³ adolescence
the period of life bounded by puberty and the assumption of adult responsibilities

puberty
the period of physical development during which sexual reproduction first becomes possible

LO⁴ Explain the physical, cognitive, moral, social, and emotional development of adults. A number of physical changes occur during the later years. The reasons for aging, however, are not yet completely understood. People can also affect the pace of their aging by eating properly, exercising, maintaining a positive outlook, and finding and meeting challenges that are consistent with their abilities. People are at the height of their cognitive powers during early adulthood. Cognitive development in adulthood has many aspects—creativity, memory functioning, and intelligence. Changes in social and emotional development during adulthood are probably the most "elastic" or fluid. According to Erik Erikson, young adulthood is characterized by the task of developing abiding intimate relationships; middle adulthood involves being productive and contributing to younger generations; the challenge for late adulthood is to maintain one's sense of identity despite physical deterioration.

Hair and nails
Hair often turns gray and thins out. Men may go bald. Fingernails can thicken.

Brain
The brain shrinks, but it is not known if that affects mental functions.

The senses
The sensitivity of hearing, sight, taste, and smell can all decline with age.

Skin
Wrinkles occur as the skin thins and the underlying fat shrinks, and age spots often crop up.

Glands and hormones
Levels of many hormones drop, or the body becomes less responsive to them.

Immune system
The body becomes less able to resist some pathogens.

Lungs
It doesn't just seem harder to climb those stairs; lung capacity drops.

Heart and blood vessels
Cardiovascular problems become more common.

Muscles
Strength usually peaks in the twenties, then declines.

Kidneys and urinary tract
The kidneys become less efficient. The bladder can't hold as much, so urination is more frequent.

Digestive system
Digestion slows down as the secretion of digestive enzymes decreases.

Reproductive system
Women go through menopause, and testosterone levels drop for men.

Bones and joints
Wear and tear can lead to arthritic joints, and osteoporosis is common, especially in women.

secondary sex characteristics
characteristics that distinguish the sexes, such as distribution of body hair and depth of voice, but that are not directly involved in reproduction

menarche
the beginning of menstruation

formal operational stage
Piaget's fourth stage, characterized by abstract logical thought and deduction from principles

imaginary audience
an aspect of adolescent egocentrism; the belief that other people are as concerned with our thoughts and behaviors as we are

personal fable
another aspect of adolescent egocentrism; the belief that our feelings and ideas are special and unique and that we are invulnerable

postconventional level
according to Kohlberg, a period during which moral judgments are derived from moral principles and people look to themselves to set moral standards

ego identity
Erikson's term for a firm sense of who one is and what one stands for

role diffusion
Erikson's term for lack of clarity in one's life roles (due to failure to develop ego identity)

LO⁴ menopause
the cessation of menstruation

crystallized intelligence
one's lifetime of intellectual achievement, as shown largely through vocabulary and knowledge of world affairs

fluid intelligence
mental flexibility as shown in learning rapidly to solve new kinds of problems

Alzheimer's disease
a progressive form of mental deterioration characterized by loss of memory, language, problem solving, and other cognitive functions

dream
in this usage, Levinson's term for the overriding drive of youth to become someone important, to leave one's mark on history

intimacy versus isolation
Erikson's life crisis of young adulthood, which is characterized by the task of developing abiding intimate relationships

generativity versus stagnation
Erikson's term for the crisis of middle adulthood, characterized by the task of being productive and contributing to younger generations

midlife crisis
a crisis experienced by many people during the midlife transition when they realize that life may be more than halfway over and they reassess their achievements in terms of their dreams

ego integrity versus despair
Erikson's term for the crisis of late adulthood, characterized by the task of maintaining one's sense of identity despite physical deterioration

Chapter in Review

LO¹ sensation
the stimulation of sensory receptors and the transmission of sensory information to the central nervous system

perception
the process by which sensations are organized into an inner representation of the world

absolute threshold
the minimal amount of energy that can produce a sensation

pitch
the highness or lowness of a sound, as determined by the frequency of the sound waves

difference threshold
the minimal difference in intensity required between two sources of energy so that they will be perceived as being different

Weber's constant
the fraction of the intensity by which a source of physical energy must be increased or decreased so that a difference in intensity will be perceived

just noticeable difference (jnd)
the minimal amount by which a source of energy must be increased or decreased so that a difference in intensity will be perceived

signal-detection theory
the view that the perception of sensory stimuli involves the interaction of physical, biological, and psychological factors

feature detectors
neurons in the sensory cortex that fire in response to specific features of sensory information such as lines or edges of objects

sensory adaptation
the processes by which organisms become more sensitive to stimuli that are low in magnitude and less sensitive to stimuli that are constant or ongoing in magnitude

sensitization
the type of sensory adaptation in which we become more sensitive to stimuli that are low in magnitude; also called *positive adaptation*

desensitization
the type of sensory adaptation in which we become less sensitive to constant stimuli. Also called *negative adaptation*

LO² hue
the color of light, as determined by its wavelength

cornea
transparent tissue forming the outer surface of the eyeball

iris
a muscular membrane whose dilation regulates the amount of light that enters the eye

pupil
the black-looking opening in the center of the iris, through which light enters the eye

lens
a transparent body behind the iris that focuses an image on the retina

LO¹ Define and differentiate between sensation and perception. Stimulation
of the senses is an automatic process. It results from sources of energy, like light and sound, or from the presence of chemicals, as in smell and taste. Perception is an active process. Perception may begin with sensation, but it also reflects our experiences and expectations as it makes sense of sensory stimuli.

LO² Identify the parts of the eye; explain the properties of light and the
theories of color vision. It is visible light that triggers visual sensations. Yet visible light is just one small part of a spectrum of electromagnetic energy that surrounds us. All forms of electromagnetic energy move in waves, and different kinds of electromagnetic energy have signature wavelengths.

In both the eye and a camera, light enters through a narrow opening and is projected onto a sensitive surface. In the eye, the photosensitive surface is called the retina, and information concerning the changing images on the retina is transmitted to the brain.

LO³ Describe how visual perception is organized. Visual perception is the process
by which we organize or make sense of the sensory impressions caused by the light that strikes our eyes. The attempt to identify the rules that govern these processes resulted in what are referred to as the laws of perceptual organization: *figure-ground perception,* and the laws of *proximity, similarity, continuity,* and *common fate.*

LO⁴ Identify the parts of the ear; describe the sense of hearing. Sound, or
auditory stimulation, travels through the air like waves. A single cycle of compression and expansion is one wave of sound, which can occur many times in a second. The ear has three parts: the outer ear, middle ear, and inner ear. The outer ear funnels sound to the eardrum. Inside the eardrum, vibrations transmit sound to the inner ear. Vibrations in the cochlea transmit the sound to the auditory nerve.

LO⁵ Describe the chemical senses. In smell and taste, we sample molecules of
substances. An odor is a sample of molecules of a substance in the air. Odors trigger firing of receptor neurons in the olfactory membrane high in each nostril. Taste is sensed through taste cells—receptor neurons located on taste buds.

LO⁶ Explain the properties of the skin senses and theoretical explana-
tions for pain. The skin senses include touch, pressure, warmth, cold, and pain. Pain results when neurons called nociceptors in the skin are stimulated. The pain message to the brain is initiated by the release of chemicals such as prostaglandins, bradykinin, and P.

LO⁷ Describe the kinesthetic and vestibular senses. Kinesthesis and the vestibu-
lar sense alert us to our movements and body position without relying on vision. In kinesthesis, sensory information is fed back to the brain from sensory organs in the joints, tendons, and muscles. The vestibular sense makes use of sensory organs located in the semicircular canals and elsewhere in the ears to monitor the body's motion and position in relation to gravity.

LO⁸ Explain why psychologists are skeptical about extrasensory
perception. One method for studying telepathy is the ganzfeld procedure. However, when Milton and Wiseman weighed the results of 30 ganzfeld ESP studies from seven laboratories, they found no evidence that subjects in these studies scored above chance levels on the ESP task. It has also been difficult to replicate experiments in ESP.

retina
the area of the inner surface of the eye that contains rods and cones

photoreceptors
cells that respond to light

bipolar cells
neurons that conduct neural impulses from rods and cones to ganglion cells

ganglion cells
neurons whose axons form the optic nerve

optic nerve
the nerve that transmits sensory information from the eye to the brain

rods
rod-shaped photoreceptors that are sensitive only to the intensity of light

cones
cone-shaped photoreceptors that transmit sensations of color

fovea
an area near the center of the retina that is dense with cones and where vision is consequently most acute

blind spot
the area of the retina where axons from ganglion cells meet to form the optic nerve

visual acuity
sharpness of vision

presbyopia
a condition characterized by brittleness of the lens

dark adaptation
the process of adjusting to conditions of lower lighting by increasing the sensitivity of rods and cones

complementary
descriptive of colors of the spectrum that when combined produce white or nearly white light

afterimage
the lingering visual impression made by a stimulus that has been removed

trichromatic theory
the theory that color vision is made possible by three types of cones, some of which respond to red light, some to green, and some to blue

opponent-process theory
the theory that color vision is made possible by three types of cones, some of which respond to red or green light, some to blue or yellow, and some to the intensity of light

trichromat
a person with normal color vision

monochromat
a person who is sensitive to black and white only and hence color-blind

dichromat
a person who is sensitive to black–white and either red–green or blue–yellow and hence partially color-blind

LO³ closure
the tendency to perceive a broken figure as being complete or whole proximity nearness; the perceptual tendency to group together objects that are near one another

proximity
nearness; the perceptual tendency to group together objects that are near one another

similarity
the perceptual tendency to group together objects that are similar in appearance

continuity
the tendency to perceive a series of points or lines as having unity

common fate
the tendency to perceive elements that move together as belonging together

top-down processing
the use of contextual information or knowledge of a pattern in order to organize parts of the pattern

bottom-up processing
the organization of the parts of a pattern to recognize, or form an image of, the pattern they compose

illusions
sensations that give rise to misperceptions

stroboscopic motion
a visual illusion in which the perception of motion is generated by a series of stationary images that are presented in rapid succession

monocular cues
stimuli suggestive of depth that can be perceived with only one eye

perspective
a monocular cue for depth based on the convergence (coming together) of parallel lines as they recede into the distance

texture gradient
a monocular cue for depth based on the perception that closer objects appear to have rougher (more detailed) surfaces

motion parallax
a monocular cue for depth based on the perception that nearby objects appear to move more rapidly in relation to our own motion

binocular cues
stimuli suggestive of depth that involve simultaneous perception by both eyes

retinal disparity
a binocular cue for depth based on the difference in the image cast by an object on the retinas of the eyes as the object moves closer or farther away

convergence
a binocular cue for depth based on the inward movement of the eyes as they attempt to focus on an object that is drawing nearer

size constancy
the tendency to perceive an object as being the same size even as the size of its retinal image changes according to the object's distance

color constancy
the tendency to perceive an object as being the same color even though lighting conditions change its appearance

brightness constancy
the tendency to perceive an object as being just as bright even though lighting conditions change its intensity

shape constancy
the tendency to perceive an object as being the same shape although the retinal image varies in shape as it rotates

LO⁴ hertz (Hz)
a unit expressing the frequency of sound waves; one hertz equals one cycle per second

decibel (dB)
a unit expressing the loudness of a sound

cochlea
the inner ear; the bony tube that contains the basilar membrane and the organ of Corti

basilar membrane
a membrane that lies coiled within the cochlea

organ of Corti
the receptor for hearing that lies on the basilar membrane in the cochlea

auditory nerve
the axon bundle that transmits neural impulses from the organ of Corti to the brain

place theory
the theory that the pitch of a sound is determined by the section of the basilar membrane that vibrates in response to the sound

frequency theory
the theory that the pitch of a sound is reflected in the frequency of the neural impulses that are generated in response to the sound

LO⁵ flavor
a complex quality of food and other substances that is based on their odor, texture, and temperature as well as their taste

olfactory nerve
the nerve that transmits information concerning odors from olfactory receptors to the brain

taste cells
receptor cells that are sensitive to taste

taste buds
the sensory organs for taste. They contain taste cells and are located mostly on the tongue

LO⁷ kinesthesis
the sense that informs us about the positions and motion of parts of our bodies

vestibular sense
the sense of equilibrium that informs us about our bodies' positions relative to gravity

Chapter in Review

5

LO¹ selective attention
the focus of consciousness on a particular stimulus

direct inner awareness
knowledge of one's own thoughts, feelings, and memories

preconscious
in psychodynamic theory, descriptive of material that is not in awareness but can be brought into awareness by focusing one's attention

unconscious
in psychodynamic theory, descriptive of ideas and feelings that are not available to awareness; also: without consciousness

repression
in psychodynamic theory, the unconscious ejection of anxiety-evoking ideas, impulses, or images from awareness

suppression
the deliberate, or conscious, placing of certain ideas, impulses, or images out of awareness

nonconscious
descriptive of bodily processes such as growing hair, of which we cannot become conscious. We may "recognize" that our hair is growing, but we cannot directly experience the biological process

LO² circadian rhythm
a cycle that is connected with the twenty-four-hour period of the earth's rotation

alpha waves
rapid low-amplitude brain waves that have been linked to feelings of relaxation

nonrapid eye movement (NREM) sleep
stages of sleep 1 through 4

rapid eye movement (REM) sleep
a stage of sleep characterized by rapid eye movements, which have been linked to dreaming

theta waves
slow brain waves produced during the hypnagogic state

delta waves
strong, slow brain waves usually emitted during stage 4 sleep

activation–synthesis model
the view that acetylcholine and the pons activate the reticular activating system, which stimulates the cortex, but not to the point of waking; the cortex then pieces together (synthesizes) the cognitive activity into a dream

narcolepsy
a "sleep attack" in which a person falls asleep suddenly and irresistibly

apnea
temporary absence or cessation of breathing

sleep terrors
frightening dreamlike experiences that occur during the deepest stage of NREM sleep; nightmares, in contrast, occur during REM sleep

LO¹
Define consciousness. The concept of consciousness has various meanings. One meaning is *sensory awareness* of the environment. Another aspect of consciousness is *selective attention*. Selective attention means focusing one's consciousness on a particular stimulus. We are conscious of—or have *direct inner awareness* of—thoughts, images, emotions, and memories. Sigmund Freud, the founder of psychoanalysis, differentiated between the thoughts and feelings of which we are *conscious,* or aware, and those that are preconscious and unconscious. *Preconscious* material is not currently in awareness but is readily available. Still other mental events are *unconscious,* or unavailable, to awareness under most circumstances. Some bodily processes, such as the firings of neurons, are *nonconscious.* They cannot be experienced through sensory awareness or direct inner awareness. In the sense that the *self* forms intentions and guides its own behavior, consciousness is *self.* The word conscious also refers to the *waking state* as opposed, for example, to sleep.

LO²
Explain the nature of sleep and various sleep disorders. When we sleep, we slip from consciousness to unconsciousness. When we are conscious, our brains emit waves characterized by certain frequencies (numbers of waves per second) and amplitudes (heights—an index of strength). Brain waves are rough indicators of the activity of neurons. The strength or energy of brain waves is expressed in volts (an electrical unit). When we sleep, our brains emit waves that differ from those emitted when we are conscious. Sleep disorders seriously interfere with daily functioning and include insomnia, narcolepsy, and apnea. The less-common sleep disorders—sleep terrors, bedwetting, and sleepwalking—occur during deep (stage 3 or 4) sleep.

Awake — beta waves (low amplitude, high frequency)

Drowsy — alpha waves (higher amplitude, slower frequency)

Awake

Stage 1 sleep — theta waves (low frequency, low amplitude)

Sleep spindle   K complex

Stage 2 sleep — sleep spindles and the K complex

NREM Sleep

Stage 3 sleep — beginning of delta waves (low frequency, high amplitude)

Stage 4 sleep — delta waves continue to increase in amplitude

REM Sleep
Occurs when we reenter Stage 1, about 90 minutes after falling asleep (frequently called *paradoxical sleep*)

REM sleep — brain-wave patterns are very similar to those of initial NREM stage 1

LO³ hypnosis
a condition in which people are highly suggestible and behave as though they are in a trance

role theory
a theory that explains hypnotic events in terms of the person's ability to act *as though* he or she were hypnotized

response set theory
the view that response expectancies play a key role in the production of the experiences suggested by the hypnotist

transcendental meditation (TM)
the simplified form of meditation brought to the United States by the Maharishi Mahesh Yogi and used as a method for coping with stress

mindfulness meditation (MM)
a form of meditation that provides clients with techniques they can use to focus on the present moment rather than ruminate about problems

biofeedback training (BFT)
the systematic feeding back to an organism information about a bodily function so that the organism can gain control of that function

electromyograph (EMG)
an instrument that measures muscle tension

LO⁴ depressant
a drug that lowers the rate of activity of the nervous system

stimulant
a drug that increases activity of the nervous system

substance abuse
persistent use of a substance even though it is causing or compounding problems in meeting the demands of life

substance dependence
loss of control over use of a substance; biologically speaking, dependence is typified by tolerance, withdrawal symptoms, or both

tolerance
habituation to a drug, with the result that increasingly higher doses of the drug are needed to achieve similar effects

withdrawal symptoms
a characteristic cluster of symptoms that results from sudden decrease in an addictive drug's level of usage

opiates
a group of narcotics derived from the opium poppy that provide a euphoric rush and depress the nervous system

narcotics
drugs used to relieve pain and induce sleep. The term is usually reserved for opiates

opioids
chemicals that act on opiate receptors but are not derived from the opium poppy

barbiturate
an addictive depressant used to relieve anxiety or induce sleep

amphetamines
stimulants derived from *alpha-methyl-beta-phenyl-ethylamine*, a colorless liquid consisting of carbon, hydrogen, and nitrogen

hydrocarbons
chemical compounds consisting of hydrogen and carbon

second-hand smoke
smoke from the tobacco products and exhalations of other people

hallucinogen
a substance that causes hallucinations

marijuana
the dried vegetable matter of the *Cannabis sativa* plant

LO³ Explain various uses of hypnosis, forms of meditation, and biofeedback techniques in altering consciousness.

Hypnosis—an altered state of consciousness in which people are highly suggestible and behave as though they are in a trance—is derived from the Greek word for sleep. Hypnotism can be used as an anesthetic in dentistry, childbirth, and medical procedures. Some psychologists use hypnosis to help clients reduce anxiety, overcome fears, or lessen the perception of chronic pain. One common form of meditation, transcendental meditation (TM), was brought to the United States by the Maharishi Mahesh Yogi in 1959. People practice TM by concentrating on mantras—words or sounds that are claimed to help the person achieve an altered state of consciousness. Mindfulness Meditation (MM), as opposed to TM, makes no pretense of achieving spiritual goals. Instead, MM provides clients with mantra-like techniques they can use to focus on the present moment rather than ruminate about problems. Biofeedback is a system that provides, or "feeds back," information about a bodily function to an organism. Through biofeedback training, people have learned to gain voluntary control over a number of functions that are normally automatic, such as heart rate and blood pressure.

LO⁴ Explain the concepts of substance abuse; identify categories of drugs and how they alter consciousness.
Substance abuse and dependence usually begin with experimental use in adolescence. People experiment with drugs for various reasons, including curiosity, conformity to peer pressure, parental use, rebelliousness, escape from boredom or pressure, and excitement or pleasure. Use of a substance may be reinforced by peers or by the drug's positive effects on mood and its reduction of anxiety, fear, and stress. Many people use drugs as a form of self-medication for anxiety and depression, even low self-esteem. For people who are physiologically dependent, avoidance of withdrawal symptoms is also reinforcing. Psychoactive drugs include depressants (alcohol, opiates, and barbiturates), stimulants (amphetamines, cocaine, and nicotine), and hallucinogens (LSD, marijuana, PHP, and mescaline).

How Cocaine Produces Euphoria and Why People "Crash"

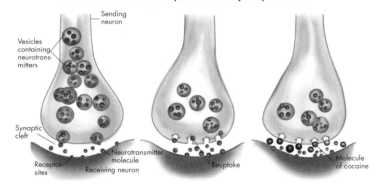

LSD
lysergic acid diethylamide; a hallucinogen

flashbacks
distorted perceptions or hallucinations that occur days or weeks after LSD usage but mimic the LSD experience

mescaline
a hallucinogen derived from the mescal (peyote) cactus

phencyclidine (pcp)
another hallucinogen whose name is an initialism for its chemical structure

LO¹ learning

(1) according to behaviorists, a relatively permanent change in behavior that results from experience (2) according to cognitive theorists, the process by which organisms make relatively permanent changes in the way they represent the environment because of experience

classical conditioning
a simple form of learning in which a neutral stimulus comes to evoke the response usually evoked by another stimulus by being paired repeatedly with the other stimulus

stimulus
an environmental condition that elicits a response

unconditioned stimulus (UCS)
a stimulus that elicits an unconditioned response

unconditioned response (UCR)
a natural, usually unvarying response elicited by a stimulus without learning or conditioning

orienting reflex
an unlearned response in which an organism attends to a stimulus

conditioned stimulus (CS)
a previously neutral stimulus that, after repeated association with an unconditioned stimulus, elicits the response elicited by the unconditioned stimulus

conditioned response (CR)
a response that becomes associated with a previously unrelated stimulus as a result of pairing the stimulus with another stimulus that normally elicits the response

extinction
an experimental procedure in which stimuli lose their ability to evoke learned responses because the events that had followed the stimuli no longer occur

spontaneous recovery
the recurrence of an extinguished response as a function of the passage of time

generalization
in conditioning, the tendency for a conditioned response to be evoked by stimuli that are similar to the stimulus to which the response was conditioned

discrimination
in conditioning, the tendency for an organism to distinguish between a conditioned stimulus and similar stimuli that do not forecast an unconditioned stimulus

higher-order conditioning
a classical conditioning procedure in which a previously neutral stimulus comes to elicit the response brought forth by a *conditioned* stimulus by being paired repeatedly with that conditioned stimulus

counterconditioning
a fear-reduction technique in which pleasant stimuli are associated with fear-evoking stimuli so that the fear-evoking stimuli lose their aversive qualities

LO¹ Describe the learning process according to classical conditioning.

Classical conditioning is a simple form of associative learning that teaches animals to anticipate events. When a neutral stimulus (like a bell ringing) and one that evokes a response (like dog food) are paired together repeatedly, the conditioned neutral stimulus will begin to trigger a response (like salivation) on its own.

KIND OF LEARNING: Classical conditioning
Major theorists: Ivan Pavlov (known for basic research with dogs); John B. Watson (known as the originator of behaviorism)

WHAT IS LEARNED
Association of events; anticipations, signs, expectations; automatic responses to new stimuli

HOW IT IS LEARNED
A neutral stimulus is repeatedly paired with a stimulus (an unconditioned stimulus, or UCS) that elicits a response (an unconditioned response, or UCR) until the neutral stimulus produces a response (conditioned response, or CR) that anticipates and prepares for the unconditioned stimulus. At this point, the neutral stimulus has become a conditioned stimulus (CS).

LO² Describe the learning process according to operant conditioning.

Under operant conditioning, animals learn to engage in behavior because of the way it is reinforced. Positive reinforcement encourages the learner to repeat a behavior more frequently. Negative reinforcement discourages the learner from repeating a behavior.

KIND OF LEARNING: Operant conditioning
Major theorist: B. F. Skinner

WHAT IS LEARNED
Behavior that operates on, or affects, the environment to produce consequences

HOW IT IS LEARNED
A response is rewarded or reinforced so that it occurs with greater frequency in similar situations.

Water   Light   Screen
Food pellet dispenser
Food tray   Lever

flooding
a behavioral fear-reduction technique based on principles of classical conditioning; fear-evoking stimuli (CSs) are presented continuously in the absence of actual harm so that fear responses (CRs) are extinguished

systematic desensitization
a behavioral fear-reduction technique in which a hierarchy of fear-evoking stimuli is presented while the person remains relaxed

LO² reinforce
to follow a response with a stimulus that increases the frequency of the response

operant behavior
voluntary responses that are reinforced

operant conditioning
a simple form of learning in which an organism learns to engage in behavior because it is reinforced

positive reinforcer
a reinforcer that when *presented* increases the frequency of an operant

negative reinforcer
a reinforcer that when *removed* increases the frequency of an operant

primary reinforcer
an unlearned reinforcer

secondary reinforcer
a stimulus that gains reinforcement value through association with established reinforcers

conditioned reinforcer
another term for a secondary reinforcer

reward
a pleasant stimulus that increases the frequency of the behavior it follows

punishment
an unpleasant stimulus that suppresses the behavior it follows

discriminative stimulus
in operant conditioning, a stimulus that indicates that reinforcement is available

continuous reinforcement
a schedule of reinforcement in which every correct response is reinforced

partial reinforcement
one of several reinforcement schedules in which not every correct response is reinforced

fixed-interval schedule
a schedule in which a fixed amount of time must elapse between the previous and subsequent times that reinforcement is available

variable-interval schedule
a schedule in which a variable amount of time must elapse between the previous and subsequent times that reinforcement is available

fixed-ratio schedule
a schedule in which reinforcement is provided after a fixed number of correct responses

variable-ratio schedule
a schedule in which reinforcement is provided after a variable number of correct responses

shaping
a procedure for teaching complex behaviors that at first reinforces approximations of the target behavior

LO³ Describe cognitive factors in learning.
Learning is often more complex than association and reinforcement; it involves searching for information, weighing evidence, and making decisions. Cognitive psychologists study mental structures, schemas, templates, and information processing to prove that learning can occur without conditioning. Latent learning—like a cognitive map of a maze—may not be revealed without motivation. Contingency theory suggests that learning occurs when a conditioned stimulus provides information about the unconditioned stimulus. Finally, observational learning makes it possible to acquire skills and knowledge by watching others rather than through direct experience.

KIND OF LEARNING:
Observational learning
Major theorists: Albert Bandura; Julian Rotter; Walter Mischel

WHAT IS LEARNED
Expectations (if–then relationships), knowledge, and skills

HOW IT IS LEARNED
A person observes the behavior of another person (live or through media such as films, television, or books) and its effects

successive approximations
behaviors that are progressively closer to a target behavior

LO³ latent
hidden or concealed

contingency theory
the view that learning occurs when stimuli provide information about the likelihood of the occurrence of other stimuli

observational learning
the acquisition of knowledge and skills through the observation of others (who are called *models*) rather than by means of direct experience

model
an organism that engages in a response that is then imitated by another organism

Chapter in Review

LO¹ explicit memory
memory that clearly and distinctly expresses (explicates) specific information

episodic memory
memories of events experienced by a person or that take place in the person's presence

semantic memory
general knowledge, as opposed to episodic memory

implicit memory
memory that is suggested (implied) but not plainly expressed, as illustrated in the things that people *do* but do not state clearly

priming
the activation of specific associations in memory, often as a result of repetition and without making a conscious effort to access the memory

retrospective memory
memory for past events, activities, and learning experiences, as shown by explicit (episodic and semantic) and implicit memories

prospective memory
memory to perform an act in the future, as at a certain time or when a certain event occurs

LO² encoding
modifying information so that it can be placed in memory; the first stage of information processing

storage
the maintenance of information over time; the second stage of information processing

maintenance rehearsal
mental repetition of information to keep it in memory

metamemory
self-awareness of the ways in which memory functions, allowing the person to encode, store, and retrieve information effectively

elaborative rehearsal
the kind of coding in which new information is related to information that is already known

retrieval
the location of stored information and its return to consciousness; the third stage of information processing

memory
the processes by which information is encoded, stored, and retrieved

LO³ sensory memory
the type or stage of memory first encountered by a stimulus

memory trace
an assumed change in the nervous system that reflects the impression made by a stimulus

icon
a mental representation of a visual stimulus that is held briefly in sensory memory

LO¹
Define memory and differentiate between types of memories. Memory is the processes by which information is encoded, stored, and retrieved. *Explicit memory*—also referred to as declarative memory—is memory for specific information. Two kinds of explicit memories are identified according to the type of information they hold: episodic memories are memories of the things that happen to us or take place in our presence ("I remember…") and semantic memory refers to general knowledge ("I know…") *Implicit memory*—also referred to as nondeclarative memory—is memory of how to perform a procedure or skill; it is the act itself, doing something, like riding a bike.

Retrospective memory is the recalling of information that has been previously learned. Explicit and implicit memories involve remembering things that were learned. *Prospective memory* refers to remembering to do things in the future.

LO²
Explain the process of memory. The first stage of information processing is changing information so that we can place it in memory: encoding. When we encode information, we transform it into psychological formats that can be represented mentally. To do so, we commonly use visual, auditory, and semantic codes. The second memory process is storage. Storage means maintaining information over time. The third memory process is retrieval. The retrieval of stored information means locating it and returning it to consciousness. The phrase below might be more easily recalled if you think of it as an acronym of the first two letters of the name of a nation (hint, hint).

THUNSTOFAM

LO³
Explain the stages of memory. The Atkinson–Shiffrin model proposes that there are three stages of memory: (a) sensory memory, (b) short-term memory, and (c) long-term memory. Part a shows that sensory information impacts on the registers of sensory memory. Memory traces are held briefly in sensory memory before decaying. If we attend to the information, much of it can be transferred to short-term memory (STM). Part b: Information may be maintained in STM through maintenance rehearsal or elaborative rehearsal. Otherwise, it may decay or be displaced. Part c: Once information is transferred to long-term memory (LTM), it may be filed away indefinitely. However, if the information in LTM is organized poorly, or if we cannot find cues to retrieve it, it can be lost.

Three Stages of Memory: The Atkinson–Shiffrin Model

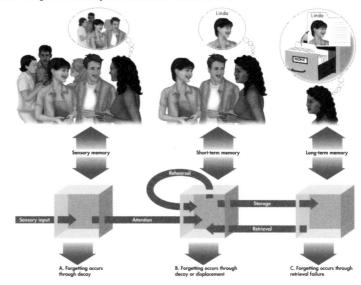

iconic memory
the sensory register that briefly holds mental representations of visual stimuli

eidetic imagery
the maintenance of detailed visual memories over several minutes

echo
a mental representation of an auditory stimulus (sound) that is held briefly in sensory memory

echoic memory
the sensory register that briefly holds mental representations of auditory stimuli

short-term memory
the type or stage of memory that can hold information for up to a minute or so after the trace of the stimulus decays

working memory
another term for *short-term memory*

serial-position effect
the tendency to recall more accurately the first and last items in a series

chunk
a stimulus or group of stimuli that are perceived as a discrete piece of information

displace
in memory theory, to cause information to be lost from short-term memory by adding new information

long-term memory
the type or stage of memory capable of relatively permanent storage

repression
in Freud's psychodynamic theory, the ejection of anxiety-evoking ideas from conscious awareness

schema
a way of mentally representing the world, such as a belief or an expectation, that can influence perception of persons, objects, and situations

tip-of-the-tongue (TOT) phenomenon
the feeling that information is stored in memory although it cannot be readily retrieved

context-dependent memory
information that is better retrieved in the context in which it was encoded and stored, or learned

state-dependent memory
information that is better retrieved in the physiological or emotional state in which it was encoded and stored, or learned

LO⁴ nonsense syllables
meaningless sets of two consonants, with a vowel sandwiched in between, that are used to study memory

paired associates
nonsense syllables presented in pairs in experiments that measure recall

method of savings
a measure of retention in which the difference between the number of repetitions originally required to learn a list and the number of repetitions required to relearn the list after a certain amount of time has elapsed is calculated

savings
the difference between the number of repetitions originally required to learn a list and the number of repetitions required to relearn the list after a certain amount of time has elapsed

interference theory
the view that we may forget stored material because other learning interferes with it

retroactive interference
the interference of new learning with the ability to retrieve material learned previously

LO⁴ Identify contributors to forgetting. Recognition, recall, and relearning are three basic memory tasks that have been used by psychologists to measure forgetting. Nonsense syllables have been used in studying each of them. According to interference theory, we forget material in short-term and long-term memory because newly learned material interferes with it. The two basic types of interference are retroactive interference and proactive interference. According to Sigmund Freud, we are motivated to repress painful memories and unacceptable ideas because they produce anxiety, guilt, and shame. Freud also believed that young children repress memories of aggressive impulses and perverse lusts toward their parents, which would explain why people could not recall episodes in their early childhoods (infantile amnesia). Adults also experience amnesia, although usually for biological reasons, as in the cases of anterograde and retrograde amnesia.

Ebbinghaus's Classic Curve of Forgetting
Recollection of lists of words drops precipitously during the first hour after learning. Losses of learning then becomes more gradual. Retention drops by half within the first hour. It takes a month (thirty-one days), however, for retention to be cut in half again.

LO⁵ Describe the biological aspects of memory. Psychologists assume that mental processes such as the encoding, storage, and retrieval of information—that is, memory—are accompanied by changes in the brain. Much research on the biology of memory focuses today on the roles of stimulants, neurons, neurotransmitters, hormones, and structures in the brain.

One Avenue to Long-Term Potentiation (LTP)

LTP can occur via the action of neurotransmitters such as serotonin and glutamate at synapses. Structurally, LTP can also occur as shown in Parts A and B, when dendrites sprout new branches that connect with transmitting axons, increasing the amount of stimulation they receive.

Part A   Part B

proactive interference
the interference by old learning with the ability to retrieve material learned recently

dissociative amnesia
amnesia thought to stem from psychological conflict or trauma

infantile amnesia
inability to recall events that occur prior to the age of two or three; also termed *childhood amnesia*

hippocampus
a structure in the limbic system that plays an important role in the formation of new memories

anterograde amnesia
failure to remember events that occur after physical trauma because of the effects of the trauma

retrograde amnesia
failure to remember events that occur prior to physical trauma because of the effects of the trauma

LO⁵ engram
(1) an assumed electrical circuit in the brain that corresponds to a memory trace (2) an assumed chemical change in the brain that accompanies learning (from the greek *en-*, meaning "in," and *gramma*, meaning "something that is written or recorded")

long-term potentiation (LTP)
enhanced efficiency in synaptic transmission that follows brief, rapid stimulation

Chapter in Review

8

LO¹

thinking
paying attention to information, mentally representing it, reasoning about it, and making decisions about it

concept
a mental category that is used to class together objects, relations, events, abstractions, or qualities that have common properties

prototype
a concept of a category of objects or events that serves as a good example of the category

exemplar
a specific example

algorithm
a systematic procedure for solving a problem that works invariably when it is correctly applied

systematic random search
an algorithm for solving problems in which each possible solution is tested according to a particular set of rules

heuristics
rules of thumb that help us simplify and solve problems

means–end analysis
a heuristic device in which we try to solve a problem by evaluating the difference between the current situation and the goal

mental set
the tendency to respond to a new problem with an approach that was successfully used with similar problems

insight
in Gestalt psychology, a sudden perception of relationships among elements of the "perceptual field," permitting the solution of a problem

incubation
in problem solving, a hypothetical process that sometimes occurs when we stand back from a frustrating problem for a while and the solution "suddenly" appears

functional fixedness
tendency to view an object in terms of its name or familiar usage

representativeness heuristic
a decision-making heuristic in which people make judgments about samples according to the populations they appear to represent

availability heuristic
a decision-making heuristic in which our estimates of frequency or probability of events are based on how easy it is to find examples

---

LO¹ Define thinking and the various concepts involved in thinking. Thinking entails attending to information, representing it mentally, reasoning about it, and making judgments and decisions about it; thinking means making conscious, planned attempts to make sense of our world, as well as categorizing new concepts and manipulating relationships among concepts. Three factors that affect problem solving include: level of expertise; whether you fall prey to a mental set; and whether you develop insight into the problem.

LO² Describe how language develops. Language is the communication of thoughts and feelings by means of symbols that are arranged according to rules of grammar. True language is distinguished from the communication systems of lower animals by properties such as semanticity, infinite creativity, and displacement. Language development reflects the interactions between the influences of heredity (nature) and the environment (nurture). Learning theorists see language developing according to imitation and reinforcement, where parents serve as models.

LO³ Identify the concept of intelligence and the techniques used to measure intelligence. Intelligence is broadly thought of as the underlying ability to understand the world and cope with its challenges. Intelligence allows people to: think, understand complex ideas, reason, solve problems, learn from experience, and adapt to the environment.

Approximate Distribution of IQ Scores

Range of IQ scores

Primary Mental Abilities, According to Thurstone

Ability	Definition
Visual and spatial abilities	Visualizing forms and spatial relationships
Perceptual speed	Grasping perceptual details rapidly, perceiving similarities and differences between stimuli
Numerical ability	Computing numbers
Verbal meaning	Knowing the meanings of words
Memory	Recalling information (e.g., words and sentences)
Word fluency	Thinking of words quickly (e.g., rhyming and doing crossword puzzles)
Deductive reasoning	Deriving examples from general rules
Inductive reasoning	Inferring general rules from examples

anchoring and adjustment heuristic
a decision-making heuristic in which a presumption or first estimate serves as a cognitive anchor; as we receive additional information, we make adjustments but tend to remain in the proximity of the anchor

framing effect
the influence of wording, or the context in which information is presented, on decision making

LO^2 language
the communication of information by means of symbols arranged according to rules of grammar

semanticity
meaning; the quality of language in which words are used as symbols for objects, events, or ideas

infinite creativity
the capacity to combine words into original sentences

displacement
the quality of language that permits one to communicate information about objects and events in another time and place

linguistic-relativity hypothesis
the view that language structures the way in which we view the world

holophrase
a single word used to express complex meanings

overregularization
the application of regular grammatical rules for forming inflections (e.g., past tense and plurals) to irregular verbs and nouns

psycholinguistic theory
the view that language learning involves an interaction between environmental factors and an inborn tendency to acquire language

language acquisition device (LAD)
in psycholinguistic theory, neural "prewiring" that facilitates the child's learning of grammar

LO^3 intelligence
a complex and controversial concept; according to David Wechsler (1975), the "capacity . . . to understand the world [and] resourcefulness to cope with its challenges"

g
Spearman's symbol for general intelligence, which he believed underlay more specific abilities

s
Spearman's symbol for *specific* factors, or *s factors,* which he believed accounted for individual abilities

primary mental abilities
according to Thurstone, the basic abilities that make up intelligence

creativity
the ability to generate novel and useful solutions to problems

LO^4 Describe the controversy surrounding intelligence testing. The role that nature and nurture play in intellectual functioning is a controversial topic in psychology. Education contributes to intelligence. For example, Head Start programs enhance IQ scores, achievement scores, and academic skills of disadvantaged children. Adoptee studies suggest a genetic influence on intelligence. But they also suggest a role for environmental influence. All in all, studies generally suggest that the heritability of intelligence is between 40% and 60%. Intellectual functioning would appear to reflect the interaction of genetic, physical, personal, and sociocultural factors.

Findings of Studies of the Relationship between IQ Scores and Heredity

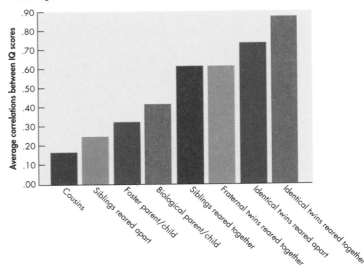

The Complex Web of Factors That Affect Intellectual Functioning

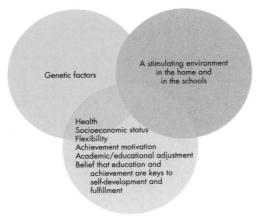

convergent thinking
a thought process that narrows in on the single best solution to a problem

divergent thinking
a thought process that attempts to generate multiple solutions to problems

mental age (MA)
the accumulated months of credit that a person earns on the Stanford–Binet intelligence scale

intelligence quotient (IQ)
(1) originally, a ratio obtained by dividing a child's score (or mental age) on an intelligence test by chronological age (2) generally, a score on an intelligence test

LO^4 heritability
the degree to which the variations in a trait from one person to another can be attributed to, or explained by, genetic factors

Chapter in Review

LO¹ motive
a hypothetical state within an organism that propels the organism toward a goal (from the latin *movere*, meaning "to move")

need
a state of deprivation

drive
a condition of arousal in an organism that is associated with a need

physiological drives
unlearned drives with a biological basis, such as hunger, thirst, and avoidance of pain

incentive
an object, person, or situation perceived as being capable of satisfying a need

LO² instinct
an inherited disposition to activate specific behavior patterns that are designed to reach certain goals

drive-reduction theory
the view that organisms learn to engage in behaviors that have the effect of reducing drives

homeostasis
the tendency of the body to maintain a steady state

self-actualization
according to Maslow and other humanistic psychologists, self-initiated striving to become what one is capable of being

LO³ satiety
the state of being satisfied; fullness

ventromedial nucleus (VMN)
a central area on the underside of the hypothalamus that appears to function as a stop-eating center

hyperphagic
characterized by excessive eating

lateral hypothalamus
an area at the side of the hypothalamus that appears to function as a start-eating center

aphagic
characterized by under-eating

anorexia nervosa
a life-threatening eating disorder characterized by dramatic weight loss and a distorted body image

bulimia nervosa
an eating disorder characterized by repeated cycles of binge eating and purging

activating effect
the arousal-producing effects of sex hormones that increase the likelihood of sexual behavior

estrus
the periodic sexual excitement of many female mammals, as governed by levels of sex hormones

LO¹ Define motivation including needs, drives, and incentives. The psychology of motivation concerns the *whys* of behavior. Motives are hypothetical states that activate behavior toward goals and may take the form of needs, drives, and/or incentives. *Needs* come in two types: physiological (needs necessary for survival) and psychological (needs for achievement, power, self-esteem, etc.). Physiological and psychological needs differ in two ways: psychological needs are not necessarily based on deprivation; psychological needs may be acquired through experience. Needs give rise to *drives* that arouse us to action. *Incentives* are objects, persons, or situations viewed as capable of satisfying a need or as desirable for their own sake.

LO² Identify the theories of motivation. Psychologists do not agree about the precise nature of motivation. The evolutionary perspective holds that animals are naturally prewired to respond to certain stimuli in certain ways. The drive reductionism and homeostasis perspective holds that primary drives trigger arousal (tension) and activate behavior. Organisms engage in behaviors that reduce tension and are motivated to maintain a steady state (homeostasis). Other theorists hold with the stimulus motivation perspective—that an organism is motivated to increase stimulation, not reduce a drive. Stimulus motivation provides an evolutionary advantage: Animals that are active and motivated to learn about their environment are more likely to survive. A humanistic theorist, Abraham Maslow believed that people are motivated by the conscious desire for personal growth. Maslow's hierarchy of needs ranges from physiological needs such as hunger and thirst through self-actualization (self-initiated striving to become whatever we believe we are capable of being). Critics argue that there is too much individual variation for the hierarchy of motives to apply to everyone.

Pyramid (top to bottom): Self-actualization / Esteem needs / Love and belongingness / Safety needs / Physiological needs

LO³ Describe the biological and psychological contributions to hunger. Biological mechanisms that regulate hunger include stomach pangs associated with stomach contractions, the functions of the hypothalamus, blood sugar level, and receptors in the liver. The ventromedial nucleus of the hypothalamus is the "stop-eating" center of the brain; the lateral hypothalamus is the "start-eating" center of the brain. Some psychological factors that influence hunger include the aroma of food, because a person feels anxious or depressed, or bored.

Problems associated with unhealthy weight are on the upswing. The origins of eating disorders aren't entirely clear. Exposure to cultural standards and role models that emphasize excessive slenderness plays a major role. Eating disorders are also more common when the family environment is negative—possibly a history of child abuse or exposure to high parental expectations. Genetic factors might not directly cause eating disorders but are likely to involve obsessionistic and perfectionistic personality traits.

LO⁴ Explain the role of sex hormones and the sexual response cycle in human sexuality. Sexual motivation, although natural, is also strongly influenced by religious and moral beliefs, cultural tradition, folklore, and superstition. What is considered "normal" depends on the society in which one lives. Level of education is connected with sexual behavior. Much about the development of sexual orientation remains speculative. Sex hormones

LO⁴ organizing effect
the directional effect of sex hormones—for example, along stereotypically masculine or feminine lines

sexual response cycle
Masters and Johnson's model of sexual response, which consists of four stages or phases

vasocongestion
engorgement of blood vessels with blood, which swells the genitals and breasts during sexual arousal

myotonia
muscle tension

excitement phase
the first phase of the sexual response cycle, which is characterized by muscle tension, increases in the heart rate, and erection in the male and vaginal lubrication in the female

clitoris
the female sex organ that is most sensitive to sexual sensation; a smooth, round knob of tissue that is situated above the urethral opening

plateau phase
the second phase of the sexual response cycle, which is characterized by increases in vasocongestion, muscle tension, heart rate, and blood pressure in preparation for orgasm

ejaculation
propulsion of seminal fluid (semen) from the penis by contraction of muscles at the base of the penis

orgasm
the height or climax of sexual excitement, involving involuntary muscle contractions, release of sexual tensions, and, usually subjective feelings of pleasure

resolution phase
the fourth phase of the sexual response cycle, during which the body gradually returns to its prearoused state

refractory period
in the sexual response cycle, a period of time following orgasm during which an individual is not responsive to sexual stimulation

heterosexual
referring to people who are sexually aroused by and interested in forming romantic relationships with people of the other sex

homosexual
referring to people who are sexually aroused by, and interested in forming romantic relationships with people of the same sex (derived from the greek *homos*, meaning "same," not from the latin *homo*, meaning "man")

sexual orientation
the directionality of one's sexual and romantic interests; that is, whether one is sexually attracted to and desires to form a romantic relationship with members of the other sex or of one's own sex

LO⁶ emotion
a feeling state with cognitive, physiological, and behavioral components

sympathetic nervous system
the branch of the autonomic nervous system that is most active during processes that spend body energy from stored reserves, such as in a fight-or-flight reaction to a predator or when you are anxious about a big test

have activating effects: they affect the sex drive and promote sexual response. Sex hormones also have organizing effects: they motivate lower animals toward masculine or feminine mating patterns.

LO⁵ Describe achievement motivation. Henry Murray developed the Thematic Apperception Test (TAT) in an attempt to assess motivation. The TAT contains cards with pictures and drawings that are subject to various interpretations. Subjects are to construct stories about the picture.

Performance goals are usually met through extrinsic or intrinsic rewards. Examples of extrinsic rewards include praise and income, while self-satisfaction is an example of an intrinsic reward. Extrinsic, or tangible, rewards can serve as an incentive for maintaining good grades. An intrinsic goal—e.g., feeling capable and intelligent—tends to have more long-lasting effects.

LO⁶ Identify the theoretical explanations of emotions. Emotions are feeling states with physiological, cognitive, and behavioral components. A physiological reaction can involve the sympathetic nervous system and result in rapid heartbeat, breathing, sweating, or muscle tension. Behavioral tendencies occur with emotions. For example, fear leads to avoidance or escape, and anger may lead to "pay-back" behaviors. Parasympathetic nervous system arousal can also occur. Joy, grief, jealousy, disgust, and so on all have cognitive, physiological, and behavioral components.

Various perspectives hold that cognitive processes—or a combination of arousal and thoughts—may determine the emotional response (see graphic below). All three theories have aspects of correctness but none fully explain emotions.

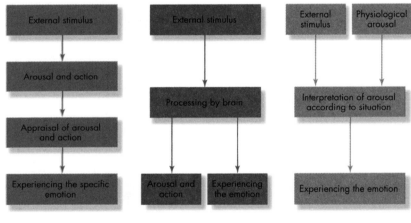

A. James–Lange   **B. Cannon–Bard**   **C. Cognitive appraisal**

parasympathetic nervous system
the branch of the autonomic nervous system that is most active during processes that restore reserves of energy to the body, such as relaxing and eating

positive psychology
the field of psychology that is about personal well-being and satisfaction; joy, sensual pleasure, and happiness; and optimism and hope for the future

facial-feedback hypothesis
the view that stereotypical facial expressions can contribute to stereotypical emotions

Chapter in Review

10

LO¹

personality
the distinct patterns of behavior, thoughts, and feelings that characterize a person's adaptation to life

psychoanalytic theory
Sigmund Freud's perspective, which emphasizes the importance of unconscious motives and conflicts as forces that determine behavior

id
the psychic structure, present at birth, that represents physiological drives and is fully unconscious

ego
the second psychic structure to develop, characterized by self-awareness, planning, and delay of gratification

superego
the third psychic structure, which functions as a moral guardian and sets forth high standards for behavior

identification
in psychoanalytic theory, the unconscious adoption of another person's behavior

psychosexual development
in psychoanalytic theory, the process by which libidinal energy is expressed through different erogenous zones during different stages of development

oral stage
the first stage of psychosexual development, during which gratification is hypothesized to be attained primarily through oral activities

anal stage
the second stage of psychosexual development, when gratification is attained through anal activities

phallic stage
the third stage of psychosexual development, characterized by a shift of libido to the phallic region; (from the greek *phallos,* referring to an image of the penis; however, Freud used the term *phallic* to refer both to boys and girls)

Oedipus complex
a conflict of the phallic stage in which the boy wishes to possess his mother sexually and perceives his father as a rival in love

Electra complex
a conflict of the phallic stage in which the girl longs for her father and resents her mother

latency
a phase of psychosexual development characterized by repression of sexual impulses

LO¹ Describe the psychoanalytical perspective and how it contributed to the study of personality.

Focus of Research
- Unconscious conflict
- Drives such as sex, aggression, and the need for superiority come into conflict with law, social rules, and moral codes

View of Personality
- Three structures of personality—id, ego, superego
- Five stages of psychosexual development—oral, anal, phallic, latency, genital
- Ego analysts—or *neoanalysts*—focus more on the role of the ego in making meaningful, conscious decisions

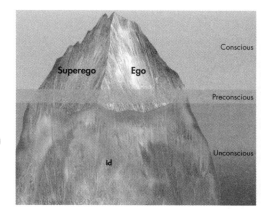

LO² Explain the trait perspective and the "Big Five" trait model.

Focus of Research
- Use of mathematical techniques to catalogue and organize basic human personality traits

View of Personality
- Based on theory of Hippocrates and work of Gordon Allport
- Eysenck's two-dimensional model: introversion–extraversion and emotional stability–instability
- Current emphasis on the five-factor model (the "Big Five")—extraversion, agreeableness, conscientiousness, neuroticism, openness to experience

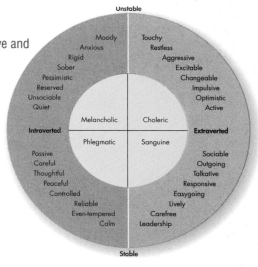

LO³ Identify the contributions of learning theory in understanding personality.

Focus of Research
- Behaviorists focus on situational factors that determine behavior
- Social cognitive emphasis on observational learning and person variables—competencies, encoding strategies, expectancies, emotions, and self-regulation

View of Personality
- Watson saw personality as plastic and determined by external, situational variables
- Skinner believed that society conditions individuals into wanting what is good for society
- Bandura believes in reciprocal determinism—that people and the environment influence one another—and in the role of making conscious choices

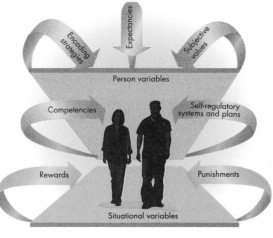

genital stage
the mature stage of psychosexual development, characterized by preferred expression of libido through intercourse with an adult of the other gender

analytical psychology
Jung's psychoanalytic theory, which emphasizes the collective unconscious and archetypes

collective unconscious
Jung's hypothesized store of vague memories that represent the history of humankind

inferiority complex
feelings of inferiority hypothesized by Adler to serve as a central motivating force

creative self
according to Adler, the self-aware aspect of personality that strives to achieve its full potential

individual psychology
Adler's psychoanalytic theory, which emphasizes feelings of inferiority and the creative self

psychosocial development
Erikson's theory of personality and development, which emphasizes social relationships and eight stages of growth

ego identity
a firm sense of who one is and what one stands for

LO⁴ Describe the humanistic perspective on personality.

Focus of Research
- The experience of being human and developing one's unique potential within an often hostile environment

View of Personality
- People have inborn drives to become what they are capable of being
- Unconditional positive regard leads to self-esteem, which facilitates individual growth and development.

LO⁵ Describe the sociocultural perspective on personality.

Focus of Research
- The roles of ethnicity, gender, culture, and socioeconomic status in personality formation and behavior

View of Personality
- Development differs in individualistic and collectivist societies
- Discrimination, poverty, and acculturation affect self-concept and self-esteem

A. Independent view of self   B. Interdependent view of self

LO⁶ Describe the different kinds of tests psychologists use to measure personality.
The two most widely used types of personality tests are objective tests and projective tests. Objective tests present respondents with a standardized group of test items in the form of a questionnaire. Responses are limited to a specific range of answers. The MMPI is the most widely used objective test. It is usually scored for four validity scales and ten clinical scales. The validity scales suggest whether answers actually represent the person's thoughts, emotions, and behaviors.

In projective tests, people are shown ambiguous stimuli such as inkblots or drawings and asked to say what they look like. People project their own personalities into their responses. The Thematic Apperception Test (TAT) is an example of a projective test.

LO² trait
a relatively stable aspect of personality that is inferred from behavior and assumed to give rise to consistent behavior

introversion
a trait characterized by intense imagination and the tendency to inhibit impulses

extraversion
a trait characterized by tendencies to be socially outgoing and to express feelings and impulses freely

LO³ social cognitive theory
a cognitively oriented learning theory in which observational learning and person variables such as values and expectancies play major roles in individual differences

gender-schema theory
a cognitive view of gender-typing that proposes that once girls and boys become aware of their anatomic sex, they begin to blend their self-expectations and self-esteem with the ways in which they fit the gender roles prescribed in a given culture

LO⁴ humanism
the view that people are capable of free choice, self-fulfillment, and ethical behavior

self-actualization
in humanistic theory, the innate tendency to strive to realize one's potential

unconditional positive regard
a persistent expression of esteem for the value of a person, but not necessarily an unqualified acceptance of all of the person's behaviors

conditional positive regard
judgment of another person's value on the basis of the acceptability of that person's behaviors

conditions of worth
standards by which the value of a person is judged

LO⁵ sociocultural perspective
the view that focuses on the roles of ethnicity, gender, culture, and socioeconomic status

in personality formation, behavior, and mental processes

individualist
a person who defines herself or himself in terms of personal traits and gives priority to her or his own goals

collectivist
a person who defines herself or himself in terms of relationships to other people and groups and gives priority to group goals

acculturation
the process of adaptation in which immigrants and native groups identify with a new, dominant culture by learning about that culture and making behavioral and attitudinal changes

validity
in psychological testing, the degree to which a test measures what it is supposed to measure

reliability
in psychological testing, the consistency or stability of test scores from one testing to another

LO⁶ standardization
in psychological testing, the process by which one obtains and organizes test scores from various population groups, so that the results of a person's completing a test can be compared to those of others of his or her sex, in his or her age group, and so on

objective tests
tests whose items must be answered in a specified, limited manner; tests whose items have concrete answers that are considered correct

response set
a tendency to answer test items according to a bias—for example, to make oneself seem perfect or bizarre

projective test
a psychological test that presents ambiguous stimuli onto which the test taker projects his or her own personality in making a response

Chapter in Review

LO¹ stress
the demand that is made on an organism to adapt

eustress (YOU-stress)
stress that is healthful

health psychology
the field of psychology that studies the relationships between psychological factors (e.g., attitudes, beliefs, situational influences, and behavior patterns) and the prevention and treatment of physical illness

pathogen
a microscopic organism (e.g., bacterium or virus) that can cause disease

conflict
being torn in different directions by opposing motives; feelings produced by being in conflict

catastrophize
to interpret negative events as being disastrous; to "blow out of proportion"

type A behavior
behavior characterized by a sense of time urgency, competitiveness, and hostility

LO² self-efficacy expectations
our beliefs that we can bring about desired changes through our own efforts

psychological hardiness
a cluster of traits that buffer stress and are characterized by commitment, challenge, and control

locus of control
the place (locus) to which an individual attributes control over the receiving of reinforcers—either inside or outside the self

internals
people who perceive the ability to attain reinforcements as being largely within themselves

externals
people who perceive the ability to attain reinforcements as being largely outside themselves

LO¹ Define stress and identify various sources of stress.
Psychological factors such as stress, behavior patterns, and attitudes can lead to or aggravate illness. People can cope with stress, and in fact there is such a thing as healthful stress (eustress). Small stressors, such as daily hassles, can threaten or harm our well-being and lead to nervousness, worrying, inability to get started, feelings of sadness, and feelings of loneliness. Hassles can predict health problems such as heart disease, cancer, and athletic injuries.

Conflict is the feeling of being pulled in two or more directions by opposing motives and can be frustrating and stressful. There are four types of conflict as illustrated in the figure below: *Approach-approach conflict* (A) is the least stressful type. Each of two goals is desirable and both are within reach. *Avoidance-avoidance conflict* (B) is more stressful. A person is motivated (M) to avoid each of two negative goals. Avoiding one of them requires approaching the other. In *approach-avoidance conflict,* (C), the same goal produces both approach and avoidance motives. *Multiple approach-avoidance conflict* (D) occurs when each of several alternative courses of action has pluses and minuses. Decision-making can be stressful—especially when there is no clear correct choice.

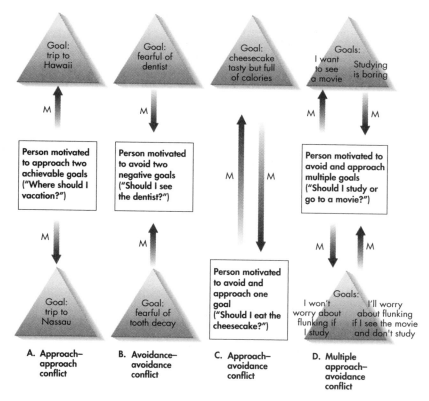

LO² Identify the psychological moderators of stress.
Psychological factors can influence or moderate the effects of stress. For example, self-efficacy expectations affect our ability to withstand stress (high self-efficacy expectations are accompanied by relatively lower levels of adrenaline and noradrenaline in the bloodstream). People who are self-confident are less prone to be disturbed by adverse events. Humor, laughter, and feelings of happiness may have beneficial effects on the immune system. On the other hand, there is a significant relationship between negative life events and stress scores, although the ability to predict a stressor apparently moderates its impact. Control and even the illusion of control can also moderate impact. Social support also seems to act as a buffer against the effects of stress. Sources of social support include: emotional concern, instrumental aid, information, appraisal, and socializing.

LO³ Describe the impact of stress on the body. The General Adaptation Syndrome, proposed by Selye, is a cluster of bodily changes that occur in three stages—alarm, resistance, and exhaustion. The alarm reaction is triggered by perception of a stressor. The reaction mobilizes or arouses the body. This mobilization is the basis for the instinctive fight-or-flight reaction. The alarm reaction involves bodily changes that are initiated by the brain and regulated by the endocrine system and the sympathetic division of the autonomic nervous system (ANS). If the stressor isn't removed, we enter the adaptation or resistance stage, in which the body attempts to restore lost energy and repair bodily damage. If the stressor isn't dealt with, we may enter the exhaustion stage—the body is depleted of the resources required for combating stress.

Stress suppresses the immune system. Feelings of control and social support can moderate these effects. The immune system has several functions that combat disease. One function is production of white blood cells (leukocytes). These cells recognize and eradicate foreign agents and unhealthy cells. Foreign substances are called antigens. The body generates specialized proteins or antibodies to fight antigens. Inflammation is another function of the immune system. This is increased blood supply, which floods the region with white blood cells. One of the reasons stress exhausts us is that it stimulates the production of steroids. Steroids suppress the functioning of the immune system. Persistent secretion of steroids decreases inflammation and interferes with the formation of antibodies. We become more vulnerable to various illnesses.

The hypothalamus secretes corticotrophin-releasing hormone (CRH)

CRH causes the pituitary gland to secrete adrenocorticotrophic hormone (ACTH)

Hypothalamus

Pituitary

Stressor

Adrenal cortex

ACTH then causes the adrenal cortex to secrete corticosteroids

The adrenal medulla releases a mixture of adrenaline and noradrenaline

Adrenal medulla

LO⁴ Explain the relationships between psychology and health. The biopsychosocial approach to health recognizes that there are complex factors (biological, psychological, and sociocultural factors) that contribute to health and illness and that there is no single, simple answer. Biological factors such as pathogens, inoculations, injuries, age, gender, and a family history of disease may be the most obvious cause of disease, although genetics certainly plays a role. Coronary heart disease (CHD) is the leading cause of death in the United States. Risks for CHD include: family history, physiological conditions, patterns of consumption, Type A behavior, hostility and holding in feelings of anger, job strain, chronic fatigue and chronic emotional strain, sudden stressors, and a physically inactive lifestyle. Cancer is the number-one killer of women in the United States and the number-two killer of men. Cancer is characterized by the development of abnormal, or mutant, cells that may take root anywhere in the body. If not controlled early, the cancerous cells may metastasize—establish colonies elsewhere in the body. Risk factors for cancer include heredity and behaviors such as smoking, drinking alcohol, eating animal fats, sunbathing, and prolonged psychological conditions such as depression.

Chapter in Review

LO¹ schizophrenia
a psychotic disorder characterized by loss of control of thought processes and inappropriate emotional responses

delusions
false, persistent beliefs that are unsubstantiated by sensory or objective evidence

affect (AFF-ekt)
feeling or emotional response, particularly as suggested by facial expression and body language

psychological disorders
patterns of behavior or mental processes that are connected with emotional distress or significant impairment in functioning

hallucination
a perception in the absence of sensory stimulation that is confused with reality

ideas of persecution
erroneous beliefs that one is being victimized or persecuted

flat affect
a severe reduction in emotional expressiveness, found among many people with schizophrenia or serious depression

predictive validity
in this usage, the extent to which a diagnosis permits one to predict the course of a disorder and the type of treatment that may be of help

LO² stupor
a condition in which the senses, thought, and movement are dulled

positive symptoms
the excessive and sometimes bizarre symptoms of schizophrenia, including hallucinations, delusions, and loose associations

negative symptoms
the deficiencies among people with schizophrenia, such as flat affect, lack of motivation, loss of pleasure, and social withdrawal

paranoid schizophrenia
a type of schizophrenia characterized primarily by delusions—commonly of persecution—and vivid hallucinations

disorganized schizophrenia
a type of schizophrenia characterized by disorganized delusions, vivid hallucinations, and inappropriate affect

catatonic schizophrenia
a type of schizophrenia characterized by striking motor impairment

waxy flexibility
a feature of catatonic schizophrenia in which people can be molded into postures that they maintain for quite some time

mutism
refusal to talk

LO¹ Define psychological disorders and describe their prevalence.
Psychological disorders are characterized by unusual behavior, socially unacceptable behavior, faulty perception of reality, personal distress, dangerous behavior, or self-defeating behavior. The American Psychiatric Association groups disorders on the basis of clinical syndromes and factors related to adjustment. About half of us will experience a psychological disorder at one time or another.

Past-Year and Lifetime Prevalences of Psychological Disorders

	Anxiety Disorders	Mood Disorders	Bipolar Disorder	Substance Use Disorders	Any Disorders
Prevalence during past year	18.1%	9.5%	2.8%	3.8%	26.2%
Lifetime prevalence	28.8%	20.8%	4.4%	14.6%	46.4%
Median age of onset	11 years	30 years	21 years	20 years	14 years

Sources: Kessler et al., 2005a; Kessler et al., 2005c; Merikangas et al, 2007.

LO² Describe the symptoms, types, and possible origins of schizophrenia.
Schizophrenia is characterized by disturbances in thought and language, perception and attention, motor activity, mood, and social interaction. Schizophrenia is connected with smaller brains in some people, especially fewer synapses in the prefrontal region, and larger ventricles. A genetic vulnerability to schizophrenia may interact with other factors, such as stress, complications during pregnancy and childbirth, and quality of parenting, to cause the disorder to develop. People with schizophrenia may also use more dopamine than other people do.

LO³ Describe the symptoms and possible origins of mood disorders. Mood disorders involve disturbances in expressed emotions. Major depression is characterized by persistent feelings of sadness, loss of interest, feelings of worthlessness or guilt, and inability to concentrate. Bipolar disorder is characterized by mood swings between elation and depression. Genetic factors may be involved in mood disorders. Research emphasizes possible roles for learned helplessness, attributional styles, and underutilization of serotonin in depression. People who are depressed are more likely than other people to make internal, stable, and global attributions for failures. Most people who commit suicide do so because of depression.

LO⁴ Describe the symptoms and possible origins of six types of anxiety disorders. Anxiety disorders are characterized by feelings of dread and sympathetic arousal. They include phobias, panic disorder, generalized anxiety, obsessive–compulsive disorder, and stress disorders. Some people may be genetically predisposed to acquire certain fears. Cognitive theorists focus on ways in which people interpret threats.

LO⁵ Describe the symptoms and possible origins of somatoform disorders. People with somatoform disorders display or complain of physical problems, although no medical evidence for them can be found. They include conversion disorder, hypochondriasis, and body dysmorphic disorder. Somatoform disorders may reflect the relative benefits of focusing on physical symptoms or features rather than life problems that most people would consider to be more important.

LO 3 major depressive disorder (MDD)
a serious to severe depressive disorder in which the person may show loss of appetite, psychomotor retardation, and impaired reality testing

psychomotor retardation
slowness in motor activity and (apparently) in thought

bipolar disorder
a disorder in which the mood alternates between two extreme poles (elation and depression); also referred to as *manic depression*

manic
elated, showing excessive excitement

neuroticism
a personality trait characterized largely by persistent anxiety

rapid flight of ideas
rapid speech and topic changes, characteristic of manicky behavior

learned helplessness
a model for the acquisition of depressive behavior, based on findings that organisms in aversive situations learn to show inactivity when their operants go unreinforced

attributional style
the tendency to attribute one's behavior to internal or external factors, stable or unstable factors, and so on

LO 6 Describe the symptoms and possible origins of dissociative disorders. Dissociative disorders are characterized by sudden, temporary changes in consciousness or self-identity. They include dissociative amnesia, dissociative fugue, and dissociative identity disorder (multiple personality). Dissociative disorders may help people keep disturbing memories or ideas out of mind, especially memories of child abuse.

LO 7 Describe the symptoms and possible origins of personality disorders. Personality disorders are inflexible, maladaptive behavior patterns that impair personal or social functioning. Genetic factors may be involved in personality disorders. Antisocial personality disorder may develop from some combination of genetic vulnerability (less gray matter in the prefrontal cortex of the brain, which may provide lower-than-normal levels of arousal), inconsistent discipline, and a cynical worldview.

LO 4 specific phobia
persistent fear of a specific object or situation

claustrophobia
fear of tight, small places

acrophobia
fear of high places

social phobia
an irrational, excessive fear of public scrutiny

agoraphobia
fear of open, crowded places

panic disorder
the recurrent experiencing of attacks of extreme anxiety in the absence of external stimuli that usually elicit anxiety

generalized anxiety disorder
feelings of dread and foreboding and sympathetic arousal of at least six months' duration

obsession
a recurring thought or image that seems beyond control

compulsion
an irresistible urge to repeat an act or engage in ritualistic behavior such as hand washing

post-traumatic stress disorder (PTSD)
a disorder that follows a distressing event outside the range of normal human experience and that is characterized by features such as intense fear, avoidance of stimuli associated with the event, and reliving of the event

acute stress disorder
a disorder, like PTSD, that is characterized by feelings of anxiety and helplessness and caused by a traumatic event; acute stress disorder occurs within a month of the event and lasts from two days to four weeks

LO 5 somatoform disorders
disorders in which people complain of physical (somatic) problems even though no physical abnormality can be found

conversion disorder
a somatoform disorder in which anxiety or unconscious conflicts are "converted" into physical symptoms that often have the effect of helping the person cope with anxiety or conflict

la belle indifférence
a French term descriptive of the lack of concern for their (imagined) medical problem sometimes shown by people with conversion disorders

hypochondriasis
a somatoform disorder characterized by persistent belief that one is ill despite lack of medical findings

body dysmorphic disorder
a somatoform disorder characterized by preoccupation with an imagined or exaggerated physical defect in one's appearance

LO 6 dissociative disorders
disorders in which there are sudden, temporary changes in consciousness or self-identity

dissociative amnesia
a dissociative disorder marked by loss of memory or self-identity; skills and general knowledge are usually retained

dissociative fugue
a dissociative disorder in which one experiences amnesia and then flees to a new location

dissociative identity disorder
a disorder in which a person appears to have two or more distinct identities or personalities that may alternately emerge

multiple personality disorder
the previous term for *dissociative identity disorder*

LO 7 personality disorders
enduring patterns of maladaptive behavior that are sources of distress to the individual or others

paranoid personality disorder
a personality disorder characterized by persistent suspiciousness, but not involving the disorganization of paranoid schizophrenia

schizotypal personality disorder
a personality disorder characterized by oddities of thought and behavior, but not involving bizarre psychotic behaviors

schizoid personality disorder
a personality disorder characterized by social withdrawal

borderline personality disorder
a personality disorder characterized by instability in relationships, self-image, mood, and lack of impulse control

antisocial personality disorder
the diagnosis given a person who is in frequent conflict with society, yet who is undeterred by punishment and experiences little or no guilt and anxiety

avoidant personality disorder
a personality disorder in which the person is unwilling to enter relationships without assurance of acceptance because of fears of rejection and criticism

METHODS OF THERAPY

Chapter in Review

LO¹ psychotherapy
a systematic interaction between a therapist and a client that brings psychological principles to bear on influencing the client's thoughts, feelings, or behavior to help the client overcome abnormal behavior or adjust to problems in living

asylum
an institution for the care of the mentally ill

LO² psychoanalysis
Freud's method of psychotherapy; (also the name of Freud's theory of personality)

catharsis
release of emotional tension, as after a traumatic experience, that has the effect of restoring one's psychological well-being

free association
in psychoanalysis, the uncensored uttering of all thoughts that come to mind

resistance
the tendency to block the free expression of impulses and primitive ideas—a reflection of the defense mechanism of repression

transference
responding to one person (such as a spouse or the psychoanalyst) in a way that is similar to the way one responded to another person (such as a parent) in childhood

wish fulfillment
a primitive method used by the id to attempt to gratify basic instincts

ego analyst
a psychoanalyst therapist who focuses on the conscious, coping behavior of the ego instead of the hypothesized, unconscious functioning of the id

interpersonal psychotherapy (ITP)
a short-term dynamic therapy that focuses on clients' relationships and direct alleviation of negative emotions such as anxiety and depression

LO³ client-centered therapy
Carl Rogers's method of psychotherapy, which emphasizes the creation of a warm, therapeutic atmosphere that frees clients to engage in self-exploration and self-expression

Gestalt therapy
Fritz Perls' form of psychotherapy, which attempts to integrate conflicting parts of the personality through directive methods designed to help clients perceive their whole selves

LO⁴ behavior therapy
systematic application of the principles of learning to the direct modification of a client's problem behaviors

systematic desensitization
Wolpe's method for reducing fears by associating a hierarchy of images of fear-evoking stimuli with deep muscle relaxation

LO¹ Define psychotherapy and describe the history of treatment. Psychotherapy uses psychological principles to help clients overcome psychological disorders or problems. Throughout most of history it has been generally assumed that psychological disorders represent possession, and cruel "treatment" methods such as exorcism have been used. Asylums, mental hospitals, and community treatment are relatively recent innovations.

LO² Describe traditional psychoanalysis and short-term psychodynamic therapies. The main method of a Freudian psychoanalysis is free association, but dream analysis and interpretations are also used. Modern approaches are briefer and more directive, and the therapist and client usually sit face to face.

LO³ Define humanistic therapy and contrast its two main approaches. Rogers' client-centered therapy uses nondirective methods: The therapist shows unconditional positive regard, empathy, and genuineness. Perls's directive method of Gestalt Therapy provides exercises aimed at helping people integrate conflicting parts of their personality.

LO⁴ Define behavior therapy and identify various behavioral approaches to therapy. Behavior therapy relies on principles of learning to help clients develop adaptive behavior patterns and discontinue maladaptive ones. These include flooding, systematic desensitization, and modeling. Virtual therapy is a new method for desensitizing patients to fears. Operant conditioning methods include token economies, successive approximation, social skills training, and biofeedback training.

LO⁵ Define cognitive therapy and describe Beck's approach and REBT. Cognitive therapy aims to give clients insight into irrational beliefs and cognitive distortions and replace them with rational beliefs and accurate perceptions. Beck notes that clients may develop depression because they minimize accomplishments and catastrophize failures. Ellis originated rational emotive behavior therapy (REBT), which holds that people's irrational beliefs about events shape their responses to them.

LO⁶ Identify advantages, disadvantages, and types of group therapy. Group therapy is more economical than individual therapy. Moreover, group members benefit from the social support and experiences of other members. However, some clients cannot disclose their problems to a group or risk group disapproval. Specialized methods include couple therapy and family therapy.

hierarchy
an arrangement of stimuli according to the amount of fear they evoke

modeling
a behavior-therapy technique in which a client observes and imitates a person who approaches and copes with feared objects or situations

aversive conditioning
a behavior therapy technique in which undesired responses are inhibited by pairing repugnant or offensive stimuli with them

rapid smoking
an aversive conditioning method for quitting smoking in which the smoker inhales rapidly, thus rendering once-desirable cigarette smoke aversive

eye-movement desensitization and reprocessing (EMDR)
a method of treating stress disorders by having clients visually follow a rapidly oscillating finger while they think of the traumatic events connected with the disorders

token economy
a controlled environment in which people are reinforced for desired behaviors with tokens (such as poker chips) that may be exchanged for privileges

successive approximations
in operant conditioning, a series of behaviors that gradually become more similar to a target behavior

biofeedback training (BFT)
the systematic feeding back to an organism of information about a bodily function so that the organism can gain control of that function

self-monitoring
keeping a record of one's own behavior to identify problems and record successes

behavior rehearsal
practice

feedback
in assertiveness training, information about the effectiveness of a response

LO⁵ cognitive therapy
a form of therapy that focuses on how clients' cognitions (e.g., expectations, attitudes, beliefs) lead to distress and may be modified to relieve distress and promote adaptive behavior

rational emotive behavior therapy (REBT)
Albert Ellis's form of therapy that encourages clients to challenge and correct irrational expectations and maladaptive behaviors

cognitive-behavior therapy (CBT)
an approach to therapy that uses cognitive and behavioral techniques that have been validated by research

LO⁷ meta-analysis
a method for combining and averaging the results of individual research studies

specific factors
those factors in psychotherapy that are specific to a given approach, such as free

LO⁷ Explain whether psychotherapy works and who benefits from it. Statistical analyses such as meta-analysis show that people who obtain most forms of psychotherapy fare better than people who do not. Psychoanalytic and client-centered approaches are most helpful with highly verbal and motivated individuals. Cognitive and behavior therapies are probably the most effective. People from various cultural backgrounds may profit from different kinds of treatment.

LO⁸ Describe methods of biological therapy and their benefits and side effects. Antipsychotic drugs help many people with schizophrenia by blocking the action of dopamine. Antidepressants help many people by increasing the action of serotonin. Lithium often helps people with bipolar disorder. The use of antianxiety drugs for daily tensions is controversial because people build tolerance and do not learn to solve their problems. ECT, another controversial treatment, induces a seizure and frequently relieves severe depression. The prefrontal lobotomy attempts to alleviate agitation by severing nerve pathways in the brain but has been largely discontinued because of side effects.

association in psychoanalysis or systematic desensitization in behavior therapy

nonspecific factors
those factors in psychotherapy that are common to many approaches, such as the "therapeutic alliance" with the client

LO⁸ rebound anxiety
anxiety that can occur when one discontinues use of a tranquilizer

antidepressant
acting to relieve depression

selective serotonin-reuptake inhibitors (SSRIs)
antidepressant drugs that work by blocking the reuptake of serotonin by presynaptic neurons

electroconvulsive therapy (ECT)
treatment of disorders like major depression by passing an electric current (that causes a convulsion) through the head

sedative
a drug that relieves nervousness or agitation or puts one to sleep

psychosurgery
surgery intended to promote psychological changes or to relieve disordered behavior

prefrontal lobotomy
the severing or destruction of a section of the frontal lobe of the brain

SOCIAL PSYCHOLOGY

Chapter in Review

LO¹ social psychology
the field of psychology that studies the nature and causes of people's thoughts and behavior in social situations

LO² attitude
an enduring mental representation of a person, place, or thing that evokes an emotional response and related behavior

A–B problem
the issue of how well we can predict behavior on the basis of attitudes

elaboration likelihood model
the view that persuasive messages are evaluated (elaborated) on the basis of central and peripheral cues

fear appeal
a type of persuasive communication that influences behavior on the basis of arousing fear instead of rational analysis of the issues

selective avoidance
diverting one's attention from information that is inconsistent with one's attitudes

selective exposure
deliberately seeking and attending to information that is consistent with one's attitudes

cognitive-dissonance theory
the view that we are motivated to make our cognitions or beliefs consistent

attitude-discrepant behavior
behavior inconsistent with an attitude that may have the effect of modifying an attitude

effort justification
in cognitive-dissonance theory, the tendency to seek justification (acceptable reasons) for strenuous efforts

stereotype
a fixed, conventional idea about a group

attraction
in social psychology, an attitude of liking or disliking (negative attraction)

triangular model of love
Sternberg's view that love involves combinations of three components: intimacy, passion, and commitment

intimacy
close acquaintance and familiarity; a characteristic of a relationship in which partners share their inmost feelings

passion
strong romantic and sexual feelings

commitment
the decision to maintain a relationship

LO¹ Define social psychology.
One area of social psychology studies the ways in which people can be goaded by social influences into doing things that are not necessarily consistent with their personalities. Social psychology studies the nature and causes of behavior and mental processes in social situations. Topics covered in social psychology include: attitudes, conformity, persuasion, social perception, interpersonal attraction, social influence, group conformity, and obedience.

LO² Define attitude and discuss factors that shape it.
Attitudes are comprised of cognitive evaluations, feelings, and behavioral tendencies. A number of factors influence the likelihood that we can predict behavior from attitudes: specificity, strength of attitudes, vested interest, and accessibility. Attitudes with a strong emotional impact are more accessible. People attempt to change other people's attitudes and behavior by means of persuasion. According to the elaboration likelihood model, persuasion occurs through central and peripheral routes. Repeated messages generally "sell" better than messages delivered once. People tend to respond more to fear appeals than the purely factual presentation. Persuasive communicators tend to show expertise, trustworthiness, attractiveness, or similarity to the audience.

LO³ Define social perception and describe the factors that contribute to it.
The primacy effect refers to the fact that we often judge people in terms of our first impressions. The recency effect appears to be based on the fact that recently learned information is easier to remember. The attribution process is the tendency to infer the motives and traits of others through observation of their behavior. In dispositional attributions, we attribute people's behavior to internal factors. In situational attributions, we attribute people's behavior to external forces. According to the actor–observer effect, we tend to attribute the behavior of others to internal, dispositional factors, but we tend to attribute our own behavior to external, situational factors. The fundamental attribution error is the tendency to attribute too much of other people's behavior to dispositional factors.

consummate love
the ideal form of love within Sternberg's model, which combines passion, intimacy, and commitment

romantic love
an intense, positive emotion that involves sexual attraction, feelings of caring, and the belief that one is in love

LO 3 social perception
a subfield of social psychology that studies the ways in which we form and modify impressions of others

primacy effect
the tendency to evaluate others in terms of first impressions

recency effect
the tendency to evaluate others in terms of the most recent impression

attribution
a belief concerning why people behave in a certain way

dispositional attribution
an assumption that a person's behavior is determined by internal causes such as personal attitudes or goals

situational attribution
an assumption that a person's behavior is determined by external circumstances such as the social pressure found in a situation

actor–observer effect
the tendency to attribute our own behavior to situational factors but to attribute the behavior of others to dispositional factors

fundamental attribution error
the assumption that others act predominantly on the basis of their dispositions, even when there is evidence suggesting the importance of their situations

self-serving bias
the tendency to view one's successes as stemming from internal factors and one's failures as stemming from external factors

LO 4 social influence
the area of social psychology that studies the ways in which people influence the thoughts, feelings, and behavior of others

foot-in-the-door technique
a method for including compliance in which a small request is followed by a larger request

LO 5 social facilitation
the process by which a person's performance is increased when other members of a group engage in similar behavior

evaluation apprehension
concern that others are evaluating our behavior

diffusion of responsibility
the spreading or sharing of responsibility for a decision or behavior within a group

social decision schemes
rules for predicting the final outcome of group decision making on the basis of the members' initial positions

groupthink
a process in which group members are influenced by cohesiveness and a dynamic leader to ignore external realities as they make decisions

deindividuation
the process by which group members may discontinue self-evaluation and adopt group norms and attitudes

altruism
unselfish concern for the welfare of others

LO 4 Explain why people obey authority figures and conform to social norms. Other people and groups can exert enormous pressure on us to behave according to their norms. In fact, classic experiments have demonstrated that people influence others to engage in destructive obedience or conform to social norms. For example, the majority of subjects in the Milgram studies complied with the demands of authority figures, even when the demands required that they hurt innocent people by means of electric shock. Factors contributing to obedience include socialization, lack of social comparison, perception of legitimate authority figures, the foot-in-the-door technique, inaccessibility of values, and buffers between perpetrator and victim. Asch's research in which subjects judged the lengths of lines suggests that most people will follow the crowd, even when the crowd is wrong. Personal factors such as desire to be liked by group members, low self-esteem, high self-consciousness, and shyness contribute to conformity. Group size also contributes.

Overbearing experimenter

"Learner" who appears to be receiving shocks

"Teacher" with "aggression" machine

LO 5 Describe how and why people behave differently as group members than as individuals. The concept of social facilitation refers to the effects on performance that result from the presence of other people. The presence of others may facilitate performance for reasons such as increased arousal and evaluation apprehension. Anonymous group members, however, may experience diffusion of responsibility and performance may fall off, as in social loafing. Social psychologists have identified several decision-making schemes, including the majority-wins scheme, the truth-wins scheme, the two-thirds majority scheme, and the first-shift rule. Group decisions tend to be more polarized and riskier than individual decisions, largely because groups diffuse responsibility. Group decisions may be highly productive when group members are knowledgeable, there is an explicit procedure for arriving at decisions, and there is a process of give and take.